O N W A T C H

ON WATCH

A MEMOIR

Elmo R. Zumwalt, Jr.

ADMIRAL USN (RET.)

Quadrangle | The New York Times Book Co.

Second Printing June 1976

Library of Congress Cataloging in Publication Data

Zumwalt, Elmo R   1920–
  On watch.

  Includes index.
  1. Zumwalt, Elmo R   1920–2. United
States. Navy. 3. United States—Military policy.
I. Title.
V63.Z85A33   1976   75–8301
ISBN 0–8129–0520–2

To beautiful, steadfast Mouza, whose patience and understanding made possible her husband's career in the Navy;

To Elmo, Jim, Ann, and Mouzetta, whose performance and character have survived their father's preoccupation with the Navy;

To the men and women, enlisted and commissioned, whose love of country, bravery in action, and questioning minds made it a duty and a pleasure for their service chief to try to modernize and humanize the Navy;

To those who fell in battle and suffered stoically in hospitals and enemy prisons, whose unquestioning sacrifices made it an honor and an inspiration to be their colleague in the Navy;

I very respectfully submit this report.

The man who is just and firm of purpose can be shaken from his stern resolve neither by the rage of the people who urge him to crime nor by the countenance of the threatening tyrant.

Horace, *Odes,* III, 1, 1–4

Contents

ACKNOWLEDGMENTS x
PREFACE xi

PART I   THE CUT OF MY JIB   1

1. My Favorite War Story   3
2. The Cutting of My Jib   23
3. The Summons   43

PART II   PLATFORMS AND WEAPONS   57

4. High-Low   59
5. The Rickover Complication   85
6. Congressional Dispositions   123

PART III   MEN AND WOMEN   165

7. Programs for People   167
8. Mickey Mouse, Elimination Of   182
9. Sailing Second Class   197
10. Blowoff   217
11. Z-NAVOPS 01 Through 121 Are Hereby Cancelled   261

PART IV   FRIENDS AND FOES   273

12. Into the Tank   275
13. A United States Day and a NATO Day   292
14. The Assistant   308
15. Up to Speed   329
16. Tilt!   360
17. A Last Hurrah in Vietnam   377
18. Kissingerology   395
19. Troubled Waters and Oil   424
20. Changing the Watch   461

CHRONOLOGY   513
APPENDIXES   516
Appendix A   Department of the Navy—Washington
Headquarters Organization   516

Appendix B   Organizational Chart of the National Security
Council   518

Appendix C   Comparison of U.S. and USSR Naval
Capabilities   519

1. U.S. vs USSR General Purpose Naval Ship Construction
1966–1970   519

2. U.S. vs USSR Merchant Fleets   519

3. Growth in Soviet Missile Launch Platforms   520

4. Age/Type of Active Merchant Ships U.S. vs USSR   520

5. U.S. Estimates of Soviet Naval Forces for 1975   521

6. U.S. Naval Strength 1970 and 1974 522

7. U.S. vs USSR Total Combat Surface Ships 523

8. Ratio of Air Attack Anti-ship Systems to Combat Ships 523

9. Ratio of Air Attack Anti-ship Systems to AAW (Including AIC Fighter) Defenders 524

10. Ratio of ASW Vehicles to Submarine Targets 524

11. U.S. vs USSR Submarine Forces 525

12. U.S. vs USSR Naval Ship Construction 1966–1970 525

13. Applications of Relevant Power 526

14. The Strategic Nuclear Balance U.S. vs USSR 528

Appendix D Z-grams 530

Appendix E U.S. Navy First-term Reenlistment Rates 533

MAPS 534

1. The Mediterranean 534

2. The Pacific 536

3. The North Atlantic 538

4. The Indian Ocean 539

GLOSSARY 540

INDEX 545

(Illustrations follow page 272.)

ACKNOWLEDGMENTS

This book is dedicated to the memory of Malcolm Scott Wine, who entered the lives of the Zumwalt family as a volunteer in a political cause in which he deeply believed, and who was taken from us ten months later, loved as a friend, respected as a colleague, and cherished for what he taught us.

I am grateful to many for the successful completion of this book:

My associate, Robert Rice, for his patience, counsel and research and for teaching me how to write a book.

The following friends and loved ones:

for their diligence, valued professional assistance and sound advice: Roger Jellinek, Jim and Lisa Zumwalt, Rear Admiral Bill and Dorothy Thompson, Elmo and Kathy Zumwalt;

for the improvement generated by their thoughtful review of the several versions of the manuscript: Mouza Zumwalt, Admiral Worth Bagley, Captain Jack Davey, Dave Halperin, Bill Norman, Rear Admiral Charles Rauch, Vice Admiral Rex Rectanus;

for their painstaking and detailed research: John Mendiola, Bernard Cavalcante, Nancy Jenkins, Norman Polmar, Dominic Paolucci, T. K. Jones;

for permission to print a brave letter: Anne Swanson;

for their hard-working technical assistance: Mae Counselman, Judy Casey, Jeannine Zimmerman, Peter Lowe, Carolyn Ball, Ann Zumwalt.

PREFACE

Most high-ranking military officers practice in retirement the same reticence they necessarily practiced while on active duty about the details of what they saw and did in the course of official business: the controversies they participated in, the political maneuvering they witnessed, the personal eccentricities they encountered, the frustrations they suffered, the mistakes they and others made. Such a rule of reticence is both useful and honorable. It would be difficult either to preserve the military subordination to civilian authority that the Constitution demands or to foster the civilian reliance on military candor, objectivity, and expertise that the security of the nation requires if generals and admirals habitually used retirement as a signal to begin telling tales out of school. I have consciously and, I am bold to say, conscientiously departed from the useful and honorable custom of reticence in writing this book. I shall try to explain why.

When on 30 June 1974, in the middle of my fifty-fourth year, my four-year term as Chief of Naval Operations expired, I walked out the door of the United States Navy, my much-loved professional home for thirty-five years, with as much relief as regret. Technically, I did not have to leave the Navy. Secretary of Defense James Schlesinger had urged me to stay on in any four-star job other than CNO (to which by law I could not be reappointed) that I desired. I felt morally obliged to retire, because I had decided at the beginning of my watch that I was duty-bound to apply to myself the same "up and out" policy I intended to apply to every flag officer. But I did not have to leave the government. Alexander Haig had asked me to become Administrator of Veterans Affairs. I refused because by then I had become so sure that certain continuing national policies and procedures were inimical to the security of the United States that I no longer wanted to be associated in any capacity with an Administration responsible for them. Indeed I wanted to be far enough outside to be free to criticize those policies and procedures.

I am not speaking primarily of the Watergate scandals, which were within a few weeks of reaching their climax when I hung up my uniform. Naturally I was ashamed of being a member of an Administration capable of such misdeeds, even though I was a sailor without political ties or duties and could not possibly be suspected of having had any part in perpetrating them. I am speaking of a species of immorality that I found, if not as spectacularly repugnant as eavesdropping, breaking-and-entering, perjury, and obstruction of justice, at least as damaging to the nation's well-being, and about which I had first become concerned many months before the June 1972 burglary. I refer to the deliberate, systematic and, unfortunately, extremely successful efforts of the President, Henry Kissinger, and a few subordinate members of their inner circle to conceal, sometimes by simple silence, more often by articulate deceit, their real policies about the most critical matters of national security: the strategic arms limitation talks (SALT) and various other of the aspects of "détente," the relations between the United States and its allies in Europe, the resolution of the war in southeast Asia, the facts about America's military strength and readiness. Their concealment and deceit was practiced against the public, the press, the Congress, the allies, and even most of the officials within the executive branch who had a statutory responsibility to provide advice about matters of national security. The result, which I am sure was the one intended, was to foreclose outside and inside the government alike, almost all frank and sensible discussion of major policy issues. Indeed the result was to remove the formulation and conduct of policy from the very ken of both the public and those who were presumably members of the government's inner councils.

My surprise and then my dismay were intense as I gradually came to realize that affairs were being managed in that way. I had assumed office on 1 July 1970 both with enthusiasm for what I believed were the political-military policies of Richard Nixon and Henry Kissinger and with definite views about how the government should arrive at major decisions. I had formed the latter in the course of serving directly under civilians near the center of affairs during the Eisenhower, Kennedy, and Johnson Administrations. Though on more than one occasion each of those Administrations was less open with the Congress and the public than was strictly consistent with the democratic ideal, all three were almost unvaryingly open within. Because the appropriate members of the bureaucracy were encouraged to have their say about matters that concerned them, there was an extensive exchange of views and often vigorous debate. The decision-makers skillfully used the inevitable rivalries between agencies and the competing parochial interests within agencies to stimulate the adversary give-and-take that is essential to sound decision-making. My participation in this process, which included being a junior member of the team that managed the Cuban Missile Crisis, convinced me that on the whole the penalties of slowness, unimaginativeness, and compromise that may be incurred by an Administration that allows its members to express themselves freely are worth paying. In such an Administration in the long run almost everyone is likely to get educated. And because officials down the line understand the basis for the decisions made at the top, those decisions receive the active support down the line that is indispensable if they are to be carried out.

On the other hand, the Nixon-Kissinger "system" of bypassing and often deceiving the bureaucracy is almost sure to short-circuit itself eventually, as the record of the Nixon years testifies. One thing that happens is that conscientious officials, when they find that the direct channels through which they are accustomed to transact their business have been blocked, inevitably and properly seek other, circuitous ones that make it possible for them to meet their responsibilities. At the same time, less conscientious officials sometimes respond to the intrigues in the parlor with below-stairs intrigues of their own. And so luncheons prolong themselves, late evening bull sessions proliferate, telephone conversations become portentous, photo-copying machines hum day and night, leaks appear in the press, Congressmen come into possession of papers that were presumably under lock and key, and everyone looks askance at his neighbor. In sum, men and women who ordinarily would spend all their time straightforwardly performing their duties are forced to spend much of their time puzzling over whether they can perform their duties at all and if so how, and governmental inefficiency becomes far greater and more damaging than anything a bureaucracy working by the book could perpetrate.

All of that happened in the Nixon Administration, but it was not the worst thing that happened. Worse yet was that the momentous issues of the day could not receive the kind of objective, painstaking, detailed scrutiny that is the only safeguard against potentially disastrous strategic or technical mistakes. As a result there were many mistakes of both kinds. And of course under the grotesque system of management that prevailed, those bold enough to point out the mistakes found themselves at once on a written or unwritten "enemies list." Then came Watergate and the President felt compelled to seek for foreign-policy "successes" to distract the country from his domestic misbehavior, and all pretense that issues were being dealt with honestly was abandoned. The only advice that was acceptable was advice custom-made to support predetermined goals of the President or his principal advisors. If it could not be custom-made, it was discouraged. If it could not be discouraged, there were threats. If threats did not enforce silence, they were sometimes carried out. I know. It happened to me, and more than once, for I had decided by the middle of my watch that I could not remain on the "team"—it was more like a suicide squad—and I did not.

But I am probably dwelling too long on matters of bureaucratic style and procedure. What is important to record is the inextricable relationship the Nixon Administration's perversion of the policy-making process bore to its ignoble outlook. Its contempt for the patriotism and intelligence of the American people, for the Constitutional authority of the Congress, and for the judgment of its own officials and experts reflected Henry Kissinger's world view: that the dynamics of history are on the side of the Soviet Union; that before long the USSR will be the only superpower on earth and the United States will be an also-ran; that a principal reason this will happen is that Americans have neither the stamina nor the will to do the hard things they would have to do to prevent it from happening; that the duty of policy-makers, therefore, is at all costs to conceal from the people their probable fate and proceed as cleverly and rapidly as may be to make the best possible deal with the Soviet Union while there is still time to make any deal. The political-military policies of the Nixon Administration flowed quite logically from that view of the world, which the President certainly went along with whether or not he had arrived at it independently of Kissinger. I think what I learned during four years in the thick of that miasma made it my duty to write a book.

I

THE CUT OF MY JIB

CHAPTER 1

My Favorite War Story

Herewith most of a letter I wrote my father thirty years ago on the way home from war. I was a twenty-five-year-old lieutenant three years out of the Naval Academy, the executive officer of the destroyer *Saufley,* sailing across the Pacific from China to the United States. I reproduce what I wrote Dad during that voyage almost as written, but not quite. I have deleted certain racial slurs against the Japanese. I doubt that they were pardonable even in 1945, though they certainly were common coinage; they are unfit to print in 1975. Additionally, in a handful of places, I have indulged myself by correcting lapses of syntax, punctuation, or spelling that resulted from haste or carelessness. I have not changed substance by an iota.

10 NOVEMBER 1945

Dear Dad,

When the war ended, my ship, the *Robinson,* was at Ulithi Atoll, in the Western Carolines. We were nursing our wounds and preparing for the grand finale—the invasion of Kyushu.

Peace changed the plans. The same orders that sent Admiral Halsey's forces into Tokyo with General MacArthur's crowd sent a small but compact group of us to Okinawa and thence to Shanghai —as best we might get there.

We left Okinawa with one destroyer *(Robinson)* and a dozen

minesweepers. We got to the outlet of the Yangtze River—some thirty miles from land and fifty miles from Shanghai—before we ran into the first minefields. The *Robinson* dropped her anchor for several days while the minesweepers swept back and forth, exploding mines and creating a path for us and future forces through the Japanese sown fields.

On the fourth day we were amazed to behold a Japanese vessel— a troop transport, similar to our LST, standing out of the Yangtze. We overhauled him, put a shot across his bow and made him strike his colors.

I was selected to be the prize crew captain. I picked a crew of eight men and two other officers. We went aboard at 1400 with each man armed to the teeth. The procedure had been rehearsed on the way over so that the ship became a beehive of activity as soon as we stepped over the gangway.

One sailor pulled down the Japanese colors and hoisted the U.S. flag above. Two of us took station on the bridge overlooking the foc'sle while the others searched the ship for sabotage (opened sea cocks, fire, bombs, etc.), driving all Japanese onto the foc'sle under our guns.

Two men stood guard with Tommy guns while two more searched the crew and passengers (a total of two hundred). Two men took a party of twenty disarmed Japanese aft to the powder magazines to throw all ammunition over the side. One officer and one man spiked each gun. Another officer and man inspected the engine rooms. I took the Japanese Captain, a mild and deceivingly innocuous man of fifty, into his cabin for a conference. He knew no English until I indicated that he was of no use to Americans and would be turned over to the Chinese at which point he became quite coherent. He had been to America twenty-five years earlier it seems and he was remembering more of the language minute by minute rather than face the Chinese.

At the conclusion of a busy four-hour period, we had completely disarmed and secured the ship. I had taken charts from the Captain's sea cabin giving us all the Japanese mine fields and learned that the ship had left Shanghai that day. These two facts cut down the time of sweeping by at least two weeks since heretofore we had had to guess at the position of the fields. We sent these charts back to the *Robinson* on the last boat. No sooner had it left than a violent storm hit us. All U.S. ships got underway and steered out to sea to weather the storm. We were left at anchor all by ourselves.

It was a novel situation to be miles from shore and friendly ships, in an unseaworthy vessel (built only for calm sea traffic) with only ten Americans to rule two hundred Japanese. But each of us wouldn't have traded places for the world. We locked all Japanese except key engine and anchor personnel in a big cargo hold. Two sailors stood guard over the hatch. The others slept on the bridge under guard of one officer and one sailor. The unexpected storm lasted four days. We had brought food and water for one day. We appropriated several cases of beer and soda pop which we used instead of Japanese water as the latter liquid appeared to be extremely unsanitary. We also appropriated all the Japanese boxed crackers (much like our hard tack) and canned goods. This gave us ample healthy rations. We let the Japanese eat rice.

When the storm cleared, the U.S. vessels returned from sea and picked us up; the Japanese vessel having been rendered harmless was ordered to anchor near us.

A day or two later several more Japanese vessels came out of the river apparently trying to escape to Tokyo once more to avoid the Chinese. We captured all of them. The largest was a 1200 ton river gunboat about the size of our old destroyer—a trim, sleek craft with 8 cm guns, carrying a crew of about 190 officers and men.

I was selected to become prize crew skipper of this vessel. I took two other Naval Academy officers (ensigns) and fifteen men for the job. Profiting from our earlier experience, we carried, in addition to arms and radio gear, sufficient U.S. water for several days and rations for longer. We found our new command (HIJMS *Ataka*) to be a veritable treasure chest. Rare silks, expensive wool yarn, leather goods, cases of liquor (including good U.S. Scotch and bourbon), beer, soda pop, billions of Chinese dollars, not to mention all manner of trophies and personal valuables, were among the hastily collected loot. The Japanese skipper, this time no obsequious reserve, was a stern-faced militarist of the old school. He had been Damage Control Officer of the Japanese carrier *Shikoku* during the attack on Pearl Harbor. His actions throughout the war were among the thickest fighting. At the time we intercepted him he was proceeding at his elusive best with his squadron of five ships.

We drove the Japanese out of "officers country" which was the after part of the ship. Our sailors and officers moved into these comfortable quarters—two to each stateroom. A large wardroom became an armory, galley for preparing food, and a guard station to protect the sleeping Americans in the officer rooms. All Japanese, stripped of their valuables, were kind enough to move forward into two cargo spaces.

We had come aboard with exciting orders. First, we were to search and disarm the vessel, which we did in the same manner as in the previous vessel. Second, we were to force the Japanese skipper to take us to Shanghai up the Yangtze and Hwangpoo Rivers to establish contact with the handful of Americans who were supposed to have flown in from the guerilla territory of West China. Our primary task was to learn which parts of the river were mined and which were navigable, what wrecks were in the way, where buoys were located, etc. We were to return with sufficient information to enable other vessels to safely make the journey.

We had boarded the *Ataka* late in the afternoon of 11 September. By midnight the ship was secure. Early on 12 September we got underway with U.S. sailors guarding the Japanese as they worked the engines, anchor, helm, etc. One of the ensigns commanded the engine rooms. The other recorded all the navigation information. I interrogated the Japanese skipper, Captain Terihese, about all his courses and speeds. Whenever he refused to explain a situation, we found that we could make him talk by steering the vessel directly for the area he seemed to be trying to avoid. He would then quit refusing, explain that mines or wrecks made that area particularly dangerous. The system worked well because we had all the Japanese officers and men who were unoccupied, lined up on the foc'sle where a mine or wreck could do the most harm.

The trip which ensued was the beginning of the most fascinating chapter of my life. We went north of the famous Saddle Islands, passed lonely Gutzloff Island in filthy mud saturated water—the Yangtze river silt which carries for miles to sea. Shortly after we passed the entrance buoy, from which it is thirty-five miles to Woosung at the entrance to the Hwangpoo, we sighted our first Chinese junks. Hundreds of them, high-sided graceful sailing junks which in symmetry and lineament at a distance—outside of olfactory range—resemble the old Spanish galleon of the Panama-Spanish Main run. These are the merchant junks that carry the produce of China along her coast and up her rivers. Here the river was wide, the banks being long faint traces on either horizon.

Up and up we steamed. As the river narrowed, the wrecks became more frequent and the navigation more circuitous. Villages came into view—small farms with the typical Chinese farm hut of straw—thatched roof leading down to the ground. The most common comment was that China was one place which lived up to preconceived notions. The river banks were green and beautiful.

At one in the afternoon, we turned to port leaving the wide Yangtze for the tricky, narrow Hwangpoo. At the confluence of these two rivers on the western or Shanghai side of the Hwangpoo is the Shanghai port of Woosung. This grew up as a seaport for Shanghai to handle those large ocean-going vessels which couldn't be sailed up to the city itself. A good road runs along the west bank of the river from Woosung to Shanghai and the entire fifteen-mile stretch is dotted with towns and metropolitan areas. In America when we come to a river we build a bridge; in China, the progress goes no further than the first bank. As a result, we saw the phenomenon of a metropolitan west bank with a rural east bank directly opposite.

At the exact confluence of the rivers there is a long breakwater and channel-preserving wall past which the current flows in tricky eddies making the ascent tense for the first few hundred yards.

Just as we rounded the difficult bend, we sighted two Japanese PT boats speeding down on us at thirty knots. Now we had heard rumors that China's Japanese had not quit, but we little dreamed of the adventures we were to encounter. Our orders had commissioned us to learn as much as possible of the situation in Shanghai. Our first lesson was fast unfolding.

We had a Chinese-American sailor as part of the prize crew for prospective interpreting. We put him on the telescope to make the decision as to whether the occupants of the boats were Japanese or Chinese. As soon as he called out "Japs," we put a dozen shots across the leading PT's bow. My order had been to fire ahead of him. With typical American exactness, the eleven men who fired put their shots into the bow ahead of the occupant, thereby rendering pro facto a too literal interpretation of the command. My marksmanship was bad, too, Dad! As a result we had the pleasant sight of a Japanese making rapidly to shore with a badly leaking boat. The second boat disappeared from where it came.

The Hwangpoo is only 500 yards wide. On that day it was lined with literally thousands of junks, sampans (the lizardlike oar-propelled craft on which Chinese are born, live and die by the thousands). Our shots broke a tranquil silence. Almost as though it had been prearranged, the Chinese multitudes sent up a cheer and shout of welcome that was a roar. Small steam launches sounded their sirens, all craft twisted and turned like happy animals showing their pleasure. Crowds waved and whistled. This, remember, was the first American vessel—the first U.S. flag to fly on that river for four years. For the next hour and a half our triumphal entry continued with undiminished celebrating along the fifteen-mile stretch to Shanghai.

Here and there in sullen groups we saw Japanese troops well armed and equipped, cynical watchdogs to the procession. Our shooting of their PT boats seemed to have stunned them. Military logic dictated caution on our part but we were too exuberant to follow that course—which, later events proved, was fortunate.

Halfway up the river a Japanese signal tower sent us a blinker order to lie to for inspection—as interpreted by our obliging hosts. We were flying the U.S. flag over the Japanese flag. Our answer was to lower the Japanese pennant to the deck. We emphasized the negative by shooting out the blinker light. The little fellows came flying out of the tower from all directions. There were apparently no "divine winds" blowing that day.

Entering Shanghai itself gave much the same sensation you would have sailing a ship down Market Street in San Francisco. It is a modern city of tall buildings, streetcars, paved streets, and electric lights. The Bund is the famous drive that follows along the river in the city's heart. Pedicabs (a bicycle device which pulls a passenger cart for two passengers) and ginrickshas thronged this avenue along with a few antiquated autos. Here and there a shiny new car indicated Japanese Army or Navy headquarters.

In normal times Shanghai itself is a thriving port. However, so effectively had our Army and Navy mined the river and sunk their ships that no Japanese commerce had gone on over this waterway in months. As a consequence, the excellent dock was crowded three and four deep with the saddest shipping spectacle I have ever seen. There were hundreds of ships, large and small, steam and sail, Chinese and Japanese. Most of them had become shelter for the sampan people. It was obvious that to tie our ship up near any of these craft would be to invite theft, filth, and worst of all, disease.

As we proceeded up the river, we tried to contact by radio and by signal light any building or tower that looked as though Europeans might be in control. We got plenty of answers, but all in Japanese. It began to be painfully obvious that the Japanese were not only in control of all facilities but that Allied forces didn't exist as a cohesive unit. You can picture the scene—afternoon wearing on, an American ship appearing in the Hwangpoo after four years' absence—Japanese gnashing their teeth in eloquent frustration—Chinese cheering—a sullen Japanese crew lined up with a handful of expectant sailors guarding them. And you can visualize our predicament—docks with no available space, no contact with any Allies—surrounded by 175,000 armed sentinels.

We saw an open dock. The chart confirmed our opinion that this was Japanese Naval Headquarters reserved for Japanese men-of-war. Barracks around the place were full of Japanese troops; Japanese soldiers stood guard along the wharf, Japanese flags flew; expensive cars lined the area.

We decided that the only way out was the "Damn the torpedoes" approach. We pulled into the dock and forced the Japanese captain to order the dock personnel to take our lines and tie the ship up.

We could hear the angry growls of the hundreds of Japanese in the area as we lined the *Ataka* crew up on the dock side of the ship to act as a screen for our sailors.

Just as it had been necessary to use the only existing organization on the river—the Japanese naval facilities—to dock our ship, so was it imperative to use them to establish contact with the American forces rumored to be in the city. We had a small YMS, an American minesweeper which had followed us up the river to learn where and why we blew up if we should do so. I ordered him to tie up astern. Leaving one of the ensigns in command, I took the skipper of the YMS and an armed guard of three sailors through Japanese guards. The three sailors were a handpicked lot. One was the Chinese-American sailor, one Loo Lim, son of an American citizen who had returned to Canton, China. He was one of four boys of the family sent to San Francisco for his education. Leaving China in 1938 at fifteen years of age, he had learned of the gradual degradation of his country through the personalized spectra of family letters. He had seen the family fortune wiped out, security lost, and finally actual starvation among his relatives. He loathed the Japanese with a depth of feeling that was something to behold.

The second sailor was a Texas farm boy. One of three brothers in the service (one paratrooper, one flying sergeant), he had run away from high school to enlist. He was a boy of keen intellect and amazing presence of mind as he was to demonstrate many times. His courage was phenomenal. On three occasions in the next few days, he saved my life.

The third sailor was a Modesto, California, boy—a handsome kid who had been a flying cadet, washed out for daredevil flying. He, too,

was cool and nerveless. We marched across the dock in the form of
a staff—two officers abreast followed by the three men. The sailors
carried submachine guns. We carried pistols. At the first line of
guards, one attempted to stop us. In a beautifully executed double
play, the lad from Texas disarmed him. We marched in, covered
from the rear by the guns of the Americans on the *Ataka* and YMS
and from the front by the Japanese.

We entered the Japanese headquarters building demanding an
interpreter. One hurried out. We informed him that we were the
vanguard of a vast horde (keeping fingers crossed) and that he was
expected to obtain fullest cooperation for us. As an initial demonstration of good faith, he was to carry out the following orders
immediately: (1) Fuel the *Ataka*. (2) Provide water and provisions. (3) Supply a suitable car and driver to take us to our desti-
nation. (4) Keep all Japanese away from our ship.

We saw him enter the office of the #1 and followed him in. The
#1 was a very practical man who, seeing our guns, ordered that all
items be provided. Leaving #1 under guard until the completion of
fueling-provisioning, to prevent any tricks, the original party of five
set off in a beautiful 1941 Packard with a Japanese sailor driving and
an English-speaking Japanese officer as interpreter.

Our information was that Admiral Milton E. ("Mary") Miles, the
dare-devil Commander of U.S. Naval Guerilla Forces in China, the
one American more loved by the Chinese and hated by the Japanese
than any other, had set up temporary headquarters on the Yu Yuan
Road which was several miles from the docks on the other side of
the metropolitan area. Our ride to find him was a land-borne reenact-
ment of the celebration coming up the river. As soon as we were
recognized by the first of thousands of curious Chinese, the news
seemed to spread with electrifying rapidity throughout the city. At
one crowded street corner we witnessed a fitting tribute to the amo-
rous generosity of the prewar U.S. sailor when a bevy of young girls
threw themselves on the car shouting, "Hey Joe, Meg Wa (American) can do for free." Old and young, rich and poor turned out to
greet us. And here and there sullen and armed Japanese pushed their
domineering way through the crowds or drove into crowded throngs
on horseback injuring and scattering them.

Never, as long as I live, will I forget the look on the face of one
old Chinese woman who, broken and bent, lurched onto the running
board and rode for several blocks, combining the only three words
of English she apparently knew into an inane and joyous litany,

"Hello—thank you." "Hello—thank you," "Hello—thank you." It was almost as though this woman, in her withered cackle, was providing the symbolic lyrics for the stark melody of the multitude.

We reached the building on Yu Yuan road and met Commander Heagy—the flag "lieutenant" for the Admiral. Here then was the first contact—the meeting of East and West—the joining of the foremost rivulets—preceding the two vast rivers of men and equipment which, leaving America, had fought their opposite ways around the world. The one through India over the Hump into China and across that tortured land. The other through all the famous mileposts of the Pacific. And with our handshakes, like the golden spike that joined the Transcontinental Railroad, the rivers met and the old job ended, giving way to new, less tragic ones.

Commander Heagy is one of those military characters who seems to spring up to fill unique posts just where they are most needed. An old Navy pharmacist, enlisted twenty-eight years ago, he had gone on to become a Warrant Officer. As a hobby during all those years, he had tinkered with radio, becoming so expert that he was listed by the Office of Strategic Services on their card file as an outstanding authority. When Admiral Miles was given the job of picking his guerillas, he went through the files and selected this man to be his "fly by night" Communications Officer. For three long years this man of fifty years had endured all the hardships of Chinese guerilla warfare, rising to the rank of lieutenant commander—still listed in the non-military branch of the service, the Hospital Corps.

He talked to us, learned our story, and rapidly became a good friend to us. He took us to see the Admiral's Flag Secretary—a Captain Bouman. The two of them ordered Japanese beer for all of us and we told our story a second time. By this time evening was over and the YMS skipper was obviously as eager as I was to get away to return to our vessels lest they be in trouble with the Japanese at the docks.

Nothing would do but that we all load into cars—they were impressed with our Hirohito-given vehicle—and go to see the Admiral's number two man—Navy Captain Byersly. This stern but kindly officer was so surprised and pleased to see us that we were immediately taken to see the Admiral.

Admiral Miles was comfortably ensconced in a huge manor appropriated from a Japanese overlord.

Sent to China in 1941 as a full Commander, this officer was instructed to organize the whole of Western China into guerilla units, using Navy personnel to train and lead them. For the next four years he and his men carried on in "Lawrence of Arabia" fashion, being responsible for 70 percent of the effective guerilla activities.

He offered us our first Scotch in months. When we pointed out that we were in a duty station, the Admiral replied that there were tears in his eyes and he couldn't see what we should do with the drinks.

Here finally we were able to point out the explosive situation at the dock. Instantly sizing up the situation, the Admiral ordered all the enlisted men in Shanghai to be rushed down to the docks to guard us. Having heard me mention a Lieutenant Commander, two Captains, and one Admiral, you must have the impression that the town was jammed with Americans. However, only the top echelon had arrived, consisting of thirty-odd officers and fifty men, all of whom had been kept well secluded to prevent accidents.

Here then was a moment for decision. With two ships to be protected or left to the Japanese, the solution had to be bluff. I don't believe that the Japanese ever discovered that the fifty guards who reinforced our fifteen sailors were 100 percent of the naval personnel in Shanghai.

The Admiral further ordered us to give 50 percent of our crew liberty each day. We were to remain in armed bands and to let everyone know the Navy was in town. This was carried out with great zest. There was reason to believe that Japanese bigshots might be on the ship disguised as ordinary seamen since several had disappeared about that time. Accordingly, we were to shift down the river early next morning to a dock which was to be taken over that day by the Chinese from the Japanese.

We left the Admiral, sped back through the crowds to the dock to find that there had been considerable excitement in our absence. As soon as we had left, the Japanese presented a demand to my executive officer that the *Ataka* crew be allowed to go on liberty. Imagine the situation—the vanquished presenting terms to the victor. My executive officer felt pretty certain there would be a massacre if he gave a flat no and so he tempered with the answer that he would confer on the matter. As soon as the Japanese envoys left, he gathered up all the guns and men, lined up the Japanese on the weather deck and had all Americans withdraw to the YMS astern of the *Ataka.* That left the *Ataka* crew alone on their vessel under the three-inch guns of the YMS. It was a risky but good position. With all the Americans concentrated on the gunboat she was now able to fire into either the disarmed *Ataka* or the dock troop barracks. We had agreed on this ahead of time knowing that if the Japanese on the *Ataka* tried to break away we would have to sink her and get away from the rifle fire of the barracks in a hurry.

I believe that another half-hour would have seen all hell break loose. We arrived with the extra guards just as the sides were all set to go.

About two hours later as we were preparing our supper, we were amazed to see the Admiral drive onto the dock. It is characteristic of the man that he came in full uniform, a beautiful target for all those who had been seeking him for months. He inspected our ship, ate some spam with us, appropriated a couple of hara-kiri knives and samurai swords and then, satisfied that we were secure, he departed.

Next morning we slipped the cables from the dock, swung the ship around, and went back down the river one mile to a big Japanese dock famous amoung merchant seamen—NYK or Wayside Wharf. Our orders had been to get there early and that the Chinese would have seized the dock and posted guards. We coasted our 1200 tons of river craft gently alongside a dock that had only Japanese on it —regular army troops. Had we been veterans of China, we would have known that early morning is about noon.

At any rate there was no choice but to seize the dock ourselves. I ordered the skipper of the YMS to give me one officer and twelve men (he had followed us down the river). I took three sailors from my prize crew. We deployed as follows.

Ten of us took the three-story Godown (Chinese for warehouse) which had a thousand beautiful windows for snipers. The others took the two-story shed—open toward the river. We disarmed a total of forty-five Japanese soldiers and collected them on the dock under the *Ataka* crew's guns. They had hidden in niches all over the area and had to be dug out. We learned later that they had expected to be ordered to resist. As a matter of fact, one Army officer jumped up and attempted to use his sword on me. Before I could shoot him, the priceless sailor from Texas knocked him down—to make the second time he had saved me.

Just after we finished the job of disarming and had posted our own guards on the gate of the stockade around the docks, the Japanese Army sent two powerful automobiles with envoys to demand that we release the Army troops. The guard had allowed one car with one envoy to pass through with his armed chauffeur. They drove onto the dock next to the ship. The envoy, an Army captain bedecked in full regalia including Luger pistol and samurai sword, stalked up the gangway demanding to see the Captain of the *Ataka*. I came out to see him. On hearing his truculent demands made in the presence of many of our Japanese prisoners, it became obvious that much depended on the quota of "face" with which we should come out of the conference. Accordingly, the following episode occurred. I reached for his pistol and took it, handing it to one of our sailors. The other hand spun him around the gangway. Using the grip on the seat of his pants, I rooster-walked him onto the dock. The story to tell it sounds much like that of a bully but you must consider that he, a gamecock dandy in all his military regalia, posed a challenge which couldn't be overlooked if our minority control in the Japanese area was to be maintained. It was the CO that he had demanded to see. It had to be the CO who degraded him. We were on our own in this part of Shanghai. The handful of American guerillas were five miles away in Frenchtown (French Concession). Only 3000 Chinese soldiers were in town and those were pitifully armed. One of my sailors, again Rufus Fowler, the Texan, followed me with a Tommy gun. When we reached the Japanese driver, obviously aghast at the treatment his lord was receiving, he suddenly raised a pistol and pointed it at me. In my novel situation, with both hands in use holding Mr. Tojo off the deck by pulling on his trouser seat, my only defense was to raise him in front of me as a shield which you can bet I did in negative time. In the quickest reflex action, Rufus ducked around the car unseen by the driver who was trying to get a shot at me without creating a blowhole for the divine winds through his master's chest. Using his submachine gun as a lance, he lunged into the driver from the rear, knocking him out and giving me my third excuse to wonder at the benevolence of Providence.

The dock, which we had captured, became Naval Operating Base, storage center for tons of gear and barracks center for many men, and the Americanized *Ataka* was a forerunner of a marvelous medley of ships tied up to her dock.

Then we carried out the last phase of the Admiral's orders. We took our first real liberty in eighteen months. Shanghai base was selling liquor diluted with everything imaginable. We took a couple of quarts of special stuff from the *Ataka*. We each tucked a bundle of money under our arms—about 2,600,000 Chinese dollars apiece ($20 U.S.) and away we went—two officers and eight men in a train of two-man pedicabs. The two officers wore 45s as protection for the gang.

As we drove the mile and one half down Yangtzepoo Boulevard

leading into the Bund, I passed in rapid succession a beautifully decorated Chinese wedding procession with a gorgeous bedecked bride riding in a sedan-type, lace-draped carriage; a coolie lying dead from starvation on the sidewalk; a Japanese mule train with a hundred well-armed soldiers; a thousand beggars; a well-dressed Chinaman in an expensive pedicab; a hundred Chinese prostitutes; a hundred Chinese street vendors selling from open hearths of coal the myriad doughy concoctions of starch ridden China; an opium den; a Chinese church. And as a measure of their respective frequency of occurrence, no one noticed the dead man—they all watched the bride.

Our marathon led us from place to place, through the old Chinese city, the English concession and back to the ship at four in the morning. We were met at the gangway by the remaining ensign who informed us that we had orders to get underway at first light for the Yangtze River mouth to rejoin our ships. The adventure appeared to be over.

Without an hour's sleep, we raised the Japanese at 0500 to commence the trip down the river.

Arriving at the outer anchorage at noon, I went aboard the *Robinson* to report to my Squadron Commander—a full Captain. I recommended that ships be sent to Shanghai as soon as reasonably safe from mines in order to alleviate the tense situation. We submitted a full report on this situation and on all the navigational dope for the two rivers. All this info was used, and the recommendation to rush ships in was taken. We were grateful to receive a "Well done" from the Squadron Commander.

Our next surprise was the receipt of orders to return to the *Ataka*, to prepare for returning to Shanghai in the early morning and to take Admiral Kinkaid up the river. He was to follow the *Ataka* in a YMS so that we could run mine interference for him.

The second lap of our adventure was uneventful. We tied up at our captured dock while the Admiral's YMS went downtown to the Customs Dock now guarded by Chinese.

Naval Operating Base (NOB) was in name only. No American forces had any trucks or cars because all of us had flown or sailed in hurriedly and lightly. It was obvious that during the hectic free-for-all interim, before the main body with all its jeeps and command cars and gasoline sailed up the river, it was a case of every unit for itself. Moreover, my *Ataka* was under orders to move further down river about five miles from Shanghai proper to the old Standard Oil docks on the uninhabited side of the river directly across from the Shanghai Power Company to supply protection to the Standard Oil Company and Shanghai Power Company officials—all of whom, recently released from Japanese prisons, were striving to put their respective companies back into operation and were subject to attack from Japanese and Chinese guerillas. The immediate problem was to work out a satisfactory system of quick transit so that our eighteen-man defense could aid both companies on opposite sides of the river.

We persuaded the Chinese to loan the *Ataka* a steamer about sixty feet long with a three foot draft. We broke in three of our Japanese engineers as engine crew for the launch. A Japanese quartermaster became helmsman, and two Japanese "deck apes" became line handlers.

Our sailors took turns acting as Captain of it, much to their delight. This launch made it possible to get from one bank to the other within five minutes. We learned the channel through the mud banks at the sides of the river so that before long we could come alongside docks on either side at full speed.

A day or two after we moved we learned that a particularly vicious garrison of Japanese about a mile from the Power Company had been left unmolested by the Chinese. You will remember that upon our arrival there were an estimated 150 Americans, 175,000 Japanese, and a few thousand Chinese troops in Shanghai. Each day the situation had eased as more Chinese were flown in and more Japanese disarmed. By now there were probably only 15,000 Chinese in town, but probably 40,000 Japanese had been disarmed. At any rate, there were many of the enemy still loose in our vicinity. This unit controlled several nice looking cars, one of which we decided could make a welcomed addition to the *Ataka* transportation pool.

In the dead of night I took my trusted bodyguard and friend, Rufus Fowler, and we stole away from the ship, dressed in Japanese raincoats. Skirting the Power Company, we came to a barricaded bridge guarding the camp.

We jabbered a Japanese word which we had learned in answer to a challenge from the guard, who opened the barricade gate and let us pass. We turned left along the canal which was lined with undergrowth and, as soon as out of sight and earshot of the bridge, cut to the right to the vehicle park.

Then came a half-hour of stumbling and fumbling while we examined each car for keys and gas or alcohol (sniff test). We finally ruled out all alcohol burners (very poor starters) and selected the only three gas burners. Of these, the newest was a 1940 Plymouth. None of the cars had keys. Over in a corner of the garage we found a mechanic sleeping. We awoke him, muzzled him and had him provide us with tools with which we cut the ignition wires and bypassed the key switch.

Just as we started the car, the mechanic whom we had counted on using as a hostage to get clear of the barricade broke away and ran. Fowler was driving and I was on the running board to do the shooting. I decided that the shooting of this particular Japanese would merely sound the alarm sooner than if we let him live to awaken the garrison himself. Accordingly, we executed the well known naval manuever of "getting the hell out of there." We figured we'd have to knock down the barricade with the car. Just as we were accelerating to do so, the guards swung open the gate and saluted smartly. Ten seconds later bullets were zinging overhead but fifteen seconds after that the car was outrunning them.

About a week after we first entered Shanghai, I was invited to a dinner party by a Navy lieutenant, ex-Chinese guerilla, who had met some members of the Russian community. The dinner was to be at the home of one of these Russian families. We drove out into the Russian district in two cars—Lieutenant Martin, Lieutenant Champe, yours truly, and a Russian boy whose name I won't attempt. We stopped in front of the Shanghai-type apartments which are right on the sidewalk facing toward an inner court.

We entered a room on the second floor above the court—a dining room empty of people but beautifully decorated. The table was covered with delicious and artistic Russian dishes—meats, liver paste, zakushka (salad), and a host of other preliminary dishes whose names I never learned.

No sooner had we absorbed the background of the setting when the Russians entered from another room. First, a stout and jovial looking man. Second, a tiny woman about the same age (forty-five) who walked with a regal manner as though a person of importance. After that came four girls. The first one was a gorgeous blonde, lithe and well-formed with a lovely soft complexion and the same air of regality—almost aloofness—as the older woman. The second one entered and my heart stood still. Here was a girl I shall never be able to describe completely. Tall and well-poised, she was smiling a smile of such radiance that the very room seemed suddenly transformed as though a fairy waving a brilliant wand had just entered the room.

I never saw the remaining two girls. This girl was, it developed, the hostess. There we stood, the four men arrayed in a line opposite those who had just entered. For a long moment there was utter silence. And then, as though to relegate the magic of the spell to a more subdued level, the one whom I shall call the Queen (the second girl) waved each member of the party to his seat. All this time I had stood staring, and it was perhaps for this that I was waved to a seat next to this young hostess. We sat down to the most memorable meal of my life. Dish after dish and course after course came by—so delicious that the mind refused to acknowledge the stomach's defeat. The men drank vodka and the women drank wine. After each course, a toast had to be prepared by a member in succession. The strength of the vodka was only overwhelmed by the size of the meal we had eaten.

After my preliminary dumbness, I opened a conversation with this girl who had struck me so. And as we talked I studied her. Beyond being pretty, she had a radiant air that was enchanting. She spoke English poorly with a delightful Russian accent and a too literal use of English phrases. For several weeks previous to our Shanghai visit, I had been studying Russian. I knew enough words to intrigue her into a discussion of the subject. It developed that she had instructed in the Russian language. She agreed to teach me. I learned that the older couple were her aunt and uncle; the blonde her cousin, and the other girls, their friends.

After the next to last course, the Russians have what is apparently a seventh-inning stretch during which the Russian boy opened an accordion. He played and sang a series of beautiful and poignant Russian songs. Then two of the girls did a lovely Russian folk dance.

This was the beginning of a new period for me. Each morning for ten days I came for an hour's Russian lesson. After that I was allowed a date at night. There was a picnic in Hungjau Park, a dance at the Russian Club, and many suppers at home. I learned more about the family. The girl was Mouza Coutelais-du-Roche. Her father, a French national, had come to Russia and married one Anna Mihailovna Habarova—a member of the White Russian society. Forced to flee during the Revolution, they had escaped over the border to settle down in Harbin, Manchuria, along with thousands of others. There a daughter, Mouza, was born in 1922. Harbin became a predominantly White Russian community. There people nearly all had recovered from poverty and gradually saved money which was invested well. They had nice homes, schools, churches, and lived an autonomous existence for many years. They were happy in this little bit of Russia they had recreated. In 1932 the Japanese moved in handling the Russians gingerly, not knowing the strength of the Soviet bear or her inclination to protect her people without a country. In 1940, just after Mouza graduated from high school, her mother was diagnosed as cancerous (stomach) and required an operation. Mouza brought her mother to Peking for an operation, leaving her father in Harbin. After the operation, they were sent to her mother's sister's home in Shanghai for better weather for recuperating. The operation was not successful. Her mother died a lingering death in 1941. By this time, Shanghai had been severed from the Manchuria connection by the war. For the next four years, Mouza was marooned from her father and to this day has not seen him. Her aunt and uncle cared for her.

Mouza's aunt was the wife of one Colonel Gorbunova in the Czar's Army. She saw him killed along with her brother in the Revolution and hated the Soviets with a venom in strange contrast to her usual demeanor. Her second husband, Mouza's uncle, was a young Captain in the Zabakailsky Cossacks. His wife was killed, his baby son taken from him never to be seen again, and he escaped to Shanghai. He is a wonderful old Rock of Gibraltar with a basic optimism that reminds me of you. He is a lover of music, speaks Chinese, Russian, English, Japanese, and a sprinkling of other tongues.

He loves to talk of the carefree Cossack days. He grew up in an area much like our dairy country which was in the vicinity of Lake Baikal. He lives content with the memories of the richness of that earlier life.

As the days wore on, Mouza and I saw more of each other. The pace grew faster—one hour, two hours, three hours each day. After five weeks, I asked her to marry me. After another two days, she agreed.

About a week before this important personal milestone, we witnessed a striking historic one—the fleet return to Shanghai. One cold morning we looked out from the decks of the *Ataka* and saw, stretching down the river as far as the eye could see, meandering like an apparition through the flat fields of the river basin, a grim grey dragon of masts and guns and superstructures. The fighting fleet was back. Driven from Shanghai in early 1941 by the vacillating directives of a confused democracy and later by the overwhelming force of surprise attack all the way to Guadalcanal, these powerful survivors of the long trek back were symbolically saying "We're here to stay." Among the sea monsters looking strangely out of their element in this narrow river was the *Robinson* with the sister ships of her division—*Saufley, Philip, Waller.* As she steamed by, we pulled a steam launch up beside her and stepped aboard to report to the Captain. It was a thrilling moment for all of us. We had our Japanese lined up at attention for the fleet.

Upon deciding to get married, we found that our troubles had just begun. Mouza is a member of the Russian Church which resembles our Catholic or Episcopalian service. The bishop subjected me to the works—everything but the third degree. I had to have two witnesses swear that they had known me for five years and that my family was respectable. Lieutenant Ed Martin and Lieutenant Commander Fairbrother of Los Angeles stretched the truth to attend to this. We then were to be required to wait for two weeks before the wedding could be held.

The American Consul pointed out that for visa purposes an American wedding ceremony would be more practical. We found a Presbyterian minister (just released) who was willing to perform the ceremony only if we were not married by the Russian Church before-hand. Both he and the church required a statement from the CO that permission was granted. The Captain said "NO!"

Some of my friends on the beach—the same ones who had been at the original dinner party and had served as witnesses later—framed a party to which we invited my CO and XO. It was a lovely affair at the Palace Hotel. I brought Mouza. Next morning the CO invited me up and said "Yes!"

At this happy point, the ship got orders to sail, presumably for the U.S. We turned the *Ataka* over to the Chinese as follows:

I had left the ship at 1000 to call on the Admiral and determine our status. At 1330 I met a Flag Lieutenant who informed me that Admiral Kinkaid himself was to be on board the *Ataka* at 1400 to turn it over to Admiral Chen of the Chinese Navy (the world's senior Admiral—having been Fleet Admiral for sixteen years). I had five miles of crowded traffic to drive through, a river to cross, and a ship to get ready in thirty minutes.

The ride that ensued was more frightening than the games of "ditch" we used to play in those plush high school days. Leaving a stream of scattering rickshas and pedicabs in our wake, we arrived at the Power Company in fifteen minutes. Our launch was not expecting me so I had to hop a sampan. Standing up like Washington crossing the Delaware (an ignominious version), I mused on the strange spectacle the two Admirals would see if they should arrive at that moment. Just after I arrived on board, they rounded the bend in their launch—the luck had held good. The "gang" had had all our gear removed to the launch; the ship was clean and bright. Everything was ready.

The bands played; Admirals spoke; sailors saluted; the U.S. flag came down; the Chinese flag went up; the U.S. crew marched off. The adventure was ended.

Being once more attached to the *Robinson* and no longer my own boss made planning more awkward. The wedding date was to be 1 November 1945. We were to sail 23 October. Finally, I talked the old Russian bishop into a special waiver on the two week wait and we scheduled the wedding for 22 October.

On the morning of the 22nd, the Chinese driver took me to Mouza's at 0800. We picked up a Russian priest and went to the cemetery for a traditional pre-marriage ceremony at the grave of the bride's mother. We then proceeded to the American Embassy where Dr. Boynton, a Presbyterian minister, married us in a brief, simple ceremony. My witnesses were F. M. Lalor, an Academy ensign, XO of the *Ataka,* and C. R. Fitzgerald, the Modesto sailor.

After the ceremony, the bride was taken away to prepare for the Russian wedding which was to be the real one for her. My best man, Lalor, and I went to Lieutenant Commander Champe's room at the Palace Hotel where most of the ship's officers collaborated in a diabolical attempt, safely thwarted, to have me drunk before the Russian ceremony.

At 1030 I left the hotel and proceeded to the Russian Church. As I stepped into the courtyard of the church, I was amazed to find about 100 sailors lined up in two ranks standing at attention. Our ship had 300 sailors on board. One hundred fifty were ashore each day. This meant that two-thirds of them had come to the wedding. I felt very honored at this and at the formation of honor. These men saluted each member of the ceremony as he passed through them— the Captain, the officer ushers, bridesmaids, bride, etc.

According to tradition, I entered the church portals alone with a bouquet in my hand. All the guests gathered within stood facing me. A carpet was placed for me to stand upon while a Russian choir sang for fifteen minutes. Next came the bridesmaids—with the bride being the last to enter on the arm of the best man. I met her at the portals, handing her the bouquet. She was dressed much like our American brides, only lovelier, of course. We faced the music which continued for another fifteen minutes.

This letter was mailed as a first installment. The second was to have completed the account of the wedding and reported on the honeymoon and my trip home, but one duty or another always interfered and I never wrote it. I do not repine about that. On the contrary, from my present vantage point in time I see that all the letter lacks is a short postscript:

P. S. I was wrong. The music never stopped.

CHAPTER 2

The Cutting of My Jib

Considering how consistently fulfilling my thirty-five years of naval service were, it is curious to remember that a yearning to be a professional sailor was not among the considerations that prompted my decision to seek admission to the Naval Academy in 1939. I was planning to be a doctor like both my parents, and I saw a term in the Navy as a useful and, if I was lucky, an adventurous prelude to a lifetime of practicing medicine in a small town. My father, whose World War I service as an Army doctor had been one of the memorable experiences of his life, had brought me up to consider it a duty to serve my country and to expect, besides, that there would be a great deal of fun in connection with performing it. Moreover, at the time of my graduation from high school in 1938, the European scene was dark enough to lead me to believe, along with most other people, that it was possible, if not probable, that the United States before long would be fighting a war.

Beyond those inducements to applying to the Academy, and doubtless more influential, was the attraction of finishing off my education at no expense. My family, though never in want, was not affluent. My school years had been the years of the Great Depression, and a country doctor of my father's school did not dun patients who were having difficulty in feeding, clothing, and sheltering themselves. A good many of his patients were in that fix. Our town, Tulare, in the San Joaquin Valley of California not only suffered the ills that afflicted agricultural communities everywhere during the thirties, but the extra ones brought by the arrival in the Valley of a large number of destitute "Okies," refugees from the Oklahoma Dust Bowl. On top of that, my mother, a pediatrician, contracted an incurable malignancy and the family's savings and a good deal of borrowed money as well were put into making the last agonizing months before she died in 1939 as easy on her as possible. And so, after a year at Rutherford Preparatory School in Long Beach had filled such gaps as Tulare High School had left in my secondary education, I took the competitive examination Senator Hiram Johnson sponsored each year for candidates for the service schools and won his appointment to the Naval Academy as a member of the Class of 1943.

I did reasonably well at the Academy. I finished in the top 5 percent of my class academically, and won two gold watches for public speaking. Militarily I ranked seventh, behind the regimental five-striper and five four-stripers. However, I have no recollection that my years there were especially thrilling. For one thing, the education the Academy offered did not impress me. It was a trade school rather than a college, and I did not emerge from it with a feeling of intellectual satiety, or even fulfillment, though I did have time to do a lot of reading. For another thing, the events in the outside world during those years were bound to pale anything that happened within academic walls. Germany invaded Poland early in my plebe year. France fell as that year was ending. The Battle of Britain was fought during the first part of my second year, and Germany attacked Russia at the end of it. And halfway through my third year, the Japanese bombed Pearl Harbor. As a result, the Class of '43 had no fourth year. To our delight, we went to sea in June 1942.

That my personal experiences in the war were marvelously exciting and romantic and that, in addition, I had reason to believe that I had some aptitude for a naval career no one who has read the first chapter of this book can doubt. Before the experiences that chapter relates, I had risen from ensign to full lieutenant, from a know-nothing assistant engineer whose chief petty officer had cautioned him to stay out of the engine room to Battle Evaluator, the third ranking officer of a destroyer. I had been in half a dozen major engagements, including the Battle of Savo Island, the Battle of Surigao Strait, and the invasions of Attu and Kiska in the Aleutians, during the last of which I had had the odd experience of being aboard the destroyer that led to the landing beach (fortunately unopposed due to a last-minute Japanese evacuation) the wave of boats carrying the field hospital in which my father was serving. Nevertheless, in each of the three years that followed the end of the war, I applied for admission to medical school and law school—for by now I was in doubt about which civilian profession to pursue. Each year I was accepted. And each year I postponed resigning from the Navy for one more year.

I suppose the most powerful argument against staying in the Navy was that doing so would inflict on a young wife totally unfamiliar with American ways, and on the children we started having in 1946, when Elmo III was born, the itinerant life and the long and frequent absences that are a condition of service. Economic calculations pulled in both directions: in the long run I would certainly earn more as a doctor or lawyer than as a naval officer, but in order to go to school I would have to give up such income as I had and at the same time contrive to support a growing family for at least three years. My personal predilections pulled in both directions: the enjoyment I derived from naval service was almost evenly balanced by my desire to follow in the professional footsteps of my parents. The state of the Navy pulled in both directions: it was obvious that serving in a peacetime Navy that was rapidly getting smaller and was the object of a decreasing amount of popular and official concern would not be the thrill that three years of triumphant wartime duty had been, yet it was precisely during this post-war letdown that the Navy needed most whatever talent and dedication I—or anyone—could give it. One strong force that pulled in only one direction, that of staying in, was the Soviet Union.

During the many hours of leisure aboard my destroyer during the last year of the war (leisure that was the product of the virtual annihilation of the Japanese Navy in the big battles of earlier years), I had started studying Russian and reading about Russia in as systematic a fashion as the books available in the western Pacific allowed. Then came my personal encounters in Shanghai with victims of the October Revolution, each of whom had vivid stories to tell. And when the war was over the Soviets, of course, did not follow the American policy of rapid and drastic demobilization, but maintained their armed strength and used it to turn the nations of eastern Europe into abject satellites. I concluded then that the USSR's purpose was to achieve world hegemony as soon as possible and as brutally as necessary, a purpose the United States and its allies could thwart only if they stayed militarily strong. In the years since I have not found cause to alter that conclusion. My conviction that the survival of our republic depends on its military strength always has been, as it was thirty years ago, what has chiefly motivated my career.

As often happens, the passage of time and a change of circumstances painlessly resolved the dilemma over which I had been fretting for three years. In 1948 I received my first shore assignment, as Assistant Professor of Naval Science in the ROTC program at the University of North Carolina. (The then Secretary of Defense, Louis Johnson, had decreed for reasons best known to himself that a tour of duty with the reserves was a prerequisite for promotion, so we all sought such hitherto unappealing billets eagerly.) Thus, after three years as the executive officer of the destroyers *Saufley* and then *Zellars,* years that had seen me away for long spells, leaving Mouza on her own, with her still imperfect English and incomplete acclimatization, in the Navy towns of Newport; Portland, Maine; New London; Portsmouth, Virginia; Norfolk, and Charleston, I was able to settle myself and my family into the pleasant university town of Chapel Hill, where for two years we were able both to lead the kind of family life that is taken for granted by most Americans and to broaden our social and intellectual horizons by daily contact with people whose interests and pursuits were much different from ours. In this unwontedly stable and relaxed environment I reviewed my career and discovered, somewhat to my surprise, that by now I was close to being a ten-year Navy veteran—counting the three years at the Academy. My professional achievements and standing were on a par with those of the most successful third of my class. And I enjoyed the life; the elements of order and clarity that inhere in military organization and military activity suited my personality. I suddenly realized how foolish it would be for me to trade away ten years of experience, a substantial fund of hard-won professional skill, a way of life that gave me great satisfaction, and a deep sense that what I was doing was important for a new career that, at best, could hardly be more rewarding except in a material way.

Any doubt I may have had still about remaining in the Navy vanished on a memorable day in 1950, which Mouza and I had the privilege of spending with General George C. Marshall and his wife at their home in Pinehurst. Our visit to the Marshalls had been arranged by a remarkable woman named Christina Wright, everybody's "Aunt Tina," and the real aunt of Caroline Caldwell who, with her professor husband Jim, was a Chapel Hill neighbor and good friend of ours. Aunt Tina was on cordial terms with an extraordinarily large number of notable people, and she apparently considered it an obligation to introduce to them youthful acquaintances of hers whom she thought might benefit from such encounters. General Marshall and I talked for several hours that day. I was in a pessimistic mood. Those were the days when Secretary Johnson was cutting the military budget to a level that made me feel that America's conventional fighting forces would have little chance of emerging victorious from the confrontation with the Soviets I considered an ever present danger. To make matters worse, the public evidently approved this course. I voiced my doubts and fears to General Marshall, who at the time was in temporary retirement between his tour as Secretary of State and his tour as Secretary of Defense. In reply, he spoke at length and in much detail of the amazing way the American people, apparently indifferent to the nation's military posture throughout the thirties, suddenly had sprung to life and in an incredibly short period of time done all the things that were necessary to turn back the challenge of Germany and Japan when the challenge had become plain to them. He said, "Young man, don't ever sell the American people short. They have vast reserves of hidden strength ready to use when the crisis is clear." He peered at me over his glasses and added, "And when that time comes your country will need dedicated career men like you." Obviously General Marshall did not mean that as an order, but I unreservedly and gladly took it as one.

During the next dozen years my career went well. I had three commands, first of a destroyer escort, then of a destroyer, then of a guided-missile frigate, the first ship of a new class. Between those assignments I spent a year at the Naval War College and had two fruitful tours in Washington, one in the Bureau of Personnel, the other mostly as the aide to the Assistant Secretary of the Navy for Personnel, so I was well up to speed on personnel matters. In pace with the leaders of my Academy class, I rose to the rank of captain. In appropriate contexts later in the book I shall touch on some of the highlights of those years. In this chapter my purpose is to sketch those few decisive experiences that made me the man I was when I became Chief of Naval Operations. Therefore I shall skip to 1962 when I was a student at the National War College in Washington and my work came to the attention of Paul Nitze, an individual with

whom I was to be associated intimately for the next three years as
an assistant and, I venture to say, working partner, and who has been
both my mentor and close friend ever since.

The most important piece of work each student has to do in the
course of his year at the National War College is to write a thesis
based on original research. I had maintained my interest in Soviet
affairs over the years and I chose as my subject "The Problem of the
Next Succession in the USSR." With a view toward illuminating the
dynamics of the struggle for power that was sure to occur when
Nikita Khrushchev died or retired or was deposed, I examined in as
much detail as available sources permitted the four-year struggle that
had occurred following Stalin's death in 1953 and the four-year
period of consolidation of Khrushchev's power that followed the
struggle. This research not only gave me an opportunity to do a great
deal of fascinating reading, but to engage in correspondence with
such eminent Sovietologists as Robert Conquest and Myron Rush,
and get to know Ambassadors Charles Bohlen and Llewellyn
Thompson, the American diplomats who knew the Soviet Union the
best. It is appropriate to note here that the opportunity the National
War College gives fairly senior military people to take a year off from
the daily pressures of operational or staff work and stretch their
minds in a reasonably leisurely and contemplative setting is of very
great benefit to them and to the country.

In any case, when my project was near completion my turn came
to speak to the student body about what I had been doing and what
I had found. As it happened, the day after I gave my talk, which was
extremely well received, Paul Nitze came to the college to deliver a
lecture. Except during the Eisenhower years, Nitze had occupied
policy-making positions in the Government since 1942, when he left
the investment banking firm of Dillon Read & Company to work for
the Board of Economic Warfare. At the time I am writing of he was
Assistant Secretary of Defense for International Security Affairs, the
Defense official directly responsible for liaison between State and
Defense and for dealing with other governments on matters affecting
security and defense. The day of his War College lecture, Secretary
Nitze reported to the College's commandant and was rather annoyed, he said later, that the commandant showed less interest in
discussing his imminent performance than in telling him about my
presentation of the previous day. Always on the watch for people
who might strengthen his staff, Paul instructed his executive assistant to review my record and on the basis of the resulting evaluation

—without ever interviewing me—offered me a position in ISA. The Navy's mind set then, and I fear to a large extent even today, was that working in ISA was not especially "career enhancing," to use a much-used Service phrase. No job under civilians was considered to be. The most prized Pentagon assignments were in "Op-06," the division of the CNO's staff that dealt with plans and policy. The next most prized were in "J-5," the division of the Joint staff responsible for the same area, where I was slated to go after War College. After those two, numerous Navy and Joint Staff jobs had more prestige than ISA. Consequently, when my detailer—the officer in BuPers responsible for helping me manage my career—sent for me and told me about Secretary Nitze's request for me, he urged me strongly not to go to ISA. However, I had been a detailer myself some years before, and I had also worked for civilians, and on the basis of those experiences I had arrived at much different priorities than the conventional ones. By pulling a tactful string or two in the upper reaches of BuPers, I managed to override my detailer's objection and go with Paul.

I have never made a better decision. Under the tutelage of Paul Nitze I earned what I think of as a Ph.D. in political-military affairs. When I first went to work for him I was one of a number of efficient and rising young officers with a keen interest in the world's power relationships and a bent for strategic analysis. When I left him I had firsthand experience of how political-military affairs were managed, conceptually and tactically, at the top level of government. I was at Paul's side during the Cuban missile crisis, in whose management he played a leading part, during the negotiations that led to the Nuclear Test Ban Treaty, in which he was a central figure also, and in half a dozen other important, if less dramatic, situations. As far as I know, this experience was unique among naval officers of my generation—though in the Army Alexander Haig was having a similar one. It could not have been surpassed as a preparation for the duties I was to assume subsequently as a member of the Joint Chiefs of Staff and as principal naval advisor to the President.

When I reported to International Security Affairs in August 1962, I was made the desk officer for France, Spain, and Portugal. It was a good introduction to the work at ISA, familiarizing me with the always delicate subject of U.S. naval and air bases in Spain and Portugal and with the inner dynamics of our rather stiff relations with France, particularly with respect to nuclear matters. As I have said, Secretary Nitze drew me into the center of the work on the

Cuban missile crisis when it developed in October, and thereafter I continued to be his Cuba contingency planner. In addition, because my year of research at the War College had given me some insight into the moods and intentions of the Soviet leadership, and when his better trained Soviet analyst Colonel Tom Wolfe of the Air Force was not available, Paul consulted with me often about what their latest actions or utterances might portend for the United States. Meanwhile Paul had promoted me, within a few weeks of my arrival in ISA, to Director of the Arms Control Division in ISA, a surprising testimonial to his confidence in me, since the job usually was reserved for a flag officer. Arms control was a particularly live issue at that time. Not only were years of negotiations with the Russians on the subject finally producing tangible results in the form of the Nuclear Test Ban Treaty, signed 5 August 1963, which outlawed all nuclear tests except underground ones, but this success had raised hopes that progress toward arms reduction might be possible. Within the Government there was much discussion of this subject, and many more or less analytical papers were written. I venture to include in the "more" category a study Paul Nitze and I collaborated on and circulated in October of 1963, "Considerations Involved in a Separable First Stage Disarmament Agreement." ("Separable First Stage Disarmament" presently became known by the less forbidding name of "Strategic Arms Limitation," whence, by adding "Talks," came the acronym SALT.) Because I think it stands up well even after thirteen years of dramatic arms buildups and dramatic arms-limitation negotiations, and because it presents the philosophy that underlay my arguments and actions about arms limitation during my four years as a member of the Joint Chiefs of Staff, I shall quote a few brief excerpts from that paper here. Its opening words are still cogent:

> The discussion within the Administration concerning a Separable First Stage Disarmament Agreement (hereafter referred to as SFSDA) has been unsatisfactory because the parties to the debate have started from divergent positions. One school has tended to look at the problem primarily from the standpoint of what appears to be negotiable with the Soviets judged primarily in the context of the Geneva negotiations [the Eighteen Nation Disarmament Conference] or, if not negotiable, of what would have favorable propaganda implications for the United States. Another school has become convinced that none of the Separable First Stage proposals so far suggested are to the U.S. interest but has tried to accommodate (within the limit that no such SFSDA be actually agreed

to) to the propaganda demands of our situation at Geneva. A third school has held that the USG should seek out and analyze the substantive elements of potentially desirable SFSDAs, ones the U.S. could live with, before considering the tactical and propaganda issues of negotiation (whether at Geneva or in other forums). This paper endeavors to continue the evaluations of the third school.

The last words of the paper also are to the point:

> Whether great power rivalry is yet . . . susceptible to amelioration and sublimation—even though the impulse for common interest . . . settlements is certainly increasing in the kind of world we live in—remains moot. This paper attempts to raise the issues, decision on which is necessary for the conduct of those negotiations required to determine whether that rivalry can be circumvented. Nothing in this paper should give cause for great optimism. But the problems delineated should not be a cause for undue pessimism or abatement of our efforts. The seventeen years of apparently meaningless propaganda exchanges in the arms control field finally gave birth to two arms control agreements. The fact that these agreements came about at a time when political détente suited the needs of the Soviet leadership should not obscure the fact that a great body of common language and dogma in the arms control field made it possible for relatively quick agreement when the political circumstances were appropriate. A future struggle to succeed Khrushchev could well result in the seizure of arms control issues by one of the aspiring lieutenants as a tool for the winning of possible support necessary to achieve power. Or increasing problems in the allocation of economic resources or with the Chinese Communists could drive the Soviet leadership toward the accepting of such packages. The detailed, painstaking, yearslong spelling out of the details of a mutually acceptable first stage agreement with the USSR . . . should continue.

Between the paper's opening and closing paragraphs were many pages of detailed consideration of the tradeoffs among numbers, sizes, yields, and deployments of weapons, strategic and tactical, nuclear and conventional, that might be in the interest of the United States. For as the opening paragraph just quoted states, and as I continue to believe, until the United States arrives at well-considered positions about what is safely negotiable and what is not, negotiations are bound to be unproductive at best and counter-productive at worst. In those pages of analysis, just one sentence is underlined, and if its advice had been heeded, the strategic arms agreement with the Soviets we are living with today might have been far less prejudicial to U.S. interests than I believe it to be: *"Control over super-weapons . . . seems indicated."* I shall have a good deal more to say on this subject of the Soviets' great advantage over us in missile throw weight in those parts of this book that discuss the progress of SALT during my term as Chief of Naval Operations.

In the early fall of 1963 Fred Korth resigned as Secretary of the Navy and President Kennedy nominated Nitze to replace him. Three members of the Senate Armed Services Committee, Barry Goldwater, Strom Thurmond, and the late Harry F. Byrd, took extreme offense at this nomination for reasons I have never altogether understood. I assume a principal one was that Paul had been associated closely for many years with Dean Acheson, a mighty cold warrior but a man those particular Senators nevertheless could not forgive for "losing China" and for saying he "would not turn his back" on Alger Hiss. It seemed that there might be a nasty confirmation fight. Paul had signified that he would like me to come with him as his executive assistant and naval aide in his new job. Consequently two of Secretary of Defense Robert McNamara's associates, whom he had detailed to try to push through Nitze's nomination, consulted with me about how to do it. Their notion was to take on the three objecting Senators publicly and vigorously. However, they wanted soundings taken in the committee first to make sure that that was a promising tactic. They asked me to take those soundings. It was unusual and very likely inappropriate to request a Navy captain to get that deeply into partisan politics, but I was eager enough to see Nitze heading up the Navy to accede to it without reluctance. I am particularly glad I did because that was the occasion when I first met Henry Jackson, who knew and admired Nitze and whom I called on as the man most likely to give me the advice we sought. We have been good friends ever since; I have always found his grasp of military-political issues to be the surest of any senator's, and I shall always be grateful for the advice and support he gave me and the Navy during my term as CNO. He was as sensible as usual at that first meeting. He said that the votes to confirm Paul were there and that there was no use stirring up the three dissenters. He advised me instead to collect affidavits from all those who were in a position to defend Paul Nitze from thoroughly unfounded charges, which affidavits Senator Jackson could put in the record, together with a strong supporting speech at the strategic moment. Shortly after the nomination had gone to the Senate, President Kennedy was killed, and the Committee chairman, the late Richard Russell, who reportedly sympathized with the opposition to Nitze, sat on the nomination for a time. But presently Lyndon Johnson made one of his highly successful telephone calls to Russell, and the Committee approved the nomination with only Goldwater, Thurmond, and Byrd voting "Nay," just as Jackson had predicted. The Senate immediately ratified the action of the Committee. That was my first involvement with what the bureaucracy grandly calls "legislative affairs." I was to have many more.

As a rule the Secretary of the Navy mostly concerns himself with personnel administration, weapons development, procurement, budget-making, and Congressional relations. Matters of strategy and crisis management are the realm of the Secretary of Defense and his Assistant Secretaries and of the Joint Chiefs of Staff, and routine, day-by-day naval matters that of the Chief of Naval Operations. The managerial side of the Navy was one I had little experience with and I welcomed the opportunity to acquire so much so fast. Like the ISA work, it gave me a background that was of immense value to me when I became CNO. Moreover the McNamara years were unusually interesting ones in which to be in a Service Secretary's office, because Secretary McNamara used his Service Secretaries pretty much as Assistant Secretaries of Defense for their military departments. He involved them in strategic and operational matters beyond their normal administrative roles. For example, when Fidel Castro cut off the water of the naval base at Guantanamo, McNamara, through Nitze, sent me down there with orders to produce within seventy-two hours a U.S. plan for retaliation and logistics independence.

In addition to teaching me everything they did, my three years with Nitze changed my working habits—or compulsions—for the better or the worse, depending on your point of view. I had always worked long hours, but I had also led an active social and family life. The association with Paul, by showing me how much people working at the top of their bent could accomplish, gave me an insatiable appetite for work. It was in those years that I began bringing home full briefcases almost every night and poring over their contents instead of going to parties, that I began to spend more Saturdays at the office than with Mouza and the four children, Elmo, Jimmy, Ann, and five-year-old Mouzetta, as we called little Mouza. In this respect, too, I was in training for CNO, though of course I was not aware of it at the time. A CNO cannot avoid working twelve- to sixteen-hour days—six days a week if he's lucky and seven if he's not.

The final benefit Paul Nitze conferred upon me, and it was no small one, was the two stars of a rear admiral two years earlier than the members of my class technically became eligible for promotion to flag rank. Normally before a captain is selected for flag rank he must have had a capital command—generally a destroyer squadron or perhaps a cruiser in the case of a surface sailor like me. (Aviators get the carriers.) However, Paul wrote a final fitness report about me that described my service with him in such laudatory terms and so strongly recommended that the capital command tradition be waived in my case that it persuaded the selection board (the board gave the same waiver to two other officers) to give me my stars in July 1965. Because rotation between staff and operational billets is part of the routine of a military career, that promotion sent me to San Diego in September as the commander of a cruiser/destroyer flotilla in the First Fleet, a tour that was cut short in 1966 when Paul and the CNO, Admiral David MacDonald, set up a Division of Systems Analysis in the Navy and called me back to Washington to head it.

If the years with Nitze greatly expanded my intellectual scope and sharpened my administrative skills, the command of the naval forces in Vietnam, which I was given in 1968 along with a third star of a vice admiral, matured and molded me in an equally significant and perhaps more fundamental way. For one thing it gave me the opportunity to work intimately with the late General Creighton Abrams, the most impressive military man I ever have been professionally associated with. For another it enabled me to become personally acquainted with hundreds, if not thousands, of fighting sailors at a time when being a fighting man entailed not only facing the fire of the enemy in the field but the indifference or even the contempt of an all too large segment of the public at home. The profound and indelible feelings of fellowship, admiration, and respect the performance and sacrifices of those men inspired in me had much to do with the "Mod Navy" I strove for as CNO. I often thought of my efforts to improve the Navy's relationship with its people as a testimonial to these courageous men and women. Beyond these important influences on me, a fighting command is the ultimate test of how good at his profession any professional soldier or sailor is. The Compleat Admiral should be able to conduct in action the campaign he has planned at his desk. The ability to motivate, direct, and control men and women in situations of stress and danger is the quality above all others the nation needs and looks for in its military leaders. And so I welcomed the assignment to Vietnam as an essential step forward in my profession. I welcomed it also because I had strong convictions about the nature of the American involvement in Vietnam that I hoped I could translate into action there.

The issue of large-scale involvement of American fighting forces in Vietnam first had arisen in the government in a major way in 1964, when I was working for Paul Nitze in the Navy Secretariat. At the time I, like Paul, was a "dove" in the sense that I opposed massive American intervention on the ground in southeast Asia. We argued that, undesirable as a Communist takeover of the whole of Vietnam surely was, it did not pose an immediate or direct threat to the safety of the United States, nor did we have a treaty, or any other commitment to fight for South Vietnam, that would make a failure to send troops a failure to keep a promise. We argued that if a Presidential decision were to be made to assist South Vietnam in a major way, it should be through sea and air forces mostly, with only a small number of advisory ground troops. We argued further that the rules of engagement, if we did provide large-scale help on the ground, almost certainly would preclude major ground action north of the Demilitarized Zone and thus would make a decisive victory over the North Vietnamese unlikely. Under all those circumstances we considered it highly imprudent to embark on an enterprise that might drain a substantial portion of the military strength of the United States at a time when the USSR was furiously building up its own. Paul presented all those arguments on more than one occasion to his superior, Robert McNamara.

Between 1964 and 1968 the war in southeast Asia, as we had feared it would, indeed did gobble up many of the resources the Services needed to keep up to date. The Navy not only obsolesced, but lost a significant portion of the forces it needed to control the seas, particularly anti-submarine vessels, planes, and weapons of many sorts. The delivery of air strikes against targets in Vietnam and Laos was what the war demanded insatiably of the Navy and it had to concentrate its resources on the attack carriers and their escorts and planes that were needed for those strikes. Thus, in addition to the sorrow every American felt over the casualties, the destruction, and the political rancor that the war had wrought, I had a professional motivation for wanting to see America's commitments to Vietnam reduced. And of course by the fall of 1968, when I arrived in Vietnam, those commitments, which had been tenuous in 1964, were enormous and inescapable. We had made reiterated and solemn pledges of support to the government of South Vietnam and as a result we shared with it the responsibility for the fate of some seventeen million Vietnamese. Moreover, our allies, though some of them found it politically prudent to decry publicly U.S. involvement in southeast Asia, privately made it clear that they would be extremely distressed if we "bugged out" and abandoned an ally. Yet anti-war sentiment at home, on the eve of a presidential election, was strong and getting stronger. Under the circumstances, the program that Secretary of Defense Melvin Laird later was to call "Vietnamization," turning over to the South Vietnamese as much of the war as possible as soon as was consistent with military effectiveness, seemed to be the only way to disengage honorably. And indeed shortly after I arrived in the country, President Johnson called General Abrams home to instruct him to get just such a program under way. Vietnamization is generally thought of as an initiative of the Nixon Administration, but in fact Lyndon Johnson ordered the first steps in that direction just before he relinquished the presidency.

Nothing could have suited my own inclinations more than Vietnamization. Very soon after I took over the command my colleagues and I devised a program I called ACTOV, a labored acronym for Accelerated Turnover to Vietnam that I chose because it sounded like "active," which was what I wanted the program to be. However, my desire to turn the in-country U.S. naval operation over to the Vietnamese was accompanied by an equally strong desire to increase the scope and effectiveness of that operation. I had nothing to do, of course, with the air sorties being flown off the Navy carriers in the Gulf of Tonkin. Those activities were conducted by the Seventh Fleet, whose commander reported to the Commander in Chief Pacific Fleet. As Commander Naval Forces, Vietnam, I reported to CinCPacFlt with regard to purely naval matters, but I was the operational subordinate of General Abrams. My command had no carriers or submarines or destroyers. It was made up mostly of small craft that patrolled coastal waters, rivers, and canals. Its primary mission was to interdict water-borne infiltration of troops and supplies from North Vietnam into South Vietnam. An important secondary mission was to give whatever support it could to Army operations in the watery terrain of the Mekong River delta.

By the time I arrived on the scene, the interdiction mission had pretty much been accomplished as far as the coast and the main branches of the Mekong were concerned. Since 1965 the Navy had been conducting an operation code-named Market Time, whose essence was to maintain three barriers to infiltration from the sea. Farthest out, 100 to 150 miles offshore, was an air barrier set up by big, long-range patrol planes flying out of Vietnam and the Philippines. They were part of the Seventh Fleet but they came under ComNavForV's operational control while participating in Market Time. Closer in was an outer surface barrier that generally consisted of six or eight medium-sized ships—destroyer escorts, minesweepers, Coast Guard cutters, LSTs, and the like—also assigned by the Seventh Fleet to ComNavForV for Market Time. Finally there was an inshore barrier maintained by about 100 heavily armed, 50-foot aluminum PCFs, known as "swift boats." Early on those three barriers cut down to a trickle the flow of supplies by sea to the delta, where the Viet Cong were furthest away from the stockpiles in the north. The Communists thereupon resorted to a readily available, if slower and more arduous, alternate route: down the Ho Chi Minh Trail through Laos and Cambodia to the Mekong and then down the Mekong's main branches into the delta. We had responded effectively to this with "Game Warden," an operation that sent into the Mekong a fleet of little 28-foot fiberglass PBRs, which carried grenade launchers, .50 caliber machine guns and four-man crews armed with M-16 rifles; plenty of fire power to handle most rivercraft carrying supplies.

I inherited one other operation in the delta, which, unlike the plains and mountains north of Saigon, was a countryside where boats could play a significant part in the fighting, being intersected by the many branches and tributaries of the Mekong, crisscrossed with canals and dotted with swamps. That operation was a sort of transportation and escort service for the Army's 9th Division, which had the formidable assignment of searching out and destroying enemy concentrations in the delta's treacherous terrain. The Navy's Mobile Riverine Force had a substantial number of old LCMs, shallow-draft landing craft with armored sides, each of which could carry upward of fifty infantrymen in its well deck. It had modified those LCMs in several ways. Some had flat fronts with big guns on them, 40-millimeter machine guns or 105-millimeter howitzers. Some were crammed with communications equipment. Some had little flattops that could hold medical evacuation helicopters. Eight or ten of these, escorted by an appropriate number of PBRs, made a sort of mini-armada that could carry perhaps 500 9th Division troops to remote locations, give them heavy artillery support as they landed and withdrew, and provide them with far better command, control, and communications than they could possibly have carried on their backs.

I think the reader will have gathered from these brief descriptions of some of the Navy's activities in Vietnam that conducting riverine ("brown water") warfare requires ingenuity and improvisation. There is no body of accepted doctrine on the subject; the Naval Academy does not offer courses in it; indeed there is little empirical experience from previous wars to draw upon. You have to make up riverine warfare as you go along.

I was fortunate to have on my staff just the man I most needed to help me find places in Vietnam where the Navy could make contributions. Captain Rex Rectanus, then my Assistant Chief of Staff, Intelligence, and now a Vice Admiral and Deputy Assistant Secretary of Defense for Intelligence, one of the few three-star intelligence specialists in naval history, had been in the country for several months before I arrived. He had completed an analysis of the entire Viet Cong logistics system that proved to be more accurate than anything either CIA or DIA had. He was the first person to conclude that Cambodia had become the major logistics depot for the Viet Cong delta operations and that this depot was being reinforced by Communist shipping into Sihanoukville and then by truck to the Cambodian border. Just across the border was an interconnecting series, almost a network, of streams and canals that extended some 250 miles from Tayninh south to where the Cambodian "Parrot's Beak" juts into Vietnam, then southwest to the Gulf of Siam. Since we had choked off the main rivers, all supplies and reinforcements from the Ho Chi Minh Trail to the Viet Cong in the delta were ferried across or sometimes even carried on those remote waterways. I saw no reason why some combination of our versatile assortment of small craft could not penetrate them, perhaps even carrying South Vietnamese or 9th Division troops, and at worst force the Communists to bring in their supplies overland on their backs, which would make the exercise a great deal slower and more difficult. I tried my ideas out on Major General (later Lieutenant General) Julian Ewell, a brilliant tactician who commanded the 9th Division. His reaction was favorable. We conducted our penetration in several stages; the first major one we called Giant Slingshot. The key was to establish in this hostile territory a series of little bases where a few dozen men could eat and sleep and where fuel, ammunition, and spare parts for up to four dozen boats could be stored. There were considerable risks in this operation and indeed during the first stages of Giant Slingshot, casualties ran at the unwontedly high rate for the Navy of 6 percent a month. However, by dint of sailors adopting some of the routine of ground troops, like standing perimeter guard and sometimes foregoing hot food and dry beds, we did manage to seize about 2000 tons of Viet Cong supplies and greatly reduced the Communists' control of a piece of country where they had been traditionally unchallenged. By the spring of 1969, the Navy was blockading the entire river-and-canal system along the Cambodian border and as a result, General Abrams told me, Viet Cong activity in the delta was much reduced and overall U.S. casualties were considerably reduced.

Another place where Rex and I thought the Navy was uniquely suited to play a part was on the Cau Mau Peninsula, a place of streams and mangrove swamps, hard to get to and even harder to get into, at the extreme southern tip of Vietnam. For years the Viet Cong had been using the peninsula as a sort of surge tank, taking sanctuary there when our forces in the neighboring areas of the delta had the upper hand and sallying forth when the fortunes of war shifted. The U.S. command had regarded the peninsula as so irremediably enemy country that it had evacuated as many of the inhabitants as possible and then bombed it with B-52s. As a result a normally fertile and industrious region was virtually without activity. It occurred to me that if the Navy could gain control of a section of the principal river in the area, it might be possible for a resettlement effort to begin on the river banks and gradually spread up and downstream and inland as the foothold expanded. The local Army judged a riverside base in that part of the country to be foolishly risky so I hit upon the expedient of setting a base up on pontoons anchored in midstream. The local Army people judged that to be even more foolishly risky but General Abrams, overruling the IV Corps Senior Advisor, approved it. From Sea Float, as we called it, swift boats and PBRs could range up and down the river and it had a pad for helos as well. We supported it with three-inch gunboats so it had sufficient fire power to dominate the river banks on both sides to a distance of several miles. It was protected from mines floated downstream or swimmers carrying demolition charges by nets and various warning devices. We defeated several enemy attempts to destroy Sea Float. Under Sea Float's protection, resettlement did begin. Pineapples were planted once again, pottery kilns were rebuilt, shrimping and fishing began anew, and more and more old inhabitants returned to the area. The memorandum slips I used in Vietnam to pass along to my staff ideas that I thought would expedite the U.S. departure from Vietnam and that I wanted to have investigated were headed "ZWI" for "Zumwalt's Wild Ideas." Sea Float was one of my favorite ZWIs and I visited it every month or so, often bringing with me an Army or Air Force bigwig who had expressed skepticism about the practicality of such a venture.

However, of all the pieces of work I participated in in Vietnam, the one closest to my heart was ACTOV; indeed I am as proud of it as of anything I have ever done. A chief source of my satisfaction is that the program was not a mere exercise in military planning and operation, but was effective principally because it combined the military elements with improvised social action of many kinds. The first requisite for its success was for the Americans connected with it to believe in it. This meant a concerted attempt to obliterate an all too prevalent notion that the Vietnamese were congenitally incapable of operating or maintaining mechanical equipment or mastering military tactics or preserving discipline. Beyond this general but all-important attitudinal effort the program contained a number of features that I like to think were innovative, or at any rate uncommon.

We devised an English curriculum that in a matter of weeks equipped thousands of Vietnamese sailors with enough language to work side by side in boat crews with Americans. (We taught the Vietnamese English rather than teach Americans Vietnamese because Commodore Tran Van Chon, the Commander of the Vietnamese Navy, looked on his Navy as an international service and wanted the men and women in it to speak an international language.)

We established a small facility for building ferro-cement boats and taught the Vietnamese to use it, thus giving their Navy a capability to replace small craft over the long haul. (The sea worms in the coastal waters off Vietnam will rot a wooden boat inside of five years no matter what kind of paint is applied to the wood.) The first boat the Vietnamese built was an exact copy in ferro-cement of one of their wooden junks, huge keel and all. It worked out fine, though later they designed a somewhat more manageable "coastal raider" to replace their wooden junks.

We initiated a rather intensive sensitivity training program for both American and Vietnamese sailors to ensure that when Vietnamese joined the crews of American boats—and their doing so one at a time was the heart of our technique for turning over the boats to the Vietnamese—each party understood the culture and habits of the other well enough to minimize the possibility of personal conflicts based on unfamiliarity or misunderstanding.

We built homes and provided subsistence for the families of Vietnamese sailors at the little coastal or riverside bases I have already mentioned. One part of this effort was a pilot "long-line" program for fishing the rich coastal waters. Another was a "pigs-and-chickens" program that involved, among other things, bringing a large number of brood sows into Vietnam from the Philippines. The first two were named "Chon" and "Zumwalt." I was flattered, of course, though I'd rather my namesake had been a boar.

ACTOV was not only a wonderfully satisfying program to work with but, by one of those pieces of luck that anyone who aspires to high position needs, gave my career an unexpected boost. When I received the Vietnam command, it was not at all regarded as a plum, but rather as something of a dead end, a brown-water command in a blue-water Navy. I have been privately told, and I am inclined to believe, that the Chief of Naval Operations, Admiral Thomas Moorer, worried that the prolonged and close relationship between Paul Nitze and me betokened the formation of some kind of power center that might frustrate programs he cherished—he was an aviator and I was a surface sailor—and therefore he thought it well-advised to send me a long way from the Pentagon and such intrigues as might be in progress there. Certainly the fact that the command was elevated from a two-star to a three-star billet when it was offered to me is evidence that someone wanted badly for me to take it, though that someone may not have been Tom Moorer at all, but the new Secretary of the Navy, Paul Ignatius—Nitze had just moved up into the post of Deputy Secretary of Defense—who, the conventional wisdom to the contrary notwithstanding, thought the Vietnam command an important one.

In any event the whole thing worked out quite differently than I thought it might. However much the Vietnam command might have put my predecessors in the wrong place at the wrong time, it did the opposite for me. In February of 1969, only weeks after the Nixon Administration had taken office, the new Secretary of Defense, Melvin Laird, paid a visit of inspection to Vietnam. The idea of greatly accelerating the process of turning the war over to the Vietnamese already was simmering in his head. One afternoon during his visit, in the briefing room at 9th Division headquarters in the town of Dong Tam, I had an opportunity to brief Secretary Laird on AC-TOV. I have every reason to believe that that unspectacular, indeed routine, occasion was, from the point of view of my career, one of the major events of my life.

C H A P T E R 3

The Summons

On 12 April 1970 I was eating breakfast in my headquarters-home in Saigon with the Deputy Commander of the Pacific Fleet, Vice Admiral Walter H. Baumberger, and members of my staff, when a messenger came over from the communications office to tell me that I had a telephone call from the Secretary of the Navy, John Chafee. Red Baumberger said to me, "Bud, my guess is that that's your summons to the top job in the Navy." I offered to bet that it wasn't, that being the kind of bet a man is always willing to lose, and walked over to the communications office. Secretary Chafee—formerly the governor of Rhode Island—instructed me to get on the next commercial flight for Washington without telling anyone I was leaving. I pointed out to him that it simply was not feasible for the Commander of the U.S. Naval Forces in South Vietnam to leave his wartime theater without checking out with his theater commander and his Navy boss, the Commander in Chief of the Pacific Fleet. I further pointed out that since the Deputy Commander of the Pacific Fleet had been with me when the Secretary called, I would in any case have to give him some information about the call. Secretary Chafee agreed that I could tell those three, but no others.

After passing the word to Red Baumberger, I drove out to see the theater commander, General Creighton Abrams, at his headquarters. I told him about my summons home and that I supposed it was for the purpose of giving me my next assignment. I had been in South Vietnam for only twenty months and had expected to stay until the summer of 1971. I very much wanted to see ACTOV into its final phase. I said to Abe, therefore, that I would like to be able to quote him as desiring me to stay on for another year. Abe thought for a minute and then said, "Sure, Bud, you can tell them that, but first listen to what they have to say. You never know when those civilian fellows are in trouble and might decide you're the only man who can do a certain job for them." I agreed that this was good advice, and left to catch the plane.

My somewhat mystifying instructions from Secretary Chafee were that I should wear civilian clothes on the flight home, that I would be met at Dulles airport by a chauffeur and driven directly to the home of the Under Secretary of the Navy, John Warner, and that I was to remain incommunicado there until the Secretary got in touch with me. When I arrived at Warner's home, in the Georgetown section of Washington, he reaffirmed the Secretary's instructions. Then he left for his office and I sat down to await Secretary Chafee's call.

As I waited I recalled my first meeting with the Secretary a month earlier, on 9 March. On that occasion, too, I had flown from Saigon to Washington at his request, to be interviewed in connection with, presumably, my next assignment. Like this trip, that one had made me wonder about what was in store for me. On the one hand I was worried that I would not be permitted to finish the work I had begun in South Vietnam. On the other hand, I had heard that Vice Admiral Isaac (Ike) Kidd, commander of the First Fleet, was to be given command of the Sixth Fleet, and this had turned my aspirations in another direction.

Let me explain. Years before, when the Navy began its post-World War II deployments, it created four numbered fleets. In the Pacific there was the First Fleet in the east and the Seventh in the west; in the western and occasionally the eastern Atlantic there was the Second Fleet; in the Mediterranean there was the Sixth Fleet. The commands of the two overseas fleets, the Sixth and Seventh, were considered by all of us to be the real plums among Navy jobs afloat. Originally command of those fleets had rotated from officers who were aviators to officers who had come up through the surface fleet. However, the three admirals, George Anderson, David McDonald, and Thomas Moorer, who followed Admiral Arleigh Burke, a destroyerman, in the job of Chief of Naval Operations all were aviators, and during the nine years of their incumbency, the overseas fleets had been under the command of aviators exclusively. This had provoked some hard feelings among surface officers, including me. That is why, with the report that Ike Kidd, a non-aviator, was going to receive the command of a traditional aviator's fleet—at the insistence of Secretary Chafee, the rumor was—I began to entertain the hope that I would be given the opportunity to be the first non-aviator in more than a decade to command the other overseas fleet, the Seventh. This was an even more demanding job at the time than commanding the Sixth, since the Seventh Fleet was then heavily involved in the fighting in southeast Asia.

And so, entering Secretary Chafee's office that March morning, I had mixed emotions: regret at the possibility that I might be required to leave my wartime command before my mission was complete; hope at the possibility that I might be given command of an overseas fleet; and concern at the possibility that I might be assigned to a new job less challenging than either of those two. Secretary Chafee, a man of great personal warmth and charm, had begun the interview by telling me that he was in the process of interviewing a large number of flag officers in connection with future assignments. He did not specify the assignments he had in mind, but he did stimulate my hopes about the Seventh Fleet by asking, as his first question, what my attitude was toward the new tradition of aviators being given the exclusive right to command the overseas fleets. That had enabled me to speak my piece on that subject to the man who, by law, made the decisions for the Department of the Navy.

The Secretary then had asked me to describe the problems of the Navy as I saw them, and discuss how I thought they should be dealt with. Since those subjects are what this whole book is about, I need not summarize here what I told Chafee that day. When I had finished, he told me that his boss, Secretary of Defense Melvin Laird, wanted to see me. My meeting the following day with Laird, whom I had first met more than a year before in Vietnam, was brief. He had limited himself to asking me for a quick review of affairs in South Vietnam. He then had called Henry Kissinger, the Presidential Assistant for National Security Affairs, and had asked him to meet me, which was part of a continuing process to get Kissinger acquainted with senior members of the military. I had been cleared through the White House gates in the late afternoon and ushered into the reception room of Kissinger's West Wing office suite. Kissinger's deputy, Colonel Alexander Haig, whom I had known since we had served together as junior members of the task force that handled Cuban affairs after the missile crisis, had come through the office and we had talked about the war for several minutes. My summons to Dr. Kissinger's office had ended our conversation. Kissinger and I shook hands. I sat down. After two or three minutes of discussion the telephone rang. He talked for about fifteen minutes with great fluency and charm, evidently to an inquiring journalist. He hung up and said that he had hoped to get me in to meet President Nixon, but that the President was all tied up. He said that he had enjoyed talking with me and I left. When I later asked Secretary Laird what part, if any, Kissinger or the President had played in picking me for Chief of Naval Operations, the Secretary replied that when he first put my name before Kissinger, the latter had said that on the basis of the meeting just described, he concurred in the choice. Evidently he had expressed that "well-founded" concurrence to the President, which persuaded the President he did not have to interview me for the job himself.

I spent two hours or so musing in John Warner's living room on Monday, 13 April, before Secretary Chafee showed up. He wasted no time getting to the point. He said, "Bud, you are the one Mel Laird and I have nominated to the President to relieve Tom Moorer as Chief of Naval Operations when the President appoints Tom to relieve General Wheeler as Chairman of the Joint Chiefs." The transition was to take place on 1 July. The Secretary went on to say that I was the candidate they had settled upon after he had interviewed me the month before and had learned my thoughts about the Navy's future. He added that in addition to agreeing with my views about the Navy, they wanted a non-aviator as CNO for the first time in nine years, and that they also wanted someone younger than the norm in order to help bring the Navy "into the modern age." I was 49, which may not be young for most positions in life, but is for a Chief of Naval Operations.

Secretary Chafee told me frankly that I had not been Tom Moorer's first choice for the job among the six candidates they had discussed seriously. Moorer felt I was too young to be accepted by the majority of the Navy's higher officers at that time and had strongly urged that I be saved for the top slot for four more years. The Secretary said that, despite this advice, he and Laird had decided on me. He asked me whether I would take the job. I said that I, along with Tom, would have preferred a four-year postponement, which would have allowed me to complete my Vietnamization program and then to command a numbered fleet. But, I said, I also believed so deeply in the need for the changes in the Navy that I had discussed with him that I could not refuse the job.

The Secretary expressed his satisfaction and told me that I would meet with the President in the Pentagon, privately, on Wednesday, and that day or the next the announcement would be made. He said that he and John Warner joined in the suggestion that I should remain at Warner's house until the public announcement was made and then, to symbolize the transition and to indicate Admiral Moorer's support of my selection, I should move to Moorer's quarters at Admiral's House at the Naval Observatory for the rest of my stay in Washington. I agreed. The Secretary left and I spent another day in the Warner home where his shy, but very hospitable, wife did her best to keep me from feeling I was a prisoner.

Wednesday came. I was picked up again by Warner's chauffeur, and driven to the basement of the Pentagon, where I was spirited up the Secretary of Defense's elevator to his private office. I waited there a few moments in conversation with the Executive Assistant to Laird, Brigadier General Robert Pursley, an old friend. Bob congratulated me on my prospective appointment and said that in his view Laird had been a key factor in the decision to nominate me. Some four months later, when Laird and I were returning from a visit to Turkey and Greece, he confirmed this. He reminded me that when he had visited South Vietnam, soon after assuming the job of Secretary of Defense, I had given him a briefing on the Navy's strategy in the delta and coastal war and on our ACTOV program for the Vietnamese Navy. He said that it had served to demonstrate to him that Vietnamization, as he was to call it later, could be made a viable program much more rapidly than conventional wisdom was inclined to accept. He said that following the briefing he had asked General Abrams about my competence, and that Abe had given me very good marks. Laird had thereupon decided, he said, that I had the necessary qualifications for the job of Chief of Naval Operations, and had instructed his assistant, Bill Baroody, to insure that my name was on the list of candidates submitted to him by the Secretary of the Navy.

I spent only a few moments with Bob Pursley before I was summoned to the office of the Secretary of Defense. Laird introduced me to the President, who rose and shook my hand. He congratulated me on my appointment and said that the announcement would be made the next morning at 1100. He went on to say that he knew from Mel that I was relatively young for the job but that he personally considered that an asset. He asked me where I was from. I told him that I had grown up in a small town called Tulare in the San Joaquin Valley. He brightened and said, "Oh yes, I know where that is. I picked lemons right near there at Lindsay one summer when I was a kid. It's very hot." I agreed. The President observed that he was quite concerned about the growing Soviet maritime capability, and that he understood from Laird that one of my strong points was that I had a healthy appreciation of that fact. I told him that I did, and that one of my principal objectives was going to be to try to persuade him and the Secretary to do more with regard to the Navy's budget in the years ahead. He smiled and said he "hoped that I would be successful." He went on to make the point that the decision-making process was a very complex one that involved more than the support of the Secretary of Defense in order to get a favorable presidential decision. He reminded me that the Director of the Office of Management and the Budget (OMB) and many others on his personal staff "made inputs into the decision-making process," and suggested that I would have a better chance of success if I kept in touch with all of them. I told him that I was planning to do so and would take his advice as a directive. I asked him whether Laird had informed him that I also had some very strong ideas with regard to changes in personnel administration. He said that he knew of them and would look forward to reading about them. I told the President that I was aware of the fact that the Chief of Naval Operations, beyond his responsibility to the Secretary of the Navy and to the Secretary of Defense, was, under the law, Naval Advisor to the President and that I visualized that this gave me a very special obligation, one that normally could be carried out by reporting through channels but also required me to insure that the President was informed of my views. The President stated that he understood this. That concluded the meeting, which had lasted no more than five minutes. I was not to see him again until some three months later, after many of my principal projects had been set in motion.

I returned to seclusion at the home of John Warner. That night I told John that the next morning at a quarter to eleven, fifteen minutes before the President made my appointment public, I proposed to telephone my seventy-eight-year-old father to break the news to him before he heard it on the radio or television. After a career as country doctor in Tulare, Dad had retired at the age of seventy, and left Tulare to live in Indianola, Washington. Within a year he came down with a stomach ulcer, which he diagnosed as being the result of inactivity. About that same time I had learned that the Naval Ordnance Test Station at China Lake, on the desert a hundred miles or so from Tulare, was having difficulty in filling the position of head of the Industrial Medicine department. I put the Test Station people in touch with my father who accepted the appointment immediately and had been an immense success in the ensuing eight years. As a matter of fact, I have been told that he was so popular that when I was selected for rear admiral in 1965, the China Lake newspaper carried the headline "Dr. Zumwalt's Boy Selected for Rear Admiral." Warner readily agreed that Dad deserved the courtesy of being informed ahead of time. I called him at 1045 next morning and broke the news to him. At 1050 John Warner called breathlessly to say, "Bud, don't call your father, there has been a delay in the press release." "I've already called" was my answer. "Get him back and tell him not to talk," Warner instructed. At 1055 I had Dad on the phone and asked him, "How many have you told?" "Only five so far," he responded. "Button them up," I said. He did. At 1115 the press release went out. Then I called Mouza, who was in the Philippines with our two daughters, and who did not yet even know that I had left South Vietnam. The telephone was not a very private one at her end and I felt that my news would get to other ears if I called her before the announcement was made, so I waited until after. I told her that I was in Washington and that I was "taking her to the house that Aunt Tina had predicted we would live in." She shrieked with delight. With her second breath my beloved, ever cautious Mouza said, *"Boschi moi,* that means in four years you have to retire."

The "Aunt Tina" reference was to a favorite story in our household. Aunt Tina, you may remember, was Christina Wright, the remarkable aunt of one of our neighbors in Chapel Hill where I served from 1948 to 1950. She was the good friend who took us to see General Marshall but we temporarily lost touch with her in the course of the next few years of moving from job to job. In 1954 I was assigned to the Bureau of Naval Personnel in Washington and we bought a house in the suburbs. I was in the basement one evening pounding on something with a hammer when Mouza came downstairs and said, "Some woman who calls herself Grace Carney is on the phone saying that she wants us to come to dinner with a Mrs. Wright, but I don't think that we know either of them and she must have the wrong party." Grace Carney was merely the wife of Admiral Robert Carney, then CNO. You can believe that the news that the wife of the Chief of Naval Operations was on the phone brought a lieutenant commander, who had never been invited to dinner in the home of an admiral, up the stairs two at a time.

I accepted the invitation, of course. We studied all the rules of etiquette and arrived at exactly the appointed hour, comforted by the thought that there would be many people there and we could shrink into anonymity. It turned out we and Aunt Tina were the only guests. Admiral and Mrs. Carney were extremely gracious. Aunt Tina regaled us throughout dinner with funny stories and considerably embarrassed the young lieutenant commander and his wife by calling the Carneys "you kids." After dinner, and a proper interlude for coffee, Mouza and I made our manners. The three of them walked us to the door and Aunt Tina said, as we were departing, "I'm so glad that you kids were able to come, because I was very anxious for you to see your future home." Mouza and I looked apologetically and speechlessly at the Carneys. Mrs. Carney put the matter in proper context by smiling and saying, "Now isn't that a sweet thought," whereupon we left and went to get something to eat, having both been so awestruck that we had not eaten adequately at the very hospitable Carney table. Through the years we had told this story with great relish and so it was the obvious way of letting Mouza know what had just happened to me.

I spent that afternoon in a temporary office in the Pentagon, receiving congratulatory visits and telephone calls, and making at least one important call, to General Abrams in Saigon, to let him know I would be back on Saturday morning. Abe received the news in his usual laconic fashion, and did not congratulate me on my appointment. I was hurt but I said nothing. The next day I got a message from him that meant a great deal to me:

1. When you talked with me by phone this morning, I was at that time unaware of the public announcement that the President had nominated you to be CNO.
2. I was at [General] Julian Ewell's farewell today and the place was buzzing with the news of your nomination. The atmosphere was like a small town where news has come that one of "their boys" has made good. I join with your many friends in acclaiming this selection. More than this, I am aware of the awesome burden of leadership that will soon be yours. For this I pray that God will bless you with the health, the patience and the wisdom you will need to fulfill this responsibility.

Wednesday evening, as scheduled, I reported for the second time in my career to Admiral's House, or more properly Quarters A, at the U.S. Naval Observatory. This pleasant Victorian house, which soon would be my home for four years, and which at the end of my term became the legal residence of the Vice President, is situated on a wooded hill in the center of the Observatory grounds off Massachusetts Avenue in the heart of the District of Columbia. Tom Moorer was out of town that day, but his wife Carrie made me welcome and gave me a good dinner. Tom got back the next day, Thursday, and I had a long talk with him in his office, during which he dispelled whatever trepidation I may have felt about working closely for four years with the man who had "exiled" me to Saigon. At our meeting he confirmed what Secretary Chafee had told me; that he thought it was a shame to use up my naval service so rapidly by becoming CNO at the age of forty-nine. However, he expressed himself as solidly in support of my nomination, and offered to make himself available at any time to help me with the transition. He was as good as his word.

That same Thursday the Senate Committee on Armed Services held hearings on my nomination that with all respect—and indeed satisfaction—I must describe as perfunctory; the hearing began at 1005 and adjourned at 1030. I made a brief statement ad lib and so did Secretary Chafee. Three or four Senators made generally laudatory comments, notably the committee chairman, John Stennis of Mississippi, and Henry Jackson of Washington, with whom I had worked from time to time in the past. In addition, Senator Stennis read the subsection of the law that defines the duties of the Chief of Naval Operations:

> The Chief of Naval Operations is the principal naval advisor to the President, and to the Secretary of the Navy on the conduct of the war, and the principal naval advisor and naval executive to the Secretary on the conduct of the activities of the Department of the Navy.

And he cautioned me that the Committee expected the CNO to be "responsible to the President of the United States, and also to this Committee," to "be frank and full of candor, sound counsel, and advice." I took this warning seriously, though I might have been better advised to consider it mere senatorial rhetoric. I will have occasion to describe how my candor before the Committee gave me more grief than anything else.

That evening I was on my way back to Saigon. My nomination was approved unanimously by the committee on 7 May and by the Senate as a whole five days later. A month to the day after my nomination went to the Senate, on 15 May, I was relieved in Saigon by Vice Admiral Jerry King. My wife and two girls flew in from Clark Field in the Philippines for the change of command ceremony, at which General Abrams awarded me the Distinguished Service Medal. My elder son, Elmo III, a Lieutenant Junior Grade in command of PCF 35, a "swift boat," part of the brave and proud mini-fleet that patrolled off the coast and in rivers of Vietnam, also was able to be there.

Mouza, the girls, and I then traveled home in a circuitous manner that enabled me to get to know, or get to know better, a variety of important personages, military and civilian, American and allied, and to meet a large number of junior officers and enlisted men in the Seventh and Sixth Fleets as well. We visited Japan where its senior military officer, Admiral Itaya, Chairman, Joint Staff Council, Japanese Self-Defense Force, and I exchanged reminiscences about the Battle of Surigao Strait in which we both had fought more than twenty-five years before, he as a commander and I as a young destroyer lieutenant. He had ended up swimming, so you might say his reminiscences were saltier than mine. I conferred briefly with Generalissimo and Madame Chiang Kai-shek on Taiwan. I received the most professional briefing I have ever heard on the military-political situation in Asia from Prime Minister Lee Quan Yew in Singapore, who made it clear that the U.S. entry into South Vietnam had kept Indonesia, Singapore, Malaysia, and Thailand from going behind the bamboo curtain and that their future rested on the final outcome there. In Naples we called on "CinCSouth," the commander in chief of NATO's southern forces, Admiral Horacio Rivero, the highest ranking Spanish-American in the U.S. military. In Stuttgart we called on Air Force General David Burchinal, Deputy Commander in Chief in Europe, and in Brussels on General Andrew Goodpaster, Supreme Allied Commander, Europe. Also in Brussels, Air Force Lieutenant General Royal Allison, the delegate representing the Joint Chiefs of Staff in the Strategic Arms Limitation Talks, briefed me on SALT. I had wanted to go to Vienna, the site of the talks, to confer with my old mentor, Paul Nitze, the American delegate representing the Secretary of Defense, but Secretary Chafee suggested that I should not in order to spare Admiral Moorer any additional concern about a Nitze-Zumwalt axis. From Brussels we went to London, where we saw the British naval chiefs. We got back to Washington early in June and I plunged into an attempt to learn in less than a month just what the job was that I was about to assume.

As far as clearing the ground for the next four years of work went, perhaps the most important meeting in the pre-assumption period took place on 24 June. It was the first get-together of my personal staff, the officers who would have daily access to me and would speak with my voice to the Navy. Since many of these people will crop up repeatedly in my story, let me introduce them here by their names and numbers—numbers because all staff billets have numerical, or in some cases numerical/alphabetical, code designations. The CNO is "00." The VCNO is "09," and the Deputy CNOs are "Op (for OpNav, meaning office of CNO) 07, 06," etc. These designations are the prefixes for the people who work in the lower echelons. Thus the members of the CNO's staff are "002, 3, 4," etc., or "00A, B, C," etc. Similarly, the members of Op-07's staff are "Op-072, 3, 4, or A, B, C."

Very well. 002, my executive assistant, the officer who knew all my business and transacted a great deal of it, was one of the most profusely decorated aviators in the Navy, Captain Burt Shepherd. When he left in 1972 to assume command of the carrier *America,* another brilliant flyer, Captain Don Pringle, succeeded him. Lieutenant Commander Ray Inman, 002B, was Burt's Assistant who screened thousands of papers per week in order to pass only the most important hundreds to Burt. Captain H. B. Robertson (and later Jim McHugh), 00L, did the endless legal work connected with the CNO's responsibilities. I had two aides, Marine Lieutenant Colonel Mike Spiro (later Lieutenant Colonel Dick McDonald), 006A, and Navy Commander Jerry Wages (later Dave Woodbury), 005. They managed long-range schedules, made the arrangements for trips, supervised the details of running Admiral's House and its grounds, supervised drivers, stewards and so forth, and served as personal aides. They were assisted by Lieutenant Commander Bobbie Hazard, 005A, a woman line-officer, who was the manager of the public side of the office and had to deal with countless administrative emergencies. Captain Jim Strong, 004, was my in-house expert on Joint Chiefs of Staff and National Security Council matters. Captain Ray Tenant, 00E, represented me on all the boards CNO must sit on and never has time to: Navy Mutual Aid, Naval Institute, Navy Relief Society, etc.; and he was my liaison with the Red Cross, the American Legion, the Boy Scouts of America and dozens more. Commander Arie Sigmond, a riverine warfare expert from my Vietnam staff, was chief speech writer and a splendid all-purpose man. Lieutenant David Halperin, OOP, also from my Vietnam staff, did special work for me in the personnel field.

My first public affairs officer in Vietnam had been Commander, later Captain, Jack Davey, who then went on to the Naval War College, which he finished that June. He returned to my staff as OOD. In addition Captain Bill Thompson, who had been the Secretary of the Navy's public affairs officer for years and who came out to Vietnam to escort me home public relationswise, sat in on most of my personal staff meetings as Deputy Chief of Information for the Navy, 007B. He presently became the first public affairs admiral in the Navy's history.

Dr. William Narva was staff doctor and a thoroughly professional naval officer on all our trips.

I have saved for last two of my closest associates from Vietnam. Captain Charles (Chick) Rauch, OOG, an ex-Polaris submarine skipper, originally was supposed to be a sort of all-purpose assistant, with special responsibility in such areas as Vietnam, strategic systems, nuclear power, and submarine operations. The way things worked out, though, personnel reform became such an urgent and complicated activity, and Chick displayed such an enormous gift for working in that field, that it became his full-time activity. He is still in it. As a rear admiral he works in the Bureau of Naval Personnel as "Pers-P," a position I created that to all intents and purposes is that of the Navy's ombudsman.

I gave Captain Emmett Tidd, by that time already a rear admiral designee, a unique job, that of Decision Coordinator. In creating this new job on the CNO's staff—for Emmett had done it for me in Vietnam—I was acting in accordance with advice Arleigh Burke had just given me. Admiral Burke had said, "If you really want a decision carried out, send for the action officer after you have made it and convince him it's a good idea." As Decision Coordinator, Emmett was technically a member of the VCNO's staff, Op-09C, because administration is the VCNO's responsibility. His job was twofold. The first part was to see that all matters requiring decisions by the CNO or the VCNO came before us in an orderly fashion: i.e., that all points of view were fairly presented, that all options were laid out, that brevity was stressed, that when briefings were necessary all the right people attended them. The second part of the job was to convince the action officer. As the first step in the latter process Emmett hit upon the device of putting a green stripe on the edge of any piece of paper that contained a CNO/VCNO decision. Thus anyone receiving a paper with a green stripe on it knew he had better act promptly on it. Because my first few weeks on the job were a period of rapid and voluminous decision-making, "Green Stripers" from which there was no place to hide cascaded upon the members of the operations staff. I think it is fair to say that during that period Emmett Tidd was not the most popular figure in the Navy. Emmett did not win every battle. One day I called him to check on the status of a particular decision that had gone by "Green Striper" to the Material establishment. Emmett came back later in the day and said he had finally located the missing "Green Striper" in the back of a certain commander's file drawer. When Emmett called him to account, the commander replied, "Why, hell, nobody's in favor of that but Admiral Zumwalt." Subsequently Emmett distinguished himself as the Commander of the Recruiting Command, in which capacity he effected a revolution in Navy recruiting operations. He is now a vice admiral in command of Surface Forces, U.S. Pacific Fleet.

At the first staff meeting I tried to tell my new staff what kind of a guy I was. A tape-recorder was running in plain view as I spoke:

> . . . I am action oriented and tend to think better when explaining the problems to the person who is taking action. My basic philosophy is, if a proposed change is in doubt, make it and see what happens. It is easy to get a thousand reasons why you shouldn't do something. If the odds are even 40 in favor and 60 against, my reaction is to change it and see how loud the screams are. . . . Nothing goes beyond our immediate group while still in the idea stage. In addition everybody should be eyes, ears, and funnel to 002 when we have gotten wind of hurt feelings, made mistakes, etc., so we can change as necessary. I am very good at *not* revealing how we got information. Will not blow your cover. Don't worry about being exposed. Navy makes greatest progress when CNO and SecNav work together. We run into too many problems when we don't. There will be times when the Secretary will overrule. . . . It is terribly important that I keep SecNav informed of everything that happens before he gets a call from SecDef or Congress. No memos on things which are extra sensitive. Will pass most of these things verbally. No written record. . . . All of you here are just an extension of CNO. CNO is one taking action. . . . Guard CNO against rumors. . . . Want to ensure that I receive public relations and operational incidents reports prior to

their reaching SecNav/SecDef/Congress. . . . Do not wait for me to depart [at the end of the day]. Go on home. We can call you if we need you.

The Change of Command Ceremony took place at 1100 hours on 1 July 1970 at the U.S. Naval Academy. En route to it, in the middle of U.S. Route 50, three miles from Annapolis, my limousine broke down. Mouza and I, dressed in full regalia, got out and stood on the shoulder of the highway. A young sailor in uniform stopped his car and offered us a lift. He turned out to be a member of my personal staff who was en route to the ceremony himself. If the breakdown appeared for a moment to be a hex, this welcome offer of assistance was obviously a powerful counter-hex and we promptly accepted it. We arrived at the ceremony unceremoniously, but on time.

The ceremony took place in a cobble-stoned open space in front of Bancroft Hall, with the stage facing the legendary statue of Tecumseh. After the Navy Band played the National anthem, and the retiring Chief of Chaplains delivered an invocation, the Secretary of Defense, the Secretary of the Navy and the retiring CNO spoke briefly. Admiral Moorer then read the orders detaching him as CNO and ordering him to the chairmanship of the Joint Chiefs of Staff. His flag was hauled down, and he received "full honors," four ruffles and flourishes and a nineteen-gun salute. It was my turn. I read my orders and was sworn in by the Judge Advocate General. I ordered my flag broken out and received those same full honors. I turned to Admiral Moorer, who rose, saluted him and said, "Admiral Moorer, I relieve you." He returned the salute and replied, "Very well." I saluted Secretary Chafee and said, "Sir, I report for duty as Chief of Naval Operations." He replied "Very well." I saluted Secretary Laird, and said, "Sir, I report for duty as a member of the Joint Chiefs of Staff." He replied, "Very well." I spoke briefly of my family, of my predecessor, of my aspirations for the Navy. The incoming Chief of Chaplains gave the benediction. The Navy Band struck up *Anchors Aweigh.*

II

PLATFORMS
AND
WEAPONS

CHAPTER 4

High-Low

The accelerating obsolescence of the U. S. Navy since the end of World War II as opposed to the impressive growth and modernization of the Soviet Navy during the same period was a contrast I emphasized and dwelt upon in the long interview I had with Secretary of the Navy John Chafee when he was searching for a new CNO. Since he chose me I assume he agreed with what I said then on that subject, and I shall summarize it here. I said that, given the Nixon administration's determination to reduce military budgets, the only way I could see for the Navy to free funds for developing up-to-date ships and weapon systems that could cope with the new Russian armaments was to retire immediately large numbers of old ships and aircraft. That meant that the price the nation would have to pay for sufficient and appropriate naval capability in the 1980s would be seriously reduced naval capability during at least the early seventies, while the new systems were being designed, built, and deployed.

I said that this was true of both general-purpose (conventional) forces and strategic (nuclear-missile) forces. In the former case, some of our carriers and their escorts had seen service in World War II; in the latter case, the oldest Polaris-Poseidon submarines would, by 1980, reach the end of the twenty-year life for which they had been built. I said that three sets of delicate decisions would have to be made. One was how far to reduce current capability so as to get the most money possible for modernization without becoming so weak as to tempt the Soviets into rash action. A second was how to bring the Navy into balance by supplementing the high-performance ships it was building in small numbers, because they were so expensive that small numbers were all it could afford, with new types of ships that had adequate capability for many missions and at the same time were inexpensive enough to build in the larger numbers required for an American naval presence in many parts of the oceans. The third was how to allocate resources between general-purpose and strategic forces so that the enormously important and enormously expensive strategic forces would neither starve nor consume so much as to reduce conventional capability to a point at which a major conventional threat could be countered only by a threat to escalate to nuclear war.

My colleagues and I made our decisions in those three areas against a background of asymmetrical U.S. and Soviet maritime development, which in turn had resulted from the great dissimilarity of the maritime situations of the two nations. To begin at the beginning, the Soviet Union is a land power in both an economic and a political-military sense, while the United States is, as I like to put it, a "world island" whose every activity is bound up with use of the seas. If it had to, the Soviet Union could feed itself and keep its industry going without ever sending a ship beyond its coastal waters. In addition, all the Soviet Union's most important political relationships, except the one with the United States, are with nations that also are situated on the Eurasian land mass. Russia can protect its most important client states or attack all but one of its most likely enemies without going to sea. By contrast, the industry and trade of the United States depend on ocean traffic in both directions and most of its important allies are on the far side of broad oceans as well. The economy of the United States requires that it have a large maritime capability. The political interests and commitments of the United States require that it be capable of having a large military influence overseas. Both of those exigencies, in turn, make a powerful U.S. Navy imperative. Even more to the point, they define the double mission of the U.S. Navy: to keep the seas open for commercial and military traffic of all kinds, which we call "sea control," and to make it possible to apply military power overseas, which we call "projection." In World War II the U.S. Navy was called upon to perform both missions and at the end of that war it was the best balanced, most powerful Navy the world has ever seen. The Soviets on the other hand had virtually no Navy at all; they never had had much of one, and most of it had been destroyed or captured during the fighting.

In the late forties and early fifties, when the Cold War and their aspirations to become a world power led the Soviets to begin a naval buildup, they found that having to start from scratch was in one way a great advantage, for it allowed them to "optimize," that is build a Navy to precisely the specifications that would make it most capable of showing strongly against its only likely opponent, the United States. That meant a Navy that could challenge U.S. sea control— for it is obvious that without sea control the projection mission is impossible to carry out. In choosing this as their top priority mission, the Soviets gave themselves a second advantage. Denying sea control to an enemy is a far easier task than maintaining sea control oneself. Denying sea control means cutting lines of communication, which requires fewer ships, less sophisticated equipment and smaller risks than maintaining lines of communication, since a line of communication has to be maintained throughout its length, but can be cut anywhere.

The Soviets went about giving themselves the capability they judged they needed in a completely logical way. First they built a very large number of submarines until they had three times as many as we. They were diesel-powered, torpedo-carrying boats and as individual vessels they were not in a class with ours, but their numbers made them capable of inflicting a good deal of damage. Then the Soviets began improving their submarines. They made their diesel boats quieter, and thus more difficult to detect, since the primary means of detecting a fully submerged submarine are acoustical. They began building nuclear-powered boats, with the virtually unlimited range and the ability to stay submerged indefinitely that nuclear power confers.

At the same time as these submarine developments were proceeding, the Soviets were developing a wide variety of types of surface vessels, from little missile attack boats to big heavy cruisers. As befitted their mission, which was to attack convoys and carrier task groups in the waters near Eurasia, those ships tended to be more heavily armed, faster and with a shorter range than our ships of similar types, which were designed to cover the whole reach of the oceans. What was most troublesome about the Soviet surface ships was one notable item in their armament, cruise missiles, which also began appearing in submarines. Not having the capability to fly planes off ships and not being willing to wait until they developed it, the Russians devised these air-breathing vehicles, which are rather like pilotless planes. They are offensive weapons directed against surface targets. They can be fired from the surface, from the air, or from underwater. They can be controlled, even redirected, in flight. Their typical range is longer than that of conventional artillery and shorter than that of planes, from twenty miles to a couple of hundred, say, depending on type. They have enough explosive power to inflict heavy damage on any ship in our fleet, except carriers, with one good hit. To disable a carrier seriously would take a large number of hits. Thus the Soviets gave themselves the capability to mount heavy attacks on our surface ships from positions outside the range of our gunfire. One other threatening expedient they devised to compensate for their lack of sea-based air was to develop bases from which long-range land-based air—also equipped with cruise missiles as well as more orthodox armament—could reach ships almost anywhere in the Indian Ocean, the Mediterranean, the Red, the Norwegian, and the North Seas. By 1970, scores of Soviet ships had cruise missiles, which meant that scores of Soviet ships had long-range offensive capability.

To counter the Soviet naval threat, the United States and its allies have one great geographic advantage: no major Soviet ports or naval bases front on the open ocean. Whether from Murmansk or Vladivostok, the Black Sea or the Baltic, Soviet warships must come through straits or narrow water to engage an enemy. This fact, it is important to note in passing, is one of the reasons the U.S. government over the years has found it necessary to give strong support, whatever their regimes, to the straits nations: Greece and Turkey, Spain and Portugal, Norway and Denmark and Iceland, South Korea and Japan, Indonesia and the Philippines. The most effective way to neutralize the Soviet naval threat in a war situation would be to seal off the straits, through which Russian warships not only would have to sail to join in battle, but would have to return eventually for replenishments. However, this task of sealing the straits— and of course coping with the substantial number of ships that would be bound to get through under the best of circumstances—is one that calls for deploying U.S. ships around the world from the Sea of Japan to the Norwegian Sea. Thus it calls for a very large number of ships. It also calls for types of ships that became increasingly scarce as the war in southeast Asia proceeded.

In the war in Southeast Asia, as in the Korean War, the enemy could not dispute U.S. control of the seas and so the Navy's main business became projection: amphibious landings, air strikes, and occasional episodes of naval shore bombardment. Not only did the Navy's share of the budget shrink during those wars because the Army and the Air Force underwent greater attrition of equipment, but under the circumstances the Navy had to put a disproportionate share of the money it did receive into maintaining its capability for projection—its carriers and attack planes, its amphibious vessels, its ships with the weapons for bombardment. Sea-control forces—antisubmarine planes and their carriers and ships suitable for patrol and escort duty—were allowed to obsolesce and, finally, retire without replacement. More damaging yet, work on future sea-control requirements—new types of ships from which planes or helicopters could operate, new techniques for combating submarines, new vessels to escort convoys, new kinds of weapons with which to fight on the surface was postponed for many years. The one exception was nuclear-powered attack submarines, which through Admiral Hyman Rickover's special influence on Capitol Hill got built in ample numbers.

Internal forces in the Navy had contributed to unbalancing it in the 1960s. I no more intend to suggest that George Anderson, David McDonald, or Tom Moorer, the three aviators who preceded me as CNO, deliberately allowed the surface Navy to deteriorate than I would welcome a suggestion by them that I deliberately neglected air during my watch. The point is, and it is a difficult one to make clear to an outsider, that for the last quarter-century or more there have been three powerful "unions," as we call them, in the Navy—the aviators, the submariners, and the surface sailors—and their rivalry has played a large part in the way the Navy has been directed. (The submariners have not had a CNO in recent times, but they have had the aforesaid Admiral Rickover, who most of the time is more than a match for most CNOs.)

The intense competition for resources and recognition among the three unions—for there is never enough of either to satisfy everybody, or even satisfy anybody—has had both constructive and destructive consequences. It tends to lead the Navy's civilian masters, who presumably are not parochial, to examine alternatives far more rigorously than they would if there were no push-and-shove. It develops a pride in service that is invaluable not only in combat situations, but as an antidote for the routine hardships of peacetime naval duty. It stimulates professional expertise. On the other hand it almost inevitably breeds a set of mind that tends to skew the work of even the fairest, broadest-gauged commander if he is given enough time. Whichever union such a commander comes from, it is hard for him not to favor fellow members, the men he has worked with most closely, when he constructs a staff or passes out choice assignments. It is hard for him not to think first of the needs of his branch, the needs he feels most deeply, when he works up a budget. It is hard for him not to stress the capability of his arm, for he has tested it himself, when he plans an action. I am not the person to evaluate the extent of my own bias, but I think it fair to point out that following three air CNOs in a row, as I did, I was bound to have some redressing to do. Regular rotation of the top jobs among delegates from the respective unions seems to me to be a prerequisite for institutional stability.

The union system has one other curious side effect. Certain crucial activities are outside the jurisdiction of all the unions and therefore tend not to concern them very deeply. No union has a vested interest in mines, which have no bridges for captains to pace. No union has a vested interest in the increasingly great variety of electronic surveillance instruments that operate independently of ships or planes. All the unions should have a vested interest in secure, high-speed communications, but somehow they too have been in no-man's-land. Such adjuncts to fighting, important as they are, receive no automatic institutional protection. Thus, the Navy was far behind the USSR and our own Air Force and NASA with regard to use of satellites, computers, and modern communication management techniques. I resolved to do my best to protect the non-union shops from the indifference of the unions.

A final malady that afflicted—and continues to afflict—the whole Navy, though the surface Navy was and is the greatest sufferer, can be described in one word, a word I have used already: Rickover. By virtue of the force of his personality, his apparent permanence in office, his intimate relations with key members of Congress and his statutory independence of the Navy as Director, Division of Naval Reactors, Atomic Energy Commission, Admiral Rickover for years had been able to tilt the Navy toward relying exclusively on nuclear propulsion. If nuclear power is not the earthly paradise that "Rick" makes it out to be, it is surely an excellent way to propel warships, chiefly because a nuclear-powered ship can steam at high speed without refueling for ten or twelve years. Thus nuclear power is particularly appropriate in strategic submarines, and advantageous in attack submarines and a limited number of big carriers and their escorts.

However, it has a vice that outweighs its virtues in many kinds of vessels. Nuclear-propulsion systems are so big and heavy that making some types of ships nuclear means making them much bigger and hence much more expensive than conventionally powered ships that fight almost as well, as much as five times as expensive in the case of certain types. The sea-control mission, as I have just explained, requires a large number of platforms from which weapons can be fired and planes launched, a large number of ships. In most cases seven or five or even three ships of moderate capability would contribute far more to the success of this mission than one supership, as a series of analyses ordered by Robert McNamara, when he was Secretary of Defense, decisively demonstrated. For twenty years Rickover has been working successfully toward a supership Navy, and so it is partly his doing that for twenty years the Navy has been getting smaller except of course in the item of nuclear-propelled submarines. Occasionally, someone outside the Navy has made the obvious case for numbers of lower cost ships. One of them during my watch was U. Alexis Johnson, an entirely professional foreign service officer, who at the time was Under Secretary of State for Political Affairs. Twenty-seven days after I became CNO Alex wrote a letter to Deputy Secretary of Defense, David Packard, expressing his concern that the Navy was not adequately addressing the cost-numbers trade-off in going for fewer large expensive systems rather than large numbers of lower cost systems.

I was no stranger to problems of the kind I had to solve in order to "reoptimize" the U.S. Navy to meet the Soviet threat. Every officer who has been in battle is bound to have a store of practical knowledge—and a set of strong opinions, too—about the adequacy and the balance of the systems he has fought with, and I had seen action as a junior officer in World War II, a middle-level officer in the Korean War, and a force commander in Vietnam. Beyond that I had served from 1963 to 1965 as Paul Nitze's executive assistant when he was Secretary of the Navy, and from 1966 to 1968 as the first Director of Systems Analysis for the CNO. In both those jobs the stuff of daily life had been carefully weighing the probable effectiveness of various kinds of ships and weapons against their costs and the time it would take to develop, build and deploy them, and then deciding which ones to invest in. As soon as the President announced my appointment, in the middle of April, a month before I was relieved of my Vietnam command, I began to create machinery to produce a long-term plan that I hoped would reconcile the dilemmas I had discussed with Secretary Chafee.

The first thing I did was to persuade the commander of the Seventh Fleet to lend me one of my successors as Nitze's executive assistant, Rear Admiral Worth Bagley, then commanding a destroyer flotilla, to serve as my principal assistant in this project. Worth Bagley, who later in my watch became Commander in Chief, U.S. Naval Forces, Europe (CinCUSNavEur), and thus supplanted me as the youngest naval officer ever to win his fourth star, comes from a remarkable naval tribe. One of his uncles, a namesake, Ensign Worth Bagley, was the only naval officer killed in the Spanish-American war. Another of his uncles, Josephus Daniels, was Secretary of the Navy under Woodrow Wilson throughout World War I, and, as such, Franklin D. Roosevelt's immediate boss. A third uncle, Fleet Admiral William D. Leahy, was F.D.R.'s chief of staff during World War II. Worth's father, Vice Admiral David Bagley, fought at Pearl Harbor in command of battleships. And his older brother, David, whom I promoted to three stars and made Chief of Naval Personnel, now has four stars as CinCUSNavEur. That gives the family sixteen stars and one seat in the Cabinet in two generations, and provides U.S. Naval history with its first four-star brothers. Another extraordinary fact about these two brothers and their uncle, Ensign Worth Bagley, is that all three failed their plebe year at the Naval Academy and had to repeat.

I picked Worth for his brains, but it was no accident that I picked a brainy destroyerman rather than a brainy aviator or a brainy submariner, as the reader of the preceding pages will understand. The first imperative as far as I was concerned was for the program to be conceptually ready in the shortest possible time. I had been around Washington long enough to have a clear idea of what was involved in bringing a program from concept to reality through the competitive office holders in the Department of Defense, through the cheeseparers in the White House budget apparatus, through the political parochialists on four Congressional committees and the political opportunists in two Houses of Congress—and I had only four years. I named what Worth and I were starting to do "Project 60," to signify my determination to have something to put before John Chafee and Mel Laird by the time I had been in office no more than sixty days. Actually there was a lot more to Project 60 than the modernization program that this chapter deals with. Project 60 was nothing less than a comprehensive plan for my four years as CNO, and included a variety of programs for meeting the two other principal issues the Navy confronted in 1970: how to maintain a high-quality all-volunteer force when the draft expired, which it clearly was about to, and how to maintain sufficient capability during the modernization process for the Navy to continue to perform its assigned missions. Subsequent parts of the book will deal with those endeavors.

Worth was Project 60's full-time man. From the middle of April to the middle of May, I still had my wartime command responsibilities in Vietnam. Then I took the long trip home I have described already. The trip made an important contribution to Project 60 because it gave me an opportunity to exchange ideas about it with most of the Navy's top commanders. Worth could not join me in Washington immediately; he was unable to leave his flotilla until August. However another destroyer officer of high intellect was available during the interim period, Captain Stansfield Turner, Secretary Chafee's executive assistant. Stan, a Rhodes Scholar, had just been selected for flag rank, but his new command would not be ready for him until Worth was ready for me, and the Secretary graciously relinquished him to me for six weeks or so. Stan, incidentally, got his fourth star not long ago as Commander in Chief of NATO's Southern Forces—CinCSouth. First Stan, then Worth, drew into the work on Project 60 on an ad hoc basis whichever other staff members they needed. I estimate I spent an average of two hours a day on it myself. At the time I also was spending about two hours a day on my new personnel program, about two hours a day on Joint Chiefs' work, and about two hours a day making myself known on Capitol Hill. That left the other eight hours of my working day for running the Navy.

I have often been asked—I have often asked myself—whether a working schedule like that makes sense. I can only answer "yes and no," or perhaps "no and yes" is more accurate. I never have been a nine-to-fiver. Since I began working in earnest my habitual work day has been dawn to dusk, with weekends included if they had to be. The hours I put in as CNO obviously were physically and mentally fatiguing, but they were not beyond my strength. I was even able to summon up enough philosophy to bear Mouza seeing me off to work one morning after a family breakfast during which I studied urgent messages with, "So long Daddy. We'll see you in four years." What frustrated me was that there were so many things to do that

I could rarely do any one of them as well as I wanted to; the price of performing creditably overall was to fall short of excellence in many specific instances.

Mostly my day consisted of fifteen-minute blocks, with a separate task assigned to each. Matters of importance might occupy two blocks; matters of great importance might even occupy four or five. Even so I rarely had the time to go deeply into the details of anything. This constant pressure was not the result of insufficient help, Lord knows. I had a Vice Chief who handled the bulk of the office's administrative work, ran the OpNav (CNO) Staff of several hundred people and served as my alter ego. I had nine Deputy Chiefs or their equivalent, each one with a large staff, each one responsible for an important segment of naval activity. I had ten special assistants, each one with a small staff, each one in charge of a project in which I had a particular interest. I had an ample complement of chauffeurs, aides, and the other factota a busy executive uses to fend off the too numerous phone calls and visitors, to keep track of his appointments and transportation, social obligations, and clothes.

Nevertheless, there were sixteen-hours-a-day-worth of things only I could do. It takes a Chief to sit on the Joint Chiefs. Congressmen, particularly senators, are seldom satisfied to talk with anyone but the top man. Project 60 and my personnel program were too important to be left entirely to others, indeed too unorthodox to win support unless my personal participation was clear to all. And then there was the mass of routine—sailing orders, promotions and job assignments, procurement problems, contingency plans—that the CNO must concern himself with, however fleetingly. Worst of all, this strenuous routine allowed me almost no time for detailed reflection on many issues, though I was by law "principal naval advisor to the President," and as such obliged to have well-thought-out opinions about a host of situations and contingencies. Most of my thinking about important but non-urgent matters had to get done between 0610 and 0624 in the morning, while I was running my daily two miles on the Naval Observatory grounds, or on those frequent enough occasions when I had to ride somewhere in a plane.

Perhaps I was more aware than another man would have been of the limitations a fragmented attention imposes on good work because I had once taken part in a piece of work that had gotten done brilliantly because the attention of the people who did it was not fragmented. In 1962 I was an assistant to Paul Nitze, then Assistant Secretary of Defense for International Security Affairs. It was in

October of that year that the Soviets were discovered emplacing missiles in Cuba. Immediately a dozen or more top executives, beginning with the President and several cabinet members and including Paul, dropped almost everything else they were doing to consider how to deal with those missiles. They cancelled all but the most urgent meetings not concerned with Cuba. They attended only those social events they had to for fear the Russians would draw conclusions from their absence. For once the most senior officials of the government, meeting almost continuously, themselves did the kind of detailed, laborious, analytical work that generally falls to staff people of the rank I held then. They—we, for I was a junior participant—explored meticulously each possible course the U.S. might adopt, each possible Russian response to each of those courses, each counter to the Russian responses. The policy that all of us thus carefully and collectively developed proved to be a good one. I doubt that it could have been developed in any other way or by people of any lower position. Of course, when the Soviets began to remove the missiles from Cuba and the emergency abated, the team broke up and its members resumed their ordinary round of activities. Ever since I have been more or less reconciled to the fact that our democratic system is like a sleeping giant, its slumber unperturbed by early warning signals, but capable, when the signals herald great and imminent peril, of compensating for this lethargy by springing almost instantaneously into action.

Speaking of the inherent difficulty or reluctance of a democracy, absent a crisis, to keep its attention on military possibilities and contingencies, another of its effects is to preclude the kind of comprehensive planning and optimal use of assets that occur routinely in the Soviet Union. To speak only of the Soviet Navy, its chief, Admiral Gorshkov, has control of land-based long-range aircraft that can attack our naval platforms with bombs and cruise missiles; in lay terms, he has a piece of the Air Force. Every Soviet merchant ship serves as a surveillance and intelligence collection platform for the Soviet Navy. Many Russian merchant ships are configured so as to be readily useful as naval auxiliaries in the event of war, which they are. Even in crises short of war, these ships can be promptly diverted from commercial to military activity. Every Soviet fishing vessel, every space support ship, every oceanographic and survey ship contributes to the Soviet naval mission. From time to time over the years the U.S. Navy has tried to persuade the government to acquire similar assets in order to enhance the total power it might bring to bear in a crisis. However, under our system, with the co-equal Congress and its associated lobbies working outside the Defense Department, and with each agency of the executive branch applying parochial pressure on Congress, it has not been possible to achieve the total maritime strength of which this country is capable. But this field of effort is potentially so fruitful that I decided during our Project 60 evaluation to see what I could do to make available the resources of outside agencies.

We examined the use of Army helicopters on merchant ships and on escorts on the theory that unless the Navy could control the seas, the Army could not be deployed anyway. This effort did not emerge from the bureaucratic jungle. We asked the Air Force to broaden its contingency plans to include the use of its strategic bombers for mining important waters. That was approved in 1971. We asked the Air Force to install our new Harpoon cruise missiles in its bombers so that it could give the Navy long range support of sea lines, similar to the assistance Admiral Gorshkov was getting. This initiative finally began to bear fruit in late 1975 in a training agreement between the Navy and the Air Force.

I personally believed that the Defense Department was making a great mistake by not requiring some, if not all, of the Air Force's tactical air wings to be carrier capable so that the United States could have optimal air power to use in a typical crisis. In three of the four crises during my watch—Jordan, September 1970; Indo-Pakistan, December 1971; Yom Kippur War, October 1973—the U.S. Air Force was totally incapable of playing a role due to lack of access to airfields, and only carrier aviation could be brought to bear. I brought this up personally with General Jack Ryan, Chief of Staff of the Air Force. After studying the problem, he declined to take it on. I gave the Secretary of the Navy a copy of a proposed directive for the Secretary of Defense to forward to the Secretary of the Air Force and the Secretary of the Navy on the subject of "employment of Air Force aircraft on carriers," that "died on the field of honor." I then went to Melvin Laird and his deputy David Packard and urged that they get it done. Both of them thought it was a good idea, yet both declined to touch it. Their reason was probably a good one, that the Congress and its lobbies would not permit it, and a jurisdictional wrangle would hurt the Defense budget. On the other hand, General Leonard Chapman, Commandant of the Marine Corps, readily agreed to use Marine aircraft to help augment carrier wings as necessary, recognizing that the Marines must be able "to get there" and had better help the Navy to do so, given our dramatic reduction in power.

We tried using merchant ships for refueling at sea and found they could do it. But we never could get the leverage within the Executive Branch to get the merchant ships being built in this country properly configured during construction so that they would be most efficient in that role. We examined the feasibility of using commercial container ships for replenishment of ammunition and other logistics in conjunction with a heavy lift helicopter. This proved practicable but no program was approved. We examined the feasibility of giving super tankers the capability to handle Very Short Takeoff or Landing (VSTOL) aircraft and anti-submarine helicopters during wartime, together with the necessary shipboard equipment so that they could provide their own fighter, anti-missile, and anti-submarine capability. The answer was that it was technically but not politically feasible to bridge the jurisdictional differences between DoD and the Maritime Administration.

On 28 June 1971, after nearly ten months of efforts of this kind, I suggested the following to Admiral Moorer in connection with a forthcoming Secretary of Defense management conference, which all the top authorities would attend:

Service Roles and Missions—The current fiscal and domestic political climate makes it more and more important that we break away from rigid boundaries established by traditional service roles and missions. To a limited degree, this has already begun. Examples are cooperation in ocean surveillance and the USAF mining role. These represent a beginning—much more can be done; for example, the Air Force can contribute to ASW and to the Navy's sea control requirements (both of which are essential to providing the logistics for deployed tactical AF units). What makes each service avoid this kind of thinking is that if accepted, it may result in de facto alteration of relative funding profiles. Actual changes in relative funding allocation is a subject we'll have to address eventually. Expansion of cross service missions now might be a good way to begin. It may even make the pill easier to swallow later.

Again, the problem was put in the "too hard to" file.

As I have said, the underlying theory of that segment of the project dealing with modernization was to accelerate the retirement of obsolete ships in order to free as much money as possible for new development and construction. We then worked out a concept we called "High-Low." I first advanced this concept in 1962 in an article in the Proceedings of the U.S. Naval Institute entitled "A Course for Destroyers," in which I had used the terms "The Complete Mainstream" for certain kinds of destroyers and "The Simplified Mainstream" for others. Obviously "High" and "Low" expressed the idea more clearly. "High" was short for high-performance ships and weapons systems that also were so high-cost that the country could afford to build only a few of them at a time; there are some missions the Navy cannot perform without the great flexibility and versatility of such ships. "Low" was short for moderate-cost, moderate-performance ships and systems that could be turned out in relatively large numbers; they would ensure that the Navy could be in enough places at the same time to get its job done. In sum, an all-High Navy would be so expensive that it would not have enough ships to control the seas. An all-Low Navy would not have the capability to meet certain kinds of threats or perform certain kinds of missions. In order to have both enough ships and good enough ships there had to be a mix of High and Low.

The innovative part of this program was the Low. In contrast with the Soviet Navy, which always has operated on the principle epitomized by a quotation hanging above Admiral Gorshkov's desk that "better is the enemy of good enough," the U.S. Navy has traditionally insisted on traveling first class. There was more than enough High, more than enough Too High, already under construction or under contract when I began Project 60, and almost no Low at all. This was true especially in the case of ships. A new group of too sophisticated, too expensive attack submarines, the SSN-688 class, was being built at what would soon approach $300 million a copy. I knew something about that submarine because the concept for it had been sprung upon me as a fait accompli when I was director of the Division of Systems Analysis, the office where all concepts for new weapons systems were supposed to be worked up first. Somehow Admiral Rickover had gotten the work done elsewhere and without my knowledge. I protested, but my immediate boss, a submariner himself, approved the concept anyway.

Similarly, the Marines were in the process of getting something they had long wanted, a big modern amphibious ship, the LHA, which also was too expensive at $133 million a copy in 1973 dollars, but at least had the virtue that each one could carry as many troops as the several smaller landing vessels it replaced. (We used 1973 dollars in all Project 60's Low calculations because the Fiscal Year 1973 budget would be the first in which Low projects were funded.)

The day before I took command, but with my assent, the Navy signed a contract for thirty 8000-ton $100 million 30-knot destroyers of a new class, DD-963 or Spruance, to replace the almost obsolete 2100- and 2200-ton World War II destroyers that were still serving as escort vessels for carriers and convoys. At that time the Navy had in operation or under construction only 150 of the 250 escorts its studies showed were needed for the future. The 963s would raise that figure to 180. The genesis of DD-963 is a story of some interest because it typified the Navy's institutional resistance to modest programs. When Paul Nitze was Secretary of the Navy he pushed vigorously for the development of a new class of inexpensive escorts to succeed the DE-1052, an escort that began to join the fleet in the early sixties. The DE-1052 had been a breakthrough for advocates of Low. It was a modestly equipped single-screw vessel that many sailors of the old school predicted would be unable to keep up with fast carriers, and in any case would forever be under tow because one propeller, one engine, and two boilers were obviously not enough for a warship. These forecasts proved to be almost entirely wrong. DE-1052 was no star, but she performed adequately and since her cost was low, the Navy could afford probably twice as many of her as of a more brilliant performer. It was a ship of this character, with somewhat improved performance, that Paul wanted as the next class of escorts. However, the admiral he put in charge of the project, together with the engineering duty officers on the development staff, found a host of technical reasons to recommend a larger, more expensive ship. Paul fired that admiral and got a new one to manage the project. The new admiral came up with the same findings. My guess is that both of them thought they were speaking for the CNO. Anyway, three project managers later, when the new escort finally got designed, it was the far too expensive DD-963.

There were two other very High programs under way. One involved nuclear-powered aircraft carriers (CVANs), the most expensive ships there are. CVAN 68, *Nimitz,* was under construction. CVAN 69, *Eisenhower,* was being developed; that is, work was going forward on its long-lead-time components, the reactors particularly. CVAN 70, *Vinson,* was on the drawing board, but no money had yet been authorized. The second program involved DLGNs, nuclear-powered guided missile frigates, used to escort the nuclear carriers. A class of five was being planned by Admiral Rickover.

On most of those High ships, SSN-688, LHA, DD-963, CVANs, DLGNs, implementing decisions had already been made. Congress had authorized them and appropriated funds for them and the Navy had signed contracts for them. Moreover there was no question about their quality. The trouble with them was that they were too good in the sense that the Navy had given up too much to get them. They came within the purview of Project 60 only to the limited extent that we could increase or decrease the construction tempo, or the total number of each ship delivered. And that narrow option was narrowed further by the absence from even a drawing-board of any Low types. We would have to start on Low from scratch. That meant that for at least two years, while preliminary design work was proceeding, practically all the Navy's construction money, that which had been provided by my predecessor and that which we hoped to add by early retirement, would of necessity go into the High. Another of Project 60's theoretical underpinnings, to correct as rapidly as possible the tilt toward projection and away from sea control that the Korean and Vietnam wars had produced, dictated how the High money should be spent. We cut back the LHA program (projection) from nine ships to five, as the contract allowed us to, a decision made easier by the cost overruns and construction delays that were occurring at the Litton shipyard in Pascagoula, Mississippi, where DD-963 also was to be built. Since we wanted to get an inexpensive escort into the fleet as part of our Low, we resolved not to expedite DD-963. However, escort vessels are a critical component of sea-control forces, so we resolved not to slow down DD-963 either but simply to proceed with the program as it had been planned. We put DLGN in the same category. We decided we would try to expedite work on the fourth nuclear carrier since for reasons of both obsolescence and operating costs the carrier forces were dwindling fast. As for the SSN-688, like everything in which Rickover has a hand, it had complications leading to ramifications resulting in shenanigans, all of which I shall sketch in the next chapter.

Project 60 visualized starting work on four new classes of ships, all of them designed primarily for sea-control duty. Three of them were inexpensive and well within the means of existing technology, and one was a long-range research and development project. The simplest and cheapest was a high-speed 170-ton hydrofoil patrol boat, PHM, armed with a new weapon I shall describe later in this chapter, the Harpoon cruise missile. Its purpose is mainly as a strike vessel against enemy surface craft. It will patrol narrow or coastal waters like the Gulf of Tonkin or the Mediterranean or the Red Sea, or serve as a low-value trailer of high-value Soviet ships in such waters. We found this concept so attractive in Project 60 that we made a decision immediately to deploy two gunboats (PGs) with three-inch guns to act as interim trailers in the Mediterranean. PHM's advantage to the Navy is that in those places where it can operate, it will replace on a one-to-one basis much larger ships, with much larger fuel consumption and big payrolls, thus freeing those ships for essential deepwater duties, and more important, making it possible for the larger and more valuable ships to be outside the range of surprise Soviet cruise missile attack.

Second there was the patrol frigate, PF, another attempt to get that modest escort vessel that Paul Nitze had seen miraculously metamorphosed into DD-963. Like DE-1052, PF is a single screw ship of about twenty-eight knots and, at 3400 tons, about half the tonnage of DD-963, with a somewhat smaller crew, and about half as costly to build. We insisted on a top limit of fifty million 1973 dollars. Yet it is almost as heavily armed as DD-963, since Harpoon is the basic weapon in each and each carries two anti-submarine helicopters. PF may have some limitations as an escort for carriers, particularly nuclear carriers. Part of its low cost comes from forego-ing some speed and range and part from using certain less sophis-ticated kinds of sensing and communications equipment. However, it is quite adequate as a patrol vessel or as an escort for convoys of merchantmen or naval auxiliaries and, like the DE-1052, can serve as an escort for carriers in a pinch. The surface union was at first no more enamored of the PF than it had been of the DE-1052. That the program is on track and has turned out so well is a tribute to Vice Admiral Frank Price, who was the deputy (now retired) charged with preventing a repetition of the DD-963 growth problem.

The third "Low" component, and the one nearest my heart, was an extremely austere carrier we first called the "Air Capable Ship," then the "Sea Control Ship." She was to be a 17,000-ton twenty-five knot ship with endurance of 7500 nautical miles at twenty knots. She was to be capable of carrying fourteen helicopters and three Harrier VSTOL planes. She could handle only such aircraft because she would have no launching catapults or arresting gear for landings. Her price was to be 100 million 1973 dollars, about one-eighth the cost of a nuclear carrier. Her principal peacetime purpose was to show the flag in dangerous waters, especially the Mediterranean and the western Pacific where the Sixth and Seventh Fleets operate, so that the big carriers that are the Navy's most important ships could withdraw from the front lines and deploy out of reach of an enemy first strike, thus putting themselves in a favorable position to respond to such a strike—and therefore to deter it. To use the undoubted vulnerability of carriers to Soviet cruise missiles as an argument for getting rid of carriers, as some Defense critics do, seems to me a classic example of throwing out baby with the bath water. The solution to the problem is to deploy big carriers out of reach of cruise missiles and replace them with low-value ships that at the same time have some defensive capability, to wit Sea Control Ships.

In a wartime situation the positions of the two kinds of carriers would be reversed: the big, powerful ones would fight their way into the most dangerous waters, destroying opposition beyond cruise missile range with their planes, and the Sea Control Ships would serve in mid-ocean. The Navy's twelve or at best fifteen big carriers would be needed in wartime for the large, complicated tasks of conducting air strikes against enemy vessels or shore installations, searching out and destroying submarines over long distances and at high speeds, providing air support for the land battle, interdicting land- or sea-based enemy air and cruise-missile attack against ships and ports. They had far too much offensive capability to waste on convoy duty. Yet in any real war situation there might be at sea as many as twenty convoys of merchantmen, troop transports, and naval auxiliaries in need of air protection from the time they left the reach of land-based air until they entered areas where the deployed carriers were operating. Providing this protection would be the chief wartime mission of the Sea Control Ships. Eight vessels capable of that mid-ocean job could be built for the price of one full-fledged carrier, which in any case, if it was assigned to convoy duty, could protect only one convoy instead of eight. Moreover the SCS would be fast and easy to build because all of her systems—propulsion, weapons, sensing, communications—had already been proved out in other vessels and needed minimal modifications. Clearly SCS was a good investment. Unfortunately when it was first proposed it was seen as a good investment by no union but my own. Both the nuclear folk and the aviators saw it as infringing on their turf. Later the aviators got behind it.

Finally, for the future, there was the "surface-effect ship." This would be a four-or-five-thousand-ton vessel that could skim just above the surface of the ocean at 80 to 100 knots. Such a ship, which could cross the Atlantic, say, in not much more than a day, virtually immune from underwater or surface attack, could revolutionize naval warfare. At that speed, it need not be equipped with a launching catapult and arresting gear; it could carry four or five carrier planes, even the big F-14s, and turn them virtually into VSTOLs. Thirty-five such ships, a member of my staff once calculated, could carry two divisions of troops to Europe in three days. The ramifications of such capability in anti-submarine, anti-aircraft, and other kinds of warfare are endless. We put the development of this ship—for which the basic propulsion technology already was in existence—in a ten-to-fifteen-year time frame. As of this writing two promising 100-ton prototypes have been built. I have ridden on one. It's quite a thrill.

In addition to these measures for increasing sea-control capability in the future, we hit upon one expedient for increasing it overnight, as it were. This idea, originated by then Rear Admiral Jim Holloway, was to make all carriers, which customarily had been designated either as attack carriers (CVAs) or anti-submarine carriers (CVSs) into dual-purpose vessels. This increased sea-control capability because CVAs outnumbered CVSs by almost two to one. All that this involved was modifying the deck loadings so that each ship carried both attack and anti-submarine planes instead of one or the other, adding some minor command-and-control apparatus and, of course, installing the spare parts and the maintenance equipment that such change in deck loading necessitated. The cost of thus changing a carrier over was $975,000, a sum miniscule by comparison with what almost anything else in Defense costs nowadays. Of course, modifying carriers in such a way dissatisfied some people. They pointed out (correctly) that making a carrier capable of two dissimilar missions made it less capable than it had been of either one. They also pointed out (again correctly) that on the record of recent wars and crises a carrier was more likely to be called on for projection than for sea control. However, a twelve-carrier Navy with as much water to cover as the U.S. Navy has would simply be incapable of keeping the sea lines of communication open in a major war if those carriers had no sea-control capability, and I thought that was too big a risk to run. Fortunately, the majority of my colleagues, including the most important sachems in the aviators' union, agreed with me.

As might be expected in a Navy that aviators had presided over for a decade, we were in good shape as far as types of planes were concerned. During the latter years of the southeast Asia war, CVAs had carried two types of modern attack plane, the workhorse A-7, a light, relatively inexpensive machine that performed most strike and ground support missions, and the heavier, costlier A-6, which had similar armament but was built and equipped to operate effectively in bad weather and at night. Both were recent additions to the fleet: I remember that when Paul Nitze moved from ISA to the Navy in 1963, taking me with him, his first official act as Secretary was signing off on the Research and Development program for the A-7. Both planes had proved their value in Vietnam. Both, with technical modifications, would be serviceable for another decade at least. The aviation admirals were content with them. There was no reason for me not to be.

On the sea-control side a new anti-submarine plane, the S-3, was about to go into production at Lockheed. It contained up-to-the-minute equipment that enabled it to drop sonar buoys over large areas, monitor the signals of those buoys and fire Mark 46 torpedoes at whatever enemy submarines the buoys—or other localizing sensing devices—find. There was every reason to believe that this plane would be serviceable for many years. The problem it presented was that at $13 million a copy it was not inexpensive, to use a cautious double negative, and Congress was showing some reluctance to buy as many as the Navy needed. The S-3 came into Project 60, therefore, as an action item for the Navy's legislative liaison people.

Somewhat further from production than the S-3, though already contracted out to Grumman, was the plane most of us thought of as the new star of the Navy's air arm, a fighter, the F-14. It was to replace the F-4, which had been designed in 1954 and had proved itself a superb one-on-one machine in fighting MIGs over Vietnam. However, with the massive deployment of cruise missiles by the Soviets, the day of the one-on-one fighter was ending; it was not capable of defending ships against a massive cruise missile attack. The F-14 was. In addition to excellent flight characteristics, it had a new missile system, the Phoenix, able to intercept Russian Foxbat aircraft at altitudes above 80,000 feet. And it had an extraordinary fire-control system that could track 24 targets simultaneously, automatically choose the six most threatening and fire at them simultaneously. Such equipment comes high. The F-14 is a very expensive plane, to use a well-justified double positive, even when you consider that the multiplied capability it gives a carrier makes operating with a reduced number of carriers feasible. The precise price of a single plane is harder to state than that of a ship, since planes are bought by the hundreds rather than by the fives or tens, and the unit price goes down sharply as the size of the buy goes up. However, it is pretty hard to find a way of stating F-14's price that makes it less than $14 million in 1973 dollars, and pretty easy to find a way of stating it that makes it a lot more.

I had become convinced that the F-14 was the world's best fighter plane long before becoming CNO. In 1966 when I came back to Washington from San Diego after a year as a new rear admiral in command of a destroyer flotilla to set up the Navy's Systems Analysis Division, my first assignment from Secretary of the Navy Paul Nitze was to study the cost effectiveness of the F-111B plane in comparison with all competition. The reader may recall that there had been quite a controversy in the Pentagon several years earlier when Robert McNamara had ordered that there be as much commonalty as possible between the new land-based fighter plane the Air Force needed and the new carrier-based fighter plane the Navy needed. Thus was born the swing-wing plane that first was called the TFX, then the F-111, the Air Force's version being F-111A and the Navy's F-111B. Despite heroic efforts by the Secretary of Defense and Secretary of the Navy to make F-111B successful, the compromises that had to be made to develop an air frame capable of performing two different missions led over time to greater and greater weight, and it presently became a close question as to whether the plane would be able to land on and take off from a carrier.

It was while this weight question was still in doubt that Secretary McNamara asked the Navy to examine again the cost effectiveness of the plane, assuming for the purpose of the study that it *could* land on and take off from a carrier. I soon learned that an earlier generation of analysts had done their work well. The fire control and missile system had been brilliantly designed to deal with the Navy's special problem—to crowd into a small airfield at sea a few fighter planes with the capability to search the air surrounding a carrier task force for hundreds of miles and provide a very long range capability to kill many airplanes and cruise-missiles coming from several directions simultaneously. The study concluded that if the F-111B could use a carrier, it was by all odds the most cost effective aircraft for fleet air defense and other fighter roles.

However, by the following year it had become almost certain that the F-111B would not be able to use a carrier. Meanwhile, four companies had sent in bids to produce a fighter that put the F-111B's engine, fire control system, and missile in a new airframe. I did another study that showed that this new airplane, subsequently known as F-14A, was probably the way to go. The Navy decided to go that way. By March of 1973, to get ahead of myself, I was able to report to Congress that our calculations showed that when we compare a thirteen-carrier force carrying 301 F-14s with a sixteen-carrier force carrying 903 of the old F-4s we found the smaller force to be militarily more effective; $2.5 billion cheaper in procurement costs; $500 million a year cheaper in operating costs; and requiring 17,000 fewer sailors.

Helicopters are coming into increasing use in naval warfare. They have been used for many years as rescue craft on carriers, and for some time troop-carrying helicopters have been an important element in the amphibious forces. Project 60 demonstrated that we could achieve high payoff if escort vessels carried one or two helos on their decks to use as aids in detecting incoming aircraft, cruise-missiles, and submarines. We had available in inventory over 100 SH-2s, a sort of all-purpose helo that was not highly satisfactory for the new mission, being too light to load with all the equipment the mission calls for, but it was adequate and inexpensive and available, so we decided to adapt the SH-2 for the near term and at the same time begin Research and Development (R&D) on a more advanced machine. We called the new helo, together with its embarked detection and kill equipment, LAMPS, for Light Airborne Multi Purpose System, a combination of sensors to find submarines and equipment to fire Mark 46 torpedoes at them. Expediting LAMPS, which was already in the design stage, was one of the high priority items in Project 60. The SH-3, the carrier rescue helo, which is bigger than the SH-2, is the one we planned to put on the sea-control ship. The third important component in Project 60 that involved helicopters was to economize on and modernize minesweeping techniques by retiring almost all our surface minesweeping vessels and adapting the big CH-53 helicopters the Marines were using for amphibious operations for minesweeping. In the mid-sixties, helicopters had successfully demonstrated a modest capability to sweep moored mines and a study had recommended they be used for this task. By 1970 helos had doubled their rates of sweeping mechanical mines and had demonstrated a significant potential to sweep magnetic mines. Our cost analyses showed that shifting the emphasis to helos for minesweeping could achieve significant savings on both operation and maintenance costs. In addition helicopters had the operational advantage over ships of being able to deploy rapidly to any location in the world. Developing the equipment and techniques took time and money, and meant going almost entirely without minesweeping capability for more than two years, which was a pretty big risk. Fortunately we got away with it. The new system was in operation by 1973, when the Navy was called upon to sweep the mines out of Haiphong harbor as part of the Vietnam cease-fire agreement, and the force that did that job proceeded almost immediately thereafter to repeat its performance in the Suez Canal. In these operations the ability of the helicopters to sweep areas much faster than surface ships and with less manpower demonstrated that this concept was a winner.

When it came to weapons, all of us who worked up Project 60 felt strongly that the most urgent task by far was to develop and deploy a proper cruise missile as rapidly as possible, in surface vessels, particularly escorts, first, then as soon thereafter as possible in planes and submarines. To my mind the Navy's dropping in the 1950s of a promising program for a cruise missile called "Regulus" was the single worst decision about weapons it made during my years of service. That decision was based on the theory that our carriers were so effective that we did not need cruise missiles, though some have suspected that the reluctance of the aviators' union to give up any portion of its jurisdiction played a large part in the decision. In any case, without cruise missiles practically all our long-range offensive capability was crowded onto the decks of a few carriers. Even those pets of Rickover's, the enormously expensive nuclear-propelled guided-missile frigates (DLGNs) remained almost purely defensive ships without cruise missiles. It was another case of numbers being more to the point than quality.

Fortunately, while I was heading the Division of Systems Analysis, the Secretary of the Navy had in effect rescinded the Regulus decision by directing my office to do a study that would lead to a program for a new cruise missile, Harpoon. The most significant string attached to this order was the verbal message relayed to me through the aide system that the missile was to have a range of no more than fifty miles if it was to be acceptable to the CNO. Evidently the aviators' union was still nervous about its prerogatives. We did the study, it was accepted, and a development program got under way, in the course of which Harpoon's range increased a few miles. However, the program was not proceeding at a rapid enough pace to suit the needs of a Navy that was in the process of divesting itself of much of its other offensive capability. Expediting Harpoon to the maximum extent possible was one of Project 60's most urgent proposals. And to fill the gap until Harpoon became operational, we directed interim programs adapting various surface to air missiles into a short range surface role temporarily.

One other weapon whose development we proposed to accelerate was Captor, a rather spooky mine that, when it detects an approaching submarine, releases a Mark 46 torpedo to make a run against it. This was one of the cases of a program proceeding slowly for no other reason than that no union was pushing it; it clearly was a weapon that could be of great importance in fulfilling the mission of denying straits to the Soviets.

Finally, to round out only the most important of Project 60's fifty-two separate points, there were several kinds of "non-union" electronic systems that badly needed strengthening. These had been heavily on my mind since 1966, the year I commanded a destroyer flotilla in the First Fleet, and took part in four fleet exercises designed to test, among other things, communications, detection, and deception systems. Those exercises showed serious deficiencies in at least four areas where the Soviets were known to be extremely effective. The most important was in battle-condition communications within the fleet. In order to fight a modern battle successfully it is necessary to transmit and receive rapidly and securely—in other words without deciphering or jamming by the enemy—a staggeringly large volume of data about the rapidly changing speeds, courses and ranges of hundreds of ships, planes, and missiles, and about changes in the intentions of our own forces and in the estimated intentions of the enemy. Otherwise ships will not perform the correct maneuvers, planes will not go where they're supposed to, missiles will not hit their targets. Technological development in electronics has been so rapid that it is almost impossible to keep up with. When the World War II battleship *New Jersey* was recommissioned for shore bombardment duty during the southeast Asia war, it turned out that her communications systems, the finest that could be produced when she was built, were so far out of date that she was virtually out of communication with the fleet. The communications systems in a modern front-line ship are probably a hundred times more effective and complicated—and expensive—than *New Jersey*'s, yet they still have a hard time handling the amount of work they are given to do, reliant as they still are on High Frequency transmission with manual transmission methodology. We proposed to increase our investment in this critical field by almost three-quarters. It is a large sum if you do not compare it with the cost, say, of one SSN-688 class submarine.

Besides this general problem in communications, a special, particularly difficult one was communicating reliably with submerged submarines. Historically submarines in naval engagements have operated almost entirely on their own because there was no way to control their activities, minute by minute, and fit them into a battle plan. But of course their effectiveness would be greatly enhanced if such coordination were possible. We wanted to work harder on this problem. A similar, and perhaps even more critical, problem is maintaining communications with strategic submarines without, of course, giving away their positions. The most persuasive criticism made of the effectiveness of the Polaris-Poseidon system is that sometimes it is difficult to stay in touch with the boats and that in a nuclear exchange situation a breakdown in communications would have major consequences indeed. This was an aspect of communications in which there was intense union interest; the reason progress was slow was the inherent difficulty of the problem.

In sensing and detection, acoustic and electronics, our equipment was quite good, but this is a field in which there always is need for improvement, especially in the electronics field where the Soviets were clearly ahead of us. We needed higher probabilities of detection in order to reduce the losses we would take in wartime from the undetected platforms which would get through. Much of the newest sensing and detection equipment operates out of buoys or satellites or other kinds of devices that no union cares much about, so it always is necessary for top management to take special care that work in this area is not neglected. The same can be said about the deception devices designed to frustrate the enemy sensing and detection system, with the addition that this is one of the several places where the Russians are well ahead of us. One of Project 60's most potentially worthwhile innovations was to call for a central office with the responsibility for overseeing and coordinating all electronic warfare and command-and-control projects, instead of leaving them to the mercy of individual project managers as in the past. High energy laser development was accelerated as a result of Project 60.

I hope it is clear from this perhaps too discursive account of the main features of Project 60 that it had a central theme: to reoptimize the Navy so that it was equipped to meet the specific threats that the Soviet Navy posed. While we had been engaged in Vietnam, the Soviets, driven by the lesson of the Cuban missile crisis, had built a force that came close to being able to challenge our control of the seas. They had two-and-a-half times as many attack submarines as we. They had cruise missiles in many of these submarines and in many ships in their rapidly growing surface fleet and in their land-based naval aircraft. They had superior electronics. Meanwhile Korea and Vietnam had tilted the U.S. Navy dangerously away from sea control. Project 60 was an effort to begin to redress the balance. It was completed almost on schedule. I briefed the Secretary of Defense on it on 10 September, seventy-two days after I had been sworn in. The Secretary of the Navy had approved it earlier. Laird appeared to be pleased with it. My own attitude probably is reflected best in some comments I made to the very first meeting of my CNO's Executive Panel (CEP), whose function I will describe later, on 24 October 1970.

> I haven't really met my original objective. I had hoped that we could get going very quickly with Project 60 as a pilot effort toward changing direction, and by the end of that period we would have this group [the CEP] up to speed so that we could pass the baton without any significant missteps. As is so often the case we were just not able to get it set up that quickly. The Project 60 effort has been completed, and it expresses some changes of direction, but not as many as I would have liked. However, it represents the best we could do with a reasonable degree of consensus. This was also all we could manage in time to have much impact on this year's budget.
>
> I find myself with a great sense of impatience in that I have been in the job for four months (and that represents 8 percent of my time) and as yet I have only gotten the rudder over about 10 degrees. I am really looking forward to the fruit of this effort. I advised all flag officers in distributing the presentation to them on 16 September 1970 [that] I considered that [it] set forth "the direction in which we direct the Navy to move in the next few years"

CHAPTER 5

The Rickover Complication

The fact that from the start of my watch to the end of it Vice Admiral, and then Admiral, Hyman G. Rickover was a persistent and formidable obstacle to my plans for modernizing the Navy did not at all surprise me. I had expected him to be. Over the course of my service I had encountered Admiral Rickover a number of times. I knew that he would stop at nothing, bureaucratically speaking, to ensure that nuclear-powered ships received priority over vessels of any other kind. I knew that he had enormous influence on Capitol Hill, far greater than that of any other military man, so great that one student of the scene remarked to me, "Congress doesn't really think of Rick as an admiral at all, but kind of as a Senator." I knew that his Division of Nuclear Propulsion was a totalitarian mini-state whose citizens—and that included not just his headquarters staff but anybody engaged in building, maintaining, or manning nuclear vessels—did what the Leader told them to, Navy Regulations notwithstanding, or suffered condign punishment. In sum, I knew as soon as I was designated CNO that developing a productive working relationship with Rickover was among the toughest nuts I had been called upon to crack. In my exuberance over being chosen to head the Navy, I believed I could do it. I was wrong.

The first time I ever met Admiral Rickover face to face was on a Friday in May 1959, when I was a commander and the executive assistant to Richard Jackson, the Assistant Secretary of the Navy for

Personnel. It was so remarkable an experience that I wrote an account of it as soon as it was over:

In April I received the exciting information that I was one of a group of commanders with destroyer experience slated for interviews with Admiral Rickover. Admiral Rickover was to select two from this list to fill the billets of CO of a nuclear frigate and XO of a nuclear cruiser.

In the latter part of April I was informed by Captain Dunford of Admiral Rickover's shop to stand by on a Friday to be interviewed by Admiral Rickover. I appeared at about ten o'clock. A receptionist sat in a barren corridor of the very austere cubicles assigned to Admiral Rickover and his people. Having been identified I stood at the desk until she obtained a telephone permission to have me enter the waiting room. Within the waiting room, which also served as a conference room, consisting of a table and chairs with no reading matter, professional or otherwise, there were six or seven other officers, mostly young lieutenants of the line and supply corps, standing by for interviews for prospective jobs in nuclear submarines. There was a general atmosphere of guarded conversation. Responses to questions gave one the feeling that at least some of the officers felt their conversations were being recorded or that their general demeanor was being photographed by a hidden camera. After a wait of an hour or an hour and a half, Captain Dunford, an extremely pleasant and affable, as well as a highly intellectual gentleman, escorted me from the waiting room to the first of three interviewers through whom I must pass prior to seeing Admiral Rickover. These were Captain Lancy, Captain Dunford, and Commander Crawford. All of them were highly intelligent and capable; all of them conducted interviews in accordance with the finest administrative procedures and psychological techniques. Their questions were thorough, searching, and friendly. In all cases I felt that they left nothing to be desired. They covered the gamut of professional background, professional interests, family background, extracurricular affairs, outside reading, etc. In between interviews I returned to the conference room and waited under the sign which admonished "after having been interviewed by Admiral Rickover no one is to return to this room except to pick up his personal possessions and leave immediately without talking of interviews," or words to that effect. During the course of waiting in between interviews various members of the staff who were known to me made it a point to come in and make me feel more at home there than might otherwise have been the case. By the end of my three interviews, about five o'clock, I was informed that Admiral Rickover would interview me later in the afternoon. About 7:30 I was informed that Admiral Rickover had left about five o'clock and told to stand by the following day. By special dispensation of Captain Dunford I was permitted to stand by in my own office rather than in Admiral Rickover's shop. Late in the day Saturday I was informed that Admiral Rickover would not be able to interview me that day but would do so later in the week.

This routine, plus the fact that I was not actually called in for the Admiral Rickover interview for nearly a month, added a great deal of excitement and suspense.

In May, on a Friday, I received a call from Captain Dunford inquiring whether I would be available for an interview that day. I informed him that I would be able to get away any time after ten o'clock. Fifteen minutes later, at 8:30, I received a message that Admiral Rickover wanted to see me immediately. With the friendly consent of my under- standing boss I left his important affairs and rushed over in company with my classmate Ray Peet, who had received a similar urgent sum- mons. On arriving and going through the same identification procedures we were escorted to Captain Dunford's office. This gentleman informed us both that, should we be fortunate enough to be selected by Admiral Rickover, he (Admiral Rickover) would insist that we get some addi- tional engineering experience. Both of us had been assistant engineers on destroyers early in our careers. Admiral Rickover's proposal was that (should we be selected), we would be ordered immediately to jobs as assistant engineers on carriers (a job usually assigned to a lieutenant or lieutenant (JG). One gained the impression that this was a part of the hazing considered necessary to put one through the plebe year in nuclear college. However, it could not be denied that both of us could use more engineering experience. I pointed this out but also gave my conviction that as CO of a broken-down WW II built DD, from 1955–1957, during which time I had to qualify three different chief engineers, one of whom held a Physical Education degree and another of whom was an ensign of ten weeks experience, I felt that I had in effect been my own chief engineer for two years. Subject to this reclama I agreed that I would accept orders as assistant engineer of a carrier if it were determined necessary.

At this point Captain Dunford escorted me to Admiral Rickover's office. I should state at this time that I believed, as I was walking down the long corridor toward the experience I had been anticipating, that I was as nearly qualified for the interview as I could be. As Lieutenant Detail Officer I had sent many lieutenants to be interviewed by Admiral Rickover. I had talked to numbers of them after their experiences were over. I knew something of his personality, style, and interview tech- niques. I also knew that in my judgment a great deal of luck was also involved in his judgment as to whether or not a particular type of individual was acceptable to him. But with this qualification I well knew that one must neither rise up and smite him nor be accommodating and obsequious.

We entered a swinging door which looked into a narrow, ugly office consisting of a desk, behind which sat the gnomelike figure, and in front of which were two chairs. Admiral Rickover motioned for me to sit in one of these chairs. Captain Dunford took a seat behind me at a table which was the only other piece of furniture in the room (Admiral Rickover has made it a practice always to have a witness in the room). After I sat down Admiral Rickover looked through the notes that the three interviewers had made on me. He then looked up and with a very serious expression which to me resembled a sneer and which expression did not leave him (with two exceptions) throughout the entire period I was with him, said, "Everyone who interviewed you tells me you are extremely conservative and have no initiative or imagination." I sat silent.

ADM. R.: What do you have to say about that?

CDR. Z.: I need a few seconds to reflect on that, Admiral. It is the first time I have received a charge like that about me.

ADM. R.: This is no charge, God damn it. You're not being accused of anything. You are being interviewed and don't you dare start trying to conduct the interview yourself. You are one of those wise Goddamn aides. You've been working for your boss for so long you think you are wearing his stars. (I had been briefed ahead of time that Admiral Rickover was death on aides and told to remove my aiguillette before coming over to his office.) You are so accustomed to seeing people come in and grovel at your boss's feet and kiss his tail that you think I'm going to do it to you. Now, (turning to Captain Dunford) get him out of here. Let him go out and sit until I think he is ready to be interviewed properly. And when you come back in here (turning to me), you better be able to maintain the proper respect. Do you understand?

CDR. Z.: Yes, sir.

Captain Dunford escorted me to a barren room, apparently referred to as the "tank," in which there was a table and chair, but no reading matter. The chair faced a blank wall. The occupant had on his side a small square window opening onto the passageway, through which people walking by could peer; after a while one began to feel much like an animal in the zoo. After about thirty minutes of cooling off in the tank, I was sent for and escorted back to Admiral Rickover's office by Captain Dunford. Again Admiral Rickover motioned me to the chair. At this point the phone rang and Admiral Rickover began to harangue his caller about something that he considered terrifically wrong in the future construction program. It was the kind of information that could probably be classified confidential. After talking about three minutes Admiral

Rickover stopped, pointed to me and with a greater degree of anger (despite the fact that he would have known that I had a Top Secret clearance) said to Captain Dunford "Get him out of here, I don't want him listening to this." Captain Dunford and I retreated to the passageway. About ten minutes later we were sent for again and the interview continued.

ADM. R.: Now what is your answer to my question?

CDR. Z.: I think that my record shows . . .

ADM. R.: Answer the question.

CDR. Z.: I believe I have . . .

ADM. R.: Answer the question.

CDR. Z.: I have initiative, imagination, and I am not conservative.

ADM. R.: Humphhhhh.

ADM. R.: Where did you go to high school?

CDR. Z.: Tulare Union High School.

ADM. R.: Where did you stand in high school?

CDR. Z.: I was the valedictorian.

ADM. R.: I said where did you stand?

CDR. Z.: Number one.

ADM. R.: How many in the school?

CDR. Z.: (Pause) About . . .

ADM. R.: Answer the question, approximately.

CDR. Z.: 300.

ADM. R.: Aside from the summers, did you work or did your family support you? (Grimacing)

CDR. Z.: (Having in mind the answer, "I worked in the summers, during the school year, and my family supported me.") I worked in the summers . . .

ADM. R.: Listen to my questions, God damn it. You've been an aide too long. You're too used to asking the questions. You are trying to conduct this interview again. I said aside from the summers. Now do you think you can answer the question or do you want to stop the interview right now?

CDR. Z.: My family supported me.

ADM. R.: What did you do after high school?

CDR. Z.: I went to prep school for a year.

ADM. R.: Why? To learn what you should have learned in high school?

CDR. Z.: I didn't have an appointment to the Naval Academy yet.

ADM. R.: Why didn't you go to college?

CDR. Z.: I had a great awe of the Academy and wanted to have a better background.

ADM. R.: In other words, you did go to prep school to learn what

	you should have learned in high school? Where did you stand at the Naval Academy?
CDR. Z.:	In the top 3 percent.
ADM. R.:	Did you study as hard as you could?
CDR. Z.:	Yes, sir.
ADM. R.:	Do you say that without any mental reservations?
CDR. Z.:	Yes, sir.
ADM. R.:	Did you do anything besides study?
CDR. Z.:	Yes, sir.
ADM. R.:	In other words you didn't study as hard as you could?
CDR. Z.:	I gave my answer in the context of what I thought was the balance between academic and extra-curricular . . .
ADM. R.:	Stop trying to conduct the interview. You're acting like a damn aide. I told you for the last time I am conducting this interview. Now, shall we go ahead on that basis or do you want to get out of here?
CDR. Z.:	I'm ready to go ahead on that basis.
ADM. R.:	Now what were these special extra-curricular affairs you are so proud of?
CDR. Z.:	I was a debater, an orator and . . .
ADM. R.:	A debater (sneering). In other words you learned to speak equally forcefully on either side of a question. Doesn't make a damn bit of difference what you believe is right—just argue the way someone tells you to—good training for an aide.
CDR. Z.:	No sir, I consider that debating taught me logical and orderly processes of thinking.
ADM. R.:	(Voice rising to a shout) Name one famous man who was able to argue on either side of a question.
CDR. Z.:	Clarence Darrow.
ADM. R.:	Darrow, Darrow, what case?
CDR. Z.:	Leopold and Loeb case.
ADM. R.:	(Still shouting) You are absolutely wrong. I warn you here and now you better not try to talk to me about anything you don't know anything about. I know more about almost anything than you do and I know one helluva lot more about Darrow than you do. I warn you, you better stop trying to snow me.
CDR. Z.:	In my mind Darrow believed in the right of every man to have counsel and, believing that, he could take either side of a case.
ADM. R.:	You're wrong. Absolutely wrong. Darrow believed in fundamental dignity of the human life and there was only one

side of any case that he could take. (Turning to Captain Dunford) Get him out of here. I'm sick of talking to an aide that tries to pretend he knows everything.

Captain Dunford returned me to the tank. After about an hour's wait an old friend of mine, now working for Admiral Rickover, stopped by and, knowing it was after lunchtime, handed me a sandwich. After I had the first big mouthful, a most personable commander came running in to tell me I must now go back. As I walked into the Admiral's office still chewing the balance of the bite, Admiral Rickover looked up and said, Don't you even have enough sense not to chew gum when being interviewed?

CDR. Z.:   I am not chewing gum, sir.

ADM. R.:   Then what in the hell are you chewing?

CDR. Z.:   I had a bite of a sandwich in my mouth when sent for.

ADM. R.:   (A very slight, faint trace of a smile showing) All right, now are you ready to talk sensibly about Clarence Darrow?

CDR. Z.:   Yes, sir.

ADM. R.:   Do you still think he could take either side of a question?

CDR. Z.:   Yes sir, having in mind his fundamental belief that everyone deserves counsel.

ADM. R.:   I give up. (Pause) Suppose you were the Superintendent of the Naval Academy (anger deepens), what would you do with the curriculum?

CDR. Z.:   In these troubled times with the midshipmen's course as crowded as it is, I would eliminate some English and history to provide more math and science.

ADM. R.:   Thank God you are not the Superintendent. Its just the kind of stupid jerk like you who becomes Superintendent. That's what's the matter with our curriculum today. Do you mean that you would graduate illiterate technicians?

CDR. Z.:   No sir, I would expect the midshipmen to acquire their extra history and English on their own after finishing school. In fact, I would insist on it.

ADM. R.:   Did you ever read anything after you graduated?

CDR. Z.:   Yes, sir.

ADM. R.:   Any philosophy?

CDR. Z.:   Yes, sir.

ADM. R.:   Name one.

CDR. Z.:   Plato.

ADM. R.:   Now I warned you not to try to impress me. I told you I was sick of having an aide trying to impress me. I proved

how stupid you are on Darrow. I know more about this
subject and almost any other subject than you do. Are you
sure you want to go on on Plato?

CDR. Z.:   Yes, sir.

ADM. R.:   What did he write?

CDR. Z.:   *The Republic.*

ADM. R.:   Did you read it?

CDR. Z.:   Yes, sir.

ADM. R.:   (Extremely contemptuously) What's it about?

CDR. Z.:   (Realizing that it had to be in six words or less) The ideal
man or the ideal democratic state.

ADM. R.:   (Turning to witness) You see what kind of stupid jerk this
guy is? Trying to pretend he knows about *The Republic.*
I can tell you what *The Republic* is about. It's about
justice. How long did you study *The Republic?*

CDR. Z.:   About twenty hours.

ADM. R.:   Twenty hours, twenty hours (shouting)—you mean to tell
me that a guy like you could learn all about one of the
great works in twenty hours?

CDR. Z.:   No sir, I am sure I could have put more time in it.

ADM. R.:   How many?

CDR. Z.:   Probably a hundred.

ADM. R.:   A hundred (shouting again)—much more like a thousand
for a guy like you. (Pause) Do you think Plato would have
advocated eliminating history and English from the curriculum?

CDR. Z.:   No sir, but Plato was postulating a perfect world and we
don't have one.

ADM. R.:   Stop trying to conduct the interview. (turning to witness)
I am getting sick of this guy. He is trying to act like an
aide again. Get him out of here.

As we returned to the tank this third time, I found myself so angry
that I was actually unable to speak. The Commander obviously had
much experience with symptoms like mine and merely put his arm
around my shoulder and said very soothingly, "Don't let it get under
your skin, we all have to go through this."

I remained in the tank about forty-five minutes before being resum-
moned. Upon returning to the Admiral's office again, I was again
severely dressed down for trying to conduct the interview and being an
aide and for being too used to seeing people cravenly bow down to the
Secretaries, and then he asked whether there was any point in continuing
the interview.

CDR. Z.:	Yes, sir.
ADM. R.:	How long have you been interested in nuclear power?
CDR. Z.:	Five years.
ADM. R.:	What have you done to prepare yourself for nuclear power?
CDR. Z.:	I have watched for various . . .
ADM. R.:	Answer the question.
CDR. Z.:	Very little.
ADM. R.:	Miss Jones, come in here. (Secretary comes running with pad and pencil). Take a letter. To the President of the Chase National Bank, New York, New York. Dear Mr. President. For five years I have wanted a million dollars. Please send me a check for same today. Yours very truly. H. G. Rickover. P.S. I have done nothing whatsoever in the last five years to earn this money but send it anyway. (Turning to me) Do you get the idea?
CDR. Z.:	Yes, sir.
ADM. R.:	Why haven't you done anything?
CDR. Z.:	My modus operandi has always been to study intensely the background of the specific area in which I am currently operating.
ADM. R.:	What is your current area?
CDR. Z.:	Personnel.
ADM. R.:	How much do you study?
CDR. Z.:	I average about four hours per night.
ADM. R.:	Just on personnel?
CDR. Z.:	Two hours a night on the important papers of my office and two hours a night on background studies.
ADM. R.:	God help us, that's what is wrong with our personnel when we have guys like you working on it. How long have you known that you were going to be interviewed?
CDR. Z.:	About four to six weeks.
ADM. R.:	Four times seven is twenty-eight times four is 112. That's 112 hours at least since you've known that you had available for study by your own admission. Now why haven't you studied anything about nuclear power in this period?
CDR. Z.:	I have.
ADM. R.:	What?
CDR. Z.:	The BuPers booklet on Nuclear Physics.
ADM. R.:	Are you ready to take a test on it?
CDR. Z.:	No sir, but I think I could pass.
ADM. R.:	I doubt it. I understand you are pretty proud of your leadership capacity.

CDR. Z.:	I expect the note refers to a definition I gave of leadership.
ADM. R.:	What is leadership?
CDR. Z.:	It is knowing your own job well, knowing the job of your subordinates, and inspiring them to do theirs better.
ADM. R.:	(Sneer stiffening) Where did you learn that kind of leadership, from a book?
CDR. Z.:	No sir.
ADM. R.:	Well then you must have been born with it. Was your father a great leader?
CDR. Z.:	Yes, sir.
ADM. R.:	What did he do?
CDR. Z.:	(Still angry and knowing Admiral Rickover's distaste for those who engage in extracurricular affairs) He is a country doctor. He has practiced for forty years in his small town, has been mayor, member of two school boards, president of Rotary, Scout chairman and ran as Republican nominee for Congress. He has been the kind of outstanding citizen that makes a small community go. (I said this with more force and vigor than I had said anything throughout the interview.)

Admiral Rickover stopped, nodded, and for the second time showed the slightest trace of a smile and changed the subject. At this point his questions became more rapid, he having achieved his objective of forcing all my answers to be in short phrases and not more than six words.

ADM. R.:	Where did you stand in math?
CDR. Z.:	About the top 3 percent.
ADM. R.:	In science?
CDR. Z.:	The same.
ADM. R.:	English?
CDR. Z.:	Within the top seven.
ADM. R.:	And you want to eliminate it?
CDR. Z.:	Curtail it.
ADM. R.:	What did you do when you graduated from the Naval Academy?
CDR. Z.:	Went to a Pacific destroyer.
ADM. R.:	Which one?
CDR. Z.:	*Phelps.*
ADM. R.:	What did you do?
CDR. Z.:	Assistant Engineer.
ADM. R.:	Assistant Engineer, are you sure?
CDR. Z.:	Yes, sir.
ADM. R.:	How many in the Engineering Department?
CDR. Z.:	Three officers.

ADM. R.:   Oh, then you weren't the Assistant Engineer. You were
                just a flunky. There you go again trying to act like an aide
                again. Trying to impress me. The Assistant Engineer is
                the number two officer.
CDR. Z.:   We called all officers Assistants other than the Chief Engi-
                neer.
ADM. R.:   Don't start trying to conduct this interview.

This pattern continued throughout the balance of the delineation of
my professional career at which time we shifted to discussion of family.

ADM. R.:   Are you married?
CDR. Z.:   Yes, sir.
ADM. R.:   Children?
CDR. Z.:   Yes, sir.
ADM. R.:   How many?
CDR. Z.:   Four.
ADM. R.:   What ages?
CDR. Z.:   Thirteen, ten, five, and one.
ADM. R.:   (Shakes head sadly from side to side with the look on his
                face which seemed to say "Will this never cease?") What
                are you going to do when you get back to the Pentagon,
                run up and down the E ring and tell everybody about this
                interview?
CDR. Z.:   Admiral, I'm going to say it was the most fascinating
                experience of my life.
ADM. R.:   Now you're being greasy. Get out of here.

I left and returned to the office to call my detailer in BuPers. I reported
that I had completed the interview, that I was sure I had not been
selected, that I had set a new record of four trips to the tank, and that
he should go ahead and issue my originally slated orders to USS *Dewey.*
    One hour later I received a telephone call from BuPers informing me
that Admiral Rickover had picked me for one of the two nuclear jobs.

When my boss, Secretary Jackson, asked how the interview had
gone, I showed him that account. He showed it to his boss, William
Franke, the Secretary of the Navy, who in turn passed it along to
his boss, Thomas Gates, the Secretary of Defense. The reaction of
the three men was about the same. They shook their heads and
sighed. Nobody ever could figure out what to do about Rick. I did
not accept the summons to join the nuclear Navy. The two open jobs
were commanding officer of the guided-missile frigate *Bainbridge*
and executive officer of the cruiser *Long Beach.* Ray Peet, an Acad-

emy classmate, was the other young commander Admiral Rickover picked. Ray and I agreed that each of us needed a command of his own, not an exec's job, at that point in his career. Since Rickover did not care which of us went to which job, the choice was up to the Bureau of Personnel, and it picked Ray for *Bainbridge.* Therefore I went to the command I was originally slated for, the guided-missile frigate *Dewey,* almost a twin of the *Bainbridge* except that she was conventionally powered.

One result of this was that Ray was selected for captain two years early, a year ahead of me, along with three other classmates, Bill Anderson and Jim Calvert, the first two nuclear submariners to sail their boats across the North Pole under the ice, and Carl Holmquist, an aeronautical engineer who had been considered the class genius. (Bill Anderson retired from the Navy as a Captain, was elected to Congress for two terms and was subsequently defeated. Carl Holmquist became a rear admiral in his technical branch. Jim Calvert became the Three Star Superintendant of the U.S. Naval Academy and Commander First Fleet before he retired.) However, Rickover's terms for giving Ray—or anyone else—the command of *Bainbridge* were that he remain in the nuclear program for five years, starting with those eighteen months as an assistant engineer I referred to in the account of my interview. Fate thus enabled me to overtake Ray. I commanded the *Dewey* for two years. I spent the next year at the National War College. I then served under Paul Nitze, first as his Director of Arms Control when he was Assistant Secretary of Defense for International Security Affairs, then as his executive assistant when he became Secretary of the Navy late in 1963. Jim Calvert and I were the first of our class to make rear admiral, in 1965, a year ahead of Ray, so my failure to get a job I wanted badly turned out to be one of the lucky breaks in my career.

The next time I encountered Admiral Rickover was toward the end of 1963 when he came to pay his respects to the new Secretary of the Navy. On the way in to see Paul Nitze, he looked into the cubicle where I sat and said, with no greeting or other preliminary, "Now remember, Captain Zumwalt, I didn't reject you, you rejected me." He is not one to leave a bureaucratic flank unprotected. I came to appreciate what a formidable problem Rick was for the Navy during my tour in the Secretariat, though you would never know it from looking at an organization chart. The box he occupies there, and occupied then under a slightly different title, is the fourth-echelon one of Deputy Commander for Nuclear Propulsion, Naval Ship Systems Command, who reports to the Chief of Naval Material, who reports to the CNO. However that was not the only organization chart he had a box on. He also was a fourth-echelon official of the Atomic Energy Commission as Director of the Division of Naval Reactors, a presumable subordinate of the Assistant General Manager for Energy and Development Programs, who reported to the General Manager, who reported to the Commissioners. The AEC was, of course, entirely outside the Defense chain of command and the jurisdiction of the Congressional Armed Services Committees. It reported to the President directly and to the Congress through the Joint Committee on Atomic Energy. As an AEC official, Rick was responsible for the research, development, manufacture, and safety of nuclear reactors for naval vessels. As a Navy officer he was responsible for the design, production and maintenance of the engineering plants of nuclear-powered ships. He was a master at blurring the line, pretty fuzzy to begin with, between the two jobs.

For example, while I was working for Paul Nitze we received an inquiry from the Dutch Navy which asked whether the U. S. Navy was willing to join in a certain undertaking that would involve naval reactors. Paul and I judged that it probably should not be done, but in accordance with sound staff procedure Paul solicited the comments of Rickover, the admiral responsible for nuclear propulsion. Rickover always has been vehemently against sharing American nuclear technology with anybody, ally or not. He sent back a strong negative reply, not on Navy stationery as it should have been but on AEC stationery. That was his standard practice whenever a Navy request irked him, since it enabled him to distribute copies of his reply to his Congressional friends without going through the Navy chain of command. Within a couple of days Paul's phone was abuzz with angry Congressmen threatening to investigate his dastardly plan—actually only a routine question—to give away America's atomic secrets. In short, Rick doffed his admiral's suit whenever he found himself in conflict with Navy policy, and sniped at the Navy in his civvies.

Of course any other officer who behaved that way would have been no more than a temporary annoyance or embarrassment. Even if, for reasons of law or policy, he could not be disciplined or banished, his tour would soon be over and he would be retired or sent to command the shore patrol in Western Samoa or supervise the acquisition of office supplies in Omaha. However Rick's tour never ended—never ends. He has been doing the nuclear job since 1949; he had already put in fourteen years when Paul Nitze moved into the Secretariat twelve years ago. That was and is flatly unprecedented. There may be cases I am not aware of, but I myself never have heard of a naval officer other than Rick who stayed in a major billet for more than six years, the record length of Arleigh Burke's watch as CNO, for instance. Two-, three- and four-year tours are the Navy standard. Rickover's tour never ends because Congress will not let it. Early on he successfully cultivated important members of the Joint Committee on Atomic Energy and of the Armed Services committees. He was able to do this both because he headed an innovative and glamorous program of a kind Congressmen like to have their names associated with, and because he is a master of public relations who, by providing certain influential Congressmen with publicity that delighted them, developed an image as one military man with the courage to speak plainly enough to make headlines and candidly enough to be worth inviting to testify at all sorts of hearings, in his field of expertise and out of it.

Rick's narrowest escape came in 1953 when he was still a captain. In 1951 and in 1952 selection boards had passed him over for promotion to flag rank, and ordinary Navy procedure is that any captain who is thus passed over by two successive boards and reaches thirty years commissioned service must retire. Because selection board proceedings are secret an explanation of the reason Rickover was passed over is necessarily speculation. My own speculation is that he was not considered to be enough of a generalist even as an engineer to merit flag rank. However, there was much sentiment in Congress that, with the new nuclear program in its infancy, Rickover's career should not end that early—a sentiment that many of us middle-grade officers shared, I must add. Evidently the Secretary of the Navy, Robert B. Anderson, a very competent man, also shared it. Therefore, he included in his instructions to the 1953 selection board the requirement that it select for rear admiral one nuclear-qualified EDO (engineering duty only) captain. Since there was only one nuclear-qualified EDO captain in the Navy at the time, and his name was Hyman G. Rickover, you can safely say that this requirement left little to the board's imagination.

In 1962 Rick reached the mandatory retirement age of sixty-two, but President Kennedy, as was his prerogative under the law, extended him on active duty for two years. However, no extension beyond age sixty-four is permissible. On 1 February 1964, unless there were a change in the law, Rick had to retire, the Congress, the President, or anyone else notwithstanding—which by no means meant he had to disappear, I hasten to make clear. Nitze's predecessor as Secretary of the Navy, Fred Korth, had promised the Congress that Rickover would continue on the job, and that promise was one of Paul's legacies when he took over in November 1963. It was our understanding that Rick was looking forward eagerly to retirement in the hope that he would be rehired immediately in the same job as a civilian. I think he calculated, first, that being a civilian would ensure his tenure, second, that it would free him from whatever restraints his occasional wearing of the uniform imposed on him and, most important, that it would convert his Navy position from a uniformed to a civilian one and thus enable him to pass it along to one of his long-time civilian assistants. Since the tours of the military members of his staff, like all other military tours except his, did have fixed terms, he had no long-time uniformed assistants. However, he had developed to a fine art the technique of inducing military assistants he liked to retire at the end of their tours with him so that he could rehire them as civilians and keep them forever. Retirement means the end of an officer's career in the sense that he is no longer eligible for normal promotion or subject to routine assignment. However, a retired officer, if he is one of no more than ten in his Service, can be recalled to active duty, with his consent, to perform a specified job for a specified term. This is what the Chief of Naval Operations, Admiral David McDonald, wanted done in Rick's case and this is what Paul Nitze decided was proper to do. Rick was furious when Nitze called him in to give him the decision. I remember him coming out of Paul's office hollering, "My parents have both lived to ripe old ages, so don't think you'll get rid of me soon."

Of course, Rick was right that nobody would get rid of him soon. He is now seventy-five years old and beginning his seventh two-year term as a retired officer recalled to active duty. By now the biennial campaign to make sure that he is recalled another time, which generally starts almost a year before his term expires on 1 February of even-numbered years, has assumed something of the formal character of a minuet. It is likely to begin with this or that Congressman writing to the Secretary of the Navy that it had "occurred to" him—which means Rick has put a flea in his ear—that "it might be appropriate" to make an early announcement of Rick's reappointment. Memos and letters then fly hither and yon: from SecNav to the chairman of the AEC and the CNO; from the CNO to the Chief of Naval Personnel;

from the CNP to the CNO; from the CNO to SecNav; from the Chairman of AEC to SecNav to VAdm Rickover; from VAdm Rickover to SecNav; from SecNav to SecDef; from SecDef to the inquiring Congressman—in the days I am writing of it usually was L. Mendel Rivers of South Carolina or F. Edward Hébert of Louisiana, successive chairmen of the House Armed Services Committee and dedicated Rickover fans—who then rises in the House to commend the Defense Department for retaining "the father of our nuclear Navy." This event can occur as early as March, eleven months before the end of Rick's term, or as late as the late fall. But it always occurs. Just one time was there a serious attempt to dematerialize Rick, and it failed ignominiously. That was in 1967. Paul Nitze, still Secretary of the Navy and increasingly disenchanted with Rickover's behavior, and the Secretary of Defense, Robert McNamara, an early "High-Low" man and therefore an opponent of Rickover's "All High" programs, had President Johnson convinced that if the concept of civilian control meant anything, Rickover must go. Lyndon Johnson was no Rickover fan himself. But the rumor that Rick's extension was in doubt came to the attention of Rickover stalwarts like Senators Everett Dirksen and Richard Russell. LBJ met such a storm of protest that he hastily changed his mind. Since then no one has made more than a token effort to question Rick's reappointment. I didn't the two times it came before me, much as I would have liked to. I was fighting too many hard battles I had a chance of winning to waste my time on one that was an almost sure loser.

I have one other vivid Rickover recollection from my days with Nitze. Once, while he was meeting with Paul, Rick began bragging about how strongly he encouraged dissent and debate in his shop, how he ran it on the basis of an adversary process, in fact. When Paul expressed polite skepticism, Rick offered to send over some officers in training for top nuclear command, to give their account of how his personnel system operated. Sure enough, a few days later two such officers did call on the Secretary. They told Paul essentially the same story Rick had. On their way out, one of them took me aside and said, "Bud, I have now carried out my orders from Admiral Rickover to say exactly what we have just said to the Secretary. However Admiral Rickover did not tell me what to say to *you*. Be sure to tell the Secretary that we said to him what we were told to say to him, and that the Rickover system doesn't work that way at all." Crude, you say? Well, Rick is not subtle, just devious.

My last pre-CNO lesson in the Rickover *modus operandi,* and the most important, came in mid-1967, not long after I became the first occupant of a newly created staff position, "OP-96" Director of Systems Analysis. Alain Enthoven, the Assistant Secretary of Defense for Systems Analysis and Robert McNamara's premier "whiz kid" had been urging Secretary Nitze to justify the large number of destroyer-type ships the Navy judged necessary. We agreed that the proper course was for me to do a Major Fleet Escort Study whose purpose would be to determine with as much accuracy as possible what the fleet's requirements for escorts of various types would be in the mid-1970s. The study did not deal directly with propulsion systems, but since it recommended a very large building program that ultimately would bring the Navy's total number of escorts to a minimum of 242, and since a nuclear-powered escort—a DLGN like *Bainbridge*—costs two-and-a-half times as much as a big, high-performance destroyer and five times as much as a relatively austere patrol vessel that is entirely adequate for many purposes, the study did come down by implication on the side of conventional propulsion for almost all escorts. It thus brought into focus a professional disagreement that was, and continues to be, one of the most divisive in the Navy. Reduced to its simplest terms, it is whether the Navy can better perform its mission with a large number of ships, many of which (but not all, I emphasize) would have to be rather small and austere, the fiscal situation being what it is, or with a small number of big, powerful, sophisticated ships.

All the worthwhile analytical studies that have been done over the years in this field conclusively demonstrate that the additional conventionally powered escorts that can be bought in comparison with nuclear escorts for a given number of dollars improve the odds for a U.S. victory in a conventional war at sea. All anyone has to do is look at a map of the world and see the vast expanses of water that America's commitments to her friends and allies make it necessary for the United States to use freely to conclude that a large number of platforms is the critical need. They are needed to protect carriers and amphibious forces, to track down and destroy enemy submarines and aircraft, to escort troop and supply convoys, to patrol narrow or coastal waters. I would like to be able to present the argument of those who take the opposing view but, frankly, I do not think they have one. They iterate and reiterate what marvelous ships the nuclear-powered ones are, the CVANs, the DLGNs, the various classes of submarines, which no one can or does deny. They then go on to say that since America can produce such marvelous ships, she should settle for nothing less, which of course does not meet, much less answer, the point that a Patrol Frigate can perform *certain missions* as well and that a Spruance class destroyer can perform *nearly all* missions as well as a DLGN. For the price of one DLGN, as I have said, you can buy five Patrol Frigates or two and a half "gold-plated" Spruance destroyers, either of which alternative gives more fighting power than one DLGN. In 1972 Arleigh Burke, a great CNO and naval strategist, in commenting on the tradeoffs between nuclear ships and conventionally powered ones, said it with typical terseness: "You need numbers." I can only conclude that the opponents of High-Low—and the Major Fleet Escort Study was, of course, an early try of mine at pushing the High-Low concept—are either gadgeteers, people who like to play with expensive, complicated toys, or parochialists, people who are so involved and absorbed in one aspect of naval activity that they do not or will not see any other. Admiral Rickover is an archetypical parochialist. Indirectly the Major Fleet Escort Study said that strategically the Navy could not afford as many nuclear-powered escorts as Rickover wanted. Neither it nor I ever suggested there should be none. He was not about to endure that conclusion meekly.

Rick's efforts to stultify the study were both overt and covert. One member of my study team was Forrest Petersen, a captain who was awaiting the command of the nuclear carrier *Enterprise.* As soon as Rick got wind of the way the study was going, two or three months before it was officially complete, he made it implicitly clear to me, through others, that unless support for nuclear propulsion turned up somewhere in the study, Pete could kiss *Enterprise*—which meant his career—goodbye. As I said, Rick is not subtle. I alerted my boss, Vice Admiral Eph Holmes, the very experienced and professional Director of Program Planning, on whom Rick undoubtedly would lean next. Then we tried to devise a strategy that might defang Rickover without compromising the integrity of the study. It is worth noting that Rickover's power was such that we took it as given that he could, and would if crossed, carry out his threat against Pete, and Pete was too good to lose. Presently the idea came to us that an "Endurance Supplement" to the study might be a useful exploration of an interesting subject. It could address itself to the relative cost-effectiveness of DLGNs and DLGs (like my *Dewey*) as escorts for nuclear carriers, the setting in which nuclear escorts might be expected to show up best, since DLGs that are the same size and have the same armament and equipment as DLGNs are only 3 percent cheaper than DLGNs over a ten-year period of operations. To be fair, it also was the setting in which Rickover chiefly envisioned DLGNs. His nuclear-propulsion compulsion did not at that time extend to suggesting that DLGNs escort freighter convoys or patrol coastal waters, just that they be built in large numbers ahead of anything else. He has subsequently broadened the Rickover doctrine by persuading the Congress to enact a law that requires a special Presidential finding if any important escort without nuclear power is recommended to Congress. I put Pete in charge of working up the supplement, which took him off the hook on which Rickover was threatening to impale him. Ironically, though we bent the supplement in Rickover's direction as far as our professional scruples allowed us to by using the assumptions favorable to his case, it still made a case for nuclear propulsion that was "underwhelming." Rick wanted something like twenty-five DLGNs. The supplement said that from sixteen to nineteen *could* be justified—with all sorts of questionable assumptions.

Forrest Petersen, at my request, to help him stay on Rick's team, kept Rickover up to date on the progress of the Endurance Supplement, and as soon as it began to produce results that could be interpreted as favoring nuclear propulsion Rickover arranged to have lunch with the CNO, Admiral David McDonald. The Vice CNO, Admiral Horacio Rivero, and I as the chief hero or villain of the Major Fleet Escort Study, also attended. I was puzzled by the affair, which took place on 5 July 1967 and appeared to be largely a social occasion. We chatted about this and that, and every so often Rick delivered a boiler-plate theological harangue about the beauties of nuclear power, but we engaged in no real discussion and transacted no business. It was not until three years later, when a member of my staff found in the CNO files the point paper Rickover had given McDonald, that I understood why he had bothered to come over at all. The only surprise in the point paper is its circular reasoning:

> The very large escort building program recommended by the Major Fleet Escort Study . . . is probably larger than any program the Secretary of Defense is likely to approve. . . . All things considered, including the present attitude of the Congress, the Navy should concentrate its efforts concerning escorts for the next few years on attaining approval for a nuclear escort building program that will give us five all-nuclear carrier task groups by the late 1970s.

What he said meant to me: "Since the Navy will not have enough money to carry out the very expensive construction program the Fleet Escort Study proposes in order to increase the size and effectiveness of the Navy, it should devote itself to carrying out the equally expensive construction program Admiral Rickover proposes in order to decrease the size and effectiveness of the Navy." He was, of course, not interested in displaying logic, but power. The words of art in that quotation are "all things considered, including the present attitude of Congress." He was going to make sure that "the attitude of Congress" was to favor his program, not anybody else's. In the event, he did not get everything he wanted, but he got more than I, the action officer on how to get the most for the Navy's money, would have given him if the gift had been mine.

On the basis of all these experiences with Admiral Rickover, his attitudes and programs were, as you can well imagine, an important part of the calculus when I began working with Worth Bagley, Stan Turner, and the others on Project 60.

With his disproportionately large amount of influence, through his Congressional friends, over a disproportionately large part of the Navy's budget, Rickover had the power to skew any plan for modernizing the Navy that did not give his programs what he considered to be their due. There was nothing to be gained by antagonizing him, not to speak of fighting him head-on. The only tactic with any promise was to try to negotiate a quid-pro-quo deal with him; to give him, in return for his support of High-Low, or at worst his neutrality toward it, something he dearly desired. Actually that was not hard to do. Though Rick always tried to make it appear that everybody except he and the Congressional sages who supported him opposed nuclear propulsion, the fact is that within the Navy there was almost universal support for most of the nuclear-propulsion program.

Speaking for myself, I heartily favored nuclear propulsion for both attack and missile submarines, for a certain number of carriers, and for a certain number of their escorts, agreeing with Rickover that in *some* situations the kind of performance only nuclear ships could deliver was indispensable. Our differences were two: over how many nuclear ships should be built how fast, in other words, how large a portion of each year's budget should be spent on nuclear vessels, and over what fraction of the surface fleet we could afford to have nuclear-powered given the importance of numbers of ships. Those were the areas in which I hoped we could reach an accommodation.

With a view to exploring this subject as soon as possible, I arranged a meeting with Rick shortly after my return to Washington from Vietnam, a month before I officially took over my new duties. Since it is advisable to prepare carefully for a summit, a few days before it was to occur one of my closest colleagues, Captain (now Rear Admiral) Charles F. Rauch, Jr., an ex-Polaris skipper who knew his way around nuclear propulsion, paid a visit there. Chick spent the better part of a day talking with Rickover's principal assistants, and at the end was granted a fifteen-minute audience by the man himself. Rickover played the codger that afternoon. He gave Chick avuncular advice about how to do his job as a member of my personal staff. He commented knowingly that I would have some trouble because I had jumped over so many people into the job of CNO. He insinuated that I owed my elevation to Paul Nitze and "the systems-analysis crowd." (Rick has always hated systems analysis, doubtless because its analyses often have been unfavorable to his systems. As I noted in the previous chapter, he managed to smuggle his Class-688 submarine into the budget before Navy Systems Analysis knew there was such a vessel.) He ventured the thought that aviators were running the Navy, to its disadvantage, and asked Chick what my opinion on that subject was, which was simply trying to make trouble since he knew perfectly well what my opinion on that subject was. Chick ducked the question. Rick said that the Navy didn't have enough submarines or good enough submarines, that present-day officers were a sorry lot, and that American submarine design capability was nonexistent. He said that if the United States were to get into a conventional naval war today with Russia, it would lose. Rick and I always did see pretty much eye to eye on the relative naval strength of the US and the USSR, though at that particular moment I was 10 percent more optimistic than he. I thought we had a 55–45 chance of winning such a war on 30 June 1970. Chick concluded his report of the interview with, "I would predict that he will be very honest but very friendly with you since he will know that he got all of his little barbs and petty concerns to you through me."

The tone of our meeting, which took place on 2 June 1970, was much as Chick had predicted. Even that early, the outlines of Project 60 had emerged and I was able to lay the High-Low concept and my feelings about ongoing construction programs before Rick, including the tentative decisions to continue DLGN construction at its present rate, to continue expeditiously to work on the two CVANs that were authorized to join *Enterprise,* and to push for authorization for a fourth. Then I made my pitch. The Class-688 attack submarine program called for the delivery of three boats a year. I proposed to increase this to five a year for the first three years and reduce it to two a year thereafter. The advantage of this arrangement to Rickover was obvious: I was promising him nineteen boats instead of fifteen during the five budget years of my tenure. The advantage to me was pretty clear, also. Creating new ships is a time-consuming process. I calculated that even if my Low projects were approved rapidly, it would be three years before I could spend much money on them. Once that time came, I would grudge the $300 million a year the *third* 688 boat would cost, but until that time came I would have available the extra 600 million a year for a fourth and fifth boat, and at the rate Soviet submarine building was going, the Navy had a real need to speed up its own program.

I told Rickover all that. What I definitely did not tell him was that I hoped my offer of extra 688s would head off, for a time at least, a new class of even more luxurious attack submarines that he had begun to campaign for and whose design doubtless would burst from his brow full-blown whenever he thought the time was propitious. I was successful in preventing that from happening. He also had begun to campaign for a new class of ballistic-missile submarine to replace Polaris-Poseidon. On that subject I said that if the Soviet advances in missile technology and numbers continued at their present pace for much longer, I, too, would consider a new strategic submarine a necessity and would fully support it. In return I asked him to support my Low program for inexpensive Sea Control ships, Patrol Frigates, and hydrofoil craft in substantial numbers. At the risk of appearing repetitious, I point out and emphasize that I did not propose—nor did I desire—to cut back any ongoing nuclear-propulsion projects; with respect to the carriers, indeed, I desired and proposed to expedite them. All I wanted Admiral Rickover to do was go along with, at the very least tolerate quietly, my new programs. On 2 June 1970 he agreed to do so.

I am not entirely gullible. I did not think I had exorcised Rickover that easily. CNOs before me had used similar expedients, such expedients being the only ones available to them (as to me) because of Rickover's power on the Hill, and despite them Rickover's power had continued to grow at the expense of a balanced Navy. That power was the heart of the matter. Inextricably entwined with the important professional question of how many ships of what types should be nuclear-powered was the crucial institutional question of whether a fourth-echelon corner of the Ship Systems Command should exert the enormous, if not preponderant, influence it did on the Navy's budget, the Navy's strategic posture and the careers of thousands of the Navy's men and women. There is almost no way for a CNO not to find himself in an adversary position to Rickover, because Rickover brazenly—though seldom openly—challenges the duly constituted authority of every CNO and indeed every Secretary of the Navy, every Secretary of Defense, and every President. After my summit with Rick I had a small hope for the best and a large expectation of the worst.

The first signal from Nuclear Propulsion indicated that my expectation had a firmer foundation than my hope. Toward the end of August I circulated a draft of Project 60 to senior officers along with a request for their comments. Rickover's response filled me with foreboding about his intentions toward High-Low. He did not condescend to submit a point-by-point analysis or critique of the various programs I have sketched in the preceding chapter. Instead he came forward with an eight-page pamphlet that contained theology, exhortation, and innuendo in about equal parts. The theology reiterated the virtues of nuclear power. The exhortation called upon all good men to come to the aid of nuclear power. The innuendo suggested that no naval officer but H. G. Rickover, and especially no CNO, had the wit to grasp the importance of nuclear power. Since almost all this material has appeared in Rickover's Congressional testimony or speeches or interviews or books or magazine articles, and can be found in his collected works in any public library, I shall not trouble to quote it here. I passed it along to my staff with a note telling them, in effect, that if they could find anything in it worthwhile to include in the Project 60 report, they should do so.

For two and a half years thereafter, Rick and I coexisted more or less peacefully, though I suppose at bottom we acted like two wary old dogs who keep circling each other because neither dares lunge first. We conferred regularly on the telephone and face to face. I delivered the submarines I had promised. Together we got the CVAN program moving a little faster and, far more important, sold a skeptical Congress the proposition that the May 1972 strategic arms limitation (SALT) agreements made a new class of missile submarine, the Trident, necessary. And as I have said, I made no objection early in 1971 and even earlier in 1973 when Rick's biennial campaigns for reappointment got under way, though I confess that I made certain that before giving my assent each of the two Secretar-

ies of the Navy involved was aware of the ritualistic pattern of
Rickover-inspired Congressional pressure for biennial reappointment. Nevertheless the hair on the backs of our necks always seemed
to bristle when we encountered each other, especially when Congress
was working on the budget. I suppose that was inevitable, given
Rickover's status as an independent baron within the Navy. The
budget, a Presidential document that presumably arbitrates among
the competing claims for money, never gave Rickover everything he
considered necessary in the nuclear power field and never gave me
everything I considered necessary in either nuclear or conventionally
propelled ships. Consequently Rickover always was nudging Congress to give him a piece of my balanced program and I was constantly fighting to maintain the balance within inadequate budget
allocations. Henry Kissinger, no lover of independent baronies,
asked me at least twice about the possibility of retiring Rickover for
keeps. Both times I reminded him of what Congress had done to
LBJ, and Henry dropped the subject.

What finally impelled me to tangle with Rickover had nothing to
do with shipbuilding programs or the budget, but with what was
about to befall Captain Charles O. Swanson, the Commander of the
Pearl Harbor Naval Shipyard. I first heard about Captain Swanson
some time in April 1973 when a routine paper indicating that he
would be relieved of his command on 1 June crossed my desk. I gave
Captain Swanson a second thought on 1 May when I received a long
and touching letter from his wife, Anne. The letter, after summarizing Captain Swanson's Navy career, which was impressive, and
touching on the poor shape the Pearl Harbor yard was in when he
took it over on 1 July 1972, which I knew to be true, continued:

> In February it became increasingly evident that a political battle was
> brewing, with Admiral Hyman Rickover making greater demands and
> often questionable ones on all U.S. Navy shipyards, but Pearl Harbor
> Naval Shipyard in particular. Chuck realized less and less support from
> the "corporate office" of Naval Ship Systems Command in spite of the
> improving performance of the yard, and the response and obvious loyalty
> to him and what he was attempting to do here on the part of labor and
> management, and the growing professionalism of his military group.
> ... Finally last Monday, April 23rd, Chuck flew to Washington to see
> [Rear] Admiral [Robert] Gooding [Commander of the Ship Systems
> Command]. When he arrived in Washington, and prior to seeing Admi-

ral Gooding, he was made aware of the fact that many in NavShips knew that his relief had been selected, even was making plans to be in Pearl Harbor by 28 May, and that he, Chuck, would be relieved on 1 June. Losing a political battle is shocking, disappointing, temporarily defeating, but acceptable. The manner in which Admiral Gooding [and] his deputies . . . handled themselves with respect to a man of Chuck's career reputation, integrity, and loyalty to the Navy and the EDO community in particular—to say nothing of the morale and the career aspirations of the other officers on his staff here—was totally . . . unacceptable. . . .

It is not my intention to request your help in any interceding action —Chuck sees his usefulness as an active duty EDO at an end and plans to submit his request for retirement—but rather that your inquiry and interest in this might stem the possibility of further intimidation and further breakdown of morale within the EDO community itself. I feel strongly these events must relate to the atmosphere of fear in which the civilian managers in shipyards working on nuclear ships are forced to function. . . . My almost twenty-three years as a Navy wife have been happy and rewarding ones and I do not want to see the total breakdown of something I hold so dear. Please, Admiral Zumwalt, can you help?

A student of the bureaucracy might find it worth noting that on 2 May, the day after I received and read Anne Swanson's letter and directed my staff to make a preliminary inquiry into what was behind the premature relief of her husband, I sent off a memo to the Superintendent of the Naval Academy whose first paragraph read as follows:

In accordance with the recent decision of the Secretary of the Navy and the Chief of Naval Operations, the academic building which is being constructed to comprise the Naval Engineering Studies Complex of the U.S. Naval Academy is hereby named Rickover Hall. This is considered to be a fitting tribute to Vice Admiral Hyman G. Rickover, U.S. Navy, and will provide additional inspiration to our future naval officers.

Ironies like that appear regularly on any desk like the one I was sitting at. Indeed I am glad that the Navy has honored Rickover's early achievements. I only wish that he had managed to augment them with that sense of Platonic justice about which he lectured me in 1959.

My involvement with the Swanson affair lasted a year and two days; my final memorandum on the subject was dated 3 May 1974. The course the affair took, in outline, was that my preliminary inquiries convinced me that there was enough doubt about the propriety of relieving Captain Swanson after only eleven months of a tour that normally would last three years, and thereby irrevocably foreclosing any chance he had for further advancement in the Navy, to warrant an investigation by the Inspector General, Vice Admiral Means Johnston, Jr. On 29 May I so ordered. Means, a man of much fairness, listened to fifty or sixty hours of testimony in Hawaii, and consulted with a number of senior officers there who were familiar with the work of the yard, including Admiral Noel Gayler, Commander in Chief Pacific, and Admiral Chick Clarey, Commander in Chief Pacific Fleet. Both of them had a favorable impression of Swanson. In fact both of them had alerted me soon after Anne Swanson had about what was, in their judgment, the unwarranted relief of Captain Swanson. When Means returned to Washington he spent a day and a half with Rickover's files. An extract from a memorandum my executive assistant wrote me on 21 June after a long conversation with Means—whose job is designated "008" in Navy code—is relevant here:

> 008 said he saw Rickover and described Rick as terribly emotional and unstable. He said Rick screamed and yelled at him and was extremely upset. Rick is apparently worried about a Congressional investigation. . . . Rick finally and reluctantly allowed 008 to see the letter reports sent to him by Commander Taylor [the AEC inspection head in Pearl]. 008 said that he was not allowed to copy the letters or take the letters out of the room. He could read the letters and take notes . . . and he was under observation at all times during this day and a half period. . . . Rick would call him periodically and have another tantrum.

Means' report, submitted the first week of July, was that there was no cause to relieve Captain Swanson of his command.

At that point, of course, I had to give Rear Admiral Gooding and his boss, Admiral Isaac Kidd, the Chief of Naval Material, an opportunity to respond to the IG's report. (Rickover managed to avoid official involvement as a principal in the Swanson affair. He maintained both in person and through Kidd and Gooding that he had nothing to do with the proposed dismissal of Captain Swanson. A carload of salt would not have enabled any of us to swallow that claim.) Admirals Kidd and Gooding dissented from the findings of Admiral Johnston, in detail and at length, so Captain Swanson had to be given a crack at them. He wrote a reply that ran to two volumes, each of two hundred pages or more when all enclosures, exhibits and other addenda were added in. That was mid-August. An inspection of the Pearl Harbor yard by a Rickover team was scheduled for early October, and I decided that it would be prudent to await its findings before taking final action. The package that arrived on 17 October contained a sixty-seven-page report with as many or more additional pages of charts, graphs, enclosures etc., a thirteen-page covering letter from Bob Gooding and a two-page covering letter from Rickover containing a couple of characteristically snide remarks: "[This report] is in contrast to the practice of sending people to a shipyard or any industrial activity who are not technically knowledgeable of the subject to be inspected which can only result in superficial findings." (Take that Admiral Johnston!) "On the basis of this inspection I extended Pearl Harbor's authorization to handle radioactive material associated with naval nuclear propulsion plants for six months. . . . Under normal circumstances I would have extended the yard's authorization for a much shorter period of time. However, because of the political situation surrounding the Shipyard Commander I decided on the six-month extension in order for the situation to 'cool' and with the hope that this period of time would permit the Navy to make a decision on the Shipyard Commander's tenure without having a short-time deadline to consider." (Take that Admiral Zumwalt!) To relieve Rick's painful uncertainty about the Shipyard Commander's tenure, I dictated the following memorandum for the record on 24 October and sent copies to the Chief of Naval Personnel, the Chief of Naval Material and Vice Admiral Rickover: "It is planned that Captain Swanson will remain in command of the Pearl Harbor Naval Shipyard. There are no plans to relieve him." And on 29 October I wrote to the Secretary of the Navy about Rickover's endorsement: "In reviewing subject memorandum I note an implication—that the situation is simply being allowed to 'cool' for political purposes. This is not the case—his retention in command was an equitable decision based on the merits of the case." (Take that Admiral Rickover!)

The evidence that led me to retain Swanson fills half a dozen legal-size file folders. The most limitations of space allow me to do, then, is sketch in the broadest outlines the conclusions Means Johnston and the rest of us reached on the basis of that evidence. The first conclusion was that Swanson had been marked by Rickover before he ever assumed command of the yard, which meant his dismissal had little to do with his performance there. On 13 June 1972, while being briefed in Washington for his new assignment, Swanson had spent fifteen minutes with Rickover. Rickover had concluded the conversation with his customary charm and sensitivity. "You'll never make it," he had told Swanson. "You worked for that son of a bitch, Name Deleted," Name Deleted being a distinguished engineering duty officer who was reluctant to go along with Rickover's methods of personnel administration. Additional evidence that Swanson was a marked man appeared in various cantankerous and cautionary letters Rickover sent him before he had had an opportunity to settle into his job. And any doubt I may have entertained that it was Rickover who had marked him was dispelled after my inquiries started when Admirals Gooding and Kidd offered him a wide variety of choice engineering jobs in non-nuclear situations if only he would leave Pearl Harbor quietly.

A second conclusion was that the management system that Captain Swanson had opposed to incur Rickover's wrath was, to use words I used at the time and not carelessly, un-American and autocratic. It was, to be blunt about it, a system of spying and intimidation. Members of Rickover's AEC shipyard inspection team walked around the yard, clipboards in hand, making notes on who was smoking or drinking a soda or talking with friends, on how much time workmen spent on lunch breaks or in the head, and of course on which supervisors were allowing such deeds to be done by their people. They even went so far as to invade the parking lot of a popular restaurant just outside the yard to take down license-plate numbers of the cars with shipyard stickers parked there, because Rickover did not approve of his folk eating lunch off base. On one occasion when the skipper of a ship that had been overhauled in the yard sent out letters of commendation to the workmen he thought had done an exceptionally good job, Rickover ordered them withdrawn. In May 1973, a team from the civilian Manpower Action Council, an advisory group working out of Ike Kidd's office, inspected the Pearl Harbor Naval Shipyard and reported:

We . . . became immediately aware of the aura of fear among the workers and management alike. It was apparent in our discussions with the engineers and mechanics who are associated with nuclear work in their hesitancy to talk with MAC representatives for fear of retribution from the "gestapo" which management has created. Our presence was looked on as another attempt to pin down the "troublemakers" or as a waste of time (we were quoted the cost per man-hour which we were wasting by one enthusiastic manager). However once we had established a rapport with the employees they spoke of their deliberate attempts to get out of nuclear work, including mishandling of their work so that the "spies" could require their removal.

The report also spoke of the unwillingness of workmen in the nuclear shops to accept promotion to foremen, and the steady exodus of middle managers in nuclear work. When Captain Swanson took over the yard he tried to mitigate this "Orwellian system," as he repeatedly called it in his defense, being sure that the watchfulness of Big Brother was one of the major reasons for the yard's poor record of completing nuclear jobs on schedule and within the contracted price. (The yard had always had an excellent record in non-nuclear work, it is interesting to note.)

A third conclusion was that what made possible the existence and the persistence of such an obnoxious system of management was abuse by Rickover of the authority his position with the Atomic Energy Commission gave him. As an AEC official Rickover was the safety czar over all work on or connected with naval reactors. He had authority to prescribe rules and procedures governing the handling of radioactive materials in the course of such work. He had authority to conduct periodic inspections to determine whether or not those rules and procedures were being followed. He had authority to withdraw permission to handle radioactive materials from any facility he —and he alone—judged was mishandling them. He also had authority to remove individuals from nuclear work on safety grounds. As a result of this very large grant of authority, which extended onboard nuclear vessels and which clearly should have been invested in some sort of board or committee rather than in one man, or subject to automatic careful review, Rickover was able to put into every nuclear facility a team of subordinates who were officially attached to the AEC, though they usually were naval people, and who reported directly to him. Clearly stringent inspection systems are mandatory in any facility involved in nuclear safety. But, going beyond safety considerations, Rickover used those teams to govern every aspect of a nuclear facility's activities and to bend every employee of such facilities to his will, which he was able to do by brandishing "safety" whenever he met opposition. Let Means Johnston describe how this system affected Captain Swanson:

> . . . at Pearl Harbor Naval Shipyard there is a Commander Taylor plus four naval officers and one civilian (Navy payroll) wearing AEC hats. These people are all experts in the radiological field, probably the best

the Navy has. Unfortunately they work directly for Vice Admiral Rickover in his AEC hat and not for the Navy. My investigation revealed that instead of really helping the Commanding Officer of the Shipyard, Commander Taylor was actually harrassing the Commanding Officer involving himself in every facet of management, and submitting reports (no copy to the CO) direct to Vice Admiral Rickover in his AEC hat. Vice Admiral Rickover then used this information in his NavShips-08 position to write official letters to the Commanding Officer. This procedure violates the chain of command completely and, furthermore, it constitutes a vicious spy system, alien to normally accepted tenets of Navy management. As a related matter, COs of submarines also are required to submit secret reports to Vice Admiral Rickover concerning yard performance. When one CO was asked if the reports were balanced, that is, did he include favorable comments concerning management, he replied in the negative, that only unfavorable comments were desired. Again the CO of the Shipyard is not provided a copy of these informal letter reports. My recommendation is that Commander Taylor and his staff be withdrawn from the AEC and put to work helping the Navy. Commander Taylor should report to the Commanding Officer of the Pearl Harbor Naval Shipyard. I would further recommend that all other AEC representatives in all other yards work directly for the Shipyard Commander.

I think I had ample reason to come to Captain Swanson's defense.

In December—"as a Christmas present," Swanson subsequently noted—Rear Admiral Gooding struck again, way below the belt in my opinion. He filed not just an unfavorable but a vehemently adverse fitness report on Swanson for the period 1 February to 30 September, thus turning 180 degrees away from the fitness report he had written for the previous period, from Swanson's assumption of his command to 31 January, which had given Swanson high marks. (One of the things Means Johnston had wondered about when he made his inspection was why on 31 March Bob Gooding had decided to fire an officer he had reported to be outstanding as of 31 January.) Furthermore two other superiors of Swanson's, Commander Fourteenth Naval District and Commander Service Forces Pacific, had filed fitness reports on him for the period beginning 1 February, and both had given him superb performance ratings and had recommended that he be selected for admiral as soon as might be. Once again Swanson was put to the labor of composing a lengthy defense, which he delivered in two installments, the first on 31 January, the second on 15 February. Gooding lingered over this package for almost a month before replying to the reply, then bucked it along to Ike Kidd who apparently considered it such an exceedingly hot potato that he whipped it over to me without wasting a moment or indulging in a word of comment. When I put my staff to analyzing it, I made it clear that I was in no great hurry. Whatever final action was taken would have to be taken by the Secretary of the Navy, and the incumbent, John Warner, had stated that he was not about to tangle with a man of Rickover's clout on Capitol Hill. I left him a copy of Means Johnston's memorandum to buck him up but he made it clear he would not act on any recommendation. However, John was about to be relieved by his Under Secretary, J. William Middendorf II—who at this writing still holds the position—and it was to him I decided my recommendations must go. My principal recommendation, which I sent to Secretary Middendorf along with the rest of the package on 3 May, was that Gooding's adverse fitness report be stricken from Swanson's record. Bill Middendorf had the courage to direct that this action be taken.

The denouement of the Swanson story is bittersweet, though more bitter than sweet. On 30 October 1974, Captain Swanson relinquished command of the Pearl Harbor Naval Shipyard and retired from the service. In a way he had won his fight. He had faced down Rickover & Company and kept his job for a year and a half longer than they had wanted him to. He had left Pearl Harbor Naval Shipyard a better place than he had found it despite their lack of support. He had retired with a record that shows he was vindicated by the highest naval authority and with the satisfaction of having made it a good deal harder for Rickover to mistreat future shipyard commanders. But he had had to retire. The system, alas, does not forgive anyone who takes it on as vigorously as Charles Swanson did. If he had not fallen afoul of Rickover his ability almost certainly would have won him flag rank, and his Naval career might well have been a brilliant one. The Navy also lost much when Charles Swanson was compelled to leave it. It lost his ability. Beyond that it lost his integrity, a quality in shorter supply and of more worth.

Rear Admiral Gooding is now Vice Admiral Gooding by dint of his command having been elevated from a two-star to a three-star billet. Admiral Kidd is Commander in Chief of the Atlantic Fleet and just missed being picked for CNO. And old man Rickover, he just keeps rolling along.

The first budget in which Rickover, according to our June 1970 understanding, was to give me some *quid* in return for two years of *quo* was the one for Fiscal Year 1974, which began on 1 July 1973 and was half over when the Congress, behind schedule as usual, enacted the Defense appropriation just before the Christmas recess. In FYs '72 and '73 Rickover had received his extra submarines and my help in securing authorization and the first funds for the fourth nuclear carrier. Now I expected him to accept fewer submarines in the 1975 budget plan and to support the Low parts of the High-Low mix on the Hill in 1974. The FY '74 budget was the critical one for the Low end of the mix because it contained the first significant sum for the vessel that was the critical component of Low, the Sea Control Ship. The Sea Control Ship, you may remember, was an austere little (17,000-ton) carrier, carrying fourteen helicopters and three VSTOL planes, that would cost about $100 million, or about an eighth as much as a big carrier.

By the fall of 1973, the SCS concept had been thoroughly tested and had worked out better than even I in my enthusiasm had expected. The testing had been conducted by Guam, an amphibious ship designed to put Marines ashore in helicopters. Guam was slightly bigger than SCS but similar in speed, endurance and air capability. We had sent her into strategically important waters in various parts of the world to carry out exercises that simulated the situations SCS might find herself in: defending convoys in the United Kingdom-Iceland gap against land-based, long-range bombers; repelling submarine attacks in mid-ocean; alerting task forces to incoming aircraft, submarines, and surface ships. The favorable results of those exercises had won over a number of skeptics within the Navy, including those aviators who customarily insisted on traveling first class. James Schlesinger, the Secretary of Defense, was for it, overruling John Warner who told me that he had committed himself to Rickover to slow the program down. Secretary Schlesinger had approved a construction schedule that called for the delivery of one SCS in FY '75, three in FY '76 and two a year for two years thereafter, a total of eight. The first $29 million of construction money had been in the budget the President sent to Congress and had cleared the two Armed Services Committees. By Thanksgiving all that remained to make SCS a reality was action by the two Appropriations Committees.

Meanwhile, throughout the fall, I had been receiving loud and clear signals that Rickover was fulminating against SCS. One of the loudest and clearest came in September from Nelson W. Freeman, the Chairman of the Board of Tenneco, the parent company of Newport News Shipbuilding, one of the principal contractors for nuclear ships. Freeman, bringing with him his lawyer, Thomas Corcoran—"Tommy the Cork" of New Deal fame—had come to Deputy Secretary of Defense Bill Clements and me to tell us that unless Rickover was restrained somehow from interfering in Newport News' operations, the company would have to seriously consider giving up Navy business. I quote from my memorandum of the meeting:

> Mr. Freeman then proceeded to describe at length the inspection system which Admiral Rickover and the Navy use in Newport News. He stated that it has become so onerous and the management approach so abusive that he has ordered Newport News to "throw Admiral Rickover's ass" out of the plant if he shows up. . . . I said that in my view we were dealing with a problem in which, as a result of Admiral Rickover's management system, we were about to kill the goose that laid the golden egg. Admiral Carr, [Clements' Executive Assistant] . . . stated that Admiral Rickover was only responsible for the nuclear part of it. Mr. Freeman said that anybody that thinks that doesn't know how the system works. I gave my view that Admiral Rickover does get beyond nuclear power and does really run the entire shipyard involved in constructing a nuclear plant and indeed the Ships Systems Command with regard to nuclear ships.

During that same conversation, this piece of disagreeable news came out:

> Under questioning from Mr. Corcoran, Mr. Freeman confirmed that Newport News had submitted a bid for a design of the Sea Control Ship which was about three and a half million dollars and that they had been "blackmailed" out of it by Admiral Rickover and it had gone to National Steel for seven million, even though National Steel didn't have the expertise and had to hire architects. Mr. Clements appeared puzzled at this. I pointed out to him that Admiral Rickover's policy is to work against any non-nuclear-propelled large (war) ship. Mr. Freeman confirmed that Admiral Rickover was vehemently against non-nuclear propelled ships.

I cannot resist quoting the last paragraph of the memorandum as well:

Mr. Corcoran made the point that there is nothing as dangerous as an old man with a dream, that Admiral Rickover is trying very hard to accomplish his vision for a nuclear-propelled Navy before he dies; but that he, Tommy Corcoran, sees much evidence on the Hill of great concern about the corners that Admiral Rickover is now cutting.

In the first part of October, when most of us were spending most of our time on the Yom Kippur War in the Middle East—and Mr. Nixon was spending most of his time "massacring" Archibald Cox, Elliot Richardson, and William Ruckelshaus and then enduring the storm of public outrage the Saturday Night Massacre provoked—I got wind of anti-SCS machinations in another quarter. In describing a day he spent on the Hill pressing the Navy budget, John Warner said that in the course of a call he had paid on George Mahon, the Chairman of the House Appropriations Committee, members of the Committee's staff openly attacked SCS in front of Mahon and him as "Zumwalt's Gold Watch." The Secretary did not identify the staff members, but I knew that Ralph Preston, the chief counsel and thus head of the staff, was in close touch with Rickover. Of the four Congressional committees I dealt with, Mahon's always was the most difficult because the Chairman, a charming and courtly gentleman and one of the grand old men of the House, left much business to his staff. Some members of that staff seemed to me to abuse the confidence Mahon placed in them by promoting hobby horses and pursuing small private vendettas. One year the Committee reduced the funds for the Center for Naval Analyses which had refused to fire a staff member who had marched in a peace demonstration; a Committee staff member told me that had been the reason for the cut.

Incidentally, though the phrase "Zumwalt's Gold Watch" has a Rickoverian ring, I never discovered whether or not Rick actually coined it. I never even discovered whether the phrase was meant to describe Sea Control Ship as a ceremonial, over-expensive, and essentially pointless gadget, or as a bribe the Navy was giving me so that I would keep quiet after my imminent retirement.

Rickover and I talked often about his programs and mine in October, November, and December. The tone of our conversations was not improved by the high feelings the Swanson affair was generating at the time, but I doubt that their substance would have been much different if Charles Swanson never had existed. Some excerpts from my notes of one of these conversations, on 30 November, give an idea of how they generally went, and also show Rick playing one of his favorite roles, the elder statesman—Polonius maybe. Rick began:

"There are—hell of a lot of rumors—I can say one thing, I think if we work together—can do something for—Navy. If [we] don't there will be lot of trouble. Rumors are [around] that you want to kill frigate and you want to kill four submarines. Two out of FY '73 program and two out of FY '74. My feeling is you're against nuclear power—I have that feeling." [I responded] "I think we've settled things pretty good Rick—I've guaranteed three after five." [By this time Bill Clements had arbitrated the battle between Rickover and me over whether to go down to two subs in the '75 budget as we had agreed three years before. Bill had decided on three every other year and two every other year.] [R. said] "Well, we've been through that and my feeling is that you want to reduce submarines—but that's all right you can have that feeling—you're CNO —you're boss—but I don't agree we ought to reduce [them]." [I replied] "My perception is that is not way it works—my perception is I'm trying to get nuclear-propelled ships and non-nuclear-propelled ships and you're on Hill killing my non-nuclear ships." [R. said] "No, I'm not killing your non-nuclear ships. I don't care what people have told you —I told you that [on phone] this morning. . . . I did not mention any other ships—and I'm not going to do that—I'm going to assure you of that. I would like to say—I think we'd better get together." [I said] "I do too, Rick." [R. said] "I think dealing with intermediaries bad. If all right with you, sir, I think we ought to make definitely these points. I can talk now as old guy. I can't gain anything further. I think you know, all I'm trying to do whatever I can for U.S." [I said] "I feel same way." [R. said] "OK, but I see it in a different way because you have whole life ahead of you. You have things you can do—certainly with a man of your ability there are plenty opportunities. I don't have that—all I can do now is whatever I can for U.S." [I said] "I think that's a good idea." [R. said] ". . . something can be dispelled right at moment instead of going on and on and on and on!—and I don't like it either [because] when we started out you used to come thru me—and then all of a sudden it changed. Doesn't do any good for the Navy."[I said] "We waste a hell of lot of [collective] effort." [R. said] "Right—I've got my people all kinds of people doing nothing except this goddamn crap. . . . If issues were settled between us we could knock off all that and get to work. It takes up lot of your time too. I'll make [a] deal with you—I'll help you lobby for your goddamned stuff too. Not against your stuff, [I'm] only against killing nuclear ships. [I am] no expert on other ships, I don't have time—I can't do it. I'll help you. . . ."

After that theatrical preamble, which of course was entirely mean-ingless since Rick not only did not help me but continued to work actively against me, the conversation got down to what it was sup-posed to be about, an effort on my part to ensure that the sudden deadline with which I had been confronted by Rick on awarding a contract to provide drydock facilities for a private yard to build submarines in would withstand the scrutiny of propriety and legality. It did.

In December Rickover's views prevailed on the Mahon Commit-tee to knock SCS out of the budget. However the Senate Appropria-tions Committee, whose Chairman, John McClellan, and senior Re-publican, Milton Young, were both strong supporters of the High-Low mix, left it in and the matter went to conference. The Senate conferees, including the doughty Senator John Pastore, fought hard for SCS, but Mahon is a powerful Congressional figure and they had to give him something. The compromise kept the twenty-nine million dollars in the budget but froze it pending an evaluation of SCS for the Mahon Committee by the General Ac-counting Office. In effect that killed SCS. Even if the evaluation was favorable, which was unlikely, since the GAO is a creature of Con-gress and more often than not acts according to its perception of its master's desires, the delay would effectively postpone the project long enough to give Rickover and its other foes time for several more cracks at it. To no one's surprise, the evaluation, which came in after my watch had ended, was unfavorable. However, I suspect, the need for such a ship being so urgent and obvious, that sooner or later Congress will approve something like the SCS. Jim Schlesinger tried in the fall of 1975 and saw his "small" carrier become just as expen-sive as *Eisenhower* and *Vinson,* but only half as big.

Nevertheless, the Sea Control Ship lives. The Soviet Navy has two in operation and has begun construction on a third.

Rickover and I had one more go round in 1973, between the adjournment of Congress in mid-December and the new year. That is always a frantic time of year in the Executive Branch because the next fiscal year's budget, which goes to Congress in January, is getting its final jiggering. By that time the amount of money each agency is to get is pretty much settled, but it is still possible, if your footwork is fast and you have plenty of peripheral vision, to rear-range the spending within an agency. During those last two weeks of December Rickover made a crafty and determined effort to get $244 million of construction money allocated to two of his guided missile frigates (DLGNs). Since that would have meant not building at least eight and probably ten patrol frigates that the Navy badly needed, I fought him tooth and nail. Rickover's repertoire of wiles ranged all the way from the almost sublime one of trying to slip the delivery date of the desperately needed third nuclear carrier by more than a year so that Newport News would be able to make room for DLGN work to the totally ridiculous one of getting himself invited to the Schlesingers for dinner so he could make his pitch to the Secretary in the privacy of his home on the day after Christmas. When Jim Schlesinger called me up to find out if I agreed with Rickover's pitch to put the nearly quarter of a billion dollars into the budget for the next increment of nuclear frigates, I took the position that he should be given 100 million and that it should be added to the budget, not put in by taking out conventional ships. I also urged that Rick be made again to pledge active support to the conventional ships program.

On Monday, 31 December, Secretary Schlesinger informed Rickover that he would add the 100 million onto the budget provided Rickover promised full active support of the Sea Control Ship and Patrol Frigates. Rickover said, "In other words you are blackmailing me." Schlesinger, smiling, said, "Yes." Rickover said, "I accept." I consider that I won that fight and lost the war. Although Rickover got, with my support, his $100 million add-on, which was less than half what he wanted, and it did not come out of the hide of non-nuclear ships, he did not keep his bargain with Secretary Schlesinger, but continued to work against any and all Low construction programs.

While all this was going on, the Congress gave Rickover his fourth star, and we had a little ceremonial breakfast in my office so that I could formally commission him. As we finished breakfast there was the following conversation, as I reconstructed it:

Rick asked what I was going to do about his commission. I said we were going to deliver it to him, about two minutes worth, with a photographer. I don't know if you want a picture, I said, but I do. R. said, Oh, I want one too.

R. asked me what I was going to do when I got out. I said I don't know, I haven't given it any real thought. R. said, I hear rumors that you are going into politics. It would take you too long. By the time that you get so that you could carry your weight around, it would be a long time. I said it would drive me crazy to get a job where I couldn't get anything done. R. said, I wouldn't wait because you will have a let down. I said probably after two weeks I would be climbing the walls. He said you would, you're not that kind of guy. My advice is to go right into something or you will have a hell of a let down. I mentioned something about going on a trip—go to the mountains, fishing or hiking.

Ceremony then held and Rick departed.

CHAPTER 6

Congressional Dispositions

Every program of the Navy's, like every program of every executive agency's, needs Congressional approval before it can begin. Consequently lobbying—"Congressional relations" is the official euphemism—is an activity a naval executive must engage in assiduously, particularly if he proposes to strike out in a new direction as I proposed to do. One cannot lobby the Congress as an institution; one lobbies individual members of the Congress, each with his or her distinctive intellect and interests, principles and prejudices, talents and habits of work. It is difficult to overstate the importance of establishing some sort of working relationship with a substantial number of these widely assorted men and women. I have tried to show the enormous influence on the balance and the capability of the Navy as a whole Admiral Rickover has exercised for almost a generation, chiefly by virtue of the relationships he has established with certain powerful figures on Capitol Hill. In succeeding chapters I shall describe how the inbred cultural attitudes or the parochial political calculations of a handful of Congressmen put personnel reform in the Navy in jeopardy. I shall also touch on the way the handling of a number of critical international matters, among them strategic arms limitation and the winding down of the war in southeast Asia, suffered from the failure of the administration to take into its confidence members of Congress most intimately concerned with them. In this chapter I shall try to give some of the flavor of the day-to-day encounters between the Navy and the Congress over proposed or ongoing programs.

The Navy deals, as a matter of routine, with fewer than 100 of the 535 members of the Congress: the members of the leadership hierarchy of the Senate and the House, the members of the Armed Services Committee of each body, the Chairman of the Appropriations Committee of each body, and those members of Appropriations whose duties or predilections have led them to concern themselves with military affairs. When I assumed office, a senior admiral told me that I need not worry about Congress beyond those members. However, I conceived my role to be not only hortatory but educational and I resolved to see as many members as I could at least once each year in order to keep them up to date on the shifting strategic and maritime relationships in the world. I suppose I saw an average of 85 senators and 350 representatives every year. I found they fell into three categories of almost equal size. A third were sincerely what can be called in shorthand "pro-Defense." A third, for whatever reason, were sincerely "anti-Defense." The members of the middle third were the ones who really fascinated me, for they appeared to be entirely without convictions or principles. Let me relate what a couple of them told me. A representative: "Admiral, I'm as worried about our defense posture as you are, but if I vote for the Defense budget, I won't be here next term." A senator: "Look, I've got to have a 30 percent pro- and a 70 percent anti-defense voting record to get reelected in my state. You tell me which 30 percent to vote for." The members of this group gave me some important votes when I needed them badly, but I never learned to love them.

Throughout my watch the relations between the Navy and the four committees were, on the whole, businesslike and unambiguous. Of course each of the committees had its own way of looking at things. House Armed Services, under F. Edward Hébert of Louisiana, had the character—developed during the long chairmanship of Carl Vinson of Georgia and maintained during the short turbulent chairmanship of L. Mendel Rivers of South Carolina—of being the Navy's best friend in Congress when it came to construction programs. Hebert and a few of the committee's other members took a very dim view, though, of my efforts to loosen up the Navy's personnel administration and especially to achieve racial integration. House Appropriations, under George Mahon of Texas, tended to listen harder to Admiral Rickover than I thought it should, as I have noted, to the considerable detriment of my "Low" programs for relatively inexpensive ships. Senate Appropriations, under the tenacious John McClellan of Arkansas, aided by the committee's senior Republican, Milton Young of North Dakota, was an extremely businesslike group that did what it did with a minimum of fuss or bluster.

Senate Armed Services was the most unpredictable and therefore, I suppose you could say, the most colorful of the four committees. Its chairman, John Stennis of Mississippi, was a staunch supporter of a strong national defense, a man of integrity and patriotism whose earnest search for consensus made him one of the Senate's most respected members. However, in my opinion he lacked the intellectual breadth to preside over the momentous national issues that were his responsibility—not to say over the strong-willed group of men and women who sat on his committee. (Until she failed to be reelected in 1972, Margaret Chase Smith of Maine was the committee's senior Republican.) Senator Stennis was difficult to engage in objective discussion about defense because he had little grasp of the details of programs and tended to take criticisms of current programs or reservations about the budget as reproaches directed at him. Moreover, he did not exercise the control over the activities of members of his committee that the run of southern Senatorial patriarchs do. This was all to the good in the case of a committee member like Henry Jackson, with his sure grasp of national security issues, but it was singularly unhelpful in the case of a committee member like Stuart Symington, whose inability to grasp an issue has never prevented him from discussing it at length.

Additional to these regular and on the whole amicable and productive Congressional relations were the mostly hostile and futile encounters that took place when a senator or representative suddenly perceived in this or that naval situation an opportunity to do his country or himself a service and thereupon plunged toward the headlines as rapidly as the importance of the issue and his skill at public relations could carry him. The most diligent of these plungers, as we shall see, was Senator William Proxmire of Wisconsin, who felt he had a license to inquire into military affairs any time he chose in his capacity as chairman of the Subcommittee on Priorities and Economy of the Joint Economic Committee, of which he was also chairman. Another thorn was Representative Benjamin Rosenthal of New York, also the proprietor of a subcommittee, the Subcommittee on Europe of the Foreign Affairs Committee. That office enabled him to conduct a two-year campaign against homeporting a carrier task group in Greece.

To "homeport" a ship overseas simply means to move the families of the ship's crew to the port out of which that ship operates when it is deployed overseas, and to install some modest medical, educational, and commissary facilities for them if none exist already in that port. This expedient makes it unnecessary for the ship to return to the United States for the two or three years between major overhauls; ships not homeported have traditionally returned to their U.S. homeports every six months or so for another six months, if for no other reason than to allow families to spend time together. The Navy has long homeported a few ships overseas. Homeporting as many ships as possible overseas was an important element in the plan for modernizing the Navy that Project 60 produced. That plan envisioned a Navy with as few as twelve carriers in the near future. Yet there was no likelihood of reducing the Navy's commitment to maintain five carriers overseas at all times, a minimum of three in the western Pacific and two in the Mediterranean. On the contrary, the western Pacific commitment was irreducible for at least as long as the war continued in southeast Asia, and probably longer in view of the shaky situation in Korea and the need to keep Japan covered. And in the course of a conversation we had in the Sixth Fleet in September 1970, just after the Jordan crisis ended, President Nixon personally told me that he considered that the unstable situation in the Middle East made the Mediterranean commitment irreducible also.

Maintaining five carriers overseas without homeporting required a force of fifteen carriers, nine based on the west coast and six on the east coast. The rough calculation is that, in order to keep overseas deployments no longer than six months, each forward ship must be backed up by two ships stateside, one of them probably undergoing major overhaul, the other being routinely refitted and retrained in preparation for relieving the forward ship. Thus a Navy with twelve carriers can deploy five overseas continuously only by either extending the length of deployments beyond six months, which would damage morale and discourage reenlistments, or basing two or three on overseas ports. Overseas homeporting reduces the number of back-up ships needed in peacetime and greatly increases the time the crews of the homeported ships spend with their families, since there are no more six-month separations but several days of port visits every two or three weeks. It also increases the time the men of the ships based in the U.S. spend at home by about 15 percent, since each ship deployed permanently overseas means that a relief ship will not have to make a round trip across the ocean twice a year, a saving of some eight weeks a year per ship in the Mediterranean and twelve in the Pacific. The personnel issues were the overriding ones in the decision to homeport. Long family separations are the biggest single deterrent to enlistment and reenlistment in the Navy; reenlistment rates were at a disastrously low level; quality and number of enlistments threatened to go the same way as draft pressures decreased due to the drastic reduction of American forces in Vietnam. Keeping up the quantity and the quality of naval personnel was a prerequisite for any modernization plan.

My records show that I raised the question of homeporting as soon as I got back from that trip to the Mediterranean during which I spoke with the President. On 5 October, the day of my return, I sent a memorandum to Admiral Chick Clarey, the Vice CNO:

> Based on the President's obvious conviction in the utility of the Sixth Fleet, and in order to retain force levels for our credibility, I believe we need to recommend much more homeporting in the Mediterranean than has been the case in the past—to include carriers, escorts, and service ships.

Two days later I had another meeting with the President, during which he reaffirmed his desires about the Sixth Fleet. On 12 October I sent Chick a second memo on the subject:

> 1. As you know we are on the horns of a dilemma by the President's commitment that the force levels in the Sixth Fleet will not drop and the urgent budgetary requirement to start dropping force levels.
> 2. I consider it mandatory to come up with a homeporting scheme for SecNav to submit to SecDef ASAP.

On 6 November I had an informal meeting with Henry Kissinger to which I carried a large number of point papers about matters that concerned me at the time. One of them read:

> It is critical to personnel retention that long family separations be reduced.
>
> Homeporting of U.S. Navy ships in Sixth Fleet area (Rota, Malta, Naples, Athens) and in Seventh Fleet area (Sasebo, Singapore) would accomplish this in a way that would not require expensive support facilities ashore since families could live on the economy.

I wanted to get the White House's machinery moving as well as the Pentagon's.

Neither set of machinery operated at what anyone could call high speed. However, in this instance bureaucratic sluggishness was less to blame than the vexing political problems homeporting appeared to present. The one that most concerned my two immediate superiors, Secretary of the Navy Chafee and Secretary of Defense Laird, was that the recently proclaimed Nixon Doctrine, which both of them heartily approved, called for a reduction, if possible, in military presence overseas and in any case a low profile wherever there was such a presence. It seemed evident to the two Secretaries that there was a discrepancy between a program that would put more American servicemen and their families on foreign soil and the requirements of the Doctrine. They still believed, as we all did, that the Doctrine was a serious program for dealing with our allies rather than what all of us were to recognize it to be within a couple of years, a piece of political rhetoric aimed at American congressmen and voters.

I never envisioned homeporting as being a high-profile operation. Indeed I considered one of the prime requisites for an overseas homeport to be a sufficiency of services, housing above all, to take care of the crews and their dependents. The Navy had neither the money nor the wish to construct elaborate new facilities overseas. As we finally worked out the cost of homeporting in Athens, the original outlay was to be between $13 and $18 million and the annual expenses between $10 and $15 million—the cost of one F-14 plane. The figures are variable because opinions differ about whether certain expenses should be charged to homeporting or should not because the Navy would have incurred them anyway. Nevertheless, the only real answer to the Nixon Doctrine argument against homeporting was the one I touched upon in my second memorandum to Chick Clarey on the subject: there was also a discrepancy between the Presidential requirement that the overseas fleets be kept up to strength and the Presidential requirement that the Navy reduce its budget, and homeporting could reconcile it.

The Supreme Allied Commander in Europe, General Andrew Goodpaster, endorsed the idea of homeporting ships in Europe—in England or the Netherlands as well as in the Mediterranean—as soon as I broached it to him, but it took many months to win Secretaries Chafee and Laird over. Meanwhile, my staff had been reviewing the topography and demography of every Mediterranean port that seemed even remotely capable of supporting a carrier task group. By the middle of 1971 we had concluded that Athens offered the best combination of a situation that made access to the eastern Mediterranean easy; a harbor large enough for the eight or ten ships that usually make up a task group; adequate facilities for ship upkeep and repair; nearby air fields for plane maintenance and pilot training exercises; available local housing that met American standards, and shopping and educational facilities for the families of the task group's men. There was a NATO air base just outside Athens and some 8000 Air Force personnel and their dependents had been living in and around the city for a number of years. Since the responsibilities and concerns of Secretaries Chafee and Laird were almost exclusively military, the choice of a country that played a critical role in the defense of NATO's southern flank did not bother them. However, it did bother many officials, including those who favored homeporting as a general idea, in the Department of State, which had the ticklish job of dealing with the so-called colonels' junta that had overthrown the elected government of Greece in 1967.

Action officers at State, caught between the military imperative of maintaining a warm relationship with Greece and the political imperative of seeking to turn the Greek regime away from its repressive domestic policies, felt that homeporting in Athens, by increasing U.S. military dependence on Greece, would weaken U.S. pressure to liberalize the regime. Those State people urged the Navy to do new, elaborate, on-site surveys of various Italian ports. Of the Mediterranean countries, Italy had the least complicated and troublesome political relations with the U.S. The new surveys, which of course delayed homeporting by more months, confirmed the results of the old ones. They found, specifically, that Naples was the equal or superior of Athens in every respect but the most critical one. Naples could not comfortably absorb some 9000 more Americans—6000 sailors and 3000 dependents. The large numbers of American servicemen and their families living there—for Naples in addition to having ships homeported there already was the site of NATO's southern headquarters—had saturated the available housing and had created enough anti-Americanism in the local population to make many resident Americans uncomfortable and uneasy. Since the central idea of homeporting overseas was to reduce family separations, a city that could not accommodate families in comfort was clearly unsuitable for homeporting.

Meanwhile, a retrospective analysis of the Jordan crisis of September 1970 had driven home to senior-level State and National Security Council officials the need for two carrier task groups in the eastern Mediterranean and the critical importance of maintaining good relations with Greece. These senior officials overruled their reluctant subordinates. State approved Athens and on 21 January 1972 Ronald Spiers, chief of State's Political Military office, and I appeared at a closed session of the Senate Foreign Relations Committee to tell its members about the homeporting plan before we broached the subject to the Greeks. To have gone to the Greeks before informing the Congress would have been an unforgivable piece of *lèse majesté.*

Our reception by the committee was not enthusiastic, nor had I expected it to be. Many of the committee members, in addition to viewing the colonels with dismay, as we all did, supported William Fulbright, the chairman, in his argument that the U.S. should seek to reach an agreement with the USSR to pull naval forces out of the Mediterranean altogether. The military believed that such a withdrawal would give the Soviets a decisive advantage in any non-NATO conflict in the area—to be specific, an Arab-Israeli conflict in which our allies would not let us use their airfields—because in the absence of the planes of the Sixth Fleet, Soviet land-based planes, flying out of airfields in the USSR or Arab client states, could dominate the eastern Mediterranean. In short, the views of the committee majority and the views of the Administration were diametrically opposed on this issue, and the next day the predictable occurred. The press, quoting "sources," carried reports of what had transpired behind the Committee's closed doors. Since those reports dwelt at considerably greater length on Senator Fulbright's views than on mine I think I can be believed when I say the "sources" were not Navy sources. It was at this point that Representative Rosenthal made his presence known. Rosenthal's Subcommittee on Europe had held a hearing the previous summer that had excoriated the colonels' junta and had led to the passage by Congress of an amendment to the foreign aid authorization bill banning all assistance, military and economic, to Greece unless the President certified that giving it was necessary to the national security of the United States. Naturally the press asked his opinion of homeporting in Greece. He said it was "insane."

These pleasantries having been exchanged, the U.S. government on 25 January officially signified to the government of Greece that it desired to homeport a carrier task group in Athens and within a matter of days the government of Greece agreed in principle to the idea. At that point, according to the terms of a 1953 Military Facilities Agreement between the United States and Greece, it was up to the U.S. Navy to work out specifics with the Hellenic Navy. Those negotiations began on 11 February, closely monitored by the State Department and the office of the Assistant Secretary of Defense for International Security Affairs, both of which were anxious to keep the inevitable Congressional rumblings to a minimum.

Our desire was to deploy the task group to Athens in installments, with the staff of the rear admiral commanding the entire Mediterranean carrier task force (two task groups) arriving in Athens during the summer of 1972, a squadron of eight destroyers following within a few months, and a carrier, along with a dependents' support ship (the hospital ship *Sanctuary*) rounding out the group a year or so later. While the navy-to-navy talks about these matters were in their first stage, the President announced on 3 March that selling $70 million worth of military equipment to Greece, including tanks and fighter planes, was necessary to national security of the United States. Representative Rosenthal promptly charged that this action was connected with the homeporting negotiations—which it was not —and that he would hold hearings on homeporting the following week.

That first round of hearings on homeporting in Greece, held jointly by Rosenthal's Subcommittee on Europe and the Subcommittee on the Near East, under the chairmanship of Lee Hamilton of Indiana, was tame. As far as I could tell no member of either subcommittee questioned the validity of the idea of homeporting Navy ships in the Mediterranean. Almost all the questioning of me and my fellow witness Warren Nutter, the Assistant Secretary of Defense for International Security Affairs, was aimed at demonstrating that there was a better country than Greece to homeport in—"better country" boiling down finally to Italy. The only feasible Mediterranean countries beside Italy were Spain and Portugal, whose regimes were no more attractive to the objecting Congressmen than Greece's and which were at the wrong end of the Mediterranean to boot. Once we had cited our surveys showing that Athens was the most desirable port, and offered assurances that we had no intention of violating the Congressional ban on aid for Greece by building the Greeks any new facilities, the hearings fizzled out. Rosenthal and his allies were not satisfied, but for the nonce, at least, they evidently could think of no further way to give practical effect to their dissatisfaction.

Consequently we were able to complete our negotiations with the

Hellenic Navy and in September Destroyer Squadron 12 (DesRon 12), manned almost 90 percent by men who had volunteered for the planned three years of overseas duty, sailed for Athens, while a support ship was transporting many of the wives and children as well. This sealift of the families, which we called Operation Pegasus, saved the Navy a certain amount of money, but its real purpose was to increase morale. A cruise across the Atlantic and into the Mediterranean on Navy ships was something of an adventure for most of the wives and children and their weeks at sea were profitably used to brief them on some of the details of their new situation. Meanwhile, with no outcry at all from the Congress, just with the usual fretting over possible and impossible consequences by State, preparations also had been going forward to homeport a carrier task group in Japan; two months before DesRon 12 sailed for Greece, DesRon 15 sailed for Yokosuka. In addition I succeeded in homeporting two stores ships in Japan, at Sasebo, and a submarine tender at La Maddelena in Sardinia, and I kept pushing for homeporting a carrier group in northern Europe and a destroyer escort in Australia, though nothing ever came of the last two efforts.

In December Representative Rosenthal, who evidently had been smoldering since spring, asked the General Accounting Office to conduct a cost study of the Greek homeporting program. I inquired of the Navy's Office of Legislative Affairs what this might portend, and was informed in reply:

> Rosenthal has not been convinced that the Navy made the right decision to homeport in Greece. Should the GAO report be critical, it is my opinion that Rosenthal will continue to harrass the Navy. Yes, he is still on the warpath.

Certain people in the State Department were still on the warpath, too. During the spring of 1973, while the GAO was conducting its study, State did an on-the-scene survey and reached the conclusion that it would be a mistake to implement what we called "Phase II" of the plan, sending the carrier and its air wing and the *Sanctuary* to Athens to join the destroyer squadron. One reason for reaching that conclusion was that an informal poll among the destroyer squadron's crew members and their families showed that only about 60 percent of them found Athens a desirable place to live. I immediately had similar polls taken in Norfolk and Newport, the alternative

U.S. homeports. They showed that fewer than 50 percent found those cities desirable places to live.

Fun and games aside, the State Department study did make legitimate criticisms of several of the details, political, logistical, and operational, of the program, but in my opinion those faults were so far overbalanced by the benefits that homeporting in Athens conferred that I had no hesitation in continuing to push for it. The most immediately obvious of those benefits was an increased retention rate. During its first six months in Greece DesRon 12 had a first-term reenlistment rate of 21.3 percent, compared with a 15.7 percent rate for similar ships in the Atlantic Fleet. The figures for DesRon 15 in Yokosuka were even more impressive: 34.2 percent compared with 18 percent for the rest of the Pacific. Even though one would expect better than average reenlistment in ships whose crews were four-fifths volunteers, the figures were significant and encouraging. In addition there were rapidly improving reenlistment rates on destroyers homeported in the U.S. that must have had something to do with the 15 percent greater family togetherness their crews were enjoying.

The GAO completed its review of the progress of the program at the end of the spring of 1973 and Congressman Rosenthal called new hearings in July. The review found what no sensible person ever had doubted: that the basing of a large number of ships, sailors, and their dependents in a foreign country was too complicated to be planned or executed flawlessly. A few things had gone wrong in Athens. Some families had prepared themselves or had been prepared by the Navy badly for living in an unfamiliar culture and had been surprised or frightened or affronted by the local sanitation, cooking, shopping facilities, and manners and, particularly, by the overt anti-Americanism of some Greeks. Pier space for the destroyers had not been available as soon as the Navy had hoped. The government had suddenly decided to close the best harbor in the vicinity to all warships—including Greek ones—and reserve it for tourist ships. The nearest available air field for carrier pilots to practice proficiency was at Souda Bay in Crete, a 300-mile round trip from Athens.

These and other problems the review mentioned were real and troublesome. They were also of a kind that no amount of planning would have eliminated. Many of them, indeed, were endemic to homeporting ships anywhere. For example, some aircraft squadrons assigned to carriers based in Norfolk are regularly based in Jacksonville, a round trip of considerably more than 300 miles. When I saw a preliminary draft of the GAO review I found one fundamental flaw in it, that the program as it was going forward in Athens was being evaluated on the basis of projections the Navy had made before it had had the opportunity to discuss them with the Greeks. Other than that, with the exception of a number of technical mistakes about purely maritime matters that were to be expected from nonprofessionals, it was an unobjectionable, if undistinguished, piece of work. If I may quote what I said at the hearings, "I think that their [the GAO's] work, like that of every agency, ranges from very good to very bad and that this particular study was neither the best nor the worst I have seen."

However, a funny thing often happens to a GAO interim report on its way to becoming a GAO final report. Here and there on the objective, factual body of the interim report accretions appear in the form of conclusions that support the opinions of the Congressman who called for the report in the first place. The principal such accretion to the report on homeporting in Greece, as the GAO delivered it during a hearing before Representative Rosenthal's subcommittee on 16 July, was "the major conclusion . . . that the Navy's planning for the whole project was inadequate." There were minor accretions, too, that cast doubt on the relevance of homeporting to retention of personnel. And so when it came my turn to testify on 19 July, I was not feeling particularly warm toward either the GAO or the subcommittee.

The hearing started, in customary fashion, with my making a short preliminary oral statement that was a precis of a longer written one I submitted for the record. Then Rosenthal, to the surprise not only of the Navy people but of many of the members of his subcommittee as well, read off what he described as "some brief comments" of his own. They were a tirade that questioned the Navy's truthfulness and candor about almost every aspect of the Greek homeporting operation and concluded, "I am personally appalled by the Navy's whole performance before this subcommittee. . . . [T]he testimony of the Navy last year is now revealed by the GAO report and my own conclusions on that report to have been a calculated pattern to render disservice both to the State Department and to this subcommittee. For that performance, the Navy must take full responsibility next week when the State Department testifies and it must explain the consequences of relying on your information last year when it accepted the political consequences of homeporting." (Earlier he had said that "adding a major American presence to Greece while that country was under an illegal dictatorship was a fundamental political error.") I should say here that Benjamin Rosenthal in private conversation is a pleasant and reasonable man. It is only when he dons his statesman's toga and mounts the rostrum that he becomes intemperate and abusive.

I was not about to accept that kind of talk about the Navy in public without responding, so I delivered a counterstatement—it might not be too strong to call it a counterattack—that began, "Frankly, I find myself appalled by this statement, Mr. Chairman; I think that it contains allegations that are disgraceful to the Navy quite apart from any allegations you may be making to me as a person." Congressmen are not accustomed to retorts by witnesses from the executive branch who, no doubt rightly, usually calculate that it is imprudent to bite the hand that feeds them. Rosenthal was obviously taken aback by the forcefulness of my reply but, even on the unlikely assumption that he realized that he had gone too far, there was no way for him to back down in a public hearing. And so the hearing developed into no more than an overheated version of a typical kind of sparring match between legislative interrogators and executive witnesses.

By himself Representative Rosenthal was unable to put an end to homeporting in Athens, but events later in the year came to his assistance. In November, the Papadapoulos (the colonels') government, which had been moving indecisively toward liberalization, fell victim to its indecisiveness. Colonel Demetrios Ionnides, the head of the secret police, led a coup that overthrew it and established an even more repressive regime, one that, rhetorically at least, took even more umbrage at U.S. "interference" in its domestic policies than the colonels' had. Congressional opponents of homeporting of course used this, to considerable effect, as a demonstration of how right they had been all along. As a matter of fact I myself decided at this point, the Ionnides regime being as unsavory as it was, to delay Phase II of the program—sending the carrier Independence and its air wing to Athens. Phase II was postponed and then abandoned. And as I write this, DesRon 12 will not be replaced in Greece when its tour there is over, despite the restoration of democracy to Greece, and despite an impressive Fiscal Year 1975 first-term reenlistment rate of 46 percent, the highest in the destroyer force.

The Yokosuka homeporting, to which no one in Congress ever objected, continues smoothly. The carrier Midway joined DesRon 15 there on 5 October 1973, with markedly beneficial effects on both naval operations in the Pacific and reenlistment rates. I think it is fair to say that Representative Rosenthal's fulminations against home-porting in Athens did more harm to the men of the Atlantic Fleet and their families than it did good to the cause of democracy in Greece. However, he is not the first Congressman, nor will he be the last, to allow his repugnance for undemocratic and repressive regimes, which we all share, to make him forget that the United States often has critical national interests in those parts of the world where such regimes flourish. If the defense of NATO and Israel are essential to the welfare of the U.S., which I know Benjamin Rosenthal would maintain, a working alliance with Greece, whatever its government, is a policy that must be considered, especially with an ever-worsening free world maritime capability.

Senator Proxmire's righteousness came into its fullest flower toward the end of the spring of 1972. For some time before that he had been fulminating against the Navy. Beginning the previous summer he had taken frequent potshots at the F-14, the most spectacularly effective fighter plane that has ever been produced, calling it a "lemon." Then, on 28 March 1972, in the course of hearings the subcommittee was conducting into the costs of shipbuilding, he produced a directive I had sent the previous month to the Chief of Naval Material, Admiral Isaac Kidd. The directive had made suggestions to Ike, and solicited suggestions from him, about ways to meet an increase announced by the Office of the Secretary of Defense of more than $400 million in the Navy's Fiscal Year 1972 "outlay target," with the end of the fiscal year only five months away.

To explain what this was about it is necessary to wax somewhat technical. To begin with, annual "outlays"—the amount of cash money an agency spends in a year—are pretty much outside the province of the Congress, especially with an agency like the Navy that cannot possibly spend all the money Congress appropriates for it during the year it is appropriated. For example, Congress gives the Navy in one year almost all the money for a major warship that will take eight or ten years to build. This money is given in the form of "obligational authority," that is, authority to enter into contracts for the construction of the ship. A rough schedule of when and in what amounts money will be paid to the contractors—of the outlays—is one of the important points that must be negotiated when the contracts are being drawn. There is no way for Congress to participate in this process. All it can do is insist that the Navy, or any agency, demonstrate that it really needed the money it asked for by negotiating contracts promptly and seeing to it that work gets under way as soon as possible. An agency that does not use its obligational authority in the year it was given that authority ordinarily is suspected by Congress of having asked for more money than it needed or could use at the time, and runs a great risk of having its next year's budget cut back.

When I said that a construction contract provides a "rough" schedule of outlays over the duration of the contract, I meant that so many variables enter into a major construction project that there is no way of planning its timing with real precision. Anything from strikes to last-minute changes in design, from inflation to breakdowns in machinery, from a subcontractor's bankruptcy to inclement weather can change the pace of the project and therefore the rate at which money is laid out. In addition to these, as it were, natural ebbs and flows, outlays can be manipulated in a number of ways and for a number of reasons. A shipyard can work eight hours a day or twenty-four; construction priorities can favor long-term or short-term, expensive or inexpensive projects; contractors' just claims can be settled at an accelerated rate. Often an agency needs to control outlays in such ways for internal managerial reasons, but each year, as well, the national Administration gives the agencies "outlay targets" as one way of tuning the economy as a whole. The Treasury needs outlay targets to help it calculate how to time its collections and borrowings and generally control its cash position. In addition, the Administration for all sorts of reasons may want to slow down or speed up the economy; increase or decrease the deficit; justify higher or lower taxes; placate hawks or doves. I have no inside information about why the White House at the beginning of February 1972 decided to raise the military's outlay targets for FY '72, which ended on 30 June. My guess is that Mr. Nixon wanted to have the economy humming by Election Day the next November and at the same time set outlay targets for FY '73 that looked frugal.

One thing I am quite sure of is that such orders always are given with the utmost discretion for both economic and political reasons. Juggling outlay targets is not something that looks good in the press, as Senator Proxmire took pains to demonstrate. As far as I know there was no "documentation" in the instance under discussion— except mine. The order about the extra $400 million for the Navy was given orally by Secretary Chafee who, I assume, got it orally from Secretary Laird who, I assume, got it orally from someone in the White House. If I had not thoughtlessly broken this chain of discretion by sending a written directive to Ike Kidd, I would have saved us all a lot of trouble. In any case, the order would have been easier to execute if it had come near the beginning of the fiscal year instead of near its end, because in the former case we would have had time to enter into new contracts, if necessary, instead of being limited to manipulating the terms of existing ones. The lateness of the order was more Congress's fault than the White House's. The Administration cannot set its final outlay targets until it knows precisely how much money it has and it cannot know that until Congress acts. In FY '72, Congress did not pass the military appropriations bill until January 1972, which was running pretty late even by Congressional standards. It was because I felt a considerable sense of urgency over the time bind the Navy had been put in that I fired off a directive to Ike—and let me confess that in that directive I committed another bureaucratic sin: I mentioned 30 June. Washington decorum dictates that all executive agencies pretend that they are spending their money with no regard for when the fiscal year ends or begins. William Proxmire quickly made me aware of my mistake. "The notion of getting rid of money in a hurry is playing a most unfortunate game with the taxpayer," he said.

Coming from Proxmire, that was a cheap shot, of course. Doubtless there are many members of Congress who are ignorant or confused about budgetary matters, which after all are fearfully complex, but Proxmire is not one of them. He was then the ranking majority member of the Senate Banking Committee—he is now its chairman —and he was chairman of the Joint Economic Committee. He knew as well as anyone in Washington why the Navy—or any agency— "gets rid of its money in a hurry," and he also knew perfectly well that the Navy, with its large budgetary carryovers from year to year, was, of all agencies, the least driven to get rid of money in a hurry. His tears over the "most unfortunate game" the Navy was playing with the taxpayer were decidedly crocodilian.

Another member of Congress, Representative Les Aspin, also of Wisconsin, an ex-Army officer who had worked in the Pentagon and who can be counted on to chime in whenever military spending is under discussion, promptly issued a press release that said, among other things, "Admiral Zumwalt's memorandum reads like instructions to 'spend, spend, spend' so that the Navy can obtain the same large outlays for next year. It notes no specific program that is needed to counter the Soviet threat." Leaving aside the fact that the entire Navy program—and much more—is needed to counter the

Soviet threat, I certainly did not need to teach Ike Kidd a lesson on that threat; he had come to Washington from the command of the Sixth Fleet in the Mediterranean during the Jordan crisis and knew about it firsthand. Indeed during the Jordan Crisis Ike had sent me a strong personal message describing the Fleet's shortages of spare parts and other equipment. A curious result of all this was that my directive, to the extent that it was remembered at all, was remembered as the "spend, spend, spend" memo, though of course those words were put in quotes in Aspin's release not because I ever used them—I didn't—but because Harry Hopkins had used them, preceded by "tax, tax, tax," and followed by "elect, elect, elect," to describe Franklin Roosevelt's electoral strategy thirty years before.

Apparently my insistence that the Navy needed, and should obligate and eventually expend, every dollar the Congress authorized and appropriated angered Senator Proxmire, for he set about to prove forthwith that the Soviet maritime threat was not what the Navy made it out to be. He enlisted the assistance of the Center for Defense Information, an organization, headed by a retired rear admiral, Gene La Roque, that disseminates to the media and legislators military facts of various kinds, most of them selected and arranged in such a way as to encourage their use in an anti-military context. On 19 May Proxmire wrote me announcing his intention of making a "full presentation" to the Senate on 25 May of the facts furnished by the Center and other sources that made him believe that "the present balance of naval forces is dramatically weighted on the side of the U.S. and NATO countries." He continued, "I invite you to comment on the following points which I will make, and I will submit your reply to the Senate at the same time so that comparisons can be drawn. It is imperative that you respond no later than noon Wednesday, May 24th." Thereupon followed two pages of comparisons of numbers, sizes, and fire-power of U.S. and Soviet naval vessels of various types, and a pair of Center for Defense Information tables from which most of those comparisons were drawn. Though the facts those tables contained were accurate on the whole, such gross comparisons between naval forces with entirely different missions are, as I have tried to point out in my discussion of world maritime strategy, an inappropriate, if not a misleading, way of trying to determine which force is better able to carry out its mission.

Moreover, even if in the five days the Senator vouchsafed me I could have put together the comprehensive philosophical, strategic, and statistical reply his evident lack of knowledge about maritime affairs called for, I would have been debarred from doing so that week. The President was in Moscow preparing to sign the first set of strategic arms limitation agreements. All officials of the executive branch had been ordered not to make comments about foreign affairs while the President was out of the country. A public statement, which would have had to have been cleared by the Secretary of Defense, about the relative strengths of the U.S. and the Soviet navies would certainly have been a comment about foreign affairs, and it would have been judged doubly inappropriate in view of where Mr. Nixon was and what he was doing. Therefore, while my staff worked on a detailed analysis of Proxmire's data to send him after the President's return to Washington, I sent off a brief reply in which I stressed my disagreement with his assessments, referred him to my testimony that spring before the Senate Armed Services and Appropriations Committees and urged him to postpone his presentation to the Senate until I had had an opportunity to brief him personally. He did not postpone his presentation, of course, but gave a speech that added little to the substance of what he had written to me but much abusive rhetoric. He waxed particularly eloquent over my offer to brief him:

> I am writing back and insisting that he reply to my facts in writing. I was briefed by Admiral Zumwalt on the F-14. First of all he brought a flotilla of admirals, captains, and commanders to my office. There was so much gold braid that I calculated that almost half the funds for Navy pay and allowances must go to these gentlemen.
>
> Then he gave me a "selected" briefing. He justified that biggest lemon of all lemons, the F-14 fighter plane, which will cost at least $16 million a copy. The way he did it was take some relatively unimportant factors to try to show that it was superior to the F-4 in those facets.
>
> It reminded me of the way baseball records are kept. They now talk about the record for left-handed catchers who hit singles in the fourth inning of the fifth game of a seven-game World Series against a rookie left-hander.
>
> It was that kind of "selected" information the briefing used to justify the F-14. I am therefore refusing a briefing which, if like the last one, never would produce any solid answers and which was largely a gold-braided snow job.

He also made a point of denouncing the fourth nuclear carrier and the proposals for Trident—the latter, will you believe, on the day after the President had signed an agreement that froze U.S. inferiority in numbers of submarine-launched ballistic missiles for five years, ample time for the Soviets to eliminate the technological advantage of our strategic force over theirs if we did not go to Trident, among other strategic modernization programs.

It is both difficult and distasteful to conduct any kind of exchange with a person who speaks as loosely and discourteously as William Proxmire did on that occasion. However, one of my firmest political convictions is that it is incumbent on any Administration to provide Congress with the information it must have if it is to fulfill its Constitutional role as a coequal branch of the government. One of my great quarrels with the Nixon Administration was that it deliberately withheld or suppressed information about our military posture relative to the USSR's that would have enabled—indeed impelled— the Congress to treat the Soviet threat with the seriousness it deserved. Therefore, it ill-behooved me to take offense at a Senator who, however loosely and discourteously, was making inquiries into precisely the subject I thought Congress most needed to know about.

We continued working on a detailed reply to Proxmire's assertions. Meanwhile, I had to fly to Naples to attend a change-of-command ceremony at which Admiral Richard Colbert, "Mr. International Navy," was to relieve Admiral Horacio Rivero as NATO's southern commander in chief. If I may digress for a moment, Admiral Colbert had been responsible for the establishment of our naval command course at the Naval War College in Newport, which had trained a whole generation of foreign naval officers, many of whom had gone on to become flag officers in their respective navies, and some to become chiefs. His continuing contacts with these individuals had served to make him one of our most outstanding NATO commanders. Early in 1973, he developed a malignancy and was operated on unsuccessfully. Knowing that he was a terminal case, he had come to me and said that he wanted nothing in life now except to be permitted to return to his command and serve as long as he could. Although it was an unusual procedure, I insisted that Admiral Colbert be given this opportunity. He performed magnificently throughout his final months and readily agreed to return home when it became apparent that the end was approaching. Within a week from the time he marched proudly off the plane at Andrews Air Force Base in Washington, where Mouza and I greeted him, and after a final chat at Bethesda Naval Hospital during which he instructed me carefully on all the things he wanted me to carry on for him in the NATO command and finally asked me whether or not there was anything more that he could do to help me, Admiral Richard Colbert passed away, loved and mourned.

Just before I left for Naples the mail brought me another communication from the Senator, dated the day after his Senate speech. As he often did, he had seen to it that the media got this letter before I did. It demanded a reply to fourteen questions, most of which began "Is it not true that . . . ?" or "Do you deny that . . . ?" Though I did not think that this prosecutorial approach to a complicated subject like the relative strengths of two navies was likely to prove edifying, there was nothing for it but to start the mill grinding on replies to the fourteen questions.

Three years later, rereading the two letters I sent Proxmire the first week in June 1972, I am glad he put me through that drill. Exasperating as it was in the midst of a too-busy life—at that particular moment the Navy's conventional forces were being stretched thin by escalated fighting in Vietnam, the SALT agreements were threatening the credibility of its strategic forces, and its budget was being subjected to election-year hanky-panky—exasperating as it was to be required to take time out from pressing day-to-day affairs to write a strategic treatise, it was a worthwhile exercise. The two letters to Proxmire, though they were composed in haste and in an adversary spirit, remain as persuasive non-technical statements as have ever appeared over my signature of the conceptual framework within which an assessment of relative military strength must be made. The first letter, dated 2 June, which went out immediately upon my return from Naples, began by pointing out the bias in some of the Center for Defense Information's figures, but its burden was the differing missions of the two navies as I lay them out in the "High-Low" chapter of this book. The second letter, dated 8 June, the reply to the fourteen questions, began by offering half a dozen "Is it not true . . . ?" questions of my own, designed to demonstrate that it would have been as easy for us to be misleading about Soviet strength as it was for the Senator to be about Soviet weakness: "Is it not true that the Soviet Navy's superiority in anti-ship missiles is virtually absolute?" for example. It then objectively answered the fourteen questions one by one. Its answer to the fourteenth and the letter's concluding paragraph are I think worth quoting:

> Question: Is it not true that our Navy is Number One? Is it not true that under present plans and programs we will continue to be Number One for the forseeable future?

Response: An examination of the record will show that I have not said that *total* Soviet inventories have been growing in number. Rather I have asserted that the essential composition and employment policies of the Soviet Navy have been changing in ways which make it a significantly more capable and challenging force. I cited the growth of its nuclear submarine forces and its cruise-missile capabilities from air, surface, and subsurface platforms as the central features of this change in capabilities. Its long-range, steady-state deployments have imposed the requirement for new strategies and programs for our Navy. It is my considered judgment that the *trends* in the net capabilities of the two navies have been running rapidly against the U.S. The President's budget is, as Mr. Laird has pointed out, the baseline from which to build.

If I were sure that we would be permitted to move forward with our plans and programs, as your question suggests, there would be no doubt in my mind that we would be able to have superiority at sea against the Soviet Navy. However, the entire thrust of your correspondence and the purported study your questions are based upon, clearly provides no justification for such an optimistic supposition. [Subsequent Congressional defense budget cuts have validated my forecast to the Senator.]

I made sure that the media were briefed on this letter in time for them to report on it before Proxmire received it. Turnabout seemed to me to be fair play.

Before the Proxmire-Zumwalt correspondence was consigned to the small type in the Congressional Record, Senator Proxmire had a last few thousand words. On 12 June he spoke to the Senate again in somewhat more measured tones. Though he did not change his view that the Navy needed no new building programs, he appeared to be better educated about the facts of maritime life than he had been when he first took the Navy on. Indeed my advisors and I took this second speech, which added nothing to the first one, to be a signal that the Senator was dropping the whole thing in a familiar Proxmirian manner: blusteringly.

I have noted that Senator Proxmire skirmished intermittently against the F-14 interceptor plane. In fact he got the General Accounting Office to do a study of its effectiveness that found the plane to be deficient in "dogfighting" capability, a finding that in addition to being mostly erroneous entirely missed the point that the F-14's missiles were so deadly at long range that they would destroy most enemy planes before they got close enough for a dogfight. The study and the conclusion that Proxmire drew from it that the F-14 was a "lemon" were fully reported by the media, like most of Proxmire's activities, and were without much significance, like most of Proxmire's activities. Proxmire, for all his conspicuousness, has little influence on the opinions of his colleagues or the business of the Senate, and the GAO, however acute it often is when it examines costs, has neither competence nor credibility in technical military matters.

However, an F-14 drama of serious and significant character did take place in the Congress during my watch. It is worth summarizing here because it contained most of the elements that make large-scale long-run military procurement programs so hard to understand and manage.

To recapitulate in a sentence or two the genesis of the F-14 as I described it in an earlier chapter: it was developed after the Navy version of Robert McNamara's favorite, the F-111, proved incapable of carrier takeoffs and landings. It used the F-111's superb Pratt & Whitney engine and Hughes fire-control and missile systems in a new carrier-capable airframe built by Grumman Aircraft, which had been doing high quality work for the Navy since before World War II. The Navy signed the contract with Grumman at the beginning of 1969. It gave the Navy the option of purchasing, over a period of seven years, between forty-eight and ninety-six planes a year. The top number of over 700 would allow the Navy to replace all its F-4 fighters, two 12-plane squadrons on each of fifteen modern carriers, with F-14s. The F-4s were excellent planes, as they had proved repeatedly over Vietnam, but they dated from the fifties, so they were not only physically old but were on the verge of being made operationally obsolete by the most recent Soviet classes of both fighter planes and larger aircraft carrying anti-ship (cruise) missiles.

By the time I became CNO, the research and development phase of the F-14 program was nearing completion. However, inflation and the quadrupling of personnel costs caused by the end of the draft had skewed the budget and reduced to 313 the number of planes the Navy could afford. That meant one squadron per carrier instead of two—and in a Navy that those budgetary realities had scaled down to twelve carriers—plus four squadrons for the Marines. The rest were for training and backup, of course. This reduction in total numbers to be bought also meant a rise from less than $10 million to more than $12 million in the unit price of the planes. The more planes a company manufactures, the less it costs to manufacture each one because of economies of scale and because overhead and R & D charges are distributed more widely.

Congress had so far acquiesced with little objection to this program. There had been a brief flap about it just before I took office, at the time of the Cambodian incursion, but nothing had come of it. The Congress had appropriated enough money through Fiscal Year 1971 to buy the first thirty-eight planes. The very first one made its first flight three days before Christmas 1970. It made its second flight on the last day of the year and crashed, with the test pilots bailing out safely. The crash was caused by a malfunction in the hydraulic controls. It was a problem that was relatively minor and easy to solve, and of a sort that occurs in developing any new piece of equipment. However, happening as it did on the second flight, it was something of a public relations disaster. Moreover, the loss of the first plane delayed the program by some six months.

Meanwhile the cost to Grumman of building the plane had been rising precipitously. Three major factors were responsible for this. The first was that the plane proved more difficult to build than Grumman had planned for in its proposed price to the Navy. This is such a normal part of any military procurement program that one can almost call it built-in. Under a system of competitive bidding every company tends to take the rosiest possible view of its managerial and technical capabilities. It is rare piece of military hardware indeed that is as easy to develop as either the contractor or the Pentagon hopes it will be, given that each such weapon system presses the state of the art. The second was an annual rate of inflation —and therefore of the cost of labor and materials—about twice as large as had been expected and specified in the contract. The third was the Administration's decision to drastically curtail the space program, in which Grumman was heavily involved. The termination of its NASA contracts meant that Grumman had to charge a much larger part of its overhead to Navy contracts than it or the Navy expected it to. As is true of most government-industry contracts, there was a considerable amount of elasticity in the F-14 contract, which envisioned a "target price" for the planes but provided a top price of some 20 percent more than that to protect the company against future rises in costs that could not be anticipated at the time the contract was signed. However costs had risen even more than that, and Grumman claimed it was faced with a loss of a million dollars or more a plane on a Fiscal Year 1972 order of forty-eight planes. Ordering fewer would have constituted a Navy breach of the contract, and that would have meant dropping the program or signing a new contract at far higher prices. In the spring of 1971, as Congress began its consideration of the FY '72 budget, Grumman began lobbying for relief both on Capitol Hill and in the Pentagon. And so in both places that spring there were fairly bitter disputes about whether to drop the contract, renegotiate it or go ahead with the program and try to do it under the existing contract.

There was no doubt in my mind that we should go ahead with it. For one thing combat over Vietnam was wearing down the F-4s of the carrier force at a rate that made their replacement an increasingly urgent matter. For another it seemed to me the height of irresponsibility to abrogate a contract that was turning out to be economically favorable to the government rather than to the contractor. My understanding of the free enterprise system is that a corporation that stands to make a handsome profit if things go well should have to run the risk that they won't go well. John Chafee shared my view. However the czar, so to speak, of military procurement, Deputy Secretary of Defense David Packard, whose approval was necessary if the program was to come before Congress in the first place, had reservations about the type of contract the Navy had entered into with Grumman, about one aspect of the plane's capability and about forcing Grumman to take big losses. Dave was a strong proponent of a principle that Secretary Laird called "fly before buy." It went against his grain to approve and authorize money for forty-eight planes before even one had been thoroughly tested—and as the result of the December crash, test flights of the F-14 did not resume until May 1971, the very time when the purchase of the forty-eight was under consideration. Since the actual payment of money to Grumman by the government would not occur until the planes were delivered, and every aircraft off the line would have to meet stringent Navy standards before it was accepted and paid for, the "fly before buy" issue was not hard to resolve.

The capability issue centered on the plane's power plant, which was the cause of the doubts about its dogfighting ability that Proxmire was later to make so much of. The program called for Grumman to build F-14As, that is, F-14s powered by the existing F-111B engine, until such time as a new more powerful engine that was being developed for the Air Force's F-15 and, in modified form, for the F-14, was ready for production; then the Navy would switch to the new engine and build F-14Bs. The F-14Bs would be better than the

F-14As in maneuverability and speed at high altitude, the so-called dogfighting capability. Otherwise the two versions were identical. The thing that was hard to put across to people who were used to the idea that an interceptor plane was necessarily a dogfighting plane was that the F-14's primary mission is not dogfighting. Its primary mission is intercepting the large Soviet aircraft that carry air-to-surface missiles capable of sinking ships, or of intercepting those missiles after they are fired. Neither those Soviet planes nor those Soviet missiles are capable of dogfighting but they certainly are capable of doing heavy damage to the United States fleet if they are not intercepted. To perform this mission the F-14 is uniquely equipped with the Phoenix missile and the AWG-9 fire control system, and those two pieces of hardware are an important element in the high cost of the plane. The Air Force F-15, to which the F-14 was repeatedly and irrelevantly compared, is primarily intended for dogfights. Its armament is the same as the F-14's, except it does not have Phoenix or AWG-9 because Soviet ASM missiles are not the same kind of threat to land targets as they are to ships at sea. That is why F-15 is cheaper to build than F-14, a point some Congressmen kept bringing up, and lighter and therefore F-15 is more maneuverable than F-14, a point other Congressmen kept bringing up. We managed to convince Dave Packard that their comments were beside the point.

Meanwhile various amateurs were having their say in the press on this professional matter. The most this criticism of the F-14s did, coming on the top of talk about "overruns" and "bailouts," was further confuse the issues in the public mind and occupy Navy leaders and the program managers dealing, of necessity, with these irrelevant arguments. The responsible Congressional committees were not impressed. They continued to await Dave Packard's decision and in June he made it. He signified to the committees that, though the Grumman contract was not one he would have negotiated, he calculated that breaking it would be far more costly to the Government than going along with it. A few months later Congress decisively defeated a Proxmire-led attempt to drop the F-14 and appropriated $801 million for it. Thus ended round one.

Round two commenced the following spring when Congress began considering the FY '73 budget. It followed pretty much the same scenario as round one but was a great deal more intense. Grumman, its costs still going up and the banks it relied on for credit becoming increasingly reluctant to advance funds, beseeched the Congress and the Pentagon for relief in ever more urgent tones. Indeed in May the company made something of a show of omitting its quarterly dividend. Senator Proxmire, now armed with that GAO report I mentioned earlier, rampaged week in and week out in the public prints about the "Navy cover-up" of the cost of the plane and even went so far as to charge the Navy with practicing "goldplated unilateral disarmament" by committing itself to a plane so expensive that it could not afford enough of them. (The fact is that one F-14 is as effective a weapon as three F-4s, so that a carrier with F-14s embarked has deck space for more attack and anti-submarine planes than one that relies on F-4s as interceptors, and thus becomes a more effective ship.)

Dave Packard had left the Department of Defense and had been replaced by Kenneth Rush, who was neither as decisive a man nor up to speed on the F-14 situation, so guidance from the front office was less firm. I stuck to my position that Grumman should be held to its contract and pressed for the Navy to exercise its option for forty-eight planes in FY '73. I had no animus against Grumman; on the contrary I and many other people in the Defense establishment did whatever we could to ease the company's cash-flow problem by making such advance payments on the contract as were legal and by bringing such influence to bear as we ethically could on the banks that were reluctant to advance credit. But I thought that during a period when shrinking Defense budgets and increasing weapons costs were putting the Navy in a very tight corner that it was important to squeeze every dollar as hard as possible. Grumman did have friends in the Navy who advocated something that I suppose could be called a "bailout" for the company, but no one in the top leadership was among them, William Proxmire's insinuations to the contrary notwithstanding.

In this situation, the F-14 program's most effective defender was a senator whose face is not often seen in the press or on television, Howard Cannon of Nevada. Senator Cannon is the chairman of the Senate Armed Service Committee's Subcommittee on Tactical Aviation, and is recognized by his colleagues as the Congressional expert in that field. In response to Grumman's complaints and the GAO report that Proxmire was making so much of, he held public hearings on the F-14 program in April at which both the performance of the plane and the financial plight of Grumman were discussed by, among others, the chairman of Grumman, Clint Towl, and me. These hearings satisfied him about the program and he remained committed to it. His standing is such that he carried not just his committee but the whole Senate along with him and that year's purchase of forty-eight planes was ultimately approved by both the Senate and the House with little trouble. Meanwhile the plane itself was beginning to come off the production line and complete its tests. It successfully made its first landing on a carrier in June. It was exhibited to the media in October. It was proving to be every bit as good a plane as we thought it would be.

Round three was under way before round two was over. The Department of Defense's preliminary work on the FY '74 budget determined that the original plan to complete the F-14 contract with purchases of ninety planes each in FYs '74 and '75 would have to be altered, in view of the pressures that were being put on the budget, so that the 180-plane purchase would extend over four years instead of two. For reasons that I have already touched on, that skyrocketed the cost of each plane—by four million dollars according to Grumman's calculations. Grumman had gone along with the production of the forty-eight FY '73 planes—"Lot V," the contract called them —with great reluctance, claiming that the eighty-six planes in Lots I through IV had lost the company something like a million dollars per plane and that Lot V would double that unit loss. It flatly refused to have anything to do with Lots VI and VII at the contract price, announcing that it would close down production if the contract was not renegotiated, and that it would take legal action against the Navy to recover its losses.

There were months of agonizing and maneuvering, but the Department of Defense's ultimate decision was that Grumman, after five years of losses, totaling $85 million after tax recoveries, had enough of a case, morally and legally, to make a revision of the contract appropriate. By then Ken Rush had been replaced as Deputy Secretary of Defense by William Clements. Clements, Navy Secretary John Warner, and I agreed that if the Navy was to get the F-14, the contract would have to be revised. However, our long hold-out saved the taxpayers well over $100 million. A new price that was announced, some people think charitably, as almost $17 million per plane was reached for the remaining 180 planes. That really ended the story. In the budget discussions during 1973 and 1974 there was the usual gnashing of teeth and bandying of epithets, and at one point two gentlemen from Missouri, Senators Stuart Symington and Thomas Eagleton, earnestly advanced the proposal that the F-14 be replaced by the Air Force's F-15, which is manufactured in St. Louis, but the responsible members of both legislative bodies, of whom there are a lot more than are sometimes visible to the naked eye, saw to it that the program went forward. F-14 squadrons started to be embarked on the fleet's carriers, beginning with the nuclear-powered *Enterprise,* early in 1974, and by late 1976 or early 1977 the planes will be fully deployed, some ten years after designs were called for and eight after a procurement contract was signed. Incidentally, the quality of the F-14 has been confirmed by one of the world's most knowledgeable students of weapons systems, the Shah of Iran. The Shah had planned to buy some F-14s and some Air Force F-15s for the Iranian Air Force. A demonstration of the two planes was arranged for him. After he observed the performance of both, he changed his plans and went with F-14s all the way.

I am not a technical procurement man. I have told the F-14 story both because it shows how deeply a service chief gets involved in the technical area and to get across one big, general point: a major military procurement program can go wrong in many ways without any of the parties being in the wrong. If that much went wrong with what was probably the most conservatively conceived and straightforwardly managed of the major procurement programs during my watch, you can be sure that much more went wrong with others throughout the Defense Department. An especially rocky one was the contract with the shipbuilding division of Litton Industries to build the new amphibious landing ship (LHA) and the new Spruance class destroyer (DD-963). Most of the adverse economic factors that affected Grumman affected Litton too. In addition Litton had technical problems and gave the Navy political problems. Litton never had built ships before. Moreover, nobody in the United States ever had built ships the way Litton proposed to build these ships. Litton was proposing to introduce into this country a kind of "automated shipyard" that constructs ships by fitting together prefabricated modules and that had proved both economical and efficient in such places as Sweden and Japan. It was altogether proper for the Navy to underwrite to a degree a promising new technique of shipbuilding, but obviously it was also risky.

The risks were not diminished by the ambiance, if that's the word, in which Litton set about trying to build ships. That ambiance was highly political. The new shipyard, across the river from an existing old-fashioned yard Litton had acquired, was to be in Pascagoula in Mississippi, the home state of John Stennis, the chairman of the Senate Armed Services Committee, and a portion of the cost of setting the yard up was to be financed by a state bond issue. (Unsurprisingly, this arrangement annoyed the senior Republican on the committee, Margaret Chase Smith, in whose home state of Maine is situated one of the Navy's oldest and most reliable builders of escort vessels, the Bath Iron Works. However Senator Smith was able to do no more than generate an inconclusive GAO report on the subject.) The other powerful political factor was that the president of Litton was an active and generous Nixon supporter, Roy Ash.

With this combination of ingredients, two things were almost certain to happen and did. Litton took a lot longer time and spent a lot more money getting into production than it had expected to, or could recover from the Navy, under the contracts, and there was heavy pressure to rescue the company from the consequences of its optimism and lack of know-how. Though Congress, particularly Proxmire again, did plenty of chewing on this situation, most of the action was in backrooms where Ash and Litton's chairman of the board, Tex Thornton, exerted whatever pressure they could for even more time and money. The atmosphere of irregularity that surrounded the program thickened when Ash was made Director of the Office of Manpower and the Budget. I shall not attempt to sketch even the highlights of the Litton v. Navy scenario except to note that Litton's justification of its performance seemed to me to be unpersuasive and I insisted until the day of my departure that the company live up to its contract. The Navy appears to be coming out of the deal with at least some gain. Though the first LHA (three years behind schedule) or 963 has yet to join the fleet at this writing, and they are extremely expensive, at least all indications are that the ships themselves are first class.

There is one last thing I want to say on the general subject of military procurement. An almost universally recognized factor that works against economy is the great difficulty both the Administration and the Congress have in considering programs whole rather than year-by-year. If the almost 350 F-14s the Navy ultimately will have acquired had been purchased within four years, say, instead of spread over seven, the Government might have saved more than $500 million. Such a program was well within Grumman's manufacturing capability, but the government operates on annual budgets that it considers one at a time. Its inevitable tendency, therefore, is to postpone all possible expenditures until the next year or the year after that, even though that inevitably increases their total amount. I do not know how this problem is to be solved, given the enormous political ramifications of budget-making. I do know, though, that economic clichés and political rhetoric, whether they emanate from Capitol Hill or the White House, do not contribute to the solution.

The most dramatic legislative struggle I took part in, and I am sure the most significant as well, occurred in September 1973 when the Senate, in the course of considering the military authorization bill, came within two votes of cutting that year's funds for Trident, the new strategic submarine, by more than half. Ninety-six senators turned out for the vote, so I was not alone in considering the issue a great one. It was great in a fiscal sense, for one thing. It takes half a billion 1973 dollars to build a Trident submarine, which is some 600 feet long and has a huge 60,000 horsepower reactor, and another half a billion to equip it with its twenty-four missiles, which have a 4000-mile range and many nuclear warheads each. And since the size and the character of the boat requires that a new base be built for it, the final bill for the ten-boat program will be no less and most likely more than $13 billion. Of course no such sum was under consideration in September 1973. The President's FY '74 budget included a request for $1.7 billion for Trident, but that much money in one year for one type of ship is clearly enough to justify a certain amount of Senatorial interest, not to say concern.

However, I daresay the country could better afford spending too much on Trident than it could the political/military consequences of delaying it, for at bottom the decision about Trident was a decision about what the strategic arms limitations agreements we had entered into with the Soviets the year before signified and portended. Those who saw the SALT agreements as evidence that the USSR no longer sought world hegemony—if it ever had—and was ready to pursue a moderate and unthreatening course in both its political relations with other nations and in its arms buildup, believed that the development of new strategic weapons systems by the United States was a dangerous provocation that might undo détente. Those who saw the SALT agreements as an adroit attempt by the Soviets to give an appearance of moderation and accommodation in order to be better able to pursue their longstanding political and military objectives, believed that only by continuing the modernization of strategic weapons could the United States avoid being surpassed militarily and thus outmaneuvered politically by the USSR.

I scarcely need say I took the latter view. The five-year interim agreement on offensive weapons that had been signed at the Moscow summit meeting in May 1972 froze Soviet superiority in numbers of missiles, land-based and sea-based, and in total throw-weight and megatonnage, but it did not freeze what presumably offset those Soviet advantages, American technological superiority, notably in multiple warheads (MIRVs) for missiles and in the quietness, hence the invulnerability, of submarines. In other words, during the life of the agreement, which expires in 1977, the United States is forbidden to try to catch up with the USSR in number of missiles while the USSR is at liberty—and certainly has the capability—to try to catch up with the United States technologically. Since the Soviets announced that they intended to exercise this option, and at this writing are continuing to improve their submarines and work up MIRV capability, the argument that the safety of the United States demands that we keep our technological lead over the Soviets as long as we can seems to me unassailable. Doing this with respect to the sea-based deterrent meant developing a new class of submarine.

The reason for a new submarine was simple enough. The Polaris boats were getting old. The first ten had been built with an estimated life of twenty years and the next thirty-one with an estimated life of twenty-five. There was a reasonable chance that some of them could operate five or possibly ten years longer than that, with increased risk of loss. However the first Polaris had joined the fleet in 1959 and the newest dated from 1967, so it was certain that by the early 1980s at the latest the old boats would start retiring and that by the middle nineties few if any would be fit for service.

Moreover, replacing the old hulls with new ones built to the same design would not do because Polaris was beginning to obsolesce technologically as well as age physically. The critical characteristic where this was happening was in the quietness of its operation. It is impossible to overstate the importance of quietness in modern submarine and anti-submarine warfare. The mission of a strategic submarine is to lurk undetected deep beneath the surface of the ocean, ready to fire off its missiles if worse comes to the worst. Its ability to remain deeply submerged for months in remote areas pretty much ensures its safety from detection from the air or the surface of the ocean, but its safety from enemy submarines and other noise detection sensors depends ultimately on its quietness. The mission of an attack submarine is to find enemy ships, including strategic submarines, and be ready to destroy them. To find them, it must hear them, and to hear them it must itself be quiet. The noise a submarine emits is a double hazard: it can be heard by the enemy and it blocks out the noise of the enemy. Thus, in a contest between submarines the quieter one is almost sure to win. And since the last Polaris had come down the ways, both U.S. and Soviet submarines had gotten a lot quieter, and will continue to become quieter yet in the seventies and eighties. Thus, in this time frame, the Polaris/Poseidon boats could become vulnerable. But a class of U.S. missile submarines that were as quiet as our new 688-class attack boats, and that included in addition recent technological advances in such important areas as communications and command-and-control, could be expected to be an invulnerable strategic deterrent well into the twenty-first century.

When my watch began there was a research and development effort, under the name of ULMS (for underwater long-range missile system), going forward in both Vice Admiral Rickover's nuclear propulsion shop and Rear Admiral Levering Smith's strategic weapons shop. As befitted a project that was not expected to deliver hardware to the fleet until 1980 or thereabouts, it was rather low-key and shapeless, but there was no question about its ultimate importance. In my September 1970 briefing of Project 60 to Secretary Laird I said, "We are confident that the Navy can design and build a secure, effective ULMS. If the national decision is to rely more heavily on sea basing—that is, to have ULMS operating before 1980 —we must soon decide to accelerate."

There was no doubt in my mind that the national decision should, and probably would, be to rely more heavily on sea basing of strategic missiles. The USSR has a visibly increasing ability to knock out a large number of our land-based missiles and bombers in a first strike and shoot down a large number of whatever bombers were in the air at the time of the strike if they attempted to retaliate. That the Russians evaluated the situation in much the same way was evident from the reports Paul Nitze brought back throughout late 1970 and early 1971 from the SALT talks, to which he was the U.S. delegate representing the Department of Defense. He told Secretaries Laird and Packard that the strategic questions about which the Soviet delegates to the talks were most curious and concerned were whether we were planning to replace Polaris, and if so when and with what. It was Paul's opinion that the prospect of a new American strategic submarine bothered the Russians a great deal, as the greatest threat we could offer to their ambition to achieve strategic war-winning capabilities, and that a decision to build one would give the United States considerable leverage at the talks.

And so in 1971 ULMS began to take shape—a Rickover shape.

When Secretary Laird, responding to the urgings of Paul Nitze and others, began to bring ULMS front and center, Rick, as usual, was prepared to capitalize on the opportunity. He had a design for a new reactor ready to lay on the table, a reactor so big and heavy that only a huge hull could accommodate it, and that huge hull, in turn, would have to be fitted with an unprecedentedly large number of missiles to justify its size and cost. Designing a ship from the power plant out never has struck me as an ideal procedure, but practically all nuclear-powered ships have been designed that way because Rickover, the power-plant man, has always been first on the scene with a design.

My first response to Rick's new reactor was to question whether something that big, or even something new, was necessary. The reactor being installed in the 688-class submarines was big—some 35,000 horsepower—and new, and it seemed to me prudent, before committing the Navy to a prolonged and vastly expensive program of developing a new reactor, to explore the possibility of using the 688's existing one, or an adaptation or variant thereof, in the new strategic boat. Levering Smith was also unenthusiastic, arguing with reason that the size and number of its missiles should have as much to do with the design of the hull of a missile submarine as the size and weight of its reactor, and that no determination about missiles had yet been made. And so for several months there was a certain amount of internal controversy over ULMS. The more we studied the problems the more I concluded that the issue of Rick's huge new expensive reactor was a subset of a problem much more important and harder to resolve. That problem had to do with the entirely unpredictable chance that the Soviets would acquire some significant breakthrough in submarine detection technology. We saw no evidence that they were close to such a breakthrough. In the absence of a breakthrough a given number of missiles in ten boats would clearly be cheaper than the same number of missiles in twenty boats, even though the smaller boats would be individually cheaper. On the other hand, if we were to assume a highly effective Soviet detection capability, the twenty boats would permit many more of the missiles to survive to arrive at Soviet targets.

Most of us were prepared to gamble that the ability of new strategic submarines to survive would remain so great that we should build big boats. This logic led us to address the question of the 35,000 versus the 60,000 horsepower reactor in the context of a big hull. I convened a board of submarine commanders to explore the question of whether all that extra horsepower was necessary. They unanimously declared it was, on the ground that it would give a strategic submarine that discovered itself being trailed the capability of taking swift evasive action. No such trailing had yet occurred, and the prospects for it occurring were pretty remote in the case of a boat with missiles with a range of 4000—and in their second version 6000 —miles, since with missiles of that range it would have all the water in the northern hemisphere, and then some, to hide in. More persuasive was the argument of these same commanders that the extra horsepower would give the boat a chance to avoid sinking below the depth its structure will stand and being crushed in the event of a major casualty. In any event whatever impulse I had to spend a year or two battling Rick in behalf of a more modest design for the new strategic boat was effectively squelched as 1971 drew to a close by the developments in SALT, which made it imperative to get the project going at once.

Three things were happening in SALT that made ULMS a high priority. One was that, as I have already pointed out, we were evidently going to cede the Soviets' superiority in numbers and throw-weight of offensive missiles, which meant that it was of extreme importance for us to keep well ahead of them technologically. A second was that the impending limitations on anti-ballistic missile systems (ABMs), combined with the Soviet deployment of gigantic super-missiles, greatly increased the vulnerability of our land-based deterrent, Minuteman, and to a lesser extent the B-52s. The third was that there was an increasing probability that offensive weapons would be covered by a short-term interim agreement while negotiations aimed at drawing up a permanent treaty went forward; however, it was clear that no acceptable treaty could be negotiated later if one side leaped ahead of the other during the life of the interim agreement, and since the Soviets were developing a huge submarine-building capacity and improving their boats, attack and strategic, yearly, and of course improving their land- based missiles as well, it would be prudent for us to be ready with ULMS by the time an interim agreement expired.

To meet this clear need, Secretaries Laird and Packard had to make the basic design decisions before the end of 1971 if they were to get adequate funding for the project in the FY '73 budget that the President would present to the Congress in January 1972. They agreed with me that ULMS should be powered by Rick's big reactor and decided it should carry twenty-four missiles, the first generation of which would have a 4000-mile range and fit also into the Polaris boat, whose recently deployed MIRVed Poseidon missiles had a range of about 2000 miles. Also, in order to soften the financial impact of the program in that year, Secretary Laird decided that the target date for deploying the first boat should be 1980 rather than 1978. On 16 May 1972, a few days before the SALT summit, the Secretary gave a public signal that ULMS had moved from the realm of speculation to that of reality, by giving it a name, Trident.

At the time of the signing of the SALT agreements at the end of May the Armed Services Committees of the two houses were marking up the military authorization bill. New strategic initiatives always provoked controversy in the committees, particularly the Senate's, and the freshly signed Moscow agreements gave the advocates of less strategic spending what they thought was an additional argument. Laird arranged to appear before closed sessions of both committees the first week in June in order to tell them he was supporting the Moscow agreements only on the assumption that the United States would continue to modernize its strategic forces, as the agreements allowed both sides to do. The President had announced that the Russians had signified in so many words that they intended to exercise this option. Laird stressed that if the United States did not follow suit, it would find itself hopelessly behind. ("Strategic Arms Limitation," as this book will have frequent occasion to note, may sound to some people like arms reduction and, of course, should be arms reduction, but as it has been and is being negotiated with the Russians, it simply is a codification of the rules of the arms race the Soviets are winning.) I never have known anyone who was better than Melvin Laird at the delicate business of winning Congressional votes that appear doubtful. His extensive legislative contacts and great powers of persuasion, combined with the Administration's prestige in the field of foreign policy, which in the spring of 1972, a euphoric time whose mood is not easy to evoke these days, was enormous, secured almost a billion dollars for Trident that year without unusual delay or fuss.

In the summer of 1973 the situation was different, to say the least. The smallest of the differences was that the able new Secretary of Defense, James Schlesinger, was a less effective Congressional lobbyist than Laird. The biggest was Watergate, which by then had become a galloping malignancy that had half-paralyzed the Administration's conduct of affairs and had made its relations with Congress particularly indecisive. The President had asked for $1.7 billion for Trident in his FY '74 budget request, which represented a return to the Navy's original intention to deploy by 1978, though Congressional enemies of the program preferred to call it "acceleration." This was largely development money for "long lead-time items"—the reactors, the missiles, the fire-control system. The actual start of construction was still a couple of years away. Therefore the request was referred to the Senate Armed Services Committee's Subcommittee on Research and Development, headed by Thomas McIntyre of New Hampshire. In July that committee unanimously voted to cut the Administration request by almost $900 million. It is relevant to point out that only a few weeks before this vote, Congress had enacted its prohibition on further military action of any kind in Indo-China. Defense was not the darling of Capitol Hill in the summer of 1973.

I do not know whether or not it was the prevailing anti-military mood that impelled the McIntyre subcommittee to act as it did. I am sure, though, that the specific arguments it advanced to support slowing down Trident were unconvincing, not to say specious. The cut did not represent a saving of $900 million, of course. I have tried to show in my discussion of the F-14 program that spreading out a program greatly increases its final cost. "Saving" $900 million thus in FY '74 would inevitably have entailed spending much more than that in years to come, assuming the Trident boat was ultimately built, as McIntyre said he wanted it to be.

Another argument the subcommittee relied on heavily was that the Trident program as it had been presented would mean that construction would be well under way before testing had been completed and that this would violate the "fly before buy" principle Secretary Laird had proclaimed. The fact was, of course, that "fly before buy" was, as its wording suggests, a principle meant to apply to aircraft and weapons, not ship procurement. It is possible, without losing many months, to build a prototype of a plane or a missile and test it thoroughly before starting up a production line. But to build one Trident submarine and put it through all its tests before starting to build a second would mean a loss of as many as eight years. Moreover there was little risk in going ahead. I have taken occasion to dwell on the ways I think Rickover's long tenure has affected the Navy, but one thing no one can say about him is that he ever sponsored a lemon. Without exception his products had been excellent ships—too excellent, I believe I have mentioned several dozen times—and there was no reason to fear that Trident would be an exception.

A third argument several members of the subcommittee advanced with much earnestness and obtuseness was that the entire $900 million cut had been in funds for developing the boat itself; none of the cut had been in funds for developing the 4000-mile missile, which was the more pressing matter because once it was deployed—and it could be deployed in Polaris—it would give missile submarines four times as much ocean to cruise in as before and would eliminate the need for the overseas Polaris bases in Rota, Spain, and Holy Loch, Scotland. In short, the substance of this argument was that the Trident boat could be delayed without risk as long as the Trident missile was put to sea speedily. Beyond the fact that there was no economic advantage, but on the contrary an economic penalty, in delaying the development of the boat, this argument failed to come to grips with the fact that the interim agreement on offensive weapons expired in 1977 and that unless we did something in the meantime to offset Soviet superiority in numbers and throw-weight, we would find ourselves in 1977 with the choice of signing a new instrument, interim or permanent, that reconfirmed our inferiority or signing nothing and embarking on a game of strategic catch-up that might never end or end in disaster. As I saw it, the time to play catch-up was right then before the interim agreement expired. If we moved wisely there was hope that a permanent treaty imposing parity in offensive weapons, and even reduced numbers, might be negotiable as the successor to the interim agreement.

On 1 August the McIntyre subcommittee's proposal to cut Trident came before the full Armed Services Committee, then under the temporary chairmanship of Stuart Symington; John Stennis was still recovering from the bullet wounds he had received a few months earlier in a street robbery outside his house. To the astonishment and dismay of the Navy, the committee upheld the subcommittee's action by an 8–7 vote. One vote recorded for the cut was the proxy of Barry Goldwater, who I was sure was solidly pro-Trident; Goldwater himself was in a fishing boat off the coast of California at the time the vote was taken. I telephoned his administrative assistant the following day to ask what had gone wrong. The AA replied that he, too, was certain that Goldwater favored the full Trident program. I thereupon succeeded in reaching the Senator in his fishing boat and he told me that the instructions he had left about how his proxy was to be voted must have been misunderstood. On 3 August, at Goldwater's insistence, the committee voted again and rejected the Trident cut by 8–7. Incidentally, Stennis's proxy, which he had given to Henry Jackson, was cast for Trident both times.

The full Senate did not take up the military authorization bill until late in September, at which time Senator McIntyre and his subcommittee's senior Republican, Peter Dominick of Colorado, who departed in this instance from his usual support of strategic programs, offered the Trident cut as an amendment to the bill. The debate on the amendment was scheduled for 26 and 27 September, with the vote to follow. I considered this vote to be of critical importance to the security of the United States. Beyond the clear need for Trident to be deployed as early as possible in view of the SALT situation was the fact that those numerous senators who opposed Trident altogether at any time were clearly hoping to use this vote as the first step toward killing the program. I calculated that if we won this vote Trident would be nailed irremovably into the strategic program, but if we lost it we would have the same battle to fight next year and who knew how many years after that. And so during the week or so preceding this debate and vote I must have called on thirty or forty senators, and Rickover and Secretary of the Navy John Warner were similarly active.

On the assumption that there are no certainties when it comes to Congressional votes, I made a point of approaching a number of Senators whose votes I had next to no hope for: George McGovern, Hubert Humphrey, Edward Kennedy—Humphrey and Kennedy always listened carefully when I gave them my views—and Mike Mansfield. William Proxmire refused to see me. My sessions with Senator Mansfield always amused me. On this occasion, as on all the others when I met with him, he was a model of courtesy and graciousness during the small talk that preceded my making my pitch. Once I had started he listened attentively, but never said a word. When I had finished he rose and said politely, "Thank you very much." Obviously he did not want to waste my time in discussion that would have been futile, inasmuch as his mind already was made up.

I think my most productive piece of lobbying occurred on 25 September, the day before the debate began, in the office of Senator Bennett Johnston of Louisiana. Johnston, a newcomer to the Senate, was of two minds about Trident and he got the idea of staging a debate between an opponent and a proponent of immediate construction of the boat to which he could invite half a dozen of his colleagues who also were undecided. I was the logical proponent, of course, and

I suppose the opponent Johnston picked was logical too: Dr. Herbert Scoville, a former official in the CIA and the Arms Control Agency, who writes voluminously on strategic matters from the general standpoint that the Soviets are anxious to reach an accommodation with the United States about arms and other matters, and that the U.S. military's hard line tends to frustrate such an accommodation. Among the senators who attended the Scoville-Zumwalt debate I remember John Tunney of California, Gaylord Nelson of Wisconsin, and Sam Nunn of Georgia.

The burden of my argument followed what I have written in this chapter and elsewhere in the book about SALT, détente, and related matters, and the burden of Scoville's is equally easy to imagine. However, it is worth mentioning two specific points that arose because, several of the senators present told me later, they pretty much destroyed Scoville's credibility as either a strategic or a political expert. One was that he had published a paper in July predicting that the Soviets would not attempt to MIRV their missiles and in August the Soviets had started testing MIRVs. You can be sure I did not neglect to mention that. The other was a charge he was foolish enough to make that the Navy had decided to base Trident on Puget Sound, near Bangor, Washington, in order to get Henry Jackson's vote. Every senator in the room knew that was absurd, that constituents were every bit as likely to be enraged as delighted by (a) situating nuclear installations in their immediate neighborhood and (b) condemning various parcels of choice waterfront property to make room for those installations. Indeed when Scoop Jackson first heard that Bangor was the site for the Trident base the Navy preferred, he told me that he would prefer the base not to be in his state. He added that if we could convince him that it was in fact the best site for the country he would withdraw his objection, though it would cause him some political problems. We pointed out to him that the Pacific coast was the proper place to base Trident because the Pacific was the strategically logical ocean for the longest-range missiles and the West coast was harder for Soviet ships or planes to reach than the east coast, and that Puget Sound was the logical place on the Pacific coast because its great depth would make it possible for the boats to put to sea submerged and therefore unobserved. He made no further objection.

The session with Scoville not only got the Navy two or three thitherto doubtful votes on Trident, but a small extra bonus. Midway through the session the bell that signifies the imminence of a vote on the Senate floor rang. It turned out to be a vote on one of the periodic attempts to cut funds for the F-14. A couple of the senators, on the way to the door, indicated that they were not exactly sure what the F-14 issue was. I gladly volunteered to dispel their confusion on that point, and walked them to the elevator, dispelling confusion fast as we walked. I got their votes. However, there was another incident that afternoon that was less productive. John Cochran, a reporter for NBC Television News, was outside the office when the session broke up to learn how the debate had gone. He asked me whether it was accurate that the Navy had said Soviets were lobbying against Trident on Capitol Hill. I said, in effect, that the Soviets had been lobbying against it, and went on, "The Soviets, in a host of ways, including the use of employees here, do make a concerted impact upon U.S. policy. This is a courtesy that they're afforded in our democratic way and a courtesy they don't afford in the Soviet Union." Cochran put that quote on the "Today" show next morning and preceded it by saying "Zumwalt says Soviet agents have lobbied on Capitol Hill against Trident," which in essence was what I did say with the important exception that I never used the word "agents."

The reaction to this in the Senate next day, as the Trident debate began, would scarcely have been greater if I had charged the pro-Amendment members of the Senate, individually and collectively, with ancestry of a disreputable canine variety. The thunder still reverberates in my ears. Senator McIntyre: "Mr. President, I was shocked, dismayed, angered and I do not know what when I received a report made by the Chief of Naval Operations. . . ." Senator Hughes: "Mr. President, in other words by implication and innuendo, Admiral Zumwalt implied to the nation on a nationwide television show that members of the Senate, as yet unnamed, have been lobbied by Communist agents, as yet unnamed, which action may influence their votes on a U.S. defense system." Senator Abourezk: "I do not believe that any U.S. senator would allow a Soviet lobbyist in his office to try to talk about the Trident submarine. I do not believe it for a minute. It is that kind of military red-baiting, fear, and emotionalism that we have seen too often in debates on defense procurement." Senator Fulbright: "As I understand it, Admiral Zumwalt has now warned that the Congress is in danger of being misled by a swarming army of Soviet agents racing through the halls of the Capitol and lobbying members of this body. . . . I resent the insinuation that Communist agents are effectively lobbying members of the Senate." Senator Symington: ". . . of particular concern is the manner in which the Congress and the American people have been and are being lobbied with respect to this rushed program. You have just heard the latest—a member of the Joint Chiefs of Staff talking about Communist agents working against the Trident here on the Hill." Finally Henry Jackson was impelled to address himself to the matter:

> The Soviet Embassy does have a staff assigned to the Hill. They often come in and out of my subcommittee office, getting material and literature. If any senator is so naive as to think that the Soviets are not active up here, he is just not keeping up with what is going on. . . . So we ought not to react as though there is something startling about the situation Admiral Zumwalt referred to.

There were perhaps two or three minutes of colloquy between Jackson and various of his colleagues on this point, in the course of which Hubert Humphrey said *he* was not aware that Soviet embassy employees were active on Capitol Hill. Then the matter pretty much got dropped, though Symington did send me a telegram demanding that before next day's vote I supply the Senate with a list of Soviet agents and the senators they visited. I replied, "Reference your telegram, I assure you I see no Soviet threat on Capitol Hill . . ." and added the transcript of the Cochran bulletin. I rather suspect that my tendency to say what I think cost the Navy one or two votes. Since the Scoville debate won the Navy two or three, the net effect of my work on 25 September 1973 was plus one vote. On 27 September the Senate voted 49–47 against the McIntyre-Dominick proposal to cut Trident. It was too close for comfort.

III

MEN AND WOMEN

CHAPTER 7

Programs for People

I am certain that what finally decided Secretary of Defense Melvin Laird and Secretary of the Navy John Chafee to risk jumping me into the position of Chief of Naval Operations over the heads of thirty-three of my seniors was my advocacy of rapid and drastic changes in the way the Navy treated its uniformed men and women. I do not mean to suggest that my ideas about modernizing the Navy's ships and weapons to meet the mounting Soviet maritime threat was of no consequence to the two Secretaries. Obviously it was of great consequence. However every officer being considered for CNO had a more or less vigorous program to deal with that situation. Where I was virtually alone among those being considered was in viewing existing policies and practices in the field of personnel administration as an even greater immediate danger to the Navy's capability—though a far easier one to avert—than its obsolescing physical plant. After all, the best warships in the world are of no avail without crews to sail and fight them. And in recruitment, and especially in the retention of men and women who had completed their first hitches, the Navy was approaching a crisis. For many years the goal for reenlistments after the first hitch had been 35 percent. In 1970 the actual figure was 9½ percent.

Moreover, there was little prospect that this trend would reverse itself soon. The anti-militaristic mood that the seemingly futile and endless Vietnam war had created in an entire generation was at its most intense in the wake of the "incursion" into Cambodia, which

had occurred soon after I returned to South Vietnam from the trip
to Washington during which the President had designated me CNO.
And with troops coming home from Vietnam in increasing numbers
and Army draft calls, as a result, getting lower every month, the
Navy stood to lose whatever benefit the preference of many prospective draftees for the Navy over the Army had conferred upon it.
Indeed the end of the draft itself looked to be no more than a year
or two away, so that all too soon the Navy would have to compete
head on for able young people not only with the other military
services but with the civilian economy. Obviously these social deterrents to serving in the Navy were beyond the Navy's power to abolish
or alter. That was precisely the reason I thought initiating prompt
and forceful action to increase the inducements to naval service in
those areas where the Navy did have the power to act to be as
pressing as any task facing the incoming CNO.

It seemed to me that there were four kinds of things the Navy
could do to make the service more attractive and more satisfying.
One was to reexamine the regulations and practices dealing with
personal behavior—dress, grooming, and so forth—with a view to
bringing them into line with the customs and tastes of the seventies.
A second was to develop operational schedules, job rotation systems,
and homeporting facilities that would lighten what always has been
the heaviest burden of naval service, long separation from family.
The third was to find ways to give bright and talented young men
and women more responsibility and greater opportunity for advancement than they were getting, to increase "job satisfaction," in Secretary Chafee's phrase. The fourth, and most important, was to throw
overboard once and for all the Navy's silent but real and persistent
discrimination against minorities—not only blacks, the chief victims,
but Puerto Ricans, American Indians, Chicanos, Filipinos, orientals,
and, indeed, women as well—in recruiting, in training, in job assignment, in promotion, even, I was to learn, in stocking commissaries
and ship's stores. Whether or not the specifics of my ideas about
personnel were just what Secretaries Laird and Chafee had in mind,
there was no doubt that they were looking for a CNO who shared
their conviction that, however desirable gradual reform in the field
of personnel administration might have been if it had been instituted
in time, it was too late for that now and the Navy would have to risk
the resentment of the traditionalists that rapid reform was bound to
inspire. I need to record that Secretary Chafee had seen this situation

in the same way and had been struggling for a year to get personnel reforms underway.

It was my command of the U.S. Naval Forces in Vietnam that had brought my feelings about the backwardness of many of the Navy's personnel policies and practices, which had been simmering lightly throughout my career, to a rolling boil. Like most—though unfortunately by no means all—officers who have exercised command, I had always found that the style of leadership that accorded best with both my own inclinations and operational efficiency was one of treating subordinates with consideration and respect. I had not found that a "tight" ship had to be an "uptight" ship. And I had hoped that sooner or later the Navy would give institutional recognition to this principle, which guided the performance of most of the best commanders, by overhauling such of its procedures and jettisoning such of its traditions as encouraged martinetism or martinets.

In Vietnam this rather amorphous hope became a conviction that the Navy's fate might hinge on how soon and thoroughly it was done. In the course of exercising command over a far-flung coastal and delta area I spent perhaps half my days there visiting ships, boats, bases, and hospitals and during such visits I always spent some of my time "rapping" with the officers and men. The thing that stood out above all else at those sessions was that the men's complaints almost never were about operational or logistics problems nor about fighting an unpopular war far from home. Almost always they were about the myriad of restrictions the Navy imposed on their personal behavior, restrictions that made them feel that the Navy, at a time when they were risking their lives in a venture many of their contemporaries thought was dubious, was asking them as well to fly in the face of their generation's style of life. Hair and beards were the burning issue, but there were complaints, too, about leave and promotion policies, about the treatment of dependents, about the gamut of Navy personnel practices. Moreover, it was not just 18- or 19-year-old recruits who complained, but seasoned petty officers and junior officers of several years' experience. Here were patriotic men who understood the need to fight and who fought very well, men of the kind the Navy most needed to attract and keep, who were ready to quit because of the high-and-mighty tone the Navy took toward their personal habits and tastes and their individual needs.

I could not help but consider it a major responsibility of mine to act as an advocate for those men. Soon after I took command in

South Vietnam I had sent boats up and established bases on or along the narrow rivers and canals in the interior of Vietnam to increase pressure against enemy infiltrators from Cambodia. I had required thousands of sailors to shift from the relatively safe duty of coastal or big-river patrol to the rigors of front-line life and the perils of enemy fire. As I wrote in an earlier chapter, for one short period Navy casualties were 6 percent a month, which meant that if that period had lasted a year—which mercifully it did not—a sailor staying on duty that whole year would have had greater than a 50 percent chance of being killed or wounded. Compared with what I was asking of those men, the beards and sideburns they were asking of me were not much. On my long trip back home to assume the duties of CNO, I made a point of spending as much time as I could with the sailors of the fleets I visited. I got the same message from those blue-water sailors as from my brown-water sailors in Vietnam: they too were ready to quit when their time was up.

My sense of urgency about personnel reform led me to seek urgently for mechanisms that would permit that reform to occur faster than the normal pace of bureaucracy permitted. I had had a lesson about this when I was Executive Assistant to Paul Nitze, when he was Secretary of the Navy. In 1964 we set up a Personnel Retention Task Force. It produced a set of dramatic recommendations along precisely the lines of the ones I was planning to initiate as CNO. However, we entrusted those recommendations to the "system" for implementation with the result that so few of them were put into effect, and so slowly, that the impact on morale and retention that the whole package would have had was lost. I was determined not to let this happen a second time.

My staff and I hit upon one technique for coming to grips with the problem before we left Vietnam. We decided to call into Washington for consultation a series of "retention study groups." Each of these would consist of perhaps a dozen officers and/or enlisted men from a particular part of the Navy. Each board would spend four or five days reaching a consensus about the working and living conditions that made serving in the Navy difficult or disagreeable and forming recommendations for improving those conditions. It would then deliver those recommendations to me personally so that both the group's members and I would be sure that the system had not laundered their views. A NAVOP (a message to the entire Navy) establishing the retention study group program went out on 14 July 1970, just two weeks after I began my watch. The first group, junior aviation officers, convened in the Marriott Hotel near the Pentagon on 20 July and reported to me on the 25th. It had plenty to say. It came up with a total of sixty-three specific recommendations, some of them with an many as eight sub-recommendations, divided into seven separate categories: Command/Promotion Policies; Detailing Policies; General Personnel Policies; Pay/Fringe Benefits; Education/Communications; Aviation Policies; and Fun and Zest Recommendations ("fun and zest" is a phrase I use a lot because naval service has provided me with a lot of it). The recommendations ranged from beer machines in all barracks, a twenty-four-hour mess line on carriers, squash courts on all bases, and permission to wear flight suits anywhere on a naval air station, to establishing a goal of six months at home between deployments, giving aviators more opportunity to learn seamanship by assigning them as navigators to cruisers or destroyers, establishing a Navy-wide career counseling program, and requiring that fitness reports on all officers of the rank of commander and below be read and signed by the officer reported on before their submission to higher authority.

That this group and the groups that followed it came up with coherent and useful recommendations rather than mere gripes was largely to the credit of Lieutenant David Halperin, an innovative young officer who had been a valued member of my personal staff in Vietnam. I made Dave one of my special assistants when I got back to Washington, with the primary responsibility of working with the retention study groups. His technique was to let each group blow off steam for the first day or two so that each of its members had an opportunity to articulate all of his or her complaints. Then he sent them on a search for practical remedies for the ills they were complaining of, remedies that I might reasonably be expected to administer: a change of regulations here, a pilot program there, a new staff responsibility somewhere else. The night before each group was to have its hour with me, Dave put it through a dress rehearsal, making sure that each recommendation was framed in the most persuasive way and each member of the group had a part to play in the presentation. Dave rightly calculated that the members of the groups were so delighted to have the opportunity to give the top man, in person, their ideas about how to improve the Navy that no amount of preparation or rehearsal would damp their spontaneity and enthusiasm. For myself, a meeting with a retention study group was likely to be the high point of my week, a more than welcome opportunity to insert into the routine of paper work and VIP meetings an encounter with sailors from the fleet. I tried to get Secretary Chafee to those meetings as often as he had the time and I made a point of bringing in senior members of my staff who I was sure would benefit as much as I from a first-hand glimpse, however fleeting, of the Navy we were busy running from our air-conditioned offices.

Almost all of the work of the retention study groups was done during the first part of my watch. The aviation officers were followed in 1970 by destroyer and mine force officers, amphibious and auxiliary officers, submarine officers, POW/MIA dependents, aviation enlisted, service force enlisted, amphibious enlisted, black officers, medical department personnel, black enlisted, submarine enlisted, and destroyer and mine force enlisted. In 1971, by which time Dave Halperin had gone over to the White House as Henry Kissinger's aide, and Lieutenant Bill Antle had taken over the job, eleven groups met, including WAVEs, civil engineers, ROTC midshipmen, and minority women. Ten groups met in 1972, some of them to make sure that no Navy community had been overlooked, some of them for the purpose of providing me with first hand reports about how well the many new personnel programs by then in effect were working. During the first half of 1973, the last three groups met. By that time almost every conceivable point had been covered, most of them many times.

While the retention study group program was getting under way, my staff was working on various personnel problems that sailors in Vietnam and in the fleet had told me about. By the end of July the staff had prepared or was preparing a score or more of NAVOPS initiating new personnel policies or altering old ones. At that point we decided that all NAVOPS that contained, in the words of the message I sent to all commands on 22 July, "policy or guidance emanating personally from the CNO . . . will be identified with a 'Zulu' series message designator immediately following the originator, e.g., 'fm CNO Z-01', 'fm CNO Z-02.' " Those Zulu NAVOPS were messages that the fleet presently took to calling "Z-grams." The 1 July NAVOP containing my words to the fleet upon assuming office became, retroactively, Z-01 and the 14 July NAVOP establishing the retention study groups became Z-02. Z-03, an inconsequential message about certain cryptographic procedures, appeared on 22 July, the day Zulus became official. The real beginning of Z-grams came on 30 July with the appearance of Z-04 and Z-05, both of them of much moment to the people they concerned.

Z-04 gave all officers in receipt of PCS (permanent change of station) orders what enlisted personnel in receipt of similar orders already got—an automatic thirty-day leave between leaving the old job and reporting to the new one. Z-05 addressed itself to a grievance that was a particularly sore one among enlisted men on sea duty. It initiated a pilot program on three ships of the Sixth Fleet in the Mediterranean and three ships of the First Fleet on the Pacific Coast under which first class petty officers would be allowed, as only officers and chief petty officers had been until then, to keep civilian clothes for use on leave or liberty aboard ship. That this issue should have inflamed the passions of certain Navy traditionalists may be hard for a civilian reader to believe, but it did, and that was why I felt it necessary to proceed in such a gingerly fashion. The reasons cited by those who opposed the change were that there was too little storage space aboard crowded ships to carry the civilian clothing and that the right to wear civilian clothing was a perquisite of rank and seniority. Of the two, the second was the more deeply felt. In any case, I hoped that Z-05's circumspect forecast that this reform "eventually may be extended to embrace entire crew" would give second and third class petty officers and non-rated men heart. And indeed, on 23 December I found it possible to proclaim in Z-68, "In view of the enthusiastic response to pilot program authorizing first class petty officers to maintain civilian clothes aboard ship for wearing ashore on leave and liberty, privilege is hereby extended to all petty officers on all ships." Six months later, on 29 July 1971, Z-92 extended the "privilege" to non-rated men. It is an example of how difficult reform in the real world is that it took a year and three pieces of guidance by high authority to establish that a sailor can always find a place to stow something he really wants to stow, and that "civvies" for all hands are not excessively egalitarian.

Z-04 and Z-05 were the harbingers of a flood of Z-grams, most of them inspired by the reports of the retention study groups. There were ten in August, twenty-three in September, fourteen in October, eleven in November, and six in December. Then things slowed down. There were only twenty-three altogether during the next six months, ten between the end of June and the end of December 1971, and eleven in the first six months of 1972. The number of Z-grams I sent out during my first two years as CNO was 113. During the next two

years I sent out just eight. By then the easy job of issuing directives
had pretty much been done and the hard job of enforcing them
occupied my attention. Probably the two most publicized Z-grams
during the hectic first six months were Z-57, Demeaning or Abrasive
Regulations, Elimination of, which went out 10 November, and
Z-66, Equal Opportunity in the Navy, which went out 17 December.
I will discuss them at some length in subsequent chapters. Meanwhile, a sample of the titles of others will convey an accurate notion
of the extent of the ground I was covering.

Z-09 Meritorious Advancement in Rate of Superior Performing Career Petty
      Officers
Z-12 Civilian Clothing on Naval Shore Establishments
Z-17 Personal Check Cashing Ceilings at Naval Activities
Z-20 Lockers and Wash Facilities for Personnel who have to Work in Dungarees
      Ashore
Z-24 Wives Ombudsman
Z-25 Forces Afloat Liberty Policy
Z-31 Type Command Shiphandling Competition
Z-34 Uniform Changes
Z-38 Holiday Routine at Sea
Z-39 Extended Commissary Hours
Z-41 Command Excellence Forum
Z-45 Assistance to POW/MIA Families
Z-49 Medals and Awards
Z-51 Small Craft Insignia
Z-55 Human Resource Management
Z-60 Action Line Telephone
Z-65 The Vietnamization Challenge: Naval Advisors to do the job
Z-72 Quarterdeck Watches
Z-76 Outstanding Recruiter Awards
Z-83 Motor Vehicle Transportation for Forces Afloat
Z-85 Legislation Status Report
Z-86 CNO Scholars Program
Z-88 Advances of Pay
Z-94 Navy Drug Exemption and Rehabilitation Program

One among the early Z-grams deserves more than cursory mention, Z-48, issued on 23 October under the title Programs for People.
It established in the Bureau of Naval Personnel a new office, "Pers-
P," the "P" standing for people. This undramatic action actually was
of the first importance, because it was the first step toward institu-
tionalizing the new practices and programs the Z-grams kept pro-
claiming. As Z-48 said, "It is one thing to promulgate new programs,
but quite another to sustain and nourish their forward progress." It

defined the duties of Pers-P as "to provide impetus to and coordination of our programs for people." The importance I attached to this
new office is indicated by the man I chose to fill it, Rear Admiral
David Bagley, the elder brother of Worth Bagley and a prep school
classmate of mine, whom I regarded as one of the most forward-
looking and capable officers in the Navy. He performed so capably
as Pers-P that in 1972 I recommended him for the three star office
of Chief of Naval Personnel. At the same time I placed my staff
assistant for personnel, Chick Rauch, an old Vietnam colleague who
had just been selected for flag rank, into the Pers-P spot. Thus the
two positions in BuPers most critical to the success of personnel
reform were occupied for more than half my watch by officers who
enthusiastically supported such reform.

One of the first personnel programs I initiated came directly out
of my experiences as a junior officer on destroyers. I first called it the
"Young Turk Squadron," but the men in it soon gave it the much
catchier name of the "Mod Squad." It was a destroyer squadron—
Destroyer Squadron 26—in which every officer billet was assigned
to a man one rank below the one its occupant ordinarily held. Thus,
the commanding officers were lieutenant commanders instead of
commanders, the executive officers were lieutenants instead of lieutenant commanders, and so on down the line. I thought of this not
as a pilot program, since there was no way it could fail if the men
were chosen with even approximate accuracy, but as a demonstration program, a program that would demonstrate to the entire Navy
the benefits of giving outstanding young officers more responsibility
than was traditional early in their careers. Not the least of such
benefits, of course, was an increased likelihood that such men would
stay in the Navy, for it was precisely the most promising young
officers whom the slow pace of advancement galled the most. To
make the program doubly foolproof, I put Squadron 26 under the
command of Captain Richard Nicholson, an officer whom I think I
can describe without being patronizing as a protege of mine.
    Dick Nicholson had been a lieutenant commander assigned to the
office of the Secretary of the Navy at the time Paul Nitze was Secretary and I was Paul's executive assistant. During that period Dick
became eligible for promotion to commander, but the selection board
passed him over. For an able, enthusiastic, and ambitious young
officer like Dick, being passed over, even only once, means the end
of his Navy career because it virtually eliminates the chance of

reaching flag rank. There may have been others, but at that time I myself had heard of only one officer who had made admiral through normal selection after being passed over for promotion, and that had been many years before. Dick Nicholson was about to resign his commission and seek a line of work that offered him advancement. But first he asked my advice. I told him that if he didn't get discouraged, but kept charging ahead the way he had been, he had a good chance of becoming the second officer in history to overcome the handicap of being passed over by a selection board. It was risky advice, of course, but not quite as risky as it appears. For one thing I knew how good Dick was. For another, I had a good idea of why he was passed over. Since he worked in the Secretary's office, the Secretary had to make out his fitness report, and the Secretary in question, Nitze's predecessor, Fred Korth, evidently did not know the code in which fitness reports are written. He had described Dick as an "excellent officer," meaning that he was an excellent officer. However, to convey the idea an officer is excellent in fitness-report dialect you must say he is "outstanding." To say he is "excellent" merely means he is adequate. In short, "excellent" is the kind of word that makes a selection board think, "Oh-oh. That guy must have fouled up somewhere. We can't select him."

Dick took my advice and stayed in the Navy. He made commander the next time around, was given command of a destroyer and proceeded not only to get every battle efficiency award, "E", for his ship that was obtainable, but to win that year's Arleigh Burke Award for the best ship in the entire fleet. He moved from that command to a staff position with me in Vietnam, and then to command of the Market Time coastal surveillance task force, where I had the pleasure of presenting him with the fourth stripe of a captain. Under him the "Mod Squad," which first trained on the Atlantic Coast and in the Caribbean, and then joined the Sixth Fleet in the Mediterranean, was the outstanding destroyer squadron in both places. And, finally, Dick did become the second man ever to be selected normally for admiral after having been passed over for promotion; he now commands a destroyer flotilla. As for the Mod Squad, it proved what it was bound to prove and my successor, Admiral James Holloway, dissolved it and is now assigning responsibilities above their rank to outstanding young officers fleetwide.

A perennial personnel problem in the Navy has been the inordinate amount of sea duty, i.e., duty away from home and family, that men holding certain "deprived" ratings have had to serve. My first encounter with this problem came during my first Washington tour, from 1953 to 1955, when I was a lieutenant commander assigned to the Bureau of Naval Personnel. At that time, to cite the most flagrant case, a radarman could expect two years on shore after every twenty-six years at sea, and the ratio was only a little better for machinist's mates, boiler tenders, quartermasters, and a number of other specialists who could practice their specialties only aboard ship.

The conventional wisdom at the time was that because those specialties could be practiced only aboard ship, the men holding them could serve only aboard ship. It occurred to me that there must be a large number of shore billets calling for rated men that did not require a specific skill, jobs in base maintenance, in security, in the shore patrol, and the like. Sure enough, when I studied the lists of authorized billets, I found that there were something like 9000 of the kind I was seeking. Traditionally they had been occupied by yeomen or storekeepers or some such rate, but there was no reason why radarmen or boiler tenders could not fill them just as satisfactorily. When I called this discovery to the attention of my superiors, they were interested. Indeed the matter got all the way up to Vice Admiral James L. Holloway, Jr., father of the present CNO, who then was the Chief of Naval Personnel and who did me the favor of asking me to brief him on my findings. Admiral Holloway arranged for those billets to be opened up to the holders of the deprived ratings, which reduced a radarman's sea-to-shore duty ratio from twenty-six and two to seven and two, and had equivalent impact on other specialists.

However, that reform stretched the existing system as far as it would go, and not much more was done about the plight of the deprived ratings after 1955. I was determined to relieve that plight further. I did not think it was either productive or fair to require anyone to serve seven years at sea to two ashore. Three and three seemed to me to be the proper objective, as an August 1970 point paper in connection with Project 60 stated. This was not a matter that could be solved by composing a Z-gram. First, shore billets had to be found or new ones created. Second, a sufficient number of extra men had to acquire specialists' skills so that those at sea could be relieved to come ashore. We found or created new billets in several different ways, among them by converting some civilian jobs to uniformed jobs, and by expanding some of the activities that the 1955 reform first put deprived ratings into. The principal way was creating a new type of billet, that of fleet maintenance assistance expert, in the home ports out of which ships operate between deployments. This not only enabled the Navy to utilize the expertise of certain specialists ashore for the first time but, in my opinion, increased the efficiency of overhaul and maintenance operations by introducing into the process the skill and experience of men who had been responsible for various kinds of equipment at sea. In other words, I think it likely that the creation of those new jobs will save the Navy money in the long run. Because this concept never had been proposed, much less tried, it encountered the predictable suspicion of those Pentagon folk whose function is to give innovations that affect the budget the fish eye. As a result it took some three years for the plan to go fully into effect. And even so, a radarman is not all the way to three and three; four and three is about what he can expect right now.

Some who favored my personnel reforms as reasonable and long overdue were troubled by the public, not to say theatrical, manner in which I proclaimed them. They maintained that those reforms could and should have been initiated without creating a showy apparatus of retention study groups and Z-grams, without inspiring public jokes about "the Mod Navy" and getting the CNO on the cover of *Time*. I think they missed the point. "Going public" was a deliberate tactic based on my conviction that the Navy had to do more than to treat its people better in many big and little ways. It had to change, and change fast, the opinion, widespread among both sailors and civilians and having some basis in fact, that it was a humorless, tradition-bound, starchy institution owned by and operated for the benefit of white males. This change would cause controversy. It seemed to me to be both right and necessary that I set up a system which made me personally the lightning rod for such controversy.

I do not think that my program would have had much of a chance if I had not made that first, all-out effort to tell the world about it. For basically it was not I, but the sailors in the fleet, and their families, and the media, and even certain members of Congress who overcame the inertia, or in some cases the opposition, of the system and forced the reforms through. What I did, in a sense, was to unleash those forces by seeing to it that the commitment to reform by the Navy's top leadership was posted on every ship's bulletin board, was featured on the evening news, and in the pages of *Time*. Once Z-68 got on the bulletin boards, I did not have to send emissaries around to make sure that petty officers were being permitted to keep civilian clothes in their lockers. The petty officers made sure of that. Once the media had reported that the Navy had committed itself to equal opportunity, they felt obliged to keep track of whether or not that commitment was being carried through, and thus helped keep up the pressure for it to be carried through.

I made the decision to go public knowing that it entailed risks and could arouse opposition among that perhaps 10 or 15 percent of officers and senior petty officers who felt that undisputed control of every aspect of a subordinate's life was a prerogative of military seniority. And indeed there was a considerable outcry about "going over the heads of commanders" and "washing dirty linen in public" from this small group of petty tyrants or, more commonly, sincere paternalists, though more often than not they spoke not with their own voices but through the retired community. All that did not surprise me. One could not spend a quarter of a century in the Navy without having numerous encounters with such folk; one of the first captains I served under as a young destroyer officer treated his entire crew, commissioned and enlisted, like backward and unreliable children, which once and for all set my mind against that style of leadership. My own philosophy about reform in the Navy was best stated by the first chief petty officer I worked with on board USS *Phelps* in 1942. He said, "Ensign Zumwalt, the Navy ain't what she used to be, and never was."

What did surprise me somewhat was how much confusion my way of doing things created among some of the members of the Navy's "middle management." Looking back now, I can see why some of those captains and commanders and lieutenant commanders out in the field were confused. They had no experience of receiving directives about matters like beards and motorcycles directly from the Chief of Naval Operations, directives moreover that were couched in language as plain and simple as my staff and I could make it and took a tone as urgent as was consistent with common politeness. These individuals evidently took the Z-grams personally, as reproaches directed against them for past misdeeds and warnings to sin no more, rather than as the announcements of changes in policy that they were intended to be. Some concluded that since higher authority was taking such an unprecedented interest in the details of personnel administration, the best thing for them to do was wash their own hands of further responsibility of such matters. Others really did feel that their rightful authority was being diluted and diminished, that I was going straight to the men without regard for the chain of command. My one regret about the way I handled my personnel program was that I did not consult sufficiently at the beginning with middle management, and did not bring its members up to speed on my ideas and plans at the outset. The great majority of them supported the program from the outset; most of the others did too, once they understood it, and no permanent harm was done, but for the first year or two their confusion was painful to them and it did slow things down somewhat.

My first attempt to deal with this confusion, which I became aware of within days of the despatch of the first Z-grams, was to send, on 26 September, a six-page letter on the subject of "Command" to all flag officers, commanders, commanding officers, and officers-in-charge. Its fundamental message, which it elaborated in detail, was, "To accomplish what I have in mind, I think you need to achieve the very finest balance between the following: . . . a relaxed attitude and a responsible attitude, challenging your officers and crew and being considerate of them, adequate rewards but with proper restraint, polish and performance. . . ." A month later, on 23 October, I felt compelled to send to the same addressees Z-52, from which I quote the relevant passage.

Through my visits to various fleet units and bases and through literature and personal letters, I am aware of systems in use by some of you to widely distribute the policy set forth in the standard Z-numbered NAVOPS. However, from almost every source possible I have also received information that the Z-numbered NAVOPS have not received the wide dissemination that is so necessary if we are to implement these policies and keep our people informed. Since I have chosen these as a vehicle for the announcement of many new initiatives and of significant policy changes, it is important to disseminate these NAVOPS as widely as possible. Whether they are read at quarters, placed on the plan of the day, posted on a centrally located bulletin board, or published by any other scheme, is of course a matter to be treated according to the style and desire of you in command. The important thing is that those already issued and those yet to come be distributed so that all hands have an opportunity to read them.

In the wake of this rather peremptory communication I felt it necessary to include in one form or another in every Z-gram of even a faintly controversial nature a statement that I had no intention of undercutting or bypassing the authority of commanding officers, but rather relied on those officers to implement, in their own style, the new policies. I usually added to this that the relaxation in specific existing regulations or practices I was ordering did not imply that I favored relaxing traditional military discipline and obedience to orders. The reason for this last stricture, of course, was that just as there was a small minority of martinets who were reluctant to treat people like people, so there was a small minority of loafers who could be counted upon to abuse whatever added latitude they were given. I did not intend to have personnel reform in the Navy stultified by such people.

In any case, more than three-quarters of naval personnel of all ages and ranks were enthusiastic about the personnel program from the beginning. The Navy's senior admirals, too, either actively approved or loyally went along. I regard as notable, for example, the comment on the draft of Z-52, quoted above, by my Vice CNO, Admiral Chick Clarey, a man considerably senior to me who had been one of the three finalists when I was chosen for the top job and who therefore, had he been a lesser man, might have harbored considerable resentment against both my programs and me. Chick wrote, "From remarks we have heard on several occasions this is needed. Agree. Well written to get message across." I received this kind of support from almost all the senior admirals, and it helped a great deal. In the forefront of the opposition was an ex-CNO, Admiral George Anderson, who had an office in the Executive Office Building as Chairman of the President's Foreign Intelligence Advisory Board. Admiral Anderson not only opposed the liberalization of personnel administration in the Navy, but tried his best to run the Navy from the sidelines. Admiral Thomas Moorer, my predecessor, with whom Admiral Anderson had interfered often enough, described him as "a dead hand on the tiller." I was aware of his activities from the beginning: such things do not go unremarked in Washington. But it was not until two years later that he almost found his target.

Mickey Mouse, Elimination Of

During my four years as CNO, there must have appeared over my signature thousands of documents: letters, memoranda, orders, studies and analyses, posture statements, speeches, and what not. Of them all, none created more of a stir, inside the Navy and outside, than Z-57, issued on 10 November 1970. Its original title—my title —was "Mickey Mouse, Elimination of," but three days before it appeared, my superlative new Vice Chief, Admiral Ralph Cousins (who had just relieved Chick Clarey in that job), fearing that this would be considered flippant, changed it to "Demeaning and Abrasive Regulations, Elimination of."

Z-57 was an order specifically liberalizing Navy regulations or practices in twelve areas: styles of hair, beards, sideburns, and civilian clothing; uniforms for trips between living quarters and work sites ashore; uniforms for visiting service facilities like snack bars, commissaries and disbursing offices; requirements for officers and enlisted men to shift into uniform of the day for evening meals; attire for enlisted and officers' clubs; the meaning of the traditional phrase "optional uniform"; preparing ships or stations for visits by senior officers; conditions of leave; the operation of motorcycles; conditions for overnight liberty; uniforms for certain kinds of conspicuous sea duty; procedures for processing requests from individuals to higher authorities. It amuses me a little that I am known mostly as the CNO who allowed sailors to grow beards, wear mod clothes, and drive motorcycles. In truth, I spent almost all of my time pondering upon and seeking to make a contribution to American policy with respect to the U.S.–Soviet maritime balance, strategic arms limitation, naval modernization, and a number of other matters that most people would agree have more bearing on the fate of the nation than what a sailor wears to supper. There even were some Z-grams that ordered changes more profound than any in Z-57. Nevertheless, Z-57, because its subject matter was easy for servicemen and civilians alike to understand and because it dealt with practices that for years had unnecessarily irritated thousands of men and women every day, came to symbolize the Navy's effort to attune itself to the times. It caused great joy and great controversy and so it is worth discussing.

"Mickey Mouse"—or "chicken regs," as they are called just as often—is a term that covers, for one thing, those self-serving regulations and practices by which some commanders attempt to give an appearance of efficiency or smartness but which in fact make no contribution to either of those desirable conditions. Hastily painting over rust spots the day before inspection is that kind of Mickey Mouse, and so is making a sailor change out of dungarees into liberty uniform before going to the commissary for a candy bar. For another thing, the term covers those niggling, or even deliberately harrassing, regulations and practices that don't even purport to affect efficiency or smartness, but seem to derive from an institutional notion that everyone below the rank of commander, say, is immature. Requiring a person going home on leave to prove he or she had the money for a round-trip ticket is that kind of Mickey Mouse, and so is refusing to provide parking spaces on naval stations for motorcycles on the ground that motorcycles (unlike nuclear submarines or guided missile frigates or helicopters) are too dangerous for sailors to ride.

My own first experiences with Mickey Mouse actually were experiences with its absence, for I went on active duty early in World War II. Then, with the tremendous influx of civilian sailors and reserve officers, the Navy perforce knocked off most of the Mickey Mouse. This was certainly true on destroyers, in which I served. Consequently, I had nearly three years to see that it was possible to maintain a dedicated, enthusiastic, well-disciplined, well-trained crew without chicken regs. It was after the war, as the civilian sailors departed and the regulars took over again, and the Navy lost the motivating thrust of the war, that Mickey Mouse began to come back. It involved such things as a requirement that a crew be in blue or white uniform for evening meal, although this could mean that a hard-working machinist's mate would have to leave a pump repair, come up and change clothes to have a meal, and then get back into his dirty clothes to finish the job. Such idiocies are not only an inefficient use of time, but very hard to explain to conscientious sailors who are trying to get their work done. Whereas during the war it had been commonplace to permit beards and moustaches, in the post-war Navy some skippers would not permit them—even though, according to Navy regulations, neatly trimmed beards and moustaches always have been authorized. In other words, a commander often usurped the prerogative of deciding whether or not on his ship the crew could do what Navy Regulations said sailors might decide for themselves.

My concern about these practices in the years immediately after World War II was intensified by the fact that we were in an era of severe budget constraints. As a result, working conditions deteriorated and many of the best sailors and officers, those who took the greatest pride in their work, were leaving the Navy. Meanwhile, Stalin—who had not demobilized—was overrunning Eastern Europe. I was executive officer of a destroyer at the time, and it seemed to me that if we were going to retain enough of our experienced people to get through what appeared to be very dangerous times, we had to improve conditions on each individual ship.

In those days there were two sets of personnel problems with which we had to deal. One was that most sailors, after going all the way through the war with almost no leave, had great amounts on the books. They not only didn't believe the Navy was going to give it to them but they didn't even believe the Navy was going to give them all the leave they accumulated in peace time. As executive officer of my ship I initiated the practice of giving every man sixty days leave a year if he wanted it. This was what Regulations allowed, but granting it was an almost unheard of practice. To do it the ship had to keep about one sixth of the crew on leave throughout periods of operation at sea as well as ashore. My captain, Commander Leon S. Kintberger, a great seaman, agreed that it was important to accept the reduction in readiness during that period in order to get the benefit of better morale and a higher reenlistment rate. And in fact we got an immediate payoff in a reenlistment rate that was impressively high for that era.

The second major set of problems had to do with the demeaning and abrasive regulations with which Z-57 was to deal twenty-five years later. As exec on two destroyers immediately after World War

II, I was able to experiment with the elimination of these regulations at the shipboard level, and found that doing so worked wonders on morale. That is, within the ship we eased off wherever and however we could. We allowed our people to go to dinner in dungarees when they were working. We addressed sailors by their titles, not their last names. We delegated more responsibility than was traditional. These practices and many more of a similar kind made a clear and large contribution to morale without reducing good order and discipline. By the time I left sea duty in 1948 for my first shore tour, I knew from experience the impact of treating sailors like the grown men they were, and I enlarged that experience in the course of my next three tours of sea duty, during each of which I had command of a destroyer-type ship.

I was not unique. In each of my tours, I discussed styles of command with other officers, almost all of whom had served both under those who went strictly by the book and under those who made reasonable exceptions. Most of them, not surprisingly, preferred the latter style of leadership. The martinets always were a minority. But of course they were a conspicuous minority, and some of them were in high enough positions to affect not just individual ships or stations, but whole flotillas or even fleets. A vivid example of this occurred one Armistice Day during the sixties in the Sixth Fleet in the Mediterranean. Many of the ships in the Fleet were anchored in Augusta Bay, Sicily, while the commanders held an all-day conference. The admiral commanding the fleet permitted no liberty in the fleet that day though it was a holiday and the majority of the men had no duties to perform.

The sea tour that convinced me once and for all of the effectiveness of a trusting rather than a suspicious style of leadership was my second command, the old World War II destroyer *Arnold J. Isbell,* from 1955 to 1957. My first command, the destroyer *Tills,* was not completely conclusive because it lasted only ten months. I was detached from that command when the Korean War began and assigned as navigator to the recommissioned battleship *Wisconsin.* In that capacity I spent most of my waking hours on the bridge with the skipper, and had little to do with the administration of the ship, which the executive officer carried out, I gathered from wardroom conversation, very much in the old tradition. My third command was USS *Dewey,* the first guided-missile frigate. Because she was the first ship of this new type, she was manned with handpicked officers and sailors, and personnel administration was easy. *Dewey*'s problem was her weapons system, not her spirit nor morale, but that's another story.

Arnold J. Isbell's problem was her spirit and morale. The year before I took command of her, she had stood last in battle efficiency (which is the best measure of a ship's readiness to perform missions) in a squadron of eight. At the end of my first year, she stood number two, and at the end of the second, number one. We accomplished these results in a milieu in which, to the extent that it was within my power, I had eliminated the demeaning and abrasive regulations. During this two-year tour the ship spent every other six months in overseas deployments and averaged only about half of the remaining time back in our home port so that we were away from our families 75 percent of our time. What I tried hardest to do was insure that every officer and man on the ship not only knew what we were about, not only why we were doing each tactical evolution, however oner-ous, but also managed to understand enough about how it all fitted together that he could begin to experience some of the fun and challenge that those of us in the top slots were having. Our tech-niques were not unusual. We made frequent announcements over the loudspeaker about the specific event that was going on. At the begin-ning and the end of the day, I discussed with the officers who, in turn, discussed with their men what was about to happen and what had just happened, what the competition was doing and what we should do to meet it. We published written notes in the plan of the day that would give the crew some of the color or human interest of what the ship was doing. I had bull sessions in chief petty officers' quarters, where I often stopped for a cup of coffee. More important than any of these details, of course, was the basic effort to communicate a sense of excitement, fun and zest, in all that we were doing.

One initiative that was surprisingly helpful in raising *Isbell's* spir-its came close to being frustrated by Mickey Mouse of a bureaucratic front-office kind. Every Navy ship is assigned a "voice call sign" by which it is addressed over voice tactical radio nets. The theory behind the use of this nickname is that the enemy won't know what ship is calling or being called. In actual fact, in enlisted and officer's clubs, in liberty areas, wherever sailors from the fleet gather, ships, and by extension their crews, are known as often by the voice call names as by the ship's real name. Voice call signs are invented and assigned by civil servants in a remote recess of the Pentagon who, one sometimes suspects, view their work with a certain amount of irony if not downright malice. In any case, *Arnold J. Isbell,* when I took command, had the voice call sign "Sapworth." Things were bad enough aboard the *Isbell* without her being addressed in this fashion a hundred times a day. Most sailors want to be proud of their ship, and it is not easy to be proud of a ship called Sapworth. Consequently, on 26 October 1955, shortly after taking command, I sent off the following letter:

From: Commanding Officer A. J. Isbell
To: Chief of Naval Operations
Via: (1) Commander Destroyer Division ONE HUNDRED TWELVE
       (2) Commander Destroyer Squadron ELEVEN
       (3) Commander Cruiser-Destroyer Force, U. S. Pacific Fleet

Subj: Change of voice radio call: request for

1. Since recently assuming command of ISBELL this Commanding Officer has been concerned over the anemic connotation of the present voice radio call. When in company with such stalwarts as "FIRE-BALL," "VIPER," and others, it is somewhat embarrassing and completely out of keeping with the quality of the sailormen aboard to be identified by the relatively ignominious title "SAPWORTH."

2. In order that ISBELL may carry on in the "31 knot Burke" tradition and proudly identify herself to all and sundry consorts, it is requested that our voice call be changed to "HELLCAT," which call is currently unassigned in JANAP 119(B).

JANAP 119(B), the reader doubtless will have figured out, is the published list of calls. The first endorsement on this request on 22 November, by the commander of Destroyer Division 112, was "1. Forwarded." In other words, "I'm not going to take a position on a matter as controversial as this." The second endorsement, dated 13 December 1955, from the Commander Destroyer Squadron 11, was "1. Forwarded recommending approval." My squadron commander was a man of courage and perception. The third endorsement, on 17 December, from the Commander Cruiser-Destroyer Force, U. S. Pacific Fleet, was:

1. Readdressed and Forwarded.

2. COMCRUDESPAC concurs in the recommended change provided it is in consonance with call sign assignment policies of the Joint Communications Electronics Committee.

In other words, "I can't find it, but there's bound to be a catch in this." The fourth endorsement, on 12 January 1956, from Commander-in-Chief U.S. Pacific Fleet, was:

1. Forwarded.

2. CINCPACFLT is aware that many voice calls assigned to the ships of the U.S. Navy are not indicative of their qualities and/or capabilities. This is due to the limited number of words in the English language that are suitable for voice calls. No objection to the subject request is interposed providing that a precedent is not established and the voice call "HELLCAT" is available for assignment to the USS ISBELL.

In other words, "Zumwalt may be right, but he's certainly pushy."

With all those caveats on the record—for of course I received copies of them—I was not at all sure that the request would be approved. Therefore, on 30 January, I wrote to Rear Admiral H. C. "Chester" Bruton, who had been my commanding officer on the *Wisconsin* and was now Director of Naval Communications and, as such, the final arbiter of voice calls. I wrote:

Dear Admiral Bruton:

Although I would not consider writing to you, direct, in search of any personal favor, I have decided that I might be forgiven for enlisting your assistance in the official request, copy enclosed, concerning my ship.

I should imagine that something so simple as a request for a change in voice radio call would not normally come to your attention. I should further imagine that the logical thing to do would be to disapprove the request from the standpoint of time, expense, and precedent involved.

Therefore I wanted to make the following points to you, unofficially, in the hope that you might see your way clear to provide an affirmative decision.

When I took command of Isbell four months ago she had one of the lowest reenlistment rates in the force and no reserve officer had requested regular Navy in over one year. With the help of a fine group of officers we have succeeded in raising the reenlistment rate by 2.5 times in four months. In the last month two reserve officers have requested augmentation and retention, respectively, and have specifically asked to remain aboard Isbell. We are doing everything humanly possible to provide motivation, incentive, and esprit de corps. We are making progress. The approval of the requested voice call, in my opinion, will lend a great deal of impetus to the surging team spirit.

My apologies for soliciting your time for what is after all a small matter but I am encouraged to feel that you might take an interest in what is important to me and my ship.

On 3 February Admiral Bruton wrote on the bottom of this letter, "Let's do this if possible. If not let's give him something better than SAPWORTH. Pls return with necess info," and sent it on for action. On 3 March the following message arrived at the ship:

1. Reference (a) requested that the voice call sign of the USS ARNOLD J. ISBELL be changed from "SAPWORTH" to "HELLCAT."

2. The limitation of the number of words available has dictated the current joint practice of assigning voice call signs at random and without consideration of the actual word meanings. Therefore, certain voice call signs which appear undesirable from a personal viewpoint are often assigned.

3. Voice call signs are currently being assessed for the purpose of reassigning those which may be objectionable. The reassignment will be published in the next changes in JANAP 119. At that time the voice call "HELLCAT" will be assigned to the ARNOLD J. ISBELL.

That meant, "You didn't have to make such a fuss. We were planning to do it all along."

The voice call Hellcat proved immensely popular. *Arnold J. Isbell*'s officers and men proudly wore sleeve patches and baseball cap patches showing a black cat with a forked tail stepping out of the flames of hell and breaking a submarine with its paws. The impact on morale was remarkable. I should add that, operating on the stitch-in-time principle, when three years later I received command of *Dewey,* I went to that Pentagon recess to make sure I was getting an acceptable voice call sign. The people there remembered my name from the *Isbell* episode and, evidently wanting no further intervention in their affairs from their admirals, gave me the book and let me pick the sign I wanted from among those not then in use. *Dewey* became "Sea Rogue."

My next sea tour after *Dewey* was a brief year (1965–1966) as a flag officer commanding a destroyer flotilla based on San Diego. In that job, of course, I had neither the direct daily contact with sailors nor the direct responsibility for their morale and welfare that a ship's captain has, though I did try to see to it that command style within the flotilla was flexible, not rigid. As I wrote in the previous chapter, my hope that the Navy would bring its personnel policies up to date became a conviction that it must take drastic steps to do so while I commanded U.S. Naval Forces in Vietnam from 1968 to 1970, a conviction that was hardened by the message from the fleet on my way home, that second only to low pay scales and long separations from family as deterrents to a Navy career was the conglomeration of chicken regulations and practices under which they were compelled to live. Consequently, when I took over as CNO, I was in a mood to act against Mickey Mouse as rapidly and summarily as possible. I so signified to the brilliant Captain Chick Rauch, my "mini-staff" man for personnel and other projects.

However, it turned out that the Navy could contrive directives about haircuts and uniforms only at the speed that the Supreme Court, in another context, once called "all deliberate." On 21 July 1970, CNO/VCNO Action Sheet #195–70, which meant it was the 195th Action Sheet of its kind to be issued during my twenty-one days in command, went to Vice Admiral Charles Duncan, the Chief of Naval Personnel, and to Delbert Black who, as Master Chief Petty Officer of the Navy, was the Navy's top ranking enlisted man, and who also served in BuPers. Over the signature of Chick Clarey, who was still VCNO, though he was soon to move to the command of the Pacific Fleet, this action sheet asked its two addressees to provide, by 15 August, comments and recommendations on thirteen specified examples of Mickey Mouse that might be eliminated, and any others that occurred to them.

The replies came back on 21 August. Charlie Duncan whom I was about to have promoted to the four-star job of Commander in Chief, Atlantic, and is now retired, was one of the Navy's most expert operations officers, an experienced personnel man, someone for whom I feel a strong personal attachment, and a traditionalist. He wrote a reply that, though it ran to six single-spaced pages, added no new items to the list of thirteen. Its tone was cautious. He devoted almost a full page to arguing against the idea that dungarees should be the standard uniform for the crews of liberty boats, and almost as much space to a closely reasoned refutation of the proposal to allow sailors in Navy towns like Norfolk or San Diego to wear dungarees between home and work. He favored letting sailors' dependents wear what clothes they pleased on Navy bases except in "cases where decency and cleanliness are involved, or where there is a demonstrated case of demoralizing the active duty personnel (e.g. Abbie Hoffman's American flag shirt)."

Chief Black's four-and-a-half page response tersely approved all thirteen suggested changes and proposed twenty-one more. One recommendation of his that dramatized the character of certain Navy traditions was "Eliminate usage of the term 'officers and their ladies and enlisted men and their wives.' " (I was pretty sure that by now most commanding officers had dropped this ungracious distinction without being ordered to, and that I need take no action.) The Chief's first recommendation was, "Issue a clear and concise directive concerning the growing of beards. Many commanding officers' pettiness in this matter, i.e., restriction for thirty days while growing a beard, is unreasonable and works a hardship on the individual." Beards had not been one of the items in the original Action Sheet, because we believed that issue had been settled for good by my predecessor, Admiral Moorer, in a personal letter to commanders sent out on 28 May—thirty-three days before I relieved him—on the subject of "Standards of Grooming." Its six paragraphs (1) reaffirmed the Navy's long-standing policy of allowing beards and mustaches; (2) specifically allowed sideburns; (3) discouraged any attempt to regulate civilian clothes; (4) reiterated the need for neatness; (5) directed commanders to modify any regulations of theirs in conflict with the letter; (6) said, "It is not desired that any public announcement be made of this matter or that it be highlighted." I'm sure it was (6) that made it possible for some commanders to behave as if (1) through (5) never had been written. Chief Black's first recommendation became Z-57's first directive.

In response to Admiral Duncan's and Chief Black's comments, the staff dropped some of the items from the original list and added others, leaving the number, by coincidence, at the original thirteen, and drafted a proposed Z-gram. At that point I considered it prudent, in deference to Admiral Duncan and in view of the fact that grooming and uniform standards evidently rubbed sensitive nerves in everyone from fleet commanders to deckhands, to solicit advice and consent from the most exalted quarters possible, the five four-star admirals with operational commands. On 18 September I sent a personal and confidential message asking for their reactions to the "Mickey Mouse" draft. I also sent a copy to Admiral Moorer for his information. The first two paragraphs of that message accurately express what I thought I was doing:

1. I feel strongly that we must make a concerted effort to restate our personnel policies in a way which reflects greater confidence in the responsible judgment of the majority. I am not suggesting that a more

lenient attitude toward irresponsible offenders be adopted, but I do feel that we cannot permit general policies to be dictated by the need to constrain those few individuals who do not respond to the trust and confidence implied by more flexible and less restrictive regulations.

2. Demeaning and abrasive regulations have, in my judgment, done at least as much to depress Navy retention rates as have extended family separation and low salaries. For this reason, shortly after taking office, I requested a comprehensive review of current Naval policies and regulations. Based on recommendations submitted from a variety of different sources, and in furtherance of policies initiated by Admiral Moorer, I desire to eliminate many of the most abrasive naval regulations and practices, standardize others which are inconsistently enforced throughout the fleet, and provide some general guidance reflecting my conviction that declining Navy retention rates will not be reversed until the worth and personal dignity of the individual are forcefully reaffirmed.

By 9 October the replies from the Commanders in Chief were in, fifteen pages of them in all. I have been told, and I am ready to believe, that never has there been as much four-star input into one NAVOP. The CinCs concurred in general with the proposed order, but with a number of reservations and a marked lack of enthusiasm. An admiral commenting on another admiral's plans is wont to signify the precise degree of his approbation by how he concludes his message. One of my associates, after reviewing the file, said to me, " 'Warmest regards' means 'Hooray!'; 'Warm regards' means 'Okay'; 'Regards' means 'If it were up to me'. . . .' Four of the messages ended with 'Warm regards' and one with 'Regards.' Boss, draw your own conclusions." Some excerpts from those thoughtful, not to say solemn, replies are worth quoting to show how deeply embedded in the minds of the most able and experienced officers some kinds of institutional bias can be:

- While sideburns may be in vogue in many locales, in Morocco, for example, they represent to the local populace, I am informed, a definite identification as a "hippy." Therefore, in such circumstances some rules must be stated, carefully explained to all hands, and then complied with for the sake of the "greater good."

- In general, the relaxation of traditional rules and regulations must be approached with due consideration for the less evident yet inherent aspects of military life and organization. Discipline and cohesion require, for psychological reasons, if none other, visible manifestations which traditionally and conceptually have included elements of regimentation not immediately obvious in civilian life.

• My only reservation is that if we prescribe too much in detail from the top the manner in which these high standards are to be preserved and observed, we remove some of the authority of the individual commanding officer of a ship to exercise his judgment based on the particular circumstances of his command.

• Not everyone is in the habit of sitting at table in sports shirts or without a coat and tie.

• I believe your objective is highly laudable, but my recommendation is that you express your desires in the form of a personal letter of guidance to commanding officers rather than as a directive. I believe it is most important not to undercut, or give the public appearance of undercutting, the authority traditionally given to commanding officers.

• The officers and men we wish to retain I believe would voluntarily shower and shift into a clean uniform for the evening meal. A regulation may be required to protect them from the unpleasant sight and odor of others.

• I recommend we be careful not to let freedom of choice with regard to civilian clothing styles carry over into degraded standards in the wearing of the uniform itself.

• I am concerned only about the possibility that in pursuit of the very desirable goal of changing personnel policies to reflect greater confidence in the responsible judgment of the majority we might lose a little class. With this in mind I recommend we use caution and handle the subject in low key.

• We have had women in Washington several times nude in the reflecting pool—or wandering topless—I don't think you want this for the Waves. I don't think you want a dirty, barefooted man wearing cut-off jeans, a sweat shirt with a four-letter word on the front, and beads round his neck, leaving or returning to a Navy ship or station. Your paragraph would permit it and I assure you it will happen if you set no limits. The ACLU would have the commanding officer in court if he tried to stop him.

Many of the admirals' specific comments were well taken and incorporated into the final product. But one general recommendation they all agreed upon, that eliminating Mickey Mouse should be done quietly and privately, was one I had already considered and rejected. It was clear to me that the recruitment and retention situation called for a public and authoritative signal from the man in charge. I had heard a message from good sailors everywhere, whose reenlistments we had to have and whose peers from civilian life we had to attract in a future without draft pressure. The message was that, galling as certain specific abuses were to the men and women of the Navy, they were less galling than the widely held conviction that the Navy's top echelon was indifferent to these abuses, if not actively engaged in perpetrating them. I knew that was not so, but it seemed to me that the only way I could prove it was to make so personal and public a commitment to change that it would be impossible for anyone in or out of the Navy to mistake my intention, and extremely difficult for me, or my successors either, to diminish that commitment or turn away from it. President Lincoln once put a critical issue to his Cabinet for a vote and got all "Nays." He then voted "Aye" and announced, "The Ayes have it." In a small way I chose to do the same thing when I overruled the unanimous advice of men I had respected and followed for many years. I knew that the large majority of commanding officers would have no real problem with the changes. I also knew that a handful would and that among them would be some who would seek to prove that the changes would not work by washing their hands of the responsibility for administering them. Finally, I knew that the Navy could not be manned unless these changes were made. I must add that my strategy had the full support of Secretary Chafee and Secretary Laird.

However, the admirals' comments did make it clear that the greatest possible precision in the wording of the directive was necessary, and so another month passed before a final draft was ready. This delay derived from more than mere word chopping. For example, one of the doubts several of the CinCs entertained was whether beards were compatible with gas masks, and so it was necessary to unearth documentary evidence that they were. This took a certain amount of esoteric research, and therefore time, but it was finally done. The staff dug up a report from the Naval Safety Center in Norfolk to the Chief of Naval Personnel with the title, "Beard Growth and Respiratory Protection, Comments Concerning," which concluded that beards and masks could coexist.

On 5 November Chick Rauch started a final (we hoped) draft of Z-57 on its rounds through the mini-staff, where it received the bureaucratic treatment of an "almost" being inserted here, a "reasonably" being inserted there, "shoulds" being changed to "wills" and "will bes" to "are," a "not expect" being fortified by being made into a "not countenance" and a "working uniform" being honed into a "clean, neat, working uniform." On 7 November it arrived on the desk of Admiral Cousins, and he made two major changes. He dropped one of the thirteen items, a somewhat confusing one about senior petty officers having the right to sign leave papers. And in the interest of bruising as few high-level feelings as possible he changed "Mickey Mouse" to "Demeaning and Abrasive Regulations." I hated to see "Mickey Mouse" go because I knew what that would signal to all hands, but at that point I preferred not to prolong the saga.

The same day that "Mickey Mouse" died, we decided to temper the impact of the directive further by sending out a confidential NAVOP to all commanders announcing the imminent arrival of Z-57 and explaining its implications and intent. Sending out a NAVOP to herald a NAVOP was an unusual, if not unprecedented, thing to do, but it had become increasingly evident that some commanding officers would tend to regard Z-57 as undercutting their authority, and I felt it necessary to assure them that this was just not so. That message went out on 9 November. Z-57 went out on 10 November (at 1757 Washington time). The three and a half months of staffing that had gone into it had not noticeably watered down its language. "I will not countenance the rights or privileges of any officers or enlisted men being abrogated in any way because they choose to grow sideburns or neatly trimmed beards or mustaches . . ." it said. "No one will be denied entrance [to a commissary, exchange, snack bar, etc.] for being in 'improper uniform . . .'" it said. "I not only do not wish to see fresh paint applied strictly because of my visit but consider that rusted surfaces hastily painted over are a reflection of poor command discretion," it said. "No motorcycle operator should in any way be penalized or denied entry because of the color of his headgear," it said.

On 11 November the media told the world about the "Mod Navy." I was content; the message had gotten through.

Eighteen months later the first naval aviator to be shot down over North Vietnam after bombing in the north resumed entered prison camp to join those courageous colleagues who had languished there for four years already. The commander of the long-term captive U.S. personnel, by seniority and by inspiration, was Captain (now Rear

Admiral) Jim Stockdale. Starved for news for himself and his fellow prisoners, Jim tapped a message through the walls that was relayed to the new POW from cell to cell, "What news?" From cell to cell the answer came back, "Got a new CNO, named Zumwalt. No more Mickey Mouse or chickenshit." The message had gotten all the way through—and in the original vernacular.

CHAPTER 9

Sailing Second Class

Eliminating Mickey Mouse, relieving some of the pressure naval service puts on family life, and creating new opportunities for fun and zest were deeds that were difficult to perform only in a bureaucratic sense. They required much prodding and tweaking of long-established regulations, routines, and mind-sets and constant monitoring of the system to make sure the prods and tweaks were having the intended effect, but they presented no attitudinal problems to the great majority of the men and women of the Navy. On the contrary, that majority, as I had been sure it would, welcomed the initiatives in these areas as steps toward bringing Navy norms and practices into closer conformity with those of the rest of American society. Of a far higher order of difficulty and importance was bringing the Navy's treatment of members of ethnic or racial minorities, particularly blacks, into conformity with stated national policy and the law of the land, not to say common fairness and decency. It goes almost without saying that this presented profound attitudinal problems to many people, including some at high levels of authority.

There was no one of my duties as Chief of Naval Operations that I had had less practical experience with than race relations; in fact, when I took office I had no inkling that dealing with race relations should or would be among my most important duties. The most I can say for my appreciation of the problem was that my heart was in the right place. In Tulare, California, where I grew up, there had been many Mexican-Americans and a few blacks. I had gone to school with them, played football alongside them, and become good friends with some of them. My parents, who as practicing physicians dealt not just professionally but personally with people of all kinds, bequeathed me their knowledge that color of skin or racial origin provided no clue to a person's character or worth. However, when I left home and took up a naval career, that knowledge proved to be on the whole more academic than immediately useful for the simple reason that the Navy systematically excluded, except for menial service, people with dark skins and non-European ancestries. I can remember only three instances in thirty years when I personally had to contend with what I can only call the institutional racism of the Navy. On each of two ships that I commanded a Filipino sailor asked me to help him get transferred out of the stewards' department into the line Navy. Both were well qualified for the jobs they sought and I succeeded in helping them, but only by dint of applying on the Bureau of Naval Personnel an amount of pressure that, considering the reasonableness of the requests, I found both embarrassing and uncalled for. The third, and by far the most upsetting, instance occurred when I was about to take over the job of detailer for lieutenants in BuPers in 1957. In the course of briefing me on my new duties, the officer I was relieving told me that the routine for assigning minority officers was to send them to dead-end billets so that their promotion beyond middle rank would be unlikely. I did not follow that prescription, but I cannot say that beyond not following it I could think of a way that a junior commander could alter a policy that, evil though it was, was clearly winked at or even encouraged by the captains and admirals he worked for.

In any case, when I took over as CNO my almost total lack of personal contact with minority people in the Navy led me to perceive their problems much more from a managerial than a human viewpoint. I thought in terms of the recruitment effort that would be appropriate in view of the end of the draft and the imminence of an all-volunteer Navy, for example. The statistics showed that, at the time my watch began, blacks accounted for just 5.5 percent of enlisted personnel and a shameful 0.7 percent of officers. That seemed to me to be making extremely poor use of a large reservoir of valuable manpower. The figures also made it clear that as far as breaking down racial barriers was concerned, the Navy was marching in the rear rank of the military services, which was not the position in which I wanted to see an institution I respected and loved. Thus, attracting more members of minorities to the Navy and providing better opportunities for them once they entered were items that were on my agenda for personnel from the beginning. However, they were not at the top of it, and I had not yet done much about them by October 1970 when my young assistant in charge of the retention study groups, Lieutenant Dave Halperin, who had a knack for discovering people of unusual ability, suggested that I see a certain Lieutenant Commander William Norman with a view toward making him a special assistant for minority affairs.

Bill Norman was about to leave the Navy. After seven years of distinguished service as a navy flight officer aboard carriers, an instructor at the Naval Academy, a White House aide, and a member of just about every committee or council or commission on race relations or minority affairs the Navy had set up in the previous half dozen years, he had decided that the unceasing strain of the conflict between being black and being Navy was greater than he was willing to bear any longer, and he had resigned his commission. He was in California when he received my invitation to come to see me and, he has since told me, he responded to the invitation with reluctance, having heard by then more than enough high-ranking pledges to implement the racial policies that, after all, Harry Truman had ordered the military to put into effect in 1947. And so what happened at our first conversation, whose ostensible purpose was for me to check him out, was that he checked me out. Evidently I passed his inspection, for he agreed to join my personal staff. I am not being facetious. Knowing what I know now, but did not know then, about the experience of minority people in the Navy, I think Bill Norman had every reason to look hard and skeptically at my motives and my intentions. I will add that I can't think of anyone who did more during my watch to make the Navy a better place to live in than Bill did in the two and a half years he was a member of my staff, first as "OOM," my special assistant for minority problems, then as "OOG", my special assistant for all personnel matters, when the original occupant of that position, Chick Rauch, made rear admiral and moved into the Bureau of Naval Personnel as "Pers-P" to replace Dave Bagley, who had become Chief of Naval Personnel.

During Bill's first month or so on my personal staff, he put me through a most upsetting cram course in what it was like to be a member of a minority group in the Navy. Only a few of the lessons came in the short weekly meetings we had. Most of those were all business. Among his other qualities, Bill is a model of managerial conciseness and efficiency. My records show that my first purely

business meeting with him—the first meeting after he had interviewed me and decided I might be possible to work with—took place
on 5 November, and lasted the usual fourteen minutes. He did not
waste time on the "good morning, Admiral, how are you today"
routine, but whipped out a one-page checklist and laid it on the desk
between us:

I. ADMINISTRATIVE MATTERS
  1. Weekly memos to CNO
  2. 15 minute meeting/week with CNO—Can ride to or from work
  3. Propose trip to each Navy District for separate meetings with
     minority personnel, unit commanders, and community leaders as
     "kick-off."
     a. Announce appointment and itinerary by NAVOP. . . .

"I. ADMINISTRATIVE MATTERS" contained three more points
and then there was "II. MAJOR PROBLEM AREAS (with selected, specific problems)" that consisted of a "1," a "2," and a "3,"
each of which consisted of an "a," a "b," a "c," a "d," and an "e."
Every so often there were spaces for me to put my initials next to
"Approved," "Disapproved," or "See me." It is the technique of
doing business I like the best; an awful lot of work can get done in
fourteen minutes that way. Actually the business routine between
Bill and me soon settled down into a breakfast a week, which, since
it also included the trip from my home to my office, came to a good
deal more than fourteen minutes. However, he always brought along
one of those checklists. There's a stack of them an inch thick in my
files.

As I have said, those sessions were pretty much all business and
it was only months later, as our friendship became close, that I
learned of Bill's own experiences as a black officer in a white Navy:
of the fact that as a young officer he had rarely received a voluntary
salute; of the time in Meridian, Mississippi, when the commander of
the naval air station asked him not to come to the officers' club that
night because his presence there would embarrass some local dignitaries who had been invited as guests; of the time he was returning
to his ship from an evening in town in civilian clothes and the officer
of the deck told him sharply that the enlisted men's gangplank was
at the other end; of the time ashore in Japan when he intervened
between a Japanese and a white chief petty officer who was abusing
him and the chief had called Bill a "goddam nigger" and punched

him, and when Bill had put the petty officer on report, the captain
of the ship had declined to punish him because the man had a
"perfect record"; of the time he was assigned to the faculty of the
Naval Academy and could not find anyone in Annapolis who would
rent a black man decent living quarters and an Academy official had
told him that was Bill's problem, not the Academy's; of the eternal
temptation when he was with his own people to apologize for the
uniform he wore. But if it was not until later that I learned those
personal things about Bill, I learned right away that things like that
were a matter of daily occurrence for the black men and women of
the Navy. By the time Bill and I had our first business meeting on
5 November there was already in session a retention study group of
black officers and their wives, which Bill and Dave Halperin had
convened at only a few days' notice and which delivered its report
on 6 November to as big a roomful as I could assemble of high-
ranking officers and civilians, including Secretary of the Navy John
Chafee.

The October conversation with Bill Norman, when we first met
and he told me, in effect, "j'accuse," convinced me intellectually that
I had underestimated by far the seriousness of the Navy's racial
problem. The 6 November retention group report, and a similar one
delivered by black enlisted men and their wives two weeks later, hit
me in the gut. Let those who will call me naive, but it was at those
sessions that I came to realize for the first time that the Navy did
even worse things to its minority people than give them demeaning
jobs and stunt their careers. Day after day it inflicted upon them,
sometimes without even knowing it was doing so, personal slights,
affronts, and indignities of a peculiarly humiliating kind. Though I
suppose one could regard it as a small thing, I was especially moved,
because I took it as symbolic of the Navy's pervasive uncaringness
for its minority people, by the fact that Navy exchanges did not carry
any of the lines of cosmetics black women used, or the styles of
clothes young black people wore, or the records and tapes young
black people listened to. But perhaps the most revealing incident at
the officers' meeting came in the course of a discussion of housing
for black Navy families. One of the members of the group had just
delivered an eloquent description of the difficulties he had had
finding decent living quarters for his family as he had moved around
the country, and of the lack of help he had received from the administrative people at the bases to which he had been assigned. An
admiral demurred. I cannot quote him exactly but I can come close.

He said, "Now when I was commanding in Charleston I had this boy working for me who was having a little trouble getting located and I found him a right nice place to live." One of the wives asked, "How old was this boy?" The admiral answered, "Oh, thirty or thirty-five, I reckon." "I see," the wife said, and the discussion resumed at the point at which it had been interrupted. I saw, too, and I know John Chafee saw. As much as anything that exchange showed me how urgent it was to get started on the long hard way we all had to go.

On 17 December 1970 I sent out Z-66, "Equal Opportunity in the Navy," which was probably the most important and certainly the most heartfelt of the 121 Z-grams. I'm proud enough of it to quote it almost in its entirety:

> 2. Last month Secretary Chafee and I, along with other senior officials of the Navy Department, met on one occasion with representative black Navy officers and their wives and later with a group of black enlisted men and their wives. Prior to these meetings, I was convinced that, compared with the civilian community, we had relatively few racial problems in the Navy. However, after exploring the matter in some depth with these two groups, I have discovered that I was wrong—we do have problems, and it is my intention and that of Secretary Chafee to take prompt steps toward their solution.
>
> 3. What struck me more than anything else was the depth of feeling of our black personnel that there is significant discrimination in the Navy. Prior to these meetings, I sincerely believed that I was philosophically prepared to understand the problems of our black Navymen and their families, and until we discussed them at length, I did not realize the extent and deep significance of many of these matters.
>
> 4. There are two keys to the problem. First, we must open up new avenues of communication with not only our black personnel, but also with all minority groups in the Navy so that we may learn what and where the areas of friction are. Second, all of us in the Navy must develop a far greater sensitivity to the problems of all our minority groups so that we may more effectively go about solving them. Our meetings here in Washington were a beginning, but no more than that. Much remains to be done.
>
> 5. For example, I am particularly distressed by the numerous examples of discrimination black Navy families still experience in attempting to locate housing. This situation and others like it are indicative in some cases of less than full teamwork being brought to bear by the whole Navy team in behalf of some of our members and failure to use existing

authority and directives to enforce their rights. In some places housing personnel are tacitly contributing to discrimination in housing.

6. Secretary Chafee and I have asked our staffs to begin work with other members of the Navy Department to make an in-depth investigation of this problem and present to us within sixty days proposals which will help alleviate the most acute housing problems. Meanwhile there are many things that can be acted upon immediately. Therefore, by 15 January 1971 I expect action to be taken as follows:

A. Every base, station and aircraft squadron commander and ship commanding officer shall appoint an aware minority group officer or senior petty officer as his Special Assistant for Minority Affairs. This officer or petty officer should have direct access to the commander/ commanding officer and will be consulted on all matters involving minority personnel. . . .

B. All shore based commanders shall ensure that a minority group wife is included in the Navy wives' ombudsman concept. . . .

C. The programs already begun by ComNavSupSysCom to ensure that the special needs of minority groups are recognized and provided for shall be expedited, namely:

(1) Suitable cosmetics and other products for black personnel and their dependents will be stocked in Navy exchanges.

(2) Ship's stores will stock black grooming aids.

(3) Every base and station will employ, as soon as possible, at least one qualified barber/beautician in major barber and beauty shops, and will work toward the goal of having sufficient barbers/beauticians qualified in hair care for black personnel to provide service for all black patrons.

(4) All major commissaries shall stock foods and produce frequently requested by minority groups. As a minimum, specific recommendations should be solicited from minority personnel and their families and acted upon by local commissary managers.

D. Special services offices which deal in discount tickets for various entertainment programs will also obtain discount tickets to events of special interest to minority groups whenever such tickets are available.

E. A representative selection of books, magazines, and records by and about black Americans will be made available in Navy libraries, wardrooms, clubs, and other reading areas.

Any of the above which cannot be accomplished within the time specified above will be reported via chain of command together with a summary of circumstances preventing timely implementation.

7. In order that I may reach a more complete understanding of the problems experienced by our minority personnel, in addition to SecNav/ OpNav/BuPers team visits I am directing my special assistant for minority affairs, LCdr Norman, to visit major naval activities within ConUS to meet with individual commanding officers and with minority military personnel and their dependents. By learning in depth what our problems are, I believe we will be in a better position to work toward guaranteeing equal opportunity and treatment for all of our Navy people.

8. This is the first of my reports to you on minority affairs. Secretary Chafee and I will be looking into all areas of minority affairs and will be issuing further reports as our problems become more clear and their solutions become more apparent. It is evident that we need to maximize our efforts to improve the lot of our minority Navymen. I am convinced that there is no place in our Navy for insensitivity. We are determined that we shall do better. Meanwhile, we are counting on your support to help seek out and eliminate those demeaning areas of discrimination that plague our minority shipmates. Ours must be a Navy family that recognizes no artificial barriers of race, color or religion. There is no black Navy, no white Navy—just one Navy—the United States Navy.

There were a number of innovative features in Z-66, but its last sentence, necessary as it was, was not one of them. For twenty years or more Secretaries of Defense, Secretaries of the Navy and CNOs had been expressing that sentiment one way or another and nothing much—or, to be charitable, not nearly enough—had come of it. Where Z-66 broke new ground was in ordering that certain highly visible things be done by a specific date; in licensing a black lieutenant commander to make official visits to all kinds of places and ask all kinds of people all kinds of questions; in confessing in the most public way possible—to every member of the Navy, to their relatives and friends, to the press, to the public—that the Navy had until then been insensitive to the problems of minority groups; finally and probably most controversially, as subsequent chapters will reveal, in setting up a network of Minority Affairs Assistants from whom before long Bill Norman, by making half a dozen telephone calls, could secure the information about racial matters that would enable the top of the chain of command in my office to act promptly when the bottom of the chain, on the scene, failed to act. To put the matter succinctly, Z-66 told the world that when it came to racial affairs Secretary Chafee and I meant business. This was the year 1970, twenty-three years after President Truman ordered an end to racial segregation in the armed forces, sixteen years after the Supreme

Court had handed down *Brown* v. *Board of Education,* fourteen years after the Montgomery bus boycott, seven years after Martin Luther King spoke of his dream, five years after the march from Selma, five years after Watts blew up, two years after Dr. King had been murdered. It was not too soon for the Navy to mean business.

While Z-66 was being drafted and, during the weeks after its promulgation, while various administrative steps to give it force were being taken, the Naval Investigative Service Office (NISO) in the Philippines, at the behest of the base commander, was conducting an investigation into the racial situation at the Subic Bay Naval Base and the Naval Communication Station at nearby San Miguel, the two principal naval installations in the Philippines. Subic Bay, only two days' steaming from Yankee Station in the Gulf of Tonkin, where the ships of the Seventh Fleet were deployed during the Vietnam war, was a large and well-appointed base where those ships most commonly put in for replenishment, upkeep, and maintenance, and a spell of rest and recreation for their crews. The Communication Station at nearby San Miguel was the Navy's most important facility of its kind in the western Pacific. The Subic Bay base and, to a far greater extent, Olongapo City, which was just outside the base's gates, had been the scenes of periodic flareups. The "recreation"— if that's the word—area of Olongapo was divided between a section of white bars and whorehouses, "The Strip," and a section of black bars and whorehouses, "The Jungle." It was in those tawdry, not to say sordid, neighborhoods that trouble most often broke out. Marijuana and narcotics were almost as freely available all over Olongapo as liquor. On Thanksgiving night there had been a flareup in the Jungle and, newly preoccupied as I was then about racial matters, I asked for a report on the situation there. The report was completed in the middle of January but, moving through channels at the usual measured pace, it did not reach my desk for another month. It was a document, submitted by the very fine flag officer Rear Admiral George Muse, of extraordinarily high quality, thoughtful, sensitive, and thorough, and it provided, from out in the fleet, the final, damning proof that Bill Norman and the black retention groups had not been telling me fairy tales. I will venture the further opinion that the quality of the report, remarkable as it was, was less remarkable than the fact that a report that candidly critical of the Navy arrived on my desk intact after passing through as many admirals as it did. For that near miracle I must credit the loyalty and sense of commitment these reviewing authorities had given to the strong language of Z-66.

I wish I could reproduce that report in full here, for it not only painted a vivid picture of how minority people lived in and felt about the Navy, but it foreshadowed events that were to occur almost two years later at Subic Bay. However, it runs to fourteen pages, so I must be content to quote only a few of its most significant paragraphs.

4. A surface inquiry approach to the question: "Do we have a racial problem within the Subic Bay/San Miguel area?" would have led to an assumption that only a few vocal, first-enlistment, young, militant black troublemakers, poorly adjusted and spreading dissension, are responsible for isolated instances and that, in fact, a racial problem does not exist. This would have been a felonious assumption. There are those who refuse to reason, to accept responsibility, to cooperate, or to understand the need for military discipline; those who are unable to adjust to military life; those who are paranoid; and those who will grasp at any straw to rationalize their own shortcomings. Such persons are found in all races. As a rule, these men are generally on their first enlistment or have achieved little progress in the course of a second enlistment. Commands can cope with this type best by first recognizing the type, identifying the man, and requesting transfer or separation for the individual.

5. The in-depth inquiry conducted by NISO Phil indicated that while the outspoken, the militant, and uncompromising are found primarily among first-enlistment blacks, those on the second enlistment and those dedicated to a career will, when questioned after proper rapport has been established, in the vast majority of cases, voice complaints of prejudice and discrimination. They rationalize to some extent for the black who becomes involved in trouble; and they exhibit marked hostility toward those who are offensive in language toward other blacks. These older blacks, however, explain that for the most part they have learned to live with discrimination and prejudice, and accept it as a fact of life. One CPO put it, "Just being black is the biggest problem." Petty officers in this group pointed out, however, that the younger blacks in the vast majority of cases do not share this attitude. The younger ones who feel that acceptance and integration are not proceeding fast enough are rigid and impatient in their demands. They refuse to understand or accept any reason for results short of "NOW."

6. There was some pattern noted in the interviews of blacks, in that early in the session complaints pertained to such things as availability of cosmetics, black publications, barbers skilled in the Afro haircut, and in rare cases food appealing to blacks. It became apparent, however, in the course of numerous interviews that the interviewee merely found these

problems easier to talk of than those about which he had deeper feelings, that is those affecting his personal sensitivities. Even the more articulate appeared to show an inability to set forth and illustrate with meaningful examples that it was the "hurt feelings" that troubled him most often when he experiences prejudice or discrimination. More than one black man referred to his desire to be treated like a "human."

7. Examples of types of prejudice and discrimination centered in some eight general categories: . . .

h. A rather nebulous group of experiences that can best be described as "attitudes," "indications," or "insinuations" on the part of whites which make blacks feel uncomfortable and appear to subtly convey prejudice. It should be noted that it was with the last type that the NISO Phil special team had the greatest difficulty in collecting illustrations and assessing. While valid beyond doubt, illustrations offered by blacks interviewed appear to fail to properly depict to whites the significance and emotional value, when brought to light divorced from the setting and circumstance in which they occurred, of voice inflection, glances, and personalities involved. In command briefings on the inquiry, the team likewise felt it had inadequately conveyed its impressions on this particular facet. These illustrations by blacks included such complaints as "the manner in which an individual looked at them," "inflection in voice during comments," "the application of a dual or sarcastic meaning to a remark," "the tendency of a given white to be noncommunicative or to be unpleasant," and "the manner in which service is rendered to blacks by Filipinos." . . .

9. Social activity of blacks, USNB Subic area: . . . Several blacks interviewed offered that they avoided frequenting the clubs on base or the bars in town patronized by whites because they have found that even whites who normally appear to be devoid of prejudice when sober display symptoms of deep-seated prejudice after having a few drinks. Numerous blacks related that under these circumstances they find the conversation degrading, belittling, or insulting when their white drinking companions begin to relate that he "is not prejudiced," "understands colored people," "had a good friend one time who was a Negro," "had a Negro maid in the family that they were very fond of," "finds Negro women sexually desirable," or "thinks that 'niggers' deserve a fair break." A great many blacks clearly conveyed the impression that they feel the mixing of alcohol and integration at today's level of interracial maturity frequently spells trouble and will continue to until more whites have a sincere change in basic attitudes toward blacks. . . .

10. White reaction, USNB Subic area:

a. Interviewers had difficulty in identifying whites who were conversant with racial matters as related to their present environment, USNB Subic

Bay. While most had black acquaintances by virtue of assigned barracks spaces or duty assignments, few had black associates or black friends. Whites quartered in the barracks offered that blacks tended to show a preference for the company of other blacks to the exclusion of all whites. Whites noted a strong social pressure, more evident in the last six to nine months, that drew blacks into the black circle and excluded whites. Many whites offered that they found offensive the Afro haircut, Afro costuming, and the black power salute. They found the dialect with which blacks communicate among themselves difficult to comprehend. Many of the whites who claimed black associates disclaimed any communication with the more militant blacks who most whites regard as "troublemakers." These whites, who professed to "take a man for what he is regardless of color," offered that they avoid the company of white troublemakers, likewise. Very few whites interviewed had read any black literature and few had discussed racial matters with blacks. In answer to a query on the latter point, most whites responded in essence that they have given the racial matter little thought and felt that the initiation of such a discussion would be considered offensive.

b. The majority of whites interviewed professed a belief that commands were "giving in to" the blacks, were establishing dual standards (the hair cut being the most frequent example), and were "afraid" of the blacks. Many whites expressed a fear of the blacks and noted that while blacks were united at times of violence, whites fled or at least did not come to the aid of another white. Whites as a group expressed resentment and some fear over the "black power salute" or "black power check." Almost all whites interviewed regarded the black power salute as a symbol of militancy, whereas the blacks profess it to be a symbol of unity. . . .

12. Based on this inquiry to date, the following observations and conclusions are offered:

a. Most whites of all rates and ranks are practically oblivious to the racial issue or to the feelings of blacks concerning prejudice and discrimination.

b. Both blacks and whites profess an attitude of non-prejudice, but it was noted by interviewers that most interviewees exhibited some varying degree of prejudice in the course of the interviews.

c. A great many blacks and whites exhibited a reluctance to initiate a discussion with a member of the opposite race on racial matters. Few whites are familiar with black literature or contemporary black thinking.

d. The vast majority of white petty officers of all rates show an inability to discuss racial matters within the perspective of the 1970s.

e. White officer and petty officer personnel at all levels of management have not apparently been trained to handle problems with racial overtones.

f. Both white officers and petty officers display a lack of sensitivity concerning what produces feelings of offense, irritation or hostility among the blacks.

g. There has been a serious breakdown of communications within the division officer/petty officer system. Grievances which could and should be handled and resolved at the division officer or petty officer level are too frequently elevated to the executive officer or at times the commanding officer level. Rather than attempt to develop and exercise junior officer and petty officer personnel in the rudiments of management, some commands are inclined to open doors all the way up the line and bypass these key individuals. Emphasis on the "open door policy" while dramatically democratic; at times self-satisfying to the senior advocate; and effective at quickly getting at the apparent problem of the moment, can in the long run impede the development of managers at the lower echelons. It can, if carried to extremes, undercut middle management and create future disciplinary problems.

h. All officers and men interviewed called for a consistent discipline policy and enforcement of regulations.

i. While nearly all stated a recognition of the need for military discipline, many blacks in varying terms either requested, felt the need for, recommended, or demanded a recognition of black subculture within the American culture.

j. There is a distinct lack of black officer personnel assigned to the local area.

k. Officers of all grades, especially commanding officers, would benefit from having the opportunity to take part in discussions with blacks of various points of view from militancy to complacency.

Those eleven points in the report's Paragraph 12 defined in as terse a way as I could imagine the formidable agenda of racial matters the Navy was morally obligated and pragmatically obliged to act upon. Its urgency was underscored by the single comment attached to the report by the Commander in Chief Pacific, Admiral John McCain. The report had mentioned in passing a Human Relations Council that had been set up at the San Miguel Communication Station in accordance with a suggestion to consider organizing such councils issued by my predecessor, Tom Moorer. "It would be remiss not to surface one reservation which it is felt must be addressed, and that is the extent to which we may allow committees to assume the prerogative of the commander," Jack McCain wrote. The fact that that was all CinCPac chose to say about the manifestations within his command of one of the great social upheavals in the history of the United States indicates the extent of the Navy problem.

Retention, which was what most of the Z-grams, particularly the early ones, were all about, and equal opportunity were the aspects of personnel administration that occupied most of my attention during the first year and a half of my watch. I paid little attention to recruitment, which seemed to me to be going reasonably well. I did not look much beyond the gross numbers, which showed that in Fiscal Year 1971, my first year, the Navy took in 102 percent of the quota it had set itself. Since first-term reenlistments during that same period rose from the dismal 10 percent of the previous year to an encouraging 17 percent, I had some reason to believe that the new policies were beginning to make a difference.

However as the monthly recruitment figures came across my desk in the fall of 1971, I became more and more alarmed. With troops coming home from Vietnam by then and draft calls down almost to zero, the Navy was falling further and further behind its quotas for incoming recruits. In December it barely made 50 percent, the worst showing of any of the four services. Moreover a look behind the gross numbers compounded the bad news. On the basis of the scores on the so-called intelligence tests—which at best measure aptitude—it gives to prospective enlistees, the Navy puts them in one of four "mental groups," and it also rates them as "school eligible" or "non-school eligible." In the modern Navy, with its complicated weapons systems, power plants, communications equipment, and sensors, a great many jobs are highly skilled and most jobs are something more than semi-skilled. If the modern Navy is to be manned properly, around four-fifths of its personnel need specialized schooling of some kind and it really cannot handle more than about 5 percent Mental Group IV, the lowest category. To make up for its failure to attract people of high quality, and with ships to man and a war to fight, the Navy began accepting a larger percentage of recruits from the low mental groups. So although for FY '72 as a whole almost 97 percent of the recruiting quota was achieved, over 20 percent of recruits were in Mental Group IV compared with an already excessive 14 percent the year before, and only 73 percent were school eligible, a drop of 11 points from the year before.

In the case of minority recruits, those percentages were enormously magnified. Over 14,000 recruits, almost 16 percent of the total, were minority members in FY '72, and fewer than half were considered school eligible. Of the almost 12,000 of those minority recruits who were black, only slightly more than a third were considered school eligible. This implied one of two things, or more likely some of each: the tests were culturally biased and so the capacity of minority people was being underrated and they were unfairly being assigned to work below their capacity, or the recruiting system was so consciously or unconsciously biased that it operated on the assumption that the proper people to fill the Navy's least desirable jobs, and generally occupy the bottom positions in the Navy's social and intellectual hierarchy, were minority people. I scarcely need add that as long as such recruiting practices persisted, much of the work on equal opportunity that was being done within the Navy was meaningless. Many months earlier I had sent a message to the Recruiting Command calling upon it for "heroic measures" in the face of the imminence of an all-volunteer Navy. At the beginning of 1972 it had become clear to me that if any heroic measures about recruiting were going to be initiated they would have to be initiated at the level of the Chief of Naval Operations.

As with most administrative tasks, heroic or otherwise, the way to begin was to put the best possible people into the critical jobs. Rear Admiral David Bagley had been outstanding in the new BuPers billet I had created, "Pers-P," and was clearly ready to take on greater responsibilities. With Secretary Chafee's enthusiastic concurrence, I nominated him for Chief of Naval Personnel, a position that included among its numerous responsibilities the general oversight and support of the recruiting effort. This move, as I have mentioned, enabled me to replace Dave as Pers-P with Chick Rauch, and replace Chick as OOG with Bill Norman, and so it upgraded superior personnel administration people all along the line. To head the Recruiting Command itself I chose a man whose abilities I had tested personally time after time, Rear Admiral Emmett Tidd. Emmett, you may recall, had been one of my principal colleagues in Vietnam and had come with me to Washington to take on the indispensable, but thankless, job of "decision coordinator" in my office, the source from whom all those hated "green stripers" flowed. He was already a rear admiral designate when he took on the Washington job and was chafing to get out to sea with the cruiser-destroyer flotilla his new rank entitled him to command, for which every good destroyerman chafes. I needed him so badly to expedite the decisions made by Project 60 that I kept him chained to his desk for almost a year. Finally I turned him loose and he went to Charleston to take command of CruDesFlot 6, where he was enjoying himself immensely. On 4 February 1972 Emmett was in Newport to give the commencement address to a graduating class of the Officers' Candidate School. When he descended from the dais he got word that I wanted to speak with him, but that I was on my way to a Joint Chiefs of Staff meeting and would call him in Charleston that night. By his account, he got back to his home in Charleston at about 2230, and as he opened the door the telephone started to ring. His recollection of the beginning of the conversation is that I said, "Emmett, I want you to come back to Washington and take command of the Navy Recruiting Command." Then there was a long pause. Then he said, "Boss, what have I done wrong?"

Unfortunately, the question was not entirely jocular. One of the troubles with the Navy's recruiting effort was that recruiting duty, especially for officers, was considered by the career planners in BuPers no assignment for first-class people. A captain put in charge of a Recruiting Area could be pretty sure he could kiss whatever hope he had of making admiral goodbye. The rear admiral given the Recruiting Command could calculate that when he put in his two or three years there, he would follow, by request, the second alternative in "up or out." And recruiting duty "enhanced the careers" of junior officers in just about the same way. This was all right while there was a draft in existence, as there had been ever since Emmett or I had been in the Navy. There always had been enough people who disliked the Army to make it possible for an unambitious or lazy Navy recruiter to do his job simply by sitting at his desk and deciding which of the people in the queue before him he would sign up. And when the huge draft calls for the Vietnam war started coming in, the main job of a Navy recruiter really became keeping people out, a function BuPers was quite right to consider one that did not require an inordinate amount of brains or talent. In short, the first step in making the Navy recruiting effort effective was to adjust the Navy's attitude toward recruiting to the new and surprising fact that the only way to obtain the high-quality people who were needed was to conduct an active search for them and an active campaign of persuasion once they were found. The lines of would-be sailors outside the post offices or in the basement of city hall were gone with the draft.

With a little help from the rest of us, Emmett Tidd did turn the entire Navy recruiting operation around. The help we—principally Dave Bagley and I—gave him was no more than he had a right to expect from people who had asked him to alter the course of his career, and at first glance not necessarily for the better. We were accessible; indeed Dave instituted a routine weekly meeting with him so that any problem of Emmett's that needed resolution by higher authority would receive it promptly. We freed additional resources of money and manpower for the recruiting effort and saw to it that those increases got written into the next budget. And we made it clear throughout the Navy that recruiting was no longer an activity to be held in low esteem. Indeed in April, only a few weeks after Emmett took over, I sent out Z-109, whose topic sentence was "Recruiting is my top priority." The message went on to instruct the appropriate parties that henceforward officers and enlisted men, both, should be assigned to recruiting duty on the basis of superior performance rather than because, as in the past, the Recruiting Command was a convenient place in which to stash people whose performance had proved to be inferior. I also said, "We must ensure that quality standards are maintained. If there must be a compromise, I will accept fewer people to meet those standards. . . ."

With this minimal amount of encouragement and support from the top, Emmett was able to use his enormous administrative skill and his gift for motivating the people who work for him to create what I consider to be a model recruiting operation. He took over close to the end of Fiscal Year 1972, so his results only began to show in FY '73, and showed fully in FY '74. In the latter year, he achieved 103 percent of his numerical goal. (Following the guidance of mine I have just quoted, he was far below his quota in FY '73.) Fewer than 4 percent of all recruits in FY '74 were in Mental Group IV. Furthermore, as the result of the emphasis Emmett placed in minority recruiting, minority personnel in the Navy rose from less than 5 percent to almost 10, and in FY '74 as high a percentage of minority recruits as of the total, some 80 percent, were school eligible. That was quite a job for anyone to do in less than two years, and he richly earned his promotion to vice admiral that I saw to it he got by upgrading his command to a three-star billet.

However, the year's delay in getting the recruiting operation squared away cost the Navy heavily. On 31 March 1972, just before Emmett took over the Recruiting Command on 12 April 1972, the North Vietnamese launched the "Easter Offensive" across the demilitarized zone that would have won them the war then if the United States had not responded with an enormous air and naval buildup in the western Pacific. By Presidential order, the number of carriers on Yankee Station in the Gulf of Tonkin was doubled from three to six, which of course meant that an appropriate number of additional escorts and auxiliaries were sent into action there. In order to do this, the average duration of an overseas deployment for a ship of the Seventh Fleet had to be increased from six to almost nine months. And in the Pacific deployments were not broken by occasional port visits to such places as Naples or Athens or Izmir or Rota, but by occasional port visits to Subic Bay, whose character I have already described. Finally, the intensity of the air activity over Vietnam that the White House demanded meant that there were more casualties, more damage to planes and ships, increasing short-ages of spare parts and equipment of various kinds, and routine sixteen-hour and eighteen-hour or even twenty-hour working days for weeks on end for many of the men of the Seventh Fleet.

It was precisely at this inopportune moment of maximum stress on personnel that the effect of the insufficient recruiting effort of the past year and more reached the fleet: the shortfalls in total numbers of recruits and the increase in numbers of underqualified recruits. I do not want to overstate the case. The shortcomings in recruiting were not a major factor in the turbulent events that the next chapter will relate. The major factor was the insistence by the Administra-tion, year after year, in cutting defense budgets without similarly cutting defense commitments. The Navy simply did not have the resources to meet the emergency created by the Easter Offensive without straining itself in many places, including the nerves of its personnel. But recruiting shortcomings did aggravate the situation, particularly when it came to minority relations. When the pressures of daily existence are so great that large numbers of people feel aggrieved, their nerves jangled, and their tempers stretched thin, the most likely objects of the hostility they feel are people they never cared for much when times were easy. For all too many Americans, including sailors, that meant and means people with skins of a differ-ent color. The relatively sudden introduction into the fleet of an unprecedentedly large number of blacks, too many of whom were unskilled, put extra strain on both them and their white shipmates at a time when strain was already excessive.

I made an eight-day visit to the western Pacific at the end of August 1972. My first day was spent in Indonesia, where I paid a ceremonial call on President Suharto, to whom I delivered a personal letter from President Nixon, and where I had discussions of more or less consequence with a number of military dignitaries. The rest of the time I spent with the Seventh Fleet, which was the primary purpose of my trip across the ocean. I wanted to observe at first hand how the Fleet was bearing up after almost five months of unremitting pressure. An important member of my party was the Navy's senior enlisted man, Master Chief Petty Officer of the Navy Jack Whittet, without whose help my personnel reforms would have had less success than they did. On 22 through 26 August we visited twenty-one ships—four carriers, *Kitty Hawk, America, Midway,* and *Saratoga;* eleven escorts, including *Dewey,* the guided-missile frigate whose first captain I had been; three amphibious ships, and three auxiliaries —as well as the Naval Air Station at Cubi Point and the Naval Station at Subic Bay. We also took a quick look at Olongapo City, which assured me that the report I quoted earlier in this chapter did not exaggerate its character. The best way for me to describe what we found is to quote the sections of "Total Numbers" and "Personnel" from a point paper entitled "WestPac Trip Observations" dated 31 August, four days after my return.

TOTAL NUMBERS

1. We now have in the Seventh Fleet 37 percent of our end FY '73 carriers (6 out of 16); 30 percent of our cruiser/destroyer—or warship —types (63 of 207); 25 percent of our amphibs (17 of 68); 51 percent of our replenishment ships (31 of 61); 24 percent of our total ships (145 of 595); and 41 percent of our VF/VA [aircraft] Sqdns (29 of 70).

2. If we should attempt to mount such a level of support at end FY '74 with the forces in our 24 June Program Objectives Memorandum: 46 percent of our carriers (6 out of 13); 37 percent of our warships (63 of 170); 27 percent of our amphibs (17 of 64); 63 percent of our replenishment ships (31 of 49); 28 percent of our total ships (145 of 525); and 45 percent of our VA/VF Sqdns (29 of 64).

3. Moreover, we cannot come close to one-in-three deployment ratios. With LantFlt carriers deploying to WestPac, all carriers are now averaging 6.6 months in ConUS between 7.6 month deployments; present deployments for both LantFlt and PacFlt are projected as an average of 8.6 months. Moreover, of 23 Seventh Fleet ships—all types—sampled, during the period FY '71 to 30 March 72, the average ship has been away from homeport 55 percent of the time. Since 30 March this has risen to at least 81 percent.

4. In FY '72 prior to 30 March, the Seventh Fleet averaged 65 percent of the time at sea; cruisers and destroyers were high with 77.2 percent

and 74.3 percent respectively. Since 30 March, this has increased to an overall fleet average underway percentage of 78.6 percent; carriers and cruisers/destroyers were high with 87.1 percent and 78.3 percent respectively.

PERSONNEL

1. Manning level in PacFlt is marginal and the trend is down. Shortages are acute in some ratings (e.g., Boiler Tender, Internal Communications), in particular pay grades, and in certain skill areas within ratings. For example, in Engineering ratings, Boiler Technician, Machinist's Mate and Interior Communications Electrician are now manned at less than 90 percent in the Pacific Fleet. Manning of pay grades E-5 and E-6 of the Boiler Technician rating—the top watchstanders—is 76.3 percent. Manning of Interior Communications Electricians trained as gyrocompass technicians is approximately 60 pecent. Overall non-rated manning is 79.7 percent. Projected Seventh Fleet losses due EAOS [Extended Active Obligated Service] are 1500 per month.

2. Have taken stopgap measures, such as reducing non-deployed unit manning below EDP [Enlisted Distribution Plan], reduced shore establishment manning, extended PRD [Prospective Release Date] for 3719 personnel and beefing up with TAD [Temporary Additional Duty] augmentees.

3. Almost 50 percent of our pilots are on their second or third combat deployments; 10 percent of the pilots in four squadrons aboard USS *Midway* are on their fourth such deployment.

4. Of the career-enlisted men in the 23 ships, 630 men (16 percent) have been at sea continuously for more than four years; in the worst case, USS *Providence,* 37 percent of the career enlisted have so served.

5. The impact of increased time away from homeport and tempo of operations is largely borne by the very group we wish to retain—approximately 77 percent of the men in the Seventh Fleet are first-termers.

6. Although morale is now very high due to a sense of purpose—or basic patriotism—I doubt that these young men would want to make a career of very hard work coupled with family separations noted previously. We will be hard pressed to convince them that their prospects are for a better lot over the next twenty years, as they listen to their career shipmates, and can see force levels declining with no concomitant decrease in commitments.

7. Summary: Prognosis is for continuing degradation, instability, lower morale, loss of readiness for units drawn down, higher travel, and maintenance costs due to stopgap measures.

CHAPTER 10

Blowoff

In previous wars, accumulated pressure on fighting men had vented in shipboard outbreaks and riots and it did in this war, too, on the night of 12 October 1972. Unfortunately, but unsurprisingly, that first and worst explosion occurred aboard CVA 63, USS *Kitty Hawk*. It was unfortunate that *Kitty Hawk* should be the scene of a major racial disturbance because she had a good Minority Affairs program and a black executive officer, Commander Benjamin Cloud, one of the Fleet's promising middle level officers. It was unsurprising because *Kitty Hawk,* which had left San Diego on 17 February, had been on the line in the Pacific for almost eight months while domestic support for the war was at an all-time low, and during that period had set a new record for number of sorties flown from a carrier during a single deployment. The trouble occurred as *Kitty Hawk* was on her way to her station in the Gulf of Tonkin after a brief stay at Subic Bay for upkeep and repair. At about 2000 hours a young black apprentice seaman was summoned to the ship's investigator's office for questioning about an allegation, arising from a brawl in Olongapo City two nights before, that he had refused to obey an order from, had spoken disrespectfully to, and had assaulted a petty officer. He brought with him nine friends from the crew when he reported. He refused to make a statement. Angry words were exchanged. The ten men stormed out of the office. On their way through the after mess deck they beat up a white mess attendant who was stacking trays.

From then until 0500 next morning *Kitty Hawk* was the scene of sporadic rampages interspersed with various kinds of cooling-off sessions that involved at one time or another perhaps 150 or 200 of the more than 5000 men aboard including the Marine security detachment. These transactions resulted in some sixty injuries serious enough for medical treatment, including three that required medical evacuation to hospitals on shore. Twenty-six men, all black, ultimately were charged with one offense or another. At 0758 hours on 13 October *Kitty Hawk* arrived on station in the Gulf of Tonkin and commenced air strike operations against North Vietnam.

Four days later, at 1400 hours on 16 October, a group of about a dozen black sailors aboard AO 145, USS *Hassayampa,* a fleet oiler docked at Subic Bay, told the ship's executive officer that they would not sail at 1600 with the ship, and indeed would attack white members of the crew, if money that allegedly had been stolen from the wallet of one of the members of the group was not returned forthwith. Mostly as the result of a series of inadequate responses to this ultimatum by the executive officer, and subsequently the captain, seven white sailors were set upon that afternoon by the group of blacks, many of whom were armed with walking sticks with Black Power clenched fists carved on their handles, a standard item in the souvenir shops in Olongapo. Five of the sailors who had been assaulted were given first aid and returned immediately to active duty. The other two had injuries so minor that they declined medical treatment. However, it took a Marine detachment, which arrived at 1500 hours, to restore order conclusively. At 2100 hours eleven black sailors who had been given the choice of voluntarily putting themselves into safekeeping until an investigation was completed, or being arrested and charged then and there, chose the former course and left the ship. Ultimately six of them were charged. At 2115 hours *Hassayampa* put to sea.

The two incidents were dissimilar in their details, and the conditions of life on the ships on which they occurred were even more dissimilar. No one could have predicted that, of all the ships in the Pacific, *Kitty Hawk* and *Hassayampa* would be the two that would erupt. And even after the eruptions no one could explain precisely why they occurred only on those two ships. The most disturbing implication of the incidents, then, was that they could have happened anywhere: on fighting ships like *Kitty Hawk* and on auxiliary ships like *Hassayampa;* on ships with enormous crews like a carrier and on ships with relatively small crews like an oiler; on ships with conscientious captains and competent executive officers like *Kitty Hawk* and on ships with not very conscientious captains and not very competent execs like *Hassayampa;* on ships with good Minority Affairs Programs like *Kitty Hawk* and on ships with virtually nonexistent Minority Affairs Programs like *Hassayampa.* Clearly racial animosity was not confined to an overcrowded or overworked or insensitively commanded ship, but was a condition that afflicted perhaps unavoidably, the entire Navy, as it finally made room for the black Americans it had systematically excluded for so long. The behavior of black sailors who hauled white shipmates out of their bunks and beat them was obviously intolerable, but their perception that the Navy was a racist institution unfortunately was all too accurate. And so the *Kitty Hawk* and *Hassayampa* incidents put the responsibility squarely on me, as the top officer in the Navy and as the initiator of the program to integrate the Navy, of seeing to it not just that discipline was maintained while integration proceeded, but that the "maintenance of discipline" did not become a euphemism for slowing down the process of integration. I faced the same challenge the Chiefs of Staff of the other three services had already faced. Similar episodes had occurred in each of those services when they took their first significant steps toward integration years before. The Navy was not leading the procession in this field. On the contrary, I am embarrassed to say, it was bringing up the rear.

The most alarming possibility that the two incidents raised, of course, was that they would set off a chain of similar outbursts throughout the fleet. Happily that did not happen. Moreover, neither *Kitty Hawk* nor *Hassayampa* failed to perform her assigned missions for all the turmoil aboard. Finally the Commander in Chief of the Pacific Fleet, Admiral Chick Clarey, a strong proponent of racial equality in the Navy and a most efficient officer, responded rapidly and ably to the outbreaks. Within days he had put three legal teams aboard *Kitty Hawk* to expedite the necessary business of identifying offenders and drawing charges. He had instructed his senior subordinates to make sure that all required programs and procedures in the "human goals" field were in effect in every ship. He had sent out strong reminders to all commanding officers that minority affairs and equal opportunity were their personal, nondelegable responsibility whether or not Minority Affairs officers or Career Counselors had been assigned to their commands. He had taken steps to give carriers, when they came off the line, enough time to get to Yokosuka and back, so they could avoid nearby Subic Bay, and he had sent his inspector general to Subic Bay to see what could be done to clean up that pesthole. He and I had a long telephone conversation about all those matters on 18 October, in the course of which we agreed that one thing the *Kitty Hawk* and the *Hassayampa* episodes had in common was that both occurred immediately after the ship's crew had been exposed for several days to Subic's questionable delights. In short, the immediate crisis appeared to be under efficient management.

However, the two outbreaks portended badly for the future. To get as precise as possible an idea of how badly, I ordered a new minority officers' retention study group to convene. Consisting of twelve ensigns, lieutenants junior grade and full lieutenants from various commands, it met from 24 to 31 October, and on the latter date delivered its report to me. It was a shocker. Its four general findings were that the Navy had failed to accept the racial situation as its problem; that being a member of a minority and a member of the Navy were incompatible; that only blacks, rather than all minorities, were represented in current policies and programs; and that the Navy's classification, advancement and placement systems selected out minorities. Here are some excerpts of what they told me that day:

> The implementation of Z-Grams that directly affect the minority members of the Navy is at the whim of commanding officers of individual units. . . . Briefings by equal opportunity and race relations personnel indicate that much of their time is spent attempting to correct crisis situations without a comparable amount of time spent in the prevention area. . . . There is no accountability for failure to implement policies. . . . Programs and policies directly affecting minorities are promulgated in the nature of requests versus command. Although you [CNO] have stated "Race relations programs cannot be sustained by fiat from Washington," the consensus of the Retention Study Group is that the programs are not being implemented. . . . It is apparent that double standards have been established. Z-Gram 113 creates the billets of enlisted Career Counselors. It is specificaly stated that these counselors will be "unencumbered by collateral duties." On the other hand Z-Gram 66 establishes Special Assistant for Minority Affairs as collateral, [which] implies that the alleviation of racial problems in our Navy is not of prime importance but is a secondary mission. . . . The recruiting slogan, "You can be black *and* Navy too" is false advertising. "You can be black *or* Navy too" more truly represents the situation in our Navy today. . . . Minority members are often detailed to billets which are not career enhancing. Crisis placement in areas such as minority recruiting, minor-

ity affairs, human relations, and race relations receives an urgent priority but when promotion time arrives they seem to lack that same urgency. . . . In the area of disciplinary procedures, non-majority Navy personnel receive a disproportionate amount of punitive discharges, non-judicial punishment and extra military instruction. Naval penal institutions house a greater proportion of minorities than their percentage in the Navy. When racial discord results in physical altercations, only minority personnel are subject to charge and punitive measures. . . . Ethnic slurs in the form of tactical callsigns are just as detrimental as name-calling. Callsigns such as "blackface" and squadron insignia illustrating a person (gray in color) in a bathtub labeled detachment "jig" indicate that such practices are sanctioned and condoned. The term "gook" can be heard frequently over tactical frequencies from aircraft on strike missions in Vietnam. Is this a RACE WAR??? . . . The look of incredulity when a white encounters a minority officer, various snubs at social functions, and the general hostility encountered by minorities, are all indications of the racism in our Navy today. . . . Navy classification tests are culturally biased. [They] not only are invalid predictors with respect to minority group members but also are a destructive mechanism since the upward mobility of personnel is dependent on them. . . . Housekeeping service functions such as the deck force, laundry, mess decks and X-divisions are overwhelmingly non-white. . . . Minority group members are vastly underrepresented in key placement positions such as enlisted distribution, detailing, placement and classification interviewing.

Following closely on the heels of that earful came a report by the Assistant Secretary of Defense for Manpower and Reserve Affairs, Roger T. Kelley, of a three-week inspection trip to Europe. Secretary Kelley said that if the Navy's race relations programs in Europe were compared with those of the Air Force and the Army, the Air Force could be said to be in college, the Army in high school, and the Navy in elementary school. He called on the Navy to make immediate improvements, which he pointed out were particularly necessary because the conditions of service in the Navy were the most arduous of those in any of the three services. While I was pondering those gloomy messages, on 3 November racial trouble broke out on another carrier, CVA 64, USS *Constellation,* engaged in training exercises off the California coast. Until then Washington had paid little heed to what had been going on. The first news of the *Kitty Hawk* trouble had made the front page of the *New York Times* and the paper had run daily follow-ups for several days thereafter. *Hassayampa* had also received modest notice in the press. However, the imminent presidential election preoccupied Washington at that point; Subic Bay seemed far away. Unfortunately, the *Constellation* flap lasted past the election. It put racial equality in the Navy in mortal jeopardy, and it did the same thing to my prospects for seeing my programs through to the end of my four-year tour. I have never been in a nastier fight or one that was more important to win.

Though the events aboard *Constellation* produced no injuries or property damage, they were more troubling than those aboard *Kitty Hawk* or *Hassayampa*. The latter had been, fundamentally, spontaneous outbursts of anger, nasty evidence of past racial injustice and of present institutional inability to cope with it, but tactically simple to bring under control. The situation aboard *Constellation* was harder to handle because it was so complex. "Connie" was a sort of floating testimonial to the more than occasional pertinence of Murphy's Law: anything that can go wrong probably will. On her decks that autumn all the Navy's most conflicting exigencies and trends, attitudes and traditions, systems and procedures seemed to converge.

"Connie" was at San Diego for retraining after a deployment on Yankee Station, in the Gulf of Tonkin, that had been extended for three months beyond the optimum six months schedule. Indicative of the high morale the ship's company maintained during that long deployment was an unprecedented 64 percent first-term reenlistment rate in the month of March. Because of the accelerated tempo that the war in southeast Asia demanded, she was due to return to the Seventh Fleet just after the New Year, giving her only six months stateside. That in turn meant that a very large package of repairs, which began on 1 August, after the crew had returned from the thirty-day leaves they had more than earned, had to be crowded into eight weeks. During that period the ship was all but uninhabitable. The air conditioning was out for most of the time; there were regular shutoffs of water and steam in various parts of the ship so that cooking and dishwashing and bathing were sometime activities; from 0600 to 2200 the din and dust were constant; and the work of the civilian repair crews had priority over that of the Navy crew members, so that the latter often had to perform their necessary duties after midnight or on Sundays.

While this was going on the new additions to the ship's company were assembling. They included a larger percentage than Connie had ever had before of non-school-eligible young blacks, who more or less automatically were relegated to those deck and engineering divisions that were repositories for sailors with low test scores. The veteran officers and petty officers aboard, quite aside from whatever conscious or unconscious racial attitudes they may have had, were unaccustomed to large numbers of such blacks since in the past the Navy had diligently excluded them. For their part, many of the recruits—and this was true of whites as well as blacks—had been given insufficient grounding, as they were hustled through boot camp and out to the fleet, in such long-established but confusing Navy systems as semiannual marks, school eligibility, mess-cook duty, non-judicial punishment, and early discharge. A group of perhaps fifty or sixty black sailors developed the notion during October, as the ship went through the refresher training exercises that were the first step in getting ready for deployment, that they were being treated unfairly in duty assignments, at Captain's Mast (where minor offenses are disposed of nonjudicially by commanding officers), in evaluations by their superiors. They began holding informal meetings in a section of the mess deck known as the "Sidewalk Cafe," and in the course of those meetings spokesmen emerged, pretty much on the basis of loud voices and intemperate language. The news of the brothers' "protest" on *Kitty Hawk* reinforced the solidarity of this group.

Meanwhile, as a result of routine last-minute changes in the manning of the ship, there turned out to be a shortage of 250 bunks for the lower ratings. Rather than increase the discomfort of an overcrowded ship by jamming in 250 temporary steel-mesh bunks, "Connie's" commanding officer, Captain J. D. Ward, decided to transfer out 250 men. The rumor swept the black shipboard community that all 250 would be black and that many of them would be given general —less than honorable—discharges. That the rumor was without foundation did not lessen its impact on "Connie's" black crew members. Indeed the exceptionally thorough official investigation of the events of those weeks that was conducted immediately after they occurred found that amost all the blacks' grievances—discriminatory treatment of blacks at Captain's Mast, discriminatory assignment of blacks to mess-cook duty and so forth—were without factual basis. However, it also found that the human goals and minority affairs program that "Connie" had initiated in response to the directives on such subjects from Washington and Chick Clarey's headquarters in Hawaii were more faithful to the letter of those directives than to their spirit. "Connie" was not unique in the fleet in that respect, of course, or even notable. Nevertheless, making the job of Minority Affairs Officer on a ship with a complement of almost 5000 men a collateral duty of a Chief Petty Officer who preferred his regular job and spent three-quarters of his time on it was not giving minority affairs what could be called top priority. Nor, indeed, was giving the chairmanship of the Human Relations Council to the dental officer, who by the nature of his job could not be intimate with the personal problems of working sailors, the way best calculated to inspire confidence in the Council among the crew.

As November began and the anger of the group of disaffected blacks showed no sign of abating, Captain Ward became understandably concerned that his already too tight schedule would be entirely disrupted by turmoil among the crew. He, too, had heard of *Kitty Hawk,* and had no desire to preside over a second such scene. He set about indentifying the principal "agitators" among the blacks, with a view to getting them off the ship if he could. By 2 November he had a list of fifteen such agitators, which he sent to his personnel officer with a request for the latter to determine whether any of them met the criteria of BuPers for administrative discharge by the commanding officer. The personnel officer reported that six of them did. The captain ordered that immediate action to discharge the six be taken. Enter Murphy's Law. Not only did one of the six have a perfectly clean record and therefore was not subject to early discharge, but he also happened to have been the most skillful and popular afro barber on the ship. I suppose one can call it a piece of good fortune—a suspension of Murphy's Law—that dropping that particular spark into a powder keg led to a slow burn rather than an explosion. Around midday on 3 November, while "Connie" was conducting air operations off the coast of California, about sixty black sailors "congregated on the forward mess decks and commenced harrassing Caucasian sailors who were eating," in the words of the report.

The report gives an almost minute-by-minute account of what happened aboard *Constellation* during the next twenty-four hours, running to fifty-three numbered paragraphs covering seven single-spaced legal size pages. However, for the purpose of this narrative, those events can be adequately summarized in a few sentences. The group continued to occupy a section of the mess decks throughout the day and early evening, though not a large enough section to interfere seriously with the service of meals. The captain took a variety of actions to bring the demonstration to an end. They succeeded in averting violence, but not in inducing the group to disband. At 2145 hours, the Human Relations Council held a previously scheduled meeting on the after mess decks. The meeting rapidly turned into the kind of exercise by black militants that urban officials throughout the country had become familiar with by then but was a brand new experience for naval officers and petty officers. The black spokesmen were loud, obscene, and threatening, and drowned out any attempt to reason with them. They demanded a meeting with the captain. He declined to leave the bridge, not only because air operations still were in progress, but because he sensibly judged that allowing himself to be cursed and threatened would not enhance his ability to control the situation.

In the early hours of 4 November, with all planes in, and a substantial group of men dug in for the night on the mess decks, with blankets, music tapes, and playing cards, Captain Ward, whether or not he knew it, was sitting squarely on the hottest spot in the Navy, with very little in either his personal experience or the Navy's corporate wisdom to guide him. After all, he was no sociologist or community organizer or city councilman, but simply a veteran and, in the phrase of the report, "mission oriented" naval flyer, whose mission was to deliver a combat-ready *Constellation* to the Seventh Fleet in accordance with a schedule that under the best of circumstances would have been difficult to meet. Moreover he was in a personal as well as a professional squeeze. A carrier command is the critical assignment of his career for a naval aviator. Its bestowal on him signifies he is being considered for flag rank; he knows that whether or not he makes admiral pretty much depends on the ship's record under his command. Finally, it is important to remember that by tradition, by regulation, and by ordinary common sense a ship's captain has unchallengeable authority over and irrevocable responsibility for the internal affairs of his ship. No one is entitled, indeed no one is qualified, to usurp or overrule the decision of a ship's captain about how best to maintain order aboard his ship. There is a Department of Defense directive, "Guidelines for Handling Dissident and Protest Activities Among Members of the Armed Forces," that is supposed to guide an officer in Captain Ward's situation, but I leave it to the reader to judge how much it does:

The service member's right of free expression should be preserved to the maximum extent possible, consistent with good order and discipline and the national security. On the other hand, no Commander should be indifferent to conduct which, if allowed to go unchecked, would destroy the effectiveness of his unit. *The proper balancing of these interests will depend largely on the calm and prudent judgment of the responsible Commander.* [My emphasis.]

In short, Captain Ward was not only sitting squarely on the hottest spot in the Navy, but he was sitting there all by himself.

By 0300 hours that morning Captain Ward had made his decision. He called in his department heads and told them he was bringing the ship back to San Diego, where the dissidents would be formed into a "beach detachment" and sent ashore in a *non-disciplinary status,* so that the ship could continue its exercises in peace and quiet. He radioed this decision to San Diego half an hour later. At 0630 he passed the word about the return to port—but not about the beach detachment—over the public-address sytem. At 0745 "Connie" docked at the Naval Air Station (NAS), North Island. A bevy of senior officers was on the dock to meet the ship: the captain in command of NAS, North Island, and the captain who was his executive officer, the captain who was chief of staff for the Commander of Naval Air Forces, Pacific (ComNavAirPac), the captain in charge of minority affairs for ComNavAirPac, and the captain who headed the Human Resources Development Center in San Diego. The five captains, along with a black chief petty officer from ComNavAirPac's minority affairs office, went aboard and into a meeting with Captain Ward and his executive officer. After reviewing the situation, the five captains and the chief unanimously recommended to Captain Ward that he not form a beach detachment but keep the sit-in strikers aboard and modify his training schedule to allow the ship to remain in port as long as was necessary to solve its personnel problems. Though hindsight gives me the wisdom to assert that Captain Ward would have been well-advised to follow that recommendation, fairness compels me to add that the case was not all that clear at the time, and, given Captain Ward's intimate knowledge of the dynamics of getting his ship ready for wartime deployment against an impossible deadline, a good case for his decision can be made.

Captain Ward and his exec were adamant about continuing training exercises as scheduled. At 1030, the captain went down to the mess deck and told the sit-ins about the beach detachment. About an hour later 144 men (a handful of them white) under the command of a black lieutenant, assisted by five black chiefs and four other black petty officers, left the ship and were taken to a barracks on the Naval Air Station. This was a considerably larger detachment than Captain

Ward had expected it to be or, apparently, that it should have been. The number of men participating in the mess deck sit-in was ninety at the most. Though the captain had thought he made it clear to his department heads that only men clearly identified as "agitators" were to be off-loaded, word was passed in some divisions that anyone who volunteered could go ashore. That foul-up never was explained satisfactorily, but it contributed to the difficulty of the problem. A group of eighty or ninety aggrieved men is hard enough to handle; a group of 144 is that much harder. The beach detachment met in the barracks with various officers—not including Captain Ward— until midafternoon, and then its members, who were still in a non-disciplinary status, were granted liberty to expire at 0800 hours on 6 November, some forty hours later. On 5 November, "Connie" was at sea again conducting air operations. She returned to North Island at about the same time the detachment's liberty expired, but only to off-load a damaged plane suspended over the side. While the plane was being removed Captain Ward did have an opportunity to confer with ComNavAirPac, Vice Admiral Thomas Walker, and to instruct the lieutenant in charge of the beach detachment to "interview those who wished to return to the ship, to evaluate their motivation, and to predict if they were possible troublemakers." At noon "Connie" left for more air operations. That afternoon I took steps to ensure that thenceforth the occupant of the hottest spot in the Navy would not be Captain J. D. Ward but Admiral E. R. Zumwalt, Jr., who was being paid to sit there.

I had first received the word that there was trouble aboard "Connie" by telephone from Admiral Clarey, in Hawaii, who himself had just heard it from Vice Admiral Walker in San Diego, in midafternoon on Saturday, 4 November, a couple of hours after Captain Ward had formed his beach detachment and put it on the beach. Of course I immediately notified Secretary Warner and Admiral Mickey Weisner, who was Vice CNO at the time, and I took steps to ensure that the Chief of Information would see to it that information would get to the press through PR channels in the Pacific fleet. I also alerted Bill Norman. Using Minority Assistant channels of communication to which he had unique access, he would be able to learn the thoughts and moods of the protesters directly. Radio messages from Chick Clarey on the night of the 4th and early morning of the 5th provided additional details. Nothing much happened on Sunday the 5th of course, with "Connie" at sea and the beach detachment on liberty. However, all of us were keeping in close touch with developments and when at noon San Diego time, on Monday the 6th, "Connie" put to sea once more with the protesters, their grievances unresolved, still on the beach and still in a non-disciplinary status, I decided it was time for higher authorities—to wit the CNO and the Secretary of the Navy—to act.

So far the "Connie" affair had been virtually unnoticed by both the press and the Washington politicians, engrossed as they were in the next day's presidential election. I judged that if it could be resolved before the election returns were in next night, it might continue to escape the attention of the ideologues and rabblerousers on both sides of the racial issue. To that end, on Monday afternoon I set up a conference call with Tom Walker and Chick Clarey, with Mickey Weisner and Bill Norman in the room with me. I asked John Warner to participate also, but he declined. When the call was over, I went to his office to tell him what we had decided, but he had left for the day. I reached him at home later in the evening and reported on what was happening.

This crisis could not have brought together more dissimilar decision makers than Bud Zumwalt and John Warner, who had succeeded John Chafee as Secretary in May 1972 when the latter returned to Rhode Island to run (unsuccessfully) for the Senate. Both as Under Secretary and as Secretary, Warner, in an effort to keep peace in the family, had been in constant touch with the senior retired officers and their supporters on Capitol Hill who opposed the changes in personnel administration that I was bringing about. Though he favored integration, he had urged me a number of times to go very slowly with it. I, of course, believed that going fast was essential. Fortunately both John Chafee, while he was Secretary, and Mel Laird supported my position, so Warner's attempts to slow me down went for naught.

I learned from the afternoon conference call that Admiral Walker, with Admiral Clarey concurring, already had decided that there was no way of getting the protesters back aboard "Connie" where they belonged unless the ship returned at once to North Island and stayed there as long as necessary. Certainly it was impossible for the ship's command to resolve grievances against it while the ship was at sea and the aggrieved were ashore. That seemed indisputable to me, even though it meant overruling Captain Ward, who insisted that changing the ship's schedule in the face of a protest was tantamount to knuckling under to the protesters. His opinion was in accordance with long and honorable Naval tradition and was logical for one whose principal concern had to be his own ship and its mission. But I had to make my judgment in the light of my responsibility to the entire Navy, a responsibility that obligated me to find a way of combining the maintenance of discipline with the maintenance of progress in racial matters. If discipline had been the only concern even within the "Connie's" small world, Captain Ward would have had the dissenters arrested at once, rather than taking the action he did take. Now, however, "Connie" and her beach detachment were on the verge of becoming a symbol of the Navy's problem with its minorities. If the Navy's progress in racial integration was not to be irreparably set back, there had to be delicate handling of this symbolic band as its members were brought back under naval discipline. My guidance was, "It is terribly important to get the division officers in their departments working with these people, hopefully in smaller groups, as soon as they get in. And polish that off with Captain Ward talking with those that continue to hold out. Start off with the presumption that those who agree to return will not only have their grievances looked into but will not have disciplinary action taken against them. Make it clear at some point before the end of the day that there is a point of no return at which time disciplinary action must be taken against them."

We spent quite a long time working out a step-by-step plan for the next day, with heavy emphasis on coaching the division officers before they met the protesters. I shall not go into that plan here since it was stultified by the refusal the next day of the men to break into small groups or meet with division officers. The three days they had spent in nobody's company but their own had coalesced and hardened them. They had elected an eleven-man committee to speak for them. That morning the committee drew up a list of its conditions for return to the ship which the captain took under advisement. Meanwhile, the men were given liberty until 0800 next morning, Wednesday. Richard Nixon was reelected President that day in the biggest landslide in history. On local (San Diego) television that night, between election reports, several of the "Connie" protesters appeared in a taped interview and stated their grievances. The *Constellation* incident had not yet become a national *cause célèbre*, but it was about to.

The first word of the protest in the eastern press appeared Wednesday the 8th in the form of a very short wire-service report in the *New York Times*. I spent virtually the entire day on the problems of *Constellation*, but to little purpose. For four days, on board ship and on shore, the Navy had been patient in taking into account past racial injustices in dealing with these men. By then, I had concluded that the Navy had not only dealt with the dissenters fairly and patiently but that it would be perceived as having done so and that the time had come to take decisive action. However, John Warner was not yet ready to agree that the only course of action consistent with military discipline was ordering the men back aboard ship and putting them in a disciplinary status if they refused to reembark. He said that he did not want a confrontation and continued to insist on further delay. Adding to the difficulty was Captain Ward's understandable reluctance to take back aboard those among the beach detachment whom he considered to be "agitators" or "troublemakers." Under orders from Tom Walker, which effectively meant from Chick Clarey and me, the captain met on Wednesday morning with the beach detachment in the Naval Air Station auditorium and asked them—John Warner's policy made it impossible for him to order them—to return to the ship. The reports I received were that his presentation to the men was "masterful," but by that time masterfulness was not good enough. When he asked for a show of hands by those willing to return to the ship, he received a near unanimous display of clenched fists from both blacks and whites. I spoke to Chick Clarey three times that day and we finally worked out what seemed a promising way to break the deadlock and at the same time abide by the prohibition against arresting the men. Captain Ward would meet again with the dissidents and tell them that the beach detachment was dissolved as of then and that it must vacate the barracks immediately, that its members were on liberty that would expire at 0800 the following (Thursday) morning aboard ship, and that after that time anyone not aboard would be considered AOL (Absent Over Leave) and thus subject to disciplinary action. At 1905 Washington time, Chick called me at my quarters to tell me that this plan had been carried out.

We had one exchange during that conversation according to my notes that shows that we were far more inclined to blame ourselves than our subordinates for inexpert management of a major national problem.

Z: Are you aware according to our reports first human relations counseling session on the ship was held within last week when first started having signs this trouble?

Clarey: No, not aware that. I suspect this not only case in the fleet. [I] have asked for report by next Monday how my orders and instructions been carried out. [I] want my unit commanders go aboard and not send messages around. Did you see message?

Z: Yes, [I] did, and [I] thought it was a good one.

Clarey: [I] would say in all honesty you that situation exists other places. [I] kick my pants [for] not putting out directives instead of suggestions. [In] reviewing my program [there are] several places down the back road [that I] could have said, "This is a directive. I have made human resources mandatory in this fleet now."

Z: All of us [have been] assuming [that] suggestion [was] all [it] took. [I am] just as guilty [of that] as you.

Clarey: With my staff here other day [I] criticized myself for not having issued orders. [I] told myself that when you created 09C [the CNO's decision coordinator] that I should have done that myself. [I] know from [my] experience [that] unless you have some follow-up system [on] what [has been] done to carry out our directives, [they] just don't get done.

At 0730 Thursday the men of what had been the beach detachment were on the dock in uniform and with their gear. There also were newspaper and radio reporters and television cameramen there. At 0800, when the colors went up, the men came to attention and saluted. At 0810 the ship's command duty officer came off the quarterdeck onto the dock and told the men that their liberty had expired and that they would be unauthorized absentees unless they reported aboard at once. The men did not do so. The captain then sent divisional officers onto the dock to try to round up their men. The men laughed at them. Some time later five lawyers representing the men appeared and the captain invited them to his quarters for a discussion. I was kept apprised of these developments almost minute by minute. We had an officer on the dock with a direct line to my office, and my executive assistant, Captain Don Pringle, was in constant touch with him. Meanwhile I was trying to get John Warner to authorize me to take action, which he continued to avoid doing. His notion was that there should be a "cooling-off period," with the men back in the barracks again—which in my view would have actually been a heating-up period—and that "Connie" should leave San Diego (and the problem) because it was a "symbol"—which of course would have been symbolically refusing to address the problem.

He offered those thoughts at 1100 hours, which was 0800 in San Diego, the time when the men on the dock were first refusing to return to the ship. My program was to bus the men back to the barracks, where they would be kept in groups no larger than busload-size; to inform them when they got there that they had been transferred from *Constellation* to the Naval Air Station in a disciplinary status; then to spread them around among the various facilities that make up the San Diego Complex, and restrict them to barracks overnight; and first thing next morning to initiate appropriate disciplinary proceedings, and to begin determining whether after the disciplinary proceedings were over, a new assignment, a discharge or some other action would be the best ultimate disposition of each case. I had this written up in the form of a "scenario" and asked four key people to comment on it, my Vice Chief, the Chief of Naval Personnel, the Deputy Judge Advocate General, and the Chief of Information. All approved it wholeheartedly.

Meanwhile the situation on the dock in San Diego was not improving. More representatives of the media were arriving. The oratory of the leaders of the protest was becoming more torrid. A series of conferences between the captain and the lawyers for the men got nowhere because the lawyers refused to advise the men to return to the ship until the captain agreed to review their grievances and the captain refused to agree to anything until the men returned to the ship. Around noon, San Diego time, Tom Walker telephoned asking for guidance. I had a note sent into Warner who was in a meeting saying, "We need you badly." When he arrived, I handed him my scenario, to which I had attached a memorandum that is worth quoting in its entirety, since it was pretty strong medicine and I would not have brewed it if I had not thought the situation a serious one.

MEMORANDUM FOR THE SECRETARY OF THE NAVY

Subj.: Need to act immediately with regard to the USS *Constellation* disciplinary problem

1. It is my strong recommendation that you rescind your verbal order to: instruct Vice Admiral Walker to detach the grievance group from the USS Constellation; permit them to return to the barracks as a group; and to withhold action to take them into custody until tomorrow.

2. It is my strong recommendation, concurred in by the Deputy JAG, ChInfo, Chief of Naval Personnel and the Vice Chief of Naval Operations, that you immediately authorize me to instruct CinCPacFlt to have Vice Admiral Walker proceed in accordance with the scenario attached.

3. It is my belief, shared by the others mentioned above, that we have reached the point where the basic structure of the Navy as a military organization will suffer grievously throughout if action is delayed longer. It is further our belief that delay increases the probability of physical violence with regard to the grievance group and weakens public confidence in the Navy.

John Warner read the memo and the scenario and refused to keep them. He handed them back. We then went round and round about the matter for almost two hours and he finally agreed to let me get on with my program. It was now approaching 1400 hours in San Diego, more than six hours after the men had assembled on the dock, plenty of time, as the evening news shows and the next morning's newspapers gave ample evidence, for the men to utter for quotation a plethora of militant statements and to pose for a gamut of clenched-fist photographs. At 1450 San Diego time, the men left the dock in buses and from then on things went pretty much according to the scenario. There was no violence or any attempt at it. Evidently both the advice of the lawyers and the prudence of the men ruled that out. During the five days of the protest a couple of dozen members of the original beach detachment had rejoined the ship, so there were 120 aboard the buses. Ultimately forty-six of them received discharges, thirty-six honorable, and seventy-four were given new assignments. The punishments they received for being AOL for six hours on 9 November were trifling.

Now Washington became the center of the excitement. Through-out the incidents I have just described, beginning with *Kitty Hawk,* opponents of integration had been fulminating about how "permis-siveness"—an obvious buzz word for "integration"—was about to destroy the Navy. One of the leaders was retired Admiral George Anderson, a man I had heard remark in the late fifties, in reference to a particularly bloody fight between rival factions of short-haired white sailors under his command in the Pacific that, "boys will be boys." From his desk in the Executive Office Building as Chairman of the President's Foreign Intelligence Advisory Board he was re-portedly on the telephone tirelessly, urging retired officers and, I was told, active duty officers as well, to do something to stop Bud Zumwalt's permissive programs before it was too late. During the *Constellation* crisis, indeed, he was in nearly daily communication with John Warner, telling him, John later told me, how concerned the President was about the whole thing, which may account in part for John's procrastinating. However, I had a formidable backer in the person of Mel Laird, who assigned two of his principal aides, the Assistant Secretary for Public Affairs, Daniel Henkin, and the Department Counsel, J. Fred Buzhardt, to help John handle these matters. Those two learned that one of my occasional meetings with flag officers in the Washington area was to take place on 10 November, and that I was planning to talk to them about the Navy's racial problems. They suggested to John that my speech be made public. John thereupon decided that he, too, would address the flag officers and that his speech, too, would be publicly released.

It was not my custom to deliver set pieces to the flag officers, but rather to speak informally with them. Moreover the Washington area flag officers, the great majority of them in staff postions rather than in the chain of command, were not an entirely appropriate audience for what I wanted to say. Nevertheless, I was delighted to be given a military forum in which to make my policies clear. Ever since the covert operations with the press and Congress had begun I had been seeking a way of bringing the whole business out in the open. I wanted the public, the press, and the Congress to have no doubt about what the Navy's policy was and what the opponents of that policy were trying to do. I wanted to put both the racists and those suffering from racism within the Navy on public notice to follow orders. I wanted to tell members of minorities within the Navy and their families and friends back home that the Navy's top leadership was committed to racial integration. I wanted to reaffirm publicly that the Navy was a disciplined organization. The issue had ceased to be a purely internal naval one that could be handled via command channels or Z-grams or the Flag Officer's News Letter or the Public Affairs messages to the fleet or Bill Norman's communications network or any of a dozen other channels readily available to me. It had become a national issue and I will be everlastingly grateful to Mel Laird for making it easy for me to go national.

I have made hundreds of speeches in my life and, if I am spared, I probably shall make hundreds more, but I doubt that I ever have made or will make a speech that meant more to me than the one I made to the Washington flag officers on the morning of Friday 10 November 1972. I am proud enough of it to reprint it in full.

Gentlemen, I have asked you to meet with me today because I find it necessary to make clear not only my position on an important issue but my conviction that programs relevant to that issue must be implemented. And by implemented I mean exactly that—down to the very lowest levels of command.

When I took office twenty-eight months ago I, together with then Secretary of the Navy John Chafee, brought to Washington men and women of our officer corps who were members of minority groups.

I went on record at that time saying how surprised I was to find so great a misunderstanding between our racial groups. I also made clear the potential explosiveness of such a misunderstanding within our Navy. And how important I considered the resolution of our racial tensions. And let me stress here as I will later on, I mean resolution within the framework of disciplined, efficient, orderly, and ethical military operations.

Approximately two weeks ago, I received the fourth in a series of retention study group reports evaluating how effectively the more than two hundred minority programs we have devised are working.

It was immediately clear to me from this report that the Navy has made unacceptable progress in the equal opportunity area. And that the reason for this failure was not the programs but the fact they were not being used.

At about the same time as I received this report, some of the very things I feared twenty-eight months ago might come to pass did, in fact, take place.

There is no point here in recapitulating the incidents which took place aboard the carrier *KITTY HAWK*, the oiler *HASSAYAMPA*, and most recently the carrier *CONSTELLATION*. For while these incidents are of great importance, a detailed discussion would only obscure, with specifics, the more fundamental issues we must face.

Let me remark, however, that these incidents are not the cause of racial pressures; rather, they are the manifestations of pressures un-relieved.

Gentlemen, even before the details of those incidents began to come to me in the message traffic, it was clear to me the time had come for me to speak very plainly. To speak without the usual cushions of jargon and without the exquisite politeness we sometimes use to mask the impact of our thoughts.

What we are talking about here is not a call for permissiveness, or a direction to coddle. Let me say again that discipline necessary for good order will and must be maintained and that each officer and man will be held accountable for failure to meet the standards of work quality we need and must have.

I am speaking to you and, through you, to the Navy's entire command structure, to emphasize again that this issue of discrimination must be faced openly and fully.

Let me begin my plain statements by saying that, in my opinion, the most destructive influence on the resolution of racial problems is self-deception.

It is self-deception to think you can legislate attitudes. You cannot.

It is self-deception to feel a program is a reality. It is not.

It is self-deception to think that the Navy is made up of some separate species of man—that Navy personnel come to us fresh from some other place than our world—that they came untainted by prejudices of the society which produced them. They do not.

It is self-deception to consider all issues involving blacks and whites solely as racial in motivation. They are not.

And, finally, it is self-deception to consider the Navy, or any military organization, as free-wheeling—"to each his own way"—civilian society. In fact, even a civilian society unbounded by military law and tradition can only exist within the system of law and custom. For a military society to fill its purpose every man must know his own role—and live within it.

There must be no substitution of one prejudice for another. The prejudice against good order and discipline is as pernicious as the prejudice of race.

We have tried—sometimes successfully, sometimes not—to free ourselves of those self-deceptions. They lead to abstraction instead of practicality. They lead to inefficiency and failure due to an over-emphasis on theory, without consideration as to the practicality of implementation.

For instance, I believe many incidents are characterized as racial only because that is their most visible aspect. They have, in fact, many causes. Men at sea for months on end, working extended hours seven days a week, with aging equipment, and escalating demands, face pressures almost inconceivable to those who have not known them.

It was recognition of the possibility that these duty pressures might burst forth in black-white confrontations that I sought, through my racial programs, to forestall such explosions.

But it was also clear that we could accomplish nothing by putting our already overworked commanding officers in the intolerable position of having every move dictated, and their every judgment questioned.

Fully aware of the realities I have just outlined, I attempted to devise programs to defuse racial and sex discrimination tension.

As you know, we promulgated programs covering everything from housing to the establishment of special minority affairs counseling, to getting black cosmetics in the exchange.

Some of the results have been gratifying—particularly the education field and the broadened entrance opportunities into the Navy for minority members.

Plainly stated, we have tended to succeed wherever the establishment of a program met a need without a corresponding need to change or dismantle an existing procedure. We have tended to fail wherever a "real" change from hallowed routine was required.

It is my view that these current racial incidents are not the results of lowered standards, but are clearly due to failure of commands to implement those programs with a whole heart.

From the soundings provided by that fourth retention study group we know that pressures have built up because of a failure to anticipate and defuse them with more equitable leadership.

That study group reported that while there was overt cooperation with Z-gram 66—which established Minority Affairs Assistants in commands —these MAAs were effectively hamstrung in all too many cases.

For example, despite clear directions for the distribution of bulletins relating to racial programs—Navy Minority Information messages (NAVMINS)—commands are not making them available as they should. It is difficult to understand but a number of minority assistants have never even seen any of these messages.

For example, despite clear direction that abilities to foster equal opportunity should be considered on all fitness reports this aspect has only been considered in a small percentage of reports—and then perfunctorily.

For example, instead of using MAAs as advisors to assist command in relieving basic causes of tensions, command has used them as action officers to slip over a "hot spot" without getting at the cause.

For example, MAAs are too often consulted only in high tension situations and not on a continuing basis.

And finally, commanding officers on the one hand direct their assistants to report directly to them, while on the other hand they allow intermediate command levels to impede this access.

In response to these problems I am now directing, via this speech and in a communication to all Flag Officers, Commanders, Commanding Officers and Officers-in-Charge, that every effort be made to:

1. Create an environment within their command that makes equal opportunity a reality and discrimination, for any reason, an unacceptable practice.

2. Ensure that NAVMINS and all other messages and letter directives

setting forth equal opportunity policy, and race relations programs, be disseminated to, and discussed with, every man and woman under their command.

3. Place equal opportunity and race relations training at the same priority level in their training programs for officer and enlisted personnel as professional performance in the operational billet tasks assigned.

4. Seek out and take appropriate action, either punitive or administrative, against those persons who are engaged in or condoning of discriminatory practices or who have violated either the spirit or the letter of our equal opportunity policy.

5. Similarly, seek out and reward those people who are particularly effective in assisting them with programs to comply with the spirit of our policy in this area.

6. Ensure that their minority affairs assistant has established a meaningful dialogue with the minorities in their command, use him as an advisor, take measures to ensure he has ready access to them, and initiate action as they deem appropriate based on his recommendations utilizing the force of their office and subordinate chain of command.

7. Implement additional policies and programs to achieve within their command the concept of one Navy.

In addition I intend to use the Inspector General of the Navy as an "on-the-scene" examiner of these problems on a continuing basis.

Equal opportunity is a stated goal of our Commander in Chief, President Nixon, and the Human Goals program of the Secretary of Defense, Secretary of the Navy, and Chief of Naval Operations.

Equal means exactly that. Equal.

Having, I hope, made my position clear on these several points, let me now speak on what I believe is the key to addressing our racial difficulties.

No program promulgated by any Chief of Naval Operations can really change an attitude. Nor can any CNO know every incident, or even respond to each incident. You cannot run a Navy, or any large organization, if the top must provide all the solutions.

Nor can you bring about real change by obeying the letter and not the spirit of a program.

Uncomprehending response or response which lacks commitment from the heart—no matter how correct—is essentially obstructionist. Just as obstructionist as a man who puts an order in a drawer and forgets it.

What I am asking for, and what this Navy must have if it is to continue to fulfill its mission—especially in an all-volunteer environment—is something more than programs. We must not administer programs; we must lead men and women.

The even handed leadership of men is what it is all about.
And it can only come with every senior *leading* every junior.
It is not a push to the far edge of the untried I am suggesting, gentlemen. It is a return to our oldest and most proven tradition.
Command by leadership.

The two weeks following the delivery of that speech were a time of frantic activity, not to mention professional concern. That my four-year term as CNO was in danger of premature burial was the least important part of it. The personnel programs that had been my first priority as CNO, that indeed had been the principal reason John Chafee and Mel Laird had selected me as CNO, were in mortal jeopardy. It would be absurd for me to maintain that I enjoyed those two weeks. However, if I had to face a time like that again, with as much at stake as was at stake then, I would be more than willing.

My schedule for Saturday 11 November, the day after I gave the speech, called for me to leave for an official four-day visit to Hawaii. However, on Friday I was notified that my eighty-one-year old father at the Naval Ordnance Test Station, China Lake, California had just had a slight stroke. I decided to leave Washington early in order to spend the night with him, and to go on to Hawaii from China Lake in the morning. Late Friday night Mickey Weisner telephoned me in China Lake to advise me to come back at once. Apparently the speech had set the town buzzing. The network evening news shows were full of it. The *New York Times* was making it the lead story and using the "Equal means exactly that. Equal" passage as its "Quotation of the Day." Some of the George Anderson crowd were storming about admirals being "chewed out" in public—even though most of the members of my audience, as far as I could tell, had not taken it as a personal attack on them. Mickey did not think that it was the right time for me to be away. Needless to say I agreed. At 0535 Pacific Standard Time I flew out of China Lake. Exactly four hours later at 1235 Eastern Standard Time I walked into my office. The telephone was ringing. Henry Kissinger was on the telephone from Key Biscayne. How right Mickey Weisner had been!

Kissinger all but shrieked at me. I made notes of the conversation and later in the day made a memorandum for the record based on them, but I was not willing, on reviewing it, to have a record of what seemed to me to be an illegal order from such a high source even in my private files. Consequently my memorandum fails to convey the full flavor of our conversation. Though we talked for five minutes or more, Kissinger really had only one thing to say: the President (as Commander in Chief) wanted the *Constellation* protesters to receive dishonorable discharges immediately if not sooner. Since under the Uniform Code of Military Justice—the law of the land—a dishonorable discharge was an impermissible penalty in the absence of a long-drawn-out general court-martial and in any event could not result from being AOL for a few hours, the conversation began on a note of unreality. I learned a little later that what had first put Mr. Nixon into a fury was seeing the "Connie" sailors giving the clenched-fist salute on the dock on the Thursday evening news. Whatever the UCMJ said, Mr. Nixon viewed clenched-fist salutes as he tended to view all disagreement, not to say opposition, as mutiny. Therefore he interpreted my speech as an expression of support for mutineers.

> Dr. K said . . . the President . . . feels very strongly that there are to be no further negotiations with people who do not carry out orders no matter what the price. He read in the newspapers that all they can get is three days on bread and water. [I] said that there undoubtedly would be a range of punishments which in some part will be based on past records of people involved. Some whose records are bad enough could well be processed out of the Navy. Others get courts and lesser offenses. Dr. K said that the *President does not feel that he can prescribe the precise penalty but that he would like the men out of the Navy if possible.* [My emphasis at the time.] He wants other sailors to know that orders disobeyed will receive the most drastic penalties. [I] said the problem was to tread the narrow line and make it clear to other sailors that justice has been exercised. . . . Dr. K said that you are the CNO and in charge of the operation of the details. [Kissinger lowers his tone a notch.] . . . [I] said you must remember that we are talking about a Navy in which the carriers have done heroic services and other ships [have been] long overdeployed and undermanned and working twenty hours a day. Dr. K said you know the President's feeling about the Navy, having been in it himself, but he feels he would like to see discipline maintained. We know what we owe the Navy in every crisis we have ever gone through —Vietnam, Mediterranean, Middle East, etc. [Kissinger lowers his tone a second notch.] . . . Dr. K said . . . the President has called me twice on the subject. . . . The details of the matter will have to be left to you and we know you must follow the UCMJ. He wants you to know that you will be backed up on any measures you think are necessary to restore discipline. [I] said let me say I don't think on the ships where these events have taken place that basic order and discipline have broken down—in all cases the breakdowns are consigned to individuals. In the recent case

there was some unartful handling by the CO . . . there was a delay in executing orders of a few hours. . . . [That was the closest I thought it proper to come to mentioning the John Warner problem.] Dr. K said he just wanted to make you aware of his feelings—you will take the strictest measures that are compatible with the situation. We will talk to you again on Monday to see where it stands.

Thus Kissinger lowered his tone a third notch. In fact—though I wished I had known it at the time—he was signing off. I never heard from him again on the subject and you can be sure I did not call him.

As you might suppose, that conversation shocked me. Even though a professional military man has been prepared by training, by habit, and by conviction to obey unhesitatingly the orders of his superiors, including specifically orders he disagrees with, he cannot but be taken aback when his Commander in Chief, of all people, relays to him a peremptory, angry, illegal order such as that which had just been given me. The fact that it was clearly illegal spared me the pain of an internal conflict between conscience and duty: conscience and duty both dictated that I not obey it. However that same fact grievously eroded my confidence in and respect for my Commander in Chief, the more grievously since it came just four days after his smashing victory at the polls, a victory which I had welcomed and which I would have thought would have made him feel secure enough to permit the Navy to solve this problem. I did not yet know Mr. Nixon. Beyond that, Kissinger's tone of voice and choice of language made it fairly clear to me that my job was hanging by a thread, though I did not find out until a few days later how thin that thread had been. Secretary Laird did not tell me when I spoke with him that afternoon that, in the course of one of the several conversations he had had with Kissinger while I was flying east, Kissinger had ordered him to fire me. He saved that news for a calmer time. Mel had enough support in Congress to be able to treat Kissinger not as an all-powerful potentate, but as a mere assistant to the President, with no standing in the chain of command and certainly no right to give orders to a member of the Cabinet whose office had been established by the Congress and whose incumbency had been approved by the Senate. He told Kissinger that if Kissinger wanted me fired he should try firing me himself. Kissinger was not up to knocking that chip off the shoulder of a man Laird's size.

I spent a good deal of the time on the telephone that afternoon going back and forth over the situation with Secretary Laird and his executive assistant, Rear Admiral Daniel Murphy. One thing we all thought to be a pity was that Al Haig was absent from the President's entourage just then. Whatever his other qualities, Al as a military man understood that the UCMJ would not permit a permanent stain to be put on the record of a hot-headed nineteen-year-old who had done, as far as what a court martial could admit as evidence went, little more than raise a clenched fist to a television camera and overstay liberty for a few hours. I wanted to fly down to Key Biscayne forthwith to see the President, and explain to him the whole course of events on *Constellation* as well as the UCMJ. Mel vetoed that, which I guess was just as well; it probably would have taken very little that weekend, no more than showing up in Key Biscayne, say, to induce the President to dispense with my services once and for all. Next I proposed that I go on the "Today" show Monday or Tuesday to explain the Navy's position not just to the President but to the public at large. My intention was the same—to put across the idea that the "Connie" incident could be an opportunity for the Navy rather than a disaster. However the Secretary was determined to keep the CNO's profile low for a while—for the CNO's sake, among other reasons, I'm sure. Hungering as I was for action, I was reduced to accumulating ammunition for the counterattack in the hope that presently I would have the opportunity to mount one.

Now that I had publicly declared racial integration to be a top priority, I put my staff to drafting a Z-gram on discipline and good order for early promulgation. I called Chick Clarey in Makalapa to ask him to send me at once his Inspector General's report on "Connie"—which he had not yet read himself—so that I could have a complete chronology of the events in San Diego. It may help put events in context to note that my notes of that telephone call show that Chick and I also talked at some length about what to do with a team of some 400 mine-sweeping experts on their way to the Pacific just then to stand by for the call to clear the mines out of Haiphong harbor. You will recall that two or three weeks earlier, uncoincidentally on the eve of the election, Henry Kissinger had announced that "Peace is at hand" in Vietnam. One of the things Chick and I were worried about was that the team would have to do their standing by in Subic Bay, with its drug problems and its racial frictions. Of course peace was not quite at hand, it turned out, so we were able to put aside that particular worry for the nonce. However profoundly preoccupying the situation I have been describing, I still had a wartime Navy to run.

It is hard for even me to believe it retrospectively, but during that hectic week I quite deliberately precipitated a real crisis—though it was a mini-crisis to be sure—that put my job on the line on a second issue. In accordance with the plans I had outlined to John Chafee before he chose me as CNO, I had been vigorously accelerating the upward movement of young officers I considered promising. I wanted as many as possible of the critical commands and staff jobs to be in the hands of such officers when I left, so that it would be easy to locate a suitable successor to me without going into left field, as Secretary Chafee had had to do to locate me. Since moving an officer from one billet to another means replacing him in the old slot and then replacing his replacement, and so down the line, these moves in the Navy have the name "daisy chains."

In the fall of 1972 I had prepared what I intended to be the last big daisy chain before my successor was chosen. The occasion was the imminent retirement of two four-star admirals who had been leading contenders for CNO in 1970, Chick Clarey, Commander-in-Chief of the Pacific Fleet, and Bush Bringle, Commander-in-Chief of U.S. Naval Forces in Europe. The daisy chain started by moving Mickey Weisner, already a four-star, from Vice CNO to the Pacific Fleet, and giving Worth Bagley, who had continued to demonstrate unique qualities, his fourth star as CinCUSNavEur. To replace those two, I proposed to bring Vice Admiral James Holloway III from his command of the Seventh Fleet to Washington as four-star VCNO, and give Rear Admiral Daniel Murphy, Mel Laird's executive assistant, a third star and move him into Worth Bagley's job as Director of Navy Program Planning. Behind these moves were a number of others, amounting to a dozen or more in all.

In any such major shuffle of senior personnel the CNO proposes the list that is to go to the Secretary of Defense and to the President, but the Secretary of the Navy disposes. For weeks John Warner declined to forward my list. Besides having various objections to this man or that, he had a general objection, he said, to the speed with which I was reducing the average age of senior officers, which was the reason, he said, he did not want to give Worth Bagley and Jimmy Holloway their fourth stars. I viewed his statements as a pretext to cover up his desire to keep Jimmy and Worth out of the running for CNO, a pretext that was necessary because no one could question Worth's or Jimmy's brains or efficiency. I was amused that the forty-six-year-old Warner professed to believe that the fifty-one-year-old Holloway and the forty-nine-year-old Bagley were too young for four stars. But I was also determined to see my daisy chain through in its entirety. Though I probably could have had all the rest of it without demur if I had been willing to pass over Worth and Jimmy, I quite simply considered them to be two of the three or four outstanding officers in the Navy, and I wanted them to be in a position that entitled them to serious consideration when it came time to choose a new CNO. The uproar over *Constellation* hardened this determination by making it clear to me how important it was that my successor share my views about personnel administration. Mickey Weisner, Jimmy Holloway, and Worth Bagley had passed every test of total commitment to equal opportunity and to the treatment of individual sailors with dignity and with respect for modern lifestyles. And so in the midst of the *Constellation* problem in November, when John Warner once again delayed the daisy chain, I told him flat out that I would consider his continuing to do so to be a proper cause for my resignation, since it effectively prevented me from carrying out one of the principal programs my appointment had been based on.

That same day, I believe, John told Mel Laird about my intention, and asked him to make me do two things: withdraw the offer of resignation and withdraw the daisy chain, an ambitious program, you might say. A day or two later Mel had us both up to his office to state our opposing views, and said he would take the matter under advisement. He then sent for me alone and, after making sure that I was serious about resigning, told me that he could not take the position of supporting me unequivocally against my civilian superior and that I would have to give a little on the daisy chain. I proposed that instead of giving Worth's 090 job to Dan Murphy, I give it to Rear Admiral Thomas Hayward of Secretary Warner's office, and send Dan instead of Tom to the command of the Sixth Fleet in the Mediterranean. I had almost set up the chain in that way in the first place, so outstanding were both these officers.

That appeared to satisfy Mel and he dismissed me and sent for John Warner. He told John that he thought I was serious about resigning, and asked him if he was prepared to take over the Navy in its present state of turbulence. Having thus softened John up, Mel said that he had induced me to make some changes in the daisy chain, and counseled John to approve it as amended, which John presently did. That ended that threat to my job.

On Monday 13 November a hard blow fell. One of the Navy's greatest friends in Congress, as far as money went at least, was F. Edward Hébert of Louisiana, Chairman of the House Armed Services Committee. Eddie had been a protegé of Carl Vinson of Georgia, whose every wish was the Navy's command during the thirty-five years when he was Chairman of the House Naval Affairs Committee and, after the Department of Defense was created, Chairman of the House Armed Services Committee, and whose name, along with those of Chester Nimitz and Dwight Eisenhower, the Navy has given to a nuclear aircraft carrier. Vinson, an autocrat of the vanishing old Southern breed, was Eddie Hébert's model. Eddie ran his committee with an arbitrary hand. Eddie was particularly partial to the Navy among the Services. And Eddie did not think long hair and beards were consistent with good discipline, did not favor women going to sea, and preferred to maintain the Navy's traditional policies toward minorities. I made no bones about disagreeing with Eddie on those issues, but we remained personally friendly.

On the day I spoke to the flag officers Eddie was in New Orleans to attend a Marine Corps Birthday Ball. At the Ball that night he was peppered with complaints about my speech and me, and the barrage continued over the weekend, with numbers of the retired officers and traditionalists who were among his closest friends and staunchest constituents telling him that he should give me my come-uppance. On Monday he announced to the world, via press release and without telling me first, that he had appointed a special subcommittee to investigate "alleged racial and disciplinary problems" on Navy ships. His statement said, among other things, "I share the concern of many, many members of Congress over the apparent breakdown of discipline. I believe it is incumbent upon the committee to determine what the facts are and determine if further action is required on the part of the Congress." As chairman of the subcommittee, Hébert named Floyd Hicks, a Democrat of Washington, with W. C. (Dan) Daniel, a Virginia Democrat, and Alexander Pirnie, a New York Republican, as the other members. Perhaps it is hard for the reader to understand why this action of Eddie's so appalled and affronted me. Well, "breakdown of discipline" is about as damning a charge as can be made against an entire military service, and to escalate incidents on three ships out of 596 in the fleet into "breakdown of discipline," incidents moreover that did not prevent any of the three from performing all her assigned missions, was to my mind neither more nor less than a hatchet job against heroic, overcommitted, underfunded, undersupported sailors.

After due consideration I telephoned Eddie Hébert in New Orleans late Monday afternoon as soon as I saw the story of the investigation on the UPI wire. From my notes:

[I told him] that the people [from "Connie"] being processed rapidly as can be. CO of Air Station has gotten through about half of 130 already going through others fast as he can. [H. said you] mean he is telling them not to be bad boys again. [I said] doing everything have authority to do with specific offense which they are charged with, AOL. In this particular case they pretty well coached. [H. said] they refused an order. [I said] they refused order to go back onboard ship. [H. said] they were ordered to do something and didn't. [I said] when a man fails to report aboard ship he gets charged with absent without leave. [H. said] reaction down here horrible. [I said] statement says "[I] share concern of many members of Congress over the apparent breakdown of discipline in the United States Navy." There are 593 ships that haven't had the problem and are fighting hell of tough war while working 18–20 hours a day. [H. said] you have got a lot more trouble in Navy. You are headed for real trouble because of so-called equality business and quota business putting people in jobs they are not qualified for. [I said we] have people deployed 85 percent of the time working 18–20 hours a day. Ships undermanned undermaintained. [We] have very critical problem on these ships. [H. said that] he thought it fantastic what they doing under conditions— equality business and inefficient men. Got to have quota of blacks just because they are black—I don't buy that. [I said] we don't say that. [H. said] now we not children, orders are not spelled out like that. [I said there has been] no attempt have jobs filled on quota basis. Have moved blacks in on all ratings. Ones in this [specific] case that AOL all non-rated people. [H. said that] it was refusal [to] obey order. I said that thing disturbing me is whole Navy gets indicted. Only outfit fighting war to major extent—Army and Marines out. [H. said that] whole Navy not broken down. [It] is breakdown of discipline in USN. Statement [further] says they don't know what facts are and that is what we going to find out. I'll tell you honestly, when I talked to you other day you gave me no indication of action you going to take. [I said] I was reporting to the Chairman on matters then in news. Speech something I thought necessary. [I] knew you [would] know that as soon as I gave it. [H. said that] he was trying to be Navy's friend and my friend. I am telling you that backlash [has been] horrible. [I] have gotten kickback from people all over. For obvious reasons, I can't identify half [of them]. [I asked if] Washington [state] had been particularly bad. [H. said] I will tell you one —Carl Vinson. [I] think [it is] pretty bad when Vinson says something. [I said that] only thing good about this was that friend was doing it. [H. said] he putting Hicks in charge—certainly can't charge bias against him. Others Pirnie and Daniel from South—I'm not going to discriminate against him. [I said] I hoped they would call [me]. [H. said that he] had no control of that and they were in charge—this other thing like cold water in face and reaction very, very bad. [I asked if] similar incidents [like this] in other services investigated. [H. said that] other Chiefs of Staff didn't eat out their Admirals. You chewed out your people on this side and didn't say anything about the other people. [I said that I] couldn't until reviewed cases. All we said to officers [is] get off your duffs and get [this] squared away. [H. said] that got them convicted in public. [I said] I saw nature of problem. [H. said] I am sure you do. They all get convicted without a trial. [I said] if you read speech they not all indicted—was for all those not with it to get with it. [H. said] we could have some discussion on equality too but I wouldn't do it in public. [H. inquired] why I wasn't on trip. [I told him that my] father had little stroke and flew out there and when this thing came up I thought better get back here.

There was no doubt in my mind about how to respond to this "investigation." Gratuitous, insulting and potentially damaging to the Navy though it was, it also was the kind of opportunity that no one in the executive branch ever could have given me to put the case for enlightened personnel policies in the armed services before the country. I judged that the Navy would be no worse off if I took the Hicks subcommittee on and lost than if I failed to take it on. In either case the clock would be turned back to before Z-57, Z-66 and all the others, back to Mickey Mouse and discriminating against blacks. But if I took the subcommittee on and won, the Navy during the next several years, at least, would be able to embark on its difficult missions with some assurance that the men and women who were being asked to perform them were a willing and united crew. I was certain to turn over to my successor a Navy in which all kinds of important business was unfinished: strategic analysis, ship construction, weapons development, relations with other parts of the government, and so forth, ad infinitum. But if it was within my power, I was determined to turn over to him a Navy that had learned to treat its men and women, enlisted and commissioned, in a manner that recognized that, regardless of the peculiar demands military life made upon them, they were the citizens of a free country in the last quarter of the twentieth century.

My decision to take the subcommittee on was put beyond dispute by what members of my staff told me after their first meetings with members of the subcommittee's staff. They told me that there was every indication that racial friction would be openly referred to as seldom as possible, and covertly referred to as often as possible under the rubric of "permissiveness," and that the Z-grams would be identified as the root of the permissiveness that was poisoning the Navy, because they had made it impossible for commanders to discipline their men. That, of course, was a direct, personal challenge to the Navy from which I could not, and certainly would not if I could, back down. Lord knows, the charge of "permissiveness" was familiar enough, and so was its source. People who didn't like beards and therefore thought nobody should lamented that Z-57 had deprived them of the "discretion" to discipline those who wore them. People who didn't like blacks and wanted to treat them worse than whites lamented that Z-66 had deprived them of the "discretion" to do so. Indeed every would-be Captain Bligh in the fleet was angry that the Z-grams collectively deprived him of the "discretion" to drive his men to mutiny. Let me hasten to add that "every would-be Captain Bligh in the fleet" was a very small number of people indeed. In the spring of 1971 I had had a poll of opinions about the Z-grams taken in the fleet. Eighty-six percent of enlisted men and 80 percent of officers had approved. (Some of the rest either thought Z-grams had made no difference or had no opinion.) Even in the most disapproving rates and ranks, chief petty officer, warrant officer, and commander/captain, the approval ran 77 percent; among ensigns and junior lieutenants it was 93 percent. With support for my personnel policies that solid at all levels of the Navy, I felt no trepidation about challenging the subcommittee's assumptions, even though the few opponents had access to many important ears.

However I was determined to be prepared for whatever Hicks and Company came up with and I set my staff to work gathering material for the hearings, which were to start in just one week, on Monday 20 November. I am astonished when I look today at the material they assembled in that week—or rather five days, since I needed it by Friday to study over the weekend. There are complete reports on the *Kitty Hawk, Hassayampa,* and *Constellation* incidents. There are all the Z-grams, of course, 117 of them up to that time. There are all the directives, suggestions, and reports about race relations and minority affairs programs that emanated from or came into my office, which stack up to three-quarters of an inch of paper. There is a *CNO Question and Answer Book,* one inch thick, that provides appropriate brief answers to possible questions about the three incidents, and about the entire Navy race and minority program. Finally, there is a large loose-leaf notebook, the *CNO Backup Book,* in three sections. The first section consists of six sets of data cards for me to read from: comparisons of Navy personnel programs with those of the Army and Air Force; quotations from previously issued policy statements about personnel administration; the Z-gram survey I have just cited; regulations and legal opinions on gatherings and assemblies in the armed services; recent instances of sabotage aboard Navy ships; and data about fleet performance—length of deployments, numbers of sorties, manpower levels and so forth. The second section consists of the documents submitted to the subcommittee. The third section consists of classified documents whose information was available to the subcommittee though the papers themselves were not. I cannot resist listing the contents of the second section because, better than any narrative, it tells how one prepares for a Congressional hearing —particularly if he has blood in his eye as I had then.

A. Department of Defense Human Goals Program
B. Full text of unclassified Z-grams with general subject of the three classified Z-grams
C. Remarks by Secretary of the Navy John W. Warner to Navy flag and Marine Corps general officers—10 November 1972 (releases)
    Remarks by Secretary of the Navy John W. Warner to Navy flag and Marine Corps general officers—10 November 1972 (as delivered)
D. Remarks by Admiral E. R. Zumwalt, Jr., CNO, to Washington area flag officers, Nov 10, 1972
E. USS *Kitty Hawk* data
    1. Racial breakdown
    2. Mental group/white-black
    3. Promotion E-2 through E-5
    4. Ship total NJP [non-judicial punishment]/white-black
    5. Ship total courts-martial/white-black
F. USS *Hassayampa* data
    [same five categories]
G. USS *Constellation* data
    [same five categories]

H. Navy equal opportunity directives: A1Nav 51–70, Subj: race relations and equal opportunity, Z-gram 66, Subj: equal opportunity in the Navy, SecNavInst 5360.6A, Subj: Dept. of Navy manual on equal opportunity and treatment of military personnel

I. Navy goals and objectives on race relations and minority affairs programs

J. Pertinent extract from speech of CNO to District of Columbia Council of Navy League, 13 October 1972

K. Statement on letters to Pers-P from crews of three ships

L. Data on recruit discharges by mental group and reason

M. List of charged individuals on three ships time-wise eligible for promotion but not promoted

N. Recent Navy studies on comparison of trouble makers and mental groupings

O. Communications released by Constellation

P. DoD directive 1325.6 of 12 September 1969, Subj: Guidelines for handling dissident and protest activities among members of the armed forces; OpNav instruction 1620.1 of 31 October 1969 promulgating the DoD directive

Q. Breakdown of recruits by mental groups, last few months

R. WSR 72–5, December 1971, Subj: Enlisted men's and officers' opinions of recent policy changes implemented through Z-grams

S. The Manpower Research Note, April 1971, titled, "Promotion Opportunities of First-Term Enlisted Personnel by Race, Aptitude, Education Level, and Military Occupation."

T. The Manpower Research Note, April 1971, titled, "Analysis of Disciplinary Actions Affecting First-Term Negro and Caucasian Servicemen."

U. The Manpower Research Note 72–7, February 1972, titled, "Factors Relating to Unsuitability Discharge and Desertion Status among Army Enlisted Accessions."

It was a weekend's light reading.

While the staff was getting ready to lay all this on me, I was talking to people around town. For one thing I called the members I could reach of what we call "The Board of Directors," the ex-CNOs (with the exception of George Anderson, I scarcely need to say). David McDonald provided helpful advice. The attitude of the others was summed up by Arleigh Burke in a funny remark: "Every once in a while I look at the scars on my knuckles which were caused by a coxswain who didn't want to take orders—but I realize it's a little tougher nowadays." The disclaimer at the end made it clear that he really didn't expect me to rush out to San Diego and punch 120 eighteen-year-olds in the jaw. I talked that week with various people on the Hill, Congressmen and members of their staffs. The Chairman of the Senate Armed Forces Committee, John Stennis of Mississippi, while disclaiming any intention to go into the matter with his committee, offered this helpful comment: "After all, you got to realize they came down from the trees a long time after we did." I got rather a heartening call of support from the President of the Navy League. Many senior admirals spoke out publicly in support of what I was seeking to accomplish at a time when concern for their own future in the aftermath of any shift in the top command might have dictated a more prudent course. Among these were Mickey Weisner, Vice CNO; Admiral Ralph Cousins, CinCLant; Admiral Noel Gayler, CinCPac; Vice Admirals Julien Le Bougeois, David Bagley, and Bill Mack. I spent a good deal of time discussing strategy and tactics with Dan Henkin and Fred Buzhardt, who were still acting as counselors to the Navy at Mel Laird's bidding, though I did not take one piece of advice they gave me: not to appear personally at the hearings. It was Laird's wish that I stay away on the understandable ground that appearing was a no-win proposition in view of the fact the subcommittee had been appointed for the specific purpose of cutting me up. On the other side of the fence, evidently Floyd Hicks did not want me to appear either, presumably calculating that my absence would lighten his load. It is odd to recall how hard I had to work to get myself invited to what was designed to be my funeral. The issue was in doubt until Friday the 17th when Vice Admiral Means Johnston, the Navy's former liaison with the Hill and by then Inspector General, leaned on Eddie Hebert and got him to agree to tell Hicks to let me appear. I must add to all the other reasons Mel Laird gave me during this period to be grateful to him, his acceptance of my desire to testify, though it was against his wishes.

One other thing I did that week was issue, on Tuesday the 14th, Z-117, the first Z-gram since August, when Z-116 opened up new opportunities in the Navy for women, the last one until June 1973, when Z-118 set a maximum of five years on all sea tours. A few excerpts will give the gist of Z-117, whose title was "Discipline, etc.," and a modicum of reflection will suggest my reasons for issuing it in the wake of the speech to the flag officers. Its primary audience was new sailors.

. . . What is required of you is self-discipline, especially in these times of extended deployments and reduced manpower. It is your duty to your shipmates and those who are responsible for your welfare in time of peace and especially in time of war to conduct yourselves in a manner that contributes to the overall good and welfare of your division, your ship, your station and, in the long run, country. You have taken an oath to do so and the Navy will expect nothing less nor will it accept anything less. . . .

I expect and will continue to insist upon the strictest possible adherence to our disciplinary standards in every respect. Those who do not accept these standards can expect to be promptly and fairly disciplined and held responsible for their actions in accordance with the UCMJ. . . .

. . . changes made during the past two years . . . are not intended nor in any way can they be construed to mean an acceptance of "short circuiting" the legitimate chain of command.

Let me conclude by addressing the matter of your personal responsibilities to the maintenance of good order and discipline, for in this matter there can be no compromise. I addressed myself to our Naval leadership on this subject on 10 November. Now let me tell you what I expect of you. . . . The Navy . . . requires complete and total obedience. It can be no other way. . . .

My opening statement to the Subcommittee on Disciplinary Problems in the U.S. Navy on Monday 20 November 1972 was a compressed version of the contents of this and previous chapters, so there is no need to quote from it here. Of the members of the subcommittee the only potential friend was the chairman, Floyd Hicks. Dan Daniel of Virginia was well known to the Navy, being the chairman of a special Subcommittee on Recruiting and Retention that had held hearings several months before. He was courteous, fond of showy phrases—"What I know now would not fill the thimble of a Black Forest elf," he remarked at one point, *a propos* of the three shipboard incidents—genuinely concerned about the welfare of the Navy's people, and just as genuinely convinced that bringing large numbers of blacks into the Navy would lead to disaster, a conviction he tried not to show in this situation but had shown clearly in his earlier hearings on recruiting and retention. Alexander Pirnie of New York, a lame duck who had not run for reelection, was a straight law-and-order man. He apparently had no interest in conditions of shipboard life or in the problems racial attitudes created or indeed in anything except whether punishments he considered sufficiently stiff were being meted out to offenders. His favorite phrase that day was "bands roaming around ships," which he declared himself against in a tone that indicated his belief that someone was for them. Hicks, who had been a judge in the state of Washington before coming to Congress, evidently was less set in his attitudes toward blacks than Daniel and less of a martinet than Pirnie. Indeed he was very much a neutral figure. Eddie Hébert later told me that he had given Hicks the chairmanship to find out whether he could handle a tough assignment. At the same time, Eddie had assigned Daniel to ride shotgun, as it were, on Hicks, and report back every evening how the chairman had done that day.

In other words, though Eddie Hébert was not present in the flesh, his spirit very much dominated the hearings, which would have been fine if the hearings had been about the Trident submarine or a pay raise for all hands, but was not quite the ticket for hearings about racial disorders. The brunt of the questioning that I and the colleagues who accompanied me were subjected to that day consisted of (a) an attempt to elicit details about the incidents themselves, which I could not supply without prejudice to the judicial process because those incidents were still under investigation and such men as had been charged with offenses were still before the disciplinary authorities, and (b) an attempt to get me to admit that I had been wrong to say what I had said to the flag officers, which I was not about to do. It was not a very productive day, but I was satisfied that we had blunted the subcommittee's most rampageous impulses.

Next day, Tuesday, the subcommittee was in San Diego listening to Captain Ward and other participants in the "Connie" affair. That day John Warner, Eddie Hébert, and I flew down to Milledgeville, Georgia, to have lunch with the eighty-nine-year-old Carl Vinson. Mel Laird, who had been a protégé of Vinson's when he had first entered the House and who continued to have filial feelings toward him, suggested I make the trip when I told him that Vinson had leaned on Hebert about the disturbances. My good friend Armistead Selden, the Deputy Assistant Secretary of Defense for International Security Affairs and an old friend of Vinson's from his own Congressional service, seconded the motion. The old man proved to be very much The Chairman still. He met us at the Milledgeville airport, shepherded John Warner into his car and Eddie Hébert and me into a second car driven by a local Navy recruiter he had pressed into service, and took us to his housekeeper's house for a meeting before lunch, since there was not time to go to his farm. One of the more entertaining aspects of the affair was that he treated Eddie, a man in his seventies, as a sort of junior aide.

We spent half an hour or so before lunch reminiscing about the days when he had been in Washington, with him doing almost all the reminiscing. I did get in one pertinent reminiscence of my own, though. In 1965, when Paul Nitze was Secretary of the Navy and I was his executive assistant, we drove Chairman Vinson to Annapolis for the Academy graduation, at which he delivered the commencement address. In the car he told us that whenever he wanted a hearing that cut somebody up, he would put Mendel Rivers on the subcommittee; when he was even madder than that, he would put Porter Hardy on it, too; and if he wanted to destroy somebody entirely, he would put Eddie Hébert on it along with Rivers and Hardy. He said that those were the three meanest members of his committee and he could count on them to deal effectively with any object of his wrath. After I had recounted this piece of history, I said that I hoped that was not the principle upon which the Hicks subcommittee had been constituted. Vinson grinned and winked at Hébert.

Just before lunch was served, Vinson contrived to get each of his three guests into a short private conversation. Eddie told me that the Chairman had told him to give the Navy a good scrubbing on this one, and also to make sure the Navy had an adequate budget. With me he made it clear that it was those black-power salutes on the dock that had first stirred him up. He then asked me a series of rapid-fire questions about the situation, to which I replied in like fashion. Our tête-a-tête lasted perhaps five minutes, and at the end of it I sensed that he was a lot friendlier than at the beginning. In any case, he changed the subject from the disturbances to the Soviet threat, about which he became quite animated, and asked me to send him reading material on it when I returned to Washington. After lunch, which was social, he had another brief private chat with each of us during which he instructed me to let him know if Hébert failed to take good care of the Navy's budget, and then escorted us back to our plane. I am quite sure that visit did something to relieve whatever pressure he had been exerting on Eddie Hébert.

Wednesday was interesting in quite a different way. I spent all day attending a seminar on race relations together with John Warner; General Cushman, the Marine Commandant; Admiral Kidd, the Chief of Naval Material; Vice Admiral David Bagley, the Chief of

Naval Personnel; and a few other officers. The one-track character of Representative Pirnie's mind had emerged in its full splendor at Monday's hearing when he heard about this seminar. "I wonder if there is going to be a seminar on obedience and conformance to good military order," he said. I did not consider it worth the breath to point out that seminars are useful only when they deal with subjects the participants know less than they should about, like dealing with racial prejudice. The seminar had been arranged a couple of weeks before, at the same time the appearance before the flag officers had been arranged. I considered it not only an appropriate time for the Navy's top people to inquire into their own racial attitudes, but that their doing so would be a model that people in less exalted positions would find it hard to ignore. The event itself was anything but symbolic. Under the leadership of June Caldwell, an impressive black psychologist who spared no one's feelings, we were at it until almost midnight, and I remember it as one of the most interesting days I spent during my watch.

Thursday was Thanksgiving. When I returned to the office Friday, after nearly four days away, things looked more promising than they had for several weeks. The day started auspiciously with a telephone call from Robert McNamara in which he told me that I was handling the racial problem I had inherited in "the most ethical and moral way," and that he was ready to give me any kind of help he could, including authorizing me to say that he had told me that he regretted not having done more about racial matters when he was running the Pentagon. There also were several friendly and supportive letters from Congressmen and influential people around the country on my desk that morning. Most of the press was taking my part. The day of the seminar Mel Laird had been in Kansas City, where he had had a press conference with Associated Press managing editors; in the course of it he had backed the Navy's racial programs completely. When I talked with Dan Murphy during the day, he told me that he had had lunch with Henry Kissinger and Al Haig a couple of days before and when he had told them how "screwy" the demand for dishonorable discharges had been, he had gotten the impression that they had been rather embarrassed about the whole thing. Evidently my job was secure until the next time I felt I had to speak out. In sum, my going public appeared to be accomplishing what I had hoped it would, which was to create so much overt support for twentieth-century racial policies in the Navy that the covert machinations of George Anderson and his coterie were frustrated.

That weekend the 27 November issue of *Time* was on my desk, with a long account of the Navy's current difficulties. Among other things, it said:

> Ever since Zumwalt took command of the Navy in 1970, the more conservative admirals have watched in horror as he set adrift one tradition after another. In their view, permissiveness and luxuries have no place at sea. They ridiculed his reforms as the "three B's—beer, beards, and broads." Armed with the ammunition provided by the race riots and sabotage, many admirals have shown their own lack of discipline by campaigning for Zumwalt's ouster.
>
> Some have made late-night phone calls to Pentagon correspondents. Administration officials and politicians have been cornered at cocktail parties. The message is the same: Zumwalt has gone too far. One of his critics is Admiral Isaac Kidd, 53, thought to be the most likely man to replace Zumwalt.

On top of the article was a handwritten note from Admiral Kidd that read:

> Dear Bud,
>
>   I've just read in Time where I'm one of your critics—it's news to me! When you and I *do* disagree, you'll be the first to know—and in private—*not* in public.
>   There will always be those wishing to stir things up.
>
>   Very respectfully,
>   Ike

In that same story John Mullikan, *Time*'s military reporter, quoted Warner as having said, "I'm not for a moment hesitant about rolling back some of those *advancements*" (my emphasis). Later John apologized to me for having said that. He told me his reason had been the one he had given *Time,* that he had been "under a great deal of pressure."

The fact that things appeared to be taking a turn for the better did not make my life any less strenuous, however. As I have said, I considered the tumult not as a warning to take a defensive posture, but as an opportunity to nail equal treatment for minorities and women so firmly into the Navy that anyone would have trouble removing it. At the beginning of the affair I had ordered my staff to prepare a comprehensive briefing on the relevance of the Human

Goals program to the Navy's mission as a whole. By the New Year it had been given to all hands in the Navy. I was on the telephone constantly, prodding type and unit commanders, with the permission of their commanders-in-chief—and I must report with pleasure and pride that every operational four-star admiral supported me whole-heartedly—to make sure that all commanding officers were implementing human goals programs. I stayed in touch with Congress. In December Senator Robert Byrd, in the course of a trip to West Virginia I took with him, concluded after hearing the facts that the shipboard incidents had not been quite the "mutinies" that some folk made them out to be.

Meanwhile the Hicks subcommittee, having finished with the *Constellation* people, had to suspend operations for ten days or so until the *Kitty Hawk* people were ready. They finally finished in San Diego on 12 December, and returned to Washington for two final days of hearings on the 15th and the 18th. I made my second appearance on the former day. It was one of those sessions devoted to seemingly purposeless bickering in which, nevertheless, there was a good deal of purpose.

The subcommittee's purpose was to euchre me into appearing to go along with what had been its—or Eddie Hébert's—unstated premise from the beginning: that the problems of racism in the Navy were irrelevant to the disturbances under investigation and, in any case, of negligible importance in comparison with the problem of "permissiveness." Since Eddie had admitted during our telephone discussion with me that his real beef was with the Navy's integration program, the subcommittee's efforts along that line were pretty transparent.

My purpose was to put into the record as emphatically as I could my belief that there was racism in the Navy, that it was damaging and relevant to the inquiry, and that despite the three incidents there was very little "breakdown of discipline" in the hard-fighting Navy. The territory on which this unacknowledged battle was fought was questions about why I had "dressed down" the flag officers; whether shipboard Human Relations Councils were "management tools" or "bypassed the chain of command;" who had or had not ordered Captain Ward to do what when; whether $25 fines were sufficient penalties for people who declined to return aboard ship; whether black-power salutes and "dapping" should be permitted aboard ship, and finally what I proposed to do about a dissenting *Constellation* sailor who appeared before the subcommittee in Navy trousers, a black silk shirt, and purple suede boots. (I refrained from suggesting to the member who asked that question that he might do well to spend a day in a race relations seminar.) I think the record of that hearing will show anyone sufficiently stoical to endure the tedium of reading it that I accomplished my purpose more effectively than Messrs. Hicks *et al.* accomplished theirs.

The subcommittee issued its report the first week of January. It contained seventeen findings, eleven opinions and sixteen recommendations. Most of them were trivial or innocuous, a few were helpful, a few were commendatory, and a few said precisely those things that I thought were the most wrongheaded things that possibly could be said:

• The subcommittee finds that permissiveness, as defined on page 17679 of this report, exists in the Navy today.

[On Page 17679:] As used in this report, permissiveness means an attitude by seniors down the chain of command which *tolerates* the use of individual discretion by juniors in areas in the services which have been strictly controlled; it means a tolerance of failure; a failure to enforce existing orders and regulations which have validity; it means a failure to require that existing standards be met, and a *sufferance* of the questioning of valid orders. Unfortunately, close on the heels of permissiveness, we often find appeasement when trouble arises.

• The members of the subcommittee did not find and are unaware of any instances of institutional discrimination on the part of the Navy toward any group of persons, majority or minority. [This "finding" could have been reached only by ignoring the mass of evidence to the contrary the Navy presented.]

• Nonmilitary gestures such as "passing the power" or "dapping" are disruptive, serve to enhance racial polarization, and should be discouraged. [Presumably rebel yells, on the other hand, simply prove that boys will be boys.]

• Because of the wording of the text [of my speech to the flag officers] it was perceived by many to be a public admonishment by the CNO of his staff for the failure to solve the racial problems within the Navy. . . . Concern over racial problems seemed paramount to the question of good order and discipline even though there had been incidents on the two ships which might be characterized as "mutinies." The subcommittee regrets that the tradition of not criticizing seniors in front of their subordinates was ignored in this case.

- The subcommittee expressed its strong objection to the procedures utilized by higher authority to negotiate with Constellation's dissidents and, eventually, to appease them by acquiescing to their demands and by meting out minor nonjudicial punishment for what was a major affront to good order and discipline.

- Both at the recruiting and recruit training level there must be a greater effort to screen out agitators, troublemakers, and those who otherwise fail to meet acceptable levels of performance. ["Agitator" and "troublemaker" are buzz words, of course.]

Everything I have just quoted supported in one way or another what Eddie Hébert evidently believed before he appointed the subcommittee. Indeed, transforming his beliefs from political rhetoric into the official Findings, Opinions, and Recommendations of an investigative subcommittee had been the object of the exercise—as that old Georgia fox, Carl Vinson, had taught Eddie to do.

The "law-and-order"—in plain words, anti-black—flavor that those key passages gave the report outraged me and my colleagues, and we labored over producing an almost sentence-by-sentence refutation. It seemed an important task at the time, but hindsight reveals it to have been unnecessary. The Hicks report received little attention. In the bureaucratic acronym, it was OBE—overtaken by events. Within the Navy the report had next to no impact for a variety of reasons. Emmett Tidd had almost entirely changed the recruiting picture. There no longer was an inordinate number of non-school-eligibles entering the Navy, and the hard cases that had come in the year before either had become accustomed to their new circumstances or were on their way back out. A variety of strong actions by the Navy's top leadership—among which I must insist on including my speech to the flag officers—evidently had reassured the Navy's black men and women that we recognized the Navy was giving them problems and we were trying to solve them. Most important, the great majority of Navy men and women of all colors and ranks, including the commanding officers and the senior petty officers whose "diluted" authority was the subject of much of the report's solicitude, had the good feeling and the good sense to recognize that the personnel changes we had made had benefitted all hands and were not a fit object for politicians to tinker with.

Outside the Navy other factors were at work. Most of the press had been with me from the beginning and, in the absence of further disturbances in the fleet, was not much titillated by the report. And

in the Congress and throughout the land a new subject, name of Watergate, was beginning to be a principal preoccupation. January 1973 was the month of the first Watergate trial. I had had a nasty month or two, but the giant torpedo that I had feared would blow my policies clear out of the water turned out to be a damp little squib.

CHAPTER 11

Z-NAVOPS 01 Through 121
Are Hereby Cancelled

It was past the middle of my watch before I was able to make a public proclamation about "Equal Rights and Opportunities for Women in the Navy." The Z-gram that bore that heading was 116 of 121 and did not go to the fleet until 7 August 1972. The main thing that made a fair and coherent program for Navy women hard to put together was that the law forbade women to serve on an equal basis with men. By Act of Congress women could not serve on fighting ships or fighting planes. That not only severely limited the number of billets for which they were eligible but even created some small risk that a program that gave women all the opportunities the law did allow would close shore billets to men who had been at sea for years and deserved rotation to shore duty. Women also were barred by law from attending the Service Academies. When Congress was considering repealing that law in the spring of 1974 I received instructions that since I supported a change in the law I should not be the Navy's spokesman at the Armed Forces Committee hearings on the subject. The provision was so generally popular among my civilian superiors and fellow admirals that I had only to turn to the newly installed number two Vice CNO Admiral Worth Bagley, to find someone who was able to testify against women at Annapolis with a clear conscience. However, the year after I retired Congress did repeal the Service Academy sex bar and there will be women in the Naval Academy's Class of 1980, Worth's clear conscience notwithstanding.

In any case the injustices suffered by the 9000 or so women in a

Navy of half a million men and women, though real enough and damaging enough to the Navy in the long run, could not be the highest immediate priority when the reenlistment rate for first-termers in the fleet was hovering at a disastrous 10 percent and the quality of the men entering the fleet was going down. Consequently it was not until the middle of 1971 that we convened a pair of Wave retention study groups as the first step toward devising a comprehensive program for making better use of women in the Navy, and for treating them better. I described what I thought were the most important findings of those groups in a couple of paragraphs in the December 1971 Flag Officers News Letter, a publication that went out monthly over my signature.

> We have been sadly enlightened—mainly through the briefing of our recent Wave Retention Study Groups—as to how frequently our Navy women are still being used as receptionists, coffee runners, and such, despite their technical training and competence. This appears to be especially true in the case of our enlisted women, although it is by no means confined to them.
>
> Assignment policies at BuPers have made great strides in recent years in this area, and our officer and enlisted women are being ordered—in name at least—to a greater variety of technically and professionally challenging billets at a greater variety of commands. But much needs to be done in the way of a change in basic attitudes at the local command level. Nothing is so demoralizing and disheartening to the young RM2 Wave who graduates at the top of her "B" school class and is then assigned at her new command to such stimulating duties as running the ditto machine and keeping the coffee mess going. There may be any number of attitudes at work here—e.g., the professional jealousy of the male supervisor who cannot admit that the woman can do the job as professionally as her male counterpart, or the complete bewilderment of the division officer who has never had a professional woman working for him before and doesn't quite know what to do with her! In the former the misuse is deliberate, in the latter it's thoughtless—but in both it adds up to a real waste of talent.

Meanwhile the program for women was delayed further by a bureaucratic impasse that developed between the Navy's senior woman, Captain Robin Quigley, Director of the Waves, and Secretary of Defense Laird. Robin took the position, which doubtless was theologically correct, that if women were going to be treated by the Navy as equals, there should be no "pope" over them, i.e., Director

of the Waves. In short she insisted that her own job be abolished. Mel took the position, which doubtless was as astute politically as his positions usually were, that making Navy women disappear as a distinct entity was the wrong way to influence the Congress, enough of whose members already were evoking such specters as "unisex showers." This was one instance in which there were certain inhibitions against the Secretary pulling his rank. It would have been as embarrassing to promulgate a program for women in the Navy that the senior woman in the Navy opposed as it would have been unthinkable to promulgate a Defense Department policy that the Secretary of Defense opposed. I should add that on the whole I sided with Robin Quigley. It took several months to work out a compromise. Its main elements were that the position of Director of the Waves would be abolished, but that many of the Director's most important functions would be transferred to Captain Frances McKee, a most capable senior woman officer recently appointed to the position of Deputy Pers-P. Since Robin herself insisted on vacating the position of Director, she would be assigned a non-papal job as Commanding Officer, Naval Schools Command, San Diego. Furthermore, one of the tasks of the Director of Waves, monitoring the assignments of Navy women to their jobs, would shift to the regular detailing machinery in BuPers, to which machinery a certain number of women would be assigned. Once these arrangements were made, Z-116 could go out.

Z-116 visualized, perhaps wrongly it now appears, the imminent passage of the Equal Rights Amendment, which would make most restrictions on female service in the armed forces of doubtful constitutionality. Its purpose, then, in addition to the usual one of articulating an official position on an important and controversial matter of policy, was to initiate a variety of administrative actions that would enable the Navy to make full use of women promptly when ERA or statutes liberalizing the terms of female service became law. The portion of Z-116 that details those initiatives is worth quoting for the light it throws on how little advantage the Navy had taken so far of the female talent available to it.

A. In addition to the enlisted ratings that have recently been opened, authorize limited entry of enlisted women into all ratings.

B. The ultimate goal, assignment of women to ships at sea, will be timed to coincide with full implementation of pending legislation. As an immediate step, a limited number of officer and enlisted women are being

assigned to the ship's company of USS *Sanctuary* as a pilot program. This program will provide valuable planning information regarding the prospective increased utilization of women at sea.

C. Pending formal changes to Navy regulations, suspend restrictions regarding women succeeding to command ashore and assign them accordingly.

D. Accept applications from women officers for the Chaplain and Civil Engineer Corps, thereby opening all staff corps to women.

E. Expand assignment of technically qualified unrestricted line women to restricted line billets. . . .

F. Offer various paths to progression to flag rank within the technical, managerial spectrum in essentially the same manner as we are contemplating for male officers.

G. Assign the detailing of unrestricted women officers to their cognizant grade detailers. [That was the big one Robin Quigley won.]

H. Increase opportunity for women's professional growth by:

    1. eliminating the pattern of assigning women exclusively to certain billets, and

    2. assigning qualified women to the full spectrum of challenging billets, including those of briefers, aides, detailers, placement/rating control officers, attaches, service college faculty members, executive assistants, special assistants to CNO, military assistance advisory groups/missions, senior enlisted advisors, etc.

I. Equalize selection criteria for naval training by:

    1. opening midshipman programs to women at all Naval ROTC campuses effective in FY '74, and

    2. considering women for selection to joint colleges (National War College/Industrial College of the Armed Forces).

Of these directives the only one that attracted much public notice was sending women to sea in the hospital ship *Sanctuary*. A certain number of Navy wives interpreted this as a threat to their marriages, and were joined in their outrage by self-appointed guardians of the public morality in the Congress, the retired military community, and other places. Indeed a principal frustration connected with getting a program for female equality in the Navy under way was that it was impossible to discuss the matter rationally with some people. In addition to the folk who feared unisex showers and floating orgies, there were the folk, many of them high military or civilian officials, from whom it was maddeningly difficult to elicit more than locker-

room jocularities on the subject. Richard Nixon was one of those. On one occasion, as a meeting he had been having with the Joint Chiefs of Staff was breaking up, the President said to me with a knowing look, "I guess I can put up with this race thing, but don't push so hard for women." Since, at most, he was barely able to "put up with this race thing," his opinion of women needs no further elaboration.

However, we did make some progress. We were able to open up to women a far wider range of jobs and billets than they had been eligible for in the past. A woman finally made admiral during my watch. The first woman chaplain in any service was commissioned during my watch. Half a dozen young women earned the gold wings of naval aviators during my watch. I am sure that the trend toward greater opportunities for women in the Navy is irreversible, if only for the reason that the Navy will have difficulty in securing the people it needs in an era of all-volunteer armed forces if it does not avail itself of the talents and skills of women. However, the inertia is great and the pace is slow. For many Navy traditionalists, it is even harder to give up the notion that their beloved service should be all male than to give up the notion that it should be all white.

By the end of 1972 most of the novelty, excitement, and controversy associated with the new Programs for People were in the past. Z-116 was the last major change in personnel policy I initiated and the Hicks Subcommittee's so-called investigation was the last major effort by opponents of the Programs for People to slow them down or stop them. Moreover, the Vietnam cease-fire in January 1973 took a great deal of pressure off the men of the fleet and created a more favorable environment for personnel programs in many areas, from race relations to ship/shore rotation. During my last year and a half on duty the chief task in the personnel field was the laborious one of making sure that the new programs were becoming an everyday part of Navy life. Early in November 1972 Secretary Laird called upon each of the Service Secretaries, among other officials, for a year-end "Taking Stock" memorandum that would describe the principal problems each Service faced and the most promising solutions to them. In connection with this effort my staff and I drafted a paper called "Taking Stock of Naval Personnel Management" that I was anxious for Secretary Warner to include in his response to Secretary Laird's request. Two of the early, general paragraphs in that paper give an accurate idea of where we thought we were as 1973 began. Since the form in which the paper was drafted was as a

memorandum from the Secretary of the Navy to the Secretary of Defense, all first-person singular pronouns in it refer to John Warner, though the paper evidently does not reflect Warner's views since he never allowed it to go forward.

> Foremost among our accomplishments, I [sic] believe, is the recognition that the sociological changes taking place in our society impact on the military and that the actions we have taken to adapt to these changes are in consonance with our personnel needs. To state a few: We have taken significant steps to abolish those traditional regulations and constraints on service life which have little or no value to the attainment of readiness and discipline; we have embarked on aggressive visible programs to abolish drug and alcohol addiction with concurrent emphasis on rehabilitation as a viable alternative to social degradation and condemnation; we have frankly and candidly espoused the abolition of all stigmas of racial bias; in short we have placed primary emphasis on the needs and aspirations of our human resources. While we have suffered some apparent setbacks in the achievement of goals in the area of race relationships, I am confident that the Navy will continue to make strides in these areas, maintaining discipline in the environment of the 1970s while stressing positive leadership in eliminating the perceptions of some that equal opportunity is not achievable.

> A prominent factor in attaining a balanced all-volunteer force is the need for maintaining a stable career force through adequate retention in all skill areas. There has been a significant improvement in first-term reenlistments from 10 percent in FY '70 to 24 percent in FY '72 and in career reenlistments from 78 percent in 1969 to 91 percent in FY '72. Although this signifies progress overall, there are still serious retention problems in many of the distinctively sea-oriented ratings. Efforts to improve retention in these skills through application of reenlistment bonuses and proficiency pay have not been successful in overcoming the major deterrent to improved retention—unfavorable sea/shore rotation and the lack of reasonable family life. Reenlistment bonuses will continue to be a necessary incentive but it is imperative that we continue to receive your support for sufficient, meaningful shore billets to provide an equitable sea/shore rotation for all deprived ratings. Complementing this requirement, and as compensation for the arduous nature of duty at sea, is the need for sea pay. I appreciate your support for our increased sea pay program. I consider it and the sea/shore rotation issue to be prime objectives for personnel management in the forthcoming year.

I doubt that those two paragraphs were what deterred John Warner from sending this paper on to the Secretary of Defense, who by then

was Elliot Richardson, Mel Laird having resigned at the start of President Nixon's second term. Rather it was a number of technical recommendations about pay and promotion that sought to alter established Defense Department and Congressional policy plus, I suppose, a desire to find out more about the views and character of the new Secretary of Defense before presenting him with controversial recommendations. Incidentally, until now I have not mentioned the issue of sea pay—extra pay for service at sea—because we never could get action on it, but it was something I tried for hard throughout my watch. It seems to me that sailors are as deserving of sea pay as fliers are of flight pay, but the Congress does not agree.

I was sorry to see Mel Laird go. The Programs for People owed much to his unswerving support for them, particularly after John Chafee, an enthusiastic supporter of those programs—and indeed the initiator of many of them—was replaced as Secretary of the Navy by John Warner in May 1972. The last two paragraphs of the farewell letter I wrote Mel were from the heart.

> Because of your loyalty up and down the chain of command and your evident concern for people, today's Navy man and woman are better trained, better housed, better paid, and more motivated than any of their predecessors.
>
> You have been a fair and inspiring boss and a loyal and faithful friend, both to me and to the Navy. I believe the legacy of achievement which you will pass on to your successors is the stuff of which greatness is made.

A few months later I lost another friend and colleague without whose help the Programs for People would have floundered, Bill Norman. The endorsement I attached to his request to the Secretary of the Navy for permission to resign his commission as of 30 June 1973 tells what I thought and think of Bill.

> 1. Forwarded, recommending approval.
>
> 2. In recommending acceptance of the resignation of this splendid officer, I should like the record to show that I do so not because I wish to but because honor will allow no other course. More than two years ago, after establishing a record of unmistakably distinguished service in a variety of challenging assignments ashore and at sea, Lieutenant Commander Norman was moved by various circumstances to resign from the Regular Navy. Before that resignation was fully processed, I had the opportunity to become acquainted with this man, to learn of his reason for resigning his commission and to ascertain his continued potential as

a career officer in the Naval Service. At my request, he agreed to defer his resignation for one year—then, later, for another year—to help the Navy.

3. No man has ever more selflessly, more completely or more productively given of himself than has Lieutenant Commander Norman during the past two years. His contributions to the Navy are beyond measure but have, unquestionably, spared the Naval Service from racially generated difficulties of unprecedented magnitude and, in fact, have helped transform the forces of division into mortar with which to build. He has, almost single-handedly, laid the foundation upon which a new Navy family that recognizes no artificial barriers of race, color, sex, or religion today is being built.

4. If, at some appropriate time, Lieutenant Commander Norman seeks to reenter the active Naval Service, I would strongly endorse his readmission and subsequent promotion, on an accelerated basis, to Flag rank.

The story of the people programs would not be complete without mentioning a few highlights that did not fit conveniently into the preceding chapters of this section. One was the work in the field of racial equality of Rear Admiral Draper Kauffman, the Commandant of the Ninth Naval District, which covers the entire center of the country and has its headquarters at the Great Lakes Naval Training Station near Chicago. Draper arrived at Great Lakes from the command of the U.S. Naval Forces in the Philippines at about the same time I arrived in Washington from Vietnam. At the time the command of a naval district was traditionally a flag officer's last tour before retirement and so some officers who found themselves in that billet sat back and made themselves as comfortable as they could. Draper did not. Soon after assuming his command he belatedly discovered, much as I did, how serious and complex the Navy's racial problem was. He promptly set about establishing as close relations as he could with both the minority officers and enlisted men under his command and minority groups in and around Chicago. In the course of this endeavor he learned that as far as the Navy was concerned, the biggest local racial grievance was the virtual unavailability of decent housing in the Chicago area for minority personnel and their families. It was a large-scale problem because Great Lakes NTS is the biggest naval training facility in the country. Draper tackled the problem head-on. He declared that any housing that would not accept minority Navy people was thenceforth off limits to white Navy people. As you may imagine, the decree was not easy to enforce. It aroused considerable indignation both within the Navy and in the civilian community, and in addition it worked some undoubted hardships on comfortably settled Navy families. However Draper stuck with it and by doing so—and making many other less spectacular efforts in the minority-relations field—he won the respect and trust of blacks both inside and outside the Navy, and of course of the many whites who felt as he did also. Perhaps because of its proximity to a city where racial animosities are acute, Great Lakes had been the scene of many racial flareups in the past and was always potentially explosive. Draper Kauffman reduced the explosiveness of Great Lakes considerably. As a rule recognition and rewards in the military are bestowed on achievements more martial than that, but it is not a rule that I consider unbreakable and I nominated Draper for a third star in recognition of his superior performance in the Ninth District. However, he was approaching retirement age and it is almost hard and fast DOD policy not to promote people with little time left to serve. The best I could do for Draper when he retired was present him with a copy of the nomination.

On 1 August 1972, less than a week before the promulgation of the Z-gram on women, Z-115, "Alcholism and Alcohol Abuse among Naval Personnel," went out to the fleet. It heralded a program that has become widely admired in its field. Alcoholism always has been a substantial problem in the Navy, a much more substantial one than drug abuse, especially among career personnel. Research has established that the typical Navy alcoholic, enlisted or commissioned, is a man with ten years of service, a first-class petty officer if enlisted, a lieutenant commander if commissioned. However it was a problem to which I had given no more than passing thought until we had a drug program under way. The drug program began officially, via Z-94, in the summer of 1971, prompted by the extreme concern of the naval commander in Vietnam, Vice Admiral Robert Salzer, over the sudden appearance there toward the end of 1970 of large quantities of high quality, low cost heroin. Modeled on existing Army and Air Force programs, the Navy program's basic feature was amnesty for drug addicts or abusers who voluntarily turned themselves in for rehabilitation. It has been approximately as successful as most drug programs, military or civilian, which is not very. Anyhow Chick Rauch, who was running the drug program, mentioned to me that it was anomalous to pay so much attention to drugs and none to alcohol, which was doing much more damage. That made sense to me and I asked Chick to explore the situation.

In the course of his inquiries Chick became acquainted with Captain James Baxter, a line officer who himself had been a practicing alcoholic while he held two successive important commands, had cured himself with the help of Alcoholics Anonymous and was eager to work on a program that might help Navy people in straits similar to those he had extricated himself from. Captain Baxter, for whom Chick was able to find a place on his staff, knew of a small but evidently effective Navy alcohol program that the Bureau of Medicine was sponsoring at the Long Beach Naval Station. This program was the creation of two men, Captain Joseph Zuska, a Navy doctor in whose family there had been a major tragedy caused by alcohol and who thereafter had spent almost all his time working with alcoholics, and retired Commander Dick Jewell, a recovered alcoholic. In an organization with as many crannies as the Navy, creative and potentially very important work can proceed without many people knowing about it. Once the men with the methodology, Joseph Zuska and Dick Jewell, joined up with the man with the combination to the safe, Chick Rauch, the program took off. At this writing there are five major naval alcoholic rehabilitation centers, each with about seventy-five beds, in various parts of the country. They are prepared to treat men or women, officers or enlisted personnel, and people from the Marines and the Coast Guard as well. The program is designed to restore a patient to active duty in six weeks, eight at the most. I suppose you can call its methodology, Joe Zuska's and Dick Jewell's methodology, eclectic since it calls upon the services, as the occasion requires, of psychiatrists, clinical psychologists, social workers, and chaplains; it uses individual counseling and group sessions conducted by recovered alcoholics, and it frequently asks AA or other community organizations for help.

The five centers are the heart of the program, but there is a good deal more to it than that. In fourteen naval hospitals there are fifteen-bed units to care for people who are in less serious shape than those who are sent to the centers or, more likely, who find themselves in the hospital as the result of alcohol abuse—with a broken leg, say, or a bloated liver. For even less serious cases there are on some seventy bases in the U.S. and overseas, alcohol rehabilitation "dry-docks," where people can confine themselves for full-time counseling for two weeks or so and then half-day counseling sessions for another couple of months while reporting for duty during the remainder of the day. Finally on several carriers and other large ships there are regularly organized chapters of AA. Altogether perhaps 5000 men and women a year go through one or another part of this system. Of them, 98 percent return to active duty when the treatment is over. More remarkably, 70 percent of them are performing those duties as well or better than their non-alcoholic peers two years after the treatment is over; the Navy keeps track of every person whom it treats for a drinking problem, so that figure is no sample. I had almost nothing to do with this program beyond signing my name to the Z-gram that announced it. Chick Rauch, Captains Baxter and Zuska, and Commander Jewell, the last three of whom are now retired, designed it and organized it. The most I can take credit for is cooperating with Secretary Chafee in creating a climate that encouraged Programs for all kinds of People.

Finally I would like to quote a passage from a staff paper that briefly reviewed the effort to retain enlisted personnel during my four years on watch. Following a statistical table that showed that first-term reenlistments had risen from a low of 10 percent during FY '70, just before I assumed office, to 32.9 percent during FY '74, the paper said:

The most significant event in the retention area is the payoff in the end FY statistics. This is one of those areas where there are no spectacular initiatives, but rather four years of hard work aimed pretty much at making what was there work. Retention cannot be separated from the incentives in the Human Goals area, and the overall human resource management thrust of the Z-grams. Specifically, there were a plethora of retention aid programs which were not doing the job because of a general lack of focus/support in the chain of command. Thus the thrust of the retention effort was to reinforce/revamp policy to:

• Make it clear that retention is a command, not a BuPers responsibility.

• Stimulate command initiative and personal involvement in retention. This was determined to be the major factor affecting successful retention efforts.

• Increase effectiveness of internal communications to overcome lack of personnel and command awareness of programs, opportunities, and benefits available.

• Review policy/programs which could provide relief for first termers in critically manned ratings.

• Derive a means of determining retention effectiveness.

• Coordinate retention efforts with the Human Goals Plan. The two could not be divorced because leadership, management, and command climate were proven directly to affect retention.

That last sentence describes in terms as understated, not to say uneloquent, as I can imagine what the retention study groups, the Z-grams, and everything that flowed from them were all about.

On 29 June 1974, two days before my term as CNO expired, I sent out a general message that read as follows:

1. Throughout the past four years, Z-NAVOPS have been incorporated into the Navy directives system whenever feasible. Of the 121 issued to date, 87 have been, or are in the process of being, incorporated into the directives system and two were previously cancelled. The remaining 32 were either informative in nature, announced a one-time program, or were statements of policy that have now been included throughout our personnel programs. The following is a listing indicating those Z-NAVOPS which have been incorporated into the Navy directives system. . . .

2. In view of paragraph 1 above, Z-NAVOPS 01 through 121 are hereby cancelled for record purposes.

We had made the changes stick.

Adm. Zumwalt with his wife Mouza and Sec. of Defense Melvin R. Laird at the change of command ceremony, 1 July 1970.

PLEBE SUMMER DRILL (HA!
PLATOON

Zumwalt (far left) as plebe at Annapolis.

Lieut. Zumwalt with Rear Adm. Miles in Shanghai, 1945. Adm. Miles had fought behind Japanese lines during the war in China.

The Joint Chiefs of Staff in Sept. 1973. Left to right: Gen. George S. Brown, USAF; Adm. Elmo R. Zumwalt, Jr.; Adm. Thomas H. Moorer, Chairman; Gen. Creighton W. Abrams, USA; Gen. Robert E. Cushman, Jr., USMC. (credit: U.S. Army Photograph)

With Adm. Hyman G. Rickover in Zumwalt's office.

A task force of heavily armed U.S. Navy river assault boats moving down a Mekong Delta canal in 1967.

Lieut. Comdr. John McCain III, who acted as the representative of returning POWs in May 1973, talking with his father, retired Adm. John S. McCain.

Artist's conception of a new class of patrol frigate.

Artist's conception of a new type of surface effect ship, combining helicopter support with amphibious assault capability.

Artist's conception of a high-speed hydrofoil patrol ship.

PHM-I, the Pegasus, prototype about to be launched at Renton, Washington, in Nov. 1974.

Artist's conception of a sea control ship.

The nuclear-powered attack aircraft carrier USS *Enterprise* underway in the Gulf of Tonkin in Oct. 1971.

President Richard M. Nixon at ceremony to dedicate the Stennis Technical Training Center at Naval Air Station Meridian, Miss., April 1973. Sen. John C. Stennis is seated at right, Zumwalt behind.

An F-14A Tomcat Fighter launched from the *Enterprise*.

Navy wives greet Zumwalt on arrival in Hawaii, Dec. 1970.

The first women naval aviators, at Naval Air Station Corpus Christi, Texas, in May 1974.

LEFT: Rear Admiral Samuel L. Gravely, Jr., first black to achieve flag rank, June 1971.

RIGHT: Zumwalt places new admiral's combination hat on the head of Rear Adm. Alene B. Duerk in the office of Sec. of the Navy John W. Warner (right). Rear Adm. Duerk was the first woman officer to make flag rank, in June 1972.

A woman sailor throws a line ashore from the Naval Hospital ship USS *Sanctuary*, San Diego, Cal., Sept. 1973.

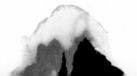

ABOVE LEFT: Rep. F. Edward Hébert of Louisiana.

ABOVE RIGHT: Gen. Al Haig in his office at the White House, May 1973. (credit: Mike Lien/NYT Pictures)

BELOW: Sen. Henry M. Jackson in his Old Senate Building office, Sept. 1971. (credit: George Tames/NYT Pictures)

LEFT: Sec. of the Navy Paul H. Nitze and Capt. Zumwalt in April 1964.

BELOW LEFT: Secretary of the Navy John H. Chafee

BELOW RIGHT: Elliot L. Richardson as Secretary of Defense

ABOVE: Adm. James L. Holloway III (right), who succeeded Zumwalt as CNO, with his father, Vice Adm. J. L. Holloway, Jr. (retired).

BELOW LEFT: Secretary of the Navy John W. Warner

BELOW RIGHT: William P. Clements, Deputy Secretary of Defense

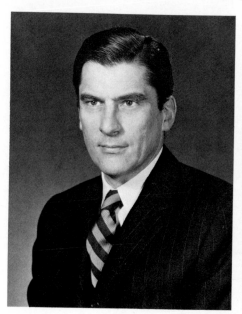

Adm. Worth H. Bagley   Adm. Bernard A. Clarey

Adm. Ralph W. Cousins   Adm. Charles K. Duncan

Adm. Noel Gayler

Vice Adm. Daniel J. Murphy

Adm. Isaac C. Kidd, Jr.

Adm. Maurice F. Weisner

Secretary of State Henry Kissinger and President Nixon, Aug. 1974 (credit: Mike Lien/NYT Pictures)

With Mouza at Annapolis for the change of command ceremony, 29 June 1974. Seated: Sec. of Defense James Schlesinger and Chairman J.C.S. Adm. Thomas H. Moorer.

IV

FRIENDS AND
FOES

CHAPTER 12

Into the Tank

When I became Chief of Naval Operations I also became a member of the Joint Chiefs of Staff, that curious committee whose members, by Congressional mandate, are "principal military advisors to the President." In that capacity the Chiefs necessarily concern themselves with every relationship between the United States and any other nation and every major event on the world scene. Each of those relationships and events, after all, has a greater or lesser military implication or consequence about which the Commander-in-Chief might need or want to hear. Both my experiences under Paul Nitze in the early sixties and my personal interests made this aspect of my new job particularly stimulating. I could not help but be enthusiastic about an opportunity to be in close consultation with the men who formulated and conducted American foreign policy, and my then admiration and respect for those men, Richard Nixon and Henry Kissinger in particular, made the prospect that much more gratifying. I was especially anxious for a chance to communicate to them my concern over the way the Navy's rapidly diminishing capability to deal with the Soviet Navy, if things ever came to such a pass, was diminishing America's capability to influence Soviet foreign policy.

On 1 July 1970 the parts of the world where developments of particular interest to the Navy were occurring were southeast Asia, the Middle East, and Vienna. In southeast Asia, the "incursion" into Cambodia, which had provoked so much distress and disturbance in America, was over, and American troops were beginning to come home from Vietnam; the truce negotiations in Paris were continuing but making no visible progress. In the Middle East, Egypt and Israel were shooting at each other across the Suez Canal, the Soviet Union was continuing to arm Egypt and Syria, the United States was continuing to arm Israel, and Palestinian guerilla operations, particularly with respect to airplane hijacking, were becoming savage. In Vienna, the second round of Strategic Arms Limitation Talks (SALT) was under way, with the United States groping vainly for proposals that the Soviet Union would even listen to seriously. Additionally, in Chile and some months later in Malta and in Iceland, elections were pending that might produce regimes less friendly to the United States and more friendly to the Soviet Union than their predecessors had been, with impacts that needed evaluation on the security of our Latin American friends in the first case, our NATO allies in the second and third, and ourselves in all three.

The setting in which the Joint Chiefs brooded over or debated these and similarly consequential matters was the "Tank," a big windowless room on the first floor of the Pentagon, just off the imposing River Entrance. There we gathered three times a week, each of us with a name plate, a bowl of rock candy, and a favorite tipple (coffee, tea, or water) in front of him on the rectangular conference table, and a three-star Deputy for Plans and Policy (Op-Dep) in a chair beside him. The first part of each meeting, with the OpDeps, and the Director of the Joint Staff and his assistant in attendance, generally was quite formal and was formally recorded. Then, more often than not, the OpDeps, the Joint Staff people, and the reporter left, and we five principals, the four Service chiefs and the Chairman, conversed in a considerably more informal and candid manner than we cared to in front of others.

My service counterparts when I first took my seat in the Tank were General Leonard Chapman of the Marines, General William Westmoreland of the Army, and General Jack Ryan of the Air Force. General Chapman, "Chappy," a thoughtful, somewhat reserved man with that indefinable quality, "command presence," was an old friend with whom I had worked before, both in Washington and when he visited in Vietnam, always happily and productively. He reminded me of General George Marshall in style and professional competence. During the two years that Chappy and I led the Navy/Marine Corps team I can recall no single instance when we failed to work out issues between us amicably and without resort to higher authority. His friendship and support are one of the high points of my professional life. The other two members of the Tank I was getting to know for the first time. With "Westy" Westmoreland I never became close and often disagreed. Two years later, when General Creighton Abrams replaced him as Chief of Staff of the Army, Army–Navy relations in the Tank took a marked turn for the better. My experience serving under Abe in Vietnam had given me such enormous respect, even veneration, for him that I never could have taken him on in the Tank as I repeatedly felt called upon to do with Westy. His untimely death from cancer in 1974 was as great a loss to me personally as it was to the country. As for Jack Ryan, he was not an easy man to figure out, being laconic by temperament or habit, and evidently more at home as an operational commander than engaged in the kind of wide-ranging speculation and analysis that is required of members of the Joint Chiefs. However, I always found what he said, when he said it, to be sensible, honest, and, mercifully, brief.

The Chairman was, of course, my predecessor as CNO, Tom Moorer. By temperament Tom, consistent with his rural Alabama background, is a cheerful and gregarious man, a good raconteur, a dedicated golfer, a mighty fisherman and hunter. It is an indication of how sorely he—like any Chairman—was squeezed between his professional judgment and the political requirements of his civilian superiors that more often than not he will appear in these pages as somber and pessimistic. Vice Admiral Nels Johnson was about to be relieved as Director of the Joint Staff, a job the Services fill in turn, by Air Force Lieutenant General John Vogt, a broad-gauged Nitze-trained man who subsequently became Air Force NATO Commander in Europe. The Director has an exceptionally tricky job, because he presides at the almost daily OpDeps meetings, and it is in the OpDeps meetings that most of the infighting among the Services takes place. As far as I could ever tell, Johnny Vogt, when he became Director, forgot he was Air Force and mediated the eternal and sometimes ridiculous parochial disputes in the OpDeps as impartially and ably as a man could. I judge Vogt's successor during the last half of my tour, Lieutenant General George Seignious, U.S. Army, the same way.

Finally, there was the colleague who for the year or so before he retired carried a big part of my JCS load, my OpDep, the Deputy Chief of Naval Operations for Plans and Policy, Vice Admiral "Champ" Blouin, an unflappable and resourceful veteran of the Pentagon wars and other wars too. Blouin was an Annapolis class-

mate and golfing companion of Tom Moorer's, who did much to help
me familiarize myself with the Chairman's way of doing things. He
had been Moorer's OpDep before I took over, which did much to
help me accustom myself to the novel world of the Joint Chiefs,
where the usual military system of a single commander making final
decisions had given way to one under which positions on the issues
were supposed to be reached by the unanimous vote of five men
whose interests and inclinations often diverged widely. Blouin was
a psychological as well as a technical blessing to me. I have always
found it helpful to my perspective for my associates to take their
work and their boss with at least one grain of salt, which Blouin
certainly did. He performed the seemingly impossible task of getting
wit into his reports of OpDep meetings, which made those reports
more attractive than most of the paper in my "In" basket. And he
did not confine his wit to his opposite numbers. I am told that one
afternoon, after I had given him fifteen or twenty complicated things
to do—by next morning at 0700 more than likely—he returned to
his desk and said to his assistant, "Bud Zumwalt wants to be CinC-
World. The only problem is, we're not staffed for it."

If the first part of that statement was, I like to think, an exaggera-
tion, the second part put the case accurately. I went to my first JCS
meeting on my first Monday on the job, 6 July, and I came away from
it convinced that the Navy could not make the significant contribution I was determined it should to the development of policy without
more resources than my Navy staff and the Joint Staff provided.
Hindsight discloses that this meeting, attended for most of its duration by Secretary of Defense Melvin Laird, was a particularly significant one in that it sounded in one or another way many of the
dominant themes of the next four years.

We talked about supplying equipment to Israel, about which there
were two problems. One was that the items in question were in such
short supply, because of financial constraints, that they could be
provided only by pulling them out of the U.S. planes in which they
were already installed. Insufficient material to meet commitments
certainly was a refrain that was to recur often. Also, there was a
difference of opinion between the Department of Defense and the
Department of State/National Security Council staff over the terms
on which we should supply Israel. State and the NSC staff were at
that time in favor of giving the aid with no strings attached. Most
of the Joint Chiefs and the Secretary of Defense thought the United
States could and should try to obtain from the Israelis, in return for

the aid, a greater willingness to make concessions to the Arabs then they had so far shown. It was a position based on a judgment that the sooner a settlement could be reached, the better its terms were likely to be for Israel, and the better U.S. interests in the Arab nations would fare. American strength in the eastern Mediterranean relative to that of the Soviets was diminishing fast. Therefore, to the extent that Israel's enemies were Soviet clients, which Syria and Egypt were then, time was on their side. The improved Arab performance in the Yom Kippur war certainly validated that judgment.

In that first JCS meeting we considered certain details incident to reducing our forces in Asia, not only in Vietnam but in Korea as well. The specifics of that discussion are not important in retrospect, but reviewing my notes reminds me that at almost every one of the several hundred similar meetings I attended during the ensuing four years, force reductions in some branch of some Service in some part of the world came up directly or by implication. Inflation, anti-militarism in the Congress and an increased rate of spending on domestic programs made force reductions an obbligato that accompanied all our deliberations.

The Chairman raised the question of how to extricate the Services from the "one-and-a-half-war concept" under which they were presumably operating. This was a theory that the Services must be—and the budget enabled them to be—at the very least prepared to fight simultaneously an all-out conventional war with a major power (one war) and a limited war like those in Vietnam or Korea (half a war). None of us thought we had such a capability, but all of us were under heavy political pressure not to let on. To my mind the most vivid illustration that the United States was not even in a position to fight two half wars, much less a half war and a whole one, was the military consensus supporting a passive American response to the North Korean capture of the Navy's intelligence-gathering ship *Pueblo*. I have heard Tom Moorer, who was Chief of Naval Operations at the time, say that there was a strong sentiment within the National Security Council for an active response to *Pueblo*'s capture but that the JCS view was that the South Vietnam half-war deprived the U.S. of the power to wage, or even plausibly threaten, a second half war against North Korea. Here again was a theme that reechoed almost weekly: how to present a true picture of America's military position to the public, or even to the Congress, or perhaps merely to the Office of Management and the Budget, without going over the heads of our civilian masters.

The Chairman reported that the President, at the urging of the Secretary, had agreed to meet soon with the Service chiefs to hear their views on the impact of proposed budget cuts of some three billion dollars. He urged us to start at once preparing for this meeting. It was the budget for Fiscal Year 1972, which would not start for another year, on 1 July 1971, that was involved. That budget had to go to Congress in January and therefore had to be put together in the summer and fall. The appointment with the President made budget discussions dominate the JCS agenda during the next several meetings. More than four years later, reviewing the notes Admiral Blouin and I made of those meetings, I am struck by the amount of heat that emanates from such customarily cool records. Evidently, the imminent opportunity to carry our protests about the proposed cuts to the President in person had started our adrenalin flowing, and the fact that each of us would probably get not much more than ten minutes to present his case made each of us extraordinarily anxious to find the words or examples or images that would most convincingly portray how prejudicial to national security we unanimously felt those cuts to be.

Secretary Laird spoke of the perils of withdrawing troops from Korea and reducing NATO commitments and, most alarming of all, of the prospect of being unable to respond to a crisis without general mobilization if forces came down below a certain level. The Chairman noted that this was the third year in a row that the Chiefs were being forced to speak of the impact of budget cuts and that by this time "we may already be at a condition of having inadequate forces." He continued to speak of the illusory nature of the one-and-a-half-war concept, and expressed the fear that we were getting to the point at which "the Soviets could blackmail us and we could have a Cuba in reverse. We're just fortunate we have not had a confrontation," he added. The Air Force pointed out that force reductions would dictate an early use of tactical nuclear weapons in any real emergency. The Army recalled how uncertain the outcome in Korea had been and in Vietnam still was, at a time when the United States had a large army and clear nuclear superiority, and wondered what would happen in similar situations at a time when the army was small and shrinking and there was at best nuclear parity. Everyone saw the Middle East as the part of the world in which America's decreasing capability relative to Russia's would have the most immediate impact.

For myself, I attempted to get acceptance from the other Chiefs for what I thought was the most graphic way of illustrating the military's plight: by numerically expressed probabilities. My calculations for the Navy, which were consistent with Admiral Moorer's non-numerical pessimism expressed above, were that as of 1 July 1970 the United States had a 55 percent chance of winning a major conventional war at sea, was heading toward a 45 percent chance as of 1 July 1971, and a considerably smaller one than that by 1 July 1972 if the budget levels under discussion were maintained because, for reasons I shall fully explain later, every budget cut of 1 percent meant a cut of several percent in the number of Navy ships and planes. When the results of my calculations first came to the attention of Deputy Secretary of Defense David Packard early in the month, he reacted strongly against looking at things in that way. Indeed, most officials had the same first reaction, particularly Secretary Chafee, who never reconciled himself to the idea. Politically, we all balked at even mentioning the possibility that America might lose a war. Emotionally, we all shrank from applying a procedure we were accustomed to associating with prize fights or football games to a life-and-death matter like fighting the Russians. Many, I am sure, simply did not want to face an unpleasant truth politically, emotionally, or any other way. Nevertheless I could see no other way than through numbers to state the case plainly; adjectives just did not do the job. And so I offered to send up to Dave Packard a paper detailing my methods of arriving at my percentages, and justifying the results. He was impressed with the paper when he got it and, fair man that he is, reported his reaction to both Tom Moorer and me and passed the paper along to Henry Kissinger.

I must stress that the mood of the Chiefs, though one of apprehension, was by no means one of self-pity or despair. On the contrary, we looked toward our meeting with the President as an opportunity to refute in the presence of the ultimate authority the arguments of those who would reduce the Defense budget further, and we were sure we had the better case. We knew—who could know better?—how unpopular the war in southeast Asia, and by extension the entire Defense establishment, was and how much political pressure the President was under to shift his emphasis to domestic problems. But we also knew Mr. Nixon's record as a consistent proponent of strong defense. Moreover, there were signs that the situation might be turning for the better. Both the Secretary and the Chairman were taking a strong line at high-level White House meetings, and Henry Kissinger on 17 July called for papers from Defense that would show the impact on both strategic and "general purpose" forces of budget cuts of various sizes. He said that we owed the President an explanation of the meaning of the shortfall between JCS-recommended force levels and existing budget programs as well as the strategic and political significance of an additional $3 billion budget cut. He emphasized that we should produce a paper that said "if we do this, these are the consequences." That gave me reason to believe that my probabilities campaign was having effect.

Actually, the FY '71 budget, the one Congress had not yet acted on though FY '71 was under way, worried us more than the one for FY '72, which we were about to discuss with the President. There was little or nothing we could do about the former, though expenditures in southeast Asia were exceeding estimates, and unbudgeted requirements for military aid to Cambodia and Israel were being imposed upon us by the White House. The President had decided that political expediency made it impossible to request more money —a "supplemental," in Washington jargon—before the November Congressional elections. Since the money for immediate commitments had to come from somewhere, this meant reductions in future procurement and in elements of the armed forces that were not involved in actual combat or support operations, but of course might be needed at any time.

One important subject that did not come up at the 6 July meeting was SALT. It came up rather dramatically three days later. The SALT situation on 9 July was that the American delegation—among whose five members were Paul Nitze, representing the Secretary of Defense, and Lieutenant General Royal Allison of the Air Force, representing the JCS—which had gone to Vienna in April with four carefully constructed alternative proposals (Options A, B, C, and D) for linking the limitation of offensive and defensive strategic weapons, had been called back to Washington for consultations after the Soviets had consecutively and summarily rejected all four. On 9 July the White House issued National Security Decision Memorandum (NSDM) 69, which set forth an Option E or, as the military called it, Option Echo. I shall not in this place expatiate on the substance of Option Echo, which later became known, in memory of the date we first offered it to the Russians in Vienna, as the 4 August Proposal. The convolutions of strategic arms limitation will receive ample attention in succeeding chapters. My point here is that Option Echo, unlike Options Alpha, Bravo, Charlie, and Delta, to which many people made contributions, was constructed speedily and privately in the White House with no consultation with Defense, State, or indeed the SALT delegation itself.

If John Newhouse, the author of the authoritative book on the negotiations, *Cold Dawn,* is to be credited, no one but the President, Henry Kissinger, and a couple of Kissinger's assistants took part in drawing up Option Echo, this despite the fact that it took away bombers from the Air Force without seeking a reduction in the several hundred Soviet super-missiles of a kind, if I may be permitted to indulge in an "I told you so," Paul Nitze and I had specified as a critical issue in our 1963 paper on arms control. Evidently Kissinger thought the ability he and his staff displayed to whip out a major policy decision so fast and so secretly vindicated his system. We in the Joint Chiefs thought otherwise. For my part, this piece of legerdemain reinforced an already strong determination to improve the quality of the Navy's monitoring of SALT and of its contribution to it. The first administrative edict signed by Emmett Tidd on my first day in office, 1 July, stated "Admiral Zumwalt desires that a competent study be undertaken on strategic arms limitations and their relation to naval forces. It is felt that inadequate analytic information and substantive analyses are available to support the current Navy rationale." By 13 July, after a long and indecisive JCS meeting on SALT, and a subsequent conversation with the Chairman, I was noting in my records that adding a development like Option Echo to all the rest of the large complicated situations needing rapid analysis and decision taxed the Joint Chiefs' machinery far beyond its capacity.

A number of things impeded the Joint Chiefs, and in fact each individual Chief, when it came to matters like SALT or Middle East policy or the Defense budget. To begin with, as far as SALT specifically was concerned, it was the traditional position of the Chiefs that they would not originate proposals to limit arms. The position was understandable but in my opinion it was injudicious. It made us eternally seem to be doing nothing but carping against those who *were* willing to make proposals. Worse yet, it made us seem to be reflexively against arms limitation in any form and therefore put us in the position of not being taken seriously, or sometimes even of not being consulted. The fact is that all of us were in favor of limiting strategic arms if limiting them without giving undue advantages to our adversaries was possible.

Strategic arms are fearfully expensive. The dollars it takes to build a Trident submarine could build eleven patrol frigates or forty F-14 carrier aircraft—and this does not include Trident's missiles, which cost as much again as the submarine. The intellectual foundation of Project 60, with its carefully balanced "High-Low" concept, was that within real-life budget constraints a high level of strategic (i.e. nuclear) capability, which in the absence of arms limitation was essential, meant a low level of conventional (i.e. non-nuclear) capability. The latter in turn left us defenseless in the face of a conventional attack unless we escalated to nuclear war. I was eager to play as large a part in achieving strategic arms limitation as my abilities and position allowed me to, and I found the stiffness of the Joint Staff's machinery in this area frustrating.

The Joint Chiefs found subjects like arms limitation hard ones to deal with in a second way: there was a tendency for each Chief's first reaction to any novel proposal to be parochial. The era of major battles over services roles and missions had passed. But when it came to SALT, the Air Force tended to be much more willing to limit the Army's Anti-Ballistic Missile systems (ABMs) than its own B-52 bombers or Minuteman missiles; the Navy tended to feel that if strategic offense was to be limited, it was far better to limit Air Force's relatively vulnerable bombers and missiles than its own almost invulnerable Polaris and Poseidon submarines (I try to be objective, but I still find the Navy position logical and convincing); the Army tended to advocate an overall strategy that stressed limiting offense (a field the Navy and Air Force had preempted) rather than defense (Army ABMs). Similarly, when it came to the Middle East, each Service had more or less plausible arguments to prove that it was best able to handle the situation. When it came to the budget, the fighting became really bloody since every major new expenditure, particularly in the strategic field, had to come out of someone's hide. In most instances, given time, the Chiefs, and even the OpDeps, for whom scoring points off each other was a game the Joint Staff system made legitimate or even conceivably necessary, finally were able to rise above parochial interests and reach a consensus, but the process was awkward and time-consuming, and too often the final position was a bit watery. And when the relationship between the National Security Council staff and the Joint Chiefs was an adversary one, which often was the case, the Kissinger team with a compact organization and one captain would have been in a better field position than we were even if it hadn't been sitting right outside the Oval Office of the Umpire.

From my point of view, there were two other inherent defects in the Joint Staff and my own Plans and Policy staff as mechanisms for dealing intelligently and promptly with complicated policy matters. One was the immense amount of routine business they were compelled to handle. Clear up to the three-star level of the OpDeps, and occasionally to the four-star level of the Chiefs themselves, the process spent much time on the awarding of medals, the selection of officers to staff the numerous joint commands, the preparation of more or less trivial reports, many of them required by law, and of course the incessant word and logic-chopping that goes with competing interests shaping half a dozen consensuses a day. The men and women involved in the process, whatever their talents and skills, worked in circumstances that with respect to both time and mood made sustained, dispassionate, analytic work difficult or impossible for them.

Secondly, and very important as far as I was concerned, the Joint Staff was almost totally useless as an instrument to monitor what other parts of the government were doing or thinking. Working, as it had to, strictly through the prescribed channels of communication and command, it was generally the last to know what was happening in Washington's bureaucratic labyrinth. One thing my years with Gates, Nitze, and the others had taught me was that the most carefully constructed position was of little value unless it came before the right person at the right time. We all needed help in keeping track of those persons and times and I did not find a place to get it in the organizational chart of either my own Navy staff or the Joint Staff.

I am getting ahead of my story, for of course I did not perceive all the defects in the Joint Staff system instantaneously on 1 July 1970. It took me months to learn the full extent of some of them and more months to learn how other interests in the bureaucracy exploited them. However, I had more than an inkling of the situation as early as 13 July, as I have said, and on 28 July I ordered the establishment of a CNO Executive Panel whose "end objective is to be a clear statement of a Navy concept suitable for use in the next four years for reshaping the Navy, using it so that civilian members of the Office of the Secretary of Defense, White House, and Congress would more clearly understand the Navy's mission, purpose and vital importance to U.S. national objectives." I stipulated that the membership of the group should be a mixture of civilian strategic and politico-military analysts, retired flag officers and active duty personnel, and I gave the job of Staff Director to one of the Navy's most brilliant officers, Captain Kinnaird McKee, with orders to "develop a concept," find a headquarters, nominate panel members, pick a staff, and be ready to begin business by 1 September. In the event, organizing the CEP took a little longer than I had hoped. It held its first meeting on 24 October, and did not develop a full head of steam until 1971, but thereafter, as subsequent chapters will relate, it served brilliantly and indispensably, analyzing and advising me about scores of complicated, scientific, strategic, and politico-military situations and problems.

On 29 July, just one day after I had ordered the establishment of the CEP, I had serious reason to regret that such a panel was not in active operation. That day the Chiefs received their periodic briefing from the Commander of the Strategic Air Command, General Bruce Holloway, on the likely results of a nuclear exchange between the United States and the Soviet Union. One of the responsibilities that goes with the SAC Commander's job is heading something called the Joint Strategic Targeting Planning System (JSTPS), a group formed by Tom Gates when he was Secretary of Defense. It integrates all the strategic capabilities of the several services into a single system that does nuclear targeting and analyzes results by playing intricate war games on computers out in Omaha. Using intelligence estimates of Russia's strategic strength and, of course, intimate knowledge of America's, JSTPS makes a range of assumptions about which weapons each side would fire at which specific targets in a variety of situations. Then it calculates the amount of damage to each side that probably would result in each case, and assesses what the effects of that amount of damage would be on each society. From time to time calculations are made as to how long, if at all, it would take each side to recover from various amounts of damage. It is an enormously complex exercise and one whose details, for obvious reasons, are kept as secret as anything in government.

General Holloway gave us an extremely nasty turn in the Tank that day. Though we all were aware that our position vis-à-vis the Soviets had been deteriorating during the last years, and the Defense budget then under discussion made it certain that this trend would continue, the picture General Holloway painted was even worse than we had imagined. In the face of the popular talk about "overkill," he made it clear that the weapons then available to the United States in a second strike—that the United States never would mount a first strike was an unvarying assumption in our discussions of the games

—could not inflict anything like the casualties on Russia that Russia already had inflicted on us, bringing into question the whole concept of "assured destruction" on which our national deterrent strategy then rested.

This briefing drove home to all of us how prejudicial to the balanced arms control we favored it was both to conduct SALT as the U. S. was conducting it and to cut the Defense budget as deeply as was being proposed. Indeed, it so strengthened the case we were preparing to make to the President that I was anxious for the Secretary, and through him the President, to receive the JSTPS briefing just as we had. If it seems odd to the reader that the results of a study so pertinent to the very survival of the republic should not have come as a matter of routine before the Commander in Chief's principal civilian advisors and executives in the field of national security, I can only report with some embarrassment that by long habit the military holds technical studies of that kind very close. The extreme sensitivity of the detailed data on which such studies are based has something to do with this, but I fear that it is mostly a matter of the military (i.e., professionals) not wanting to admit civilians (i.e., nonprofessionals) into the innermost mysteries of their calling. (One does not have to look far to find other professions where similar attitudes prevail.) There has, I believe, never been any doubt about the right—indeed the need—for the Secretary of Defense and the President to know about these matters. The problem has always been that those busy men bring in others to do the detailed examinations and that often the assistants, who do not have statutory responsibility, do not share the views of the President on strategic issues. Nor are they in all cases as circumspect with the detailed information in the plan as those of us in the military would like.

In any event, my suggestion that our civilian superiors receive General Holloway's briefing was adopted. As a result there was a discussion at a National Security Council meeting on 19 August that led to a general understanding of how different America's nuclear strength relative to that of the Soviet Union was now compared to the time of the Cuban missile crisis, and to an admission by Kissinger that it was very clear that the Soviets were aiming at strategic superiority, through SALT if possible, without SALT if necessary. Also important in the long run, the President and others in the system started asking pertinent questions like, "Under what kinds of guidance and criteria are these JSTPS studies prepared?" and "Why are certain potential targets not targeted?" Thereupon, Secretary Laird requested that the JCS, working with his office, do an analysis of the games. This was a proper reaction by the system to a major national issue, but the system grinds exceedingly slowly. Over time this civilian/military analysis, headed by Dr. John Foster, Director of Defense Research and Engineering, grew more formal. Four years elapsed before it was completed. The final study produced changes in national strategy designed to keep U.S. strategic forces effective as a deterrent under conditions of a radically altered U.S.-Soviet strategic balance that made "assured destruction" a doubtful concept. It fell to a later Secretary of Defense, James Schlesinger, to announce these changes, and they are associated with his name, but they were first formulated before his time—and have not moved from formulation to full implementation at this writing.

Actually, JSTPS kept not only civilians at arm's length, but the Joint Chiefs as well. I discovered to my surprise at the briefing that one of the assumptions of the study was that the United States would hold back no weapons as a planned strategic reserve. The idea was that whatever weapons did not get off, for one reason or another, when "the button" was pushed would be available as a reserve. This assumption seemed dangerous to me. I doubted that anyone would have the information to sort out quickly what weapons were left over and available after a catastrophic series of nuclear explosions, and I doubted even more that anyone would have the time to do so during the period when such command authority as survived would probably be seeking to negotiate with the other side. It was clear to me that if, after a massive exchange, one side had weapons left, and knew where they were and how to control them, and the other side did not, the former side would be the winning one. I set for myself the task of getting changed the assumption that there would be no reserve of weapons. I succeeded. However, another task I set myself I failed to accomplish. I could not persuade the command authority to move JSTPS from Omaha to Washington, where it could work on an intimate daily basis not just with SAC, but with the senior military people in all services, the Joint Chiefs, and the President and the Secretary of Defense, who in the interests of America's security must be willing to take the time to understand the issues involved in strategic planning and provide policy guidance for it.

To prepare for the Presidential briefing, which Admiral Moorer predicted would be the most significant meeting the JCS had had in the more than four years that he had been a member, I talked not only with Mel Laird and Tom Moorer but to two other perceptive observers, Charles DiBona, President of the University of Rochester's Center for Naval Analyses, who had spent several hours with the President recently, and Rear Admiral Rembrandt Robinson, who was the military liaison officer between the Chairman of the JCS and Dr. Kissinger, and who therefore worked in the White House. They gave me the following impressions: (1) The President was sincerely concerned about the defense situation. (2) He was not an expert in the details of the Soviet threat. (3) He was impatient with the details of the budget but wanted to understand what kinds of capability he got for various budget levels. (4) He wanted to hear opinions about priorities and was particularly interested in the future of carriers. (5) He liked strategic thinking and wanted to see the most important numbers. (6) He had a "heavily oriented gut feeling" that in cutting defense to satisfy popular opinion he should err in favor of flexibility and that Navy was the arm that provided the most flexibility. He saw the Navy as the alternative to massive retaliation.

The Service secretaries met with the President on the afternoon of 17 August, the day before the Chiefs met with him. At that meeting John Chafee told the President that the Navy was close to being in an untenable position in a way that was entirely different from mine, but perfectly logical. Starting from a "dovish" point of view he arrived at much the same conclusions I did starting from a "hawkish" one. He said, first, that we were fighting a war; second, that the Soviet Navy was expanding at a rapid rate; third, that the Nixon Doctrine required that the Navy cover the "seven corners of the world." He expressed concern that the combination of America's reduced forces and Russia's increased ones would prevent us from executing the Nixon Doctrine and since, evidently, there was no more money available, the only course to pursue was for the U.S. to reduce its overseas commitments to fit the budget. Earlier in the day Secretary Laird had cautioned the Service Secretaries and the Chiefs to give the President good news as well as bad. Evidently Secretary Chafee didn't have much good news to give.

The Chiefs briefed the President in the Cabinet room of the White House on 18 August. Sitting around the long tapering table were, besides Mr. Nixon and the five members of the Joint Chiefs, Vice President Agnew, Secretary of State Rogers, Secretary Laird, Deputy Secretary Packard, Henry Kissinger, and Alexander Haig, then a Brigadier General. Each Chief had brought a bulky attaché case containing a packet of materials for each of those in attendance. The

President did not like slides. Secretary Laird opened the meeting with a few brief comments. The Chairman spoke of the general military balance world-wide, stressing the cutbacks facing the Services and the Soviet build-up of both strategic and non-strategic military forces. His evaluation was consistent with his thesis, often stated to the JCS, that the situation was rapidly moving to a Cuban missile crisis situation in reverse. Then each of the Service chiefs had, if I remember correctly, ten minutes to discuss the objectives, plans, and programs of his service. Occasionally the President interrupted with a question, and at the end he gave a knowledgeable summary of the international picture. He obviously had a firm grasp of the military situation. The occasion was curiously bloodless. It was in no sense a working session at which the military chiefs went back and forth with the Commander in Chief. Rather, it was a ceremony, a ritual even, at which Mr. Nixon listened to things he already knew and made responses he and Kissinger had contrived beforehand. However, I was not disappointed. For one thing, like everyone in the administration, I knew that was Mr. Nixon's style. For another, I welcomed a bit of ritual that acknowledged that the President was formally seeking the advice of his senior military subordinates. For a third, putting the Navy's case in such a concise, and I hoped catchy, form was a useful exercise. There are passages that bear quoting here.

> The missions which general purpose forces have traditionally accomplished [are] sea control [which] is provided by the combined capabilities of our naval air, surface, and subsurface systems to defeat the enemy at sea, [and] projection forces, [which] are those applied to overseas land areas—aircraft from our carriers, Marine forces from our amphibious lift, the 96 percent of the logistics for all services projected from our merchant marine. In this military-political role our forces have served as a vital part of the calculus of factors that restrained the enemy—in crises like Lebanon, Dominican Republic, Quemoy/Matsu, the Chinese incursion into India, and the Cuban missile crisis. In all such cases, we had and demonstrated the capability to (1) control the seas and (2) project our forces.
>
> In Korea and South Vietnam we were forced to use our projection forces to engage the enemy. Even in these two cases, except for a brief test in the Tonkin Gulf, our sea control forces were not tested by the enemy—this was the result, I believe, of the strength of our sea control forces. The issue is whether such restraint will continue in the light of the changes in relative strengths of the two navies.

The reductions we have made in projection forces and sea control forces first from 1960 until today and second the additional cuts we would have to make . . . have come [mostly] from sea control capabilities in order to save the projection forces we needed for South Vietnam and which have the most visibility for military-political purposes. . . . in future cuts we must reduce projection forces as well as sea control forces. Today with the [existing] forces . . . and based on my review of naval warfare studies and fleet exercises, I have only 55 percent confidence that we could retain control of the seas in a conflict with the Soviet Union. With the [proposed cuts in] forces, even with our projection forces reduced to 50 percent of their present size—including the reduction of seven carriers—the loss of sea control forces would reduce my confidence to 30 percent. I believe that similar Soviet analyses will lead them to conclude that their maritime policy can be more aggressive and their risk taking can be greater than in the past and our naval forces would no longer be adequate political-military forces or even projection forces, because the Soviets would be willing to take them on in the sea control arena.

After the briefing, the President directed that it be repeated for George Shultz, director of the Office of Management and the Budget, and his deputy Caspar Weinberger. Friends on the White House staff advised me that the President, Vice President, and Kissinger all expressed the view that my presentation provided persuasive evidence that our maritime power needed bolstering. In December, the President and the Secretary of Defense restored to the Naval budget for FY '72 sufficient funds to improve my odds from 30 to 35 percent for the end of that year. I have no impulse to rewrite any of my briefing today. On the contrary, I find it an accurate description of what has come to pass.

CHAPTER 13

A United States Day and
a NATO Day

The Middle East occupied the major part of the attention of the Joint Chiefs and the Navy during September 1970. The month began with a general fear that the ninety-day cease-fire between Israel and Egypt that had gone into effect on 7/8 August was about to break down. The agreement called for both sides to refrain from strengthening or redeploying their forces, and now both sides were claiming violations. Israel had the more persuasive case. The cease-fire, which Henry Kissinger had played a principal part in negotiating, had gone into effect at midnight Suez time. (The Joint Chiefs would have recommended noon if we had been consulted, which we were not.) Under cover of that night's darkness, the Egyptians had moved a considerable number of their Russian surface-to-air missile (SAM) launchers, manned by Soviet technicians, to forward positions from which they could protect their artillery from Israeli planes. When the sun rose the next morning, there they were, and Israel could do nothing about them without flagrantly breaking the cease-fire. Israeli feelings against both Egypt and the Soviet Union had been growing hotter ever since, and by the beginning of September there seemed to be a real chance that Israel might burst across the Suez Canal. Therefore the United States was in the throes of deciding how to deter a renewed Israeli attack and how to react to it if it was undeterrable. Military ingredients were major in both parts of this problem. The amount and type of military aid that went from America to Israel week by week had a good deal of bearing on what the Israeli armed forces could and therefore would do. The amount of military strength the United States had in the eastern Mediterranean, or could rapidly bring there, had a good deal to do with the courses of action available to the U.S. in the event of renewed fighting.

During the first week in September there was a series of high-level meetings on the crisis, starting with a National Security Council meeting in San Clemente on the 1st. All these meetings covered roughly the same ground so I shall report on just one, a JCS meeting on the 4th. Admiral Moorer was especially pessimistic at that meeting. He said that when one looked at the relative capabilities of the U.S. and the USSR in that part of the world, particularly in view of the unlikelihood of the U.S. being able to use Greek or Turkish bases, the picture was "pretty grim." He said, as he had been saying for two months, that the Soviets have America in the same position that we had the Soviets in at the time of the Cuban missile crisis. He said that the Chiefs should be wary of getting committed in view of the cuts in strength the Services had undergone recently. None of us was much more cheerful. General Chapman agreed with the Chairman that the Soviets might be trying to make us back away from Israel. General Bruce Palmer, Westy's Vice Chief of Staff who was sitting in for him, said that general mobilization might turn out to be the only way to give the Soviets a clear signal of our resolution. I spoke of how important it was for the JCS not to leave the Administration with the impression that our forces were adequate to deal with the Soviets in a confrontation in the eastern Mediterranean and of the disagreeable possibility of redeploying ships and planes and troops to the Mediterranean from Southeast Asia, thus risking much of what 50,000 Americans had died for. I also suggested that this was the time to push hard for a supplemental to the budget, but I received no support on that, the others obviously regarding that cause as having been long lost. The Chairman reminded us that at our recent meeting with the President, Mr. Nixon had wondered aloud what he could do to scare the American public into recognizing the situation the Services were in and Admiral Moorer had replied that the Russians might do it for us. On that cheery note we adjourned.

The following week the shakiness of the Israeli-Egyptian cease-fire looked less foreboding than the confrontation that was occurring in Jordan between the Palestinian commandos, or fedayeen, and King Hussein's government. The previous June, provoked by the kidnapping of an American diplomat and an assassination attempt against Hussein, there had been four days of hard fighting between the

Palestinians and Hussein's forces. They had ended with Hussein making various concessions to the commandos. An uneasy truce prevailed from the middle of June to the end of August. A new crisis came to a head on 2 September when there was another assassination attempt, and daily clashes between the fedayeen and Jordanian Army forces resumed. On the 7th, Palestinian guerillas hijacked four commercial airliners carrying some 600 passengers bound for New York. On one of them, an El Al plane seized in Amsterdam, guards killed one hijacker and wounded three others and the plane was able to land safely in London. The other three planes, a Pan-American plane seized in Frankfurt, a TWA plane seized in the same city, and a Swissair plane seized in Zurich, were diverted to the Middle East. The Pan-Am plane was landed in Cairo, evacuated and blown up. The other two were set down in the desert some twenty-five miles from the Jordanian capital, Amman. About 125 of the passengers, women and children mostly, were allowed to move to a hotel in Amman; the other 150 were kept as hostages in the two planes in the summer heat on the desert.

On the evening of Tuesday, 8 September, the President ordered one of the two carrier task groups in the Mediterranean to steam east and deploy off the Syrian-Lebanese-Israeli coast. He also ordered six Air Force transport planes into our Incirclik base in Turkey, ostensibly for use in evacuating the 400 American nationals in Jordan if that became necessary. The following morning the Washington Special Action Group (WSAG), the National Security Council's subgroup concerned with crisis management, met and discussed first, how to evacuate Americans from Jordan under a variety of circumstances, second, what to respond to a Jordanian appeal for help if it came. The Chairman reported to us in the Tank that afternoon that he had taken the position that in their present state of readiness, U.S. forces would have very little staying power in the Middle East, and in view of that fact, and of the difficulty and damaging effect of reinforcing from southeast Asia, where the greatest concentration of American forces was, the United States should make every effort not to become involved in large-scale military action. There still may be some who think of the military as bloodthirsty folk who have to be restrained from coming out shooting every time a putative enemy looks cock-eyed at them or one of their friends. There were some officers like that ten years ago, but nowadays no·one talks like Curtis LeMay.

However, General Chapman and I were the only Chiefs who were willing to go the whole non-LeMay route and say outside the executive branch what all of us said so emphatically so often to each other inside: that American military capability had reached the point in several parts of the world at which the odds were that the U.S. would lose a conventional war with Russia and that there were risks, therefore, in taking a strong diplomatic line with the Russians in those places. I concluded that one of the reasons for this failure to speak out was a disagreement about the responsibilities of the JCS. Tom Moorer, as Chairman, inevitably and properly set the tone of the relations between the Chiefs as a body and the other parts of the Administration. Tom's view, a rational one, was that the JCS must not only be strictly subject to civilian authority (we all thought that) but that our official expressions must conform to the views of our civilian superiors. I remember at least three conversations during which he said that though it was necessary to give our military views with absolute frankness to the Secretary of Defense and the President, it was risky to be that frank with the Congress. Tom felt some members of Congress would use our views to embarrass the Administration. He believed further that frank pessimistic evaluations rather than encouraging Congress to do more, would lead it to feel "what's the use" and do less. Though his first proposition was unarguable, my own opinion about the second, which I believe General Chapman shared, was that Congress would react responsibly, over time, if it had the facts—and that it couldn't possibly act responsibly without the facts. This difference between Admiral Moorer and me never was resolved, and it diluted our corporate influence.

On 10 September the Palestinian commandos seized a BOAC Bombay-to-London plane carrying 117 passengers and set it down beside the other two on the desert. That day, also, the Jordanian Army shelled commando camps in northern Jordan near the Golan Heights. The WSAG meeting on the 10th was notable not for what it accomplished, which was little, but because it was an archetype of countless encounters between Defense people and Henry Kissinger. Dave Packard went to the meeting as an advocate. He wanted WSAG to recommend to the President that there be no American involvement on the ground in the Middle East, and he had prepared a paper giving a formidable list of reasons why such involvement was unthinkable. Kissinger used the meeting, as always, not to formulate recommendations that would give the President a consensus view or a range of disagreeing views, but to concoct options, every possible option, including involvement on the ground. Later, he would make a private recommendation and the President would make a decision.

And so Packard and Kissinger spent a good deal of time at cross purposes that morning. Indeed, according to the reports we received, the atmosphere became just a bit acrimonious with Kissinger complaining that Packard wasn't telling him what he wanted to know, and Packard replying, in effect, that he was telling him what he thought was important.

The day after that, 11 September, a day during which there was fighting, followed by another "truce" in Amman, the Chiefs met with U. Alexis Johnson, the Under Secretary of State, Joseph Sisco, the Assistant Secretary for Near Eastern and South Asian affairs, and representatives of Defense's Office of International Security Affairs. As far as we Chiefs were concerned, that was the most important meeting of the Jordan episode, because it was the one at which we were able to articulate the military realities most explicitly to the civilian side. Secretaries Johnson and Sisco had come to the Tank seeking information from the Chiefs on whether it was possible to establish in the Middle East a "credible deterrent"—their words— to military intervention by the Soviets. That was a question that Henry Kissinger wanted answered. The State Department and Kissinger needed such information, of course, for the talks they were conducting daily with Jordan and its neighbors and with the Russians. The only answer we could give them after much discussion was "not really." The discussion covered points I have already described: the probable unavailability of bases for aircraft in the NATO countries (Greece and Turkey) and Spain; the long, easily severed lines of communication by sea; the politically disastrous effect of putting American troops into Jordan, assuming they could be maintained there—which in any case would be intervening, not deterring; the incongruity—not to mention the vast political and social disruptions and the expense—of such slow and cumbersome processes as calling up the reserves or deploying into the Mediterranean from southeast Asia in a situation that required speedy and flexible action. Augmenting the Sixth Fleet, putting various ground and air elements in Europe on the alert, and perhaps sending a few more troops and planes across the Atlantic, which barely, if at all, added up to a "credible deterrent," were the only immediate actions appropriate to the situation that anyone could think of.

Anyone except General Westmoreland, that is. He proposed at one point sending an Army brigade to Cyprus—or maybe Turkey or Greece. What followed that suggestion was the most intensely embarrassing experience of my four years in the Tank. Secretary Johnson asked Westy with astonishment what he thought such a brigade might do—assuming Cyprus, Turkey, or Greece let it in. Westy groped for an answer and at last said that one thing it certainly could do was secure whatever base in Turkey, Greece, or Cyprus it occupied. Well, there is no need to elaborate on the ten or fifteen minutes that followed—for once Westy got hold of an idea, he did not relinquish it easily and opposition brought out the bulldog in him particularly strongly. Seeking to place the discussion back in the real world, if I couldn't end it, I expressed the Navy/Marine Corps judgment that the Navy could not guarantee to supply a brigade on Cyprus in the event the Russians intervened. Westy replied that he didn't see why not.

When the meeting got back on the track, the discussion turned to Mediterranean strategy. Ambassador Johnson made it very clear that NATO would not be with us. Admiral Moorer expressed our view that Turkey was a key country because of the Dardanelles. We might hope the Turks would close the Dardanelles to Soviet ships but we had no reason to believe they would, he said. Equally important were airfields in Cyprus and in the Mediterranean NATO nations. The net effect of the discussion was a consensus about the critical importance of Greek bases to any U.S. effort in the Mediterranean, particularly since they were the ones most likely to be available. This led to the unanimous opinion that the U.S. should improve its relations with Greece, despite the repressive nature of the Papadapoulos government. Johnson and Sisco agreed and reported that policy was already moving in that direction.

Admiral Moorer predicted that a conflict in the Mediterranean with the USSR would quickly spread to both the Atlantic and Pacific Oceans. Tom always advanced the opinion that a military conflict with the Soviets would be impossible to confine to a single theater. Ambassador Johnson asked that for the present discussion we assume the conflict would be confined to the Mediterranean, at least initially. I gave my view that the Soviets might very well seek to limit it to the Mediterranean because they knew as well as we that, with Greek and Turkish airfields closed to the U.S. Air Force, the Sixth Fleet was the only U.S. force that could engage Soviet forces rapidly, and that the Sixth Fleet could not be sure of handling a Soviet "squadron" of more than fifty ships, including twelve submarines, plus Soviet naval and long-range air, alone. (I put "squadron" in quotation marks because it actually was a fleet, containing more ships than the U.S. Sixth Fleet, but inter-service one-upmanship would not allow it to be called a fleet because that might make the Navy eligible for more money than if it was called a squadron.)

That the opinions we expressed at that meeting carried some weight is at least suggested by the fact that, though Kissinger kept talking about "keeping options open" and various elaborate contingency papers for intervention were written, the only military response the United States actually did make to the situation in Jordan was just what we told Alex Johnson was the maximum rational response: to augment the Sixth Fleet, to place an infantry and two airborne battalions in Europe on an alert, and to load two mobile hospital units into planes in Germany in case Hussein should need them, which he didn't. Moreover, even those things were not done until the risks had diminished considerably. On the 13th the commandos had released all but forty of the hostages and had blown up the three planes. On the 16th Hussein proclaimed a military government, a move Iraq and Syria promptly denounced, and under its authority his Army began mopping up the fedayeen in Amman and up north. In this context of diminished risk of direct confrontation with the Soviets, on 17 September the President ordered a third carrier, *John F. Kennedy,* escorted by two guided-missile frigates (my second son, Jim Zumwalt, was serving on one of these, USS *Leaky,* DLG 16), to join *Saratoga* and *Independence* in the Mediterranean. He also ordered a second amphibious task force, to join the amphibious force already at sea in the Mediterranean about a day and half's steaming from the Lebanese coast.

As happens more often than not when a rapid military evolution is required, the Navy was the service best able to execute it. In a memorandum to the President on 21 September Kissinger made the point that for the Air Force to have provided just half the extra air capability the Navy supplied would have taken four days longer, and that is assuming Cyprus or Greece would have provided base rights, which they almost certainly would not have. "In view of the foregoing," the memo said, "The WSAG believes we should not plan on using land based air for intervention in Jordan." Those facts should weigh for something with those who think that carriers are obsolete. Furthermore, the Navy, partly through luck but partly, also, because of the nature of its operations, was not put under immediate strain by these Presidential requirements. The carrier *JFK,* almost fully manned and equipped, was conducting post-refitting exercises in the Caribbean and needed to do little more than execute hard left rudder. *Guam,* the reinforcing amphibious ship, had been scheduled to sail for the Mediterranean that week anyway; she merely put on more speed.

On 22 September Rem Robinson gave me a copy of a memorandum that had gone to the President describing America's military posture in the Mediterranean as follows:

1. *Navy*—Two Carrier Task Groups (*Saratoga* and *Independence* with Cruiser *Springfield*, fourteen destroyers, and 140 aircraft) off the coast of Lebanon.

An amphibious task force with 1,200 Marines is ready and in position thirty-five hours off the coast.

A third Carrier Task Group (*John F. Kennedy* with two guided missile frigates) will enter the Mediterranean early Friday morning, 25 September.

A second amphibious task force (*Guam*, additional ships, seventeen helos, and a reinforced battalion of 2814 Marines) has split into fast and slow groups. Will enter Mediterranean on 27 and 30 September.

Five Navy P-3 ASW-patrol aircraft are now at Rota.

Two additional attack submarines will enter Mediterranean on 25 September and 29 September.

Four additional destroyers will depart the U.S. tomorrow for the Mediterranean.

2. *Army*—One airborne battalion and one infantry battalion ready in Europe. Another airborne battalion will be ready at noon today. Transit and load time is four hours for first rifle company, eight hours for the rest. Total force is 1600 troops. Initial company and battalion air drop; other battalions airland. 82nd Airborne Division at Fort Bragg has the initial ready force of one airborne company rigged for drop on six-hour alert. One battalion also is ready on six-hour alert; an additional battalion will be on same alert by 2:00 P.M. today . . . Remainder of division on eighty-four-hour alert.

3. *Air Force*—Eighteen F-4s and four C-130s are at Incirclik, Turkey. (Turkey has *not* authorized us to use the base to launch these aircraft in strikes over Jordan.)

This response turned out to be a sufficient American reaction for the occasion. When coupled with the strong diplomatic representations we made to the USSR and above all the strength the Jordanian Army demonstrated first against the commandos, then against the Syrians who at 0200 on 20 September, while the Sixth Fleet reinforcements were still on their way, sent a large number of tanks (Russian-built and -supplied) across Jordan's northern border. By 23

September, to the undoubted surprise of the Soviets, the Syrians had taken heavy losses from Hussein's ground and air forces and were withdrawing into Syria again, the Soviets having promised to replace their losses. The Syrians, the Iraqis, and their Soviet advisers also had to take note of the Israelis, who were moving their forces northward, clearly able to play a role. (Hussein neither needed nor desired Israeli assistance inside Jordan, and the Israelis knew it. Their plan was to march into Syria and Iraq if the need arose.)

The American forces may have been sufficient for the occasion, but they were far from formidable. In fact they were so far from it that the Chiefs and Secretary Packard expressed repeated concern about the inadequacy of U.S. naval capability in the Eastern Mediterranean. That inadequacy, to repeat a crucial though little appreciated point, arises not so much from Soviet naval superiority in that part of the world, which though real is modest, but from the fact that the Soviets could bring massive air power to bear there and the U.S. could not. My perception of American inadequacy in the Eastern Med led me to make an official recommendation that an international force (largely Anglo-American) be formed there. The British had no desire to get involved, which made my recommendation useless as a means of obtaining help, but useful in making a point I very much wanted to make about the Nixon Doctrine, and that repeatedly proved to be true during my watch: allied help was unlikely to be available in any real-world bilateral superpower crisis. Unfortunately, many members of Congress during that period justified their votes to cut Defense budgets by citing the Nixon Doctrine's assumption that we could rely on help from the allies when a crunch came.

It is difficult to evaluate just what part the Russians played in the timing of the Jordan flap. Certainly the Syrian arms were Russian, the Syrian soldiers were trained by Russians and the invasion was consistent with Soviet objectives. During the period of the most intense activity, when the Syrian armor had crossed the border, U.S. carriers had gone into the eastern Mediterranean, and *JFK* and *Guam* were on the way, the Soviets' reaction was to position their own naval forces to maintain a deterrent capability and to monitor and conduct close surveillance of U.S. fleet movements. Soviet ships equipped with cruise missiles trailed U.S. carriers around the clock, but they always did that, and for the occasion we, not having cruise missiles, assigned ships armed with rapid fire guns to trail the trailers. (All this trailing is an effort to compensate for tactical asymmetries. A carrier outside the range of the cruise missiles on Soviet ships can clearly sink them easily with her aircraft. Therefore, the Russians trail us closely in order to be able to destroy most of a carrier's planes or disable the carrier herself before aircraft can take off. We adopted the retaliatory technique of trailing the trailer so as to prevent them from preventing us from launching our planes by knocking out most of their cruise missiles before many of them took off. In the words of the poet, "Great fleas have little fleas upon their back to bite 'em/ And little fleas have lesser fleas, and so *ad infinitum*.")

The Russians, in addition to such psychological advantages as accompany turmoil in a region their adversary would like to keep calm, gained information that they presently put to good use. In a geo-political sense, the Syrian invasion was a test by a Soviet client state as to whether the massive Soviet strategic and maritime building program had sufficiently shifted the "correlation of forces"—a phrase the Soviets use to cover the political-economic-military relationships between nations—to make it possible for the Soviet Union to conduct an aggressive foreign policy in a part of the world where the U.S. writ used to run. The Soviet conclusion must have been "not yet, but soon." They learned that the Syrians needed more equipment and, especially, training before they would be militarily respectable; that Jordan was capable, if goaded, of strong and decisive action; that though the United States was deeply concerned with what happened in the Middle East, it was stretched very thin there in a military sense. The terrible danger of that last state of affairs is, of course, that in a major crisis—which the Jordan trouble was not—the alternatives become backing down (abandoning old principles and old friends) or escalation (risking a global war). The trade adjective for that is "unstable," which is as mild as possible a way of putting it.

Certainly the most dramatic, and probably the most convincing, evidence that America intended to protect her interests in the Middle East was President Nixon's visit to the Sixth Fleet on 28 and 29 September. The visit was part of a nine-day trip by Mr. Nixon, during which he held discussions with the chiefs of state and government in Italy, Yugoslavia, Spain, England, and Ireland, and had two meetings in Naples, one with senior allied NATO commanders, and one with the American ambassadors to most of the countries on the Mediterranean littoral. The trip had been planned for some time but was modified to include the Naples meetings and the visit to the fleet in order to exploit America's "political success" in the Jordan crisis. I was present during this part of the trip and I can testify that the officers and men of the fleet received the visit with enthusiasm as a most welcome show of interest in their activities and concern for their problems.

Mr. Nixon arrived aboard *Saratoga* by helicopter from Rome late in the afternoon of the 28th—later than he was expected because he had delayed his departure to greet the last of the hijacking hostages who had just been released. He had a private dinner with his staff, and then retired. (*Saratoga* was redeployed from the Eastern Mediterranean for the President's visit because the White House had indicated rather strongly that he would prefer, if possible, not to appear aboard the most conveniently positioned ship whose name was *John F. Kennedy.*) While Mr. Nixon was asleep, President Gamel Abdel Nasser of Egypt suddenly and unexpectedly died. The morning of the 29th was devoted to ceremony. Mr. Nixon received full honors on the flight deck, toured the ship, and then watched a fleet review that was scheduled to include demonstrations of refueling at sea, launching helicopters and aircraft, tracking and destroying submarines, and firing a variety of weapons. Nasser's death eliminated, to Mr. Nixon's expressed displeasure, though with his consent, the warlike firing demonstration, in order not to appear disrespectful. Representatives of the media, including the much-respected and equally feared Walter Cronkite, were there in large numbers. After lunch we all proceeded by helicopter to the cruiser *Springfield,* the Sixth Fleet flagship, for a two-hour conference. Those present included Secretaries Laird and Rogers; Admiral Moorer; Generals Andrew Goodpaster and David Burchinal, the Supreme Allied Commander, Europe, and his deputy for U.S. Forces; Dr. Kissinger; Admiral Horacio Rivero, Commander-in-Chief, Allied Forces Southern Europe (NATO); Admiral Wallace Wendt, Commander U.S. Naval Forces Europe; and Vice Admiral Isaac Kidd, Commander of the Sixth Fleet.

The President opened the meeting with a sober and persuasive statement in which he pointed out how different America's diplomatic posture had to be today than it was in the days when John Foster Dulles was able to talk about "massive retaliation," or even during the Cuban missile crisis, because of the drastic decrease of America's military strength relative to Russia's. At the same time he paid tribute to the Sixth Fleet. "Its presence gave our initiatives a chance to succeed," he said. "Without the United States fleet, I don't know what we would have done. My visit is intended to emphasize to the world that the Sixth Fleet is here and how we use it and maintain it." Secretary Rogers then spoke briefly along similar lines, emphasizing the effectiveness of taking highly visible actions like augmenting the Fleet and putting troops on alert. Admiral Moorer emphasized that the Sixth Fleet was the only way America could project its capabilities in the Middle East. General Goodpaster spoke for all of us when he said that the President's presence in the Fleet was a psychological plus for every American serviceman overseas. "This is a United States day and a NATO day," he said enthusiastically.

The President then brought up the subject of bases in the Mediterranean, which gave me an opportunity to mention my worry that Malta might slip into the Soviet sphere of influence. My thesis was that Malta was a base that we did not particularly need for our own operations, but could seriously jeopardize our Mediterranean position if the Russians got hold of it. The President agreed that action should be taken to prevent such an occurrence. General Burchinal briefed the President on the general crisis situation, including movement of forces. The President was visibly impressed by one of Burchinal's charts which showed the way in which U.S. ground forces would have had to have been flown from Germany to the Middle East in the absence of overflight rights over Austria and the NATO nations, which the State Department did not believe we would get. The troops would have had to fly north from Germany, over the North Sea, the English Channel, and the Straits of Gibraltar (or across Spain if permitted) and all the way across the Mediterranean. There were not sufficient tanker aircraft to make this long end around feasible. Hence, the Navy/Marine forces were the only ones that could be used.

I then briefed the meeting on calculations I had had made on probable outcomes of encounters between the Soviet "squadron" in the Mediterranean and the Sixth Fleet in sixteen different situations. In each of the likeliest cases, i.e., the ones in which the Russians initiated the hostilities with augmented forces, the outcome was at best a standoff, and in most instances it was clearly unfavorable to the United States.

After the meeting, the President drew me aside and said, "I take it that your conclusion is that the Soviets have overtaken the United States with regard to maritime capability."

I replied, "I think one needs to qualify that as follows. As I told you in August, as of the day I took over from Tom Moorer, a few months ago, it was my view that we had slightly better than a 50 percent probability of prevailing in a conventional war at sea with the Soviet Union. Since that time we have disposed of additional ships and are scheduled to dispose of many more in the months ahead, although we still will be able to defeat the Soviet Navy in a fair fight in the middle of the ocean. However, their mission is an easier one than ours. As a land power, they merely have to cut our sea lines of communication. On the other hand, we as a sea power must have the greater amount of maritime capability needed to keep our sea lines open, a much tougher job. Viewed in that light, I think the odds have gone down. In a critical area like the eastern Mediterranean, very close to Soviet power and very distant from U.S. facilities, when our allies stand aside and leave us on our own so that we are lacking not only their military support but even the ability to operate our aircraft from their airfields, then we are taking increasingly great risks in standing up to the Soviets."

The President said, "I agree with your general proposition. My view is that at the present time we simply can't get sufficient support from the people and, therefore, in the Congress to do what is necessary in the defense field."

"Isn't it, therefore, important that we tell the people?" I asked.

The President said, "No, I think we have to first nail down, through negotiations, our advantage which now exists in the strategic field, get ourselves out of the war in southeast Asia which is making defense expenditures so unpopular, and then, after the 1972 election, go to the people for support for greater defense budgets."

I replied that I understood his point, and it seemed to me that it was a rational approach provided we were sure we could end up getting the edge in the strategic field. I said that I thought, given the deterioration in our conventional maritime power, the world would be very risky if we granted Soviet parity in the strategic field and that it would be absolutely dangerous if we ended up giving the Soviets strategic superiority while we were in the process of surrendering our conventional capability to keep sea lines open. I concluded by saying that if either parity or Soviet superiority in the strategic field were likely, then we ought to get started on making the case for greater defense budgets now.

The President replied that he thought he could get strategic superiority, but might have to settle for parity if there was inadequate support for defense budgets. He concluded the conversation by stating that he would like my advice on what we could do within the Mediterranean in the short term and in the long term to improve our capability there as a special case. I subsequently reported this conversation to Secretary Laird, who then invited me to visit the President with him on our return to the States.

The next day, 30 September, at Naples, the President and those of us in his party attended a meeting with the senior U.S., Italian, Turkish, and Greek military commanders under Admiral "Rivets" Rivero's NATO Southern Command, and then a meeting with the American Ambassadors to all the countries on the Mediterranean littoral except France and Spain. The most interesting aspect to me of those meetings was that at the first, the NATO meeting, the President spoke of burden-sharing and emphasized that the Soviet threat to the Mediterranean was not just a threat to the U.S., while at the second, the American meeting, he stressed that the recent crisis had clearly indicated that the U.S. was virtually on its own. Both points were valid, of course, but their close juxtaposition that day gave me the distinct impression that the Nixon Doctrine was not very convincing even to its author.

At the second meeting I was most interested in my official capacity in the remarks of Henry Tasca, the ambassador to Greece, and John J. Pritzlaff, Jr., the ambassador to Malta. Ambassador Tasca reported that the Greeks had been much impressed by the show of strength the Sixth Fleet had just put on, which was good news for me because I was already thinking about the Greek homeporting idea I have described in an earlier chapter, and I needed all the Greek enthusiasm for the Navy I could get to bring it off. Ambassador Pritzlaff spoke of the Maltese elections, scheduled for the following spring, as a probable tossup between George Borg-Olivier's conservative Nationalist Party, then in power, and Dom Mintoff's Malta Labor Party, which the Ambassador described as doctrinaire Socialist. He speculated that if Mintoff won the election, he would seek economic aid from the Soviet Union, particularly since England, Malta's traditional protector and benefactor, and Italy, the other European country with which Malta had close ties, were unable or unwilling—or both—to be of much help at this point. Both the President and Secretary Rogers said that it was important for the Conservatives to win the election, and asked what the United States could do toward that end. The Ambassador suggested a number of impact items, including the loan by the Navy of a civil engineer to do a needed port survey and of two patrol boats to operate against smugglers. The Navy did provide those items presently, which did not prevent Mintoff from winning the election, as we shall see.

Naturally much of the talk at the meeting was of the effect Nasser's death would have on the Middle Eastern situation. The general and plausible but, as it turned out, entirely erroneous expectations of the U.S. experts was that there would be a prolonged power struggle in Egypt, which would relegate that country to a subsidiary role in the Middle East for some time.

From Naples, Secretary Laird, Admiral Moorer, and I went on to visit the military leaders of Turkey and then Greece, those two NATO allies whose situation commanding the narrows at the eastern end of the Mediterranean makes them strategically critical to the alliance. We got back on 5 October, and two days later, in accordance with the President's directive in the Sixth Fleet, I went to see him with Secretary Laird. This meeting in the Executive Office Building was stiffer than the one we had had on *Springfield,* perhaps because the office was a much more formal setting than the wardroom of a cruiser. In any case there was little exchange of views; it was again more a briefing than a discussion. This is one of the few important occasions when I did not take notes. My account is from memory.

Secretary Laird first reported to the President on what we had said and heard in Turkey and Greece. Then he turned the meeting over to me and I went as concisely as I could through the list of items I wanted to bring to Mr. Nixon's attention. I had three suggestions for immediate low-cost actions that might increase the potential of the Sixth Fleet in another crisis. One was to improve communications between the Sixth Fleet commander and the U.S. embassies in the Mediterranean area so that intelligence reports could be exchanged rapidly. A second was to improve U.S. base facilities at Souda Bay, Crete, and Sigonella, Sicily. The President directed that both these steps be taken. My last recommendation was to arm the gunboats that were just then being deployed to trail the Soviet trailers with the small interim missiles that were all we had in the surface-to-surface missile line pending the deployment of Harpoon. That was a matter for the Secretary rather then the President; it had been one of my recommendations in Project 60 and now it got done.

Then I gave the President a quick summary of my plans for modernizing the Navy under Project 60 so that he would be fully aware that those plans would reduce the numbers of available ships so drastically that it would be extremely difficult to keep up the Sixth Fleet's strength without homeporting. And I reverted once more to the strategic value of Malta to the Russians and urged that the United States and the United Kingdom get together on a plan to ensure, at least, Malta's neutrality. The President expressed a desire similar to mine to act on Malta. Mr. Laird and I emphasized the strategic importance of Turkey and Greece in the light of what the Soviets could have done during the Jordan crisis and the need therefore to beef up their forces. The President indicated support for higher priorities for assistance to those two countries' military programs.

The two sessions with Mr. Nixon that I have just described turned out to be, though I had no way of knowing it at the time, the only such private sessions with him I was to have during my four years as CNO. I came away from them with the conviction that the President had a firm grasp on both the generalities of our military position in relation to the Soviets and the specifics of the Mediterranean scene, and with the belief that the President was, to put it somewhat crudely, pro-Navy, and would do what he thought he could to ensure that the reductions in the Navy's size he evidently felt necessary to meet budget constraints would not seriously damage its strength. I was troubled at what he had said at both the Chiefs' briefing and aboard *Springfield* about the difficulty of alerting the American public to the dangers of the situation, but politics was certainly a field in which I had no reason or impulse at that time to question his judgment. I was willing to wait for his reelection in 1972 for him to begin, as he had promised to do in our talk in the Sixth Fleet, "to go to the people for greater support for Defense budgets." In sum, I thought the successful Presidential bluff in the Mediterranean during the preceding weeks had been a notable piece of statesmanship, I was pleased that the Navy had been able to lend the bluff some credibility, and I was no less elated at being a member of the team than I had been three months earlier.

C H A P T E R 1 4

The Assistant

Perhaps the most fascinating experience of my first months as Chief of Naval Operations—or indeed of my naval career—was learning to understand the personality, the world outlook, and the business methods of the Assistant to the President for National Security Affairs, Henry A. Kissinger. (My first glimpse of the business methods, of course, was the sudden appearance of SALT's Option Echo on 9 July, my ninth day on the job. Top-level decision-making in the Kennedy era had proceeded in a much more systematic fashion, and so I was inclined to attribute Option Echo's arbitrary and hasty emergence to remediable defects in the system, among them insufficient analysis of or attention to SALT issues on the part of the Defense establishment. As I have reported, I sought an institutional remedy in the form of my Executive Panel.) My initial impressions of Kissinger were almost entirely favorable. I have never met a person with greater powers of seduction when he chooses to exercise them, and during our first several encounters he exercised them on me. He was not only charming and witty, but he made me feel I was a person whose advice and assistance he uniquely sought. I was more than willing to provide him with as much of both as I could.

One of our earliest encounters was on the occasion of a visit to Washington by President Sese Seko (or Joseph, as he then called himself) Mobutu of the Republic of the Congo (now Zaire). President Mobutu desired to receive a briefing on the Navy's riverine operations in Vietnam with a view to instituting a lake-and-river patrol program of his own. At the request of Kissinger's deputy, Al Haig, I arranged to give him such a briefing in Blair House on the morning of 5 August, along with two members of my old Vietnam —and present Washington—staff who were experts on the subject, Captain Chick Rauch and Commander Arie Sigmond. Half an hour before the briefing Henry telephoned to ask me to report its result to him after it was over. The briefing itself was a routine affair. The political people in Defense had instructed us not to commit ourselves to anything more than advice and we followed those instructions when President Mobutu indicated that he would like material assistance in the form of boats and training for their crews. I reported all this by telephone to Kissinger and he asked me to send him immediately a point paper on the subject so that he could inform President Nixon about it before the two Presidents met at 1500 that afternoon.

A little while later he called back to say that Mr. Nixon wanted to be forthcoming on this matter and was interested in doing two of the things I had mentioned as feasible in the point paper: send an expert to the Congo to survey the scene, and set up a program to train some 200 naval personnel as boat crewmen. Though I was reluctant to spend any of the Navy's scarce money on such a project, ultimately we did set up a training program, at a planned cost of less than $50,000, in the U.S. for Congolese personnel on the basis of a plan Commander Sigmond drew up after a reconnaissance trip to the Congo. On 31 August, Henry wrote me a letter of thanks I can only call fulsome, since it said among other things that the Navy "performed in such a way as to bring smiles to Tecumseh's weathered cheeks."

What I had not yet learned at the time these seemingly trivial events took place was that one of the great conflicts within the government was between Kissinger and my boss, Secretary of Defense Melvin Laird. It was partly substantive. They disagreed about the rate of withdrawal from Vietnam, strategic arms limitation, and a number of other matters of policy. Those differences, which under other circumstances might have been reconciled, were made all but irreconcilable by a running dispute over prerogatives and authority. Kissinger insisted that as a representative of the President he had the right to deal directly, and if need be secretly, with anyone in the government. Laird insisted that as a Constitutional official and a critical link in the chain of command he was the conduit through which all dealings with his subordinates must pass, and that he could not tolerate those subordinates being given orders outside the chain of command or engaging in activities that he knew nothing about. That of course was the school I had been brought up in as a military man, and indeed I had kept Secretary of the Navy Chafee and Deputy Secretary of Defense Packard informed of the various developments with respect to the Congo as they occurred. Nevertheless, Laird was infuriated at not having been consulted in advance and he let me know it.

As a result, when I saw Henry at a social engagement of some kind early in September, I told him that I would rather receive requests from him through the Secretary's office than informally. He said he would not operate that way, nor would the President, who considered each member of the Joint Chiefs to be a military advisor to him and who intended to go directly to each of us when he wanted undiluted military advice. I said that when it came to money, as the Congo situation had, it no longer was a matter of military advice but an administrative matter about which I had to keep my superiors completely informed, as I had done in this instance. He replied that he was speaking for the President and that any information he requested from me directly was for the exclusive benefit of the President and him, and he would take responsibility for it. Incidentally, I want to stress that this conversation was not angry, or even contentious, but entirely amicable. From then on, every time we got together for business, he referred to it as a "non-meeting." Nevertheless I soon concluded that professional ethics compelled me to pass along the substance of our conversations to Tom Moorer and to Mel Laird or his executive assistant.

I next glimpsed the secret world of Henry Kissinger while the highly visible events sketched in the previous chapter were occurring during September in connection with the Middle East. That month a small, quiet negotiation over a matter of much concern to the Navy took place between Kissinger and the Soviet ambassador, Anatoly Dobrynin. Part of the Kennedy-Khrushchev understanding that ended the Cuban missile crisis had been that the Soviet Union would, in the words of President Kennedy's 28 October 1962 statement, "stop building bases in Cuba," and dismantle their offensive weapons there and return them to the Soviet Union. Our international lawyers interpreted those words to mean that the agreement forbade base facilities in Cuba out of which Soviet vessels carrying nuclear weapons would or could operate.

Soon after I took over there came to my attention a series of intelligence reports about the frequent visits of Soviet naval vessels to Cuba. On 9 September, my notes show, there were seven Soviet ships, both fighting ships and auxiliaries, in Cienfuegos, where there was evidence of the building of a base that could be of a type that the 1962 agreement forbade. I was concerned by this and I expressed my concern to Admiral Moorer and Secretary Laird, submitting on 17 September a memorandum urging that this apparent Soviet effort to establish a base not be accepted. I sent a copy of this memo to Rear Admiral Rembrandt Robinson, the exceptionally knowledgeable and efficient officer who represented the Joint Chiefs at the White House as liaison officer. A few days later Rem came to see me with the draft of a paper Kissinger had asked him to write on this subject. It was an excellent paper that stated unequivocally that the United States would not accept at Cienfuegos or anywhere else in Cuba a base that could be used by Russian ships armed with strategic weapons. I asked Rem why this paper was not being routed through the Secretary of State, the Secretary of Defense, and the JCS. He stated that Kissinger did not want this done because he did not want any policy discussion on this matter. I asked him why. He replied that Henry did not like to bring Secretary Rogers into foreign policy matters that were delicate.

A few days afterward Rem returned with a rewrite that Kissinger had done and had given Ambassador Dobrynin as an *aide-memoire*. The wording of the key section of this second draft seemed to me careless and unfortunate, as all too often happens when technical details are negotiated without consulting experts. It read, approximately, "Nuclear submarines would not be permitted to use Cuba as an operating base." This made it clear enough that nuclear-powered submarines carrying nuclear weapons were prohibited, but it left unclear the status of diesel submarines carrying nuclear weapons and nuclear submarines not carrying nuclear weapons, and it did not spell out what an "operating base" is, which was the most damaging ambiguity of all. Rem agreed with me about this. He said that he had already brought the matter up with Kissinger, who had replied that it was too late to do anything about it. He advised me that Dobrynin had promised Kissinger that the Soviet Union would find an informal way to acknowledge that the Kennedy-Khrushchev agreement had been reaffirmed.

The way the Soviets found was a typically truculent statement issued by TASS on 13 October, just one day after the JCS discussed evidence of Soviet base building in Cienfuegos, including the delivery of port equipment by a Soviet LST. The first of its eight paragraphs was: "TASS has been authorized to state that the Soviet Union has not built and is not building its military base on Cuba and is not doing anything that would contradict the understanding reached between the governments of the USSR and the United States in 1962. Any assertions on 'possible violation' by the Soviet Union of the above-mentioned understanding are a concoction. The USSR has already strictly adhered to this understanding, will adhere to it in the future, too, and proceeds on the assumption that the American side will also strictly fulfill this understanding." Along with this statement, TASS issued a commentary by one Nikolai Chigir, which began, "The TASS statement . . . leaves no doubt that definite circles of the United States have not given up the fabrication of anti-Soviet insinuations, which was so extensively practiced during the 'cold war.' " At the end of the commentary Chigir said, "The present deliberately false accusations that the Soviet Union has allegedly 'violated' this understanding were intended, according to the plans of the enemies of the Cuban people, to serve as a justification for new provocations against Cuba." One tends to think of the "language of diplomacy" as being a soft way of saying hard things. However often enough, as in this case, it is a shrill and bumptious way of hiding acquiescence—though not well enough to fool Champ Blouin. On 16 October, Champ, though he knew nothing of the Kissinger-Dobrynin talks on the subject, sensed that the TASS announcement could not have been obtained without some U.S.-USSR negotiation, and remarked to his fellow OpDeps that certain matters that properly were the business of the JCS evidently were no longer coming to them.

Moreover the Russians were not acquiescent enough to refrain from testing the *aide-memoire*'s ambiguous wording. Always on "visits" of course, never for services at a base, Russia since October 1970 has successively sent into Cuban ports first types of ships that clearly did not violate the understanding, then a tender that could service submarines; a nuclear powered submarine carrying not ballistic missiles but torpedoes that could have had nuclear warheads; and with more publicity each time, a succession of diesel-powered ballistic-missile submarines. They have done all this in the face of a statement made in the fall of 1970 by Henry Kissinger that "The Soviet Union can be under no doubt that we would view the establishment of a strategic base in the Caribbean with the utmost seriousness."

I had three reasons for attaching importance to this issue: first, the Soviets clearly had been using their Cuban naval operations to test U.S. firmness of purpose at critical times as they had done with Berlin. I believed that passive acceptance would tempt the Soviets to intransigence in other situations. Second, if the Soviets had become able to maintain nuclear-missile-carrying submarines operating out of Cuba at that time, they would have increased by half the number of submarine missiles within firing range of the U.S. Third, since SALT has begun, the Russians have been seeking to make "forward based systems" (FBS), those nuclear-armed tactical American units, essential to the defense of NATO, that are deployed in NATO nations and assigned to the alliance, and the ballistic-missile submarines at Rota, Spain, and Holy Loch, Scotland, a part of the bargaining. They have not succeeded; the United States has stuck to its position that the proper forum in which to discuss FBS is another set of talks, between the NATO and Warsaw Pact countries, that have been proceeding fitfully for a number of years under the name of MBFR for Mutual and Balanced Force Reduction. However, a real Russian foothold in Cuba could have forced FBS out of MBFR into SALT, with damaging effects on the security of Western Europe.

During the last ten weeks or so of 1970, the single largest preoccupation in the Tank was the Defense budget or, more accurately, budgets. We were drawing up the budget for Fiscal Year 1972. We were trying to get Congress to enact the budget for Fiscal Year 1971, which had started on 1 July. And until it did we were spending, under a "continuing resolution," at the level prescribed in the budget for Fiscal Year 1970. The Congressional elections the President had awaited for a clue as to how to make his final decisions on the FY '72 budget, and for which he had unleashed Spiro Agnew and his alliterative polysyllables, took place during the beginning of this period. They resulted, of course, in a Republican gain of two in the Senate and a Democratic gain of thirteen in the House, which was hardly a mandate for or against anything. Mr. Nixon remained undecided and anxious to reexplore options.

I remember the mood of that particular time, which was edgy and often acrimonious, much better than I do the budgetary and bureaucratic details that provoked the edginess and acrimony. Though the President had hinted he favored more money for Defense, the Office of Management and Budget continued to grind out a budget the military considered grossly inadequate both absolutely with respect to need and relatively with respect to what the Soviets were spending. We knew at the time what Secretary Schlesinger said later in public: that the USSR, with half of America's gross national product, has been outspending America by about 60 percent on strategic forces and from 20 to 30 percent on conventional forces.

There was a running conflict between Henry Kissinger and Mel Laird over which of them had the last word about force levels. At the same time Laird told the Chiefs that he had had to say to Kissinger that he wished Kissinger would speak up once in a while in the White House debate over the Defense budget, during which arguments Laird felt "all alone." There was a running conflict within the Defense Department between two sets of budgeteers, the "scrubbers" who have the job of combing Defense budgets for non-essential details in order to cut them to the final levels approved by OMB, and the systems analysts, who hope against hope that budgets will make sense. The Chiefs, on the whole, are on the side of the scrubbers who do not, as the analysts do, make assumptions about enemy actions, a prerogative the Chiefs tend to believe is theirs. Moreover, scrubbers do not have any illusions that under present procedures budgets can make sense. They just want them to add up right. The Chiefs find this, if not helpful, at least reasonably honest.

There was a White House meeting on the budget that totally collapsed when Henry Kissinger, who was its chairman, got the idea that one of his National Security Decision Memorandums was being criticized and simply got up and left the room. There was another one that dissolved in confusion when Tom Moorer made a passing reference to the effect of one or another budgetary decision on the economy and George Shultz, the director of the Office of Management and Budget, snapped that the economy was none of the military's business. There was a meeting in the Tank at which the Army and Marine OpDeps almost came to blows over which Service would redeploy first from Vietnam and thus save a lot of money for itself. General Abrams—then still in South Vietnam—and General Chapman had agreed much earlier that the Marines would leave first, but in the rush by the Army to save money, that deal came unstuck.

My greatest personal frustration during this time was that although everyone, beginning presumably with the President and including Kissinger, Laird, and Moorer, implored the Chiefs to come up with a paper or papers that would show vividly and succinctly the effect of various budget levels on America's readiness and capability, only Chappy dared join me in my use of probabilities, which was surely the most vivid and succinct way of showing it. This subject got its fullest airing at a meeting in the Tank on 11 December. At Admiral Moorer's direction the Joint Staff had written a paper called "Worldwide Posture of U.S. Military Forces" in order to convey to the Secretary of Defense the Chiefs' assessment of the capability and readiness of the armed forces. The assessment was gloomy and we all concurred in it. However, I had appended a footnote to it, a footnote being the prescribed way for a Service to record its reservations about a Joint Staff paper, or to express additional views. Since consensus is the eternal goal in the Tank, every Service feels for another Service's footnotes the affection it otherwise bestows on Russian missiles in Cuba, and by the same token, each Service uses the threat of footnotes to extort conceptual or verbal concessions in Joint Staff papers from the other Services. In this instance I like to think that my motive was somewhat loftier; I wanted to provoke a debate about my percentages of confidence, and that was what my footnote was about. It amended the paper by describing the Navy's posture with numbers instead of adjectives.

I succeeded in provoking a debate. I opened it by saying that the military had had a long, hard struggle to convince its civilian superiors that the Russians were achieving strategic parity, if not superiority, and that if we did not want to go through the same process to convince them that the same thing was happening with conventional forces we would have to find a way to tell our story better. I said that I thought that numbers were more forceful and more explanatory than words and since no other Service seemed interested in that approach, I would just go it alone in a footnote that would clearly show that the U.S. Navy no longer had assurance that it could carry out its mission.

General Westmoreland took the floor. His point, if I grasped it, was that since percentages showed that the U.S. Navy no longer was superior, there obviously was something wrong with percentages. In furtherance of this point he had brought along numerous excerpts from the latest edition of Jane's *Fighting Ships,* and a memorandum analyzing the Jane's data that Dave Packard had sent to Henry Kissinger. Since the memorandum contained my 1 July 1970 55 percent figure, and my forecast that that figure was on the decrease, it didn't much help Westy's argument, nor did his citations out of Jane's of a number of ships that were in mothballs. Nevertheless he persisted. I'll quote Champ Blouin's report of the discussion: "Finally, General Westmoreland again said he just could not believe that the Soviet Navy could defeat the U.S. Navy in 1971. Admiral Zumwalt endeavored to explain to General Westmoreland that it would not be a matter of lining up all of the Soviet Navy on one side of a boundary and the U.S. Navy on the other."

The other chiefs then had their say. General John Meyer of the Air Force, who was sitting in for Jack Ryan, said he, too, was surprised by the pessimism of my footnote, but that its accuracy was not the point at this time. The point was whether a narrow evaluation of the capability of the U.S. Navy versus the Soviet Navy was appropriate in a paper that he took to be a discussion of the capability of all the forces of the U.S. and her allies versus all the forces of Russia and her allies. If it was appropriate, he added, perhaps each Service should write a footnote. It was a telling bureaucratic point, not to call it a threat.

General Lewis Walt of the Marines, sitting in for General Chapman, said the Marines were even more pessimistic than the Navy about the U.S. capability to fight overseas and resupply the forces there in view of the Soviet's submarine fleet, the largest in the world.

Admiral Moorer, throwing oil upon troubled waters as was his wont, said he agreed with General Walt and proposed that the Joint Staff work on further studies that would be more specific than the one under discussion about the capabilities of each Service. He asked me to withdraw my footnote, which I did, of course. Though in a real world situation the others shared my pessimism, as my reports of our discussions of Jordan made clear, when we undertook the subjective business of dividing the inadequate defense pie into service slices, both Air Force and Army expressed high confidence in naval capability.

Just before Christmas there was respite from the struggle. A legislative conference on the FY '71 (now half over) budget agreed on a cut of $650 million instead of the billion that had been planned on, and the Secretary's office completed its work on the FY '72 budget, giving the Navy almost a billion more in total obligational authority and almost half a billion more in expenditure than it had in FY '71. That meant a saving of seventy-seven ships. Instead of a net reduction of 212 during my first two years in office, there would be a net reduction of 135. I believe that the improvement in FY '71 (going from a very bad cut to a bad cut is an improvement, I guess) stemmed largely from the strong concern over America's decreasing strength that the JCS corporately reiterated for months; I know from two close associates on the White House staff that the improvement in FY '72 had something to do with my percentages.

If the reader finds himself dismayed by the way the government draws up defense budgets, let me welcome him to my club. The beginning of the process should be to analyze, as toughly as possible, Soviet capabilities versus U.S. capabilities in the several major categories of warfare, for the present and for the future, at various budget levels. The Defense establishment as a whole has attempted such net assessments, but never completed one. However the Navy has carried through several in various significant areas of naval warfare. They are complex and they take a lot of time to absorb. Their results always are somewhat uncertain because such factors as readiness, the quality of training, performance in the most recent exercises and, of course, the tactical intentions of the other side, vary from moment to moment. This is why I express those results numerically, in percentages—odds—rather than in flat predictions. In war, as in any other human activity, there are no sure things; to say you have a 75 percent chance of winning is to imply that you have a 25 percent chance of losing and vice versa. The point is that in the absence of thoughtful net assessments, no defense budget can truly be rational, and by not producing such assessments, the executive branch has assisted in practice those it condemns in theory, the Congressional budget cutters. Henry Kissinger recognized the problem when he said at a meeting on 9 November 1970 that "he had been trying with a spectacular lack of success to get an answer to the simple question of what these [the budgeted] forces could do that another set of forces cannot do"—though Henry didn't like the answers when he did get them. Perhaps the new budget committees of the Congress will get into this field. If they do, they will get a collective shock about what has happened to this country's defense capabilities.

Early in October, Kissinger had given the press a "background" briefing on the National Security Council system. He had said that the President, in the field of national security and foreign policy, wanted to operate according to a long-term—five-to-ten-year—plan. He wanted all decisions in this field to conform to that plan. He did not feel that the traditional adversary system, under which each part of the bureaucracy made recommendations about each specific problem, was useful. He did not want to receive any specific recommendations, just a set of alternative courses of action.

We discussed this in the Tank. Admiral Moorer's view of the net effect of this system was that it did not give the JCS a chance to participate in decisions that by law we were required to participate in and so we were forced to react after the fact. I too did not feel comfortable with Kissinger's desire that there be no formal recommendations, but I was willing to try informal recommendations. Certainly mine appeared to have been considered so far by the President, and I hoped Dr. Kissinger would give them as careful a hearing.

I met twice with Kissinger during November. The first meeting, an official "non-meeting" on the afternoon of 6 November in Kissinger's office, was in a way a follow-up of my earlier conversations with the President. I was anxious to maintain momentum about Malta and the various improvements in communications, deployment, and basing in the Mediterranean that I had discussed with Mr. Nixon. I also wanted to stress the importance of Turkey, Greece, and Portugal to the Navy's continuing presence in the Mediterranean in order to influence foreign policy toward stronger support for those nations. In regard to these substantive matters, Henry said no more than that I should not worry because he spoke for the President about such things. I was content with this because his cordiality and charm, and some of the things he said, made an overwhelmingly favorable impression on me. He told me that when I had a problem I should come straight to him, not go through Al Haig, because—here his voice lowered conspiratorially—he did not trust Haig, who was always trying to go behind his back directly to the President. He told me that Rem Robinson was authorized to tell Tom Moorer and me *everything* he, Kissinger, was doing. That statement looks a little odd today in the light of all the hoopla about the so-called "admirals' spy ring," of which I shall have more to say later, but I took it then as an entirely welcome, if unorthodox, expression of confidence and cooperation.

A few days later I invited Kissinger to join the Navy party at the Army-Navy football game, to be played on 28 November in Philadelphia, and he accepted. The official military parties traditionally ride up to Philadelphia from Washington on the morning of the game in a special train. There is no such thing as a non-business occasion in official Washington, but the trip to the game generally is a relaxed business occasion, at least. Kissinger and Nancy Maginnes, now his wife, sat in a double seat at the end of one of the Navy cars and more or less held court. In my large party of friends and associates was

Lieutenant Dave Halperin, my brilliant young assistant from South Vietnam days who was now my retention-board assistant. There was only one Navy man, the fewest from any Service, on Kissinger's staff, and at our meeting on the 6th I had urged him to take on another one. He had shown interest in the idea since he was about to lose David Young, his personal administrative aide who was being promoted to the President's staff.

Kissinger had a long talk with Halperin as the train left Washington and, when that was over, I walked down to the booth where Henry was sitting with Nancy Maginnes. The notes I wrote by hand immediately after that conversation ended are the best evidence of how it went:

1. K. became very interested in Dave Halperin after talking to him at length—asked me if I thought he would make a good replacement for David Young as special assistant to K. I gave Dave top marks. Would like to get Dave into his shop ASAP. Said he had to get rid of Dave Young.

2. He stresses that he wants someone who is not Army in the above job. He says he can't trust Al Haig who is "piping" around him to get to the President. He is high on Rem Robinson.

3. Long talk on the presentation I gave President at budget time on probabilities. I gave him run-down on the President's remarks to me privately in the Sixth Fleet re his priorities. K. does not agree with the President that American people can be turned around. He states strongly that the President misjudges the people. K. feels that U.S. has passed its historic high point like so many earlier civilizations. He believes U.S. is on downhill and cannot be roused by political challenge. He states that his job is to persuade the Russians to give us the best deal we can get, recognizing that the historical forces favor them. He says that he realizes that in the light of history he will be recognized as one of those who negotiated terms favorable to the Soviets, but that the American people have only themselves to blame because they lack stamina to stay the course against the Russians who are "Sparta to our Athens." I took him on strongly on this, saying that I couldn't accept that the decision to grant the Soviets superior capability in either strategic or conventional fields should be made without putting the issue to the people. K. said, "You don't get reelected to the Presidency on a platform that admits you got behind. You talk instead about the great partnership for peace achieved in your term." He asked a number of questions about the probabilities as briefed to the President in August and in the Sixth Fleet. He said he considered it to be the most intellectual briefing the President

had gotten from the Pentagon but that it was the kind of factual information that must be concealed from the public while we negotiate the best deal we can get.

4. I went into the POW issue. He confirmed that the President is solid in his resolve to keep the pressure on Hanoi to get them back.

5. K. manifests scorn for Secretary Rogers.

6. I couldn't get him interested in the economic issues. Nor in Latin America.

Next morning, back at Admiral's house, I made the following notes:

1. Also K. stresses that he felt that MIRVs and ABMs were inevitably linked in SALT and that we must freeze MIRVs if we would freeze ABMs.

2. K. spoke again about his pleasure that he was able to overturn the bureaucracy to keep SALT going, last August. I suggested that one could always be successful in negotiating with the Russians if willing to move to their position. He smiled and said, "Only three-quarters of the way." I urged that we take longer to debate the Soviets on each position and not move too fast. K. said, "that's easy for you to say, you don't have to run for reelection."

3. K. is convinced that Soviet intransigence at Helsinki is a result of splits in the Presidium. I gave him my Soviet succession thesis and pointed out that Brezhnev is too clearly in command for this to be a likely prospect. I came out that the Soviets are waiting for us to move to them.

Lest anyone be tempted to speculate that those notes betray an anti-Kissinger bias, let me reassert that whatever bias I had at the time was pro-Kissinger. The notes convey accurately enough the substance of our conversation, I'm sure, but they cannot convey Henry's cordial manner, his plausible tone or his verbal brilliance.

However, I was not completely bamboozled. Mouza reminds me that on the train home from Philadelphia I said to her, "I have seen Henry's view of the future and I don't like it." All my instincts rejected his prophecy of American decline. Nevertheless it shook me intellectually and made me resolve to rethink my theretofore unquestioned assumptions about America's future. For several days, whenever I could remove my attention from day-to-day business, I brooded. During one such reverie there leaped vividly to mind a day I have described earlier, the day in 1949 my family and I had spent at Pinehurst—courtesy of "Aunt Tina"—with that greatest of all twentieth century soldiers, George Catlett Marshall. It was another period when the United States had voluntarily scrapped much of its military strength. The Soviets were on the move in eastern and central Europe and no doubt already were plotting the North Korean invasion of the South, which was soon to occur. As I have already reported, when I had expressed pessimism about America's will to deal with the situation, the general replied: "Don't ever sell the American people short. They have vast reserves of hidden strength, ready to use when the crisis is clear." That was a far different vision, and to me a far more real one, than the one that had been urged upon me on the Philadelphia train. It was then, I think, that the Kissinger-Zumwalt mutual admiration society began to come unglued as far as Zumwalt was concerned. My mind was as intolerant of Kissinger's intimations of American decay as my stomach was.

My changing attitude toward Henry changed my attitude toward the existing relations between the Defense establishment and the White House. I began to say with increasing force in the Tank and in the Secretary's staff meetings that the military must insist on having more of a voice in the numerous formal studies of national security matters that Kissinger ordered, and that it must strive harder, as well, to get its views into the stream of informal papers that flowed between the two offices. My success in this endeavor was limited indeed, but I surely tried.

If I had to identify the exact time and place when the Kissinger-Zumwalt mutual admiration society began to come unglued as far as Kissinger was concerned, I would probably pick Valparaiso, Chile, at 1205 on 19 February 1971, when I entered the office of President Salvador Allende Gossens during the course of an official visit I was paying to Chile as a representative of the Joint Chiefs. It is only in recent months that I have reached full understanding of why my conversation with Allende that day infuriated Henry. It is a story worth telling from the beginning, which was on 4 September 1970. That was when Allende finished first in a three-way popular election for President with 36 percent of the vote, and seemed certain to be named to the Presidency in October by the legislature, which in the absence of a candidate with a clear majority had the last word.

The victory of Allende, an avowed Marxist, was unwelcome but not surprising to the U.S. government. In expectation of it, Kissinger on 24 July had issued National Security Study Memorandum (NSSM) 97 which had called for an interdepartmental study of the probable program, domestic and foreign, of an Allende regime. The study was completed on 19 August. It presented three alternative responses to an Allende regime by the United States: "Make a Conscious and Active Effort to Reach a Modus Vivendi," "Adopt a Restrained, Deliberate Posture," and "Seek to Isolate and Hamper Allende's Chile." Largely in the light of a CIA estimate that the United States had no vital national interests within Chile and that the world military balance of power would not be significantly altered by an Allende government, the preponderant sentiment within the government was to adopt the second option. I disagreed with the CIA estimate and therefore with the preponderant sentiment. I thought that the Soviets would be able to establish air and naval bases in Chile within a few years. If they did they could inhibit the U.S. Navy's ability to move its carriers, which are too big for the Panama Canal, from the Pacific around the Horn in a conventional war. Such bases also might serve, as Cuban missile bases might have, to provide a new axis of strategic attack by land or sea-based missiles on the United States itself. I made my position known to the Chairman—who agreed with it—the Secretary of Defense, and Dr. Kissinger in a memorandum dated 15 September, which was after the Chilean general election but before the legislature had acted. In that memorandum I advocated that even if it meant taking a "moderately high political risk," the United States should attempt to stimulate enough domestic anti-Allende sentiment to prevent Allende's election by the legislature. This advice appeared to have been ignored. It was only when I read the papers on 21 November 1975 that I learned that on the very day I had sent off my memorandum, the President had directed Richard Helms to block Allende's election if the CIA could, and without telling State, Defense, or the Ambassador to Chile about it. The President did express concern about Chile more or less publicly at the 30 September NATO meeting I attended in Naples.

On 14 October the Senior Review Group, a National Security Council offshoot chaired by Kissinger that meets regularly to discuss major policy questions, took up the Chile study. Among its conclusions were that the Allende government would be hostile to U.S. interests, and that from a military standpoint, Soviet opportunity for base development was a serious problem because of U.S. counterforce requirements which would follow. On 19 October, at another

SRG meeting, Kissinger, apparently annoyed with the State Department's moderate position on Chile, decreed that "The final determination of U.S. policy with regard to an Allende or a Marxist government in Chile is more important than issues faced in the Jordanian crisis and should be resolved by the National Security Council."

On 26 October, two days after the Chilean legislature had elected Allende President, I submitted a memorandum to the JCS entitled "U.S. Policy on Establishment of Extra-Continental Communist Bases in the Western Hemisphere" which the JCS adopted and submitted to the Secretary of Defense. It was designed to devise a policy that could deal with both Chile and Cuba. And during my 6 November non-meeting with Kissinger, I stressed the importance of preventing Soviet bases in Chile and left a point paper urging that we declare privately to the USSR that we could not accept Soviet presence in Chile. Kissinger agreed we could not accept such a presence. A few days later Kissinger signed a memorandum about policy toward Chile reflecting a Presidential decision that the public posture of the United States was to be correct but cool to avoid giving the Chilean government a basis on which to rally domestic and international support for consolidation of the regime, but at the same time the United States was to try to maximize domestic pressures on the Allende government to prevent its consolidation and limit its ability to implement policies contrary to U.S. and hemisphere interests. The President also ordered a number of economic restrictions to be carried out quietly.

At a 19 November SRG meeting the decision was made that with regard to our "public position" U.S. government officials should use the following statement: "The new president has taken office in accordance with Chilean constitutional procedures. We have no wish to prejudge the future of our relations with Chile, but naturally they will depend on the actions which the Chilean government take toward the United States and the Inter-American system."

On 10 December Kissinger directed "A study of the security implications of the establishment of Soviet military bases in Chile or the use of Chilean facilities by the Soviet military."

By 30 December 1970 a whole series of unannounced economic penalties against Chile had been approved by the SRG while the U.S. continued to state publicly its respect for the Chilean constitutional process and its unwillingness to prejudge the outcome of U.S.–Chilean relations. However, during the early winter there was an apparent shift in policy culminating on 17 February when the SRG directed State to draft instructions to the U.S. Ambassador to Chile to endeavor to influence pending legislation in Chile on nationalization of foreign firms so that the new laws would permit flexibility for U.S. companies in negotiating terms for compensation. Part of that pot-sweetening initiative was a decision to release a previous hold on M-41 tanks that Chile had purchased in order to prevent the Chilean military from turning to the Soviets for equipment. Although that SRG meeting was held after I left for the trip to South America, I was informed of its decisions by the Ambassador shortly after my arrival in Chile. Thus I had reason to believe that U.S. policy toward Chile, particularly with respect to relations between military officials of the two countries, had become warmer than official pronouncements made it out to be.

I left Washington for South America on 14 February. As a stand-in for Tom Moorer, I was to meet with military leaders in Brazil, Chile, Argentina, and, as it turned out at the last minute, Uruguay. My principal traveling companion was the Deputy Assistant Secretary of Defense for International Security Affairs, Armistead Selden, who before coming to the Pentagon had served in the House of Representatives, where he had been chairman of the Latin-American subcommittee of the House Foreign Affairs Committee. That meant I had instant expertise on Latin America available at all times in case the instructions I had received before leaving proved insufficient. Selden was a good judge of the Latin American scene. The trip lasted nine days.

Our visits to Brazil, Argentina, and Uruguay were more or less routine, edifying at the time but in retrospect of no great moment: we shook many hands, exchanged many views, listened to many requests for increased military aid and, on occasion, acquired a fresh insight into the local scene. The principal object of the exercise was for U.S. military leaders to continue on cordial terms with the military leaders of those countries, and that we accomplished.

The visit to Chile was anything but routine. Our schedule for the morning of our second and last day in Chile called for Admiral Raul Montero, my Chilean counterpart, to take Selden, Emmett Tidd, who was another member of the party, and me on a tour of naval facilities in Valparaiso. He picked us up in his limousine at the American embassy in Santiago and when we were about halfway between the two cities he suddenly informed us that the President wanted to see us in the summer palace in Valparaiso for a fifteen-minute courtesy call. Though correct procedure demands that such appointments be made through or, at the very least, with the knowledge and consent of the American Ambassador, and Selden and I had rather the feeling that we had been waylaid, there was no way we could refuse to go without abandoning our "correct but cool" stance and being overtly rude. Beyond that, the opportunity to meet so colorful and controversial a figure was impossible to turn down.

The fifteen-minute meeting turned into a seventy-minute one. Despite my suspicions of Allende's intentions and my conviction that U.S. policy should have sought to prevent his accession to power—not knowing that precisely such an attempt had been made and had failed—I found him one of the most fascinating men I have ever met. Though he spoke no English and my Spanish is very limited, the words I did understand combined with his eloquent looks and gestures and the way he used the map enabled me to follow him almost completely before his interpreter translated. He described how, when he was young, he had seen many of his countrymen die for lack of adequate medical care. He spoke of his aspiration to make Valparaiso a great international port with rail links to Argentina and throughout Chile, and showed us a scale model of the plans that were being made. He spoke of the need Chile had for financial assistance from any country willing and able to give it, the United States, the Soviet Union, or whomever. He spoke of his concern with U.S. attitudes and his bad press in the U.S.; while emphasizing that he was a Socialist, he stated he was not anti-American.

When Selden and I compared impressions later, we agreed that it was easy to understand Allende's success as a politician in view of his enormous vigor and charm, and that it was impossible to doubt his sincerity when he spoke of his aspirations for his people. As for the sincerity of the attitudes he expressed toward the United States, that was harder to judge. As we were preparing to leave, Allende suggested that the nuclear-powered carrier *Enterprise*, then visiting Rio de Janeiro and scheduled to sail around the Horn on the way to California, put in at Valparaiso. He himself would very much like to visit the ship, he said. Our only possible response to this invitation, of course, was to thank him for it, promise to forward it to the appropriate authorities, and leave room for possible refusal by telling him that *Enterprise* was on an extremely tight schedule. Later in the day Admiral Montero, who prior to our visit had put Allende up to issuing the invitation, pressed for its acceptance on the ground that it would strengthen the prestige of the Chilean military and its reputation for being non-political, and would slow down the rate of erosion of democratic institutions by Allende's Marxists.

Montero's advocacy of the visit carried much weight with me. As early as October, Chilean naval officers had predicted to U.S. naval officers that the "military will not intervene as a result of the popular vote . . . or the Congressional vote," but that "military officers . . . sworn to uphold the constitution . . . [would] if Allende usurped the constitutional authority . . . be morally and legally obliged to honor their oath, and intervention would be indicated." Admiral Montero had confirmed this view on my arrival in Chile.

It was therefore more than a matter of professional courtesy to Admiral Montero that made it important to give him what support I could with regard to *Enterprise*'s visit. Moreover, all of our briefings in Washington had stressed that the Chilean military was the most promising counterweight to Allende should he attempt to turn decisively in the direction of the Soviet Union. It was in the interest of the United States to remain on cordial terms with the Chilean military. It seemed to us also that turning down a direct invitation from the chief of state would be a rebuff that departed drastically from the stated policy of maintaining formally correct, if cool, relations with the Allende government. And it surely seemed consistent with the "warmer" actions taken by the U.S. as recently as 17 February, particularly the one that unfroze the delivery of the tanks. We concluded that we should recommend acceptance of the invitation. Ambassador Edward Korry, to whom we reported the episode in all its details as soon as we were back at the Embassy in Santiago, signified his concurrence and said he would immediately send a message to the Secretary of State to that effect, in parallel with the message Selden and I sent through Department of Defense channels.

We got back to Washington five days later to find to our surprise that we had stirred up a hornets' nest, or at any rate one large and formidable hornet. All the Defense people, Tom Moorer, Mel Laird, Dave Packard, told me that they agreed with Selden and me that it would be useful and consistent with the overtly correct and currently "warming" policy to accept President Allende's invitation, and indeed a message had been sent to *Enterprise* alerting the captain to the possibility of calling at Valparaiso. And on 25 February, the day after my return and the day on which I debriefed staff members of the National Security Council on my trip, Allende issued the invitation to the *Enterprise* publicly and formally. However, the State Department and the CIA were solidly against the idea, and so was Henry Kissinger, and on the 28th the invitation was turned down, reportedly on the direct order of the President himself.

That much was easy to understand. Clearly there were two sides to the story. What baffled me was the fact that Kissinger was in a black rage at Selden and me for starting the whole thing—or so I was told by Moorer and Laird and Packard and John Chafee. He did not directly rage at me. Kissinger himself said merely that a visit by *Enterprise* was going further toward getting along with Allende than he wanted to go right then. Al Haig, who I was informed had done some raging himself, said to my face that he had sympathized with my recommendation and that the whole thing was just a difference of opinion.

In speculating about the probable reasons for Kissinger's fury, let me first say that if the whole affair had occurred after I had become better acquainted with Kissinger's bizarre personality than I was then, I would not have searched for reasons quite so assiduously. Henry was altogether capable of flying into a fury for no reason, as indeed his principal also was. As far as popularity in the White House went, being a member of the Nixon administration was not just like riding a roller coaster, but like riding it blindfolded. Not only were changes of direction precipitous, but you never knew in advance whether you were about to go up, down, or around and around. Until Chile my course had been up practically all the way. After Chile I had, to coin a phrase, my ups and downs.

At any rate, I was at a loss at the time to explain Henry's fury but I think I can explain it now that Congressional investigation has brought out something approaching the full story of CIA activities in Chile. For one thing, I think the invitation to *Enterprise* was part of a continuing effort by Allende to smoke out the real intentions of the U.S. toward his administration. Being forced into the position of turning the invitation down must have annoyed Henry because it meant blowing a little of the ". . . but correct" part of his cover, and who better to vent his annoyance on than the messenger who bore the invitation? However, that appears to have been the least of it. As I have said, another element in the issuance of the invitation was the desire of moderate officers like Admiral Montero to gain increased influence over the Allende administration in order to temper its anti-U.S. tendencies. We now know that accommodation between Allende and the military was the opposite of what the President and

Kissinger were striving for. They had set the CIA to work at alienating the military from Allende. Perhaps they never spoke directly of a coup, but certainly that was one of the most likely outcomes of CIA success in the task it had been given. Of course no one in Defense, not even Mel Laird or Tom Moorer I conjecture—I cannot be absolutely sure—knew precisely what administration policy toward Chile was because Henry had made an elaborate point of not telling them. However, that fact was not likely to mollify a man of Henry's peculiar temperament when he found his plans being interfered with. He is a master at putting people who agree with him in false positions.

I might as well append a short footnote about Chile here, since I had nothing further to do with events in that country. I saw Admiral Montero, who became a valued friend, a few more times, once on his way back to Chile from Moscow, where he had gone reluctantly at the President's order to seek military assistance. He no longer was head of the Navy in September 1973 when the military coup that overthrew Allende took place. Some months before, doubtless in preparation for the coup, the military hierarchy had replaced him with an officer of less moderate views. Raul is a fine officer and a fine man who has had the misfortune of being a moderate in a polarized world.

CHAPTER 15

Up to Speed

By midwinter of 1971 I had been in the job of Chief of Naval Operations long enough to have brought myself, in the maritime phrase, "up to speed." I had suffered through my first attack of the budget cramps. The Navy under my tenure had been called upon to play a central part in an international mini-crisis. I had sized up the Navy's friends and foes in the Congress and they had done the same for me. I had become accustomed to the routine of the Tank and to the views and idiosyncracies of my Tankmates. My program for modernizing the Navy's personnel administration was off to a running start. I had appointed a group of military and civilian experts to a CNO's Executive Panel (CEP) that had begun studying various aspects of strategy and technology of particular interest to the Navy, and whose members and staff were available to me for advice whenever I needed it, which was often. I had assembled a personal staff able to lay before me in something approaching order the maddeningly numerous details of my job. Most important, I was beginning to get the hang of the delicate and convoluted relations among the principal framers of American politico-military policy, the President, Henry Kissinger, William Rogers, Melvin Laird; their principal agents for carrying that policy out, Richard Helms and the CIA establishment, Alexander Haig and the rest of the National Security Council's senior staff, George Shultz and his Office of Management and the Budget colleagues, and my fellow workers in Defense: Thomas Moorer and the other Joint Chiefs, Hyman Rickover and the senior admirals, John Chafee and John Warner of the Navy Department, and David Packard and other Defense Department civilians in critical positions in the Comptroller's office, Systems Analysis, and International Security Affairs.

My first months on watch had strengthened my conviction that the growing maritime power of the Soviets was the most immediate and formidable threat to the ability of the U.S. to back up a foreign policy designed to fulfill the nation's commitments to allies in Europe and Asia. The more I studied the implications of the Nixon Doctrine, with its emphasis on our supplying our allies and providing them with air and naval support, rather than fighting for them with large numbers of ground troops, the more evident it became to me that the Administration was increasing its reliance on the Navy as an instrument of foreign policy at the very time when it was allowing the Navy to undergo the most rapid shrinkage in its history. The credibility of the Nixon Doctrine clearly depended on U.S. control of the seas. There is no way except by sea for arms and supplies in quantity to get to the military forces of our allies in Europe or Asia. There is no way except by sea for aviation fuel to get to American air forces based in Europe or Asia. There is no way for naval air to be used off a combatant's coast if carriers cannot cross the oceans safely and stay afloat once across. Finally the increasing size and accuracy of Soviet strategic forces suggested that, if our own missiles were to continue to be a believable deterrent, more and more of them would have to go to sea. On 10 February, in response to a request from Admiral Moorer that I comment on a draft he had sent to me of the President's proposed "State of the World" message, I put my concern in what I hoped was tactful language:

> The underlying question is whether at this juncture of history a flexible posture aimed at exploring the utility of negotiations and some sort of accommodation with the Soviet Union best serves our future interests, or whether the time has come when we should begin to gird ourselves for a harsher adversary relation with the Soviet Union, whose global power and drive for world influence appear to be still on the rise. I think it is fair to say that since the Soviet Union became a bona fide nuclear power, American policy has been tending in the first direction, with security hedges in the second. Therefore, in a sense, the policy reflected today in the Nixon Doctrine is simply a further elaboration of this trend; certainly, it seems to answer more to the mood and temper of the American people at this period of preoccupation with domestic problems

than a call for a new crusade to turn back the tide of Soviet expansion and dynamism. However, it would seem that the critical issue put before the President is not whether time is running out for a policy of "negotiation with hedges," but whether hedges already taken or contemplated are adequate to prevent further, perhaps disastrous, decline of the U.S. world position if negotiation should fail.

Obviously I did not think the hedges already taken or contemplated were adequate. Some two weeks later I went over to the State Department to give senior officials there a briefing on what the Navy was currently thinking and doing, something I was asked to do periodically. I spoke from notes, as I generally do on such occasions. The notes show that I expressed myself in quite specific terms:

The main point I want to leave with you is that the nature of the threat the United States faces is changing. . . . Soviet seapower represents a substantially new dimension in world affairs . . . that is already beginning to trigger a quite different strategic environment for the U.S. than that to which we have become accustomed since World War II. We are accustomed to think of the USSR as only a land power. Now they are also a sea power. They threaten to "outflank" us from the sea not only in NATO but in other areas where our influence has been enhanced because our principal adversary could not operate there. We must begin to think of the Soviet presence in global terms. Soviet naval and maritime power make it possible for the Soviets to move beyond revolutionary rhetoric to direct involvement and support of factions anywhere in the world.

In previous chapters I have described how well established the activities of the Soviet Navy in the Mediterranean had become and how it had begun occasionally nosing around in Cuban waters. In the next chapter I shall have much to say about the increasing scope of its operations in the Indian Ocean. In the winter months of 1971 it became evident that the Soviets also were establishing a regular presence, small in size but worrisome in its implications, in the waters off the west coast of Africa. The first Soviet naval activity in that part of the world had occurred two years earlier, but it was a one-time, *ad hoc* kind of business, an exercise, in fact, in old-fashioned "gunboat diplomacy." In October of 1968, the government of Ghana had seized and sequestered at Takoradi a pair of Soviet trawlers that presumably had violated Ghana's territorial waters. For four months the USSR tried fruitlessly by ordinary diplomatic means to secure the release of the boats. In February of 1969 the Soviets first declared economic sanctions against Ghana, then sent a task group consisting of two destroyers equipped with cruise missiles, an oiler and a submarine, out of the Mediterranean and around the African bulge, arriving on the 15th at Conakry, the capital of Guinea, just north of Ghana, whose government is a strong Soviet sympathizer. Contrary to their usual practice, the Soviets loudly announced their presence and their intended date of departure, the 20th. On the 20th they moved further around the bulge into the Gulf of Guinea, and spent fifteen days there, during at least five of which they loitered conspicuously directly off the coast of Ghana. On 3 March the Ghanaians released the trawlers and most of their crews. On 5 March the task group left the Gulf for a hastily arranged port visit to Lagos in Nigeria. On 19 March Ghana released the remaining crew members. On 26 March the task group returned to the Mediterranean. It was a trivial incident, to be sure, and one might even say that Ghana brought her humiliation on herself by her refusal to engage in pre-gunboat diplomacy. However, insofar as it was a signal intended to tell the world that the USSR was ready, willing and able to protect its interests in parts of the world thitherto inaccessible to it, it was just a bit chilling.

Toward the end of 1970, an amphibious force from Portuguese Guinea unsuccessfully attacked Conakry, presumably because Guinea had been aiding insurgents in Portuguese Guinea. Once again the USSR sent warships out of the Mediterranean into West African waters, but this time it was not a task group with an isolated mission, but a regularly constituted two-destroyer patrol, concentrated off the coast of Portuguese Guinea, for the obvious purpose of discouraging any further activities against Guinea by Portugal. It is worth noting that Portugal is a member of NATO, not because that justifies her actions against Guinea but because the Soviets did not hesitate, in a part of the seas quite remote from their sources of supply, to challenge a member of an alliance accustomed to maritime supremacy.

From that time on, the USSR has maintained a naval presence, in a number of different forms, in west African waters. In 1971 that presence amounted to 661 ship days, which was 30 percent of all the Atlantic operations of Soviet surface warships. At the same time, the Soviets have built up Conakry as a naval base, so that they now have the capability of operating a few small ships, at least, in those waters for considerable periods of time without returning to the Mediterranean for replenishment. The ultimate significance of this is that the bulge of Africa commands the route that supertankers must take on their way from the Persian Gulf to the NATO countries. This was one vital sea line of communications that seemed to many strategic planners to be unthreatened or at least defensible. With the Soviets established on each side of the African continent, in Somalia on the east and Guinea on the west, and with them trying hard to set up two more establishments in Angola and in Mozambique, that is no longer a rational assumption.

In January of 1971 the Blue Ribbon Defense Panel, a group of prominent citizens, among them Deputy Secretary of Defense to be, William Clements, issued an unsolicited supplemental statement to its main report, which concerned the organizational structure of the Department of Defense. That statement warned of a significant shift of strategic balance away from the U.S. and toward the USSR. Among the points it cited to support this contention were the Soviets' numerical superiority in intercontinental ballistic missiles (ICBMs); their far greater rate of military spending relative to their economy, and the eternal risk of a disastrous technological surprise in weaponry that an open society runs when its most dangerous potential adversary is a closed society. As for the naval balance, it said that the USSR's huge submarine-building program could within two or three years wipe out America's advantage in short-range submarine-launched ballistic missiles (SLBMs), and that the Soviet Navy now challenged U.S. naval superiority in every conventional category except aircraft carriers. It was in light of this challenge, which the Panel desired to declassify and make public but the White House refused to, that I labored on my seasonal budget tasks.

Each time of the year brings its special kind of budget work, no one of which, it is safe to say, involves less contention than any other. In the late summer and fall, you may remember, the task is to induce Congress to appropriate that fiscal year's money before the year is too far along, and to put the final touches on the proposed budget for the following year so that the President can present it soon after the Congress convenes in January. In the winter and spring the task is justifying the budget that has just been presented (FY '72's in this instance) to the four Congressional committees concerned—Senate and House Armed Services for authorization, Senate and House Appropriations for appropriation—and participating in the long, acrimonious debates within the Defense Department that lay the groundwork for the next budget in line (FY '73's). My position was that because the Nixon Doctrine increased the Navy's share of Defense's foreign policy burden, the Navy should receive an increased share of the Defense budget—or at least take a proportionately smaller cut. Needless to say, the Army and the Air Force did not agree.

In theory, budget making is a quasi-scientific discipline governed by something known as PPBS, for Planning, Programming, Budgeting System. Just before the beginning of each calendar year, the office of the Secretary of Defense issues a schedule of the events that are supposed to take place under this system. This schedule presumably represents an orderly progression from the general to the particular, from broad strategic to narrow financial decisions. It begins with the Secretary issuing a memorandum that lays out in general terms U.S. long-range military strategy. On the basis of this memorandum, the Joint Chiefs write a Joint Strategic Objectives Plan that identifies with some specificity what the several Services will have to do separately and jointly to carry out this strategy. This is usually a fairly rancorous process, involving as it does each Service's parochial view of its own capabilities and prerogatives. I, and most of my fellow chiefs, stayed out of it as much as we could, leaving it to the fangs and claws of the OpDeps. Moreover I found this particular document to be almost as valueless to read as it was fatiguing to write. Some of its prescriptions always were in the process of being falsified by events. Others were so tortured a synthesis of mutually contradictory positions that the guidance they gave was minimal. However the JSOP was considered to be an integral link in the PPBS chain, and it was produced faithfully each year. By now it was the middle of January and time for each Service and each of the other Defense agencies to come forth with a revised and updated Five Year Defense Plan (FYDP). Five-year plans are the very heart, the *sine qua non,* of PPBS. They put such matters as procurement, construction, research, and recruiting in a large enough time frame to make the shape, the progress and the total costs of programs visible.

However, all of this is mere prologue. The real action begins during the first week in February when the Secretary issues his Tentative Fiscal Guidance. This is the document that first begins to address seriously the vital questions of how much money there is going to be and who is going to be expected to do what with it. The Services and the Joint Chiefs generally have about a month to prepare responses to this paper. It is a make-or-break month for them, their best opportunity during the year to make their cases before their superiors in the Department of Defense have reached conclusions they will be reluctant to change or have announced "tentative" decisions they will find difficult or impossible to rescind. When the Secretary receives the responses of the Services he is supposed to prepare an analysis of strategies, capabilities and costs that he submits for discussion to the Defense Program Review Committee of the National Security Council. The timetable called for that meeting to occur at the end of March. Out of it presumably would come the Presidential decisions about strategy, capability, and money that govern the size and character of the budget, decisions that mark the completion of PPBS's first P, Planning.

The significance of the "supposed to" and the "presumably" in the last paragraph is that it was at precisely this critical point in PPBS that Mel Laird and Henry Kissinger, who always were more or less at odds, were most at odds. The source of the contention here was the Defense Program Review Committee (DPRC) just mentioned, which was one of several National Security Council offshoots Kissinger had set up, with himself as chairman, to make sure his finger was in every pie. The Senior Review Group routinely considered major foreign-policy decisions. The Washington Special Action Group managed crises. The Verification Panel supervised SALT. The 40 Committee, named for the order that set it up, NSDM 40, reviewed and approved clandestine activities. And DPRC was supposed to review defense programs. The only thing was, Laird seldom let it. A man with a well-developed appreciation of his own statutory responsibilities and prerogatives, he took the position—with which I agreed wholeheartedly—that decisions about the details of defense programs were by law his to make, subject to Presidential guidance, of course. He further took the position that as a cabinet member who had been confirmed by the Senate and was responsible to the Congress for his performance, he was entitled to get presidential guidance from the President, and would not accept it from a mere Assistant, however brilliant and capable, who had no administrative authority and was not publicly accountable for his actions.

I doubt that anyone but Mel Laird could have maintained that position in the face of Mr. Nixon's intimacy with and heavy reliance on Kissinger. However, Laird was almost immune from reprisal for anything less than a major dereliction of duty because of his immense popularity in Congress, where his roots are. And though his surface is all small-town hail-fellow-well-met, beneath it is a cool canny mind whose forte is bureaucratic maneuver. He is particularly good at timing, at putting off till tomorrow the battle he cannot win today.

This was how Laird managed DPRC the spring I am writing of. First he got the meeting that was scheduled for March put off until April. Then he submitted documents for the April meeting that were confusing enough to make it necessary to schedule for July another meeting to straighten things out. Then he got the July one moved back to August. By that time we Chiefs were due to give the President our annual briefing, and the work of writing a Defense budget line by line had to begin at once if it was to be ready to submit to Congress in January. The trouble was that the same exercise that frustrated Kissinger also frustrated PPBS. It wrecked the timetable and bypassed a number of essential steps. The FY '73 budget as submitted to Congress was more the product of compromises and snap decisions than of orderly management—though of course even a budget that was supremely rational when it entered Congress would as likely as not exit from Congress in a shape that made PPBS a labor mostly lost. The chief value of PPBS when it is used faithfully and intelligently is that it is an effective policeman: it cannot guarantee a good budget but it can and does prevent or deter a grossly bad one. However the choice in the Laird/Packard years was not a PPBS or a non-PPBS budget so much as it was a Laird/Packard or a Kissinger budget. The Laird/Packard anti-PPBS legerdemain effectively prevented Kissinger from becoming *de facto* Secretary of Defense as he had already become *de facto* Secretary of State. And there is no doubt in my mind that the resulting budgets were better.

But I am getting far ahead of my story, whose main point is not what Kissinger did to Laird or vice versa but what the FY '73 budget did to America's military strength. The Secretary's Tentative Fiscal Guidance came out when it was supposed to and appalled all of us. It required each Service to spend during that year one billion dollars less than the FYDP called for. In other words, it took away from each Service money needed that year for the proper execution of existing, approved programs, money that each Service had every reason to expect. The only way the Navy can reduce its expenditures that drastically in any year is by reducing the size of its forces, by cutting ships and planes.

The money cannot come out of construction programs because of the nature of such programs. Only 6 percent of the money appropriated for building ships gets spent in the first year after it is appropriated and 21 percent in the second year. Incidentally, that is a slower spending rate than Army's and the Air Force's, whose hardware is faster to build. For aircraft the numbers are 16 percent in the first year and 53 percent in the second year. In other words, to cut construction expenditure by a billion dollars means giving up from eight to ten billion dollars in authorization.

The money cannot come out of the strategic forces, intelligence, military assistance, and the like, which account for 12 percent of the Navy budget, because those programs are not only dear to strategic planners and negotiators in the White House and elsewhere, but in sober fact must have the highest priority. And so the Tentative Fiscal Guidance maintained the level of those expenditures.

Big savings could be effected by cutting bases, many of which are unproductive or redundant, or at any rate dispensable, because 95 percent of the money appropriated for them gets spent the same year; but Congress loves bases, which provide jobs and business for voters. It took five years of effort, first by Admiral Moorer when he was CNO, then by me, plus reelection of the President, plus the political courage and bureaucratic skill of Elliot Richardson when he became Secretary of Defense two years after the time I am writing about, to induce the President to beard Congress and get rid of bases that previous cuts in ships and planes had made superfluous.

That leaves cutting ships and planes, whose operation and maintenance consume more than half the budget, and where a budget cut of a dollar saves a dollar, as the only way to effect a cut of the size ordered for FY '73. I need not repeat here the arguments that convince me that numbers of ships and planes are crucial to U.S. naval capability in the face of the Soviet naval buildup. I shall simply quote some passages from a 5 March 1971 memorandum I sent to John Chafee and, I hoped, through him to Mel Laird.

I find this potential force reduction, in addition to the requirements for broad cuts in planned procurements designed to modernize our forces for the future, to be unacceptable in the face of the Soviet threat. . . . I have informed you repeatedly of my concern for the continuing degradation of Naval capabilities. In my judgment, the end-FY '70 forces gave us a 55 percent probability of success if we became involved in a conflict at sea with the Soviet Union. Since that time, naval forces have been reduced for fiscal reasons by 111 ships including four carriers; the FY '73 Base Case [the Five-Year Plan] requires a reduction of twenty-eight ships and the decrement [the billion-dollar cut] a cut of thirty-six to seventy-three ships including four to five carriers. We are confronted in FY '73, therefore, with a naval ship inventory that may be as low as 525 ships compared with 769 at the end of FY '70. . . . While I judge our naval forces today have only a 35 percent chance in an engagement with the Soviet Union, that level of confidence is reduced to 20 percent based on the potential consequences of the Tentative Fiscal Guidance. It is perfectly clear that we are unable to support the fighting of a war overseas by the U.S. or allied forces should the Soviet Union challenge the U.S. for control of the seas. . . . The decremented forces would, for all practical purposes, constitute a one-ocean Navy.

Secretary Chafee supported this position with a long memo of his own to Laird. It concluded, "I would personally be very concerned if the Navy and Marine Corps funding is reduced below the FYDP level, especially in view of the Soviet naval threat. Frankly we are not at this time, even at the FYDP funding level, buying enough new ships and aircraft to maintain the present 650-ship Navy at an acceptable rate of modernization."

After firing this salvo, Secretary Chafee, with whom by this time I had an effective working partnership, and I were compelled to divert our attention for a few weeks from FY '73 to FY '72. We spent a good deal of time in March testifying before our four Congressional committees. Though the context there was defending a proposed budget to the legislative branch rather than attacking it within the executive branch, our testimony about the magnitude of the Soviet threat was little different than what we had said in our internal memos. I can best demonstrate the tenor of these hearings by quoting from a memo describing some off-the-record testimony of mine before the Senate Appropriations Committee:

Senator Case then asked what would happen if we had a bilateral conventional naval war with the USSR in 1972.

Admiral Zumwalt replied that in his judgment we would lose.

Senator Case stated that this was a devastating reply. He went on to state that if this was an accurate assessment, the Committee was wasting its time on this budget.

Senator Young inquired of General Chapman as to whether he agreed with Admiral Zumwalt.

General Chapman stated that he generally agreed. He said he believed that the U.S. had only a marginal capability of keeping the seas open in the event of a bilateral confrontation.

Starting with the last week in March there was a lull of about a month in the program of Congressional massage and the battle over the FY '73 budget resumed full force. I am looking as I write this at a six-inch-high stack of papers, most of them typed single-space with narrow margins. They are no more than a sampling of the literature on the subject of the FY '73 budget that flowed unceasingly from office to office in the Pentagon between 23 March, when I sent an "Impact Assessment of $1 Billion Decrement on the Navy" to the Chairman of the Joint Chiefs, and 26 April, when the DPRC meeting that was supposed to be the critical one took place. Do not fear. I shall not offer even a smattering of those papers here. For the most part they simply were elaborations or emendations, technical and rhetorical, of what I have already quoted about the dire effects of reducing the budget as much as the Tentative Fiscal Guidance instructed us to. There was no disagreement among the senior military men on that subject. As always, I took the position that the strongest way of making our case was by calculating percentages of confidence. As always, only one of the other Chiefs was willing to go along. As always, I continued to use those numbers. Indeed I appended to the "Impact" paper mentioned above a handwritten last paragraph reading, "I request that my 'Jimmy the Greek' odds be provided the DPRC."

There is one paper I think worth quoting from. Admiral Moorer at the end of March asked each of the Chiefs to prepare a paper showing "Illustrative Forces" that could be maintained with the billion-dollar decrement. I sent the Navy's paper to him on 10 April. It is from the covering memorandum that accompanied the paper that I quote:

Essentially, there are three major alternatives facing our nation in the allocation of limited national resources among the many increasing and competing needs:

A. To uphold our international commitments and provide the necessary resources to sustain them. As far as the Navy is concerned, the resources were available until 1 July 1970.

B. To determine the maximum portion of our national resources that can be devoted to national security and trim our commitments accordingly. As far as the Navy is concerned, this trimming process should commence by 1 July 1971.

C. To continue the present facade of keeping the commitments without providing the forces to sustain them, but be ready to back down when

our bluff is called. As far as the Navy is concerned, this becomes necessary at the latest on 1 July 1972 under the most optimistic Tentative
Fiscal Guidance alternative.

In my judgment, all those involved in the decision-making process,
both civilian and military, must fully understand that the prospect of our
bluff being called and of the JCS having to recommend backing down
will be increasingly likely as the balance of military power shifts from
the U.S. to the USSR.

As you can see, the weeks before the DPRC meeting were filled
not only with work but, for me at least, with emotion. We in the
Navy had made a big investment of professional knowledge and
pride in Project 60. It represented to us a chance for the Navy to
regain the command of the seas it was losing fast. We feared, and in
hindsight I cannot say that our fears were much exaggerated, that
the budget cuts of the kind we were being told to take would not only
dash our best hopes for the Navy but put the country in real jeopardy.

That was my mood on 15 April when I went to the basement of
the White House for one of my periodic "non-meetings" with Henry
Kissinger. As usual I came with an attaché case crammed with point
papers, twenty-four of them in all this time, on subjects as various
as "Possible Soviet Threat to U.S. Interests in Ethiopia" and "Ecua-
dor-U.S. Tuna Boat Controversy," "Medical Care for Foreign Nationals" and "7th Inter-American Naval War College Conference,"
"Indian Ocean Strategy Studies" and "Assistance to Malta." The
one I was burning to expatiate on was "Relationship of Force Modernization to Confidence Levels," and I did. What I said to Henry
at length that day was what I have already summarized in this and
preceding chapters: that control of the seas was a prerequisite of our
meeting our commitments to our allies; that numbers of ships and
planes are critical for control of the seas; that budget reductions are
magnified in force cuts; that the most accurate, as well as the most
vivid, way to express this complex of situations and events was in
confidence percentages. I brought along charts to illustrate my point.
I think I did well that day. My feeling was that I had impressed
Henry, and later Rem Robinson confirmed my impression.

It was not surprising for Kissinger to lean in the direction of the
Navy. The swift, sudden move is a part of his diplomatic repertoire
that he places much reliance on, and the Navy is the Service most
capable of moving swiftly and suddenly in parts of the world far from

home. He often has told me that he regards carriers as probably the most important of our non-strategic weapons. However his growing inclination to recommend a greater share of Defense money for the Navy roused the Army tiger in Al Haig. Haig knew that the President would not add to the Defense budget as a whole, so that if the Navy got more the Army would get less. He was not about to let that happen, and mounted a sustained attack on the credibility of my confidence figures. Since he is a professional military man and Kissinger is not, I had to accept a stalemate downstairs in the White House as well as upstairs in the Pentagon.

As a matter of fact the Army people were even more outraged by the Tentative Fiscal Guidance than I was. They were desperate. One of the documents that has to be composed in accordance with the PPBS drill is something called the Joint Forces Memorandum. Within the fiscal guidelines, it recommends the precise makeup of the forces that will be required over a period of years to carry out the strategic objectives that previous papers have detailed. One of the more diverting turns in that year's budget vaudeville was that the Army simply refused to recognize the billion-dollar decrement in its submission for the JFM and proposed force levels that assumed the billion had not been cut. The paper sailed through several levels of the Joint Staff in that form. Evidently the idea that the Army would ignore guidance from the Secretary was so far out that nobody plugged in a calculator and added up the numbers. The discrepancy finally was discovered in the OpDeps, where on 11 June, according to Admiral Blouin, "Admiral Blouin . . . expressed concern that a Service would make a submission that did not respond to the guidance." I read that to mean that Champ was in a fury.

The OpDeps wrangled over this novel maneuver by the Army on the 11th and next day the Chiefs took it up. The discussion was long and hot. General Palmer sat in for General Westmoreland that day. Champ's minutes say, "General Palmer repeated that the Secretary of the Army and the Chief of Staff, Army, were in complete agreement that they will not respond to fiscal guidance which allows less than 13⅓ Army divisions. Anything less than that will just not support the National Strategy. The Chief of Staff, Army's, position with respect to the JFM is consistent with the Secretary of the Army's. . . . The Secretary of the Army is stonewalling." He said the same thing in similar words many times. Finally I said that since the decrement meant that the Navy would not be able to make sure the Army got overseas and would not be able to maintain it overseas if it got there, the Army would not need as many divisions as it thought it did. I confess I was needling the Army. I was tired of being told by the Army during the budget discussions that the Navy was in splendid shape and the Army had every confidence in it. Pointing out your own Service's deficiencies to get more money is fair the way the game gets played in the Tank; when Congress set up the JCS as a committee it intended that the Secretary of Defense receive the information on which he bases his decisions through two channels, the corporate Joint Chiefs channel and the adversary each-service-for-itself channel. However, praising the other fellow's Service in order to make your own appear more needy is dirty pool. Ultimately Laird had to order the Army to drop a position that Blouin wrote, in his 12 June minutes, "borders on insubordination." Feelings that spring did run high.

In that connection it is worth mentioning just one more meeting of the Chiefs on the budget because it was one of the most intense meetings I have ever attended. It occurred a month earlier, on 3 May. The occasion was a debriefing by one of the chief Defense budgeteers, Gardiner Tucker, Assistant Secretary of Defense for Systems Analysis, of that DPRC meeting that was supposed to have settled all the underlying strategic and fiscal issues but didn't because Laird wouldn't let it. We were intense this time not because we were in conflict with one another, but because we were at our wits' ends in our search for a way to convince the President that his budget cuts risked what Westy rightly called "national disaster." I did a lot of plain talking at that meeting. Champ Blouin's notes give an accurate idea of what I said:

> Admiral Zumwalt commented that . . . it does not help the President to understand the military implications of Defense cuts unless he gets the full picture. Giving him Fiscal Year '72 and '73 is not enough as it doesn't show the cuts already taken and their impact on future years. Words just won't mean enough to the President. We need to show him more graphically and we need to say very bluntly just what the effect will be. For example, in '72 he has lost his power to influence the Eastern Mediterranean. In '73, he would lose the ability to support Italy and Japan. . . . Admiral Zumwalt then posed a question, "Does anyone here think, in a conventional war, we could win over the Soviets?" General Ryan and General Westmoreland thought that it would be a tough fight, but the U.S. would not lose. Admiral Zumwalt stated emphatically to the Army and Air Force Chiefs that the Navy would not be able to guarantee their getting the necessary logistics to fight with and they'd have to fight

with what they had on hand. Further the Navy would not be able to stay in the Eastern Mediterranean. Therefore he did not see how the Army and Air Force could fight in Europe for more than a few days without the sea lanes being open. General Ryan said he was not ready to accept the statement that it would be impossible to get the logistics to Europe. General Westmoreland felt Tucker's presentation painted a better picture than the real one. The Army could not fill the NATO requirements because they would have only eight divisions available until mobilization. Admiral Zumwalt said General Westmoreland was saying just what he had finished saying; we couldn't handle the Russians with what we had on hand in Europe. Further, since the Navy could not do it on the sea, it looked like the Army and the Navy would be depending on the Air Force to bail them out. . . .

Admiral Zumwalt commented that since he has been here as CNO, he has yet to see a paper which tells the President just what he has given up since taking office. . . . Tucker felt that in August, when the presentation is made to the President, it is important to tell him just what he'll have, not just what he has given up. We have to take a positive approach and show him what his capabilities will be. Nevertheless he thought it was a good point to show the losses too. But he could not have the President adopting a program that would constitute a legacy of failure. He could not leave that with the Country. Tucker felt it was not proper to just base the presentation on what had been lost since '64, because the situation is considerably different now from what it had been in '64. We now have strategic parity or worse and the Soviet general purpose forces present a greater challenge. Admiral Zumwalt said this just proved the situation was even worse. It was important to show the President the deterioration of U.S. power. It is not only we that are examining it; the Soviets are also watching and the President has just never been told what he can and can't do. . . .

I did all I could to tell him on 10 August when the Chiefs made their annual presentation to the President. So did Jack Ryan. One of the highlights of the meeting was Ryan, who had resisted my percentages up to then, stating flatly and surprisingly but in my view accurately that he thought the U.S. had less than a 50 percent chance of winning an air war with the USSR. I spent many hours preparing my brief for the occasion. I had less than a quarter of an hour in which to summarize the entire political and military case for strong sea power, so I had to compress drastically and laboriously. Moreover, I worked hard on the tone in which I delivered my message, which I considered as important as its substance. I was determined to resist the advice of those who thought that the President wanted or needed bland and reassuring words. I made a very hard sell.

The heart of my argument was a concept I called "relevant power," by which I meant "the specific force or power that can be effective in a particular situation." I pointed out that America's strategic deterrent force, essential as it was to our security, no longer was "relevant power" in the same sense as it had been, for example, in the Cuban missile crisis. It was now balanced, as it had not been then, by the Soviet strategic force, and the two canceled each other out. I gave examples of how relevant power had been used successfully and examples of how action had been unsuccessful because the nation or nations attempting it had not held relevant power. In the former category were the Soviet occupation of Hungary in 1956, when the relevant power had been the Soviet Army, the Lebanon crisis of 1958 when the relevant power had been the U.S. Navy, Marines, and Army, and the recent events in Jordan, when the Navy and Marines had been the relevant power. In the latter category were the British-French invasion of Suez in 1956, which failed because the relevant power was the air and sea power of the U.S. and the USSR, and President Kennedy's attempt to force a resolution of the situation in Laos in 1961, which failed because the relevant power was the armed strength of the Pathet Lao.

That exposition brought me to the point I wanted most to emphasize, that it looked as if U.S. sea power, if it remained strong, would be the relevant power in all the most probable confrontations in the 1970s; on the northern and southern flanks of NATO, in the Middle Eastern conflict, in the Indian Ocean, or in a threatened war at sea. The page of my notes that dealt with the reasons for this reads as follows:

REASONS FOR THE SHIFT IN LIKELY CONFLICTS—AND RELEVANT POWER

- Strategic Nuclear Standoff
- Escalatory Potential of Central European Conflict
- Unrest in Warsaw Pact
- U.S. Popular Attitudes Toward Long Conflict
- Shifting Soviet Strategy
    —Growth of Soviet Naval Power
    —Adroit Use by Soviets of Naval Power in Mediterranean, Africa, Indian Ocean, Northern European Flank
- Shifting U.S. Strategy—Nixon Doctrine

- Possible Growth in Preference for War on Oceans—
  Soviets Are Increasing Naval Power but Would Incur
  Less Risk in a Sea War
    —Inherently More Limited
    —Militarily More Decisive
    —Easier to Control Combatants and Terminate Hostilities
- Value of Naval Power in Crisis Management

I went on to compare and contrast in some detail the strengths of the U.S. and Soviet Navies. That led me to the conclusions that two more pages of my notes set forth better than any paraphrase could.

U.S. NAVY CAPABILITIES IN NATO CONFLICTS IN THE EARLY 1970s

1. With forces provided in 1970, the Navy *could:*
   Meet NATO Commitments
   Provide Tactical Air Assistance in Central Europe
   Support NATO Flanks
   Keep Sea Lanes Open with Moderate Losses

2. With forces supported in 1971, the capabilities are *marginal*

3. With forces supported in 1972, the Navy *must:*
   Reduce NATO Commitments for Amphibious Forces
   Abandon Western Pacific to Support NATO
   Minimize Tactical Air Support to Land Battle
   Withdraw Support of Greece and Turkey
   Accept Heavy Losses in Atlantic Sea Lanes

4. With forces supported by reduced FY '73 fiscal guidance, the Navy *cannot:*
   Resist Soviet power in the Pacific
   Control Mediterranean
   Provide Any Tactical Air to NATO
   Support Either NATO Flank
   Guarantee the Outcome

U.S. NAVY'S CAPABILITIES IN EARLY 1970s FOR WAR AT SEA WITH USSR

1. With forces provided in 1970, the Navy:
   Could Back Up Unilateral U.S. Guarantee to Israel and South Korea

2. With forces supported in 1971:
   A Unilateral Guarantee to Israel and South Korea is Largely Bluff

3. With forces supported in 1972, the Navy:
   Cannot Come to the Assistance of Israel or South Korea
   Must Abandon Eastern Mediterranean and Sea of Japan
   Cannot Support Nixon Doctrine

4. With forces supported by reduced FY '73 fiscal guidance, the Navy:
   Cannot Come to the Assistance of Japan
   Must Abandon Mediterranean and Western Pacific
   Can Defend Continental U.S. and overseas Territories Only

"The net result is that 'relevant' power is or soon will be held by the USSR," I said, and went on to recommend that America's military priorities should put sea-control forces at the top, second only to strategic forces, with sea-projection forces next and land-based air and ground forces at the bottom of the list. (I didn't look at Generals Ryan and Westmoreland when I said that but I can easily imagine what color the backs of their necks were.)

WHY THIS PRIORITY ORDERING?

- Relevant Power for Nixon Doctrine (War-Fighting and Crisis Management)
- Without Sea Control, U.S. Military Forces
Cannot be Used Overseas and Allies Cannot be
Supported (Over 90% of Supplies Must Move by Sea)
- Sea Control Guarantees Survivability of the Most
Important Strategic Forces—Polaris, Poseidon
- Seapower-Heavy Mix Complements Allied Contributions Best
- Best *Hedge* Against:
  —Late Intelligence
  —Geographic Uncertainty
- Only at Sea Might We Have to Go It Completely Alone

I ended my presentation with what I called an "austere program" of modernization, whose outline I have sketched in an earlier section of this book, that called for an increase in the Naval budget for FY '73 of $1.3 billion rather than the proposed $1 billion reduction. Along with this I presented a chart I had worked on very hard that showed, I think convincingly, that the billion-dollar reduction would leave the U.S. at the end of 1973 with only a 20 percent chance of victory in a naval showdown with the USSR, whereas the $1.3 billion increase would give us over time, if later budgets were commensurate, an even chance of winning. My last words were something the President had said at a news conference the year before:

One other point I would make briefly is this; what the Soviet Union needs in terms of military preparedness is different from what we need. They're a land power, primarily, with a great potential enemy on the east. We're primarily, of course, a sea power and our needs, therefore, are different.

I was selling as hard as I could. The country had too much at stake for me not to.

Before this session broke up, the President said that he wanted George Shultz, then Director of the Office of Management and the Budget, to hear what had been said at it. However for some reason it was not possible to find within the next few days a time when all the Chiefs and Shultz were free simultaneously. I was not going to let that kind of silly problem deter me from carrying the Navy's case to the country's chief budget maker. I arranged to call on Schultz at his office to give him the briefing I gave the President. To reach Shultz's office in the White House a visitor had to walk down a corridor that passed the suite occupied by Henry Kissinger and Al Haig. As I walked down that corridor on the way to see Shultz, I met Al. We exchanged greetings and went our respective ways. He did not ask me where I was going and I did not volunteer the information. As I left Shultz's office, after having briefed him, his secretary said to me that Al had called and asked why I was there, and she had told him. When I got back to the Pentagon there was a message on my desk to call Secretary Laird's executive assistant, Rear Admiral Dan Murphy. I did and he asked me if I had just given Shultz the Navy budget briefing. I said I had, and that I had told Secretary Chafee about doing so in advance. I asked what the cause of this inquiry was. Murphy answered that Al had called to complain to the Secretary that the Navy was taking unfair advantage of the Army. The result of this complaint was that the Chiefs suddenly discovered that it wasn't all that hard to make themselves available at a time Shultz found convenient and Shultz and members of his staff came to the Tank and got everybody's briefing. That was fine with me. I thought the OMB people should hear all the military views. Besides it enabled me to present the Navy's view twice.

Al, in the words of someone who saw him do it, "hit the fan" when he heard the priorities I recommended to the President. Those priorities also upset both Jack Ryan and Westy enough to cause them to complain to Admiral Moorer, with Westy carrying his displeasure a step further, to Secretary Laird. They based their complaint on the fact that I had run some three minutes over the time that had been allotted me, but everyone knew it was my priority list that had upset them. They got no satisfaction. I had shown my presentation in advance to both Tom and Mel and had received their assent to it. Tom's was enthusiastic. He and I almost always saw eye to eye on matters of strategy and he was delighted that the President was about to hear such a strong statement of the Navy's point of view. It was typical of Laird's courage and style that he had assented: I doubt that his assent meant agreement, since I was almost directly attacking the figures he had set out in his Fiscal Guidance. But I cannot be sure. The Fiscal Guidance represented not what Laird thought he needed but what he thought was the most he could get, so he may have been glad for me to attack the figures as too low. Mel made a practice of being tight-lipped in such situations, doubtless calculating that the less he committed himself the more room he had for maneuver. His response to Westy's complaint was that Bud Zumwalt had briefed him in advance which neither Ryan nor Westmoreland had done. All of that static was beside the point, in any case, since Mr. Nixon and Kissinger evidently were impressed by the brief. Indeed in December about one billion dollars was restored to the Navy budget. In fact each year for the period 1971–74 the Navy got one percent more of the Defense budget than it had the year before.

When it came to SALT, Kissinger was wholly and uncontestedly in command, as we all had learned the previous July when he had pulled Option Echo out of his hat. We Chiefs and our OpDeps spent much time in the Tank on SALT during the winter and spring of 1971. Doubtless that prolonged contemplation of the complicated subject of arms limitation stretched our intellects, but it accomplished little else. Indeed we were purposely kept performing essentially irrelevant tasks, although we did not know that at the time, of course. For that was the winter, as John Newhouse recounts circumstantially in *Cold Dawn,* obviously working from documents that never were shown to the Chiefs, that Kissinger and Soviet Ambassador Dobrynin opened their "back channel" for talking about arms limitation. That back channel, where the real negotiations took place, was so far back that neither the members of the U.S. SALT delegation nor even those senior officials who sat on the Verification Panel knew about it. That meant, among other things, that the information about SALT that General Allison and Admiral Moorer dispensed in the Tank was at best peripheral to the day-to-day substance of the negotiations. Hence we could not affect those negotiations, which was precisely what Kissinger and Dobrynin intended.

Those who want the innermost story of SALT must consult *Cold Dawn*, then. I was aware only of what occurred in the front channel. In the front channel the U.S. was standing on the "4 August Proposal," the formal embodiment of Option Echo that had been laid before the Russians the previous summer during SALT II, as the second formal session of negotiations was called, that had remained on the table throughout the recently concluded SALT III, and that evidently was to be given another run during SALT IV, scheduled to open in Vienna on 15 March. (In some places, confusingly enough, "SALT I" is used to denote all seven sessions that led to the May 1972 Moscow agreements and "SALT II" to all the sessions since. I shall use "SALT One" and "SALT Two", when I have occasion to refer to whole series of talks.) The 4 August proposal linked offensive and defensive weapons. It set a numerical ceiling, the same for each side, on offensive missiles, with subceilings on missiles of certain types, and it offered the Soviets a choice in defense between no anti-ballistic missile (ABM) system at all and a National Command Authority ABM, National Command Authority (NCA) being jargon for the seat of government.

I never have been able to fathom the rationale for the ABM part of the proposal. The Russians just then were deploying an ABM they called Galosh around Moscow, covering besides the NCA a good deal of industry and some missile fields. We were deploying an ABM we called Safeguard around some of our Minuteman sites in the west. Whichever of the two alternatives the Russians accepted, we would have had to dismantle Safeguard, which technologically looked a lot better than the Soviet ABM. That meant, if they chose the zero ABM alternative, that we would be giving up a good system in exchange for their giving up a bad one and, if they chose the NCA alternative, that we would have had, first, to perform the almost impossible task of inducing a Congress in which the sentiment that ABMs were destabilizing was strong to approve an ABM for Washington and, second, start building it from scratch while they were improving the system they already had in place. No wonder we in the military, although as good soldiers we had accepted Option Echo when it was thrust upon us, were reluctant to play the part of enthusiasts despite the continuing pressure on us to do so from both Kissinger's office and the Arms Control and Disarmament Agency.

There were several other bothersome aspects of the SALT situation. One was the appearance in Russian ICBM fields of huge new holes, evidently for supermissiles that eventually would be able to overpower Safeguard, or for that matter any Washington ABM that conformed to the limitations contained in the 4 August Proposal. In short, the Soviets were determined to trump one of our strongest cards in the talks, our superior ABM technology. Particularly infuriating in the face of this development was a propensity of certain Congressmen and commentators to associate SALT with the Defense budget in their utterances: to press for a quick agreement with the Russians so that the budget could be reduced quickly or, worse yet, to press for reduced expenditures for strategic arms at once on the ground that limitation of such arms was in sight. Talk like that can turn into a valuable bargaining chip for the Soviets. After all, the less reason they have to fear our military power, the less reason they have to restrain their own. Their big new missiles were more than sufficient evidence that they had grasped that elementary point as it applied to them. During the negotiations for the ban on nuclear testing a few years before they had tested while they talked. Now they were building powerful new arms while talking arms limitation.

Fortunately Mel Laird and Dave Packard grasped the point too and insisted that we continue our strategic programs, particularly Safeguard, unabated until an agreement was signed and sealed. For my part, as I have already related, the new Soviet missiles hardened my opinion that the Minuteman sites were indefensible in the long run and that prudence demanded that America begin immediately to make the very large investment required to develop Trident. One of the point papers I gave Kissinger at our 15 April non-meeting was on this subject. Most of all, I was worried that mounting public pressure for a quick fix would encourage some of our SALT negotiators to lapse into a state of mind that always is tempting when negotiations are long, complicated, and frustrating: a desire to make progress for progress's sake (with "progress" in quotation marks, of course). My reading of the Russians' standard negotiating technique is that they wait patiently for evidence of such a mood among their adversaries. If the evidence appears they pounce. If it does not, they make concessions. Too often during my watch the evidence appeared.

Certainly the way they had been negotiating, if that's the word, had been calculated to try our side's patience. They had come forward with no specific proposals of their own, but had confined themselves to rejecting all of ours. They had refused to consider any limitation of offensive weapons unless our Forward Based Systems

(FBS), as they called them, were included. FBS includes two kinds of systems, tactical nuclear weapons deployed in Western Europe and Turkey and Polaris-Poseidon submarines based at Rota, Spain, and Holy Loch, Scotland. The "tac nukes" are part of the "nuclear umbrella" the U. S. is committed to provide to NATO, and as such can be negotiated away only with the Allies' approval. Moreover the Soviets have a more-than-adequate counterpart to them in the Warsaw Pact short- and intermediate-range ballistic missiles poised in eastern Europe. As for the submarines, the U.S. position always was that if any strategic submarines were a subject of negotiations, all of them should be. In any case, the Soviets indicated that what they really would like best was an "ABM only" agreement. For our part, we did not feel we could discuss FBS bilaterally with the Russians without giving our allies great offense. And we considered a defensive agreement without a simultaneous offensive agreement to be dangerous in principle and even more dangerous in practice in view of the Soviet's new massive missiles and huge construction programs for submarine and shore based missiles. As far as I know neither the President nor Kissinger, to their credit, ever considered acceding to the "ABM only" demand, despite strong pressure from various overanxious folk in and out of Congress. In short, SALT between December and March not only was in recess but appeared to be at a standstill.

The first six weeks of SALT IV did not improve matters in the front channel. Our delegation went to Vienna with a new ABM option, "four-for-one," so called because it provided for the Russians to keep their Galosh around Moscow and us to keep our four-site Safeguard around Minuteman. Four-for-one might have made good sense if we had proposed it in the first place, but coming after we had offered "zero" and "NCA," both of which were better for the Russians than four-for-one and worse for us, it was merely ridiculous and the Russians rejected it as such. For their part they laid on the table a draft treaty that chose the most uncomfortable ABM alternative of the three, NCA. That also was ridiculous because they continued to refuse to discuss offensive weapons without FBS. Therefore we were able to reject NCA without embarrassment. The fact was that the proceedings in Vienna were a charade artfully constructed by Kissinger and Dobrynin to conceal what they were doing in Washington. However, we didn't know that. We were mystified by the obtuseness of the talks.

It was not until May that, as Newhouse puts it, the front channel began to catch up with the back channel, to our further mystification. During the first week of that month the Russians in Vienna hinted, first, that they might consider a joint freeze on missile construction; second, that they might let us off the NCA hook we had caught ourselves on. The delegation was summoned back to Washington for consultation. Roy Allison, when he showed up in the Tank on 12 May to report to us, was at as much of a loss as we to explain the Soviet shift. The minutes of that meeting relate everybody's bewilderment thus: "The biggest problem will be to decide how to deal with this latest Soviet gambit. Is it bait? How shall it be handled? What effect will it have on the U.S. 4 August proposal?" Moorer asked Allison to draft what he thought might be an acceptable revision of the 4 August proposal. Kissinger still had us spinning our wheels, which we began to perceive eight days later on 20 May, when Mr. Nixon and Soviet Premier Kosygin issued a joint statement that, though it has been quoted in dozens of other places, is short enough to be worth setting down once more:

> The Governments of the United States and the Soviet Union after reviewing the course of their talks on the limitation of strategic armaments, have agreed to concentrate this year on working out an agreement on the limitation of the deployment of antiballistic missile systems (ABMs). They have also agreed that, together with concluding an agreement to limit ABMs, they will agree on certain measures with respect to the limitation of offensive strategic weapons.
>
> The two sides are taking this course in the conviction that it will create more favorable conditions for further negotiations to limit all strategic arms. These negotiations will be actively pursued.

That statement explained some theretofore mysterious things, notably the peculiar character of the talks in Vienna and the persistent disinterest in technical analyses and advice that Kissinger's office had shown. Moreover, it put everyone on notice that some kind of agreement was pretty sure to be forthcoming soon. The statement all but eliminated a "no agreement" option. Now we faced the probability, Mr. Nixon's assurances to me in the Mediterranean notwithstanding, that if we could not negotiate an agreement favorable to the U.S., we would sign one that was unfavorable. That put the military, if I may use the expression, right under the gun.

However, the statement was so general in tone that we thought we still had an opportunity to influence not just the details of the forth-coming agreement, but its outlines as well. Now we know from Newhouse that the statement was backed up by an exchange of letters between the President and the Premier. I have not seen those letters, nor has any other military man as far as I know, but New-house implies strongly that he has and that they already contained the gist of the agreement that was signed at Moscow amid so much fanfare a year later: Soviet superiority in numbers of offensive mis-siles in return for letting us keep FBS and some Safeguard. The old prestidigitator's hand continued to be quicker than our eyes.

That year, 1971, was rather a quiet year in the Mediterranean. The Israelis and the Arabs continued to glare at each other but they did not exchange major blows. Unneeded for emergency duty, the Sixth Fleet could devote itself to correcting, to the extent inadequate funds permitted, the shortcomings in readiness that the Jordan crisis had brought to light and that Dave Packard had found still existed in the course of a visit to the Mediterranean in June. Much of this effort was managerial. In an organization as large and widely dispersed as the Navy there is always room for adjustments in such fields as replacement of material, maintenance of equipment, delivery of spare parts and training of personnel. However, there is a limit to how much effect managerial tightening can have when budgets are inadequate. Dave's findings fortunately led to the allocation of addi-tional funds for readiness in later years and reversed the decade-long trend in lowered fleet readiness.

Another important part of the effort to beef up the sixth fleet was the activity I have already described in connection with homeporting a carrier task force in Greece. During my entire term as CNO the Greek situation was an embarrassment. No one I know of in the government condoned the way the colonels' junta governed the country. However the United States' only leverage against the junta was to withhold military assistance from it. That would have denied us bases that we needed not just to hedge against a theoretical Soviet threat to NATO's southern flank, but to continue to exercise our influence on the course of the very untheoretical Arab-Israeli con-flict. I had no doubt that the better of the two disagreeable alterna-tives America faced in Greece was to stomach the junta in order to keep the bases. Every reexamination of U.S. policy by the National Security Council system came to the same conclusion, and I'm sure the Israelis agreed. Under the heading "Sixth Fleet Visits to Greek Ports" I sent Secretary Laird a memorandum on 30 July that read in part,

> As you know, Greece and especially Crete provide the easternmost bases in the Mediterranean which are available to the U. S. Navy. Were these bases to be denied, it would be more difficult and costly to conduct naval operations in the eastern Mediterranean, particularly sustained operations such as occurred during the Jordanian situation in 1970 and the Arab-Israeli war in 1967. As to port access in the Mediterranean, ship visits to North African ports are made only on rare occasions; visits to France and Turkey are very limited; and, currently, Malta is not available. This leaves Italy and Greece as the only countries in the central and eastern Mediterranean which permit relatively unrestricted ship visits. To illustrate the heavy dependence on Greek ports, during the past six months 533 Navy ship visits were made to Greek ports, representing 52 percent of the total port visits made by the Sixth Fleet in the Mediterranean.

I added a handwritten note:

> During the Jordanian crisis State felt that had it come to war only the Greeks, among NATO nations in the Med, could be counted on to let us use bases.

To explain why Malta was currently not available means going back a few months to that meeting with the President during which he expressed agreement with my view that we should do all we could to prevent the island from coming under Soviet influence. Rightly, I think, I took those words of the President's as a personal directive to me to do whatever I could to strengthen the hand of Dr. Borg-Olivier's Conservative government, which was sympathetic to NATO. However, beyond the small bits of technical assistance I have already described, there was little the Navy, or the U.S. Government as a whole, or NATO for that matter, could do about the Maltese elections, which were held in June of 1971. NATO was extremely unpopular among the Maltese and Dr. Borg-Olivier judged that the surest way for him to lose was to accept large favors from NATO or a country associated with NATO. He lost anyhow, by a narrow margin. His successor, Dom Mintoff, at once demanded of the British a far higher price than they had been paying for permission to maintain their naval and air base there. In short, with the elections over, the issue changed from an ideological to a financial one, and so became one to whose solution the United States could contribute.

Sometimes the way the "system" reaches a decision makes even me sympathize with Henry Kissinger's persistent efforts to bypass or bamboozle it. The President told me at the beginning of October 1970 that he thought the United States should urge and help the British to renew their base agreement with Malta. Ten months later, on 30 July 1971, an "interdepartmental action officers group" that for several weeks had laboriously studied U.S. policy toward Malta in response to a NSSM, decided that of six options they had formulated, the one that best suited the interests of the United States was "Actively Support the Renewal of the British Agreement." If Mr. Nixon ever heard of this recommendation, which I doubt, it must have pleased him that ten months after he articulated a policy an interdepartmental action officers group solemnly ratified it.

I played an unspectacular, but I think useful, part in supporting the renewal of the British agreement. For one thing I constituted myself as an unofficial tickling committee about Malta. I raised the question at each of my non-meetings with Kissinger, and telephoned Al Haig and Alexis Johnson about it from time to time. More importantly, perhaps, I was able to use my friendship with my naval counterparts in the Netherlands and Norway to successfully urge upon them my views about Malta at a time when their governments were leading the opposition within NATO to increased payments to the Maltese government. Those views, based on a September conversation with Haig, were "that we ought to pay a little more blackmail . . . rather than risk driving Mintoff too far leftward at this time." Both Vice Admiral Johnny Maas of the Netherlands and Vice Admiral Folke Johannessen, Chief of Defense Staff of Norway, carried considerable weight with their governments, and I think their intervention helped.

The negotiations between the British and the Maltese dragged along throughout the summer and fall. Finally Mintoff set a January 1972 deadline for compliance with his demands and the British prepared to remove their forces. In March the British and the Maltese signed a new lease calling for an annual payment of some 14 million pounds, three times what the Borg-Olivier government had been getting. Of that sum, the United States agreed to contribute 3,672,666⅔ pounds. Belgium, Germany, Italy and the Netherlands (thanks to Admiral Maas) also agreed to contribute. Another troublesome problem in the negotiations, what countries would be allowed to use Malta's shipyard facilities, was resolved by barring both the United States and the Warsaw Pact countries, and giving both the United Kingdom and Malta the individual right to veto any other job. The shipyards are Malta's principal source of income, so what Mintoff gained in ideological purity from this provision, he lost in foreign exchange. For my part, I was delighted for our Navy to forego use of Maltese facilities as long as our adversaries could not get in either.

Every portentous international negotiation has its minutiae. A curious one in the Malta negotiations was that the single merchantman (owned by a Greek operating out of London) that flew the Maltese flag had engaged in trade with North Vietnam. That made Malta ineligible for AID assistance under U.S. law. I took on the unofficial assignment of finding someone in the shipping business who could arrange the transfer of the ship's registry to a country that was not getting AID money. Somalia, a client of the Soviets, was the one we hit on, but as I remember it the issue became moot before the transfer could be effected.

I devoted much effort during 1971 to establishing relations, or strengthening those that existed already, between the U.S. Navy and the navies of our allies and friends. The Nixon Doctrine, with its emphasis on "burden sharing," called for making the naval capability of the NATO allies as large as possible in order that the U.S. could devote its full attention to the sea-control mission that is its responsibility to the alliance. With a few exceptions, the naval forces of the NATO countries consisted of small ships designed to operate in coastal waters, to engage in anti-submarine patrol, to lay or sweep mines, to repel amphibious assaults, to attack with torpedoes and so forth. If the U.S. could rest assured, on the basis of joint plans and exercises, that the allies could handle that part of the job, our fleet would be free to devote itself to deepwater activities. I believed that personal contacts between top commanders was the fastest and surest way of strengthening the bonds between fleets. Therefore I enthusiastically pushed Navy sponsorship of two international naval conferences at the Naval War College in Newport and I made a number of trips abroad whose chief purpose was to make myself known to my naval counterparts in friendly countries. I described the first of those trips, to South America in February, in the preceding chapter.

There is nothing like an official trip overseas to make a person realize how restful a ninety-six-hour week in Washington is. In sixteen days during the summer of 1971, from 28 June to 14 July, I visited seven European countries. Each one of those sixteen days I was either a guest or a host at an official luncheon and an official dinner, and on most days at afternoon or evening receptions or both. I talked business at breakfast every morning, generally with American embassy or military officials. Between meals there was a regular round of military reviews and inspections. All this was in addition, of course, to the serious talks with military and civilian leaders that presumably were the purpose of the trip in the first place. The trip took me to Sweden and the six northern NATO countries—Norway, Denmark, the Netherlands, Belgium, France, and the United Kingdom. I met with the naval chief in each of the countries; with the minister of Defense and the chief of the armed forces in most of them; with General Goodpaster, the Supreme Allied Commander in Europe, and Admirals Wendt and Bringle, the outgoing and incoming Commander in Chief, U.S. Navy in Europe; with Manlio Brosio and Joseph Luns, the outgoing and incoming Secretary-General of NATO, and with Prince Bernhard of the Netherlands and King Baudouin of Belgium.

What gets said about high policy at such meetings probably could get said just as well in reports or letters or over the telephone. In fact, sometimes it is merely an iteration of what already has been said from a distance. The value to me of my strenuous official journeys —and I found making them to be among the most rewarding things I did—lay in those moments, before the guns started to fire salutes or after all the toasts had been proposed and responded to, when the talk became informal or even personal, when my counterparts and I sized each other up and began to be friends. Admiral Michael Pollack of the Royal Navy; Vice Admiral Bengt Lundvall of Sweden; Admirals Folke Johannessen and Hans Skjong, the Chief of Defense Staff and General Inspector of Norway; Vice Admiral Sven Thostrup of Denmark; Vice Admiral Heinz Kunle of Germany; and Commodore Leon Lurquin of Belgium ceased to be mere names at the top or bottom of more or less gripping official documents and became known and professional quantities.

I attached great importance to developing those friendships with my fellow sailors in Latin America, Asia, and Europe. I made a point of writing them often, once a month if possible, and of performing whatever services for them in this country I appropriately could.

They did the same for me. They remain my friends today and I trust they will—family friends, for Mouza accompanied me on most of my trips. She was an important member of the official party, meeting with Navy wives, American and allied, helping them with their problems, raising their spirits, and calling my attention to many things I had no other way of finding out about.

My friendships overseas were as good for the country as they were for me. Earlier in this chapter I related how helpful Admiral Maas of the Netherlands and Admiral Johannessen of Norway were during the Malta negotiations. Similarly, when several NATO CNOs wrote me about the impact on their ship construction programs of a decision by our Deputy Secretary of Defense to delay, unilaterally, the scheduled deployment of NATO Sea Sparrow, a missile system they needed to complete their ships on schedule, I, who had looked these professionals in the eye and assured them that we would meet our schedules, fought like a trooper and won a reversal of that decision. We could not have asked each other to do these things nor expected such wholehearted responses, if we had not taken each other's measure, face to face, man to man.

One highlight of my NATO trip was a talk with Prince Bernhard of the Netherlands. Although his position as prince consort in a constitutional monarchy is one with no legal authority or power, Bernhard evidently has operated skillfully to nudge Dutch policies in the directions he thinks they should go. My friends in the Dutch military credit him with having been a major factor in slowing the rate of decrease in the strength of the armed forces of the Netherlands in the face of considerable public pressure to reduce their size and cost. Our talk inspired me with both appreciation for his candor and informality and respect for his comprehensive grasp of the world strategic situation. Much of what I said to him appears elsewhere in this book in other contexts. He asked me for a review of the situation in southeast Asia, for my views on the world maritime balance and on the strategic effect of opening the Suez Canal, and for an account of my personnel initiatives in the Navy, about which he was informed to an extent that surprised me. The thing he said that I remember best was on the evergreen subject of American troop levels in Europe, and it told me much about both his shrewdness and the practicality of the Nixon Doctrine's wish to shift more responsibility for defense to the allies. Bernhard said that if the U.S. reduced its troop levels in Europe, the allies would reduce theirs, on the ground that what was good for one was good for all, and that if the U.S. increased her troop levels in Europe, the allies would reduce theirs, on the ground that more U.S. troops meant fewer allied troops were needed. Therefore, he said, the only thing for the U.S. to do was to keep the level just where it was which would not give any other nation an excuse for making changes. He was absolutely right.

C H A P T E R   1 6

Tilt!

The most explosive event of 1971 occurred at the end of the year, halfway around the world from America, on the Indian subcontinent. It was the short war in which India crushed Pakistan, thus enabling East Pakistan to break away and become the independent nation of Bangladesh. The war provided a vivid illustration of the thesis I had presented to the President in August. The United States "tilted" toward Pakistan, but tilt as we would, we could not affect the war's outcome. We had no "relevant power" in that part of the world, even after we had sent Task Force 74, consisting of the nuclear carrier *Enterprise* and supporting ships, into the Indian Ocean as a token of our concern. The relevant power was the Indian Army and, in the background, strongly deployed in Soviet Central Asia and able to be deployed from Iraq, the military aviation of the Soviet Union, a nation that was tilting hard in the opposite direction from us. And if, as I believe, that particular situation was not of vital consequence to the United States, it was easy enough to imagine other situations in that part of the world that would be in view of the fact that 30 percent of America's, 80 percent of western Europe's and 90 percent of Japan's crude oil emanates from countries on or near the Persian Gulf.

The power balance in the Indian Ocean changed rapidly during the 1960s. For over a century its waters had been under the firm control of the British Navy. Two other imperial nations, aligned with Britain more often than not, France and the Netherlands, also had maintained a substantial naval presence in Asian waters. The breakup of the colonial empires was accompanied by gradual naval withdrawal, with the last British warships stationed east of Suez scheduled to leave the area for good by the end of 1971. None of the newly independent nations on the Indian Ocean's shores—in east Africa, on the Arabian Peninsula and the Persian Gulf, on the subcontinent itself and, eastward, on the Malaysian Peninsula and in the East Indian archipelago—had the maritime capability to replace that of the former colonial powers, or indeed much maritime capability at all. Moreover Japan, fairly close by, no longer was a naval power and China, in a geographically similar position, never had been. The United States presence in the Indian Ocean consisted of two old destroyers and a seaplane tender, impressively named the Middle East Force, that operated out of the British base on the island of Bahrain in the Persian Gulf.

In the early 1960s the Soviets slowly and quietly began moving in. Their first point of concentration was Somalia, which has the longest African coastline on the Indian Ocean. Shortly after Somalia became independent in 1960, they offered substantial economic assistance, which meant that Soviet merchantmen, coming out of the Black Sea and through the Suez Canal, paid frequent calls at Somali ports. They followed this with military assistance. By 1965, when the Somalis experienced difficulty in repaying Soviet loans, the Soviets imposed a trade agreement under which Somalia imported only Soviet oil, with a portion of the purchase price going toward loan repayment. In 1967, in the name of facilitating future delivery of heavy equipment, but to provide bunkering for Soviet ships as well, the USSR undertook to rebuild and modernize the port of Berbera. In 1968 Russian warships, a destroyer or two one time, a submarine or two another, sailing all the way from Vladivostok because the Suez Canal was closed as a result of the Seven Days War the year before between Israel and Egypt, began turning up in the Indian Ocean and visiting Somali ports. In 1969 the Soviet-trained and equipped Somali Army overthrew the elected government and instituted a military regime. By the end of 1971, Berbera had become a storage depot for Soviet naval logistics and a regular port of call for Soviet warships, including nuclear powered submarines. Now, in 1975, a large airfield with facilities for servicing Soviet aircraft enables those planes to cover the entire Indian Ocean; a naval communications center controls all Soviet naval units in the Indian Ocean, and a missile depot provides resupply to Soviet missile-firing warships.

Similarly, when the United Kingdom relinquished control of the Arab nation that now calls itself the People's Democratic Republic of Yemen, the radical regime that seized power received assistance from the USSR that has enabled it to support an insurgency against the Sheikdom of Oman across the border. In return the PDRY has granted the Soviets bunkering rights and maintenance facilities for warships, including the permanent presence of a small number of Soviet personnel, at the old British naval base of Aden, and similar privileges for Soviet military aviation at an adjacent airfield that used to be a Royal Air Force base. In Iraq, in return for large deliveries of arms, the government has allowed the Soviets to build major airfields, capable of use by warplanes, and a facility for small naval vessels at Um Qasr at the head of the Persian Gulf. In addition an ostensibly Iraqi base in the same port is being built under the supervision of Soviet technicians and the nearby deepwater port of Basra has been used by a large Soviet Navy repair ship to support warships on patrol in the Persian Gulf, and at its outlet, the narrow Straits of Hormuz.

The pattern of Soviet expansion in the Indian Ocean was already clear when Henry Kissinger and I held our 6 November 1970 non-meeting, and we discussed its implications in some detail. On 9 November 1970 Kissinger promulgated National Security Study Memorandum 104, which called for "an assessment of possible Soviet naval threats to U.S. interests in the Indian Ocean area and the development of friendly naval force and basing alternatives consistent with varying judgments about possible threats and interests over the 1971–1975 period." That was the beginning of a year or more of governmental brooding about what, if anything, the United States could and should do in that part of the world. NSSM 104, which produced a limited exploration of military alternatives, under Defense Department chairmanship, soon was followed by NSSM 109, which decreed a study on policy for South Asia and then by NSSM 110, asking for a much broader politico/military analysis, chaired by State. A little later came NSSM 118 ordering a Contingency Study on Pakistan secession. Finally NSSM 133 required contingency planning on South Asia. This piling of study upon study resulted in what I can only call a verbal mudslide.

However, one scarcely had to wade all the way through it to be aware that, though no one thought that an emergency calling for immediate drastic action existed, there were two distinct points of view about the Indian Ocean area within the government. One group

of officials and analysts, most of them in or around State and the
Arms Control and Disarmament Agency, felt that the United States
had no vital interests in the Indian Ocean that the Russians were
likely to threaten. The other group, including the entire military,
took the opposite view. In my opinion the Soviets had three probable
strategic objectives in the Indian Ocean. One was to complete the
encirclement of China from the south. Another was to radicalize as
many Middle Eastern regimes as possible in order in the short term
to influence the outcome of the Arab-Israeli conflict and in the
long-term to secure political access to oil resources. A third was to
develop a military capability that could interfere or, in support of
political objectives, could threaten to interfere with oil deliveries to
Japan and Europe if an occasion ever arose to do so. The last two
certainly appeared to me to be direct and serious challenges to important interests of the United States.

The differing points of view led to differing strategic recommendations. Those who saw no real threat advocated a policy of negotiated
mutual reduction of naval forces in the area. Those who believed
there was a threat were vehemently opposed to such a course on the
ground that a withdrawal of the two navies would leave the area to
the mercy of Soviet long-range air, which could control it with ease.
Those of us who took the latter view advocated a continuing and
regularized U.S. naval presence in the Indian Ocean, if possible in
coordination with operations by the British, Australians, and whatever other allies had the ships for it. We advocated upgrading the
Middle East Force. And we advocated improving naval and air
facilities on the island of Diego Garcia in the Chagos Archipelago.
The two factions held their diametrically opposed views about Indian Ocean policy so stubbornly that the President evidently found
it impossible, or at least inadvisable, to decide between them.

Meanwhile, beginning in March 1971, relations between India and
Pakistan deteriorated fast, and the problem of formulating a comprehensive American policy for the Indian Ocean was becoming less and
less academic. For some time negotiations had been in progress
between the government of Pakistan and the Awami League, which
was seeking autonomy for the province of East Bengal. In March
those negotiations broke down. The Pakistani government put East
Pakistan under martial law and instituted a savage program of re-
pression there, much of it directed against the large Hindu population. That naturally aroused the indignation of the Indian government, whose wrath was augmented when refugees by the millions

began pouring into India from East Bengal. Those refugees were highly visible proof of Pakistan's iniquity. They were a threat to law and order. And they were a heavy economic burden. India took on the role of leader and supplier of a guerilla movement that was beginning to organize itself in East Bengal and whose program had gone beyond autonomy and now called for complete independence.

The first response of the United States to these events was to stop military assistance to Pakistan—India had not received any since the Indian-Pakistan war of 1965—as one way, among others, of inducing Pakistan to make concessions in East Bengal. However, the Pakistanis were stubborn and slow to respond and India was getting hotter fast.

Then, in July, Henry Kissinger astounded the world by showing up in Peking. That event was partly made possible, it is relevant to point out, by the good offices of Pakistan in helping revive communications channels between the United States and China that two decades of disuse had all but atrophied. Indeed Pakistan was the starting point for the last leg of Henry's secret journey.

The new relationship between the United States and China gave U.S. diplomacy a new dimension in many situations. It made SALT go faster. It made the Vietnam war end sooner. It eliminated a source of friction between us and our European allies. But nowhere was its impact greater—or less favorable to the U.S.—than on the subcontinent. India saw it as evidence that she could no longer count on U.S. support against Chinese intervention, which to India's mind was an ever-present threat. And so in August India signed a treaty of peace and friendship with the Soviet Union—a treaty that, as I have testified to the Congress, I believe contains a secret protocol giving the Soviet Navy base rights at Visakhapatnam—and thus became for some purposes a Soviet client. That event did not diminish the interest of the U.S. in forestalling a war between India and Pakistan, which was beginning to look likely, or even inevitable. However, it did change some feelings in exalted circles, as we shall see.

By this time the reams of paper that all those NSSMs had elicited had been OBE (overtaken by events), and policy was getting made, as it all too often does, reactively and *ad hoc*. The Washington Special Action Group began meeting regularly on India-Pakistan. It was unable to influence events. Once cold weather had closed the Himalayan passes and thus precluded any direct immediate intervention from China, India felt free to act. And once India acted, all the

President could think of to do was "tilt." It was not what you would call a decisive policy, or an effective one.

The Washington Special Action Group met on India-Pakistan on 17 August, 8 September, 7 October, 22 and 23 November, and 1, 3, 4, 6, and 8 December, a schedule that reflects accurately the administration's cycle of concern. As I reread descriptions of those events three and a half years later, I am struck most by the mood of bafflement they convey. All the principal members of WSAG were officials close to the top of the government, men presumably accustomed to and adept at influencing, if not shaping, events: Henry Kissinger in the chair, John Irwin or Alexis Johnson, both great professionals, from State, Dave Packard from Defense, Richard Helms or his deputy from CIA, Tom Moorer or occasionally one of us other Chiefs from the Joint Chiefs, one of several top officials from AID. Yet the minutes show them—us—groping for and never finding a line of action that might make America a factor in the ever more turbulent situation on the subcontinent. We were always behind events and our responses were as ineffectual as they were tardy. "Strong" diplomatic representations produced no results. Nor did appealing to Moscow to use its good offices to restrain its new ally. Nor did taking the matter first to the United Nations Security Council, then to its General Assembly. Nor, ultimately, did cutting off every bit of economic assistance to India that could be cut off. At a press conference on 21 November, Prime Minister Indira Gandhi said that India would act in her own national interests "whatever be the world opinion," and that is precisely what India did do. On 3 December Indian troops crossed the border into East Pakistan and commenced a military holding action against West Pakistan. On 16 December the Pakistanis surrendered in the East. On 17 December a cease-fire went into effect in the West. Among WSAG members only Dave Packard, as far as one can tell from the records, perceived how feckless all our initiatives were. On several occasions he suggested that since the U.S. evidently was unable to do anything effective, it should do nothing at all. That intelligent comment, the minutes show, never received a reply: the talk went on as if Dave had not spoken—and the war went on as if the talk had not.

A second notable feature of those minutes is their depiction of Henry Kissinger's increasing irritability, not to say fury, in the face of his persistent inability to divert India by as much as a hair from the course it had chosen to pursue. Doubtless a statesman shouldn't take his failures, which are bound to occur, personally, but Henry is not the only statesman who does. It was with this aspect of the WSAG meetings that Jack Anderson, in his celebrated revelations of the WSAG minutes, had the most fun.

From the 7 October meeting: "Dr. Kissinger stated forcefully that the Indians must be made aware that we will cut off all aid if they go to war, that this, in fact, would be the least the President would do. They must understand the enormously serious consequences we would attach to the initiation of hostilities." That was simply whistling in the wind since cutting off all aid was, in fact, the most the President *could* do.

From the 23 November meeting: "Mr. Van Hollen [of State] questioned the basic U.S. objective in cutting off U.S. aid to India, particularly since the war would likely be a short one. Dr. Kissinger replied that he felt it is important that the Indians not be able to face the U.S. down, and this might be the vehicle needed to show the Indians that we mean business. . . . Mr. Packard stated that we should think twice about taking action that, in fact, may do no good. He thought . . . we should think very hard about a cut in economic aid." The fact was that by doing what they wanted to do despite the cut in aid, the Indians *did* face the U.S. down.

From the 3 December meeting: "Dr. Kissinger opened the session by indicating that the President very definitely wants to tilt the present situation toward the Paks . . . According to Dr. Kissinger, the President has stated that he did not wish our presentation to be 'even-handed' in the Security Council."

From the 4 December meeting, which I attended: "Dr. Kissinger said that whoever was putting out background information relative to the current situation is provoking presidential wrath. The President is under the 'illusion' that he is giving instructions; not that he is merely being kept apprised of affairs as they progress. Dr. Kissinger asked that this be kept in mind." What the minutes of that meeting do not show, since minutes often get laundered in an effort to preserve an illusion of sweetness and light, is that I questioned the policy of tilt on the ground that it would help the Soviets cement their position in India. That infuriated Henry. In a White House corridor after the meeting adjourned I went after him again on the matter and he berated me severely and shrilly. A favorite gambit of his in such situations is to challenge his adversary to take his case to the President. I said I would be glad to if he would arrange such a meeting. That was the last I heard of that.

From the 6 December meeting: "Dr. Kissinger also directed that henceforth we show a certain coolness to the Indians; the Indian Ambassador is not to be treated at too high a level."

From the 8 December meeting: "Dr. Kissinger stated that current orders are not to put anything into the budget for India only to have the 'wicked' White House take it out. . . . Dr. Kissinger said that we are not trying to be even-handed. There can be no doubt what the President wants. The President does not want to be even-handed. The President believes that India is the attacker. We are trying to get across the idea that India has jeopardized relations with the United States. Dr. Kissinger said that we cannot afford to ease India's state of mind. 'The Lady' is cold blooded and tough and will not turn into a Soviet satellite merely because of pique. We should not ease her mind. He invited anyone who objected to this approach to take his case to the President."

On 10 December, a Presidential order that was not discussed with the Navy in advance created Task Group 74, consisting of the nuclear carrier *Enterprise* and appropriate escorts and supply ships, and sent it steaming from the Gulf of Tonkin, where the ships had been on station, to Singapore. The order did not specify what TG 74's mission was, nor could anyone, including the Chairman of the Joint Chiefs, tell me. In talking with Mel Laird and Tom Moorer I sought to be sure that these ships either had a mission or were not sent in harm's way. Tom shared my concern. The ships were held off Singapore for two days. On 12 December they were ordered through the Straits of Malacca into the Indian Ocean. Within an hour that order was rescinded. Next day it was reissued, with the additional proviso that as much of the passage through the Straits as possible be in daylight, in other words, in full view of the world. At the same time "sources" in Washington let it be known that the object of the exercise was covering the evacuation of American civilians from Dacca in East Bengal. This clearly was a cover story since that evacuation, after having been impeded by the fighting for a week, was successfully completed two days before TG 74 entered the Indian Ocean.

The naval situation in the Indian Ocean just then was complicated and confusing. Quite by chance, a large British Navy task group, including two carriers, the last ships of the British fleet to remain east of Suez, was on its way home through the Indian Ocean at the time India marched into East Bengal. Two days after that invasion a Soviet destroyer and minesweeper, whose mission had been to relieve the destroyer and minesweeper that had been on station for six months, came through the Straits of Malacca. In view of the war, the relief became a reinforcement; the original contingent stayed on. Furthermore, on 6 or 7 December, the Russians detached a cruiser armed with cruise missiles, and escorts for it, from their Pacific Ocean Fleet and sent them toward the Indian Ocean. They were sighted by the Japanese in the Straits of Tsushima on 9 December. Though those ships did not reach the Straits of Malacca until 18 December, we of course knew they were on their way.

The first orders to TG 74 had been to go on station in the Bay of Bengal, off the East Bengal coast. I argued against stationing the ships there. I felt it was taking an unnecessary risk to put a task group without a stated mission in precisely the place where harm was most likely to befall it. I won my argument, and the group was sent south of Ceylon, where the Russians, when they arrived, promptly began trailing it. Meanwhile, a second Russian task group, similar in composition to the first—a cruiser with escorts—was sent to the scene, obviously in reaction to TG 74's appearance. What prompted the despatch of the first Russian group is unclear. The best guess is that it was the presence, fortuitous though it was, of so many British ships in troubled waters. In any case, by the first of the year, when the second Russian group arrived, the American ships were put at a disadvantage by the Russians. While Soviet ships were in close trail of U.S. ships the British were no longer on the scene. As soon as Dacca had been evacuated successfully, they had continued on their homeward journey. For the first week or so of 1972, the American and Russian ships circled around each other warily, much as their counterparts had been doing in the Mediterranean for years. Then, on 8 January, Task Group 74 was ordered out of the Indian Ocean as mysteriously as it had been ordered in.

I still do not know exactly what to think about the TG 74 episode. Obviously it could not have been intended to influence the course of the war in East Bengal. On the contrary, the group was not formed until the outcome in East Bengal was perfectly clear. Perhaps the President and Kissinger, both of whom quite clearly were frustrated by their inability to influence events on the subcontinent, impulsively organized TG 74 and sent it on its way in a final effort to show the world that America was not to be taken lightly. More likely, they wanted to show China that the U.S. was a relevant military actor in that part of the world and had the will to deploy military power in a situation in which a Soviet client was defeating a Chinese ally. In either case my hunch is that the gesture was untimely and futile. But that is just a hunch. Mrs. Gandhi may have had designs on West Pakistan as well as East Pakistan, and the arrival of TG 74 may have caused her to think twice. In other words, the gesture may have been extremely timely and useful. Until the private papers of "the lady" are made public, no one will know for sure.

The strangest by-product of the Indo-Pakistan war was the "Admirals' Spy Ring," as the press dubbed it in 1974 when some of the facts became publicly known. As far as I could tell, spying admirals existed only in the paranoid imagination of Richard Nixon as stimulated by the story a certain Yeoman First Class Charles Radford told. I first became aware of the existence of YN1 Radford on 4 January 1972. That day Under Secretary of the Navy John Warner, who in the absence of Secretary Chafee was acting Secretary, called me to his office and told me that he had received orders, he did not say from whom, to get a yeoman named Radford, who had been working in the White House, out of town that day. He said his orders called for Radford to be transferred to a billet in the Pacific northwest, which was where his home was. He said further that I must arrange that Radford's orders be written in such a way that only I "would know what was going on."

When I got back to my office I learned that Radford was the yeoman assigned to the National Security Council/Joint Chiefs liaison office in the White House. Radford had been chosen by Rem Robinson, and when Rem's tour ended in May he stayed on under Rem's replacement, Rear Admiral Robert Welander. I directed a senior officer in the Bureau of Naval Personnel to write orders that day assigning Radford to the Thirteenth Naval District in Seattle, and not to ask me any questions. I reported back to Warner to tell him what I had done, and to tell him further that I did not think it proper for either him or me to permit any naval person to be treated that peremptorily without knowing why. Warner replied that he was not about to question the order of the Commander in Chief. He suggested that I not do so either.

I did not follow his suggestion. I went to Tom Moorer, whose command Radford was under, and questioned him. Tom told me that Radford was the person allegedly responsible for the leaks of top secret documents about the Indo-Pakistan war to Jack Anderson. Since 14 December Anderson's column had been carrying excerpts of such documents, including some of the WSAG minutes I have just quoted from. The publication of the news of the "tilt" toward Pakistan created a sensation. For several days the Washington *Post* moved Anderson's column to the front page from what Moorer was later to call "its natural place on the funnies page." Ultimately his exploit won Anderson the Pulitzer Prize.

Both the President and Kissinger had been beside themselves with rage over the leak. In the Tank we had had several discussions about further limiting access to sensitive documents. In short everybody had been under suspicion and a clue to the source of the leaks cleared the air considerably. I said to Moorer that to complete the job of air-clearing, as well as in fairness both to Radford and the Navy, the allegations should be presented as formal charges and that a court-martial should be convened. Tom said that he had so recommended, and that his recommendation had been disapproved. He said the White House did not want formal action taken because Radford had said that if he, Radford, were formally charged he would testify that one of his office's duties had been to forward to Moorer documents that Kissinger and the President did not want Moorer to see. Moorer reminded me of the number of times he had been given information by the White House with orders that it not be given to Laird.

I was all the way up to speed by that time on the way Henry's duplicity left booby traps everywhere, so I was not terribly surprised to find that he had laid one here. He really had put Tom in a damned-if-you-do, damned-if-you-don't position. The papers Kissinger was sending Moorer and keeping from Laird were necessary to the proper performance of the Chairman's duties. He could not refuse to accept them. I had learned firsthand during the episode with President Mobutu that the President, or at any rate Kissinger in the name of the President, insisted on his right to deal directly with the military if he chose. At the same time the Secretary of Defense is the Chairman's legal superior, and the proper channel from the Commander-in-Chief to the Chairman is through the Secretary. Furthermore, this was an issue that both Laird and Dave Packard took very personally. Moorer once told me of an occasion when he sat in a National Security Council meeting, with his briefing book before him and Packard beside him and Packard, glancing into the book, saw a document on a White House letterhead that had not been sent to the Secretary's office. From then on the Robinson-Welander liaison office made sure to cut off the letterhead before photo-copying NSC documents for Moorer. The games people play!

In such situations everyone must draw his own line. Tom drew it by not taking any action without clearing it with the Secretary. I drew it a little lower. I made a point of passing informally on to Mel or his executive assistant any information I got that I believed he did not have. But then I was not in the position Tom was. He dealt with the White House every day. I dealt with it only occasionally. Although we never discussed the matter, I believe that it is fair to say that most of us who served as members of the JCS thought that Congress had intended a somewhat different kind of service from the Chairman than from the service Chiefs. The service Chiefs serve four-year terms and by law are not eligible for reappointment. The intent of Congress in enacting that statute was to make the Chief of Staff of each Service independent in his provision of military advice. On the other hand, the Chairman of the Joint Chiefs of Staff serves only two years but is eligible for reappointment, a clear indication that Congress intended him to be "the President's man."

The question of Radford's orders boiled violently for two weeks. While I was out of the office on the afternoon of that same day, 4 January, John Warner twice called my executive assistant, Captain Burt Shepherd, about Radford. The first time Warner instructed Burt to have the orders changed from Seattle to somewhere in Oregon. The second time he refined this to anywhere in Oregon but Portland. The next day at 1405 Burt got a call from BuPers to tell him that Radford had received the orders detaching him from Washington and that a van was even then in the process of picking up Radford's household goods. At 2210 Burt got another call to tell him that Radford and the van were on their way out of town. The next day Warner called Burt to tell him that he needed to know by 1800 what the possible assignments in Oregon for Radford were. Burt provided the Under Secretary with a list of all naval activities in Oregon outside of Portland. From the list Warner selected a Naval Reserve Training Center in Salem. He instructed Burt to screen the personnel file of the commanding officer of the Training Center, and to confer with the rear admiral commanding the Thirteenth Naval District to make sure that the Training Center commander could be trusted "to follow sensitive guidance." Next day the rear admiral reported that the commander was knowledgeable, had good community relations and could handle guidance with a high probability of maintaining security.

A few days later John Warner's solicitude for Radford's peace of mind reached a new height. He called Burt to make sure that Radford, still enroute west, received word that his orders had been changed from Seattle to Salem so that he would not seek housing in Seattle when he arrived on the coast. Burt had BuPers perform this function. They reported to him that when Radford learned that he was being assigned to Oregon instead of Washington "he was pleased." Radford had asked if his security clearances had been revoked. He was assured that they had not been!!!

The curtain fell at last on this comic opera on 17 January when, before the "happy" ending, there was one more alarum or excursion. BuPers called Burt at 1330 to tell him that Radford had got the word on the specifics of his assignment, to which he was to report in two weeks, and was not happy. He did not think it provided him with the proper opportunity to be promoted to Chief. BuPers had tried to reassure him. Radford had retorted, "I know who put me here. I'll talk to him and get it changed." General consternation. Gnashing of teeth and rending of garments. Unbearable suspense. At 1830 the telephone rings. It is the Under Secretary of the Navy calling the Chief of Naval Operations to tell him that YN1 Charles Radford has agreed to obey his orders.

Sometime during this period I had a talk with Bob Welander. He told me he had been the one who had "blown the whistle" on Radford. I don't remember whether it was during that talk or at some later date that I learned what the circumstantial case against Radford seemed to be. Probably I heard some of it then and some of it later. In any case, this is a convenient place to describe it. The first of Anderson's articles contained a mistake. It referred to "guided missile destroyers, *Parsons, Decatur,* and *Tartar SAM.*" A memorandum from Welander to Haig, typed by Radford, had referred to *"Parsons, Decatur,* Tartar SAM destroyers," Tartar being the surface-to-air missile (SAM) that *Parsons* and *Decatur* carried. Welander recognized that Anderson's mistake could easily have been inspired by the wording of his memo, which was available only to himself, Haig, and Radford. He promptly relieved Radford of all duties, informed Haig and Moorer, and had the combination on his office safe changed. None of the documents Anderson printed were dated after those actions.

Moorer told me that a fast investigation disclosed that Radford had served in the office of the naval attaché in the American Embassy in New Delhi; that he had developed a great affection there for Indians and India; that the Embassy had assigned him to Jack Anderson when Anderson visited India; that the two had become friends; that when Radford returned to Washington he began attending the same church as Anderson; that two nights before the first leak appeared he had had dinner with Anderson; and that he had easy access to every one of the papers Anderson published. Radford steadfastly and emphatically denied passing any documents to Anderson.

Shortly after Radford had been relieved of his duties, Welander had been instructed to remove his own files from the White House, so when he and I had our talk he, too, was in a non-duty status. I asked both Moorer and Kissinger if there was any reason Bob should not receive the good professional assignment he was entitled to on the basis of his superior record. They both said that there was no reason at all, that the disestablishment of Welander's office had nothing to do with Welander's performance. They said that Secretary Laird always had mistrusted formal liaison between the National Security Council and the Joint Chiefs because he felt it undercut his authority, and that he had seized the leak episode as a tailormade pretext for insisting that the liaison be discontinued. I saw to it that Welander got command of the cruiser-destroyer flotilla Emmett Tidd had to leave when I put him in charge of recruiting. It was not until two years later, in January 1974, that I discovered that there was a lot more than I have just related to the Radford story. Though it means getting ahead of myself, I had better tell that part of it here, too, so that Charles Radford can vanish from the stage for good.

Early in January 1974 the "Admirals' Spy Ring" story broke in the press. Its gist was that agents of Tom Moorer, specifically Welander and Radford, had stolen National Security Council documents they were not supposed to have and passed them to the Chairman. I don't know where the press got this story. However, John Ehrlichman had just been indicted for the burglary of Daniel Ellsberg's psychiatrist's office, and some people, including James Schlesinger, thought it possible that Ehrlichman or supporters of Ehrlichman were the source of the story, with the object of demonstrating how badly needed the "plumbers" were when even the Chairman of the Joint Chiefs was pilfering documents. At a staff meeting on 14 January 1974, Schlesinger said about the "spy ring," according to my notes:

> Aha—the publicity concerning the plumbers is providing the greatest copy ever. We are sweeping from success to success. There has been manufactured a threat to national security from the JCS.

It has been blown out of proportion for various motivations—there was a group of "Plumbers" who are expecting to go to trial who need to demonstrate that there was a threat to national security.

At any rate, on 11 January in an executive session in the Tank, Tom, worried that the Joint Chiefs as an institution would be permanently discredited, told us as much of the story as he knew. Subsequently I had a number of talks about the subject with Schlesinger and with Admiral Welander, who had completed his tour with the flotilla and was back in Washington, and I saw a few more documents. Putting all these together still does not make an account that explains everything, but I offer it for what it is worth.

Two investigations of Radford apparently started immediately after Welander blew his whistle. Haig passed Welander's news on to Bob Haldeman and John Ehrlichman, and the latter began an investigation. Moorer passed Welander's news on to Mel Laird and Laird directed his counsel, J. Fred Buzhardt, to investigate. A heavy interrogation of Radford—and Welander—by both factions began. After a few days of interrogation of Radford, who had consulted a lawyer, the issue got diverted from the Anderson leaks to the allegation from Radford that he had been directed to pass unauthorized documents to Moorer. Both factions had political reasons for pursuing that line of inquiry. Haldeman/Ehrlichman always were seeking ways of embarrassing Henry Kissinger. Whether it was because Kissinger was their only real rival for the President's confidence or because Haldeman and Ehrlichman believed Kissinger was getting too independent, only the tapes can show. Laird, as I have said, probably wanted to block the direct channel of communications between Kissinger and the Chairman of the Joint Chiefs. At that point, I have been told, John Ehrlichman hustled Rem Robinson, Bob Welander's predecessor in the White House, into Washington. Apparently Rem spent a frantic day or two shuttling between the tape recorder of the investigators in the Executive Office Building and the tape recorder of the investigators in the Pentagon who had learned he was in town. His stay ended with Ehrlichman whisking him out of town before the Pentagon faction could get a last crack at him.

With the possible exception of Al Haig no military man I know of, including Tom Moorer, saw either of the reports those investigations produced, although in 1974 Martin Hoffman, General Counsel of the Department of Defense, showed me an excerpt from one. However, some of the things Radford told the investigators have become known. Indeed they have been reported so fulsomely in the media that I can skim over them here. He said that after returning from two overseas trips, Kissinger's first visit to China and an inspection tour of Vietnam by Haig, he had passed along to Welander documents he had obtained in a clearly unauthorized fashion: out of a burn basket in the Embassy in New Delhi in the first instance, directly out of Haig's attaché case in the second. (Radford had been requisitioned for those trips because he was a crackerjack shorthand man.) He said no one ever had directly ordered him to do such things, but that he had received various hints and insinuations, or thought he had, that had made him think he was expected to do them. Moorer, for his part, acknowledged that Welander had brought him papers like the ones Radford mentioned. He said that he had glanced at them, the way a man does when hundreds of papers move across his desk every day, to see if they contained anything he did not already know. When he found they did not, he put them aside without studying them to determine their source. That sounded reasonable to me because that was the way I handled the hundreds of papers a day that moved across *my* desk.

In sum, it was clear to me that Radford had done some things he clearly should not have done and that Moorer did not know he had done them; Moorer had never even met Radford. That left Bob Welander pretty much in the middle, but I had little disposition to think of him unkindly in the light of what I knew about what went on in the White House basement: Robinson believing that Kissinger expected him to keep us informed; Robinson/Welander, convinced that Haig was keeping Westmoreland fully informed, making a point of seeing to it that Moorer and I got everything Westy got; Kissinger telling me he distrusted Haig; Haig telling me and others he distrusted Kissinger; Haldeman/Ehrlichman trying to bushwhack Kissinger; Kissinger and the President using Moorer to help them make plans without Laird's knowledge and therefore pretending to keep Moorer fully informed while withholding some information from him too. I am sure there were many more convolutions than that, but those are the ones that immediately come to my mind. What I find hard to believe is that rational men could think that running things like that could have any other result than "leaks" and "spying" and all-around paranoia. Indeed they had created a system in which "leaks" and "spying" were everyday and essential elements. And so when I say Bob Welander was the man in the middle, what I mean to say is that he was in the middle of all-around paranoia, and the worst you can say about him is that, being an obedient soldier, he reflected his environment. In my opinion the most immoral participant in the affair was the person who made the decision not to court-martial yeoman Radford to prove or disprove his innocence and establish the facts. That person, Laird told Moorer, was Richard Nixon. It was a decision that led to deep personal embarrassment for two honorable public servants, Admirals Moorer and Welander, to making the Joint Chiefs as a body a laughingstock, and indeed to putting Radford himself under a permanent cloud. In a small way, as another example of the kinds of things that went on under his Presidency, it even was a nail in Mr. Nixon's coffin.

There is just one footnote to append. On 1 July 1972 Tom Moorer began his second term as Chairman. A cynic might conjecture that the President reappointed him, despite undoubted Presidential rage over being "spied on," in the expectation that the recent events would render him docile. The same cynic might add that Moorer did not receive the appointment to the third term he was anticipating because when the "Admirals' Spy Ring" made headlines he became a political embarrassment. It wasn't easy to keep hold of your integrity or honor or pride when you worked for Richard Nixon. The country owed Admiral Moorer, after his distinguished service, more than the public pillorying he got when the "spy ring" story broke and the unpublicized vindication that came six months later from the Senate Armed Services Committee—six months too late.

CHAPTER 17

A Last Hurrah
in Vietnam

During the last weekend of February 1972, I made my first visit to Vietnam since relinquishing the command there. What I wanted most to see firsthand was the progress of the naval Vietnamization program we had initiated almost three and a half years before— before the Nixon administration had taken office and Mel Laird coined the word "Vietnamization." I found that the program was right on the schedule I had set for it when I initiated it, just before the 1968 election. I had decided that the political realities were that we would have perhaps a year to complete the turnover if Hubert Humphrey became President and three to four years if Richard Nixon did. By the time of my visit, Nixon had been in office a little more than three years and American naval forces in Vietnam were down from a high of about 38,000 to 10–12,000 and were dwindling fast. Moreover, most of those remaining were headquarters or logistics people. Almost all the fighting equipment was in the hands of the Vietnamese.

Not long afterward, in the fall of 1972, when the U.S. turned the last base and ship over to the commander of the Vietnamese Navy, Admiral Chon, we had turned over to the Vietnamese Navy approximately 1000 craft of various kinds. As a result the Vietnamese Navy had grown from a 17,000-man to a 40,000-man force, and had become in terms of personnel—though not of tonnage of course— something like the ninth or tenth largest Navy in the world. Every account I receive tells me that it operated in a thoroughly professional manner to the end. In the last hours before Saigon fell, the last Vietnamese CNO, Vice Admiral Chung Tan Cang, made a decision that General Minh, the President-for-a-day, declined to make, and took twenty-seven of the seagoing ships down the Saigon River and across the South China Sea to Subic Bay in the Philippines. They carried not only their officers and men, but their families and numerous other refugees, 18,000 people in all. At Subic the ships were turned back to the U.S. Navy. It was a heroic and a sad day.

I was able to spend only two days in Vietnam but during that time I managed to visit half a dozen little naval bases in various parts of the country, meet with Admiral Chon, Ambassador Bunker, Vice Admiral Robert Salzer, the U.S. Naval commander who had served brilliantly from 1966 to 1968 as battlefield commander of the delta Mobile Riverine Flotilla, and a number of other dignitaries, take part in a press briefing and a couple of banquets, and have a long, delightful lunch with General Abrams. Though the intelligence briefing I had received before leaving spoke warningly of a heavy North Vietnamese buildup just above the Demilitarized Zone, and Abe and I agreed that the country sooner or later would have to endure another heavy offensive from the north, Abe was optimistic. He thought Vietnamization was going well. Presidential directives called for the American presence to be down to 60,000 troops by the end of May, 37,000 by 1 July and 23,000 by 1 November, but Abe thought that the South Vietnamese were well on the way to acquiring the capability to fight their own battle, and that with vigorous U.S. air and naval support against a near term enemy offensive, could acquire a long term capability to survive without U.S. help. Lest the reader think the events of the spring of 1975 have falsified this judgment, it assumed that Hanoi would need to keep in North Vietnam the ten to twelve divisions it always had kept there to defend against possible U.S. amphibious attack. It did not contemplate that Congress in 1973 would prohibit such use of American force and thus allow most of those divisions to flood South, doubling the enemy force in South Vietnam and gaining victory.

My third day in the area, 27 February, I visited the Seventh Fleet on Yankee Station in the Gulf of Tonkin. I visited sixteen or seventeen ships that day, talking to three or four groups of personnel on each and touring each ship. I finished at 2300 hours. I then boarded a plane for the five-hour flight to Tokyo, where I had an appointment with Admiral Kazutomi Uchida, the able Japanese CNO, at 0530 on 28 February. We talked for three hours. At 0830 I took off for the long flight to Washington. It is safe to assume that I slept most of the way.

The massive North Vietnamese attack across the DMZ—the "Easter Offensive"—occurred on 31 March. It was a flagrant violation of the understandings that ended the heavy American bombing of North Vietnam in 1968. That understanding called for three actions by the North Vietnamese: coming to the conference table, which they had done, ceasing the shelling of major South Vietnamese cities, which they had mostly done, and ceasing to use the DMZ as an invasion route. The President—and presumably Kissinger—reacted vigorously to the North Vietnamese attack. By some, including Secretary Laird, their reaction was judged wild. The President directed the JCS to order into the western Pacific two more attack carriers, one of which had to come from the Atlantic Fleet; 54 other ships, which increased the size of the Seventh Fleet from 84 to 138 ships; 105 more B-52s, so many that one whole runway on Guam had to be closed to operations because it was needed as a parking lot; and several more land-based tactical air squadrons. He called for intense and unremitting air strikes in support of the fighting south of the DMZ and, moved the bomb line, below which it was permissible to attack targets in North Vietnam, further and further north as the offensive continued. He even authorized bombing the up-to-then untouchable area around the port of Haiphong.

I did not see the President during this period but Mel Laird, Tom Moorer, and Johnny Vogt, the Director of the Joint Staff frequently did and they kept the Chiefs informed of his mood. From an account of the Joint Chiefs' meeting on 5 April: "The Chairman said that the President had taken a very strong position, that he felt this was an invasion in force, that the new set of rules applies, that he wanted all resources that we have on station and other available resources prepared to move forward." From the 7 April OpDeps meeting: "The President was determined to give the North Vietnamese a bloody nose in this action. He instructed General Vogt to inform General Abrams that the President wanted to know what Abrams needs, and that everything he needs will be given to him barring the reintroduction of ground forces. He said that the President had personally made the decision to send the Marine squadron to Vietnam and he said that we will use every carrier in both fleets and all our tactical air if that is what is needed to get the job done in SEASIA." From my handwritten notes of a JCS executive session on

24 April: "Laird talked about the White House. . . . The President is personally insisting on massive strikes—personally sent the carriers—the President said 'I sent them—no one else asks for them.' " Numerous other entries during April and May tell the same story.

Secretary Laird found himself in a strange position during this period. An almost totally political man, he had been from the beginning the most determined advocate of rapid disengagement from Vietnam within the Nixon administration. Not only did he read public and Congressional opinion as being ready to wreak fatal retribution at the polls on the administration if it did not disengage rapidly but, in the light of the widespread desire to reduce all military spending, he saw the country's future in jeopardy if large resources continued to be spent in Vietnam. He disagreed with Henry Kissinger about the pace of withdrawal. The two men saw Vietnam in entirely different contexts. Laird saw it in the context of domestic needs and desires plus the need to regenerate defense capability for the future, Kissinger in the context of working to keep what he considered to be the inevitable erosion of the U.S. position in the world balance of power as slow and smooth as possible.

It was as much Laird's adroitness at frustrating Kissinger's southeast Asia initiatives as any other reason that prompted Kissinger to cultivate relations with Tom Moorer that bypassed the Secretary's office. Tom would not authorize any military action without Laird's signature, of course, but he was required by Kissinger, in the name of the President, to write scenarios or prepare plans or provide advice without Laird's knowledge lest Laird find ways of avoiding or delaying a response. In a less Byzantine regime Laird would have been fired. As a matter of fact Tom Moorer informed us on at least two occasions that the President had ordered Laird fired in Moorer's presence. But Mel's strong Congressional support and the President's distaste for personal confrontations fortunately permitted Mel's survival.

All of Laird's instincts, political and administrative, impelled him to try to temper the vehement Nixon/Kissinger response to the attack across the DMZ. However, with the President taking command personally, there was little he could do but remonstrate and worry. What he worried about most he expressed forcefully at a meeting he and I had with John Chafee on 27 April. "Laird then stated that he hates to leave here in January with our readiness at an all time low because of our efforts in Southeast Asia," the memo summarizing that conversation states. (He had already signified his intention of leaving office when the administration's first term ended, whether or not the President was reelected.) He feared, quite rightly, that the Vietnam escalation would produce unrest among personnel, as well as serious shortages of material that Congress simply would not make up. Other chapters of this book have discussed at length what actually happened on the personnel readiness side—which in some ways was even worse than most of us had feared.

On the material side, the Navy, to report on the only Service I know about personally, was already feeling the pinch at the time of that meeting with Laird and Chafee. We had only enough five-inch ammunition to last through June. We were short such exotic but necessary items as electro-optical gunline sensors. We were stripping the Atlantic Fleet of certain kinds of anti-aircraft weapons so the Pacific Fleet would have enough. And we were frantically trying to borrow from the Army heat seeking anti-missile systems that might give our ships at least a rudimentary defense against cruise missiles. The worst nightmare Admiral Chick Clarey, the Commander of the Pacific Fleet, and I had was that the Soviets would supply the North Vietnamese with cruise missiles, against which our ships were almost defenseless. I could list other shortages described by other of the weekly "SitReps" (Situation Reports) on how the crisis was being managed, but that much should give the idea. What upset Laird the most about using up so many scarce resources so fast, he said during that same 27 April meeting, was that "Abe had not asked for all this support." Abe was the kind of man who trusted the JCS to make his case for him as he presented full, objective daily reports of the deteriorating situation.

I was as alarmed as Mel about what this fast attrition of resources would do to future readiness. However, I agreed with the President's response to the North Vietnamese attack. I thought the President had been right, at a time when the final crucial touches were being put on an agreement to limit strategic arms and when the Defense budget was being questioned in Congress, to signify unmistakably to the Soviets that he was willing and able to act. Moreover, my pessimistic view of the trend of U.S. military strength relative to that of the Soviets made me prefer to take our risks now rather than to be faced with an even riskier situation later. Where I faulted, and continue to fault, the President and Kissinger was that they had allowed the public to believe that the United States could defend itself in a major war, if it had to, without "going nuclear," whereas the fact was that a relatively minor conventional engagement (a "half war") like the one then in progress in southeast Asia strained our resources. I felt strongly that the responsible authorities had an obligation to tell the public that the chances of our being able to win a full-scale, non-nuclear war were small and getting smaller. In the course of one of the almost daily telephone conversations I had with Chick Clarey during the last days of April, he told me that he estimated our chances of winning right then, should the Soviets take it into their heads to unleash their forces in a worldwide war at sea, at about 30 percent. That was my estimate, too. And Tom Moorer told me that it was also his. I thought the White House should be telling the American people about such assessments by knowledgeable and responsible military professionals.

While on the subject of assessments and of Mel Laird's personality and attitudes, it is worth backtracking a couple of months to my testimony on the FY '73 budget before the Senate Armed Forces Committee, and the violent, if brief, wrath one piece of that testimony provoked in the Secretary of Defense. As I did each year, I gave the Committee my current estimate—though not in numbers—of America's ability to fight successfully a full-scale conventional war. There was no one who hated more to hear my talk of probabilities than the Committee Chairman, John Stennis of Mississippi, the man who had sternly lectured me at my 1970 confirmation hearings about my obligation to give undiluted judgments to his committee. Stennis was a consistent defender of the President's Defense budget against the efforts of the Senate's anti-Defense bloc to cut it drastically, which may be why he always took my probabilities as a reproach directed personally at him for not doing more for the military than he had done. Often he countered me with some such question as, "What have you ever asked for that we haven't given you," though obviously he knew that what we were given each year by the Congress was less than the President had asked for, that what the President asked the Congress for was less than what the Secretary of Defense had asked the President for and less yet than what the Navy had asked the Secretary of Defense for, and that I was testifying under orders to defend a budget far lower than the one I thought desirable. However, if Stennis had the impression that I was critical of him for failing to perceive what was happening to America's military capability, I cannot say he was mistaken.

In any case, at that committee session, late in February, just before I left for Vietnam, I said what I usually said about the general situation, and Stennis replied what he usually replied. However I made the mistake, and it was a big one, of departing Washington without informing Laird about one exchange the Senator and I had had about "losing the war." Laird appeared before the Committee after I had left for the Pacific, and in the course of his appearance Stennis sprang that "losing the war" exchange on him in the form of "Now, Mr. Secretary, do you agree with the testimony of Admiral Zumwalt that . . . ?" If Laird had known what I had said, he undoubtedly would have prepared a soft, if not an ambiguous, answer to such a question. As it was, outraged at being booby-trapped, he expressed disagreement furiously, and boiled for several days thereafter. I guess I should consider myself lucky to have been in Vietnam, for by the time I got back, he had pretty much recovered his equanimity. Mel often got hot, but he cooled fast and he did not keep grudges.

I went to see him as soon as I got back and he said, as I remember it, something like this: "Bud, you're doing a good job and you certainly have a right to express your opinions. Just do me one favor. Next time you talk about 'losing a conventional war,' add 'unless we go to nuclear weapons.' " It was an accurate formulation and a reasonable request, and of course I followed it thereafter. The principal reason I tell this story is for what it reveals about Mel Laird. Though, as I have said, his intellectual frame of reference was almost totally political, and therefore he turned his back on some important issues that were politically touchy, like closing bases, he is one of the "good guys" I have worked with and for. I have already related how solidly he backed me on the issue of racism in the Navy, when most members of the administration, including the top member, couldn't disown me fast enough.

The first ten days in May were the climactic ones in that round of Vietnam fighting. Despite the massive application of U.S. sea and air power, the North Vietnamese had pressed their attack with undiminished vigor through April. By 2 April they had overrun the northern half of Quangtri Province. On 15 April they were close enough to Danang to shell it. On 25 April there was fighting in Kontum. On 1 May they captured Quangtri City. On 3 May their closeness to Hue provoked panic and riots there. During the first week in May the daily assessments General Abrams and Ambassador Bunker sent the Joint Chiefs and Secretary of State were at their gloomiest, using phrases like "the battle had become brutal," "no apparent basis for confidence that Hue or Kontum could hold," "defenses around Quagtri collapsed yesterday," "virtual rout," "atmosphere of fear and anxiety."

On 2 May Admiral John McCain, the Commander in Chief Pacific (CinCPac), sent a message to Admiral Moorer reminding him of a request he had made on 23 April for approval of the mining of Haiphong Harbor so as to cut off the steady flow of military supplies, mostly Russian, into North Vietnam from the sea. McCain said that if Washington found mining unacceptable, perhaps it would consider a naval blockade of the North Vietnamese ports. As a matter of fact discussions of mining and blockading had been taking place almost daily since about 20 April among McCain, Moorer, Chick Clarey, and me. We all preferred mining to blockading. Mining was tactically simpler and politically more decisive. Ships patrolling aggressively in front of harbor entrances would be both more provocative and more vulnerable than mines lying quietly in harbor waters.

On the morning of 1 May, Al Haig on the telephone asked my opinion of these matters, presumably on Kissinger's behalf as well as his own. After I had given my opinion I had said, as a not very subtle hint that the military would like to do more to help Abe than was being done, that if the President got to the verge of deciding to lose the war through unwillingness to mine/blockade, he should meet with all the Chiefs to hear their professional assessment before making his decision final. Al said he agreed.

The theme of urgency continued to sound strongly at the meetings of the OpDeps and the Chiefs on 3 May. At the OpDeps there was discussion of a requirement the White House had just put on the Joint Staff to send still more Air Force B-52s and Marine F-4s into the battle, and of a proposal to airlift tanks to the front lines. At the Chiefs' meeting the genesis of the White House requirement was explained: "Chairman said the President wants to know why our air is not attacking Steel Tiger [Laotian] targets. He is usually told that aircraft cannot be spared for those missions; therefore he comes back and says, 'Send more aircraft over.' " My notes continue, "SecDef is concerned over the budgetary aspects and the long range impacts of our present augmentation effort. However, the Chairman pointed out that the name of the game *now* is what we do *right now.*" That was how all of us in the military felt.

On 4 May, late in the afternoon, Tom Moorer asked me to come to his office. He said he had just been instructed to produce immediately for use in briefing the President a concept for mining the waters leading to Haiphong and the other North Vietnamese ports, with the additional provision that this briefing be done without the knowledge of the Secretary of Defense. He said he was not sure he could meet that last requirement within the Joint Staff, which included members of all the Services, and asked me if I would do it in my office. I readily agreed, both because I thoroughly supported such an operation as the most promising solution to the U.S. dilemma, and because a CNO's life consists so largely of administration and liaison and paper shuffling that I welcomed an opportunity to engage once more in purely professional work.

I called for a chart of the waters off North Vietnam, a ruler and a pair of dividers, and summoned Kin McKee from the CNO Executive Panel, Captain Dave Emerson, special assistant to Vice Admiral Worth Bagley; my brilliant executive assistant Captain Don Pringle, a highly dedicated veteran of the air war over North Vietnam; Captain H. B. "Robbie" Robertson, a naval lawyer who was also a superbly qualified line officer, and Captain Stuart M. Brownell, the technical expert in mine capability on my staff. It's always nice to have an expert around. At about 2000 that evening we set to work. It is easy to mine Haiphong from the air. The only way into Haiphong Harbor is a dredged channel that is long, narrow, and shallow. The logistics are easy, too. The planes of all carrier attack squadrons are equipped to lay mines, and most pilots have been trained to do so, and the *Coral Sea,* the ship whose air squadrons we designated for the operation, even had mines on board. Before midnight we had the concept done and I was able to hand it to Admiral Moorer first thing next morning.

Friday, 5 May, was a lively day. Admiral Moorer telephoned me shortly after noon to thank me for the work of the previous evening and to discuss some of its ramifications. One of those, which afforded me some amusement, was that Mel Laird was bound to get wind of the mining/blockading discussions unless the personal liaison between the Chairman and Kissinger, which Laird had so abruptly terminated over the Radford affair, was temporarily reestablished. Tom asked me to give him someone who could represent him at the White House. I said I would let him have Kin McKee. A second ramification was that at the executive session in the Tank that afternoon Tom wanted to let all the Chiefs in on what was going on in order to get their opinions about the operation's possibilities and risks. He said he would raise the question as if it were merely a matter of contingency planning and he cautioned me, when he brought the subject up, "to be surprised as hell" so that the other chiefs would not suspect that I had been privy to something they had not been. Beyond such fun and games, though, he wanted to unburden himself about the serious military aspects of mining/blockading, over which he had lain awake brooding all night. Let my memo reconstructing the conversation speak for itself:

> He thinks looking at the possibilities of how far the Soviets will go if we in fact put the arm on one of their ships—that will put us in a contest if we go with a blockade. He said that . . . they will start lightering. He then said that if we first mine and get the ships out and demolish the pier and have the President make the statement we are going to take whatever actions are necessary to prevent any more supplies being delivered to North Vietnam by sea and we are at this moment mining—and don't say what he is not going to do—but making a hard statement we are not going to permit any more supplies going into North Vietnam. . . . Admiral Moorer said that they [the White House] can have the advantage of not turning back with this statement—but on the other hand what concerns him is what I [Zumwalt] have been saying all along that the relative balance has been going down, down, down. . . . He said that maybe we could announce that the ships operating in North Vietnamese waters are doing so at their own peril.

That afternoon at 1610 I called Chick Clarey in Pearl Harbor and we had a discussion that was, if anything, more intense than the one with Tom had been.

> [Clarey said] the CJCS called him just before I did and told Clarey they would get orders on the mining, and yesterday told him they could get orders to start doing the blockade. Clarey said that he asked him why do both—if you mine that should do the job without confrontation with the Soviets. Clarey said that due to the weakness of our forces, this project is a damn dangerous one. I asked if Tom had stressed the hold-close nature of this to Clarey—Clarey replied that he had. I then said that Tom talked to the Chiefs today in executive session. Clarey said that if the Soviets send in their ships escorted and off loaded by lighters to bring supplies into the beach and so forth, they would have more supplies than if we had gone for the blockade in the first place so they would have had to make the first move. Clarey said that the mining will do it and it will keep our ships out of danger. Clarey reiterated that a confrontation with the Soviets at this point worries the hell out of him. I stated that we are going down hill so fast, that I feel it's better to have a confrontation now than two years from now. Clarey said that the weak defense

we have against surface-to-surface missiles if they start escorting the ships in will hurt us. He suggests doing the mining and see what happens. . . .

The above is the merest summary; we talked for half an hour. The President reached his decision to mine North Vietnamese waters either that night or the next morning. At 1138 on 6 May, an alerting message went out from Moorer to CinCPac asking the mining force to be ready to begin at 0900 Vietnam time on Tuesday, 9 May, which was 2000 Monday, 8 May, Washington time. The "execute" message on the mining went out on 8 May at 1340 Washington time—0240 9 May in Vietnam. The mining itself was almost a textbook operation. The Navy and Marine attack planes from the carriers, some carrying the mines, swarmed over Haiphong and its harbor at the designated time and in less than an hour enough mines of various kinds had been sown to make the channel all but impassable. (The actual numbers and types are a secret I have no reason to believe the Soviets have learned.) Some anti-aircraft fire was directed against the planes laying the mines, but there were no casualties.

As military operations go, in fact, mining is one of the most cost effective there is. It is relatively cheap and relatively safe and extremely threatening to an enemy. One of the great concerns within NATO is that in a European war the Soviets, who have hundreds of times more mines than we do—and we have a lot—would be able relatively easily to mine every major port in western Europe. On every trip to Europe I made I stressed to the naval leaders I spoke with the importance of their developing as strong a minesweeping capability as possible in order to be sure that supplies could reach them from the sea.

At 2100 on Monday 8 May, the President went on the air to announce that just one hour before Haiphong harbor had been sown with mines that would become activated "after three daylight periods" had elapsed from the time they were laid, 0900 Tuesday Vietnam time. The President noted that there were some thirty-six merchant ships in Haiphong at the time, and he reported that the governments of the countries whose flags they flew had "already been notified" that they had that much time to leave before it was too late. At 0200 Tuesday, Chick Clarey called Tom Moorer, Jack McCain, and me to report that the pilots who had conducted the operation had reported in their debriefs "bumper to bumper traffic" leaving Haiphong, more than twenty ships in all. Actually subsequent analysis revealed that only nine, none of them flying the Soviet flag, followed the President's advice. The Soviets obviously intended their ships' continuing presence to restrain U. S. actions in Haiphong. Immediately after the speech, General Abrams sent a message from Vietnam asking that the rail lines from China, which might be used as an alternative supply route, be interdicted from the air. This was agreed to without demur, and Kissinger went so far as to authorize fighter planes, if in hot pursuit of the enemy, to penetrate the so-called buffer zone just south of North Vietnam's border with China, air space that until then had been strictly out of bounds lest a violation of China's air accidentally occur.

On Thursday morning, some twelve hours after the mines became activated, I was asked by the press office of the Department of Defense to be the spokesman on the mining on the "Today" show. I stressed that mining was a "passive" act that gave the other side the option of whether or not to accept damage and casualties. I disclosed that the ships of the Seventh fleet were on "notification," which meant they would advise every ship coming into the area about the mines; I said, "If necessary, our ships will pull right up alongside and pass the word by megaphone." I ducked all political questions. And I ended by saying, "The effect on the North Vietnamese is immediate psychologically, because they know the input of supplies to North Vietnam will be extremely limited from here on, practically a trickle or zero. They therefore must begin to decide immediately what their options are between using up their logistics in an all out massive final effort or trying for a series of lesser efforts. And so there has been an immediate effect." I took occasion to praise the performance of naval pilot Randy Cunningham and his radar intercept officer Lieutenant Junior Grade Bill Driscoll who had just become the first U.S. MIG aces of the war by shooting down their third, fourth, and fifth enemy planes in a single engagement. Later that day Mel Laird telephoned to compliment me on my performance, but I presently learned the White House felt otherwise. Several times during the show I had referred to Mr. Nixon as "the Commander in Chief" rather than as "the President." That year, 1972, was an election year, remember.

By a coincidence that is more than a little spooky, this account of the 1972 fighting is being written in March 1975, as the North Vietnamese overrun Quangtri, Kontum, Pleiku, Hue and a dozen other of the very same places they overran, or threatened to, three years before. The differences now are that there are no American

B-52s and F-4s to support the ground troops and destroy the enemy's supplies; that there are no American mines to prevent more supplies from entering the country; that there is no possibility of U. S. military equipment reinforcement, a fact that over the last year has destroyed morale at the troop level; and that statutory prohibition against U. S. air strikes against North Vietnam relieves the Communists of the necessity of keeping a reserve up north and permits almost all of their forces to invade the South. In 1972 it was the mining of Haiphong that finally turned the tide, I believe. The fighting continued for many weeks after the mines were laid, but lack of supplies finally caused the North Vietnamese to run out of steam. In 1975 no such restrictions existed.

On 7 May, the Sunday of the weekend the decision to mine was made, I had an extraordinary encounter with Henry Kissinger. From the time of my duty in Vietnam, Mouza and I had considered it a personal responsibility second to none to do whatever we could for the families of those brave Navy men who were prisoners of war or missing in action. Wherever we traveled we met with as many such families as we could. We tried to help them deal with the numerous problems people in such a plight are bound to have, and to console and encourage them as best we were able. Above all, we tried to make sure that America, and particularly America's government, remembered their husbands and brothers and sons. On the Sunday in question, two magnificent women, Sibyl Stockdale and Jane Denton, the wives of the two most senior Navy POWs—and two of the longest imprisoned—were house guests of ours. They were in town to attend a conference of POW/MIA families and at breakfast that morning they told us in no uncertain terms of their disappointment with the White House's response to their meeting. George McGovern, already a leading contender for the Democratic nomination for President, had sent a principal aide, the able Frank Mankiewicz, to speak to the meeting and answer questions. The White House had sent a junior staff member who was an undoubted expert on Vietnamese history and culture, but who knew nothing about the POW/MIA situation and, in any case, had no authority. The women took this as the latest of a series of signs that the White House did not much care about their problems. They said that morale among the families was falling fast as a result. Then they left for a Sunday morning session.

Mouza and I, much upset, conferred. We agreed that we should go to the meeting so that I could tell the families of my conviction that the President was determined to keep the pressure on North Vietnam until the prisoners were released and the missing were accounted for. On the way over to the Marriott Hotel near the Pentagon, scene of the meeting, I jotted an outline of what I planned to say to them on ruled paper with a purple felt-tipped pen. I still have it. Some excerpts: "No idea be here, first day off several months —Breakfast Sibyl/Jane learned discontent—After they left decided [to] exercise right—20 mos SVN 1 son 1 yr 3 hits, 2nd son will go —Anguish of separation, concern son husband father—Believe you should be heard further up policy totem pole—Ask questions, I don't expect be treated gently."

I was not treated gently. The questions were tough and they demonstrated that Sibyl and Jane had been right in insisting that those long-suffering families needed personal attention from the White House. Both exhilarated by the warm reception I received and indignant that I had been the only person of my rank to visit that important meeting so far, I decided to tell Henry Kissinger forthwith that the POW/MIA families, depressed by their encounter with an uninformed White House representative, needed something productive from the White House right away. Henry was the man to talk to because Henry was the man who presumably knew most about the POW/MIA situation since he had been talking about it in Paris with the North Vietnamese. I had my limousine take me to the White House and, leaving Mouza in the car, walked into Henry's office uninvited.

It was the only time I ever dropped in on Henry without advance notice. Rather than admit me to his office as in the past, he came into the reception room, obviously annoyed at my intrusion. My juices were flowing, as I say, and I told him bluntly that the White House had let the POW/MIA families down. He got red in the face and started shouting. We had quite a scene. On the way home I made more notes, not of the details of our quarrel but of the last part of our conversation, which turned philosophical as Henry tried to justify why he could not do more for the POW families. Herewith, without deletion or amendment, are those notes as handwritten in the back of my limousine on 7 May 1972:

K.:   I believe the American people lack the will to do the things necessary to achieve strategic parity and to maintain maritime superiority. I believe we must get the best deal we can in our negotiations before the

Soviets and the United States both perceive these changes in balance have occurred. When these perceptions are in agreement and both sides know that the United States is inferior, we must have gotten the best deal we can. Americans at that time will not be very happy that I have settled for second, but it will be too late.

Z.: Why not take it to the people? They will not accept the decision to become second best while we are in possession of a GNP twice that of the USSR.

K.: There's a question of judgment. I judge that we will not get their support and if we seek it and tell the facts as we would have to do, we would lose our negotiating leverage with the Soviets.

Z.: But isn't that the ultimate immorality in a democracy to make a decision for the people, of such importance, without consulting them?

K.: Perhaps, but I doubt there are one million who could even understand the issues.

Z.: But even if that presumption is correct, these one million can influence the opinions of the majority of the people. I believe it my duty to take the other course.

K.: You should take care lest your words result in a reduction in the Navy budget. There are subtle retributions available.

"Subtle" retributions! I wonder what Henry would threaten if he decided to be gross. This was not to be the last threat of revenge against "my" Navy.

If the Vietnam fighting was the most exciting and urgent of the events of the spring of 1972, the various negotiations with the Russians that led to the May summit in Moscow were probably the most significant. The principal negotiations were those that produced the strategic arms limitation agreements. Corollary to those were talks that had been going on for some six months to eliminate or minimize so-called Incidents at Sea. Incidents at Sea can be described with a fair amount of accuracy as an extremely dangerous, but exhilarating, running game of "chicken" that American and Soviet ships had been playing with each other for many years. Official Navy statements always have blamed the Russians for starting this game, but as any teen-aged boy knows, it takes two to make a drag race.

My own most memorable Incident at Sea occurred in the summer of 1962 at the end of my tour as captain of the guided-missile frigate *Dewey. Dewey,* the first ship of a new class, had been ordered into the Baltic to visit our Scandinavian friends and allies and, of course, to do a little showing of the flag in not entirely friendly waters. During previous visits of American warships to the Baltic the Russians had sometimes succeeded in embarrassing them by running collision courses with them until the U. S. ships gave way. I secured from the Commander in Chief of the Atlantic Fleet orders that made it clear that rather than suffer a U.S. warship to be shouldered all over the ocean, I was authorized to accept a modest bump or two.

Sure enough, early one morning in the vicinity of the Island of Bornholm, a Russian Riga-type destroyer escort emerged from the mist a few miles off the port bow crossing ahead to starboard. When dead ahead of *Dewey,* the Riga paralleled *Dewey*'s course, then commenced a series of S turns at slow speed. Finally at 1000 yards, now back on my port bow, the Riga settled on a collision course. I should explain here that the Rules of the Road recognized by all maritime nations provide that when two ships are on a collision course, the one to port is the "burdened" one and must give way. Therefore I was the "privileged" vessel to starboard and maintained my speed and course as required. However, I sent my crew to general quarters to be sure, among other things, that all watertight hatches were secured, and that all personnel were on the alert. I sent for my father, who was making this trip with us as a guest of the Secretary of the Navy, to watch the excitement from the bridge.

The Russian captain maintained his speed and course, too, and finally came so close that, despite my fleet commander's orders, I was about to order a radical maneuver to avoid a collision. Just then great puffs of smoke came from his stacks, indicating that he had given way at last; he was no more than fifty yards away when his forward momentum finally stopped, and the reversing of his engines, so suddenly and inexpertly done, caused him to lose power. As we steamed on, he lay dead in the water. Presently he got going again, and came up from behind us at full speed. I increased my speed to show I could run away from him if I cared to. *Dewey* in those days could do about thirty-four knots, much more than a Riga can. Then I slowed down again to show I didn't care to. For the rest of the day and all night he simply trailed us.

In the morning he moved up on *Dewey*'s starboard beam. He then began to close in on a very gradual collision course. Once again his was the burdened vessel because, although now to starboard, he had originally come up from astern and as the overtaking vessel was still required to keep clear. Evidently he was testing my resolve. He started perhaps a mile away. After an hour or so, when he was within six or seven hundred yards, I hoisted the international signal that meant "I intend to maintain my right of way." He changed course abruptly, and hoisted a signal that reads, literally, "My last course was by chance accidental." He followed us to the entrance to the Gulf of Finland and there rendered us military honors and steamed away.

Foolish episodes of this kind occurred all the time. In March of 1972 I asked a member of my staff to make a count of how many we had recorded, and how many the Soviets had complained about, since the Incidents at Sea talks began the previous October. We had recorded Soviet harassment twelve times, though we complained officially only once. They had complained to us, orally or in writing, five times. Of course, in addition to being juvenile, these incidents were terribly dangerous. Beyond the immediate damage to property and the loss of life any one of them might cause, any one could lead people to shoot at each other with results that might be by that time impossible to control. There was every reason for talks on this subject to go forward. However, since the matter was fundamentally a legalistic one and since John Warner evidently was interested, it was left principally to him.

My most dramatic encounter with the talks occurred on the evening the President went on the air to announce the mining of Haiphong, for that was a night that John Warner had invited the Soviet Incidents-at-Sea delegation, in Washington to put the last touches on the agreement to be signed at the forthcoming Moscow summit, to dinner at his Georgetown home. He also had invited me. It was originally planned as a stag party, but then he decided to invite his wife Kathy and Mouza as well, because Mouza spoke Russian and most of the Russians did not speak English. I knew as a member of JCS that the President would go on the air at just about the time the Russians arrived. I arrived a little early in order to warn John Warner. We agreed that the way to handle the situation was to invite them to watch and listen to the speech with us, rather than try to pretend nothing was happening. That was what we did, with Mouza offering a running translation of the President's words to the delegation's four military members, three admirals and a general, who spoke little or no English. The delegation's fifth member, a civilian named Bubnov, spoke English fluently. The military folk took the President's action and his words in good part, evidently recognizing the mining as something their government might well have done in a similar situation. Bubnov waxed wroth, however. He and I had a short, snappy exchange whose substance is so easy to imagine that it scarcely needs recounting, before we sat down to dine and speak of more congenial matters. It was a minor example of the anomalous "fight and fight, talk and talk" world in which diplomats and military men sometimes find themselves.

The three year agreement on Incidents at Sea, with automatic renewals, signed in Moscow was less significant for what it said, which was little more than a reaffirmation of the Rules of Road, than for what it represented, which was a desire on the part of the Soviet leadership to normalize maritime behavior, now that they were strong at sea. It was always my opinion that the leadership on both sides was less anxious to play the kind of game I have described than peppery young ship captains were. Thus the agreement can be taken, for one thing, as a public admonition to peppery youngsters in both camps to behave themselves.

Kissingerology

How vertiginous an experience it was to be an official in the administration of Richard Nixon is suggested by a list of some of the principal events that occurred between the middle of 1972 and the middle of 1973. Late May 1972: the President triumphantly visits Moscow to sign an agreement limiting strategic arms. June 1972: a "third-rate" burglary occurs at the headquarters of the Democratic National Committee in the Watergate office building. August 1972: the Senate ratifies the SALT defensive-weapon treaty and at Henry Jackson's insistence adds a proviso to the resolution approving the Interim Agreement on defensive weapons that there be "equality" in any offensive-weapon treaty to come. October 1972: Henry Kissinger declares that peace in Vietnam is "at hand." November 1972: Mr. Nixon is reelected President by the biggest margin in history. December 1972: the United States engages in the "Christmas bombing" of North Vietnam. January 1973: Elliot Richardson replaces Melvin Laird as Secretary of Defense. January 1973: the Watergate burglars are tried and are convicted. January 1973: a cease-fire goes into effect in Vietnam. March 1973: James McCord starts to sing. April 1973: Henry Kissinger declares that this is the "year of Europe." April 1973: the President asks for the resignation of H. R. Haldeman and John Ehrlichman; he replaces Attorney General Richard Kleindienst with Elliot Richardson and names James Schlesinger Secretary of Defense. May 1973: the Senate Watergate hearings begin.

At the beginning of the period, then, Mr. Nixon exercised personal control over the nation's diplomatic and military affairs. He shifted his attention to domestic politics in the months before the election. In November, safely in possession of his mandate, he turned his gaze back to the world scene. The time had arrived that I had eagerly awaited since Mr. Nixon, in his aside to me in the Sixth Fleet in October 1970, said that after his reelection he would begin to tell the American people how badly our defenses had deteriorated. Then as Watergate began to engulf him, he became increasingly unable to concentrate on anything but survival, and control passed into whatever hands could seize it, notably those of the men strategically stationed just outside his office door, Henry Kissinger and Alexander Haig. It was during this period that Haig did his quick-change act from Kissinger's two-star deputy to the four-star Vice Chief of Staff of the Army to the civilian chief of staff at the White House. It was in this setting that the practice of a discipline I call "Kissingerology" developed.

It may help make the genesis of Kissingerology clear to review here the successive stages of my relations with Henry Kissinger. At the start of my watch I felt undiluted admiration for and confidence in Henry, and was anxious only to be of as much help to him as I could in what I saw as his masterful management of American political-military policy. As the first months wore on I found myself disagreeing with a number of his ideas and discovering that a number of his methods of operation were not ones I would have chosen to employ. However I believed that as far as ideas went, he was open to persuasion and that if I established a solid personal relationship with him I might persuade him, and that as far as methods went, I could accommodate myself to a certain extent to a situation in which the issues were so important, and that I could use the "system" to correct abuses with which I was unwilling to go along. By the time the end of my first year on watch approached, I was approaching the conviction that I had been over-optimistic on both counts. One amusing early product of Kissingerology was among many pieces of evidence that led me to doubt that I could have a productive personal relationship with Henry.

SCENE: An office in the basement of the White House. HENRY KISS-INGER, smiling and gesticulating, is escorting ELMO ZUMWALT to the door.

KISSINGER: Bud, it is always a pleasure to talk to you. You are the only intellectual among the Chiefs, the only one able to take a broad view. We must have these talks more often.

(They shake hands warmly. ZUMWALT exits. KISSINGER makes sure the door is shut tightly and ZUMWALT is out of earshot.)

KISSINGER (rolling his eyes): If there's one thing I can't stand it's an intellectual admiral!

In sum, I found that I could not believe what Henry told me, that his assent to a recommendation or proposal I made to him—and he assented more often than he dissented—did not at all mean that he agreed or intended to follow my suggestion, but could very well be a mere ploy to defuse or dismiss me. To put it another way, I seldom could learn what Henry thought about a given situation, much less what he was going to do about it, from what Henry told me. As for his *modus operandi,* I discovered I had underestimated by far his bureaucratic skill. He was a master at playing off one official against another, which he could do with impunity because he had erected a fence around the President that was virtually impossible to get over or under or through. By the time the second year of my watch was drawing to an end, I knew that if I was to have any impact on political-military policy on behalf of the Navy I would have to do two things. One was to develop some kind of early-warning system that would alert me to what Henry was up to. The other was to find a way to counter Henry's near-monopoly of the President's ear by applying pressure to other parts of the decision-making machinery —the Joint Chiefs, the Secretary of Defense's staff, influential officials in other executive-branch Departments, members of Congress. In short, during the second half of my watch, the relationship between Henry Kissinger and me was almost entirely adversary.

Kissingerology had a "Haigological" branch, because the incredibly ambivalent relationship between Kissinger and Haig had a lot to do with the minutiae, the day-to-day convolutions, of the conduct of political-military affairs. As I noted earlier, Al Haig was an old acquaintance whom I first met just after the Cuban missile crisis when he was a lieutenant colonel and a special assistant to Joseph Califano, who was a special assistant to the Secretary of the Army, Cyrus Vance. After the crisis was over, Vance was assigned by Robert McNamara to head an effort to formulate a long-range policy toward Cuba and my boss, Paul Nitze, participated in that work. Al and I therefore worked together. Professionally Al was and is a man of great competence and as such was invaluable to Henry Kissinger. Henry is a non-administrator of the first order. He cannot manage details or routine. He treats the people who work for him abominably, making impossible demands on their time and energy, and often screaming and cursing and sometimes even throwing office equipment at them. Al manages details and routine expertly, and is generally even-tempered and considerate to his associates. Henry could not have run his office without Al or someone like him.

Al needed Henry for a different reason, and one Henry was well aware of. Al is extremely ambitious. He coveted daily contact with the President, and indeed he had good reason, since he rose from colonel to full general in four years without ever holding a command as a general officer, a military ascent that I am quite sure is without precedent even in wartime. Since there was no way that Henry could avoid sharing with Al his access to the President, which was his most valuable bureaucratic asset, his dependence on Al was matched by his suspicion of Al. When I say that the day-to-day conduct of affairs was partly determined by the Kissinger-Haig relationship, I mean that the decision about which one of them would take a specific trip overseas, for example, often depended on whether or not Kissinger's love of high-pressure, highly visible diplomatic activity outweighed or was outweighed by his fear of leaving the President alone with Haig for several days.

Perhaps I can illustrate the treacherousness of this particular bog by recounting the unspectacular events of 2 August 1972. I had invited Al Haig to lunch in my office. The report that he was about to be jumped from Henry's two-star assistant to the four-star Vice Chief of Staff of the Army was floating around by then, and Al must have known that I had heard it. However, he did not mention it but asked me what I thought he should do next in his career. I replied that I thought the Army's senior officers would like it if, before becoming Chief of Staff or Vice Chief, he took a command in the field for a few years. I am not above needling someone occasionally, and I said that I knew that the four-star general who had the command in Panama was anxious to retire, having in my mind as I said it an entertaining, if totally untrue-to-life, picture of Al Haig, chin in hand, thoughtfully watching the Gatun Locks slowly open and then slowly close. That ended that subject.

For the rest of the lunch Al spoke confidentially of his difficulties as the intermediary between the President, who didn't trust Henry, and Henry, who felt uncomfortable with the President. He also said that the President vacillated between a strong impulse to get out of Vietnam as fast as possible at almost any price and an equally strong impulse to "bomb North Vietnam back to the Stone Age," in Curtis LeMay's well-remembered phrase. Al said that he had to exercise considerable dexterity to stiffen the President's backbone when the President was in a bug-out mood, and that he lived in dread that some day the President would be with Henry instead of him when the bug-out mood came on and Henry would be unable to handle it. All of that was grist for the Kissingerological mill, I guess. What was grist for the Haigological mill was a report I received some time later that as soon as Al got back to the White House, evidently fearing that Henry would somehow find out where he had been, he went into Henry's office and told him, "I've just had lunch with Bud Zumwalt, the most hypocritical man in Washington." Al then gave Henry a version of our conversation that had so little relation to the facts that he might have been talking about a meeting on another day with somebody else.

Practicing Kissingerology required no "spy ring." It was simply a process of putting together systematically the bits and pieces of information that turned up during the normal conduct of business to see if they made an intelligible pattern, and then acting in accordance with that pattern. My personal staff did some of this puzzle solving for me. Papers flowed from the National Security Council in an unceasing, if turgid, stream and a careful reading sometimes provided clues to what Henry was thinking or doing about this issue or that. Two of Henry's close confidants, Helmut Sonnenfeldt of the NSC senior staff and Seymour Weiss of State, were members of the CNO Executive Panel. They spilled no beans, of course, but frequently they were able to elaborate on the official rationale and sometimes one learned a little from observing which beans they took the most care not to spill. But beyond, and more important than, such esoteric activities as NSSM or Sonnenfeldt watching were the dozens of routine encounters that occurred every day between me and my staff and Henry and his, and the friendships that sprang up out of these encounters. People who have become friends as a result of dealing with one another officially are bound to exchange information when they meet. That is the way a great deal of government business gets done; in fact it is the only way a good deal of government business can get done. One part of Kissingerology, then, really was just an intensification of the eternal effort to find out what the fellow in the office across the hall is up to, an effort that had to be intense in Henry's case both because he was up to such important things and because he put such a premium on keeping most of them secret. And the other part was just an intensification of what every bureaucrat does when he has a cause he wants to promote: he tries to rally as large a body of supporters as he can for that cause.

SALT was a prime subject for Kissingerology, and SALT was very much on the front burner—if in the back channel—during the spring of 1972. Indeed, the chief source of such American indecision as there was about mining Haiphong was its threat to the SALT summit, in whose success the administration had invested so much labor and prestige. All spring long, as American ships and planes in Vietnam were furiously trying to destroy or interdict military supplies of largely Soviet origin so that the Republic of Vietnam could survive beyond the end of May, American and Soviet diplomats in Helsinki were furiously trying to put the finishing touches on an arms limitation agreement that their Governments could sign before the end of May. Of course the arms being used in Vietnam were conventional and tactical and the arms being talked about in Finland were nuclear and strategic. All the same the simultaneous occurrence of those two sets of events on opposite sides of the world was striking, perhaps even ironic. Observing those curious goings on, even a sophisticated student of the world scene might have been hard put to say whether the two superpowers wanted to be friends or were determined to stay enemies. For myself, gratified as I would be if the former assumption proved correct, my instincts, my reading of history and my professional responsibilities all dictated that I plan for the prospect of the latter.

SALT had worked up a considerable momentum in the months since Henry Kissinger and Anatoly Dobrynin in the back channel in the spring of 1971 had made sure that there would be some sort of agreement ultimately and had given that agreement a rough shape. There would be a limitation on offensive as well as defensive weapons, with the Soviets receiving numerical superiority in the former in return for not making a fuss about our Forward Based Systems; there would be roughly equivalent defensive systems based on the realities of their existing Galosh ABM protecting Moscow and our existing Safeguard ABM protecting Minuteman sites. Within that outline there was a great deal of detailed and important filling in to be done. The numbers of offensive launchers and missiles had to be negotiated, as did the precise nature of permissible ABMs. Critical issues concerning mobile missiles, super-size missiles and ABM radars continued unresolved. Above all in importance, and not just to the Navy, was what to do about submarine-launched ballistic missiles (SLBMs), which had not come up during the back-channel talks. The only missiles considered there had been land-based ICBMs.

On the SLBM issue the Soviets appeared to be adamant: they did not want them included in the offensive agreement. There was an obvious reason for them to take that position. Their SLBM technology was inferior to ours but their submarine-building capability was greatly superior; their biggest shipyard, one among many, could turn out more strategic submarines in a year than all our yards combined. Thus, in an unrestricted sub-building race they would end up with so many more boats than we had that it would more than make up for the inferior quality of those boats. I might add that the USSR's record of catching up technologically from far behind in specific areas when they choose to concentrate their efforts is impressive, so that the U.S. faced the long-range possibility, if there were no limitation on SLBMs, of the Soviets having both many, many more boats and equally good boats. At any rate, that was the reasoning in the Tank, where the unanimous position was that if SLBMs were not included in the agreement there should be no agreement, offensive or defensive.

Some "Tankologists" professed to see in the Army and Air Force enthusiasm for a limitation on SLBMs a natural aversion to the kind of Naval "force-building" (the most pejorative of all expressions in the Tank) that a strategic submarine-building race would necessarily involve. In truth, every Chief recognized that there could be no strategic parity between the U. S. and the USSR unless SLBMs were included in any agreements. Moreover, I too had a parochial motive for advocating a limit on SLBMs. It was that the funds for force-building of the kind the Army and Air Force allegedly feared would more than likely come out of the hide of the Navy's conventional forces, which already were starving for money.

During the first months of 1972, and particularly during the first part of March, between the triumphal return of the President from China and the opening of SALT VII in Helsinki on 28 March, the SLBM issue was discussed actively within the Government, for the Chiefs' position was by no means universally held. In the Arms Control Agency, especially, there was a conviction that the Russians would not budge on SLBMs and that it would be tragic to lose the whole agreement over that one issue. The White House's position was less easy to ascertain. The impression Tom Moorer conveyed when he reported to us in the Tank on the several Verification Panel and National Security Council meetings he attended during this period was that two things were happening in the White House: the President was seriously considering the substance of the SLBM arguments pro and con, while Kissinger was searching for a tactic that would enable him to wiggle around the issue. "Kissinger said he didn't understand the logic of the Chiefs that if SLBMs are not included, the Chiefs want no treaty," reads a line in some notes I made of a telephone conversation I had with Admiral Moorer just after he had attended a National Security Council meeting on SALT on 17 March. The notes continue with what evidently was Tom's answer to Henry's comment or question: "CJCS asks what leverage the U.S. will have to curtail offensive construction after we sign an ABM deal. Moorer told the President that the JCS want to protect the security of the United States. They don't want to have an agreement for an agreement's sake." Recalling, as I often did then, Henry's observation about the USSR being "Sparta to our Athens," I can add that I thought it necessary to watch with a very keen eye any agreement being negotiated by Henry Kissinger. Unfortunately from where I sat it was not always possible to see Henry at all.

In that same conversation Tom told me. "Kissinger says the President might order the JCS to support a no-SLBM decision," but that was evidently merely Henry making a muscle. When the President made his decision on 23 March, it went mostly the other way and in support of the JCS position on SLBMs. The form the decision took was NSDM 158, a set of instructions to the delegation about to leave for Finland. The substance of the instructions was that the U.S. would consent to equality in ABMs in the defensive treaty if SLBMs were included in the offensive agreement. If they were not, the U. S. would insist on having one more ABM site than the Soviets. There was more leverage in this position than may at first glance appear because the main thing the Russians were seeking from the talks was equality in defense, where they were behind. Offensively they were ahead in both numbers and throw weight and would continue to be under any limitation formula that was under discussion. Moreover, though this Presidential directive was ostensibly for the SALT delegation, what it actually did was make it virtually impossible for

Henry to trade away a limit on SLBMs in the back channel, which was where the issue actually was decided.

The inclusion of SLBMs was the only major issue in the first phase of SALT that the Chiefs played a significant part in resolving. To be sure we had an almost Kissinger-proof case. A limit on offensive weapons that did not include sea-based ones, given the huge Soviet submarine building program and capacity, would have been an absurdity. However, the JCS did two things about SLBMs we had not always done before. We did our corporate homework and we raised our voices. Apparently our toughness on this issue caught Henry unprepared. Up to then it had always been he who had caught us thus.

Unfortunately our victory on SLBMs—if you can call winning a point within your own government a "victory"—was at best a sometime thing. The final deal was that the Soviets got 62 strategic submarines to our 44, and 950 launching tubes to our 710, on the ground that this was equality because they, having greater distances to travel from their bases, needed that many more boats to keep an equal number on station. That remained true only until the Soviets developed long-range SLBMs. In 1973, six years before the U. S. would get its 4000-mile Trident missile to sea, the Soviets began deploying SSN 8 missiles of 4000-mile range in their Delta class submarine. These missiles can be fired at us from Soviet home waters. Therefore the case can be made that the U.S. rather than the Soviets now ought to have the larger strategic submarine fleet, until 1979 at least. Anyhow, the SLBM deal could hardly be called arms limitation. If there had been no agreement at all, the Soviets could not have had in operation very many more than sixty-two boats by 1977, which is when the agreement expires.

Needless to say neither I nor any other Chief participated in a meaningful way in the discussion leading to the appalling SLBM numbers, though certain forms were observed that made it accurate for me to testify that I had been "consulted" when I was asked whether I had been by Henry Jackson while testifying before the Senate Armed Services Committee in July. The numbers had been presented to us almost a month before the summit via a 28 April Verification Panel meeting and a 1 May NSDM, which in theory gave us time to object. Even though they were presented in a manner that made it clear that objections would be unwelcome and useless, we were wrong not to have made our concern a matter of official record however futile it might have been. We were probably derelict in our statutory responsibility as military advisors as well. Until I read John Newhouse's book, I did not even know that the numbers emerged from a discussion between Kissinger and Secretary Brezhnev in Moscow during a visit Kissinger made there from 22 to 25 April. The stated purpose of the visit, which was kept a total secret until Henry's return, was to talk about Vietnam, where for one thing our bombing of Haiphong harbor had just damaged four Soviet freighters. I suspected, when I learned of the trip, that SALT also had come up, but that was just guessing; no one ever said so.

In any case, Newhouse says that the Kissinger visit had been preceded by several conversations between Henry and Dobrynin, and several written exchanges between the President and Brezhnev, on the subject of SLBMs. Newhouse says further that before Henry went to Moscow he had reached the conclusion that the only way to induce the Soviets to include SLBMs in the agreement was to concede them numerical superiority. Newhouse does not know whether it was Kissinger or Brezhnev who first advanced the specific numbers agreed upon and if he doesn't I certainly don't. I have no hesitation in saying, though, that for the President not to specifically seek the counsel of "the principal Naval advisor to the President" about something that is so clearly within the boundaries of that naval advisor's expertise and responsibility as how many strategic submarines the country needs seems to me to be a poor way for a President to arrive at a decision that vitally affects national security. And obviously the same needs to be said about his failure to obtain meaningful military advice from the JCS on a matter of over-riding national strategic significance.

The SLBM deal wrapped up the first phase of SALT to all intents and purposes. Between 1 May, when NSDM 164, containing the SLBM numbers, came out, and 26 May, when the defensive treaty and offensive Interim Agreement were signed in Moscow, there were almost non-stop negotiations about such highly technical—and important—issues as ABM radars, mobile and oversize missiles and the replacement of obsolete missiles. However NSDM 164 made it clear to me that however favorably to the U.S. those other matters were resolved, the numbers meant that we were going to subscribe to a bad bargain in Moscow. I hope I have made it clear that I think the U.S. could have gotten a better bargain if Henry Kissinger had negotiated more skillfully, but by May 1972 it was too late to repine about that. I turned my thoughts to ways of making the best of the bargain we got.

This was a subject that was much on the mind of almost everyone in Defense, particularly the Secretary. I suggested to the JCS soon after NSDM 164 was issued that we needed to insist on certain safeguards as a way of making the agreements marginally acceptable from a military point of view. I got the idea for working up such "assurances," as we were to call them, from a similar package that I, as Director of Arms Control in the Office of the Secretary of Defense, working with the Joint Staff, had put together in response to the Nuclear Test Ban Treaty of 1963. However, it was not until a meeting in the Tank on 22 May the eve of the summit, that we were able to address ourselves to it officially. During the preceding weeks the events in Vietnam had occupied most of our attention, events that many people feared would destroy the summit altogether. I have often wondered whether Henry's lopsided SLBM numbers didn't buy the Soviet's surprising indifference to our bombing and mining of North Vietnam. No one will know unless and until all the tapes from the Oval Office become open to public scrutiny. At any rate, at the 22 May meeting my recommendation became a JCS position, an action I noted thus in a memorandum for the record: "Chairman intends to have the Joint Staff put together a package of all those things that would be needed to make SALT agreement work."

On 26 May, the day the SALT agreements were signed in Moscow, I pursued the Assurance idea in a pair of draft statements, substantively much the same, that I submitted to my colleagues in the Tank. One was a statement I would have liked the Chiefs to give the President as their position about the current agreements and any subsequent ones. One of my chief concerns was that Kissinger had a near monopoly of the President's ear. The other was a statement I would have liked the President to make to the American people. The latter was a forlorn effort, I admit. Though it always seemed to me that suggesting Presidential positions on matters like SALT was a legitimate offering of military advice by a military advisor, such suggestions never got far. If they emerged from the Tank at all, they sank without a trace in the office of the Secretary. As for the JCS statement, the position that we finally sent the Secretary of Defense for recommended delivery to the President was considerably less emphatic than my draft. The proposed Presidential statement for the people was omitted. I quote my draft here as an accurate expression of how I felt then.

> The JCS have always supported the principle of an equitable strategic arms control arrangement. It is apparent that the principle of equal security for the U.S. and the USSR, which has motivated our negotiation from the outset, cannot permit a final arrangement in which the number and quality of the armaments on each side could be other than equal. The interim arrangement allows the Soviet Union as a temporary matter, large numbers of ICBMs, SLBMs and a greater aggregate missile payload as indicated by silo volume. Any final agreement, to gain the support of the JCS, must in what it permits and what it prohibits be equal in all respects for both sides. Pending such an agreement, and recognizing that the existing inequalities favoring the USSR cannot be permitted indefinitely, the JCS believe that the U.S. will have to pursue vigorously our strategic programs planned or presently underway. These include ongoing modernization of sea-based and land-based deterrent systems and the follow-on systems currently in the various stages of design and development, such as Trident, the B-1 strategic bomber, and other supporting efforts in command, control and communications.

Once Assurances began to occupy a major share of our attention in the Tank, as they did through most of the summer, the issues of SALT merged with the issues of the budget, for the Assurances were strategic programs that the Congress would have to provide money for. The general nature of such Assurances was almost self-evident. There would have to be improvements in our intelligence-gathering and monitoring systems to guard against Russian cheating. There would have to be a solid ongoing research and development program to make sure that the Russians could not secure a qualitative advantage to go with their quantitative one. And the existing programs for modernizing strategic forces—Trident, the B-1 bomber, the third generation of Minuteman, a submarine-launched cruise missile, a better command and control system for strategic submarines— would have to continue, or even accelerate, to make sure we would not be caught in 1977, when the Interim Agreement expired, with neither an agreement to limit strategic systems nor a program to build them.

Furthermore, as I have said, we in the military did not consider the limits on offensive weapons set by the Interim Agreement to be real limitations. We did not believe that in the absence of an agreement the Russians could have deployed within five years many more SLBMs and ICBMs than the number the Agreement "limited" them to. However, this was a point that many people, including quite a few members of the Senate Foreign Relations Committee, could not or would not grasp, just as they have not in 1975 grasped that the "break-through" proclaimed at Vladivostok, which gave each side 2400 strategic vehicles and 1320 MIRVed missiles, in fact gives the Soviets a 4 to 1 advantage in missile throw weight and, when they finish deployment of their MIRVs, a 2.7 to 1 Soviet advantage in MIRVs. In the course of one of the first sessions of Congressional testimony on the SALT agreement, Senator Fulbright charged Secretary Laird and Admiral Moorer with "turning SALT around" by making it a reason for asking for new programs and thus accelerating the arms race that SALT was supposed to be decelerating. The fact was that it was the unconscionable numbers in the SALT agreements themselves that virtually froze us into five more years of high spending on U.S. strategic forces. The alternative was to watch passively as the Soviets raced to build up to the huge force levels, far above what they had in 1972, set by the "limitation."

I said before that Secretary Laird was particularly keen on our JCS Assurances. He showed it during the first week in June. In a consummate political power play that few people other than he could have conceived or executed, he arranged to be summoned before the Armed Service Committees of both houses just as they were marking up the FY '73 budget. Mel strongly argued that without Assurances the SALT agreements were too risky to ratify, pointed out that the treaty limiting defensive weapons would save 711 million dollars previously earmarked for Safeguard in FY '73, and persuaded the Committee to add to the budget $168 million worth of Assurance programs that had not been reviewed—or even presented to—either Kissinger's Defense Program Review Committee or the Office of Management and the Budget. His sober and plausible explanation for resorting to such a procedure, which appeared to bypass every prescribed channel and flout every prescribed rule of budget-making, was that Congress, as a co-equal branch of Government under the Constitution, had the right and obligation to hear the undiluted views of the Secretary of Defense on critical matters of national policy. I have every personal reason to believe that he said this without guile. You may recall that back in February when John Stennis embarrassed and angered him by springing my "lose-the-war" testimony on him, he resisted his impulse to rebuke me and instead took the position that the Congress was entitled to hear *my* undiluted opinions about matters within *my* competence.

In any case, Mel executed his maneuver with great skill. He moved so rapidly that the money for Assurances was before the Congress before Kissinger or the OMB quite knew what was happening. Moreover Mel's political timing was just right. He proposed the additional $168 million at a time when it had become almost certain that George McGovern would be the Democratic Presidential nominee. Under the circumstances Mr. Nixon had shrewdly and correctly decided that the campaign strategy that would do best for him was to stay well to the right of McGovern on just about every issue—particularly Defense, where McGovern was calling for a patently absurd $30 billion reduction in the budget. Thus the President, who might have been a Defense economizer if he had been facing an opponent who was contesting the center with him, made no remonstrance against the extra funds his Secretary of Defense had asked for and an Assurances program sailed through the Congress with scarcely a demur. All that summer and fall Senator McGovern, inadvertently you can be sure, made life for us in the military a little easier than it might have been otherwise.

A National Security Council staff member told me after Congress had given Laird the extra money that Kissinger had been "distressed" both at Laird's lukewarm support of SALT before Congress and the budget add-ons he got as a result. Henry should not have been surprised at the military insistence on Assurances nor for that matter at the President's support of them. The issue had come up as far back as 19 August 1970, when the President had met with members of the SALT delegation to hear their report on the Vienna phase of the talks. According to a report of that meeting to the Joint Chiefs, Ambassador Gerard Smith, chairman of the delegation, had said to the President, among other things:

> If we were to reach agreement on the basis of the U.S. proposal, there is ample room for force improvement, modernization, and R&D. . . . Such an agreement will not solve U.S. budget problems. . . . Admiral Moorer will need to request—quite properly—force improvement, replacement and R&D action. . . . Considering these factors, U.S. needs to engage in an educational program both with the Congress and the public to let them realize that a strategic arms limitation agreement is not a panacea to all arms and budget problems.

The President had remarked at that time that "this last point of Ambassador Smith's was important and we would need to engage in such an educational program at the proper time."

The elimination of Senator Henry Jackson of Washington from the presidential race and the freedom that gave him to spend a great deal of time during June and July on hearings on the SALT agreements was another beneficial side effect of the McGovern candidacy as far as I was concerned, though unfortunate for the Senator and, in my view, the nation's political health. Of the 535 members of Congress, Scoop Jackson had—and has—the best understanding of the realities, political and military, of a host of issues, including SALT. One noteworthy example of his penetration occurred several days before the Moscow summit at a meeting at which Henry Kissinger and Tom Moorer briefed a group of strongly pro-Defense legislators about the forthcoming arms limitation agreements. According to Admiral Moorer's report to us in the Tank on 22 May, after the legislators—Senators Jackson, Stennis, John Tower, Peter Dominick, and James Buckley, and Representative George Mahon —had heard the briefing, they took the unanimous position that the agreements would not sufficiently curtail the Soviet strategic programs to make it possible for us to curtail strategic programs of our own like Trident, the B-1, et al.

All but one of them felt, in addition, that the unequal numbers in the offensive agreement would make our strategic programs easier to put through. The solitary dissenter was Scoop. He thought that the mere existence of agreements bearing the title "Strategic Arms Limitation," whatever their specific content, would diminish support for further strategic spending. He was right, of course. Though he himself has been unremitting in his efforts to put the real issues of SALT before the public, the programs necessary to keep the Soviets honest have had hard going in the Congress and in the press. This might have been all to the good if there had been a similar relaxation in the USSR once the agreements went into effect, but of course there has not been. The Soviets have continued to build and modernize to the utmost limits, and considerably beyond those limits in cases where they have been able to capitalize on loopholes in the agreements.

The hearings the Senate Armed Services Committee held on SALT intermittently during June and July were under the chairmanship of John Stennis, but they really were Scoop Jackson's show. As chairman of the Subcommittee on Arms Control, he had been monitoring SALT for three years. He had become the Committee's acknowledged expert on the subject, and as such had become more and more discontented with Kissinger's conduct of the negotiations. He was anxious, I believe, to make a record that would address those many controversial aspects of the Treaty and the Interim Agreement that he had reason to suspect the Senate Foreign Relations Committee, which had the primary jurisdiction over the agreements, would fail to perceive or would gloss over. It was Scoop who insisted that the Secretary of Defense, the Joint Chiefs and their respective SALT representatives, Paul Nitze and General Roy Allison, be pressed for their views on the agreements. It was Scoop who did most of the pressing when we took the stand.

I was one of the last witnesses because I was on a European trip during the main part of the hearings. Indeed I sat up most of the night on the plane back preparing my testimony. What I said there, I have said already in these pages: that the basis for my support of the Treaty and Interim Agreement was, first, that we continue our strategic programs full force and, second, that the Interim Agreement was only interim and that a permanent agreement must give us parity. Under Senator Jackson's skillful questioning, my views went into a public record. Finally, those hearings inspired the Jackson amendment to the resolution approving the Interim Agreement. That amendment passed the Senate fifty-six to thirty-five despite the opposition to it of most of the members of the Foreign Relations Committee and encountered no difficulty in the House. It virtually ordered the negotiators in SALT's second phase to settle for nothing less than offensive equality, and concluded by saying that "the attainment of more permanent and comprehensive agreements are dependent upon the maintenance of a vigorous research and development and modernization program leading to a prudent strategic posture." I couldn't have put it better myself. But Congress, after all, is a committee, and like any committee is often schizoid. The same Congress that passed this resolution proceeded by subsequent cuts in the President's Defense budgets to reduce the pressure upon the Soviets to accept equality in SALT.

The budgetary complications associated with SALT were minor compared with those the North Vietnamese Easter offensive created. It fouled up at least three budgets. The offensive coincided with the start of the final quarter of FY '72, which was also a time when Congress was considering the budget for FY '73 and we in the Executive Branch were planning the budget for FY '74. For FY '72, the Congress had set a ceiling for expenditures on the Vietnam war of two and a half billion dollars. For three quarters of the year we lived well within those means, but the offensive changed all that. The Navy and the Air Force especially—for the Army did not escalate its activities much—found themselves spending enormous, unanticipated amounts on combat pay, ammunition, replacement of lost equipment, spare parts, repairs, in short just about every operational category.

In the Pentagon, and everywhere else in the Government as far as I know, there are rooms full of expert practitioners of fiscal legerdemain, people who are challenged rather than inhibited by the fine print in appropriations acts. They worked hard in this national crisis at moving money, but they could not make what we spent on Vietnam that year look like only two and a half billion dollars. At the beginning of June Secretary Laird had to appeal to Congress to raise the authorization by two hundred million dollars. He got his way, which gave the prestidigitators a little more room to shuffle money in and helped solve the least of our problems.

The great one was how to make the "bare bones" FY '73 budget, already being marked up by the authorizing committees, reflect what Mel estimated would be five billion dollars worth of extra expenses if we continued our augmented southeast Asia operations until New Year, 1973—and it turned out that we continued them somewhat beyond that date. I wish I could report that someone devised a brilliant solution to this problem, but no one did, probably because it was insoluble, given the attitude of the President and his economic advisors toward inflation and budget deficits, and the attitude of the Congress and the public toward the war. What happened was typically hit-or-miss. Part of the cost was covered by supplemental funds the President asked for and received after he was reelected. Another part was made to vanish by the fiscal wizards aforesaid. And most of it was paid for by lower force levels, a slowdown in modernization and, especially, reduced readiness in all the Services.

As a matter of fact, in 1972 the Chiefs were not given even a ceremonial opportunity to justify their budget requests to the President. Largely on the initiative of Mel Laird, who feared that budget decisions before the election would be stingier than after, the date for the annual meeting between the President and the Chiefs was moved from August to November. But in November the cease-fire talks between Henry Kissinger and the North Vietnamese were at a critical stage—Henry, you will remember, proclaimed on 26 October, ten days before the election, that "peace is at hand"—and Mr. Nixon decided to use the scheduled meeting with the Chiefs to make sure that the terms of the cease-fire received military support.

I was disappointed. I very much wanted the President to hear the presentation I had prepared with a good deal of care and effort. Its theme was that the Navy was being, and increasingly would continue to be, asked to bear the major burden of responding to crises—as witness the way the nearly doubled number of ships in the western Pacific and their extended deployment were grinding down the Navy's men and machinery—and that Defense planning, programming, and budgeting should take this into account rather than keep up the traditional pretense that all the Services were equally involved in all situations. True, by a percentage point or two, the Navy was receiving the largest share of the budget of any Service, but it was also being worked the hardest and therefore was losing capability the fastest. The substance of my planned briefing, then, was much the same as the previous year's, but the impact was still more somber—or would have been if I ever had had a chance to make it. The President promised us a budget meeting later, but by the time later had come, so had Watergate.

The meeting with the President took place on 30 November. Less than three weeks before, the *Constellation*'s troubles with some of her black crew members had impelled Henry Kissinger to scold me over the telephone, after telling Secretary Laird that Mr. Nixon had wanted me fired. I had no reason to believe that he or the President had learned to love me again in the days since. I had just appeared before the hostile Hicks subcommittee. I was working day and night to win acceptance for my program of personnel reform in the Navy, but I judged that neither it nor I had much better than a fifty-fifty chance of surviving. And so for me there was a certain air of unreality about that meeting.

It took place in the Oval Office. The President, Kissinger and Al Haig already were in their armchairs when we Chiefs trooped in, sober of mien, highly beribboned and, I fear, a little like performing poodles or trained seals. Our annual meeting always included a picture-taking session and so, before we got down to business, photographers materialized and we all assumed the expressions and stances of statesmanship. The President's discussion of the status of the cease-fire increased my sense of being on a strange planet. I could not help reflecting that the crews of *Kitty Hawk, Hassayampa,* and

Constellation had not been able to deal with the Vietnam war from armchairs in a quiet study.

I had met with Admiral Moorer the day before and he had given me a preview of what the President was likely to say about the cease-fire. My handwritten notes of that meeting consist of paragraphs numbered 1 through 19. In view of past controversies and conflicts about assistance to South Vietnam, it is interesting that eleven of those nineteen paragraphs are mostly about assistance: how to use it to force President Thieu to accept the truce; whether we could afford it; which parts of which budgets to put it into; how to maneuver Congress into approving it; how to administer it in the executive branch. In other words, it was perfectly obvious to all of us at the time that the promise of massive American assistance to South Vietnam and of prompt U.S. retaliation to serious truce violations were the critical elements in securing the cease-fire and that the fulfillment of these promises would be the critical element in maintaining the cease-fire. Yet the administration never really let the American people—or Congress—in on this non-secret, apparently on the assumption that the critical element in persuading Americans to accept the terms of the cease-fire was to allow them to believe that it meant the end of any kind of American involvement in Vietnam no matter what happened there after the cease-fire was agreed to. Not even the JCS were informed that written commitments were made to Thieu. There are at least two words no one can use to characterize the outcome of that two-faced policy. One is "peace." The other is "honor."

At that meeting with Admiral Moorer I learned that Hanoi was about to accept an offer the President had made in his 8 May speech announcing the mining of Haiphong. This public offer had been that the U.S. would "cease all acts of force throughout Indochina" when the following conditions had been met by Hanoi: "All American prisoners of war must be returned," and "There must be an internationally supervised cease-fire throughout Indochina." At the 30 November meeting the President spelled out what the 8 May offer had implied: a cease-fire in place; the return of the American POWs and an accounting of the fate of the MIAs; self-determination for the people of South Vietnam without the imposition of a communist or a coalition government. It was the first point, agreed to between Kissinger and the North Vietnamese without consultation with President Thieu, that was causing all the current trouble, for it meant that

North Vietnamese troops would remain in South Vietnam. Thieu considered that intolerable—not without reason as it turned out. My notes of the meeting with the President go 1 to 23 and are far too long to quote in full, but excerpts from them may throw some light on how the President's mind was working in the full flush of his mandate. The President is speaking:

7. We're now in a position where the U.S. people know we have an agreement—Thieu is taking a strong stand—the POWs can be returned —the government of South Vietnam can retain its foreign policy insistence on free elections—the U.S. will not support a war to push the NVA [North Vietnamese Army] out—Laird agreed.

8. The President says, the President can only go so far—if we fought for two more years, we might get a marginally better deal, you don't have any options in a democracy.

9. The President insisted he must have JCS support—the left will debunk his deal—which he expects to have by the end of next week—DOD must support it—he compared the solution to that of Korea—after all the blood, the sacrifices, the military must be for it.

10. Thieu should crow—he gets continued U.S. economic and military support.

11. The President then said, we need to make the point that no paper is worth a damn, what really matters is the economic and military support and will. . . . whether the war resumes or not depends on the PRC and the USSR . . . but they've got other fish to fry and therefore we can influence them—the NVA too—they're going to need some sort of economic assistance.

20. With regard to North Vietnam troops in South Vietnam, Kissinger said that they cannot legally bring in new troops or rotate and therefore, over time, their forces would attrite. . . . Kissinger said replacement of equipment is okay, replacement of personnel is not—danger of aggression remains, but there is a full legal basis for terminating the war. . . . he said the problem was that the North has never admitted they have any troops down there so that therefore they couldn't formally agree to pull them out—the President intervened to say, they faced resumed hostilities from the U.S. and South Vietnam if they violate the deal, we have told the Soviets and the PRC of our concern—he said, of course, our will to do something is less—he urged that we not worry about the words, we will keep the agreement if it serves us—their interests require them to obey.

21. The President spoke about contingencies: (1) there were to be three-day to six-day strikes—if they get hardnosed, then we will mine and hit

more targets in Hanoi with B-52s; (2) over the longer term we need contingency planning in the event the agreement is not upheld—various plans for various levels of violation—JCS do this on their own—no ground forces . . .

23. The Chiefs expressed their concern about prospective violations under the truce, pointing out that after the '68 truce the North had proceeded to violate the terms and nothing was ever done about it.

A few days later, Admiral Moorer and Deputy Secretary of Defense Kenneth Rush met with the President at Camp David. Upon his return, the Chairman reported to us in the Tank. These are my notes on that report:

1. The President was concerned regarding the way talks were going.

2. He discussed courses of action available.

3. Since 8 May proposals were his, since Thieu is not going along, Nixon is in the position of letting Thieu block the POW release—or if he goes along with no withdrawal of NVA—and will have gotten no more than four years ago.

4. He was therefore properly concerned.

5. He asked if it was thought that Congress would support a renewal of military activity up north.

6. Moorer said it was tough to do this after saying that peace was imminent and raised the question of inadequate number of '74 dollars—he pointed out that we would have to improvise on the '73 budget and that all the services were hard hit—for the U.S. Government to make the unilateral decision, we would get opposition from all.

7. The President agreed.

8. Moorer thought that the only way we could resume in any way to make an impact would be to have an agreement—and have the other side violate—if flagrant—but wouldn't want Thieu to provoke it or for the U.S. Government to provoke it in advance.

9. The President asked Moorer the effect of the bombing and mining—CIA says no—Moorer disagreed—less than ⅓ as much is arriving including that coming in from China since 8 May—we could do better but we've had a big impact—the President agreed.

10. Since that comment made there's been some movement—the Vice President will go to Thieu on Wednesday and *reassure him concerning the full support in the event of a truce, full support economically—also that if violations occur that we will come to their assistance*—in the last day

or so there's been some break—we think one more approach to Thieu
will give us the final approval, the date will be uncertain—details remain
to be worked out, Moorer agrees it's possible that if we talk to Thieu one
more time—

It would be redundant for me to describe the foregoing italics as
"my italics," since the notes are my notes, but I did add them
retroactively in the light of the events in Vietnam in the spring of
1975. As almost everyone must remember, the President finally persuaded—I almost wrote "conned"—Thieu into agreeing to the terms
of the truce and, on 23 December, thought he had final agreement
from the North Vietnamese when the latter suddenly left the conference table. Xuan Thuy, head of the North Vietnamese delegation to
the Paris peace talks, in an interview shortly thereafter, said that he
had left because Kissinger raised all of the public demands made by
Thieu and had insisted on removing from the agreement reached in
October every mention of the Viet Cong administration in South
Vietnam.

At the same time Kissinger denied that the U.S. supported all of
Thieu's demands, specifically rejecting Thieu's insistence on the
withdrawal of North Vietnamese troops from South Vietnam. The
President thereupon ordered the famous "Christmas bombing" of
Hanoi. Immediately after New Year's day, the North Vietnamese
signified their willingness to resume negotiations. On 5 January, on
the eve of Henry Kissinger's departure for Paris, Tom Moorer re-
ported to us on a meeting that week attended by the President,
Secretaries Rogers and Laird, Admiral Moorer, Deputy Secretary
Rush and Kissinger. My notes on that report include the following.

c. President said we must focus public and Congress on what to do if
negotiations become difficult and North Vietnam does not reply.

d. Most of discussion was between Laird and Moorer, briefing on air
strikes and collateral damage.

e. Laird pointed out he must go before Congress on Monday, that it had
been set up before; it's his four-year report—he didn't want Moorer to
go with him—he intends to take a hard position concerning wheat, trade
et cetera.

f. Laird will get many questions concerning peace and air strikes.

g. Kissinger said one thing is different—we have published pictures
concerning the buildup—it is clear that the North had stonewalled and
stood mute.

h. Laird said that he feels that Congress needs something to tell their constituents. . . .

l. The President said he talked to Scott and Ford before Christmas and the Democrats after Christmas (he alerted Mansfield).

m. Not much concerning negotiations—the President confident that bombing brought them back—in fact, after agreeing on the 23rd, the NVA welched—the President returned to the 8 May policy on bombing and added to it. . . . The Chairman said that all the JCS agree that we should get the prisoners of war out on the best terms we can get.

The truce finally went into effect on 27 January and the Navy was faced with the task of sweeping the mines out of Haiphong channel. We undertook the operation under the slogan of "Slow is Good." We did not want to dispose of all the mines before all the POWs were back home. It was an operation of special importance and interest to the Navy because it was the first use of helicopters, rather than surface vessels, to tow minesweeping equipment. I had pushed the development of this new system throughout my two and a half years in office, and to pay for it I had given up most of our surface minesweeping ships in advance. Fortunately the helos became operational in time—but barely in time—to do the job in Haiphong.

In principle, the new system is much like the old one. The helos tow equipment designed to cut the mines loose and disarm or detonate them according to their type and setting. However, because helos are faster than ships and more distant from the mines, it is a lot speedier and a lot less dangerous to the men performing the operation. The one trouble we had was with the helos. We converted for minesweeping work big CH-53s, originally designed as troop carriers for amphibious forces, and since they had not been specially built to pull the heavy minesweeping equipment, there were problems of stress on certain elements of the structure. We lost a couple of helos but, fortunately, no men. Since then the system has been further improved, and we were able to use it to help the Egyptians clear the Suez Canal without even the relatively small problems we had in Haiphong.

In March a Kissingerological source on or near the National Security Council staff told me that a few days previously Henry had been heard to say that he hoped the North Vietnamese would postpone for a year or so the invasion they obviously intended to mount. If they attacked now, he said, the U.S. would be compelled to react with force. If they waited a year, he was not so sure that we would.

There were major changes in my working conditions during the first half of 1973. For one thing, soon after the end of my third year on the job, only Tom Moorer was left of the colleagues from the Tank and the Secretary's office with whom I had begun my term. To my deep regret, Leonard Chapman completed his term at the end of 1971. His successor as Commandant of the Marine Corps was Robert Cushman, a protegé of the President, who came from the job of deputy director of the CIA. To my delight, my revered boss from Vietnam, Creighton Abrams, became Chief of Staff of the Army toward the end of 1972. On 1 August 1973, George Brown, who had been the Air Force commander in South Vietnam when I was Naval Commander there, replaced Jack Ryan as Chief of Staff of the Air Force. In May of 1972 John Chafee resigned as Secretary of the Navy to run for a Rhode Island Senate seat against Claiborne Pell—and lose—and John Warner moved up into the job from Under Secretary. I have already described the difficulties this created for me in the personnel field. It made budget and procurement work harder, too, for John Warner was a Secretary who bent with every political breeze that blew, and when it came to Defense contracts especially, what blew out of such states as John Stennis's Mississippi, George Mahon's Texas, Bob Sikes' Florida and Stuart Symington's Missouri were gales rather than breezes. Dave Packard, a man of integrity and intellect, had departed as Deputy Secretary of Defense in December 1971. Ken Rush replaced him in February 1972 and eleven months later William Clements, a Texas oil man, replaced Ken. With Clements, my relations never were good. He appeared to be alarmed by my efforts to reform personnel practices in the Navy, was too easy on contractors, and seemed anxious to ingratiate himself with the White House. Finally, Mel Laird left in January according to schedule and just as his successor, Elliot Richardson, was getting accustomed to the job and beginning to demonstrate his great competence, Watergate whisked him over to the Justice Department and compelled us to start from the beginning again with James Schlesinger.

But if the turnover in associates required adjustments, it was chiefly Watergate that made the entire working environment different. January 1973 was the month the Watergate burglars went on trial and were found—or pleaded—guilty. In March James McCord, one of those burglars, began to spill the beans. In May Senator Sam

Ervin's Special Watergate Committee began its hearings. As the escalation of Watergate proceeded, the withdrawal of the President from the day-to-day conduct of affairs became more pronounced, and the intrigues among his immediate subordinates became more byzantine. In this climate people who worked in the White House sometimes felt compelled to unburden themselves of the things they had seen and heard. Occasionally one or another of them unburdened himself to me. What those people told me was rather a messy mixture of backstairs gossip and significant information about the moods and activities of the people who were running the country, and about the relationships among them. The second part of the mixture impelled me then to take notes on what I was told and impels me now to present a few excerpts from the notes—in order to recreate the surrealistic milieu of rumors flying, bureaucracy unraveling, leadership faltering, which was the historical phenomenon of that period—with as much of the gossip removed as possible. From January notes:

> Haig has backed off from Kissinger—the President now goes to Haig before Kissinger—Going back to October, Kissinger had a fast program for winding up on southeast Asia—he needed only one more session he said—Haig thought that Kissinger was going too far and giving up too much—he talked the President into backing off of his time schedule on troop withdrawals—he got himself alone with the President—Kissinger doesn't know this since Haig was supposed to be working for Kissinger —Kissinger worries about what Haig is up to while he's away—

That was when the President was still in control. From March notes:

> As a result of Haig's departure [to become Vice-Chief of Staff of the Army] there is a lot less paranoia in the office. . . . Kissinger feels a little more secure with the President now that Haig has left. . . . there is polarization in the Defense Departement between Richardson and Clements. . . . Zumwalt is considered part of the Richardson tent, Moorer and Haig are part of the Clements tent. . . . Kissinger had breakfast with Richardson. . . . Richardson is tough on insisting on these meetings and that infuriates Kissinger. . . . Clements works hard to keep in close touch with Kissinger after WSAG meetings and by telephone. . . . Kissinger says if Richardson doesn't change his tune he'll be treated the same as Rogers. . . . He'll be just cut out and action will go directly to Clements. . . . The President has said he wants to screw the universities, especially Harvard, by cutting back research and development money.

Watergate was removing the President further from the action and all plots were thickening. Then in June with Haldeman and Ehrlichman gone and Haig back in the White House as chief of staff:

> ... Kissinger was not aware of the plumber taps but did request that his own staff be tapped. .... The President wants to pull the NSC blanket over all this and to say that all Presidents did it. ... He wants to justify the motives not the act. ... Haig is running from the whole question. ... Haig puts a cover memo on each Kissinger memo. ... Kissinger says he won't put up with it and at the end of the summer he will go unless they make him Secretary of State. ... Haldeman and Ehrlichman are on one side, Mitchell and Dean are on the other. ... The President is feeling both sides out. ... Haldeman and Ehrlichman are not sure what he is doing. ... they are making implicit threats. ... there is no chance that Haldeman and Ehrlichman will come back. ... Haig will stay on until they can make him Chairman of the Joint Chiefs of Staff. ...
> ... Kissinger, Haig and Shultz are the only ones who get in to the President. ... Kissinger's resignation is what Haig would like now, however, it's necessary for Haig to keep Kissinger in line because of Watergate problems. ... Haig was involved in Watergate more than Kissinger. ... Al can't do too much if he is still interested in being Chairman of the Joint Chiefs. ... the SALT deal will be made before the JCS or SecDef get in on it. ... nobody is in on it. ... the President doesn't really care, he's so preoccupied with Watergate. ... nobody gets to the President. ... some of his old political advisors have tried to get in and he refuses to see them. ... inside the White House there are five coups a day as various power centers try to take over.

The combination of loss of control in and by the White House, the succession of new people at the top of the Department of Defense, and my distress over the way SALT, the troubles in the Middle East, the shifting maritime balance, and a host of other important issues were being handled greatly speeded up a change in my approach to my job that had been developing slowly for some time. At the beginning of my watch, keenly interested as I was in matters of global policy and eager as I was to be consulted about them, I had been preoccupied with the Navy's immediate problems: antique personnel policies, obsolescing ships and planes and weapons, outdated strategic concepts. By the middle of 1973 such programs for the Navy as I had been able to initiate were irrevocably under way for better or worse, and were being capably monitored by my staff. Hence I could devote much of my attention to an effort to secure for the Defense establishment a more influential voice, or at least a hearing, in the councils where political-military policy and programs were formulated. For the fact was that more often than not Navy or JCS positions, even when they got as far as Kissinger's office, were simply ignored.

One rather interesting product of this effort was a study of the NSSM–NSDM system by one of the most brilliant members of my staff, Commander William Cockell, soon to be promoted to captain and succeed Kin McKee as director of the CEP. (Kin is now the two-star superintendant of the Naval Academy.) Bill's study contained several suggestive findings. One was that the great majority of NSSMs called for studies of rather narrow, short-term problems, e.g., Policy toward Peru, Policy toward Malta, Policy for Southwest Africa, Program Analysis of Turkey. In other words, the system mostly generated *ad hoc* responses to immediate problems rather than the comprehensive national strategy whose lack had been a sore point with me from the beginning. Absent a national security strategy that specified what the United States would try to do where, the decisions I had to make about the structure, capability, and readiness of the Navy were a lot more the product of guesswork than I thought consistent with national security.

A second finding was that although as many as 330 people in Defense, State, the CIA, the National Security Council, and so forth, took part in gathering material for the studies and writing preliminary drafts, no more than thirty people, a large number of them members of Kissinger's staff, participated in drawing up the lists of possible alternative actions—the "options"—from which the President presumably chose when he wanted to act. In other words, the way to get one's suggestions for action before the President was not to labor over the fine print of the studies but to seek to influence those thirty people—or better yet make it a group of thirty-one by contriving to become a member of it.

A third finding, and one of particular significance at a time when the President was disappearing over the horizon, was that under the NSSM–NSDM system decision-making had been an exercise conducted in almost complete privacy by just two men, Richard Nixon and Henry Kissinger. From my observation, even the meetings of the National Security Council were relatively contrived affairs with some discussions, some set piece questions and comments by the President, but with the real summing up occurring in Nixon-Kissinger tête-a-têtes. Now that the President was paying less and less attention to any issue except one, more and more decisions were the product of tête-a-têtes between Kissinger and Kissinger. In short, most of the country's national security eggs were in one unelected, unaccountable basket.

In the light of the foregoing, the way I went about trying to secure attention within the government for my views was largely a matter of developing in various ways personal relations with other officials in the executive and legislative branches. I still broke bread on occasion with the ineffable Henry himself. I spent as much time as I could becoming acquainted with Elliot Richardson when he became Secretary of Defense, for establishing a pattern of regular and easy communication between the Secretary and me was one of my primary objectives. I have no idea of how successful this endeavor might have been if Richardson had remained in the Pentagon; he stayed only a little more than three months. He was impressive in that brief period, but fundamentally he was still learning to find his way around the shop.

My relationship with Richardson's successor, James Schlesinger, got off to an instantaneous good start thanks to the fact that I did not have a seeing-eye dog when I needed one. After a ceremony of some sort at the White House, a day or two after Jim came to the Pentagon, I lost my way in the corridors there and instead of going to the exit where my car was waiting for me, blundered to another one. As I was trying to orient myself, Schlesinger drove up in his limousine and he invited me to ride back across the river with him. We fell into conversation and he invited me to his office to continue it. We talked for another hour or more. On my way out I said to him that I was sure that this was the last time that I would have the opportunity to spend that much time with the Secretary, but I was a bad prophet. Jim Schlesinger, unlike the pragmatic Laird, is a man who enjoys intellectual exploration of the problems of his job, and during my last fourteen months in office I had many such talks with him. Though he had nothing of Laird's flair for coaxing his projects through the bureaucracy and the Congress, he had the equally important quality, which Mel Laird lacked, of formulating issues precisely and clearly and thus forcing the bureaucracy and Congress into making conscious choices.

Secretary Schlesinger came in like a lion. Early in the year the President in his "State of the World" message, and Henry Kissinger in a much publicized speech to the Associated Press, had proclaimed that the settlement in southeast Asia had made it possible for 1973 to be "the year of Europe." On 7 June, Schlesinger, who had not yet been confirmed by the Senate, offered a rather startling interpretation of the meaning of that phrase in an address, obviously blessed by the White House, to the NATO Defense Planning Committee Ministerial Meeting in Brussels. Albeit politely, he berated the Allies for a number of shortcomings military and fiscal, and strongly indicated that the United States was considering reducing the number of troops it had stationed in Europe. Though the speech contained a good deal of technical military material, it was as much of a surprise to us in the Services as it evidently was to the European ministers at the meeting. I agreed with much the Secretary-designate said, particularly his emphasis on developing a strong non-nuclear deterrent, but I was somewhat disturbed that he—or Kissinger—had chosen a time when our relations with our Allies were already edgy to take them to task. However, that issue soon became moot. Nineteen-seventy-three was not to be the year of Europe after all, despite Henry's ukase. The Arabs saw to that.

CHAPTER 19

Troubled Waters and Oil

By midsummer of 1973, Watergate had mired Mr. Nixon in the political impotence that was to remain his condition for the year in office left to him. Perhaps the most vivid illustration of how conclusively control over events had slipped from his grasp was his acceptance of Congressional manhandling of his southeast Asia policy with no more than a murmur of protest. The President who on 29 June 1973 meekly went along with Congress's ban on the use of any further American armed power in Indo-China after 15 August was a different President than the one who in April 1970 had presided over the Cambodian incursion in the teeth of angry nationwide protest; who in April 1972 had ridden roughshod over his Secretary of Defense by ordering so many B-52s into southeast Asia that the airfields there could barely hold them, and using them for the heaviest bombing campaign in the history of warfare; who in December 1972 had responded to North Vietnamese reluctance to agree to a cease-fire with a heavier bombing campaign yet. What made an easily provoked President so passive in the face of great provocations by the North Vietnamese, who were flagrantly violating the cease-fire agreement, by the Cambodian insurgents, who were intensifying their attacks on the Lon Nol government, and by the American Congress, which was foreclosing all his southeast Asia options, was of course the fact that the most pressing issue he faced no longer was the survival of the Thieu or the Lon Nol administrations, but the survival of the Nixon administration.

The final collapse of the Nixon Indo-China policy can be placed with precision on our nation's 197th birthday, Wednesday 4 July 1973. The imposition of the 15 August deadline for the cessation of U.S. action in Indo-China, which took the form of an amendment to the Defense supplemental appropriation bill, was the result of bargaining between Congressional leaders and the White House. The House had voted on 10 May to end the bombing of Cambodia and Laos "immediately," i.e., as soon as the act became law. The White House absolutely refused to accept "immediately," but made it known that it would accept a deadline a little farther away than that. But in the course of changing the amendment to read "15 August" instead of "immediately," "Cambodia and Laos" got changed to "Indo-China," which of course included Vietnam. It was a major change indeed but there was only perfunctory protest from San Clemente when, of all people, Gerald Ford brought it before the House on 29 June. Moreover, in order to get the deadline moved to 15 August, the President evidently had promised leaders of the Senate that there would be no escalation in U.S. action in the interim. Let a report of the 6 July meeting in the Tank continue the story:

> The Chairman then discussed with the Chiefs the current situation in Cambodia. He had received a call on Sunday [1 July] to bring to San Clemente a plan to ensure that the insurgents found themselves in a weakened position on 15 August. In view of the time constraints, he had gone direct to General Vogt [now Air Force commander in southeast Asia] who responded by message Monday recommending increases in B-52 and TacAir sortie levels. These increases were approved at San Clemente, but before they could be executed, the news broke of the higher sortie levels of the preceding week . . . the upshot was Fulbright's claim that the Administration had broken its "promise" not to escalate. There was a major flap on the 4th which led to a reversal of the previous White House decision. . . .

To that it may be illuminating to append an excerpt from the report of the OpDeps meeting that preceded the meeting of the Chiefs: "No one knows who made the 'no escalation commitment' in negotiating the 15 August compromise with the Congress. The Director opined that the current situation obviously made domestic political factors override the tactical situation in Cambodia." That rather feeble attempt to beat the deadline in Cambodia was the last piece of American activism in Indo-China. Whether American activism would have continued if there had been no Watergate, whether the Thieu government would have survived if American activism had continued, whether South Vietnam would have been better off if the Thieu government had survived are questions that doubtless will be debated with much heat for many years.

My own view, as an early opponent of sending American troops to Vietnam, as an opponent of the costly military strategy that followed the bad decision to go into southeast Asia, and as an early initiator and supporter of the rapid Vietnamization of the war, is in agreement with that of the counterinsurgency expert, Sir Robert Thompson. The truce agreement of January 1973, which made it possible for the United States to withdraw its forces rapidly and to win release of its POWs in exchange for a very bad deal for South Vietnam that permitted North Vietnamese forces to remain intact inside South Vietnam, could have worked. If the Nixon-Kissinger administration had kept Congressional leadership informed of the written commitments that were being made to Thieu, and if these commitments had been put forward in a public way to obtain public support for them as the only honorable way to get our forces out and our POWs home, Hanoi might have been deterred from major truce violations. But the President's preoccupation with survival and Kissinger's predilection for secrecy led to the statutory prohibition on the use of force in Indo-China that guaranteed Hanoi that it could for the first time in the long war send almost all its divisions into the South and that it could violate the truce with impunity. Further Congressional actions curtailing military assistance to South Vietnam insured that over time the South Vietnamese would lose all hope. The way the truce was achieved was the cause of the truce's destruction.

If, with respect to Vietnam, Watergate forced the President to be passive when doubtless he would have preferred to have been active, with respect to SALT it set him on a course fraught with far more peril to the country. It impelled him to be hasty in a situation that called for patience and circumspection. Bill Cockell, since spring the staff director of the CNO's Executive Panel and an inexhaustible source of wise analysis and comment, summed up the position admirably in a memorandum to me dated 30 July. It said in part:

> Perhaps I'm belaboring the obvious, but I think it's becoming increasingly evident that domestic political considerations are likely to become

the dominant influence on the U.S. SALT negotiating posture, unless countervailing pressures are brought to bear (from, e.g., Congressional sources and the Pentagon). . . . Kissinger confirms . . . the pressure to set a 1974 date came from U.S., not Soviets (who wanted a 1975 date). Implicit in the 1974 date is the hope that an agreement will be ready for signature at the (pre-U.S. election) summit in Moscow. . . . The pressures which Watergate has placed on the President to score foreign policy "spectaculars" are well known. . . . It appears that there is little he can do to recoup his reputation on the domestic front; the only hope he has for avoiding an electoral debacle in November 1974 is to score some significant achievements in the international field. . . . These circumstances suggest the most careful attention by the JCS to SALT issues and continued emphasis on their responsibility to advise, which implies foreknowledge of proposed U.S. negotiating positions.

About a week before Bill wrote this assessment, Paul Nitze had had a conversation with a young Soviet defector who had been on the staff of the Soviet Institute of World Economics and Politics. Let me quote just one paragraph from Paul's long memorandum of that conversation.

At the time of SALT One, the unanimous view of the Soviets was that their ABMs were worthless. They had second generation computers and his Institute had Bis II, which was used to run war games. It wasn't very good; certainly not good enough for ABM use. In the preparatory work for SALT One—in which the Institute had participated—the object was to control U.S. Safeguard, which they feared very much. The people at the Institute spent their time on studies analyzing what the Soviets could give in order for the U.S. to give up Safeguard. Grechko [the Soviet Minister of Defense] insisted that it was not necessary to give up anything. The Institute thought he was wrong—he turned out to be right.

This chilling evidence that the Soviets agreed with my estimate of how SALT One had turned out came on the heels of the disclosure of the provisions of what Scoop Jackson promptly labeled "the secret agreement." This was a paper entitled "Clarification of SAL Agreements," whose existence had remained unknown to anyone except possibly one or two members of the National Security Council staff for about a year. The United States and the USSR had signed it on 24 July 1972, while those SAL Agreements were before Congress still; indeed it appears to have been signed at precisely the same time Administration spokesmen were assuring the Congress that there were no "secret" agreements/understandings associated with SALT.

The "Clarification" clarified the agreement about submarine-launched ballistic missiles (SLBMs) in a way that made it even more unfavorable than it had been when it was unclarified. Once again, as in the matter of Soviet submarine visits to Cuba, it was a case of Henry Kissinger settling for language that he may or may not have known was ambiguous without, in any case, allowing those who would have known to review it. The interim agreement, you may remember, allowed the Soviets a maximum of 950 SLBMs. It provided further, "The deployment of modern SLBMs on any submarine, regardless of type, will be counted against the total level of SLBMs. . . ." That was the sentence the "Clarification" addressed itself to.

The first piece of clarification was that any missile deployed on a nuclear powered submarine counted against the 950 total, which always had been taken for granted. The second was that missiles deployed on diesel submarines—of which the Soviets still had about a score in operation—would count against the 950 total only if they were "modern" missiles. That left "modern" to be defined, and it was in the definition of "modern" that the Soviets stole—or perhaps negotiated—a march on us. A "modern" missile, the "Clarification" said, was (a) a missile of a type that had been deployed already in a nuclear submarine or (b) a missile that, though never before deployed, used a launcher compatible with a previously deployed "modern" missile.

What made all that specifically alarming was that we knew that the Soviets had developed, but had not yet deployed, a new missile that could be launched from a submarine, but we did not know whether its launcher was compatible with missiles that already had been deployed. If the new missile's launcher was not compatible, the Soviets would be permitted to deploy it on their diesel boats without its counting against the 950 total or they could install any subsequently developed different ballistic missile launcher on diesel submarines. Finally, they could have built any number of new diesel submarines on which to install these new missiles. They could thus in theory increase their numerical edge in SLBM by several hundred more than the 210 missile edge they had already negotiated. This loophole was not an easy one to account for, since what opened it up was the convoluted definition of missiles in terms of their launchers. A straightforward definition of missiles as missiles, e.g., "A modern missile is any missile of a type deployed since 1965," would have left no room for mystification or misunderstanding. The drafters of the "Clarification" had clearly created an ambiguity where none should have existed normally. Henry Kissinger had kept the agreement from the Secretary of State, the Secretary of Defense, the JCS, and the Congress so that the ambiguity was not discovered.

The status of the second phase of the talks also provided some cause for concern. Aimed at reaching a permanent agreement on offensive arms, the talks had dragged on contentiously and to little purpose for a year. The Soviets renewed their efforts to include our "Forward-Based Systems" in the discussion, which we refused to do. We continued to press unsuccessfully for special controls over the extra-large ICBMs they had and we did not have. Most mindboggling of all was the question of how to deal, if at all, with multiple warheads on missiles, a field in which we were technologically well ahead of the Soviets but could not hope to remain so for very long, and in which, therefore, it was to our interest to come as close as possible to freezing the status quo and to the Soviets' interest to permit unlimited development and deployment.

Near the end of June 1973, President Nixon and Secretary Brezhnev, meeting at San Clemente, applied summitry to the talks with results that were not altogether clear. In a joint statement, the President and the Secretary declared that they had set a 1974 deadline for reaching an agreement, and that a set of Principles first promulgated immediately after the 1972 summit in Moscow would guide the conduct of the talks thenceforward. Since presumably those same Principles had guided the conduct of the talks during their first futile year, this represented no visible substantive progress toward an agreement. Yet it was hard to imagine a deadline being set unless there was some such progress, visible or not.

The poor outcome of SALT One plus the "secret agreement" plus the dubious doings at the 1973 summit plus the President's eagerness to get SALT Two finished "before the next elections" made me resolve to give SALT the maximum possible amount of personal attention during the last year of my watch. I set up a special task force within my staff to follow SALT day by day and keep me up to date and up to speed. I harped on SALT in the Tank. I discussed SALT often with my friends in Congress, particularly Henry Jackson. As a matter of fact the entire Defense establishment by this time had developed the capability, lacking at the time of Option Echo or the mysterious SLBM deal, of making its voice heard in intra-governmental SALT discussions. The bewildering twists and turns of the talks, not to say Henry Kissinger's tactics, had impelled all of us to watch more closely and analyze more rigorously. At the same time, many members of Congress and of their staffs had also become familiar with the issues and implications of SALT, and so it became increasingly difficult for Kissinger to run the talks as if they were beyond Congress's wit to understand, and anyway none of its business. Finally, and probably most significantly, the new Secretary of Defense conceived it to be an important one of his functions to ponder on American strategic concepts and adjust them to the changing times. Jim Schlesinger infused Defense's contributions to SALT policy discussions with an intellectual breadth and rigor they had not had before.

An early and welcome indication Schlesinger gave of his abiding interest in SALT was announcing on 13 July that he was about to set up in *his* office a SALT task force to make sure that Defense policy toward the talks was formulated in a systematic way. An early, and equally welcome, indication of the direction in which his thoughts about SALT were tending came on 13 August, when he astonished us by showing up in the Tank for one of his regular meetings with the Chiefs with a set of slides, and proceeded to brief us on the strategic views he was developing. We professionals ordinarily play schoolmaster. Secretaries are almost always briefees rather than briefers, but then Jim is a schoolmaster by trade. His first slide was entitled "De Tocqueville's Challenge" and contained two quotations in which the Frenchman casts doubt on the ability of a democracy to conduct its foreign affairs in a rational or consistent manner. Having thus professorially made the point that it took more to negotiate arms limitation than an understanding of arms, he delivered a technical analysis of U. S. and Soviet strategic strengths and weaknesses, existing and projected, that showed an impressive understanding of arms for a man who had been in the Department of Defense for only three months.

He was particularly lucid on a subject that many people cannot grasp: the peril of allowing the Soviets, as the 1972 interim agreement did, a four-to-one advantage in throw-weight. If the purpose of that enormous amount of throw-weight were to fire missiles at cities it could indeed be considered "overkill," in the jargon of those who believe any further development, quantitative or qualitative, in the strategic field is superfluous. However, the threat the Soviet super-missiles pose is chiefly to U.S. missile sites and command and control centers. Unlike cities, these are small, "hard" targets, invulnerable to anything but a direct hit or a very near miss. Brute force can overcome this difficulty. The huge kill radius of the Soviet super-missiles, when they are fitted with multiple warheads and made somewhat more accurate, as they soon will be, will be capable of incapacitating U.S. missile fields. Thus, they will be able to destroy a substantial part of America's warmaking capacity in a first strike without resorting to a brutal attack on the population. Then they will be able to pause and ask, "Want to give up?" Though this is a scenario that has the Soviets taking a high risk, it is not so improbable that we can comfortably ignore it.

Because trying to match the Soviet super-missiles would cost hundreds of billions of dollars when you add together the cost of building the new missiles and the necessity, under the SALT agreements, of scrapping a small missile for each big one that was built, U.S. efforts to develop a counterforce capability equivalent to the USSR's necessarily stress qualitative rather than quantitative improvements. They aim to achieve as close to pinpoint accuracy as may be. However, as Schlesinger acutely pointed out during that briefing, qualitative, i.e., technological, gaps never remain open for long, and furthermore accuracy under combat conditions is a different matter from accuracy on the testing range. One of his slides read:

1. No nation will ever know [its] prospective accuracy under operating conditions against real world target system.

2. Each nation will know its own throw-weight.

3. Throw-weight can compensate in limited but adequate degree for accuracy degradation to be expected in real world exchange.

He went on to say that "throw-weight disparities would lead to an asymmetry of the degree of confidence in reciprocal counterforce capabilities." In less formidable words—I hope—that means that the great Soviet advantage in throw-weight, if allowed to continue, would convince everyone—the USSR, the United States, the allies of both, the third world—that the USSR was better able to cripple U.S. strategic forces than the United States was to cripple the USSR's, and that conviction, in turn, would give the Soviets room to engage in aggressive political activities of many kinds. Since Paul Nitze and I had worked on an Arms Control paper in 1963 I had considered the throw-weight issue to be a critical one. I considered further that it was one that the United States had bungled during the first phase of the talks and I was pleased to be working for a Secretary who not only shared my view but articulated it so forcefully. In Jim Schlesinger, Henry Kissinger met his superior as a strategic theorist. But since Henry is a superior bureaucrat, he was able to impose his policy positions on Jim most of the time.

In the spring of 1974 SALT would provide drama enough but in the fall of 1973 the talks, now permanently installed in Geneva instead of shuttling between Vienna and Helsinki, were laborious rather than thrilling. The impetus the San Clemente summit was supposed to have given them was invisible to the naked eye. The negotiators continued to put FBS, MBMs, MIRVs and the rest of the alphabetical stalking horses through their accustomed paces, an exercise that clarified few issues and resolved none. In any case, the events in the Middle East that fall were sufficiently startling to eclipse for a while whatever else was happening on the international scene.

Early in the afternoon of Saturday, 6 October, Arab armies massively equipped with Soviet tanks, planes, and artillery attacked Israel from across the Suez Canal and on the Golan Heights. Of all the Arab-Israeli wars, this October, or Yom Kippur, war was by far the hardest fought because for the first time the Arabs were able to make a respectable military showing. The effectiveness of the Arab attack took Israel by surprise. Though the Israelis knew the Arabs were preparing for action, they were so confident of their own progress and so intent on not appearing before the world—and more importantly before Henry Kissinger, who had warned them not to preempt—as the provoking party that they delayed mobilization until the last minute. Hence, during the first three days of the war, while they were mobilizing still and needed the bulk of available forces to stop the Syrians on the Golan Heights, the Egyptians were able to make substantial advances in the Sinai desert.

Israel always had assumed it could defeat the Arabs in a matter of days, and it had stocked military "consumables"—ammunition, spare parts, all the things that get used up fast—on that basis. However, it soon became apparent that this war would last for weeks rather than days, and that its daily costs were far greater than anyone had foreseen. Aircraft were being shot down by the dozen. Ammunition was being expended at a ruinous rate. The tank battles were on almost a World War II scale. The Israelis found they would need, in large quantities and right away, not just consumables but supplies of every description, from planes and tanks to clothing. Moreover, by the middle of the war's first week, the Syrians and the Egyptians, whose losses were of course on a scale similar to Israel's, were being resupplied by a Soviet airlift that openly flouted the words of the joint communiques that had emerged from both the Moscow and the San Clemente summits: both parties would "do everything in their power so that conflicts or situations will not arise which would serve to increase international tensions." (Of course Soviet failure to warn us of the impending attack was also a violation of those summit agreements.) And so almost every day during the war's first week the Israeli Ambassador handed a new and larger shopping list to Henry Kissinger, who by then was Secretary of State as well as National Security Assistant to the President.

It was a full week before the United States agreed to deliver supplies to Israel in Military Airlift Command (MAC) planes, which was the only feasible way to deliver the most immediate requirements in time for them to do any good. During that week the Israelis had to curtail their operations, notably an all-out offensive against the Egyptians in the Sinai, and thus lost whatever chance they might have had to win a decisive victory fast. There has been a great deal of public controversy over the causes of the delay in the American airlift. In various backstage, not-for-attribution colloquies Henry Kissinger, in his familiar role as a "senior official," has let it be known that his effort to resupply Israel fast was frustrated by Secretary Schlesinger who feared to antagonize the Arab oil producers. This tale is just a tale, and an extraordinarily disingenuous one at that. It was Henry himself who stalled the airlift. I do not mean to imply that he wanted Israel to lose the war. He simply did not want Israel to win decisively, as even his apologists, notably the Kalb brothers in their book about him, admit. He wanted Israel to bleed just enough to soften it up for the post-war diplomacy he was planning, and he probably let things go further than he intended through foreseeing as dimly as everyone else how well the Arabs would fight. In this connection it is worthwhile noting that any attempt to fine-tune the course of a battle in progress, particularly somebody else's battle, is almost laughably academic. Every professional military man knows that so many unpredictable events are bound to occur in a battle that there is no way of doing what Kissinger thought he could do: allow Israel to bleed just enough to "create a new reality" and no more.

Moreover he apparently went about achieving this fatuous and, I must say, ignoble end in a manner that illustrates graphically why, quite apart from the vices or virtues of his policy, he is an exceptionally unpleasant man to work with. According to the Secretary of Defense he ordered Jim Schlesinger, in the name of the President, to stall in responding to Israeli requests for arms. At the same time, he told the Israeli ambassador that he was exerting every effort to get Schlesinger moving but Schlesinger, concerned about Arab oil, would not act. In other words he did not scruple to deceive his allies or besmirch the reputation of his colleagues in what he doubtless thought of as "the national interest." What he told the Israelis about Schlesinger, if accurately reported, was an out-and-out lie. And what he told Schlesinger about the President's wishes might very well have been one too. More than half a year later Leslie Gelb of the *New York Times* in a retrospective piece about the first week of the October War, quoted both Kissinger and Schlesinger as saying that Mr. Nixon did not attend a single formal meeting on the War that week.

I did not know that particular fact at the time, but I was pretty sure that the President was almost totally occupied with trying to keep his splintering administration together and was paying little heed to anything else. As his reactions to North Vietnamese provocations had showed, Mr. Nixon under normal circumstances would have responded fiercely, perhaps excessively, to such an open provocation as the Soviet airlift to Syria and Egypt. It was indeed a trying week for the President, the week that Spiro Agnew, under fire for accepting bribes, resigned from the Vice Presidency. At the time the resignation was announced, Wednesday 10 October, we Chiefs were in the Tank discussing the War. As it happened, I was the first to receive the news and I passed it on to my colleagues. There was a numb silence for a moment. Then we went back to work. When an event that sickening occurs, it is a blessing to have work to do that keeps you from brooding about it.

At that meeting Tom Moorer told us, in the words of the Navy OpDep's notes, ". . . that SecDef's guidance in general about the way to respond to Israeli requests for supplies is that we are to be overtly niggardly and covertly forthcoming." That sounded to me as if Schlesinger was trying to get around Kissinger's policy of holding back rather than vice versa—as in the then private, subsequently public Kissinger version. I was a strong proponent of resupplying Israel rapidly, and I was disturbed at the mysterious delay. On the second or third day after the war's outbreak, I became convinced that in the absence of U. S. resupply, Israel was going to lose the war. I asked Jim Schlesinger directly what the reason for it was. He told me then in approximately the words he used in public later, that it was the national policy "to maintain a low profile and avoid visible involvement," and that his "hands were tied." At that point I did something I would not have done if I had been sure that Richard Nixon, and not unelected, unaccountable Henry Kissinger, was making national policy about the war. I told Scoop Jackson that I was quite sure that it was the White House, not the Pentagon, that was delaying the resupply of Israel. I told him that I believed Israel was going to lose if the United States did not get equipment aloft at once. I don't know just what Scoop did with my information, or what effect what he did had. The MAC airlift to Israel started within a very few days, on 13 October, but I have no way of knowing whether this was sooner than it would have started if I had not told my tale out of school—for there is no doubt in my mind that Kissinger planned to start resupplying the Israelis sooner or later. I believe the odds are that I forced him to do it sooner.

The themes of "low profile" and "no visible involvement" certainly were sounded loud and clear in the orders that went out to the Sixth Fleet in the Mediterranean Sea during the war's first hours— the Sixth Fleet being, as always in a Middle Eastern crisis, the only American military force in a position to react to it rapidly or in this instance, as in the Jordan crisis when our allies' airfields were not available, to react to it at all. Let me quote from an extensive account of the Sixth Fleet's actions in the October War by its commander, Vice Admiral Daniel Murphy, who before getting his third star and his fleet, had been Mel Laird's executive assistant:

> The initial guidance . . . advised that the United States would maintain a low key, even-handed approach toward the hostilities. To project this attitude, the Sixth Fleet was directed to continue routine, scheduled operations and to avoid overt moves which might be construed as indicating the United States was preparing to take an active part in the conflict. . . . There was one exception to the low-key approach: Carrier Task Group 60.1 [the *Independence*'s group] conducted a short notice sortie from Athens to join the Sixth Fleet flagship in a holding area south of Crete to provide a significant, but conservatively placed, U. S. naval presence in the eastern Mediterranean.

"Conservatively placed" is right. It is hard to imagine a less forthcoming response to the plight of a friend who has just become the victim of a bloody surprise attack than the one Dan Murphy thus described. Moreover the orders were extraordinarily rigid. They specified latitudes and longitudes and gave Dan little or no room for tactical maneuvers aimed at making his missions easier to carry out or his forces easier to protect or, optimally, both. Several times during the next few days Dan asked permission of the JCS—for in situations of this kind the CNO has control over the operations of the Navy only in his capacity as one of five members of the Joint Chiefs—to move these ships or those toward the east in order to make his surveillance of the battle scene more effective and evacuation of Americans from the Middle East, if it came to that, more rapid. Each request was turned down by Admiral Moorer, acting, he told me, on instructions from the White House, which almost certainly meant Henry Kissinger.

On 11 October, when it had become clear that Israel would not win a quick victory, when a Soviet naval buildup in the Mediterranean was beginning, and when the risks of possible evacuation had become greater, the carrier *John F. Kennedy,* three of her escorts, and an oiler were ordered from the North Sea, where they had been participating in exercises, toward the Mediterranean. However the orders specified that the group was not to transit the Straits of Gibraltar but hover in the eastern Atlantic until further notice. It remained on this station as a formal component of the Second rather than the Sixth Fleet for the entire period of the airlift.

Thus Admiral Murphy, who once the airlift began had to take on the additional missions of providing it with surveillance, warning, and sea-air rescue services, was required to operate with his Fleet widely dispersed and vulnerable. He was denied the help of *JFK*'s group outside the Straits of Gibraltar. He was denied permission to bring *Franklin D. Roosevelt*'s group eastward to join *Independence*'s group in what would have been a sound defensive deployment. He was ordered to keep his amphibious forces in the vulnerable anchorage at Souda Bay in Crete. And, worst of all from my point of view, he was not given the kind of explanation of these orders that a Vice Admiral and Fleet Commander, who after all is not a blabbermouth or a dummy, is entitled to. The amount of Arab goodwill all this restraint bought us is something to which any American who needed gasoline for his car in the winter of 1973 or paid an electric bill in the winter of 1974 can testify.

Let me quote again from Dan's report:

SovMedFlt was in a normal peacetime disposition during the first phase of the crisis [from the start of the war to the start of the American airlift]. The scheduled turnover of Foxtrot [Soviet attack] submarines was in progress and, as a result, the turnover force of at least five conventional attack boats eventually became augmentees. Almost all the Foxtrot submarines were located in the western Mediterranean during Phase I. Soviet units in the vicinity of the Task Group holding area south of Crete during this period neither represented a severe threat nor gave indications of an increased state of readiness. One conventional attack and two cruise missile firing submarines were in the general area but coordination with Soviet surface units was infrequent and sporadic. Therefore, ComSixthFlt did not perceive SovMedFlt a threat to successful completion of any of the perceived missions during Phase I.

However this situation changed markedly during what Dan called "Phase II," the period between the beginning of the airlift and the cessation of the fighting some 12 days later. On 16 October, Admiral Murphy's flagship and *Independence*'s task group were holding south of Crete. *F. D. Roosevelt*'s task group was in the western Mediterranean, *J. F. Kennedy*'s task group was in the Atlantic, the amphibious task force was in Souda Bay in Crete, and various destroyer types were strung out in the Mediterranean on radar picket duty for the airlift. That day Dan sent to Washington an assessment of the situation that paints the picture of the rather large Soviet combatant group in close proximity to TG 60.1. I paraphrase a portion of that message:

Normally just one Soviet ship trails a U. S. carrier task force in the Mediterranean. The trailer usually is a destroyer, seldom a cruiser. The Soviet fleet commander almost never appears on the scene but works out of anchorages. Since 9 October a cruiser and a submarine tender have remained near Task Group 60.1 Another cruiser and a guided-missile destroyer arrived from Kithera, after navigating the eastern end of Crete, early this morning. There are two admirals and two other command authorities on the Soviet ships. The object of this presence may simply be to let us know that they are aware of our activities and to make us aware of theirs. They show no sign of being more alert than normally.

For my part, I think that this was more than a generalized display of Soviet power; it was a specific reaction to the shifting of the fortunes of the war in favor of Israel. The airlift, which by then was delivering almost 800 tons of material a day, and the knowledge that large cargoes were en route by sea, had enabled the Israelis to stop hoarding their ammunition and equipment, as prudence compelled them to do when resupply was uncertain. They had advanced far enough east of the Golan Heights to bring the Syrian capital of Damascus under their guns and they were about to cross to the west side of the Suez Canal and put the Egyptian forces on the east side in imminent peril of encirclement and annihilation. By Saturday 20 October, the end of the war's second week, the Arabs were in so unfavorable a position that the Soviets became enthusiastic about arranging a cease-fire, something to which they had paid no more than lip service until then. They invited Henry Kissinger to discuss the matter in the Kremlin.

On the plane on the way to Moscow, the Kalb brothers tell us, Kissinger received the news that Saudi Arabia had joined Abu Dhabi and Libya, which had acted two days and one day earlier respectively, in declaring an embargo on oil shipments to the United States; the rest of the Arab countries were to follow within days. When he reached Moscow he received a message from Washington informing him of the "Saturday Night Massacre," the firing of Archibald Cox as Special Watergate Prosecutor, and the resignations of Elliot Richardson and William Ruckelshaus as Attorney General and Deputy Attorney General. Under the circumstances I am quite sure—and again Henry's spokesmen, the Kalbs, bear me out—that Mr. Nixon did not cast a very attentive eye, if he cast an eye at all, on the specifics of the agreement about a cease-fire that Kissinger and Brezhnev worked out.

The cease-fire had to be called twice by the Security Council. The first one, which went into effect at the end of the afternoon (Middle East time) of 22 October was promptly broken by the commander of the encircled Egyptian Third Army who appeared to have ignored orders from Cairo and tried to break free. The Israelis took advantage of this quixotic action and advanced on Suez City. At about noon on 23 October the hot line from Moscow delivered a message to the President signed "Brezhnev." The tenor of the message was that Israel had been involved in gross violations of the cease-fire in defiance of the United Nations Security Council resolution, and went on to say that he, Brezhnev, hoped that immediate and decisive measures would be taken to prevent further violations. By the time the flustered diplomats had called another halt, which took effect early in the morning of Wednesday 24 October, the Israelis had reached Suez City.

I return to Dan Murphy's report:

> Directive from higher authority to begin planning for return to peacetime operations received on 22 October indicated the crisis would soon be over. In a quick reaction response to Dr. Kissinger's trip, USN fighter aircraft escorted Dr. Kissinger's plane into and out of Tel Aviv on that date. These two indicators led the Fleet Commander to the conclusion that further developments would hinge on diplomatic activity and that a return to normal peacetime posture was likely. These conclusions were passed on to the TF commanders on 24 October and higher authority was informed that the Fleet could return to normal operations and meet the commitments for major exercises scheduled for the remainder of the quarter. Actions the following day drastically affected these plans.

On the day Admiral Murphy was preparing to resume his peacetime pursuits, 24 October, I received from Bill Cockell, a Sovietologist second to none, a memorandum so remarkably prescient that it is worth reproducing here in full.

1. You are probably getting this from other sources, but on the chance you are not, its importance warrants a parallel report.

2. Combining data from several sources, the following emerges:

   a. Israelis continue to squeeze the Egyptians hard.

   b. Roughly forty-eight hours have elapsed since the Russians warned the Israelis of grave consequences if they did not stop fighting.

   c. There are now indications of possibly increased alert status for Soviet airborne units.

   d. The Soviet airlift has stopped; ours continues. (Soviets might need assets—particularly AN-22 [the largest Soviet transport plane]—if they planned a troop lift.)

   e. Soviet cruiser (Moskva?) and six DD declared through the Straits [Dardanelles]. If/when they arrive, will set a new record for Soviet presence in Med.

   f. Sixteen Soviet subs in the Med; five enroute.

   g. Soviet pilots flying (possibly) Foxbats in Egypt. (If Soviets were going to introduce troops, they would want their own people doing reconnaisance in advance.)

h. This evening's CIB [Central Intelligence Bulletin] reportedly will comment on "alarming" indicators of potential Soviet military activity.

i. Press report says Al-Zayat [Egyptian Foreign Minister] will ask at emergency session of the Security Council tonight that Soviet and U.S. forces be introduced into the combat area immediately to demark/enforce a cease-fire.

3. Any inferences from this combination of data would be speculative; but it is obvious the situation bears closest watching.

As I recollect it, it was a little after noon that I received this acute piece of prognostication. I promptly forwarded it to Tom Moorer and Jim Schlesinger. I have no idea whether they, in turn, passed it along to the White House or, if they did, whether it abated the elation Henry Kissinger apparently had been feeling since his return from Moscow.

At 1000 that morning, the very time when Bill Cockell was making such a telling pattern of facts that, after all, were generally available within the government, the Washington Special Action Group was convening in the White House to hear about Henry's trip and to consider what to do next about the cease-fire and the resupply effort. The report on that WSAG meeting Admiral Moorer gave us in the Tank later in the day showed a self-satisfied Kissinger. I made notes on Tom's report. Some snatches from them: "Kissinger thinks we can reverse Arab actions," meaning the oil embargo that was to last only five more months. "Kissinger said that in general things went well for the United States [in Moscow]. The Soviets have agreed to a cease-fire. They didn't want to damage détente. Admiral Moorer is suspicious of this view. The Chiefs all agree [with him]. . . . The problem is to get Israel and the Arabs to see [the military situation] eye to eye. We have a knowledge of what's going on but the two sides are interpreting the situation differently. It is helpful that both the U.S. and the USSR are looking on, Kissinger thinks." There is no record of what he thought of the USSR's helpfulness twelve hours later.

The Chiefs met in executive session that afternoon. The notes I took show it to have been one of our more stimulating meetings, with wide-ranging discussion of a number of the issues the war had raised. However, I can detect no sign in those notes that we, any more than WSAG, had a premonition of the serious events that would occur within hours. I will quote from those notes nevertheless because they throw light on both the problems we in the military were facing at the time and on our attitudes toward them. As I have said, the meeting began with Admiral Moorer telling us how well Kissinger thought the United States was doing in the Middle East. We then turned to the vexing subject of the resupply of Israel:

> The first question is should we provide the resupply? The second question is the tempo and timing of resupply. Should we keep resupply going about as it is? . . . Should we meld it into sealift vice airlift? . . . We need a running inventory of what we've given them. Kissinger knows all the Services are below the level of their pre-war reserve stock. Each Service must . . . try for a supplement after the appropriation bill passes. Admiral Moorer agreed to continue to "ping" on Kissinger about the disastrous state of our inventory. . . . Admiral Moorer says we should put our estimate on the high side and give our estimate directly to him. . . . Yesterday the Israelis submitted a "wish list." Admiral Moorer hopes we don't give them all they've asked for. . . . Admiral Moorer finds the Israelis difficult. . . . Z expressed concern about the state of readiness of the services as the result of the loss of equipment and his further concern about what might happen if we got in a conflict now. Admiral Moorer said that the President has ordered that there be one-for-one replacement for the Israelis. . . . We are talking about large numbers of tanks and it is Admiral Moorer's thought that some tanks will go now and some will be saved to twist Israelis' arms during negotiations.

Many military men felt and feel now the same resentment toward Israel that Tom Moorer expressed at that meeting and George Brown has expressed semi-publicly since becoming Chairman. I did not and do not share it but I can understand it. America's commitment to Israel apparently involves a formidable array of military risks. It drains arms the services badly need to keep themselves in a state of readiness. It jeopardizes sources of the oil we and our allies depend on. It puts us on what might turn out to be a collision course with the USSR in a part of the world where they have almost all the advantages. It strains our relations with our NATO allies—another topic we discussed at that 24 October meeting—many of whom refuse even to allow our ships to use their ports or our planes to use their airfields if those ships and planes are engaged in helping Israel in a conflict with the Arabs. In the October War Turkey permitted the Soviet airlift to the Arabs to overfly its territory. I have no doubt that if we had asked for permission to do something similar—which we did not—we would have been turned down. Of our allies only

Portugal, which reluctantly gave us permission to refuel the airlift planes at our Lajes base in the Azores, Greece and Italy, which continued to permit the ships of the Sixth Fleet into their ports, and courageous little Holland, which spoke up in support and was singled out for Arab retaliation, did not turn their backs on us during the October war. Those who are in a hurry to condemn the U.S. for maintaining ties with the old regimes in Portugal and Greece should pause for at least a moment to reflect on what might have happened to Israel if those regimes had joined the other NATO nations in making it impossible to apply our power in October 1973.

I say that America's commitment to Israel "apparently" involves many military risks because I think the U.S. would face the same risks in intensified form in the Middle East if there were no Israel. After all, the principal fomenters of trouble in the Middle East are the Soviets, who have the long-range objective of gaining control of the oil there. They not only keep Arab hatred of Israel burning high, but provide the Arab states with the wherewithal to turn their hatred into action. I have no doubt that if Israel fell, the Soviets would find it both simple and advantageous to turn from egging on the Arabs against Israel to egging on one set of Arabs against another. In that situation the U.S. still would be threatened with the loss of Middle Eastern oil and still would be compelled to ship out arms—and to much less potent and reliable friends than Israel, at that. In sum, the democratic, militarily strong state of Israel serves, in a real sense, as a buffer between the U.S. and the USSR's long term goals of domination in the Middle East; Israel's presence is thus of great military benefit to the U.S. and the view that the Israelis are a military liability seems to me short-sighted and superficial.

Beyond and perhaps more important than this practical military fact is the perception of the whole world that of all America's international commitments, the one to Israel is probably the most deeply felt and meant. I am convinced that, even though American support of Israel does create some dissension in NATO, American abandonment of Israel would cause the virtual collapse of NATO through sheer distrust of our good faith by our European allies. And so I consider Israel's constant clamoring for arms and undoubted intransigence about the Palestinian Arabs and giving back the Arab territory it has seized to be justified from Israel's point of view and well worth putting up with from the U.S. point of view because a strong Israel plays a critical part in safeguarding America's vital interests not only in the Middle East but in Europe as well.

After the 24 October meeting in the Tank, I went over to Capitol Hill for a chat with Henry Jackson about the most recent developments. From there I went home for the strictly timed hour with the family I indulged myself in every evening, and the three or four hours of work that the contents of two overstuffed briefcases compelled me to put in nightly. Toward midnight, when I was finishing up and relishing the prospect of bed, I was summoned by telephone back to the office. The National Security Council was in session, I was told, and it was necessary for the Chiefs to stand by. As I, along with the other Service Chiefs and Deputy Secretary Clements, awaited the return from the White House of Secretary Schlesinger and Admiral Moorer, who of course were at the NSC meeting, members of the Joint Staff kept us abreast of the orders that were pouring in from the White House and the messages that were going out to American commanders all over the world. I made notes of what they told us:

At 0015 CJCS arrived at the White House. At 0030 orders went out that the *J. F. Kennedy* was to enter the Med. Carrier *FDR* was ordered east to join *Independence*. All amphibious ships were ordered to sortie [from Souda Bay] and to proceed South of Crete, arriving there about 1800. The *Iwo Jima* [an amphibious ship that can land Marines in helicopters] entered Med last night about 1750. The 82nd Airborne [at Fort Bragg, N.C.] has been put on alert. We have alerted European forces. At 0025 we went to DefCon [Defense Condition] 3 world wide. B-52s from Guam returning to the United States. DefCon 3 was set at 0041. CinC Atlantic has been informed of *JFK*'s orders and DefCon 3. The Readiness Command has been informed of the 82nd Airborne. CinC Continental Air Defense Duty Officer at 0058 was informed of DefCon 3. Continental Air Defense was not notified; we're getting ready to. At 0109 CinC Atlantic, CinC Pacific and CinC Europe were all set. CinC Strategic Air Command is in his command center. KC-135s [tanker planes] were to be moved as CinC SAC saw fit. At 0115 Military Airlift Command was alerted to provide continuous airlift. The White House reports that the Russians have notified us that the Israelis are not obeying the cease-fire and that the Soviet Union suggests the U. S. join forces in going in with the Soviets, and that if not the Soviets will go in there unilaterally. "The word is no provocative moves."

At 0130, though the Secretary and the Chairman had not yet arrived, we convened in the Tank. For my account of that meeting I rely on two sets of notes, the official record prepared by my OpDep, Vice Admiral George Talley, and a less formal minute taken down at my dictation after the meeting adjourned by my executive assistant, Captain Don Pringle. The meeting opened with the Director of the Defense Intelligence Agency, Vice Admiral Vince Du Poix, briefing us on the status of the alert, which was much as the notes quoted immediately above describe it, and on the events on the west bank of the Canal that had precipitated the crisis. From Talley's report:

> . . . The Egyptian front was quiet as of midnight, [23 October]; at 0530 [Greenwich standard time, four hours later than Washington daylight time] on 24 October Israelis occupied the naval base of Atavia; at 0615 Egypt was not allowing UN observers into the area. There were tank battles along the Cairo-Suez road; at 1907 Sadat requested a Security Council meeting and asked Soviet and American troops to come in and enforce a cease-fire. DIA estimated that the Israelis were probably in Suez City. The Soviet Med squadron has again been augmented; there are now over eighty Soviet ships in the Mediterranean. There are no Soviet flights reflected in any intelligence.

As I awaited the arrival of the Secretary of Defense and the Chairman of the Joint Chiefs, I recalled that during Project 60 in July 1970, we had analyzed the question of whether the President now could find himself in the position Khrushchev was in during the 1962 Cuban missile crisis. The study, which I later found in my files had said:

> 1. Given current and prospective force levels, in a declared confrontation situation such as that posed by the "Cuban missile crisis," the Soviet Union could place the President of the United States in a position similar to that experienced by Khrushchev in 1962.
>
> 2.a. The current most likely area of confrontation would be in the eastern Mediterranean arising from the Arab-Israeli conflict.
>
> b. Should the Soviets announce that they would militarily oppose any U.S. support to Israel, the USSR would present a significant challenge to the U.S.
>
> c. The achievement of relative nuclear parity by the Soviet Union removes one of the major edges the U.S. held over the USSR in 1962. The relative balance of general purpose forces has also shifted significantly since that period, and proposed cut backs due to budgetary constraints could result in a decisive change in the military options available to the President.

d. If the decision to deny the U.S. the opportunity to support Israel were timed to coincide with a large-scale exercise, such as exercise OKEAN, a formidable Soviet Mediterranean squadron would exist.

e. Past studies examining sustained attack carrier operations against the combined air forces of Syria/Iraq and UAR (assuming that aircraft in these countries were maintained and operated effectively) indicate that at least 4 CVAs [carriers] would be required to gain air superiority. The added capability of the Soviet forces would gravely increase the threat to U.S. forces, and would place the U.S. at the disadvantage.

I recalled also that just two months after this study had been written, during the Jordan crisis, I had personally briefed the President on my calculations of the probable outcome of a theoretical confrontation between the actual U. S. and Soviet naval forces in the Mediterranean at the time, calculations that showed the U. S. at a distinct disadvantage.

Finally, I recalled the series of advisory briefings to the President and to the Congress in which we had put forward the deteriorating odds. I was forced to conclude that there had never been in our history a naval crisis that had been so clearly foreseen as the present one, or for which we were so ill prepared.

The Secretary and the Chairman came in at 0200 and provided more details. At approximately 1930 that evening a letter bearing Secretary Brezhnev's signature had been delivered to the White House. Ominously, given the elaborate diplomatic courtesy normally used in brusque exchanges, it started "Mr. President" rather than "Dear Mr. President." It said, the Secretary of Defense and the Chairman reported, "that the Israelis had deliberately violated the understanding reached by the U.S. and the USSR and were embarked on the path to their own destruction." It suggested that the U.S. and the USSR send in troops to man the cease-fire lines. It said, they reported, "Let me be quite blunt. In the event that the U.S. rejects this proposal, we should have to consider unilateral actions of our own." From my dictation to Don Pringle:

Schlesinger, Kissinger, Moorer, and Haig met in an effort to decide whether the Soviets were up to deception all the time or had they proceeded in good faith up to original deal and then got concerned about late info about what disaster Arabs had suffered [I know the reader is as anxious as I am to know what went on in the five hours between the time of the receipt of the note from the Russians and the meeting of the four at the White House. Only Kissinger can tell us and he hasn't.] Concluded that it had been late info about how bad the defeat had been.

Z said [the reason for the Soviet letter] was . . . what [Israelis failure to stop] would lead to in terms of Soviet embarrassment.

It was agreed that Soviets felt the President was in trouble domestically over last weekend [the "Saturday Night Massacre" weekend] and [this] would be a good time to act.

Z said to Dr. Schlesinger that this sort of goes beyond détente. . . .

Decision was made that we would send a reply—now in draft form— but that we would not rush to get reply to them. Reply would say words to the effect that we don't agree to join you and would take a serious view of any unilateral intervention on your part.

Also say we think Israel is conforming to the cease-fire. (In fact they hadn't been, but Henry called and used brutal words and told Israel to observe cease-fire. Israel agreed and also offered to give up some of what they had taken since cease-fire.)

Admiral Moorer made the point at the White House that we would lose our ass in the eastern Med under these circumstances.

Z brought out to Dr. S in Tank what our confidence is [in eastern Med] —worst place to fight Soviets.

Our reason for waiting on reply to Soviets was for Soviets to see signs of what we are doing. DefCon 3 has already been leaked as expected. Friedheim [the Pentagon spokesman] has received press inquiries. . . .

K started to cover himself by saying he has been warning people for a long time that this is likely to happen—thinking of history.

K will brief [Congressional leadership] tomorrow. Originally planned to sing praises of accomplishment of cease-fire. Doesn't know what will say now.

Z pointed out that [since] one of the Soviets' feelings is that the President is domestically very weak, one of the best things we could do is to get the four chairmen and other Congressional leaders told quickly about how bad off we are and get some strong indication of support from them: i.e., move out on appropriations bills.

After an expression of support for my recommendations that it would be a good idea to ask the Soviet Navy to "stand clear" of our ships, and to head a carrier task group from the western Pacific toward the Indian Ocean, the meeting adjourned at 0320.

I doubt that major units of the U.S. Navy were ever in a tenser situation since World War II ended than the Sixth Fleet in the

Mediterranean was for the week after the alert was declared. Dan Murphy's excellent account of the situation needs no gloss from me:

> On 25 October JCS directed TG 20.1, USS *J. F. Kennedy* and escorts, to chop to ComSixthFlt as TG 60.3 and proceed to join TG 60 south of Crete. Additionally, *F. D. Roosevelt* and escorts (TG 60.2) and TF 61/62 [the amphibious task forces] were directed to join TG 60.1 south of Crete. . . . TG 100.1 (Baltic destroyers) was ordered to proceed to the Mediterranean and chop to ComSixthFlt. . . .
>
> SovMedFlt strength stood at eighty naval units in the Mediterranean on 24 October. That total included 26 surface combatants and 16 submarines, possessing a first launch capability of 40 SSMs [surface-to-surface or cruise missiles], 250 torpedoes and 28 SAMs [surface-to-air missiles]. The activities of Soviet surface combatants had been largely confined to maintaining one to three tattletales on each carrier task group and the amphibious units. Other combatants had remained primarily in port or at anchorages. At least five conventional attack submarines had also been detected in the eastern Mediterranean on 24 October. Large changes in both the numbers of Soviet ships in the Mediterranean and their actions began on 24–25 October.
>
> On 25 October a Soviet surface action group (SAG) composed of a Kynda [cruiser] and a Kashin [destroyer] joined the Soviet units monitoring TG 60.1. As other U. S. forces joined in the holding area, each task group was covered by a separate Soviet SAG which included an SSM and SAM capability. On 26 October, the Soviets began large-scale anti-carrier warfare (ACW) [exercises] against TF 60 with SSG and SSGN [guided missile submarines, diesel and nuclear] participation; this activity was conducted continuously for the six days following 27 October. A large-scale, rapid buildup in Soviet forces was also evident. By 31 October SovMedFlt strength had increased to 96 units, including 34 surface combatants and 23 submarines, possessing a first launch capability of 88 SSMs, 348 torpedos, 46 SAMs. The U. S. Sixth Fleet and the Soviet Mediterranean Fleet were, in effect, sitting in a pond in close proximity and the stage for the hitherto unlikely "war at sea" scenario was set. This situation prevailed for several days. Both fleets were obviously in a high readiness posture for whatever might come next, although it appeared that neither fleet knew exactly what to expect.

On 30 October, in accordance with a suggestion, approved by the JCS that Admiral Murphy had made a couple of days before but could not execute at once because of bad weather, the Sixth Fleet moved westward, and the tension began to abate. The Soviets began to disperse their forces on 3 November. However, as Murphy noted,

"Although other U. S. forces began relaxing their alert status on 27 October, Sixth Fleet remained at high readiness until 18 November."

It was an appalling illustration of the distrust the public felt toward Mr. Nixon by then that the news of the alert was received with widespread doubt about its necessity and speculation that it was a mere political ploy. My first personal encounter with this suspicion came shortly after noon on 25 October when a dedicated patriot, Robert Strauss, the Chairman of the Democratic National Committee, telephoned me from somewhere out west to ask, "What is going on at this time that you can tell me." I explained as best I could within the limits of security. He said, "The crisis is driving me crazy. Are we going to follow our commitments? Are we going to impeachment? Is this another move of the President's?" I replied that as far as I was concerned, the alert was just what it appeared to be. Bob Strauss honored my assurance and lent his prestige to support the U.S. action in the crisis. The next day I had lunch, scheduled long before the crisis, with Clark Clifford, a former Secretary of Defense, no less, and he too asked me whether the alert was justified.

Far from thinking that it was a political ploy by the President, I suspect the President had nothing at all to do with it. If in the account I have just given I report no words or actions of the President, it is because no such words or actions ever were reported to me. I wondered at the time whether Kissinger and Haig, protecting the Presidency and the country from Mr. Nixon's withdrawal into a total preoccupation with his own fate, had acted without him. After the JCS meeting adjourned I came upon Bill Clements alone and communicated my suspicion to him. Bill said, "I wondered the same thing and so I asked Jim if the President was in on this. Jim said he was not."

However, that does not make me question the need for the alert. The Soviets presented us with what certainly looked like an ultimatum, and it would have been negligent indeed in such a situation not to assume a posture of readiness. Some time later Helmut Sonnenfeldt, reviewing the situation from his perspective within the NSC staff put the matter tersely and accurately: "DefCon 3 was needed and was right. It was a fast moving situation and within hours it was over, but crises don't have to last to be real crises."

I myself regret that in the crunch we lacked either the military strength or the stable domestic leadership—one or the other might have been enough—to have supported the Israelis instead of forcing them to draw back from the encirclement of the Egyptian Third

Army. However, we had no choice, and because we had no choice the Soviets derived great benefits from the war. The diplomacy for which our restraint ostensibly was a prerequisite has so far produced the presence of unarmed Americans between the two armies and the legitimizing of the Palestine Liberation Organization, neither of which can be counted a gain for the United States. The Soviets achieved their long term objective of reopening the Suez Canal. The war divided Israel politically and increased Arab military strength and self-confidence. The Soviet theory—or hope, anyway—that there can be "differentiated détente," i.e., détente that prevails where and when it suits Soviet convenience, got a boost. The oil embargo and the quadrupling of oil prices exactly suited Soviet purposes— indeed the Soviets urged both actions—by shaking Western econo- mies, reducing Western defense budgets, and impelling Western gov- ernments to curry favor with both the Arabs and the Soviets.

A dramatic example of the benefits the Arab oil embargo threat- ened to confer on the Soviets came to my attention in November 1973. I learned that the Saudis had threatened to withhold from Esso a.g. of Hamburg, a subsidiary of an American company, Exxon, a percentage of oil equivalent to the percentage of fuel and lubricants going from Esso to the U.S. armed forces in Germany, and that in response Exxon had directed Esso not to deliver to those forces any products refined from Saudi crude, but to try to find non-Arab sources of oil. This evidence that an American company would bow to the Arabs even if that meant denying needed supplies to the United States Army and Air Force angered me sufficiently to impel me to fire off a strong memorandum to the Secretary of Defense:

> . . . this action raises squarely, for the first time since the Arab embargo was imposed, an issue directly impacting on NATO defense capabilities. Withholding oil supplies to U.S. forces in Europe is, in fact, an imposi- tion of an oil embargo on NATO. The threatened actions set a precedent I do not believe we should let go unchallenged. We have argued in the NATO forum that developments in the Middle East are irrelevant to alliance security interests. This case provides a graphic illustration of a threatened use of the oil weapon in a way which would directly aid the Soviets by significantly reducing NATO readiness in the central region. Under these circumstances I think two steps would be appropriate. First, I believe we should instruct Ambassador Rumsfeld to raise the issue in Brussels, pointing out the impact which the action could have on central

region capabilities. Beyond this the situation raises fundamental questions about NATO planning assumption that Middle Eastern oil will always be available for our alliance's needs in a crisis. . . . Second, I believe Ambassador Akins should bring to the Saudis [attention] the degree to which their threatened action would contribute to the achievement of Soviet goals in Europe and generally add to Soviet leverage over the alliance—with no resulting benefits, and clearly possible liabilities to the Saudis.

Bill Clements took that one for action and reported that he had read the riot act to Exxon.

That sorry episode is but one of many illustrations of how unprepared the U.S. was for the acute oil shortage of 1973–74 and the chronically high price of oil since, though many of us had foreseen just such developments for years. To confine myself to matters that I, as CNO, had a direct interest in, I can report that the lack of a long-range national policy about oil was something that concerned me from the moment I began my watch, and that I spoke about at every appropriate opportunity. On 16 January 1971 Henry Kissinger issued NSSM 114, which called for a study of the world oil situation by an already existing Inter-Agency Oil Task Force under the chairmanship of the State Department. A draft paper the task force produced two weeks later forecast accurately what eventually happened. In the words of a Defense Department summary of this draft:

> Abundant oil supplies at relatively low cost have long been taken for granted in non-Communist countries. Present world oil situation involves probability of significant increase of payments by oil companies to oil producing countries, and the possibility of interruption or cut-back in supplies, imposed by some of the OPEC (oil producers). Immediate issue for USG [U. S. government] is avoidance of serious disruption of economies of Western Europe, Japan and possibly the U.S. Longer term issues are: continued availability of oil to consumers on reasonable terms; potential threat of cut-backs in supplies by OPEC producers acting in concert; ever increasing dependence of U.S. on imported oil; and conceivably use of oil for political purposes by some producers.

The oil study was supposed to come before the Senior Review Group at the end of January. Then it was postponed until February. Then jurisdiction over it was transferred from the SRG, chaired by Kissinger, to the Under Secretaries Committee, chaired by John Irwin of State. If my records tell the story, there was little top-level work done on oil between the winter of 1971 and the spring of 1972. In April 1972 I attended the annual Bilderberg Conference, sponsored by Prince Bernhard of the Netherlands, which took place that year at Knokke in Belgium. On my return I wrote a letter to Jack Irwin that is worth quoting at length, for it foreshadows how the Allies responded when the October War precipitated the oil crunch:

> Of the subjects discussed, to my mind the most interesting was the significance of the potential energy crisis of the 1980s, an issue you have done much to put before the country. In the course of the discussion the problem was fully defined: the pressures we can expect from the producing countries and the possible incursions into the area by the Soviet Union and China were elaborated. It was even noted that perhaps more telling than these was the danger of our alliance relationship of the European Community, Japan and the U.S. having to compete with each other for ever scarcer critical resources.
>
> Once the problem was fully displayed, it became clear that few were prepared to come to grips with its broad implications—the need for a concerted response. Those who had come to discuss the Atlantic alliance continued to focus on Europe; those who had come to deliberate on the interaction among Japan, the Soviet Union, Communist China, and ourselves wanted to concentrate on the changing power relationships in the Far East. The vast territorial expanse between Europe and the Far East became blank spaces around a series of geometric figures—the Atlantic triangle and the Asian quadrilateral. When it was noted that the Soviets were pursuing an intercontinental policy and that this Eurasian policy ignored our neat designs and impacted on the oil resources of the Muslim world, where Europeans, Americans and Japanese had growing stakes, the old instinct of looking for American leadership resurfaced in fullest form. It was the general hope that we would develop ways to meet the challenge.

Let me quote one more piece of prescience that led to nothing from the Navy's precis of a Joint Staff paper in August 1972:

> The paper states (without qualifications) that by 1975 a permanent sellers' market for oil will exist, that the petroleum producing countries' bargaining strength will double 1970 revenues by 1975, that as the U.S. increases its imports it becomes more dependent on producing/refining countries, that the USSR and the PRC can be expected to remain self-sufficient, that Japan may become very competitive for Persian Gulf and Indonesian resources, and that the potential energy crisis in the U.S. is aggravated by a lack of a unified U.S. fuels policy. The paper foresees

unpopular U.S. decisions to reduce domestic consumption, increase domestic production and establish reserve inventories. . . .

Three years and several oil traumas later, "the energy crisis in the U.S. is [still] aggravated by a lack of a unified U.S. fuels policy."

Meanwhile my specific Navy responsibilities had led me to testify in my annual Posture Statement to the House Armed Services Committee in February 1972 that one among the many reasons the Navy needed a large number of escort vessels was the possibility that it would be called on to protect tankers on the long, potentially perilous voyage from the Persian Gulf to the United States, western Europe, or Japan. This suggestion aroused the wrath of one of the members of the committee, Lee Aspin of Wisconsin. He put out a press release charging me with "inventing a new threat in a desperate attempt to justify unnecessary increases in the Navy budget," and went on to say that abolishing the oil import quota, importing as much "cheap foreign oil" as national security required, and storing it in the U.S. would be far cheaper than building naval escorts. The U.S. definitely does need more oil storage capacity, and should have acted to develop it many years ago. However, beyond the fact that within less than two years after he made it, long before any importing/storing program could have accomplished much, there was no longer such a commodity on earth as "cheap foreign oil," Aspin's argument founders on the fact that protecting tankers is by no means the only duty the Navy needs escorts for.

Perhaps my most comprehensive statement on the military problems of ensuring that oil from the Middle East continued to flow is contained in testimony I gave, as the representative of the Joint Chiefs, at hearings on national fuels and energy policy conducted by Senator Henry Jackson's Committee on Interior and Insular Affairs in January 1973. Some excerpts:

. . . the major segment of our seaborne imports [are] those from the Middle East. . . . The route is a very long one, some 12,000 miles from Kuwait to New York and most of it passes through areas where U. S. forces have little operating experience and few bases. Mustering the military means to protect this long route would strain our resources severely.

But before getting into the problem let me describe the local geography of the Persian Gulf; it bears on the problem. The oil exported from the Gulf must pass through the Strait of Hormuz. The Gulf itself is quite shallow and the Straits are generally narrow. This, plus the deep drafts of the supertankers, means maneuvering room for large tankers is quite restricted. It also means that the channels are relatively easy to mine or block. Sinking just a handful of tankers in critical passages could effectively block shipments from the Gulf for a long time. . . . there is little the U.S. could now do militarily to forestall this possibility. . . .

Another possibility is that the tanker shipments might be attacked in the open ocean after they left the Gulf. Speaking in terms of capability, the only serious threat to our sea lines of communications is the Soviet Navy. In a conflict situation it must be expected that the Soviets would attack our seaborne petroleum supply. . . . While I cannot go into all of the details of this contingency here today, there are some key points you should remember.

. . . First, convoy operations would cause an immediate and major loss in shipping productivity. Ships must wait until convoys are formed and then must wait their turn to unload. These losses can equate to as much as 25 percent of our shipping capacity.

Second, the course of any confrontation would depend, to some extent, on the choices open to the Soviets. They might choose to concentrate their efforts in the north Atlantic, closer to their bases, but also closer to ours. Or they might shift to the south Atlantic. Or they might choose to conduct a low level "guerilla" campaign, using only their better subs. I will not attempt to assess such hypothetical confrontations in open hearing except to say that, at best, it would be a difficult situation. . . .

To bring any . . . naval capabilities to bear in the Persian Gulf area could require as much as a month. Our Mideast Force, normally comprising just two or three destroyers, would require augmentation to have significant combat capability. An all-nuclear task group could reach the area in nine days from Guam, but would take twice as long from the United States. An amphibious task group, operating from the continental United States, would require nearly a month to reach the Persian Gulf.

The Navy's situation in the vicinity of the Persian Gulf, touched on in the last part of the testimony just quoted, deserves brief elaboration. December 1971, the time of the Indo-Pakistan War, was also the time of the British Navy's final withdrawal from east of Suez. This withdrawal included giving up a small naval base in the island sheikdom of Bahrain inside the Persian Gulf, a base at which the United Kingdom had allowed the U.S. to homeport, since 1949, the flagship of the Mideast Force referred to above. In order to maintain its naval presence in a region where there were such large American economic and political interests, the United States early in 1972 negotiated a lease with the government of Bahrain that allowed the Mideast Force to continue to use a part of what once was the British base. At the same time we somewhat upgraded the force itself by replacing the old seaplane tender that used to be its flagship with an ex-amphibious ship that had better communications and engineering equipment. Traditionally the two or three destroyer types that comprised the rest of the force and that rotated in for a few months at a time had been among our oldest destroyers. Now we began to send in a newer one from time to time.

These improvements to the force were modest, but they were all a Navy that had to stretch its resources clear around the world, from the Gulf of Tonkin to the eastern Mediterranean, could afford. The agreement with Bahrain contained, as almost all such agreements do, a clause making it subject to cancellation by either party at a year's notice. When our airlift to Israel started in the October war, Bahrain invoked that notice in a gesture of Arab solidarity. One of the more acrimonious pieces of bureaucratic infighting that occurred that October was between those in the State Department who desired to acknowledge receipt of the message from Bahrain and those in Defense who desired to ignore it in the hope that eventually the Bahrainis would change their minds. Defense prevailed, and its position was proved in the event to have been right. After a certain amount of low-key diplomacy, Bahrain withdrew its disinvitation in the spring of 1974. Nevertheless I judge the Mideast Force access to Bahrain to be tenuous. Now that the Iranians and the Saudis are developing a strong military capability of their own, they neither believe they need, nor do they enjoy, the permanent showing of the U.S. flag in the Gulf, and of course the Iraqis, clients of the USSR, always have considered it an intrusion.

The Mideast Force always has been a symbolic force whose mission was more political than military. An American presence in the Indian Ocean that has military plausibility requires a base where fuel, ammunition, and spare parts in some quantity can be stored, where planes of all sizes can land, and where a carrier task group can anchor if need be. It happens that almost exactly in the middle of the Indian Ocean there is precisely such a place, a British Island named Diego Garcia. In 1966 we entered into an agreement with the United Kingdom permitting us to build a naval communications station there to replace one in Asmara in Ethiopia that for various reasons, political and technical, we knew we must one day give up. Congress appropriated funds for the station in 1971. Seabees had been working on the new facility ever since. Transforming it into a base that could give a carrier group in the Indian Ocean the logistics it needed to move freely was rather a modest undertaking. There already was a landing field, a small anchorage, and a certain amount of storage capacity. They simply needed enlargement. This was a project I had pushed for some time.

The October War made it a matter of great urgency. In the aftermath of that war the Seventh Fleet sent one of its three carrier task groups to cruise in the neighborhood of the Persian Gulf for several months. Keeping that group supplied with the necessities of life turned out to be an operation that both required all kinds of ingenuity and improvisation and drastically reduced the readiness of the rest of the Seventh Fleet. Almost all of the Fleet's available auxiliary vessels—oilers, and logistics ships of all kinds were needed to replenish *Hancock* and then *Oriskany,* the carriers involved, and their escorts. As a result the Fleet's other two carrier groups, on station in the western Pacific, could not replenish at sea but had to return to Subic Bay for supplies. That meant that during a ten-day period they were, roughly speaking, five days on station, two days steaming to port, one day in port replenishing, and two days returning to station. Thus, since each group could be on station only half the time, the two groups during this period were in effect only one group. Even so, the Navy had to take additional measures to keep the force in the Indian Ocean going, especially in the matter of fuel. We had to buy oil on the spot from Iran and charter merchant tankers. A Diego Garcia base stocked with supplies and capable of receiving more by air if necessary would have solved a large part of this problem.

I should add that the difficulties of *Hancock* and of *Oriskany* in the Indian Ocean conferred one unexpected benefit on the Navy. Secretary Schlesinger, with his acute strategic mind, perceived at once how important to the world balance it was for the United States to have military capability in those waters. He wanted badly to keep a carrier there permanently, which was a clear impossibility because of the strain it would put on the rest of the fleet. We—the Navy professionals, that is—finally convinced him of that, but his interest in the area was great enough to persuade him that *Hancock* and *Oriskany,* which were scheduled for immediate retirement, should be kept on for another two years until the Diego Garcia issue had been resolved and *Eisenhower,* the third nuclear carrier, was nearer completion.

The logistic difficulty the U.S. Navy had in operating freely and flexibly in the Indian Ocean was of course an old story, but as long as the Suez Canal was closed, as it had been since 1967, the Soviet Navy was under similar logistical restrictions. Soviet ships from the Black Sea or the Baltic or the Arctic Ocean had to travel slightly further to reach the Indian Ocean from the Atlantic than U. S. ships from the east coast of the United States did, and although the voyage into the eastern Indian Ocean from Vladivostok was shorter than from San Diego, it was a lot longer than from Subic Bay or Guam. To be sure, the facilities Soviets were developing in Somalia, South Yemen, and Iraq had disturbing long-run implications, but they could not support in the near future anything like the kind of fleet that, for example, had gathered in the eastern Mediterranean during the October War. The Egyptian decision to reopen the Canal in the aftermath of the war changed the equation dramatically. The trip from the Black Sea to the Persian Gulf via the Canal is some 3200 nautical miles instead of more than 11,000 through the Mediterranean and around the Cape of Good Hope. An American base on Diego Garcia became a virtual necessity to neutralize the military benefits a reopened Suez Canal gave the Soviets. Moreover a full-size landing strip on Diego Garcia would ensure that if an airlift to Israel ever had to be mounted again, there would be a place other than the Azores for big U.S. Military Airlift Command transport planes to refuel. It looked in the late fall of 1973 as if we had used the Lajes base in the Azores for such a purpose for the last time. In 1975, there is no longer doubt that that is true, as long as Portugal retains control of the Azores.

Speaking of refueling an airlift to Israel, if I may digress for a few paragraphs, some of the planes were refueled in flight over the eastern Atlantic by Air Force tankers based on airfields in Spain. This was possible because of the enormous skill of the American Ambassador to Spain, Admiral Horacio Rivero. I bring this up because I am very proud of the part I played in gaining "Rivets" Rivero's appointment to the ambassadorship. The reader may recall that Rivets was the NATO commander on the Southern Flank when my watch began. He reached statutory retirement age of sixty-two in May 1972, and on 1 May of that year he was compelled to leave the Navy. I had enormous admiration for the way he had managed his command, which was basically a diplomatic assignment. It occurred to me that his diplomatic skill, and his fluency in Spanish—he is a native of Puerto Rico—qualified him admirably for the always difficult mission of representing the United States in Madrid. The post was about to become vacant because the incumbent, Robert Hill, was returning to the U.S. to become the Assistant Secretary of Defense for International Security Affairs.

I began to talk Rivets up within the government months before he was due to retire—as early as the fall of 1971, if my recollection is accurate. I spoke with Mel Laird, who passed my recommendation along to Secretary of State William Rogers, and with John Chafee who passed it along to Peter Flanagan, the White House man in charge of ambassadorial appointments. I spoke personally with Flanagan, with Under Secretary of State Alex Johnson, and with John Ehrlichman. All reactions were favorable, and Bob Hill added his voice. However, nothing happened. Rivets retired, bought a house in San Diego, and moved in. Then in the early summer of 1972 I made one last effort. I pointed out to Ehrlichman and Flanagan, both of whom I saw again, the advantage of appointing a Spanish-American to an important position in an election year. Rivets' appointment was announced soon thereafter.

He did a fine job during his two years in Madrid, where he was able to win the friendship of Generalissimo Francisco Franco, a feat few others have accomplished. Franco was a man of very few words indeed, as I discovered when I had a meeting with him—and after the meeting Bob Hill said that the few words the Generalissimo vouchsafed me were garrulous by his usual standards. I have been told that when Secretary Rogers called on Franco, the conversation went something like this. Rogers: "Are you concerned about Soviet naval strength in the Mediterranean, Your Excellency?" The translator translates. Franco: "Si." Pause. Rogers: "Would Your Excellency care to elaborate on the reasons for your concern?" The translator translates. Franco: "No." End of interview. I have also been told that with Rivets, Franco was talkative and at ease. When the flap over the designation to replace Rivets with Peter Flanagan developed, Rivets resigned, feeling that whether or not Flanagan was approved by the Senate, his own usefulness had ended.

My records show that the first of many memoranda on the subject of the Suez Canal I sent to the Chairman or the Secretary during my term as CNO was on 14 December 1970, in the wake of the Jordan crisis. It proposed that the Joint Staff undertake a study aimed at developing a joint position by the Chiefs on the subject of reopening the Canal. The recommendation was taken up and by spring the Chiefs did agree on a position:

JCS consider a reopened Suez Canal a greater strategic advantage to the
USSR than to the U.S., but would conclude that the U.S. should support
the reopening as part of an overall or partial peace settlement. However,
JCS would also conclude that U.S. government should support a diplomatic initiative which might seek an understanding for a significant
reduction of Soviet military presence within the UAR in return for
U.S. support for a Canal reopening.

Since the U.S. already had committed itself publicly to the reopening
of the Canal without conditions, this JCS position was more a warning of the consequences of that policy than a plausible effort to
change it. I cite it to make a point that, as in the case of oil, there
was more than enough advance notice of problems and difficulties
ahead. No doubt there are numerous and complex reasons a democracy has difficulty addressing itself seriously to a problem before a
state of crisis or near crisis is reached, but surely one of them during
the period I am discussing was that the conduct of foreign policy was
far too much a one-man show. All one man can do, if he can do that,
is to keep up with the most immediately troublesome situations and
let the future take care of itself.

At any rate, though I continued to bring the subject up at every
opportunity, and the Chiefs also remained concerned, the implications of a reopened Suez Canal were on the minds of few people
outside the military until the reopening became imminent. At that
point the civilian decision makers were able to focus their attention
on the Diego Garcia issue. With comparative ease we obtained permission from the British to expand the facility there. It was less easy
to secure the consent of the Congress, particularly the Senate, in
whose craw the Gulf of Tonkin Resolution still was stuck tight.
There was much fear that extending the runway and enlarging the
anchorage at Diego Garcia implied an under-the-table commitment
to some nation or nations in the area or, worse yet, an Administration purpose to try to run the whole show in that remote part of the
world. When Congress finally did provide the funds late in 1974,
after I had departed the scene, it put unusual restrictions on spending
them; that the President could go ahead with the project only if he
made a formal finding that national security required it, and that this
finding was subject within sixty days to veto by either house of
Congress. The President made such a finding in the spring of 1975.
And in July 1975, at long last and regrettably late, Congress defeated
by a close margin a resolution to disapprove the President's finding.

Diego Garcia will thus become a poor man's counter to the facilities in the Indian Ocean with which the Soviet Navy is now richly endowed.

The annual meeting between the President and the Joint Chiefs took place at breakfast on 22 December. In preparation for it, I made up a tough, terse briefing similar to the ones I had given in 1970 and 1971, and was prevented from giving in 1972 by the use of that meeting by the President and Henry Kissinger to instruct the Chiefs on what their attitude toward the Vietnam cease-fire was to be. I showed Jim Schlesinger what I proposed to say. He urged me vehemently not to. He said, "To give a briefing like that in the White House these days would be just like shooting yourself in the foot. The President is paranoid. Kissinger is paranoid. Haig is paranoid. They're down on the Navy and to present facts like these to them will drive them up the wall." He went on to warn me that a briefing like the one I proposed to give might well get the Navy, or even the Defense Department as a whole, a budget cut in sheer paranoid retaliation.

For a Secretary of Defense to use such words about his superiors in the White House was, to say the least, extraordinary. I had to take him seriously. I reluctantly concluded that the Administration was in no mood to listen to my—or anyone's—best professional judgment and that the way to protect the Navy under the circumstances was to administer a little soothing syrup. I still have, in my own hand, the rewrite I did of my first draft, but I shall not quote from it here both because it is blander than it should have been, and because I got to deliver only a small fraction of it.

The reason I was able to deliver only a small part of my brief was that the President used the ostensible budget meeting to engage in a long, rambling monologue, which at times almost seemed to be a stream of consciousness, about the virtues of his domestic and foreign policy. He repeatedly expressed the thought that the eastern liberal establishment was out to do us all in and that we should beware. It was clear that he saw the attacks on him (to which he referred only inferentially) as part of a vast plot by intellectual snobs to destroy a president who was representative of the man in the street. It was clear that he felt pessimistic about the democratic processes in our country. It was clear he perceived himself as a fighter for all that was right in the United States, involved in mortal battle with the forces of evil.

As we left, a couple of my colleagues commented on the enormous control of himself the President had displayed, and of the brilliance of his *tour d'horizon*. Perhaps they were comparing the real Richard Nixon, whom they had not seen in person for many months, with the Richard Nixon of the Washington rumor mill, who was a haggard, palsied, drunken wreck. The President certainly was not that. But to me he did present the very disturbing spectacle of a man who had pumped his adrenalin up to such high pressure that he was on an emotional binge. He appeared to me to be incapable of carrying on a rational conversation, much less exercising rational leadership over a nation involved in a score of complicated situations, embarked on dozens of hazardous enterprises. That glimpse of Richard Nixon at the end of 1973 did not make 1 January 1974 my happiest New Year.

CHAPTER 20

Changing the Watch

As the moment for the change of the watch drew near and I prepared to leave the Navy after thirty-five years of active and deeply satisfying service, I naturally thought often of the kind of Navy I was about to pass on to my successors and of how it would fare under them. For the sake of the man who was to follow me, I wanted to leave as few loose ends as I could and for the sake of the Navy I wanted the man who followed me to be one who was able to pick up the loose ends I was bound to leave. One benefit I particularly wanted my successor to enjoy was a budget he could live with during his first months in office. Sufficient unto his watch would be the four budget struggles he would have to engage in. If there was a way I could help get him off to a respectable start as far as money for ongoing programs was concerned, I wanted to find it. Therefore, I labored longer and harder on my fourth and last Posture Statement, which I presented to the four Congressional committees early in 1974, than I had on any of the others. It discussed with a degree of precision and an amount of detail that at last satisfied me the plain question anyone judging military programs must ask: how well can the United States expect to do in the most likely kind of war against the most likely opponent?

The intellectual dimness that characterizes most public pronouncements about Defense budgets stems mainly from the failure of budget writers and budget critics in both the executive and the legislative branches to come to grips with this fundamental question.

Evidently it is not the great difficulty of answering it correctly that paralyzes them. Rather it is the fear that the correct answer will be politically explosive: the U.S. cannot expect to do well enough. Nothing goes more against my grain than blinking at plain facts. That many people in positions of responsibility were willing to do so was the most frustrating phenomenon I encountered as CNO. In practical terms, refusing to describe the circumstances that made improvements in the Navy imperative undercut the rationale for urging such improvements.

My frustration impelled me in the spring of 1973 to initiate one last large-scale effort to get the facts out. Harry Train, a brilliant young officer who, as a captain, had been Tom Moorer's executive assistant, had recently been selected for flag rank and I had moved him into my old "Op-96" job, Director of Systems Analysis for the Navy. I gave him the formidable assignment of working up a "net assessment" of the relative strengths of the U.S. and the Soviet Navies.

To produce a net assessment of any sophistication means recognizing that most of the easy ways of comparing or contrasting the two Navies—for example, counting the gross numbers of ships and planes and missiles and overseas bases—are more or less misleading. Both absolutely and in relation to their allies and likely adversaries the U.S. and the USSR are in dissimilar geographical situations. Hence their fleets have dissimilar missions. To accomplish these missions they need forces that are constituted dissimilarly. A net assessment must attempt to do what the tired metaphor about comparing apples and oranges says shouldn't be done, at least to the extent of estimating whether the side armed with apples or the side armed with oranges is the side more likely to win a fight.

It took the best part of half a year for Harry Train's people to assemble and analyze the necessary data. These presented the two navies over a ten-year period, the past five and the next five. The assessment was divided into four major areas: comparison of individual elements of naval capability, comparison of warfare areas, comparison of mission requirements, and finally probable war and crisis outcomes. The first part of the assessment compared: the modernization progress of both navies; our offensive systems with theirs; our defensive systems with theirs; each side's offensive with the other's defensive system; future capabilities; sea based air. This section demonstrated that in most cases, whatever one thought of the capabilities of either navy it was unarguable that ours was deteriorating and theirs was improving and that Congressional reductions would prevent the U.S. Navy's regaining the capability it was losing.

In the second major area, the study identified fifteen areas of naval warfare as critical ones: Anti-Shipping Missile Defense; Protection against Submarines; Anti-Air Warfare; Attrition against Submarines; Anti-Surface Warfare; Strike Warfare; Electronic Warfare; Command, Control and Communications; Combat Direction Systems; Surveillance; Amphibious Lift; Naval Gunfire Support; Mine Countermeasures; Mine Warfare; and Mobile Logistics Support. The study rated U.S. capability in those fifteen areas in two ways: as adequate, marginal, or inadequate, and as superior or inferior to Soviet capability. It found that in two of the areas U.S. naval capability was adequate, in six it was marginal, and in seven it was inadequate. It found that in five of the areas U.S. naval capability was superior to that of the Soviets and in ten it was inferior. It provided a justification for ongoing Navy programs, and then some, that was difficult to refute.

In the third major area, we described the four major types of non-strategic war scenarios in which naval forces of the two sides could confront each other: direct conflict in Europe, direct conflict at sea without war on land, unilateral military action, and crisis management.

In the fourth major area, we analyzed the potential outcomes in the above conflict situations. We concluded that the U.S. Navy's carrier and amphibious forces gave us superior capability to take unilateral action. We concluded that if a showdown came in crisis management, the outcome would depend in large part on the relative strength each side judged it had and that therefore each side's conclusion as to the perceived outcome in conflict with or without war on land was critical. We described the outcomes of specific war games, fleet exercises, etc., and after making our best judgment as to over-all war outcomes, again had to report very pessimistic odds. We explained what went into these probabilities at great length.

The result was well worth the effort. As far as I know, it is the only exhaustive military net assessment study ever done in this country.

This net assessment was presented to Secretaries Schlesinger and Clements in the fall of 1973. It had much to do with the fact that in January 1974 the President sent to Congress the best naval budget of my four years, albeit still inadequate. And it was the foundation of my 1974 posture statement. To its basic facts and estimates I appended explanations of the ways in which the specific procurement and research programs the Navy was asking the Congress to fund would improve capability in each of the fifteen warfare areas. And I concluded with my annual estimate of the probability of victory in a non-nuclear naval war against the Soviets. In view of an adjuration by Jim Schlesinger to "be optimistic," I was glad to be able to say that this was the last year when our chances of winning would be as low as 30 percent—if Congress fully funded the Navy programs, that is. I said that given those programs—the Harpoon cruise missile, the F-14 plane, the Sea Control Ship, the Captor mine, the fourth nuclear carrier, and the rest of the major systems, high and low, new and old, previous chapters have described—the Navy would improve its capability year by year henceforward until, early in the eighties, its chances would be back beyond fifty-fifty again.

To the extent that the net assessment got the facts to the four critical Congressional committees it was a success. But that was as far as the facts got. The committees heard them in closed session. A number of the members of those committees, notably Senatator Milton Young of North Dakota, the senior Republican on the Appropriations Committee, thought the facts were so important that the entire country should hear them, and pressed me to get the posture statement declassified. I was as eager as Senator Young to tell the American people what all too few of them knew, and urged the Pentagon Public Affairs people to release the statement. They pondered the matter for a few days, then sent me back a marked copy that cleared perhaps 90 percent of the statement's fifty-two double-spaced typewritten pages. All they deleted were references to adequate, marginal, or inadequate capability; to superiority or inferiority to the Russians, and to the odds on winning the war.

A similar fate befell a study of much the same kind conducted on behalf of the President by the President's Foreign Intelligence Advisory Board (PFIAB, pronounced "piffy-ab"), a panel of prominent citizens with retired Admiral George Anderson, (the leader of the movement to get me fired over my personnel policies) as chairman. On 15 October 1973 George, with whom I had few differences on the subject of our declining naval strength, telephoned to tell me that the President had just met with PFIAB and had given it the task of writing a report on the relative naval balance between the U. S. and the USSR. Earlier in the day Secretary Schlesinger had told me that he had been with the President just before the PFIAB meeting and had given Mr. Nixon a Navy graph that showed that during the current year the Soviet Navy, for the first time, would have a larger number of surface warships than the U.S. Navy. Schlesinger reported that that was what had provoked the President's order. This was at the height of the Yom Kippur War, with the big American airlift just starting and the Soviet fleet gathering in proximity to our Sixth Fleet, which had the responsibility of giving the airlift's unarmed transport planes protection. Admiral Anderson also said in the course of that call that Al Haig, no longer a general at this point, I remind you, but the President's civilian chief of staff, had said that he wanted to see the report before it got to Henry Kissinger or the President. Admiral Anderson said that he had often heard Haig expressing annoyance about the way I hammered at the shifting naval balance.

PFIAB labored for several months, gathering its information independently of Navy channels, in accordance with the President's (or Haig's) instructions, though of course it did ask for and receive our net assessment briefing. The report the Board produced was not as comprehensive as the Navy's net assessment but it came to an even more pessimistic conclusion. One member of the Board who was particularly disturbed by its findings was Nelson Rockefeller, not yet Vice President, of course. I had been invited on 7 February 1974 to discuss the report with the Board. In the course of the discussion Governor Rockefeller asked me what could be done about the very serious situation the report disclosed. I answered that increasing the annual Navy budget by five billion dollars would turn the balance around, over time. "You should be asking for a hundred billion," he said. I said, "I agree, Governor, but I won't get five." We were both right.

The Board briefed Vice President Ford later that same day and President Nixon, Henry Kissinger, and Al Haig on 8 February with the meeting, scheduled for half an hour, lasting two hours. The Board told the President that "much, much more" needed to be done for the Navy. There was discussion of a "Manhattan" type project to deal with the crisis in naval power. The President concluded that he did not want the report distributed until he could study it personally. He indicated his agreement with the general conclusions and expressed concern.

Nevertheless the PFIAB report died in the White House. For whatever reason—Watergate, Haig's hostility toward the Navy, a conviction that it was impossible to sway an anti-military Congress —its distribution was tightly controlled, and so it had no impact on policy or budgetary decisions. And as I write this, the Navy, with the sea control ship killed and patrol frigates cut from seven to three by Congress in the fall of 1974, has fewer than 500 ships, the fewest it has had since 1939. Yet the U.S. has commitments to NATO in the Arctic, the Atlantic and the Mediterranean; to Israel; to South Korea and Japan; to the Philippines and the Pacific Islands, and to much of Latin America, most of which it did not have before World War II and all of which depend heavily on naval capability for fulfillment. To continue to proclaim those commitments while refusing to maintain naval strength is a piece of flimflam that fools those who practice it more than it fools anybody else. The nations we have pledged ourselves to are not deceived.

Speaking of America's overseas commitments brings up a contribution I had the opportunity to make near the end of my watch to keeping Iceland within the NATO alliance and thereby maintaining the strength of its so-called "Northern Flank." The Northern Flank begins on the east where Norway's northernmost province of Finnmark, wrapped around Sweden and Finland north of the Arctic circle on the shores of the Barents Sea, borders Russia near Murmansk; it goes west from there to the North Cape, across the Norwegian Sea to Iceland, then across the Straits of Denmark to Greenland.

Though there is little public appreciation of the problem, having the capability to protect this line is a matter of great importance to most of the alliance's professional military men, and was of abiding concern to me. Perhaps the Northern Flank has escaped public notice because, unlike NATO's Southern Flank—the Mediterranean and its littoral—where political turmoil has been endemic for decades, it has not been the scene of spectacular events. Yet in a purely military sense the Northern Flank is potentially NATO's most vulnerable area.

A look at the map makes it clear why. Finnmark, empty of population, remote from any concentration of NATO forces, and up against the Soviet Union on one side and a sea under the absolute control of the Soviet Navy on another, is virtually indefensible. It must tempt the Soviets because occupying it would place Soviet forces in a favorable position to outflank the alliance from the north. Even if NATO has deterred the Soviets from that big much-discussed attack in central Europe that could so easily escalate into a nuclear exchange, a series of Soviet nibbles at northern Norway, with the possibility of making a large strategic gain by taking a small military risk, is a contingency that no prudent military planner can ignore.

A still more threatening feature of the Northern Flank if a European war of any kind should break out is the so called "G-I-UK" gap—the ocean straits between Greenland and Iceland and between Iceland and the United Kingdom. That is the route the big Russian submarine fleet based on Murmansk must traverse to reach the Atlantic. It is the least vulnerable route for their long range aircraft to fly over to reach these same sea lanes. Once these forces have done so they are directly athwart the alliance's most important line of communication, the sea line between the United States and northern Europe, along which 90 percent or more of American supplies and over half of the American troops must travel by sea to support a NATO war, the rest coming by the potentially even more vulnerable air routes. Thus, keeping the G-I-UK ocean gap closed in the event of war is of life-or-death importance to the alliance. And forces based in Iceland are the *sine qua non* for this closure.

Most NATO leaders, civilian as well as military, particularly those in Scandinavia, recognize these facts of life. During my first visit to Scandinavia in the summer of 1971 I found the military chiefs and civilian defense officials there concerned about the Soviet threat to the point of describing the position of their countries as being "behind the Soviet lines." As part of my trip report upon my return that summer I wrote a short paper I called "Political/Military Situation on NATO Northern Flank," which summarized what those men had told me. Under the subheading "Norway's Strategic Perception" I reported:

> Norway feels increasingly behind the Soviet line as the result of her knowledge that NATO defense initially must be across Greenland/Iceland/UK Gap and because of the very high order of recent Soviet fleet exercises off Northern Norway. Norway is particularly concerned because USSR has begun practice of announcing these exercises, leaving the USSR the option of a sudden "Czechoslovakia-type" occupation of Northern Norway. Norway believes these amphibious landings would be accomplished by helo-borne vertical assault directly from Russia and that the USSR would stop short of the Tromso area in the expectation that NATO would settle, peacefully, for this small territorial snatch.

Under the subheading "General Impressions" I wrote,

> A. USSR, over the last ten years and at an accelerated pace over the last five years, has debilitated Finland's capability to stand apart and can,

within the next five years, deal with Finland as essentially a political appendage of the USSR.

B. Over the same time frame, Sweden has been forced to make a subtle adjustment away from tacit support of NATO toward a USSR-biased neutrality, as a result of the changed conditions in Finland and the weakened military position of Norway which in turn stems from the increased Soviet maritime presence, outflanking Norway.

C. The Norwegian military position has deteriorated as the NATO capability (particularly U.S. Navy/U.S. Marine Corps) to support the northern flank has weakened and as the Soviet maritime presence off the Norwegian coast has greatly increased. Norway knows her position to be weakened. In the five years ahead, we should expect to see an erosion in Norway's willingness to work with the NATO alliance.

(When I debriefed my trip at the State Department, I compressed paragraphs A, B, and C into "Soviet strategy appears to be to make Finland into another Latvia, Sweden into another Finland, and Norway into another Sweden.")

One thing everyone I spoke with in Scandinavia on that trip agreed about was that this position, rather than merely being perilous, would be virtually untenable were it not for the allied forces based on Iceland. Those forces, whose principal defensive duties were various aspects of anti-submarine warfare and air defense, also provided the opportunity to protect and support perhaps the only believable deterrent to Soviet adventures in northern Norway, naval forces operating northeast of Iceland. However, in June of 1971, by coincidence the month during which a similar thing happened on another strategically situated island, Malta, an election had put a left-wing government in office in Iceland, a coalition government that included Communists. The new government, to the immense concern of all of us, immediately started dropping broad hints that during its tenure the lease on the base at Keflavík that the U. S. Navy maintained on behalf of NATO, would be terminated. In the same paper I quoted from above I wrote, under the heading "Recommendations":

A. Make heroic efforts to reverse the left-wing drift of Iceland . . .

B. Heroic political measures to prepare the Faroes as a fallback option in the event that the loss of Iceland occurs.

C. Greatly expanded NATO fleet exercises, including amphibious landings south of Tromso, are required on a frequent basis.

D. Greater NATO infrastructure expenditures in Northern Norway are required to provide signal of NATO resolve . . .

E. There should be homeporting of U.S. warships in UK or the Netherlands in order to show resolve on the North Flank and in order to abet increased exercises in the North Sea and off Northern Norway.

F. Endeavor to persuade Federal Republic of Germany to operate their sea going ships in the North Sea as often as possible and under the NATO umbrella.

Of those recommendations, A was carried out, as I am about to relate. That made B moot. There was moderate improvement in the fields covered by C and D. E never got through the American system, though Henry Kissinger told me at a non-meeting in 1972 that he was for it. F ran into the unwillingness of the British to encourage German presence in the North Sea; I think they were short-sighted to take that position, but it certainly was an understandable one in the light of the history of the naval relations between those two nations.

The Icelandic opponents of the Keflavík base could count on public support on a number of grounds, political, cultural and economic. In a small country caught geographically between superpowers there is bound to be neutralist sentiment. There was enough in Iceland to have imperiled the continuance of the base on at least two previous occasions, in 1956 and 1961. Moreover the sense of sovereignty of many Icelanders was offended by such visible anomalies as U.S. Marines guarding the gates of their national airport, for the military landing field at the base was also the one commercial planes used. Many Icelanders who cherished their nation's traditional values were disturbed by the mere presence on their island of upward of 3000 Americans, many of them young, single, and lonely. There was constant friction between the two governments over such matters as whether servicemen on liberty might wear civilian clothes and should be subject to a curfew. When a television station was installed on the base, the Icelandic Government insisted that it keep its signal weak and beam it away from Reykjavík so that American TV could not enter Icelandic homes. In the face of this, many nontraditionalist Icelanders, to the fury of the traditionalists, spent hundreds of dollars beefing up their sets so they could receive broadcasts from the base.

I paid a short visit to Iceland in April of 1972, both to observe the

activities of the base first hand and to try to reconcile Icelandic
officials to some of the cultural frictions the presence of Americans
in Iceland was bound to cause. I think with Ambassador Luther
Replogle's friendly collaboration I mollified some of them, but there
was no way to eliminate them all. In any case, what gave the anti-
base faction its most powerful argument was a bitter dispute that
broke out in 1972 between Iceland and Britain over fishing rights.
Fishing produces 30 percent of Iceland's gross national product and
brings in 80 percent of its foreign exchange. To protect its fishing
grounds from depletion by other nations, the Icelandic government
effective 1 September 1972 declared the waters around the island to
a distance of fifty nautical miles off limits to foreign fishing vessels.
(It is interesting to note in passing that that was 150 miles less than
the extent of the waters Ecuador claims—and invokes against
American tuna boats. International conferences on the Law of the
Sea meet regularly in an effort to solve the problem of the extent of
national jurisdiction over coastal waters, among other problems, and
just as regularly fail to do so.)

There are towns and villages in the north of England and in
Scotland that depend for their livelihood largely on fishing for cod
off the coast of Iceland. Some of the fishermen from those places
ignored the fifty-mile limit and continued their accustomed practices. The situation rapidly grew nasty. During the next nine months
there were dozens of reported incidents between Icelandic ships or
aircraft and British trawlers or Royal Navy craft, ranging from
photographs and buzzing to destruction of fishing gear to attempted
ramming to collision to ultimatums to window smashing at embassies to naval gunfire. Neither side showed an inclination to yield.
Edward Heath's British government evidently believed that Iceland
was putting on a bluff that could and should be called. The Icelandic
Minister of Fishing was a Communist, which did not contribute to
an accommodation. That was the highly charged state of affairs on
25 June 1973 when the Icelandic government, invoking one of the
provisions of the 1951 agreement between the United States and
Iceland, called for a review within six months by the North Atlantic
Council of the need for the base and of its functions. The significance
of this action was that it was the legal preliminary to renegotiating
the 1951 agreement or terminating it. With the fisheries dispute
stirring Icelandic passions to the extent it was doing, the latter
outcome appeared as likely as the former.

During the summer months of 1973, while the review was in

process and before the U.S.-Iceland negotiations, which were scheduled for early October, began, the U.S. pressed Britain, as hard as
alliance partnership permitted, to be more forthcoming about the
fisheries. The way a nation presses a friend and ally is not by composing stiff diplomatic notes, of course, but largely through the personal
contacts officials of the one government have with officials of the
other. I was on warm terms with the top professionals in the Royal
Navy, and I was able to express my views on Iceland to them, by
correspondence and in person, on a number of occasions. In their
case there was no question of trying to change attitudes or opinions.
They already agreed that the dispute should be settled promptly, not
just because they recognized the importance of the Keflavík base to
the alliance, but because they had the responsibility for the performance of the Royal Navy frigates that were conducting such embarrassing and politically risky operations in waters claimed by Iceland.
Letting them know that the U. S. Navy agreed with their professional
judgment about the risks of doing what they had been ordered to do
strengthened their hands, I hope, in their discussions with their
civilian superiors.

Later in the year, when the dispute had been settled, I wrote my
counterpart Sir Michael Pollock, the First Sea Lord, to compliment
him on the restraint the Royal Navy had showed in an extremely
touchy situation. I added, "Cooperation when national interests are
both clear and congruent is easy, but it is our cooperation when the
circumstances are more complicated which makes me convinced of
the enduring quality of the ties which bind our Services to each
other." I was not the only American who conducted similar exchanges with British friends that summer. Some of the signals we
were sending, there is no telling which ones, evidently got through
to Prime Minister Heath at last, for in quite a sudden turnabout he
withdrew the frigates and soon thereafter, on 13 November 1973,
Iceland and Britain signed an agreement that ended the dispute by
giving British fishermen rights to catch a restricted tonnage of fish
within the fifty-mile limit. With the inflammatory issue of fish
removed, the U.S.-Iceland talks began on schedule and proceeded in
relative tranquility, helped by the early removal by the U.S. of the
Marine guards from the airport gates.

But if the negotiations were tranquil, they were also tedious and
drawn out. The Icelanders insisted on a sharper reduction at Keflavík than the realities of the military situation made advisable. The
problem was not so much with the top men in the Icelandic govern-

ment as with members of the legislature, the press and the public, who were beguiled by the constant talk of détente into expecting immediate disarmament. It is an illusion many Americans cherish also, and the Soviet Union has exploited. Early in the spring of 1974, perhaps because over the years I had had a number of conversations with leading Icelanders, including Foreign Minister Einar Agusts-son, and had evidently won their confidence, the new ambassador to Reykjavík, Frederick Irving, invited me to pay him an informal visit, during which I would meet with Icelandic leaders, on my way to Brussels, where I was to participate in a NATO naval conference. I was in Iceland from 29 to 31 March. (I never did get to Brussels because I was called back urgently to Washington to testify on 1 April before Senator Mansfield's Sub-Committee on Military Construction about Diego Garcia, though when I remember how much my testimony changed Mansfield's opposition to the base, I suspect I should have gone to Brussels.) Excerpts from three documents in my files tell the story of the visit to Iceland concisely. The first is a cable Ambassador Irving sent me before I left for Reykjavík.

Events of past few days make CNO's visit timely. [Kissinger had been in Moscow from the 24th to the 28th of March and there was much speculation about the future of SALT and détente.] Much confusion exists among Icelandic politicians about the "state of the north Atlantic." There is strong streak of skepticism in Icelandic govt about the importance of the IDF [Iceland Defense Force]. Most Icelanders believe that danger of war in north Atlantic is nil; that we currently enjoy a more peaceful situation than existed in period 1949–51 when there were no foreign troops in Iceland. Icelanders resist explanation. The CNO's task is to try to make a credible argument to influential Icelanders as to why a military station in Iceland in "peacetime" is essential.

Icelanders argue among themselves as to which is more important: defense of Iceland or the ASW [anti-submarine-warfare] surveillance activity. Too many still fail to realize that they are one and the same. Icelanders feel a responsibility to NATO but they will not admit to themselves that they are an important link in the NATO defense chain. The CNO needs no coaching, but we would suggest his discussions convey the multilateral nature of the NATO defense system; the extent to which each nation's defense and credibility depends on contributions and capabilities and locations of others; importance of deterrence in discouraging attacks; extent to which all NATO allies rely upon advance warning systems and reinforcement and re-supply in case of attack; and necessity of accurately evaluating and responding to potential enemy's capability. CNO will undoubtedly be called on to compare U. S. and NATO naval strength with Soviets.

CNO will find many opportunities to field narrow questions with broad answers. He will, however, be confronted with purely local complaints such as base TV problem, imports of meat products by base, and disposal of base garbage.

The second document is a memo I wrote Jim Schlesinger upon my return. I entitled it "Iceland visit; some personal observations."

First of all, the schedule went very smoothly. Irving, who is doing an impressive job, worked hard to make sure that my time was used to maximum advantage. By the time we left, I had met with roughly a third of the Althing (Icelandic Parliament) membership, a generous cross section of the media, and a wide range of other local opinion leaders.

My message to one and all was basically threefold—I emphasized the importance of the IDF presence in the context of: (a) The defense of Iceland itself; (b) NATO solidarity: (c) movement toward East-West détente. In the process I endeavored to educate my audience to the sober realities of the still dangerous world beyond their tranquil shores. My distinct impression, as borne out by the remarks of Icelanders themselves to my accompanying staff and the Ambassador and his Country Team, was that one and all listened carefully and can be expected to retain the major thrust of my remarks.

In sum, my job was primarily to open the eyes a bit wider of a people whose native tongue does not include a word for armed conflict, much less détente. Time will be the ultimate judge of the real impact. Meanwhile the visit helped lay the groundwork for a somewhat sterner, less apologetic line, which both I and the Ambassador would advocate we take in the next round of IDF negotiations. . . .

The third document is a cable Ambassador Irving sent after my visit to Under Secretary of State Joseph Sisco, who had replaced William Porter, an expert negotiator who later became Ambassador to Canada, both in that job and as the U. S. negotiator with the Icelandic government. It may not be altogether modest to quote it, but I think it is part of the story.

1. Admiral Zumwalt's visit to Reykjavík was an outstanding success. . . . The give and take on a serious political-military level between Zumwalt and some of these politicians . . . is considered unprecedented in Icelandic political life. The Admiral talked to approximately 50 per-

cent of the non-Communist members of Parliament (and one Communist MP on Foreign Relations Committee), chairman and leaders of the opposition parties who are prominent in party policy matters.

2. We worked the Admiral hard, but to good advantage. We are still in for tough times on the IDF issue, but not as tough as before his visit. He has the thanks of all of us in Iceland. . . .

The negotiations still were going forward when my watch ended. They concluded at last, in the fall of 1974, with an agreement that permitted, with some restrictions on U.S. flexibility and with some reduction of U.S. personnel, the continuing presence of U.S. forces in Iceland. In November I received a letter from Fred Irving in Reykjavík in response to one I had written him congratulating him on the successful outcome of the negotiations. Again proudly rather than modestly I shall quote a paragraph from it:

Your chest had a right to expand . . . on the morning September 26th when the Foreign Minister and I met with SecDef Schlesinger in Washington. When the SecDef asked the Foreign Minister how he assessed your visit to Reykjavík earlier in the year, Einar Agustsson replied that it was highly successful and that it contributed to making this agreement possible. I took the occasion to second the Foreign Minister's assessment.

What remains to be said, of course, is that things look to be returning to where they were in 1972 now that Iceland has extended its territorial-water claims to 200 miles and another cod war impends. In short, my contribution was at best tactical, not strategic.

I opened this chapter by writing that I wanted the man who followed me to be able to pick up the loose ends I was bound to leave behind. I had three particular sets of loose ends in mind. I wanted a successor who would go forward with the personnel programs I had initiated. I wanted a successor who believed in the "high-low" mix and had the stamina and the wisdom to protect it from the stratagems of Admiral Rickover and to sell it on Capitol Hill. Above all, I wanted a successor with the integrity and strength of character to keep the Navy from being suffocated in the political miasma that was enveloping ever more closely the Nixon-Kissinger-Haig White House.

I knew which men fitted that description. The rapid turnover in the top leadership of the armed services that the law prescribes is no unmixed blessing, but one of its beneficial effects is that it makes each incoming Chief acutely conscious of his obligation to begin identifying and testing his most likely successors as soon as he assumes office. I had done so. I had made a point of rotating each of the officers I thought had superior potential through a variety of difficult assignments. The "daisy chain" of 1973, which I have discussed in a previous chapter, was the penultimate move in that series of moves, and my threat to resign if it was not put into effect was an accurate indication of how very seriously I took the succession. By the time Jim Schlesinger came aboard I knew that three officers, two of whom had been junior Rear Admirals and one a junior Vice Admiral when my watch began and under me had all risen to four stars, were qualified above all others to lead the Navy for the four years that would begin on 1 July 1974. They were Admirals Worth Bagley, James L. Holloway III, and Maurice Weisner.

You may recall that I brought Worth Bagley from his command of a destroyer flotilla in the Seventh Fleet to Washington as my right hand on Project 60 at the beginning of my watch. Before long I recommended him for promotion to Vice Admiral and gave him what I considered to be the most intellectually demanding three-star job in the Navy, Deputy CNO for Program Planning. The 1973 daisy chain sent him to London in the four-star job of Commander in Chief of U. S. Naval Forces in Europe, a command that has both heavy diplomatic responsibilities and operational control over the Sixth Fleet in the Mediterranean. That was where he was during the testing time of the Yom Kippur War.

Like Worth, Jimmy Holloway is from a family of admirals. He, along with Jack McCain who was CinCPac when I became CNO, shares the distinction of being a four-star admiral who is the son of a four-star admiral. His father, under whom I served during my first Washington tour when he was Chief of Naval Personnel, was the superior who most impressed me when I was a young officer. Jimmy is an experienced and accomplished operations man. He commanded the Sixth Fleet's carriers during the Jordan crisis, moved from there to the three-star job of Deputy CinC of the Atlantic Fleet, and from there to command of the Seventh Fleet in the western Pacific. The racial disturbances in the Seventh Fleet occurred when he was in command, a test of coolness that he passed with high grades. The 1973 daisy chain gave him his fourth star as Vice CNO.

Mickey Weisner, also an aviator, was Commander of the Seventh Fleet at the start of my watch. I brought him to Washington to the

476 ¶ FRIENDS AND FOES

job of Deputy CNO for Air, then promoted him to the four-star job of Vice CNO when Ralph Cousins became CinCLant. When Jimmy Holloway relieved him as Vice CNO, Mickey went to Hawaii to command the Pacific Fleet. In sum, during the three years from 1970 to 1973, all three of them had served with distinction in both sea commands and staff jobs. I had no hesitation in telling Secretary Schlesinger that each one of them had the talent, the experience and, especially, the character for the top job.

There was a fourth officer whose ability and reputation made him a candidate for the job, Admiral Isaac (Ike) Kidd, also the son and namesake of an Admiral. His father was killed on board the battle-ship, USS *Arizona,* during the Japanese attack on Pearl Harbor. Ike's name has appeared in these pages as the Commander, U.S. Sixth Fleet, during the Jordan crisis where he did a superior professional job. After he completed that term I insisted, against the initial oppo-sition of Dave Packard and Mel Laird, that he be promoted to the four-star job of Chief of Naval Material because I wanted to bring operational experience into that technical command. In the job Ike soon won the admiration and support of Dave Packard and subse-quently Bill Clements, the first and third incumbents as Deputy Secretary of Defense during my tenure, whose responsibilities brought them in close touch with service logistics commanders. But, as earlier chapters also reveal, Ike worked closely with George An-derson, when he was CNO, and being a close friend of his, came to be perceived as the senior officer who opposed my personnel policy changes. During the *Kitty Hawk* and *Constellation* difficulties, retired officers put his name forward frequently to the press as the man who would succeed me in case I was fired. His friends had made him the man whose appointment as CNO would be perceived by the fleet as heralding a return to the status quo ante. I therefore regret-fully concluded that Ike could not be on my list of CNO candidates.

I first raised the question of the succession with the Secretary in July 1973, soon after he took office. I was anxious for the matter to be settled early, six months ahead of the change itself if possible, so that the new man would have plenty of time to become familiar with the job and continuity would be assured. I had another reason for pressing for an early decision. The longer the decision was delayed, the more likely it was that there would be active campaigning for the job by several officers and their respective supporters, with unpre-dictable effects on a White House desperately in search of political leverage. The customary procedure for picking a new Chief of Naval Operations is for the Secretary of the Navy, in consultation with the incumbent Chief, to canvass the list of four-star and likely looking three-star officers, and then submit the names of the ones he judges to be the top candidates to the Secretary of Defense. From that list the Secretary of Defense chooses a name to submit to the President. When I brought up the succession with Jim Schlesinger in July, he suggested that John Warner and I get to work on the problem at once. However, John showed no interest in doing so for a couple of months. Then one day, as he and I were about to enter Schlesinger's office for one of our regular meetings, he told me suddenly, evidently hoping to catch me unprepared, that he planned to bring up the succession at that meeting.

He did not catch me unprepared. John Warner had been unhelpful to me in just about every way a Secretary of the Navy could be unhelpful to the Chief of Naval Operations: in handling the racial issue; in advancing promising young officers; in dealing with contractors; in fighting for an adequate budget; in coping with Admiral Rickover; even in managing the serio-comic affair of YN1 Charles Radford. I had long since adopted the policy of not relying on his assistance in any serious enterprise. Consequently I had been conferring about the succession from time to time directly with Jim Schlesinger, with whom I had gotten onto good terms quite soon and to whom I had relatively easy access. And so when John Warner let it be known at that meeting that his sole candidate was Ike Kidd, Schlesinger indicated a desire to canvass the field more widely than that. Later Jim asked me to consider a two-year extension of my four-year term as CNO and offered to seek the necessary legislation. I rejected this as setting an unhealthy precedent and as inconsistent with my own program to reduce the average age of flag officers.

Throughout the fall of 1973 I continued to put forward my three candidates. In December Schlesinger conferred with Paul Nitze on the matter, and Paul approved my candidates. The clincher was a poll I had taken on the subject among the four-star admirals. I asked them to name and rank their three choices for Chief. Jimmy Holloway came in first, with Bagley and Weisner virtually tied for second, close behind. When John got the results of the poll he hastily called me and instructed me not to show them to Schlesinger. I had anticipated such instructions so I was able to reply that they had come too late because I had already informed Jim. John made one last effort by saying he wondered who Rickover's choice was, and urged me to find out. I did and Rick would not commit himself, saying it was none of his business.

In February 1974, Secretary Schlesinger sent Jimmy Holloway's name to the White House. I suppose everyone in the Navy knew that the one among my three I considered the most capable of bold new leadership was Worth Bagley. However he had been so deeply involved in and had contributed so heavily to my modernization programs—including being the brother of the Chief of Naval Personnel who administered the personnel reforms I had initiated—that he was a controversial figure himself. Jimmy Holloway was not; he was popular throughout the Navy, and I was perfectly satisfied with his designation—as I would have been also with Mickey Weisner's.

Actually, it was after Jimmy's name went to the President that Ike came closest to being nominated. The recommendation remained on the President's desk for almost two months while what I had feared would happen did: an "Ike-for-CNO" campaign developed. I guess the political consideration that finally induced the President on 28 March, the day before I left for Iceland as it happened, to send Jimmy's name to Congress was that the times were unpropitious for directly repudiating a recommendation of the Secretary of Defense. In addition, and I really think this was a factor, Mr. Nixon remembered Jimmy's father from his own period of naval service. As of this writing I can report that Jimmy Holloway has kept the Navy on an enlightened course with regard to personnel and weapons systems. Meanwhile, as agreed at the time among the President, the Secretary of Defense and the incoming and outgoing CNOs, Ike Kidd has become Commander in Chief Atlantic, in which command he is not only showing himself once again a fine operational officer, but has been pushing hard the personnel programs which many of those who supported him for CNO opposed.

The long and potentially disastrous delay in nominating Holloway was just one of a myriad of pieces of evidence that the White House had fallen into almost complete disarray. During the last six months of my watch people in a position to know continued from time to time to tell me things that were happening there, and I continued to make notes of what they told me. A sampling from some of the notes, again for the purpose of recreating the surrealistic milieu of that almost unbelievable period of history:

The President in telephone and direct conversations castigates every ethnic group in the U.S. as being against him—the Jews, the blacks, the Catholics, the Wasps etc. . . . Haig works every day frequently to midnight or one o'clock and Sundays from nine to six, yet Nixon has an almost paranoid resentment of any time Haig is not available. Once in a while Haig gets off to the tennis courts and the staff has to lie about where he is and get him to scramble back to answer the telephone call. . . . Ehrlichman is the first heavy to crack and seek a deal—none previously had been willing to incriminate Nixon. Ehrlichman provided the basis for the "Plumbers" story. . . . Mr. Nixon never watches television or reads the newspapers and is therefore cut off from all except those items that his staff spoonfeeds him. . . . When it was clear that the President was emotionally incapable of acting as President, Haig did so. He was conscious of the fact that he was well above his depth. He was a frightened man but he was desperately doing his best to hold it together. . . . Nixon is so paranoid and so emotional that no one can bear to spend the long hours with him he demands. Even Ziegler tries to avoid Mr. Nixon's phone calls.

My personal encounters with the President were as always few and public, but on such occasions, many of them merely ceremonial, he seemed to me tense, easily distracted and unnaturally garrulous, as he had been at the White House breakfast with the Chiefs in December. About a month after that breakfast, on 24 January, as the senior of the service chiefs, I was acting Chairman of the Joint Chiefs in Tom Moorer's absence and in that capacity attended a National Security Council meeting the President had called. The President talked a lot at the meeting; indeed except for a Kissinger monologue about recent developments in SALT, it was pretty much a Nixon monologue. It was obvious to me that, among other things, the meeting was a staged opportunity for Mr. Nixon to show that he was still in control. The demonstration was a mixed success. Some of the things Mr. Nixon said made perfect sense. At other times he rambled, or even indulged in non sequiturs. If it was not an alarming performance, neither was it a reassuring one. By that time I had developed the routine of keeping a tape recorder running (in full view I might add) at my early morning "line-up," when I debriefed my immediate staff on the most significant things I had done the previous day. And so the following quotes are from a transcript of what I told my staff about that NSC meeting, reading off notes I had taken at the meeting.

The President . . . referred to the need to move out with regard to foreign policy in Latin America. I have never been with the President when he didn't stress our policy with Latin America over the last three and a half years and not a damn thing has ever come out of any one of the sessions and nobody has ever followed up on it. . . .

He said that it was his theory that in a second term a President ought to be sort of like an extinct volcano—the first term was the time for erupting. . . . History will record that the opening to the PRC was probably far more important than even the opening to Moscow. However . . . if we hadn't gotten the war over in southeast Asia the others would not have been possible. It was a kind of interesting formulation to me because I would have thought that he would observe that he had to have those [openings] in order to get the war in SEA over. He seems to consider it the other way around.

He said he would like to have people feed their ideas in. Then shifted abruptly: that Julie had given him a good idea recently. . . .

Then he came back to NSC meetings and said in this particular meeting as in all of them we try to make them one-subject meetings—we don't make decisions. He interpolated that he was reviewing this for the benefit of the new members, including the Vice President. [Gerald Ford had been sworn in on 6 December 1973.] He said the President made the decisions after NSC meetings as a separate function. . . . He said that [the system of conducting] foreign policy has proceeded to the point where we make like Joe DiMaggio—our hits look easy, as Kissinger's recent result in the Mideast looks routine to the people. There may not be any more superplays left to make because we have got things down to such a routine basis. . . . He said while these meetings may be dull they are most important because it's here that the background data is put together that affects the whole world's history—when we sneeze others get pneumonia and that will continue to be the case unless the U.S. recedes from the use of power. Then he urged everybody to speak up at these meetings if they sense that anything is wrong. . . .

He ended up saying that he was going to get Kissinger to describe where we were at [in regard to SALT] and he kind of made it fairly clear then that there wasn't going to be any discussion at that particular meeting. . . . The thrust of [Kissinger's presentation] was that privately Kissinger's view, which the President shares, is that there's no way we can get parity with the Soviets. The people won't support it. The President made it clear he didn't want any talk that sounded like that publicly. But that's what it amounts to. We were not given any real chance to discuss it, although Schlesinger made the point that I would have had to make, mainly that he thought we ought to insist on formal parity. Even if we can't get the Russians to come down to our numbers, we ought to first try that and then sign parity at their numbers and put the monkey back on Congress's back. If we do that there is no doubt in my mind that Congress would appropriate the money. . . .

The President . . . said he would like CIA to give him as soon as possible a look on what the Chinese Communists would look like in ten to fifteen years. He said the reason he was asking this was that when he talked to Brezhnev at San Clemente he told him in twenty-five years we are really going to have trouble with the Chinese. And Brezhnev said, no sir, in ten. Colby made the point (which I think is a very good one) that they probably both were right: that Brezhnev has to worry more in ten years and we have to worry more in twenty-five. . . .

The President turned to me at one point and said that he had asked for a net assessment on the Soviet versus U. S. Navy. He appeared to have forgotten whom he had asked. . . . He said that he knew that we probably had more numbers (which is wrong) but [our ships] are older and more tired and the Soviets have made some significant progress and he wants to know exactly what it is. He asked me what I thought of the budget this year. I told him I thought it was the best Navy budget on my watch. He said, cut it—kidding, I hope. . . .

The President discussed strategic doctrine. It was clear he didn't know anything about the new strategic doctrine that he approved. . . .

The President discussed Brezhnev's political problems: that he's got his hawks to worry about too and for that reason we've got to be sure we don't unhorse him. It is clear that the President thinks that the best he can do is count on inferiority. I am just sure that is wrong in terms of what the people will stand still for, and we have got to keep the pressure on in our positions on it.

On 11 March the Administration staged a set piece of a different kind that, if anything, was more alarming than the President's performance at the National Security Council. Henry Kissinger, wearing his State Department hat, met in the Tank with Secretary Schlesinger, Deputy Secretary Clements and the Chiefs for a long discussion of foreign policy. On the face of it what prompted this unprecedented get together was the increasing restiveness of the entire Defense establishment over what looked to be a giveaway on strategic arms, assented to if not engineered by Kissinger, at the Moscow summit scheduled for the end of June. However, I cannot help wondering whether Henry would have taken the trouble to be sweetly reasonable in the face of military opposition if the Commander in Chief had been in a political and emotional position to issue a peremptory order for obedience.

Be that as it may, Henry was at his most brilliant at that meeting. Chameleon that he is, he turned red, white, and blue for the occasion, arguing eloquently and at length that détente had increased the Defense budget, saved NATO, stabilized the Middle East and forced the USSR into a series of damaging concessions—all of which I couldn't have disagreed with more, of course. In short, confronting a group whose views of foreign policy are conservative, he became an arch conservative and cold warrior. I have no doubt that if he had been discussing the same events with liberals, he would have spoken of relaxing dangerous international tensions, slowing down the arms race, bringing China into the community of nations and restoring peace to southeast Asia. The transcript of my debrief of this meeting to my morning line-up covers more than nine single-spaced typewritten pages. Much as I would like to, I cannot reproduce it in full here. I must content myself with offering some of the more fascinating excerpts. On the reason for the détente policy:

> Kissinger . . . reminded everybody that we started in 1970 with this domestic environment in which we were under daily assault about our commitment in South Vietnam—so badly that there were tremendous anti-budget pressures. . . . we were really on our way to unilateral disarmament [and] our allies considered the U.S. intransigent and domestically headed for isolationism. Therefore . . . the Administration had to get some domestic maneuvering room in three ways: first we had to be able to get some control over our relationship with our allies; second we had to gain some freedom of maneuver with regard to South Vietnam; third—can't read my third note. As a result the U.S. invented what he referred to as its "moderate détente" policy. He suggested had we not had a moderate détente policy we could not have prevented an immoderate détente policy on the part of our European allies. If we had not taken the high ground with regard to détente, Europe would have rushed pell mell into the arms of the USSR and to covering up their interests in the Middle East. It was . . . our maneuvers, [which] have given the Europeans a lack of something to offer, that prevents Europe from taking high ground. . . . He said that there was another by-product and that is that the hatred of the liberals is so great for the President that they would give up anything to destroy him and that they therefore find themselves going right of the President. He said although he wouldn't claim . . . prescience about this, in a sense the détente policy was responsible for giving the liberals no place to go except to the right of the President.

On the accomplishments of détente:

He said that if he were in the Politburo he believed he could make a strong case against Brezhnev. [Brezhnev] lost everything in détente except for the wheat deal, which he said was a bureaucratic snafu. He can't think of a single thing that can be credited to the Soviet Union as an advantage.

On SALT:

He reminded us that we had been in a period of declining Defense budgets, that there had been . . . no support for increasing US armament. . . . And therefore we were in a position where we had to freeze a gap. He says that he thinks you can make a case that we have, by SALT One, kept the Soviet Union from building. He said, on the other hand, on the ABM side, we didn't do as well. He said we were up against a conspiracy between Congress and the Soviet Union and we gave away too much; but the alternative would have been to have given away everything and not have any ABM treaty. On the offensive side, we did get freedom to start spending more dollars for Trident and for penetration.

On the Middle East:

He said that in the Middle East the Soviet Union is beside itself, that Brezhnev has been doing his best trying to maintain his role as the Arabs' spokesman. Gromyko arrived some six hours after I [Henry] left the Middle East. In Egypt they actually ran up the U.S. flag on the U.S. Embassy [diplomatic relations between the U.S. and Egypt had just been restored] on the very day he arrived and he thought it was a particularly strong effort to infuriate Brezhnev. Syria was indifferent to Brezhnev. He said in a certain sense it's not even healthy that the Russians are so frustrated in the Middle East, that we like to keep them more restrained. But the essence of the story is that we won a great victory over the Russians in the Middle East.

On NATO:

He said that it is painful to see [the Western European nations'] domestic weakness and their anti-U.S. attitude. He said there is a great temptation on their part to use their anti-U.S. attitude, because the governments are too weak to make the difficult decisions; they are extracting what popularity they can by being anti-U.S. He said if you look at the five positions the European Common Market has taken recently, they have all been anti-U.S. and taken without consultation with the U.S. government. He was particularly furious about their recent appeal to Canada and Japan for separate declarations of principle in regard to the Common Market. . . . He said when the Russians act that way, you can't argue with it; at least they are enemies. When the Europeans act that way, you have a case of allies destroying an alliance . . . He said that we cannot tolerate the deliberate organization of Europe into anti-U.S. roles. They will become a gigantic Sweden. They will undermine us all over the world. Things will go down the drain. There will be no public support for us. . . . He said we have got to shock the Europeans in some way, and take on the French. . . . The European split is a very dangerous thing and the French policy is stupid, as it has been historically.

On China:

Kissinger talked about Communist China being the best NATO ally we have. (I've used that line a couple of times.) They are desperate with regard to our situation in Europe. They are trying very hard to help us restore the balance in Europe . . . He said that during the alert, the Chinese Ambassador came to see him (Henry) and criticized him for the alert. Then when Henry saw Mao . . . he said, by the way, with regard to that alert, you don't need to consult with us. Any time you want to call an alert on the Russians, go right ahead and count on our support. Henry told him about the position the Ambassador took and Mao said, the trouble with him is he doesn't know the difference between form and substance, and four days later they recalled him. He hasn't been back yet. He said that the Chinese pulled out of the Persian Gulf at Kissinger's request. Kissinger was now sorry that he did it because the Soviets have gone in. They are obsessed by a fear of Soviet attack. . . . They want us out there. They have a great appreciation of the need for U.S. power. We let them know every time we move B-52s, and they worry every time when they leave. . . . He said don't mistake me about the Chinese. They would kill us if they got the chance, and they would pick up Japan if they thought they could get away with it, but right now they are so concerned with the Russians that they'll cooperate.

I finally got some licks in:

I [Zumwalt] think it is dangerous to be making military deals [in the way we do] with the Soviet Union [I was referring to SALT One] when we spend months and months debating the structure of our budget domestically and then overnight make a major decision for a major impact on the structure of our forces without adequate military dialogue. He said that you already have my assurance that there will be full and free discussion on this the next time. Then I said that the final point I would like to make is that there have been great tactical successes and I agree that it is too early to say that we have lost anything in the long haul, but I believe that it is also the case that we could lose a great deal in the long haul if we are not very careful about the nature of specific terms. Since we agree that essential equivalence is something that we need at the end of this road, when we start to talk about decoupling from it in a separate mode of agreement now, [i.e., when we start talking about extending the Interim Agreement under which the Soviets got numerical superiority] this could be something that lost us all our leverage . . . or that could be modestly helpful, depending on its specific nature. Again he gave us his reassurance. When it was all over, the Chiefs all felt that he had three times committed himself for full consultation now. I said I felt much better. Admiral Moorer said, don't turn your back, Bud. I think that is about right. But at least there were a lot of people in the room that heard him say it. It is going to be harder for him to go to Moscow and sell out again. . . . Schlesinger [said] that it is his judgment that Henry is not as hungry now about the need for the deal in '74, that the President will be criticized by the left and the right for having sold out just to avoid impeachment. On the other hand if they hunker down and stand aside, and détente begins to crumble, he will be criticized for that. So it seems to be Schlesinger's judgment that what Kissinger is really up to is to keep buggering it up and not have a deal. If that is the case, then we are not nearly as badly off as we thought we might be with regard to an eleventh hour decision. I think, myself, that it really depends on how much the Russians are offering. If it is enough that he thinks he can make it look good for the President, he might grab it.

During the last three months of my watch I was able to be, to my satisfaction, pretty much a lame duck as far as running the Navy was concerned. I had made a major effort to leave in good shape the budget for the fiscal year that began the day after my departure. I had made my last trip overseas on behalf of the alliance. Jimmy Holloway and Worth Bagley, whom Jimmy had chosen as his Vice Chief, were keeping in close touch (with Worth in London), and working up speed. Hence I was free to devote the major part of my attention to my duties as a member of the Joint Chiefs and as the principal naval advisor to the President. I did not intend to relinquish until the last moment an iota of whatever responsibility or authority those positions gave me in view of the way SALT was going and of the imminence of the Moscow summit.

To state my position bluntly, I did not think that a Government in the midst of a Constitutional crisis had any business negotiating a sensitive and momentous matter like arms limitation with a potential adversary. I did not think an agreement entered into by a President in danger of repudiation by the country would have much legitimacy. Moreover I knew, as everyone in the Government did, that Mr. Nixon was paying little heed to anything but the details of his personal struggle for survival and that therefore there was no one with Constitutional authority supervising Henry Kissinger's conduct of the negotiations. Both Kissinger's low opinion of the good sense and the resolve of the American people, and the obvious ego gratification he derived from engineering foreign-policy spectaculars made me distrust him absolutely as a negotiator with the Soviets.

On 24 April, at a cocktail party given by Under Secretary of State Kenneth Rush, I received dramatic confirmation that my distrust was well placed from no less an authority than Soviet Ambassador Anatoly Dobrynin. Dobrynin had never before paid more than perfunctory attention to me at any of the affairs we attended, so when he approached me rather effusively at this party and asked for my view of how SALT was going, I assumed he was under instruction to take soundings into the American military mind. It seemed an excellent opportunity to tell the Soviets things they were not likely to hear at the State Department or from members of the tightly reined SALT Delegation. I reconstruct here the conversation from notes I later jotted on a paper from my wallet.

I answered the Ambassador's opening question by telling him that I was concerned that the Soviets did not understand that over the long haul the American people would not accept strategic inferiority. I said that if the Soviet government really wanted détente as a continuing relationship, they must agree to U.S. strategic parity; otherwise public opinion would begin to question the entire concept of détente.

Dobrynin replied that my view was not the view of Dr. Kissinger —which was hardly news to me. He said that it was Dr. Kissinger's view that the American people would not make the sacrifices necessary to maintain parity.

I reminded him that the Jackson Amendment, passed by both houses of Congress in connection with the SALT One agreements had prescribed that the U.S. must insist on offensive parity in SALT Two.

The Ambassador said, "Frankly, we were elated at the results of

SALT One. It gave us the strategic advantage in central systems necessary to offset your Forward Based Systems, and it reserved for us the right to match you with regard to warheads in the future."

I said that I had supported the Interim Agreement, which froze numbers of missiles at existing numbers as necessary to stop an ongoing Soviet building program at a time when the U.S. was not building. However, I said, the freeze was an "interim," a short-term one, that for five years froze the Soviet numerical advantage in missiles and throw-weight and megatonnage without freezing the U.S. qualitative advantage in MIRV technology. When the Soviets had narrowed that technological gap, as they were almost bound to do in five years time, the American people would no longer tolerate the great Soviet advantages in the other offensive categories. I said that Presidential election campaigns would be conducted on this basis and that ultimately, if the Soviets did not agree to parity, a heightened arms race would almost surely occur.

The Ambassador replied, "You must recognize that we consider that the numerical advantages we have been given represent relationships that must be carried forward into the future." On that unpromising note we ended the chat.

By this time my staff was supplying me with a running analysis of the developments in SALT on a day-to-day basis, relying on the inter-agency documents that circulated incessantly; and Bill Cockell continued to provide me with his incisive commentary on Soviet objectives, together with his always wise observations on our own positions. In addition, I had frequent consultations with Paul Nitze, the Secretary of Defense's representative on the SALT delegation, and with the head of Secretary Schlesinger's SALT Task Force, Fred Wikner. Fred had been General Abrams' Scientific Advisor in Vietnam and we had become friends there. We all saw a clear pattern forming. The Soviets were testing the precise extent of the White House's eagerness to sign an agreement in June by offering a series of proposals that only an extraordinarily eager White House would consider. Their most brazen package was a four-point one they presented to Henry Kissinger in Moscow in late March 1974. Its least objectionable point was amending the ABM treaty to limit ABMs on each side to one site instead of two, and even that was advantageous to the Soviets in view of their marked inferiority in ABM technology. The other three points were grossly unacceptable.

One was extending the Interim Agreement on offensive weapons for three years, until 1980, which would give additional sanction to the inequality in numbers of missiles, and make parity that much farther away in time and that much harder to attain at all.

A second was freezing the number of MIRVed missiles at 1000, with no reference to the throw-weight or megatonnage of those missiles, which would perpetuate the Soviet advantage in those areas and wipe out the U.S. advantage in MIRV technology. To accept either of those points, or any close variant of them, would clearly violate the spirit of the Jackson Amendment, though perhaps accepting them in the context of an "interim" rather than a "permanent" agreement would duplicitously preserve the Amendment's letter.

The final Soviet point was to "denuclearize the Mediterranean." That was not only a backdoor attempt to get Forward-Based Systems into the talks, but a bid for Soviet nuclear monopoly in the Mediterranean, since it proposed stripping of their nuclear weapons Sixth Fleet carriers, land-based U.S. aircraft, and Polaris submarines of the strategic forces while leaving planes based on the Soviet Union, within easy reach of the area, unaffected.

On the evening of 15 April Secretary Schlesinger met with Bill Clements, Paul Nitze, and others to discuss a Defense response to a National Security Council directive to "study" these proposals. The substance of the meeting was reported to me and I will quote my notes of Schlesinger's comments since they recall in both tone and substance the almost unanimous consternation in Defense about the way Kissinger was handling SALT.

> Letting the Soviets have 1000 MIRVed missiles does us no good. It's a facade and a farce, with no beneficial effects for us, even by Kissinger's own criteria. . . . The JCS are jumpy about an agreement that would provide for two million pounds of MIRVed throw-weight. Now Kissinger is talking about six million. . . . Kissinger is simply following what the Soviets want. If that's what we're going to do why go through the sham of negotiating. Just find out what their terms are and sign up. . . . The President may or may not be impeached. The Soviets are going to wait for the outcome. We tried out some ideas related to a permanent agreement several months back. It proved too difficult diplomatically. So we tried for an add-on to the Interim Agreement, and the Soviets didn't like our proposal there. I would have expected Kissinger to sense that the chill factor was so great the best thing for us to do would be for us to fall back and regroup for several months. What he is asking us to consider now is preposterous. At this rate we will soon be looking back with nostalgia at the bad deals of yesteryear. . . . Kissinger is at a point

where he can be boxed in by what he said before, no matter what he says now. We may be better off if we let the Interim Agreement run out and then get up and leave. To accede to the Soviets now would simply give them further expectations. The Soviets have come up with a preposterous position. We cannot let Kissinger box us in on this. He cannot say the Interim Agreement was ill advised because he was the author of it. . . . The proposed agreement is of no value to us. The President could not forward it to Congress. Even as twisty as Kissinger is, I do not see how he could rationalize it. I would have no problem going to the Senate and saying, "This agreement contains no military elements—it is a purely political document, therefore you should talk to State." People criticize the military mind but I must say I have difficulty sometimes fathoming the political mind. To have Kissinger say we would be worse off without an agreement is the political equivalent of the military "worst case." We don't serve the President by serving him up this garbage . . . Kissinger has lost his mind. He's advocating things now he rejected before. The Soviets have said in effect they don't want to give us either a permanent or a reasonable new interim agreement. The whole thing is just a fantasy. Take Kissinger's own ground rules—just as an intellectual experiment—and look at the consequences of no agreement. With the kind of agreement he's talking about the Soviets would do no less than they would without an agreement. This is like playing tic-tac-toe with a six-year-old. You always lose or draw. . . . The best approach [for Defense] is with tongue in cheek. We should play along with the game with a sarcastic smile on our face and a good sense of country humor.

The only thoughts I disagreed with were the last two. I thought playing along was too risky, even if we smiled as sarcastically as all get out. I thought the most intense resistance possible was the appropriate tactic, with the object of getting the talks deadlocked or postponed or adjourned until the U.S. Government was in a condition to talk rationally. Of course one could talk about "playing along" in the sense that it was not possible to mention Presidential impotence or Kissinger egomania in so many words. It was necessary to stick to the forms, to construct and marshal the elaborate arguments about MIRVs and Throw Weight and Forward Based Systems and Threshold Test Bans and Denuclearization and all the other elements of an agreement that would have been the substance of discussion within the Government if responsible men had been conducting the talks for the United States. Under the weird circumstances that prevailed, those arguments were pretty much a cover. The substance was, "Stop the Talks! We Want To Get Off!"

Since the propriety of conducting the exercise at all rather than the details of its conduct was the question at the heart of SALT that spring, perhaps the best way to illuminate the scene as it developed is to recount how first Paul Nitze, then I, then Henry Jackson engaged in activity that would have been untoward in most imaginable situations but in that situation was entirely justified.

Our actions were brought about by the way Henry Kissinger managed the National Security Council and its offspring, the Verification Panel, during this period of Presidential paralysis. He gave the Defense people who sat on those bodies as little opportunity as possible to state their opinions. Defense papers containing worthwhile ideas crossed the Potomac only to sink without a trace into the depths of Kissinger's apparatus. During the spring of 1974 some papers, including a dozen or more Joint Chiefs of Staff Memorandums (JCSMs) that carefully stated the military's position about various aspects of arms limitation, never even got across the river but remained in Jim Schlesinger's office. I am not sure whether Jim held back such papers because he judged that forwarding them would do more harm than good or because Henry Kissinger or Al Haig had intimidated him by more or less subtly hinting that his job was on the line. In either case, Jim did not put forward the Department's ideas, or his own, as aggressively as I thought he should.

Paul Nitze had about reached the end of his rope after five years as the Secretary of Defense's representative on the SALT negotiating team. No one knew better than Paul the way Henry Kissinger and his apparatus filtered all communications to the President so that, on the whole, Mr. Nixon only saw and heard what Kissinger wanted him to see and hear. For many months Paul had been casting about for a way to make the President aware of the disaster Kissinger was cooking up for America in Moscow. For a period of six weeks or more, beginning in April, he had spent much time on the careful drafting of a letter to the President he hoped Jim Schlesinger would sign and deliver. Knowing what we all now know about Richard Nixon, it is obvious that writing him letters was not likely to do anything but enrage him. But even as late as the spring of 1974, a few months before the end, it still seemed incredible to a veteran policy maker like Nitze that the most probable result of offering the President of the United States, in the most respectful language, a piece of thoughtful advice, would be that the author would be added to an ever growing enemies' list. Doubtless Schlesinger's perception of this extraordinary condition was one of the reasons he sat on so many papers intended for the White House. What Schlesinger did not realize was that, short of abject sycophancy, there was no way of staying off the enemies' list. Jim told me often that he was pretty much on it, too, during those last months, and that Kissinger certainly would have had him fired if he dared to.

Around the middle of May Paul finally had the letter in a shape that satisfied him and showed it, or arranged to have it shown, to various people: his boss, Jim Schlesinger, the Chiefs, Henry Kissinger, Alexander Haig, Helmut Sonnenfeldt. The Chiefs were so impressed with it that, at my suggestion, we took the unusual step of formally associating ourselves with it in a Joint Chiefs of Staff Memorandum to the Secretary of Defense. However Schlesinger would not forward the letter or the JCSM to the White House, and Kissinger, Haig, Sonnenfeldt, et al., were of no greater help. The prospects for Moscow were looking dimmer and dimmer. On 28 May Paul wrote a polite and noncommittal letter of resignation to the President, effective 31 May, coupling this with a full explanation to Jim Schlesinger of his reasons. Paul waited two weeks for an acknowledgement of his letter of resignation. He received none. Evidently the White House had decided that, in view of Paul's immense prestige in the informed circles of the U.S. and Europe, he must be kept on the team until the Moscow summit was over and that the best way to deal with his resignation, therefore, was to pretend there was no such thing. On 14 June Paul sent another letter to the President, which contained one sentence: "My request of May 28th to resign not having being accepted, I now feel compelled unilaterally to terminate my appointment effective today."

For Nitze, the finest flower of his generation in public service, a quiet, brilliant, deeply patriotic, and sensitive man, that was the equivalent of anyone else getting red in the face, pounding the table and screaming at the top of his lungs. The same day he sent that letter, Paul put out a press release that said what he had to say and left town. That press release is my favorite SALT document:

It was almost twenty-nine years ago that I supervised the on-site investigation of the effects of the atomic weapons dropped on Hiroshima and Nagasaki. Since that time much of my thought and endeavor has been directed to the twin goals of preserving the general security of the United States while lowering the risks of nuclear war.

For the last five years I have devoted all my energies to supporting the objectives of negotiating SALT agreements which would be balanced and which would enhance the security of the United States, and also of the Soviet Union, by maintaining crisis stability and providing a basis for lessening the strategic arms competition between them. Under the circumstances existing at the present time, however, I see little prospect of negotiating measures which will enhance movement toward those objectives.

Arms control policy is integral to the national security and foreign policy of this nation and they, in turn, are closely intertwined with domestic affairs. In my view, it would be illusory to attempt to ignore or wish away the depressing reality of the traumatic events now unfolding in our nation's capital and of the implications of those events in the international arena.

Until the Office of the Presidency has been restored to its principal function of upholding the Constitution and taking care of the fair execution of the laws and thus be able to function effectively at home and abroad, I see no real prospect for reversing certain unfortunate trends in the evolving situation. Time is now of the essence in establishing the preconditions for such a regeneration.

In the meantime, it is essential that the orderly process of government continue. It is the genius of the United States form of government that it has the flexibility to compensate for individual deficiencies. All those who are continuing to maintain the orderly process of government despite the tensions between their loyalty to higher authority and their loyalty to their oath of office have my full sympathy and admiration. I regret that that tension has now become too great for me to continue in office with them. As a private citizen I shall support them to the best of my ability.

My last month as a sailor was not at all what I had wanted or expected it to be. Instead of steaming serenely toward the horizon amid a chorus of "Well dones," I found myself awash in controversy and the target of recriminations that were not only acrimonious but personal. My mood was not mellow, as it should have been, but instead, a combination of gloom and impatience. The regret I could not help feeling at leaving the Navy was curdled by my relief at soon being out from under a wrecked President and an unprincipled Secretary of State. I was frustrated by having almost no time left to do all the things that needed doing for the Navy and the country. At the same time, for the first time in my life I felt—and it was a strange and unhappy feeling—that I could better serve both outside the government than inside.

After I had rejected his offer to seek a two-year extension of my term as CNO, Jim Schlesinger had offered me the choice of any four-star job I wanted if I changed my mind about retiring. Al Haig had offered me the job of Administrator of the Veterans Administration. My memorandum of conversation of that meeting on 21 May will not be as exact as Al Haig's tape of it but it is an accurate summary:

1. General Haig opened up with the following:

a. He regretted that it was just not in the cards for the Navy to keep the chairmanship of the Joint Chiefs, because he considered me to be the most qualified candidate. [The reader will join me in recognizing this as window dressing.]

b. He was quite interested in me considering a tough dirty job that badly needed doing—Director of the Veterans Administration.

c. This job would have to be done with no additional financing available, with recognition that there were many conflicting political lobbies, but with the recognition that the South Vietnam war veterans would be increasingly powerful as one approaches 1976.

d. He considered that one of the pitfalls would be that there would be a temptation of any director to get in bed with the veterans and take on the President, and that what was needed, therefore, was a military man who would remain loyal to the President and withstand the veterans' clamors for better treatment.

I had turned both offers down. I wanted to be free to say how perilous I thought the course was that Henry Kissinger had set for America. Even more important I wanted to do what I could to involve the American people in the sober consideration of national security from which the Nixon administration had systematically excluded them.

The first sour note of June should have been its sweetest one. On the 5th the President and Mrs. Nixon and Al Haig attended the graduation at Annapolis. For me it was a particularly sentimental occasion, as I noted in the very brief remarks I made before I introduced the President. In the three minutes allotted me I made six points, if I may include as a point the reference to long hair in the salutation—a funny that amused the midshipmen, who knew that those among them who had just been sworn in as Marines would promptly have to get shorter haircuts.

I give the speech here, not because it is a major public document but because the reader needs it to judge the President's reaction to it.

> Mr. President, Mrs. Nixon, Distinguished Guests, families of the Midshipmen, members of the United States Naval Academy, and that fraction of the Class of 1974 which will be permitted to wear long hair:
>
> This is a sentimental moment for me. This class and I began a four-year watch together. You here at the Naval Academy and I in Washington. And Mr. President, I think you would agree with me that they have certainly demonstrated today that there is nothing inconsistent with duty, honor, country, and having fun and zest.
>
> This is a sentimental moment because there is here today on this stage with me Admiral Chon, the Chief of Naval Operations of the gallant Navy of South Vietnam, who you have seen just commission his son, and with whom I fought in South Vietnam in support of that country's efforts to survive the onslaught of the Communist north. A great and dignified leader.
>
> And it is a sentimental moment because there is in this class the beginning of a wave which gets blacker and blacker as one goes down in classes which means that by 1976, 131 years after this great institution was built and 200 years after our nation was formed, this Naval Academy will be truly representative of the Nation at large.
>
> Mr. President, this is the class which has had the watch as those barebones defense budgets which you have submitted to the Congress, described as such by you, have been cut; as the great democratic institution, the Congress, compromised between those who would support you and those who would reduce still more, and over its four year history, this class observed defense budget cuts of two billion, three billion, five billion, and three and a half billion. And as a result, you and I have had to see this Navy reduced from 976 ships to the lowest figure since 1939, 508. But this is a class which also knows that thanks to your modernization program, if it is supported by the Congress, this U.S. Navy will begin to increase its size in the years ahead and can again regain its proper role.
>
> It is with great pride that I introduce to you Mr. President, the Midshipmen about to become Ensigns; and to this class a former naval person, your Commander in Chief, the President of the United States.

My notes show that the next day, at the end of a private meeting with Jim Schlesinger, he said to me,

> You are in the dog house again—the President is very displeased with your remarks at the Naval Academy—[it came] from Haig but it was

from the President—you commented on the fact that you were talking to that fraction of the class—which didn't have to get haircuts—on how happy you were to see the increasing wave of blackness in the descending order of year groups. And you commented on the fact that the President's defense budgets had been bare-bones budgets.

As I was suggesting to Jim that I try to recreate my words at Annapolis for him he interrupted to say, "Bud, you don't have to do that. They are so paranoid over there that it is just unbelievable." Later that same day Jim was called over to the White House to be "chewed out" about his department being out of control, so it is safe to assume that I shared the spotlight in his private meeting with the President. Sixteen days later the President was still fuming about the Annapolis speech. At a meeting of the National Security Council he said that I had taken "a cheap shot" at him for ruining the Navy. I have already made clear in these pages that as far as being in or out of favor with the front office went, serving the Nixon Administration was like riding a roller coaster blindfolded. From 5 June 1974 on, it was sickeningly downhill all the way.

TTB was the issue that next forced me to take a position that antagonized my Commander in Chief. TTB stands for Threshold Test Ban, which was something the Russians had proposed only a few weeks before for inclusion in the agreement that presumably would be reached in Moscow. The gist of the proposal was that there should be an upper limit—a "threshold"—on the size of the nuclear devices each side tested. It was a plausible idea that the Soviets doubtless calculated would be unobjectionable to the American public and easy to get through Congress. Certainly it was easy to get through Henry Kissinger, who apparently was more concerned with its political appeal than with its military one-sidedness. For there was a big catch in the proposal: the Soviets, with dozens of super-missiles deployed, already had tested the big warheads whose testing the TTB would forbid, while the United States, not having built missiles of the size of the Soviet giants, had not. Indeed, the U.S. had not yet tested warheads of the yield of those we were planning to install in the Trident submarine's second-generation missiles and, on later versions of Minuteman, systems already in the works.

In short the Soviet proposal, like most Soviet SALT proposals, aimed to freeze Soviet superiority. In what I write about TTB I purposely bypass the complicated details about seismic levels and Richter scales and kiloton yield and the comparative geological char-

acteristics of Nevada and Siberia that TTB experts discussed end-
lessly and that would have been important if the discussions had been
on the up and up.

The Verification Panel met on TTB on 4 June. At the meeting
Henry Kissinger railed against the military for its skepticism about
Soviet intentions and implied that it was to the credit of the Soviets
that they had found a relatively uncontroversial matter that it would
benefit both sides to resolve. The meeting made no recommendations. Kissinger meetings seldom did. Presumably the Panel was to
meet again in a few days to resume its discussions. On the evening
of Friday 7 June Bill Clements, Tom Moorer, for the Joint Chiefs,
and Chairwoman Dixy Lee Ray of the Atomic Energy Commission
signed a joint position paper that took a hard line on TTB, and
passed it to Secretary Schlesinger for transmission to the White
House. Schlesinger held it, saying that he did not want to "add to
the tensions." It did ultimately go to the members of the Verification
Panel which included Kissinger, of course. At the same time the
Arms Control and Disarmament Agency produced a soft-line position paper on TTB, which whether or not by his design, gave Kissinger the opportunity to "compromise." A Verification Panel meeting had been scheduled for the weekend but was called off. On 7 June
Kissinger, referring only to his own SALT proposals, which the
military thought gave away too much U.S. security, and disregarding
JCS support of various Nitze and Schlesinger proposals, said to Tom
Moorer, "Why are the JCS opposing *every* SALT negotiation initiative?" On 10 June, in a manner reminiscent of the way Option Echo,
almost four years before, and the SLBM numbers, more than two
years before, had arrived as if from outer space, and despite his
personal pledge given to the JCS in the Tank on 11 March, NSDM
256 materialized. We first learned of it when a cable from Moscow,
where a team of American experts was discussing TTB with a team
of Russian experts, reported that the Russians were talking knowl-
edgeably to the Americans of a new American approach to TTB that
the Americans had not yet heard of. The NSDM itself did not
circulate in Washington until the next day, 11 June. In short, the
Russians learned what was in NSDM 256 before the Joint Chiefs did,
which no one could believe was accidental since its contents were
entirely unacceptable to the Chiefs.

Tom Moorer was out of town that week and I was acting CJCS.
At an executive session in the Tank on Monday 10 June, before
NSDM 256's existence was known to us, I had taken advantage of

being in the chair to warn my colleagues of the false position they might find themselves in after the Moscow summit, using the AC-DA's soft paper on TTB as an example of what they might be asked to defend before Congress. An excerpt from my debrief of that meeting to my morning lineup:

> I pointed out to the Chiefs . . . that Henry had slipped the departure for Moscow until the 26th so that by the time [the Presidential party] had come back . . . Moorer, Zumwalt, Nitze and Wikner would be gone and [the Chiefs] would be going through the same thing that the Chiefs had gone through at SALT One. I described how the others had all gone over [to the Jackson hearings] while I was in Europe and had gotten pretty badly whiplashed. I had been given that word and studied in the plane on the way back and was able to do a little better only because I had the good fortune not to be with them at the outset. George Brown [the CJCS Designate] suggested that everybody get out the old hearings and read them . . . As we walked out he came alongside me and said, "Bud, if you decide to start going public on these things when you get out, I would appreciate it if you let me know." Wikner had told Brown that the President ought to be concerned about the views of Moorer and Zumwalt because they would be free agents when they got out.

When I learned about NSDM 256, I concluded that the JCS could not, if duty and law meant anything, accept that Kissingerian high-handedness passively. I immediately set in motion within both the Joint Staff and my own staff machinery to produce a JCSM protesting vigorously to the President about not being consulted in the drafting of the NSDM and requesting that he reconsider its provisions. Bureaucratically—but not Constitutionally—it was a pretty strong action to propose, but then the situation within the Government was not what one would call ordinary. There was no assurance, even, that the President had been consulted about the NSDM's contents or, if he had been consulted, that he had been able to focus his mind on it. All the Services thought it was important to try to get the President to amend the NSDM. However there was the usual wrangling over details, first among the OpDeps, then among the Chiefs. The wrangling's substance was of a familiar kind, too. Most of it was not over whether this or that paragraph was or was not true, but over whether it was or was not "counterproductive."

I particularly wanted to include a statement that there was "no military rationale" for a TTB. The Army and the Air Force particularly felt that that statement was counterproductive. I had the votes.

The Marines went along with the Navy and I, as acting Chairman, was the tiebreaker. However, the spirit of compromise prevailed, and I relinquished my "no military rationale" in order to keep some other strong expressions that made the Army and the Air Force nervous. Even I agreed that complaining about the way the NSDM had been drafted might be counterproductive if our purpose was not to make a record but to change the President's mind—or call the matter to his attention, as the case might be. We decided to make that point orally to Jim Schlesinger, through whom the paper would have to go in any case; we tried to hedge as best we could against his failing to forward it by "requesting" instead of "recommending" that he do so. There was some discussion about whether the memorandum should be from the Secretary of Defense rather than from the Joint Chiefs, but we ended by agreeing that its chances of getting across the river would be better if the Chairman's name rather than the Secretary's was signed to it and so in Admiral Moorer's absence, I signed it. (Jim Schlesinger later asked Tom Moorer to resubmit this paper over his signature as the Zumwalt signature would raise the Presidential hackles too high.) That was on Thursday 13 June. When I returned to my office my executive assistant told me that Schlesinger's executive assistant had called to say that Jim would not speak at the ceremony at which I turned my command over to Admiral Holloway. I later learned that that decision by Schlesinger had been pursuant to an order by Al Haig. Jim was also ordered not to award the already approved Department of Defense Distinguished Medal at my retirement ceremony. Mickey Mouse is not peculiar to the Navy.

Knowing I had done all I could do to persuade the Chiefs to adopt for the record a hard collective position about what I feared was going to happen in Moscow, but feeling strongly that it was not enough, I spent the weekend drafting a long personal letter to the President, in my statutory capacity as his Principal Naval Advisor. First thing in the morning on Monday 17 June I had six copies made besides the ones for the files. The original would have to go (or not go) to the White House through the prescribed channel, the office of the Secretary of Defense. There was a copy each for the Secretary of the Navy and my four colleagues on the Joint Chiefs. The remaining copy was an advance copy to go directly to the President. I wanted no hold by Jim Schlesinger. There was a meeting on SALT that day in the Tank, with Schlesinger in attendance. I signed the letter before I went to the meeting because I wanted to tell my

colleagues what I had done, not ask them whether I should do it. The
letter was long. It was also the most important letter I ever wrote,
so I shall reproduce it here in full.

MEMORANDUM for the PRESIDENT of the UNITED STATES

Via: The Secretary of Defense

Subj: Strategic Arms Limitations

I believe, as I know you do, that there is no subject of greater importance than SALT to the country's long term security—both in
terms of preserving the peace, and in terms of the impact which its
outcome will have on the perceptions of others, and on the outlook
and international behavior of the U.S. and the USSR. For these reasons, there is no subject which is more worthy of our closest and
most careful attention.

I believe that fact, combined with the circumstance of my impending
departure from the office of Chief of Naval Operations and your forthcoming summit meeting, imposes on me a special obligation—pursuant
to my statutory responsibilities as your naval advisor—to provide you
with my military judgment on the current state of the Strategic Arms
Limitation Talks.

I have found similar exchange of views with the JCS and the Secretary
of Defense to have resulted in useful insights in the past, and would have
preferred that more time were available for such exchange on this occasion. However, I have been advised that I will be called to testify before
the Arms Control Subcommittee of the Senate Armed Forces Committee
next Wednesday, June 19, on the matter, and judge it important therefore to place these views before you at this time.

I have been following the course of SALT Two with a special sense
of responsibility, since I was a member of the Joint Chiefs of Staff which
approved the SALT One agreements, on the basis of certain assumptions
and assurances relating both to U.S. programs and to the planned course
of follow-on offensive arms negotiations.

You recall that the considerations which influenced the JCS on that
occasion included the fact that the Interim Agreement placed a limit on
the potential scope of ongoing Soviet deployments, and that it was of
limited duration, to be superseded within five years by a permanent
agreement providing for equivalents in strategic capabilities. The existing
U.S. superiority in MIRV technology was deemed sufficient *temporarily*
to offset Soviet superiority in the number and throw-weight of Soviet
missile systems during the anticipated limited duration of the Interim
Agreement.

At the same time, it was recognized that the Soviets would make a maximum effort in all areas not limited by the agreement—a fact which Secretary Brezhnev emphasized to you.

It was equally recognized that a steady shift in the strategic balance to Soviet advantage would be inevitable under these circumstances unless the U.S. resumed improvement of its own strategic capabilities, while simultaneously pursuing the goal of a permanent agreement that provided for true strategic equivalence. I think it is important to keep in mind that these two objectives were interrelated, in the sense that without improvement of U.S. capabilities the Soviets would have little incentive to come to an equitable permanent agreement.

In summary, through the SALT One agreements we knowingly set in motion events which, over time, had the potential to shift the strategic balance to our disadvantage. The underlying assumptions which made this situation tolerable were that it represented a temporary phenomenon; and that we would move steadily during the next five years to a situation of agreed equivalence in strategic capabilities.

We are almost halfway through that period now, with relatively little progress toward the basic goal. In the meantime, the strategic balance, as foreseen, has continued to shift to our disadvantage.

Since signing the Interim agreement, the Soviets have proceeded rapidly to develop and test new systems, including four new MIRVed ICBMs which represent not only advances in technology but are significantly heavier than those they will replace; the new DELTA class submarine (eight already afloat, twenty-eight estimated by 1977) with its associated missile, the range of which is roughly equivalent to our planned TRIDENT missile (which will not be operational until 1978 even if the TTB permits testing to be completed); and the BACKFIRE bomber.

In this situation, time is clearly on the Soviets' side. Each day shifts the balance further to their advantage. Since the Soviets see important political gains to be reaped from strategic superiority, they can be expected to be reluctant to yield this advantage. This has been borne out by the results of SALT Two to date. The Soviets have shown almost total intransigence, and have yielded on few points in controversy. While the Soviet position has remained essentially constant, our own has moved steadily toward theirs as we have accommodated our stance in the hope of gaining an agreement.

The reasonable conclusion to be drawn from the Soviets' behavior thus far is that they are not now disposed to negotiate a comprehensive permanent agreement on terms compatible with the national security of the United States.

As a result of that Soviet behavior, recent U.S. negotiating effort has been directed toward exploring the possibility of a more limited agreement which would place some limits on the MIRV deployments of both sides, coupled with an extension of the Interim Agreement.

I believe strongly that such agreement would be contrary to U.S. interests, for several reasons:

—It would perpetuate and give an appearance of treaty-like permanence to the numerical imbalances of the Interim Agreement. By so doing, it would lend weight to the Soviets' argument that they are entitled to the quantitative advantages of the Interim Agreement in perpetuity and could defeat our arms control objective of achieving essential equivalence by encouraging already evident Soviet effort to gain a significant margin of strategic superiority.

—It would represent a deviation from the principle which made the Interim Agreement acceptable from the standpoint of U.S. security interests; i.e., that the parties would proceed directly therefrom to negotiate a permanent agreement providing for essential equivalence within a five year period.

—It would pose very serious verification risks.

And, finally, in both my judgment and that of my colleagues in the Joint Chiefs of Staff, there is no significant strategic or military rationale for such agreement.

All the analyses I have seen confirm my judgment that none of the separate MIRV agreements currently under consideration in the interagency arena is consistent with the preservation of U.S. security.

Under these circumstances, I see only two general alternatives for assuring essential equivalence. One is for the Soviets to accept in good faith the premise of the Interim Agreement—reemphasized in the 1973 "Basic Principles" for further SALT negotiations—that both sides' objective is prompt negotiation of a permanent treaty which avoids unilateral advantage. The other is for the United States to undertake now to attain in the long term and maintain a posture of strategic equivalence without extending the Interim Agreement or adding to the unequal restraints now imposed by it.

My experience as a close observer of SALT Two has led me to the conclusion that a satisfactory permanent agreement is unlikely to result unless the United States brings to bear all the negotiating leverage it can muster. Specifically, this requires taking SALT out of the narrow context of arms control negotiations and putting it in the broader framework of the entire détente relationship between the U.S. and USSR. This would require that the United States make clear to the Soviets that détente cannot survive without a stable military equilibrium, and that essentially equivalent strategic forces are the foundation of such equilibrium. Implicit in this is the proposition that prompt Soviet movement toward an equitable permanent agreement is necessary to establish the good faith of their long-term intentions.

At the same time, we should make clear to the Soviets that their failure to demonstrate good faith will inevitably jeopardize those tangible benefits which they are seeking from the détente relationship (e.g., trade, advanced industrial technology); and place on them the added economic burden of increased strategic arms competition with the United States.

In support of this broadened approach, I believe we should make absolutely clear to the Soviets that anything less than true equivalence is politically unacceptable in the United States. The U.S. public will not willingly accept a position of inferiority, with all the military risk and loss of international influence which that entails. The Soviets should be made to understand that their failure to agree to strategic equivalence will drive the U.S. in the direction of expanded strategic programs, which will inevitably destroy the atmosphere and domestic political support essential for a policy of détente.

In my judgment, failure of the United States to convey this fundamental fact to the Soviets runs the risk of producing both an unsatisfactory SALT outcome and the ultimate destruction of détente.

In approaching the Soviets, the U.S. should not be modest about what it is offering them. In the face of unquestioned U.S. economic and technological superiority, an offer of agreed, permanent strategic equality is no insignificant thing. We can legitimately represent this as a substantial concession in itself; as clear evidence of U.S. good faith concerning détente; and as something that requires a Soviet response in kind if détente is to remain viable.

For this to succeed, however, it is absolutely essential that we be totally forthright with the American public about the true state of affairs and what is required to attain an equitable agreement. If the public is accurately informed, I am confident it will appropriately respond. The signal we must convincingly convey to the Soviets is that the U.S. people will unhesitatingly support whatever programs are necessary to ensure that the Soviets do not gain permanent superiority in strategic capabilities.

At the same time, in all our behavior toward the Soviets we should consistently reflect the fact that attainment of an agreement providing for essential equivalance by 1977 remains our primary objective. We must make totally clear to the Soviets that we will not be deflected from that objective by excursions which essentially perpetuate the imbalances of the Interim Agreement (or worse, extend their life); or which ratify

Soviet gains in the area of our former technological advantage. Such excursions, especially when combined with an extension of the Interim Agreement, seriously jeopardize our prospects of ever attaining an equitable comprehensive agreement and, by actually encouraging Soviet efforts to gain permanent strategic superiority, pose grave risk to our national security.

Finally, we must clearly communicate to the Soviets our belief that their own interests are best served by prompt movement toward a permanent agreement which will remove strategic weaponry from the list of tension-producing issues between the two countries, and create the strategic balance which is essential for a true détente.

In conclusion, I would like to touch on two related matters in the arms control area.

The first is the U.S. position on the Threshold Test Ban Treaty reflected in NSDM 256. Though advice of the Joint Chiefs of Staff was not sought on the impact which that NSDM would have on our security, they have subsequently forwarded to you their collective views on the subject. I would like simply to add emphasis to those views by stating my own judgment that there is no supportable strategic or military rationale for the proposed treaty; and that the current U.S. position, as reflected in the NSDM, runs the risk both of undercutting U.S. leverage in the SALT negotiations, and of imperiling U.S. security by precluding or seriously inhibiting the development of weapons systems essential for force modernization and the support of national nuclear weapons strategy. The impact on the TRIDENT II weapons system will be particularly severe and, given the increasing vulnerability of land-based systems, restricting our ability to deploy modernized systems at sea could have especially serious consequences in the future.

We know that the Soviets have already completed most of the warhead test program for their next generation of strategic missiles. The United States, on the other hand, still has a number of tests scheduled for accomplishment over the next several years in support of its own strategic force modernization program. Most of these key test programs would be precluded or severely curtailed by the NSDM standards. In this connection, I think it is worthy of note that the TTB proposal was reportedly a Soviet initiative, for it is clear how the combination of the Interim Agreement's numerical asymmetries, the vigorous Soviet programs for development and deployment of new MIRVed systems, and now the proposed TTB all interact to accelerate the shift in the strategic balance to Soviet advantage.

The second point relates to the procedures used to develop U.S. negotiating positions in the strategic arms limitation area.

I have been impressed throughout both SALT One and SALT Two by the fact that the Soviets obviously have a well-thought-out negotiating strategy. I have been equally impressed by the lack of adequate procedures on our side to ensure that the U.S. position stems from a clear articulation of basic U.S. objectives, and that specific negotiating positions are developed in a carefully coordinated manner to support those objectives. Additionally, I think it essential that our procedures ensure that you receive in clear and undiluted fashion the judgments of both your political and your military advisers before reaching key decisions on U.S. positions. From my observation, the system as presently operated fails to assure you of such balance in the consideration of major SALT issues, hence runs the risk that positions potentially detrimental to the country's long-term security may be adopted. To rectify this situation, I would recommend strongly that you periodically confer directly with the Secretary of Defense and the Joint Chiefs of Staff and solicit their advice on these subjects of such far-reaching national importance.

I offer you these views, Mr. President, knowing that we share a deep interest in ensuring the country's future security in a world that hopefully will be characterized by reduced tensions among the major powers. My judgments stem from thirty-six years of military service, culminated by four years as a member of the Joint Chiefs of Staff, and from my deep conviction that there is no subject more important to the country's future than the successful management of the Strategic Arms Limitation Talks.

I hope these views will be useful to you.

E. R. ZUMWALT, JR.

Advance Copy to:
The President of the United States

Copy to:
The Secretary of the Navy
The Chairman, Joint Chiefs of Staff
The Chief of Staff of the Army
The Chief of Staff of the Air Force
The Commandant of the Marine Corps

That same Monday Scoop Jackson got into the act, bless him. He had become alarmed by the information he was receiving about how positions for the Moscow summit were being prepared. He summoned the Pentagon's top people, civilian and military, to closed hearings before his Subcommittee on Arms Control on Wednesday 19 June. What he wanted to inquire into was whether and to what extent the Defense establishment was being consulted about SALT. For an experienced and responsible senior Senator, on the eve of delicate international negotiations involving matters of war or peace not to say life or death, to pry into differences over national security within the executive branch was if anything more extraordinary than Paul Nitze's resignation at a delicate time, or Secretary Schlesinger's intimation that he lacked confidence in his Commander in Chief.

I was delighted with Senator Jackson for doing it. I judged that if anything would restrain the pilgrims to Moscow, it would be a written record in the files of the Senate Armed Services Committee —the parent body of Scoop's subcommittee—that suggested, without even spelling it out, that the Administration had failed to elicit in some cases, and to heed in others, the advice of those professional advisors whom the law bade it consult and listen to carefully. Scoop got his record that Tuesday. The Chiefs, who testified in the afternoon after the civilians had gone on in the morning, punctiliously volunteered no information, but the questions he and his colleagues asked were acute enough for our answers to make it clear that Kissinger saw to it that discussions in the National Security Council and its offshoots often were perfunctory, particularly when the military disagreed with him; that often JCSMs did not reach the President; and about the only chance any of the Chiefs other than the Chairman got to speak face to face with the President was at the annual budget meeting. Since not only Scoop was there but, for various lengths of time, Senators Stennis, Symington, Thurmond, Tower, Taft, Nunn, and Byrd of Virginia, I felt that a significant portion of the Senate had now been warned against the possibility of hanky-panky in Moscow.

The day after the Jackson hearings, Thursday 20 June, the National Security Council had its last meeting before the President, Kissinger, Haig, et al., left for Moscow. In debriefing the meeting afterward, Tom Moorer described it as "blah." Evidently the one exception was Jim Schlesinger's presentation of Defense's position on TTB, ABM and the MIRV option, which was full and strong, though it elicited little response from the other participants. Schlesinger, I should explain, tried manfully to get Administration acceptance of U.S. superiority in numbers of MIRVed missiles in order to compensate for Soviet superiority in megatonnage and throw-weight. Kissinger, as the Vladivostok agreement was to demonstrate later, was willing to perpetuate that Soviet superiority by granting equality in numbers of MIRVed missiles. On the morning of Monday 24

June, right after line-up, I met privately with Jimmy Holloway and
Worth Bagley. I briefed them from my notes. That conversation—
or more accurately, Zumwalt soliloquy—not only relates some of the
principal happenings at the NSC meeting, but provides background
for those happenings and gives a clear idea of how I was feeling on
my last Monday on the job:

Jim Schlesinger . . . told me that he had gotten his "ass chewed out
several times by Kissinger and Haig" and finally, early in the week before
I sent the letter, the President had sent for him and accused him of
disloyalty and not keeping the Pentagon in line and so forth. So it was
clear that he was going to have to come in with some kind of interim
MIRV. He began to talk about it both in his staff meetings and in the
Tank. So I concluded over the weekend that I just wanted to be very sure
that I make a personal effort to get my views to the President. . . .
Meanwhile Jackson got concerned and got SD and JCS over there for
hearings on Wednesday of last week. Got Nitze in Thursday and put us
all under oath, first time he had ever done that. I am sure he will give
us a next round because he is really out to get the facts and he is really
fed up to the gills with Henry, which is clear to me from his comments.
He is going to swear in Henry if he shows up. As a result he caused the
Chairman to [say] that more than ten JCSMs had not gone over. He
asked each one of the Chiefs what recommendations he had made. I said
I had had three budget meetings, I said that I signed the JCSM [about
NSDM 256] as acting Chairman. That one was the most controversial
one because we sent that directly to the President since the other thirteen
hadn't gone to him. I delivered it to Schlesinger with a piece of paper
saying, "Please send this to the President." Schlesinger still hasn't delivered that one. Schlesinger sent for me Thursday morning. He was interested in what the hearings had consisted of, so I ran through [them] for
him. He was fairly relieved that we had all handled ourselves by walking
around it without volunteering anything. He then said, "You should be
aware that the President thinks that the JCS are all 'a bunch of shits' and
that you are 'the biggest shit of all.' " My impression was that Schlesinger thought it was good that we had taken a hard-line position. This
lets him take a slightly softer line and [puts him] in a position of being
able to say to the President, "These guys feel pretty strongly." I think
that is consistent with what happened at the NSC meeting Friday. In that
meeting Schlesinger outlined his interim MIRV position. Kissinger said
. . . "I've already tried that on Dobrynin and he won't buy." Admiral
Moorer was asked to comment and he said that the Chiefs preferred no
interim MIRV. They were overruled on that and the Chiefs, less Admiral
Zumwalt, went with Secretary Schlesinger's position. Admiral Moorer

told me Friday night that the President said . . . he is the damn guy that "took a cheap shot at me down at the Academy." . . . He ended up saying, after all I have to make the decisions, not Admiral Zumwalt. I got honorable mention three times in that meeting. However, privately Schlesinger had told me that the President is every bit as upset about Admiral Moorer and he sounded off about the fact that Tom Moorer is spying on him. So it seems to me that it doesn't make much difference whether you say what you think or not.

That same day the Chiefs met in the Tank with Jim Schlesinger. The transcript of my debrief of that meeting to my morning lineup covers five single-spaced pages. Reading it a year later reveals that the Tank that afternoon was not a council room but a decompression chamber. I hope I have been able to convey how concerned we all had been for a month or more. We spent that afternoon, having done for better or worse whatever was within our power, trying to reconstruct and run through what had happened. We exchanged Kissinger experiences, and you can be sure each one of us had more than enough. We rehashed what had happened in recent weeks. We assured and reassured each other that everything was going to come out all right. We transacted no business. There was no business left to transact. In two days the President would be off to Moscow. Perhaps I can compare us to a group of defendants waiting for a jury to bring in a verdict. All we could do was wait with whatever patience and phlegm we could summon up. In the event, we won. Despite Kissinger's importunities in Moscow, the President did not sign anything. It is to Mr. Nixon's credit that he did not sign, but I have no way of knowing what produced his unexpected firmness —whether Paul Nitze's resignation or my long letter had anything to do with it, whether Al Haig found, in a moment of national crisis, his professional conscience, whether the President himself was brought temporarily out of the miasma that enveloped him by his country's peril. In any case he flatly overruled Henry Kissinger's advice to accommodate to the Soviet positions, and we back in Washington were mightily relieved.

All that remains for me to tell, then, is how I almost was court-martialed or fired three days before my watch ended. Early in June I had accepted an invitation from Laurence Spivak to appear on his network television show, "Meet the Press," on Sunday 30 June, the last day of my watch. Excerpts from memoranda I dictated for the record pretty much tell the story. On 25 June I met with Jim Schlesinger.

SecDef stated that although he did not intend to order me not to, he urged me to consider withdrawing from "Meet The Press" or terminating my tenure as CNO before that time in order that I would not be an official DOD representative at that time. He stated that he did not expect me to remain muzzled after retirement but that I should be aware that I was *persona non grata* with the President and with Kissinger, that I could well be in serious difficulties. I asked him whether my assurance that I would not discuss SALT Two, previously given, was not sufficient. He stated that he thought that anything I had to say on any subject would come as an anathema to the President and Doctor Kissinger. He asked me how I had gotten so across the breakers with them. I stated that it all began when I gave my second presidential brief and insisted that we would lose the war, on the odds, if we didn't get bigger budgets, and that the final blow came when I opted not to be Kissinger's whore: he used to call me over for lunches the first two years and [I] debriefed the Chairman and SecDef or his executive assistant on those meetings. SecDef stated that Henry was telling the President and Haig and SecDef and perhaps others around town that I had come sucking around for the job as Chairman and had turned bitter when they did not offer. I reminded SecDef that he knew first hand that I had never put any pressure on him for the job. He stated that he was not concerned about the facts, just about the paranoia of two very sick people, the President and Kissinger. He said, frankly I am not sure my own tenure will last much longer. . . . He stated that he has already received one hint from the White House the President may retaliate by reducing the Defense budget, and that he clearly was capable of reducing the Navy budget in retaliation for anything I said on "Meet The Press."

At 1415 on 28 June, I met with Jim again:

SecDef and General Wickham [his executive assistant] were in the room. SecDef asked whether I had arranged to get off the "Meet The Press" program as I had agreed to do two days ago. I told him that I had not done so and reminded him that I had said two days ago that I would consult with my people and let him know if I foresaw any difficulties. SecDef agreed that that was accurate but said that he sensed that I was leaning in favor of coming off the program when I was with him last time and he gathered that now I was leaning against it. I stated that this was correct. He asked me why, in view of the fact that he had warned me that it would hurt the Defense Department, Navy and me. I told him that it stemmed from the principle involved: that Secretary Kissinger had deceived us, lied to us and avoided consulting me, that I had taken strong positions against all of this and that was why, I believed, the White House did not want me to appear. I should be ordered. Secretary Schlesinger stated the White House "has instructed me that the Commander in Chief has ordered you to get off the program." I stated, "Do you so order me?" SecDef thought for several moments and then said how do you handle the SALT Two issue. I stated I would not discuss it. The Secretary asked, what would you do if they got into the Kissinger-Jackson secret agreement. [Remember Kissinger had kept secret from all, until the Soviets spilled the beans, his flawed agreement with the Soviets which permitted them to install new but different missiles on diesel submarines.] I stated that I would limit myself to comments on anything that Kissinger had stated in public on the secret agreement. SecDef then said, you can't possibly avoid any discussion on SALT Two negotiations. I said that I have lots of practice on not answering questions I do not want to answer. . . . I said I assumed there would be questions on the maritime balance, etc. Secretary Schlesinger said that they would keep hammering away at the SALT issue. I stated that I would hold firm and that I would honor an order. Secretary Schlesinger then directed General Wickham to contact Mr. Friedheim and tell him to contact Spivak and tell him that Admiral Zumwalt could not appear because SALT Two could not be discussed and offered Secretary Calloway on the all-volunteer Army.

I then had a long and inconclusive meeting with the public-relations and legal people on my staff about whether or not I had received a legal order to get off the show, and the various options I had or didn't have if I had or hadn't been given such an order. Meanwhile Jerry Friedheim, the Assistant Secretary of Defense for Public Affairs, had been going round and round with Spivak, who of course had been making the appropriate efforts to keep me on the show. At 1820 that afternoon, I was summoned back to the presence of Secretary Schlesinger:

SecDef, in the presence of General Wickham, read me a draft written directive that in the event I decided to appear on "Meet The Press," I was not to discuss SALT in accordance with the Presidential directive on that subject, nor any prior aspects of SALT except those that have already been discussed by the President, the Secretary of State and the Secretary of Defense. He asked me whether I needed to have this put in writing and signed. I told him that it would not be necessary but that I had one question, in that the wording of the sentence about discussing only those prior aspects of SALT that had already been discussed by the President, the Secretary of State and the Secretary of Defense would lead into discussions of the secret agreement. He therefore revised his directive verbally to me that I was not to discuss any aspect of SALT in view of the sensitive negotiations going on.

He then asked General Wickham to leave. He stated that he had received threats from the White House that they would, if necessary, court martial me if I went on "Meet The Press." I inquired whether that threat pertained in view of the guidance I had just been given. He stated that the directive was his way of making it possible for me to appear without creating a backfire, to make the White House buy off.

He stated that the White House had further stated that they would destroy me (organizing retired Navy community, and all others to ensure that I had no future.) He asked me if I intended to continue with my plan to appear. I stated that I did and would comply meticulously with my order. . . .

He stated that he had never seen such paranoia as exists in Moscow with Henry, the President and Haig feeling they are threatened by the JCS and demanding that the JCS make a public announcement that the secret agreement was *de minimis* and a non-problem. SecDef stated that he had informed Al Haig that there was no way the Chiefs could be made to back off this problem, about which they felt very strongly. He stated that even Al Haig had become paranoid. I told him that it had been my observation that Al always had been, but that he was cleverer than the other two at concealing it.

P.S. As I left, SecDef said, take care. He then followed me to the door and said, that was not said lightly.

On Sunday 30 June I went on "Meet The Press." The record of that session shows that I carried out my orders by resisting seven questions designed to get me to speak about SALT. And I even was able to use one of them to offer a quotation from Horace as my view of Paul Nitze's performance in this period: "The man who is just and firm of purpose can be shaken from his stern resolve neither by the rage of the people. . . ." As an active-duty military man I did not use that passage's final phrase, ". . . nor by the countenance of the threatening tyrant."

Because 1 July was the day Tom Moorer was to turn over his command to George Brown and no one, least of all I, wanted to detract from that ceremony, Admiral James L. Holloway III relieved me as Chief of Naval Operations in a ceremonial sense at Annapolis on Saturday 29 June. The ceremony was identical to the one four years before; only the actors were different. Vice President Gerald Ford kindly accepted my invitation to speak at this ceremony, whether or not over White House objections, I do not know. I had a little public fun with him about having to turn over Admiral's House, the traditional CNO quarters at the Naval Observatory, to the Vice President for his official residence. I introduced my four children and two daughters-in-law to the audience. I called Mouza to the platform to pay her public tribute and to present her with flowers. In accordance with the orders from the White House, Secretary of Defense James Schlesinger's name did not appear on the program as a speaker. But he was there and spoke and awarded me the medal the White House had ordered him not to. He has told me since that three days before my term ended he had been ordered to fire me and that those days were the toughest of his life. I give him high marks for them.

As always the ceremony ended with the Navy Band playing "Anchors Aweigh." Evidently the White House had forgotten to tell it not to. Mouza and I drove away. The band struck up the song that means the most to us, "The Impossible Dream." I had told it to without asking the White House.

CHRONOLOGY

9 Mar. 1970	Zumwalt interviewed by Secretary Chafee.
12 Apr. 1970	Secretary Chafee telephones Zumwalt in Saigon to summon him to Washington.
13 Apr. 1970	Chafee tells Zumwalt that he has been nominated by the President for Chief of Naval Operations.
15 April 1970	Zumwalt meets President Nixon.
7 May 1970	Zumwalt's nomination for CNO approved by the Senate Committee on Armed Services.
12 May 1970	Zumwalt's nomination approved by the Senate.
15 May 1970	Vice Admiral Jerry King relieves Zumwalt in Saigon.
2 Jun. 1970	Zumwalt has first meeting with Admiral Rickover after designation as CNO.
24 Jun. 1970	Zumwalt meets with his personal staff for the first time.
1 Jul. 1970	Change of command ceremonies. Zumwalt becomes CNO.
6 Jul. 1970	Zumwalt's first JCS meeting.
18 Aug. 1970	JCS meet with President.
10 Sept. 1970	Zumwalt briefs Laird on Project 60, seventy-two days after becoming CNO.
28–29 Sept. 1970	President Nixon visits Sixth Fleet, after Jordan crisis. Zumwalt advises him on shifting balance of naval power. Nixon says he will tell the American people how badly our defenses have deteriorated—after his reelection.
5 Oct. 1970	Zumwalt and Secretary Laird meet with President Nixon at Executive Office Building.
12 Oct. 1970	Zumwalt sends Admiral Chick Clarey memo requesting homeporting proposal.
24 Oct. 1970	Zumwalt discusses Project 60 with the CNO Executive Panel.

5 Nov. 1970	Bill Norman briefs Zumwalt on minority problems.
6 Nov. 1970	Zumwalt's first official "non-meeting" with Kissinger.
10 Nov. 1970	Zumwalt issues Z-gram 57, "Demeaning or Abrasive Regulations, Elimination of"
28 Nov. 1970	Zumwalt with Kissinger on Army/Navy train to football game. Kissinger gives Zumwalt his "Sparta to our Athens" analogy.
11 Dec. 1970	JCS meeting; Zumwalt instigates debate over Navy's readiness and capability.
17 Dec. 1970	Zumwalt issues Z-gram 66, "Equal Opportunity in the Navy."
19 Feb. 1971	Zumwalt meets with President Salvador Allende Gossens in Valparaiso, Chile.
15 Apr. 1971	Zumwalt meets with Kissinger in White House to discuss twenty-four point papers.
28 Jun.- 14 July 1971	Zumwalt visits seven European countries—Sweden, Norway, Denmark, Netherlands, Belgium, France, and the United Kingdom.
10 Aug. 1971	JCS meeting with President.
4 Dec. 1971	Zumwalt attends WSAG meeting and questions the policy of tilt.
Jan. 1972	Radford–"Admirals' Spy Ring" affair.
25 Feb. 1972	Zumwalt visits Vietnam.
27 Feb. 1972	Zumwalt visits Seventh Fleet on Yankee Station in the Gulf of Tonkin.
Apr. 1972	Zumwalt visits Iceland.
Apr. 1972	Zumwalt issues Z-gram 109, "Recruiting is my top priority."
5 May 1972	Zumwalt prepares concept for Haiphong mining.
7 May 1972	Zumwalt visits Kissinger at the White House to discuss the POW/MIA situation.
11 May 1972	Zumwalt appears on "Today Show" as spokesman on the mining of Haiphong.
22 May 1972	JCS discuss Zumwalt's recommendation for safeguard on SALT.
2 Aug. 1972	Zumwalt has Haig to lunch.
7 Aug. 1972	Zumwalt issues Z-gram 115, "Alcoholism and Alcohol Abuse among Naval Personnel."
Aug. 1972	Zumwalt visits Seventh Fleet in Western Pacific to observe overall fleet problems.
12 Oct. 1972	Riot aboard USS *Kitty Hawk*.

16 Oct. 1972	Racial disturbance aboard USS *Hassayampa*.
3 Nov. 1972	Racial trouble aboard USS *Constellation*.
10 Nov. 1972	Zumwalt speaks to Washington flag officers about Navy's position on integration and racism.
14 Nov. 1972	Zumwalt issues Z-gram 117 on discipline.
20 Nov. 1972	Zumwalt testifies before Subcommittee on Disciplinary Problems in the U.S. Navy.
21 Nov. 1972	Zumwalt, John Warner, and Edward Hebert fly to see Carl Vinson.
27 Nov. 1972	*Time* magazine story on Zumwalt.
30 Nov. 1972	JCS meet with President Nixon at Oval Office with Kissinger and Haig to discuss Vietnam cease-fire.
Apr. 73–Oct. 1974	Captain Swanson issue at Pearl Harbor.
19 Jul. 1973	Zumwalt testifies before Benjamin Rosenthal's Subcommittee on Europe/Foreign Affairs Committee.
Sept. 1973	Zumwalt participates in legislative struggle over funding of Trident.
24 Oct. 1973	Zumwalt and other Chiefs are summoned to the Pentagon at midnight to discuss Brezhnev's letter and required actions.
22 Dec. 1973	JCS meeting with President Nixon; Secretary Schlesinger urges Zumwalt not to give briefing.
7 Feb. 1974	Zumwalt goes before PFIAB to discuss its report.
29–30 Mar. 1974	Zumwalt invited to Iceland by Ambassador Irving Frederick.
24 Apr. 1974	Ambassador Anatoly Dobrynin asks Zumwalt's opinion of SALT.
5 Jun. 1974	Zumwalt addresses graduating class at Annapolis with President Nixon present.
17 Jun. 1974	Zumwalt sends President Nixon letter on SALT.
28 Jun. 1974	Secretary Schlesinger tells Zumwalt that the White House threatens court martial if Zumwalt appears on "Meet the Press."
29 Jun. 1974	James Holloway relieves Zumwalt as Chief of Naval Operations at Annapolis with Vice President Ford and Schlesinger present.
29 Jun. 1974	Zumwalt sends out general message: "Z-NAVOPS 01 through 121 are hereby cancelled."
30 Jun. 1974	Zumwalt appears on "Meet the Press."

APPENDIX A

DEPARTMENT OF THE NAVY—
WASHINGTON HEADQUARTERS ORGANIZATION

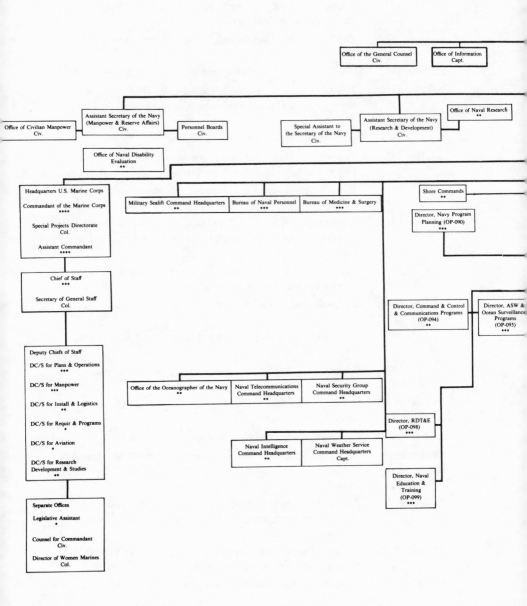

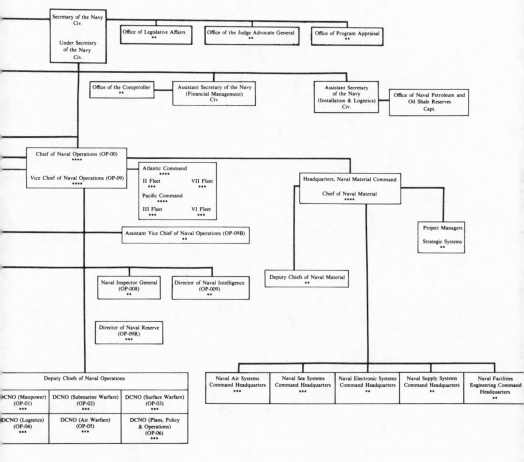

| | Secretary of the Navy
Civ.
Under Secretary
of the Navy
Civ. | Office of Legislative Affairs
** | Office of the Judge Advocate General
** | Office of Program Appraisal
** |

Office of the Comptroller
**

Assistant Secretary of the Navy
(Financial Management)
Civ.

Assistant Secretary
of the Navy
(Installation & Logistics)
Civ.

Office of Naval Petroleum and
Oil Shale Reserves
Capt.

Chief of Naval Operations (OP-00)
****

Vice Chief of Naval Operations (OP-09)
****

Atlantic Command
****

II Fleet   VII Fleet
***   ***

Pacific Command
****

III Fleet   VI Fleet
***   ***

Headquarters, Naval Material Command

Chief of Naval Material
****

Project Managers

Strategic Systems
**

Assistant Vice Chief of Naval Operations (OP-09B)
**

Naval Inspector General
(OP-008)
**

Director of Naval Intelligence
(OP-009)
**

Deputy Chiefs of Naval Material
**

Director of Naval Reserve
(OP-09R)
***

Deputy Chiefs of Naval Operations		
DCNO (Manpower) (OP-01) ***	DCNO (Submarine Warfare) (OP-02) ***	DCNO (Surface Warfare) (OP-03) ***
DCNO (Logistics) (OP-04) ***	DCNO (Air Warfare) (OP-05) ***	DCNO (Plans, Policy & Operations) (OP-06) ***

| Naval Air Systems
Command Headquarters
*** | Naval Sea Systems
Command Headquarters
*** | Naval Electronic Systems
Command Headquarters
** | Naval Supply Systems
Command Headquarters
** | Naval Facilities
Engineering Command
Headquarters
** |

KEY

Navy:
****   Admiral
***   Vice Admiral
**   Rear Admiral

Marine Corps:
****   General
***   Lieutenant General
**   Major General
*   Brigadier General

Civ.   Civilian

APPENDIX B

ORGANIZATIONAL CHART OF THE NATIONAL SECURITY COUNCIL

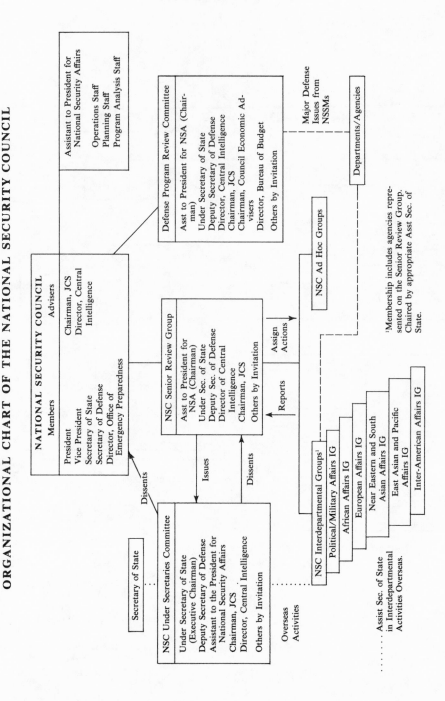

APPENDIX C

COMPARISON OF U.S. AND USSR NAVAL CAPABILITIES

1. U.S. vs USSR GENERAL PURPOSE NAVAL SHIP CONSTRUCTION 1966–1970

	U.S.	USSR	USSR/U.S.
Major Combatants	9	20	222%
Minor Combatants	28	138	490%
Amphibious Ships	24	10	42%
Attack Submarines	27	41	152%
TOTAL	88	209	237%

2. U.S. vs USSR MERCHANT FLEETS

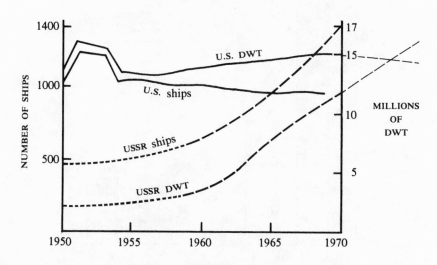

DATA FOR U.S. REFLECT ONLY PRIVATELY OWNED VESSELS

3. GROWTH IN SOVIET MISSILE LAUNCH PLATFORMS

	1960	1970
Major Missile Warships	6	20
Missile Patrol Boats	6	160
Cruise Missile Submarines	0	65
Soviet Naval Aviation (SNA) Badger Aircraft	145	282
TOTAL	157	527
Long Range Aviation (LRA) Bear Aircraft		75

4. AGE/TYPE OF ACTIVE MERCHANT SHIPS
U.S. vs USSR

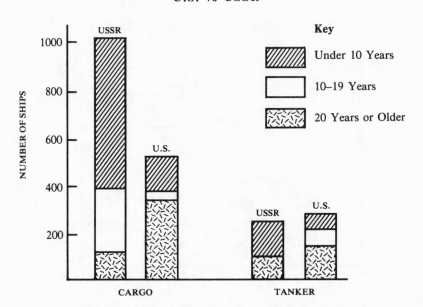

5. U.S. ESTIMATES OF SOVIET NAVAL FORCES FOR 1975

	A	B	C	D
Year Estimate Made	Missile- Equipped Surface Ships	Major Surface Force Combatants	Nuclear Subs (Incl. SLBM'S)	Conventional Subs
1967	58	178	117	232
1968	77	191	130	218
1969	83	209	139	218
1970	95	215	141	159
1971	91	224	145	142
	(157%)	(126%)	(124%)	(61%)

This chart shows the estimates made in each of the years indicated of the Soviet forces that would exist in 1975. Examination shows that, except for conventional submarines, the intelligence community constantly underestimated what the Soviets would have in 1975, and each year had to raise its estimates.

6. U.S. NAVAL STRENGTH 1970 AND 1974

	1970	1974
Total Active Fleet Ships	769	512
WARSHIPS	414	303
Battleships (BB)	—	—
Attack Carriers (CVA/CVAN)	15	14
ASW Carriers (CVS)	4	—
Surface Combatants	233	161
Submarines (SS, SSR, SSG, SSGN)	59	12
Submarines (SSN)	46	61
Submarines (SSBN)	41	41
Patrol (PG, PCER, PHM)	16	14
AMPHIBIOUS	97	65
Command Ship (LCC)	2	2
Transport Dock (LPD)	12	14
Assault Ship (LPH)	7	7
Tank Landing Ship (LST)	46	20
Assault Ship (LHA)	—	—
Other Amphibians	30	22
MINE WARFARE	64	9
AUXILIARIES	194	135
TOTAL ACTIVE AIRCRAFT	7929	6263
Attack	1644	1187
Fighter	1146	695
PERSONNEL ON ACTIVE DUTY		
Navy Military Personnel	692.4	545.5
Officers	80.5	57.2
Enlisted	611.9	478.7
Marine Corps Military Personnel	295.7	188.8
RESERVE PERSONNEL		
Navy Reserve	547.5	510.2
Marine Corps Resreve	246.3	191.1
CIVILIAN PERSONNEL (DIRECT HIRE)	376.3	323.6

7. U.S. vs USSR

TOTAL COMBAT SURFACE SHIPS

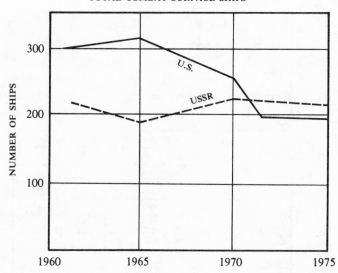

8. RATIO OF AIR ATTACK ANTI-SHIP SYSTEMS TO COMBAT SHIPS

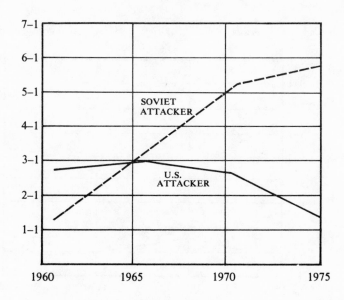

9. RATIO OF AIR ATTACK ANTI-SHIP SYSTEMS TO AAW (INCLUDING A/C FIGHTER) DEFENDERS

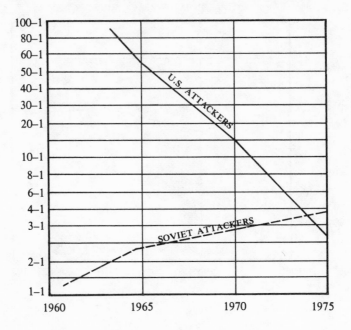

10. RATIO OF ASW VEHICLES TO SUBMARINE TARGETS

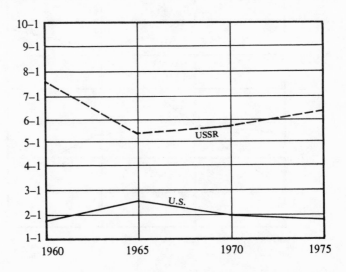

11. U.S. vs USSR SUBMARINE FORCES

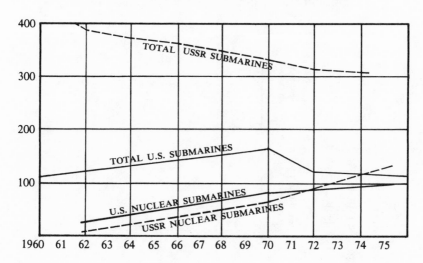

12. U.S. vs USSR NAVAL SHIP CONSTRUCTION

1966–1970

TYPE	USSR CONSTRUCTION AS % OF U.S.	
Major Combatant	155	%
Minor Combatant	387	%
Amphibious Ships	48	%
Attack Submarines	165	%
Total General Purpose	202	% [U.S.]

13. APPLICATIONS OF RELEVANT POWER

WHAT WILL BE THE "RELEVANT" POWER OF THE 1970S?

WHICH SITUATIONS REQUIRING APPLICATION OF U.S. FORCE ARE LIKELY?

LIKELY SITUATIONS		STRATEGIC NUCLEAR FORCES	GROUND FORCES AND LAND-BASED TACAIR	SEA CONTROL AND SEA PROJECTION FORCE
1950s–1960s	1970s–1980s			
NUCLEAR				
1. Threat of Strategic Nuclear Attack		X		
EUROPE				
2. Warsaw Pact Thrust Across German Central Plain		X	X	X
3.	NATO Northern Flank Endangered by Soviets; Iceland/Baltic/North Sea			X
4.	NATO Southern Flank Intimidated by Soviets; the Mediterranean Littoral			X
ASIA				
5. Large-Scale U.S. Ground Involvement in Asia			X	X
6.	Provide Help to an Asian Ally Who Helps Himself; Confidence in Our Will and Ability to Support: Japan, Taiwan, Korea, Philippines, Thailand, Etc.		?	X

7. Cuba, 1962 — X

8. Lebanon, 1958, Taiwan Strait, etc. — X | ?

			X	X
9.	Middle Eastern Conflict			X	X
10.	Countering Soviet Use of Seapower to Gain Political Influence in Indian Ocean			X	X
11.	War at Sea?	?		X	X
12.	Conflicts Arising from the Growing Commercial Importance of Ocean Resources			X	X

APPLICATIONS OF RELEVANT POWER

SITUATION	POWER HELD AND USED SUCCESSFULLY — RELEVANT POWER	RELEVANT POWER NOT HELD BY SIDE ATTEMPTING ACTION — SITUATION	RELEVANT POWER
Hungary, 1956	Soviet Army	British-French Invasion, Suez 1956	U.S./USSR Air and Sea Power
Lebanon, 1958	U.S. Sea Power (later, U.S. Army)	Laos Crisis, 1961 (Kennedy Bluff Called)	Pathet Lao
Taiwan Strait, 1958	U.S. Sea Power (Some TACAIR)	CPR Protests of U.S. Violations of Chinese Airspace	U.S. Sea and Air Power
Cuba, 1962	U.S. Sea, Air and Amphibious Forces (with U.S. Strategic Nuclear Superiority)		
Jordan, 1970	U.S. Sea Power		

14. THE STRATEGIC NUCLEAR BALANCE
U.S. vs USSR

From *Foreign Affairs,* by Paul Nitze

TOTAL STRATEGIC MISSILES

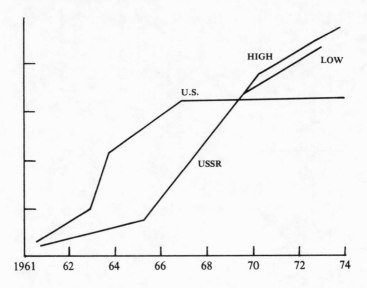

TOTAL STRATEGIC FORCE LOADING (MEGATON EQUIVALENTS)

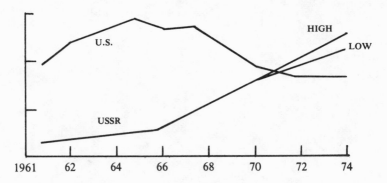

TOTAL INTERCONTINENTAL WARHEADS/BOMBS

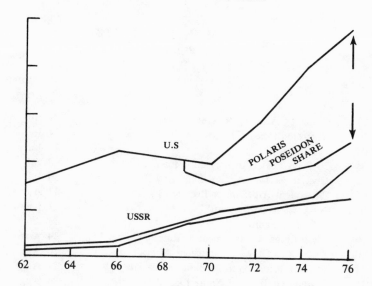

APPENDIX D
Z-grams

NUMBER	TITLE	EFFECTIVE DATE	
01	Relieving Admiral Moorer	01 Jul	70
02	Retention Study Groups	14 Jul	70
03	Classified	22 Jul	70
04	30 Days Leave Authorization for All PCS	30 Jul	70
05	Civilian Clothes Aboard Ship for POIs	30 Jul	70
06	Dependent Air Charter Program	11 Aug	70
07	Navy Sponsor Program	11 Aug	70
08	Officer Assignment	11 Aug	70
09	Meritorious Advancement in Rate of Career POs	14 Aug	70
10	Services to Crews of Transient Aircraft	20 Aug	70
11	Enlisted Requests to Remain on Sea Duty	21 Aug	70
12	Civilian Clothing on Shore Establishments	24 Aug	70
13	Post-Deployment Leave Policy	26 Aug	70
14	Collateral Duties	27 Aug	70
15	Statement of Earnings	28 Aug	70
16	Swaps	02 Sep	70
17	Personal Check Cashing Ceilings	02 Sep	70
18	Navy Finance Center 24-Hour Service	04 Sep	70
19	Below Zone Percentage Limitation Suspension	04 Sep	70
20	Lockers and Washing Facilities	08 Sep	70
21	Compensatory Time Off	09 Sep	70
22	Improving Shore Establishment Habitability	09 Sep	70
23	CPO Advisory Board to CNO	12 Sep	70
24	Wives' Ombudsman	14 Sep	70
25	Forces Afloat Liberty Policy	16 Sep	70
26	Shore Patrol Staffing and Training	21 Sep	70
27	Forces Afloat Operating Tempo	21 Sep	70
28	Retention Study Group Progress Report	21 Sep	70
29	Leave Policy for Deployed Units	22 Sep	70
30	Commissioned Officers' Mess Open	23 Sep	70
31	TYCOM Shiphandling Competition	23 Sep	70
32	Reenlistment Ceremonies	23 Sep	70
33	Navy Exchange and Commissary Advisory Boards	25 Sep	70
34	Uniform Changes	25 Sep	70
35	BOQ/BEQ Conveniences	25 Sep	70
36	Standards of Service	26 Sep	70
37	Aviation Squadron Command	26 Sep	70
38	Holiday Routine at Sea	28 Sep	70
39	Extended Commissary Hours	05 Oct	70

40	Cash/Check Option at Payday	07 Oct	70
41	Command Excellence Forum	12 Oct	70
42	Junior Officer Request for Sea Duty	13 Oct	70
43	Disbursing Claims Processing	13 Oct	70
44	Quarterdeck Watches	13 Oct	70
45	Assistance to POW/MIA Families	15 Oct	70
46	Refinement of 3-M System	15 Oct	70
47	Responsibility for Inactivating Ships	20 Oct	70
48	People Programs	23 Oct	70
49	Medals and Awards	23 Oct	70
50	Cold Iron Status	23 Oct	70
51	Small Craft Insignia	23 Oct	70
52	Classified	23 Oct	70
53	Officer Billet Summary	02 Nov	70
54	CNO Discussions with Navy Personnel	02 Nov	70
55	Human Resource Management	04 Nov	70
56	Exchange of Duty for Officers	09 Nov	70
57	Eliminating Abrasive Regulations (Mickey Mouse)	10 Nov	70
58	Acceptance of Checks in Ships' Stores	14 Nov	70
59	Professional Development Program	14 Nov	70
60	Action Line Telephone	18 Nov	70
61	Reassignment of CWO and RPS Duties	19 Nov	70
62	CNO Senior Officer Forum	27 Nov	70
63	COMTAC Publications Aboard Ship	30 Nov	70
64	Ship Conning Indication	03 Dec	70
65	Vietnamization Challenge	05 Dec	70
66	Equal Opportunity	17 Dec	70
67	Command Inspection Program	22 Dec	70
68	Civilian Clothes Aboard Ship	23 Dec	70
69	Command in the Grade of Captain	28 Dec	70
70	Grooming and Uniform Policy	21 Jan	71
71	Battle Streamers for Navy Flag	23 Jan	71
72	Quarterdeck Watches	03 Feb	71
73	Enlisted Vietnam Volunteers	18 Feb	71
74	Preferential Housing Consideration for Volunteers for Naval Advisory Duty in Vietnam	18 Feb	71
75	Sea/Shore Rotation	25 Feb	71
76	Outstanding Recruiter Awards	25 Feb	71
77	Enlisted Blue Working Uniform	27 Feb	71
78	Inspection Scheduling Policy	05 Mar	71
79	Augmentation into the Regular Navy	15 Mar	71
80	MCPOS on E-8/E-9 Selection Boards	16 Mar	71
81	Regular Navy Warrant Officer Program	14 Apr	71
82	Boards, Committees and Guidance Programs Reduction Review	29 Apr	71
83	Motor Vehicle Transportation for Forces Afloat	17 May	71
84	Copies of Fitness Reports	18 May	71
85	Legislation Status Report	24 May	71

86	CNO Scholars Program	07 Jun	71
87	Navy Uniform	13 Jun	71
88	Advances of Pay	14 Jun	71
89	SECNAV/CNO Fellowship Program	19 Jun	71
90	Responsibility Pay for Senior Naval Advisors in Vietnam	25 Jun	71
91	Limited Duty Officer Program	29 Jun	71
92	Civilian Clothing Aboard Ship for Non-rated Personnel	29 Jun	71
93	People Programs	06 Jul	71
94	Navy Drug Exemption and Rehabilitation Program	15 Jul	71
95	Master Chief Petty Officer of the Command	19 Jul	71
96	Retention Study Group Schedule	20 Jul	71
97	Commuted Rations for Hospital Patients	21 Jul	71
98	Advance Information about New Duty Stations	11 Aug	71
99	Officer Swords	18 Aug	71
100	Personnel Exchange Program (PEP)	29 Oct	71
101	Six Day Sales Operation at Designated Navy Commissary Stores	22 Nov	71
102	Responsibility for Standards of Smartness	22 Dec	71
103	Sailor of the Year Award	01 Jan	72
104	Challenge of 1972	01 Jan	72
105	Navy Drug and Rehabilitation Program	05 Feb	72
106	Quarterdeck Watch Officers	02 Mar	72
107	CNO Sailor of the Year	10 Mar	72
108	Continuation Beyond 30 Years Active Service	19 Apr	72
109	Recruiting	26 Apr	72
110	Human Resource Development	27 Apr	72
111	Classified	04 May	72
112	Collateral Duties	01 Jun	72
113	Career Counseling Program	13 Jun	72
114	Ecology Spot Rep	06 Jul	72
115	Alcohol Abuse and Alcoholism Among Naval Personnel	01 Aug	72
116	Equal Rights and Opportunities for Women in the Navy	07 Aug	72
117	Good Order and Discipline	14 Nov	72
118	Reduction of Maximum Sea Tours	28 Jun	73
119	Minority Affairs Assistants	10 Oct	73
120	Revised Master Chief Petty Officer of the Fleet/Force/Command Program	03 Apr	74

APPENDIX E

U.S. NAVY FIRST-TERM REENLISTMENT RATES

(Data from NAVSO P–3523, "Budget & Forces Survey," from
Office of the Navy Comptroller, Statistics & Reports Division)

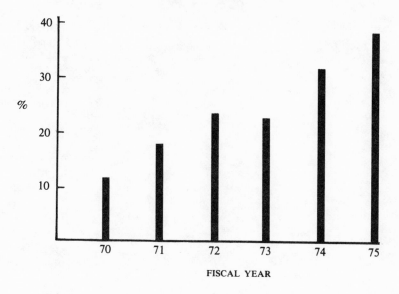

1. The Mediterranean

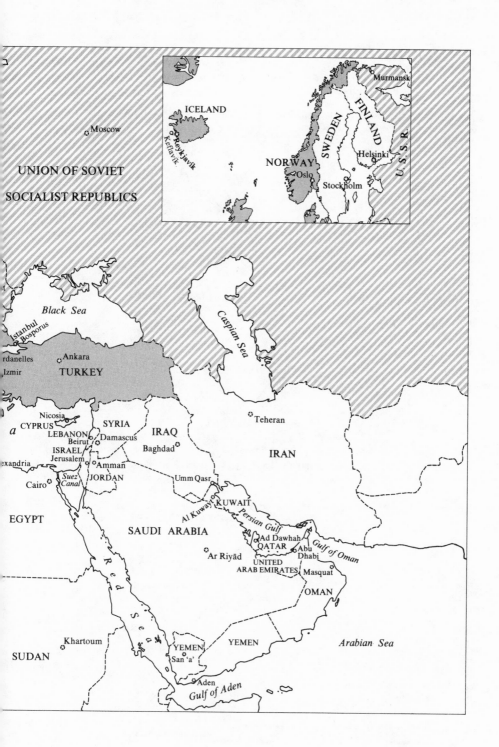

UNION OF SOVIET

SOCIALIST REPUBLICS

ICELAND

Moscow

Reykjavik

Keflavík

NORWAY

SWEDEN

FINLAND

Murmansk

Helsinki

Oslo

Stockholm

U.S.S.R.

Black Sea

Caspian Sea

Istanbul

Bosporus

rdanelles

Izmir

Ankara

TURKEY

Teheran

Nicosia

CYPRUS

a

LEBANON

ISRAEL

xandria

Jerusalem

Cairo

Suez Canal

SYRIA

Damascus

Beirut

Amman

JORDAN

IRAQ

Baghdad

Umm Qasr

IRAN

EGYPT

SAUDI ARABIA

Al Kuwayt

KUWAIT

Persian Gulf

Ad Dawhah

QATAR

Abu Dhabi

UNITED ARAB EMIRATES

Gulf of Oman

Masquat

Ar Riyād

OMAN

Red Sea

Khartoum

SUDAN

YEMEN

San 'a'

YEMEN

Aden

Gulf of Aden

Arabian Sea

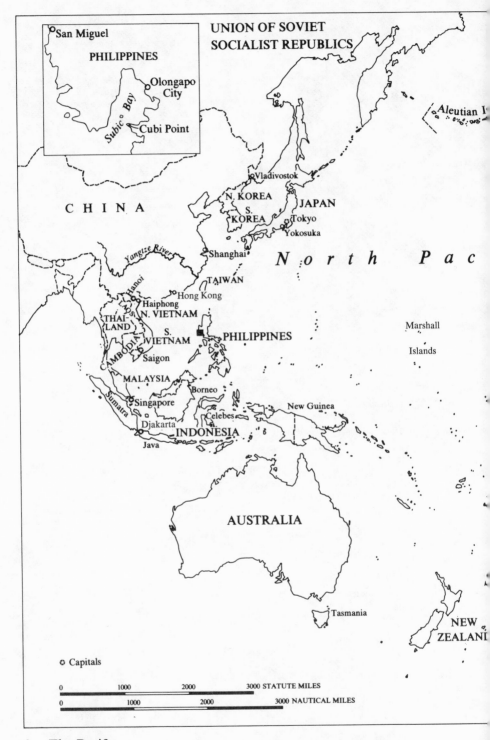

2. The Pacific

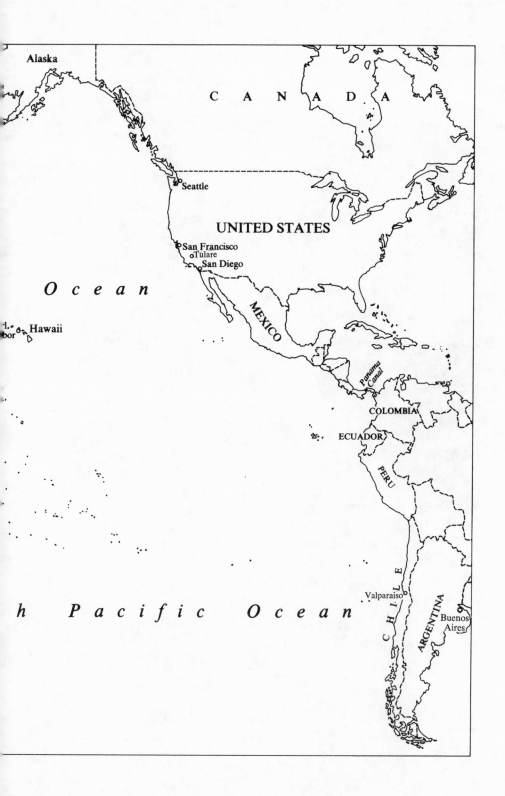

Alaska

C A N A D A

Seattle

UNITED STATES

San Francisco
Tulare
San Diego

O c e a n

MEXICO

Hawaii

Panama
Canal

COLOMBIA

ECUADOR

PERU

h   P a c i f i c   O c e a n

Valparaiso

CHILE

ARGENTINA

Buenos
Aires

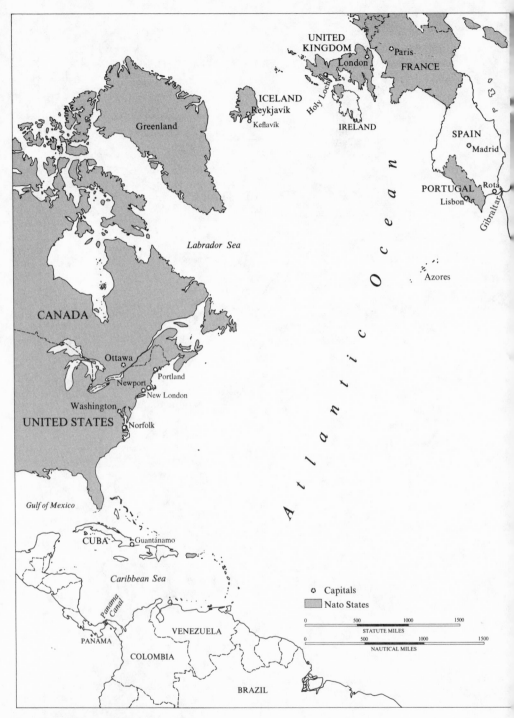

3. The North Atlantic

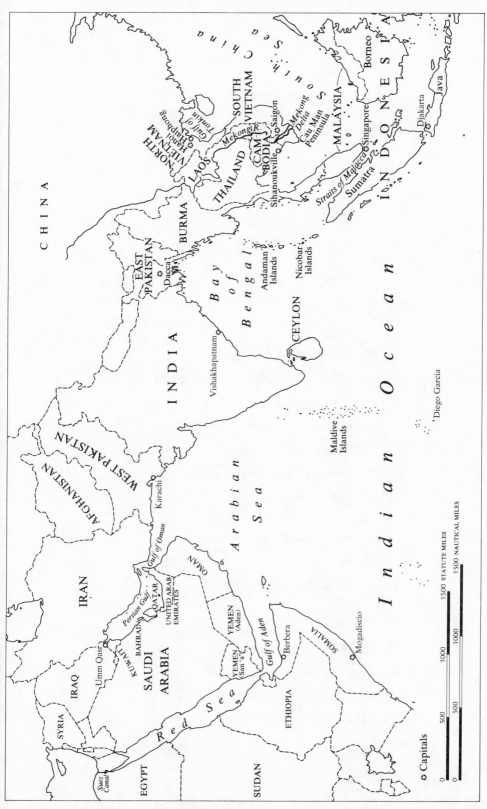

4. The Indian Ocean

GLOSSARY

ABM	Anti-Ballistic Missile
ACDA	Arms Control & Disarmament Agency
ACLU	American Civil Liberties Union
ACTOV	Accelerated Turnover to Vietnam
AEC	Atomic Energy Commission
ALNAV	All Navy (Message to Everyone in Navy)
ASAP	As Soon As Possible
BIS	Board of Inspection and Survey
BT	Boiler Tender
BuPers	Bureau of Naval Personnel
CEP	CNO Executive Panel
CHINFO	Chief of Information
CinCLant	Commander in Chief Atlantic
CinCPac	Commander in Chief Pacific
CinCPacFlt	Commander in Chief Pacific Fleet
CinCUSNavEur	Commander in Chief, US Naval Forces, Europe

CJCS	Chairman of the Joint Chiefs of Staff
CNM	Chief of Naval Matter
CNO	Chief of Naval Operations
CNP	Chief of Naval Personnel
ComNavAirPac	Commander of Naval Air Forces, Pacific
ComNavForV	Commander of Naval Forces, Vietnam
ConUS	Continental United States
CVA	Attack Carrier
CVAN	Nuclear Powered Attack Carrier
CVS	Anti Submarine Carrier
DD	Destroyer
DDRE	Director Defense Research, and Engineering
DesRon	Destroyer Squadron
DIA	Defense Intelligence Agency
DLG	Guided Missile Frigate
DLGN	Nuclear Powered Guided Missile Frigate
DMZ	Demilitarized Zone
DoD	Department of Defense
DPRC	Defense Program Review Committee
EAOS	Extended Active Obligated Service
EDP	Enlisted Distribution Plan
EDO	Engineering Duty Officer
Exec	Executive Officer
FBS	Forward Based Systems
FY	Fiscal Year
FYDP	Five Year Defense Plan
GAO	General Accounting Office
G-I-UK Gap	Greenland-Iceland, United Kingdom Gap

ICBM	Intercontinental Ballistic Missile
IDF	Iceland Defense Force
IG	Inspector General
ISA	International Security Affairs
JAG	Judge Advocate General
JCS	Joint Chiefs of Staff
JCSM	JCS Memorandum
JG	Junior Grade
JSTPS	Joint Strategic Targeting Planning System
LAMPS	Light Airborne Maritime Patrol System
LantFlt	Atlantic Fleet
LCdr	Lieutenant Commander
LCM	Landing Craft, Medium
LHA	Amphibious Assault Ship carrying helicopters
LST	Tank Landing Ship
MAA	Minority Affairs Assistant
MAC	Military Airlift Command
MBFR	Mutual Balanced Force Reduction
MRBM	Medium Range Ballistic Missile
NAS	Naval Air Station
NASA	National Aeronautic and Space Administration
NAVMINs	Navy Minority Information Messages
NAVOP	Message from the Office of CNO
NCA	National Command Authority
NISO	Naval Investigative Service Office
NOB	Naval Operating Base
NSC	National Security Council
NSDM	National Security Decision Memorandum

NSSM   National Security Study Memorandum

NVA   North Vietnamese Army

OBE   Overtaken by Events

OMB   Office of Management and Budget

OpDeps   Deputy Chiefs for JCS Matters

OPNAV   Office of the Chief of Naval Operations

PacFlt   Pacific Fleet

PBR   River Patrol Boat

PCF   Fast Patrol Craft (Swift)

PCS   Permanent Change of Station

Pers-P   Office in BuPers for People

PF   Patrol Frigate

PFIAB   President's Foreign Intelligence Advisory Board

PG   Gunboat

PPBS   Planning, Programming, Budgeting System

PR   Public Relations

PRD   Prospective Release Date

R&D   Research and Development

SAC   Strategic Air Command

SALT   Strategic Arms Limitation Talks

SAM   Surface-to-Air Missile

SCS   Sea Control Ship

SD   Secretary of Defense

SEA   Southeast Asia

Seabees   Naval Construction Battalions

SEASIA   Southeast Asia

SecNavInst   Secretary of Navy Instruction

SFSDA   Separable First Stage Disarmament Agreement

Sit Rep   Situation Report

SLBM   Submarine Launched Ballistic Missile

SRG   Senior Review Group

SSM   Surface to Surface (Cruise) Missile

SSN   Nuclear powered Submarine

TACAIR   Tactical Aircraft

TAD   Temporary Additional Duty

TF   Task Force

TFG   Tentative Fiscal Guidance

TG   Task Group

TTB   Threshold Test Ban

ULMS   Underwater Long Range Missile System

USG   United States Government

USNB   United States Naval Base

VC   Viet Cong

VF/VA   Fighter/Attack Squadrons-Aircraft Designation

VSTOL   Very Short Takeoff and Landing

WAVES   Naval Women

WestPac   Western Pacific

WSAG   Washington Special Action Group

INDEX

A-6 aircraft, 78
A-7 aircraft, 78
ABM, *see* Anti-ballistic missiles
Abourezk, James, 162
Abrams, General Creighton, 277, 314, 418
    Vietnam War, 378, 379, 383–384, 388
    Vietnamization, 378
    Zumwalt and, 34, 36, 39, 43–44, 47
Abu Dhabi, 438
Accelerated Turnover to Vietnam (ACTOV), 36, 40–42, 44, 47
"Admirals Spy Ring," 369–376
Agnew, Spiro, 289, 291, 313, 434
Aircraft
    A-6, 78
    A-7, 78
    B-52, 156, 384, 389
    BACKFIRE bomber, 500
    F-4, 78, 144, 146, 148, 384, 389
    F-14, 77–79, 136, 140, 143–152, 162, 284
    F-14A, 80, 146–147
    F-14B, 146–147
    F-15, 146, 147, 149–150
    F-111, 144
    F-111A, 79
    F-111B, 79, 146
    Foxbat, 78

    S-3, 78
    VSTOL, 71, 75, 77, 116
Aircraft carriers
    CVAs, 77–78
    CVANs, 73, 74, 101, 105, 107
    CVSs, 77
    Sea Control Ships, 75–76, 106, 116–121
    See also names of ships
Airplane hijacking, 276, 294, 295
Alcohol problems, 269–271
Alcoholics Anonymous, 270–271
Allende Gossens, Salvador, 321–328
Allison, Lieutenant General Royal, 52, 282, 348, 352, 410
Al-Zayat, Foreign Minister, 440
America (aircraft carrier), 53, 215
American Indians, discrimination against, 168
American Legion, 53
Amphibious ship (LHA), 72–74, 150–151
Anderson, Bill, 96
Anderson, Admiral George, 44, 63, 181, 239, 250, 255, 464–465, 476
    racial disturbances, 233–234
Anderson, Jack, 366, 369–373
Anderson, Robert B., 98
Angola, U.S.S.R. and, 333
Anti-ballistic missiles (ABM)

U.S.S.R., 349, 350, 352, 400, 402, 487

U.S., 284, 320, 349–352, 402, 487

Antle, Lieutenant Bill, 172

Arabs, 279, 353, 354, 423, 432
  oil embargo, 449–452
  U.S.S.R. and, 363, 432–439, 441, 442, 445–449
  See also names of countries

Argentina, 324, 325

Arizona (battleship), 476

Arleigh Burke Award, 176

Arms Control and Disarmament Agency, 349

Arnold J. Isbell (destroyer), 185–189
  voice call sign, 187–189

Ash, Roy, 151

ASM missiles, 147

Aspin, Les, 138–139, 452

Assassination attempts, 293, 294

Ataka (Japanese ship), 5–6, 9–16, 19, 20

Atomic Energy Commission, 97, 113

Augustsson, Einar, 472, 474

Australia, 363
  homeporting, 132

Austria, 303

Awami League, 363

AWG-9 fire control system, 147

Azores, 456

B-52 aircraft, 156, 384, 389

BACKFIRE bomber, 500

Backup Book, 249

Bagley, Admiral David, 66, 175, 199, 211, 212–213, 251, 254–255

Bagley, Admiral Worth, 66–67, 104, 243, 244, 261, 385
  question of Zumwalt's successor, 475, 477, 478
  Zumwalt and, 475, 478, 485, 506

Bagley, Ensign Worth, 66

Bahrain Islands, 361, 453–454

Bainbridge (guided-missile frigate), 95–96, 101

Bangladesh, 360

Barents Sea, 466

Baroody, Bill, 47

Bath Iron Works, 151

Baudouin, King, 357

Baumberger, Admiral Walter H., 43

Baxter, Captain James, 270, 271

Bay of Bengal, 368

Belgium, 52, 355, 357

Bernhard, Prince, 357–359, 451

Bilderberg Conference, 451

Black, Delbert, 190–191

Black Sea, 361

Blacks, *see* Discrimination; Racial disturbances

Blouin, Admiral "Champ," 277–278, 280, 312, 315
  budgets and, 341, 342

Blue Ribbon Defense Panel, 333

Bohlen, Charles, 28

Borg-Olivier, George, 305, 354, 355

Bornholm, Island of, 392

Boy Scouts of America, 53

Boynton, Dr., 21

Brazil, 324

Brezhnev, Leonid I., 320, 483
  Kissinger and, 404, 438
  Nixon and, 429, 445, 481, 500

Bringle, Admiral Bush, 243, 357

Brosio, Manlio, 357

Brown, George, 418, 441, 497, 510

Brown v. Board of Education, 205

Brownell, Commander Stuart M., 385

Bruton, Admiral H. C., 188–189

Buckley, James, 409

Budgets
  Blouin and, 341, 342
  Chafee and, 337–338, 347
  Haig and, 341, 347
  Joint Chiefs of Staff and, 280–282, 284, 287–291, 313–317, 333–348, 407–411, 461
  Kissinger and, 281–282, 313–317, 335–336, 340–341, 348
  Laird and, 155–157, 335–338, 342, 347, 348
  Moorer and, 337–339
  Nixon and, 281–282, 313–314, 348, 463, 494
  Packard and, 336
  SALT and, 407–410
  Schlesinger and, 116, 120, 157, 463, 464
  U.S. Air Corps, 334, 337, 411
  U.S. Army, 334, 337, 341, 342
  U.S. Congress and, 336–339, 342, 407–411, 463–466
  U.S. Department of Defense and, 116, 120, 155–157, 336, 463, 464
  U.S. Navy, 281, 284, 289–291, 315–317, 333–348, 411, 461–466, 494

Westmoreland and, 341–343, 347–348
Zumwalt and, 280–282, 284, 287–291, 313–317, 333–348, 407–411, 461
Bunker, Ellsworth, 378
Vietnam War, 383–384
Burchinal, General David, 52, 302, 303
Burke, Admiral Arleigh, 54, 98, 102, 250–251
Buzhardt, J. Fred, 234, 251, 374
Byersly, Captain, 11
Byrd, Harry F., 32–33, 505
Byrd, Robert, 257

Caldwell, Caroline, 26–27
Caldwell, June, 255
Califano, Joseph, 397
Calvert, Jim, 96
Cambodia, 37–39, 145, 167, 275, 282, 424, 425
Canada, 484
Cang, Admiral Chung Tan, 378
Cannon, Howard, 148
Captor mines, 82
Carney, Admiral Robert, 49–50
Carney, Mrs. Robert, 49–50
Carr, Admiral, 117
Case, Clifford P., 338
Castro, Fidel, 33
Cau Mau Peninsula, 39
Center for Defense Information, 139, 142
Central Intelligence Agency (CIA), 38, 329, 365, 481
Chile and, 322, 327–328
Ceylon, 368
CH-53 helicopters, 80
Chafee, John, 51, 56, 59, 66, 137, 146, 228, 235, 267, 281, 289, 327, 330, 418
budgets and, 337–338, 347
on discrimination, 201–204
on homeporting, 128, 129
on personnel policies, 168–169
Vietnam War, 380, 381
Zumwalt and, 43–46, 167–169, 172, 194, 211, 239, 243, 271, 310, 457
Chagos Archipelago, 363
Champe, Lieutenant, 17, 21
Change of Command Ceremony, 56, 510–511

Chapman, General Leonard, 70–71, 418
as Joint Chiefs of Staff member, 276, 293–295, 314–315, 338
Zumwalt and, 276–277
Chen, Admiral, 20–21
Chiang Kai-shek, Generalissimo and Madame, 52
Chicanos, discrimination against, 168, 197–198
Chief of Naval Operations, see Zumwalt, Admiral Elmo R., Jr.
Chigir, Nikolai, 312
Chile, 276, 321–328
CIA and, 322, 327–328
Kissinger and, 321–328
Laird and, 326–328
Moorer and, 326–328
Nixon and, 322, 323, 327–328
U.S.S.R. and, 322–324, 326, 328
Zumwalt and, 321–328
China, 6–22, 290, 361
India and, 364
Kissinger and, 364, 368, 482, 484
money value in, 14
NATO and, 484
Nixon and, 368, 381
oil and, 451
U.S.S.R. and, 31, 363, 484
Vietnam War, 388
World War II, 6–22
guerilla action, 11–12
Zumwalt in, 6–22, 25
Chon, Admiral Tran Van, 40, 377, 378, 494
CIA, see Central Intelligence Agency
Clarey, Admiral Chick, 110, 181, 190, 243
homeporting, 127, 128
racial disturbances, 219–220, 223, 227, 228, 230–231, 242
Vietnam War, 381, 382, 384, 386–387
Clements, William, 117, 149, 333, 419, 450, 463, 476, 481, 488
TTB, 496
Zumwalt and, 418, 448
Clifford, Clark, 448
Cloud, Commander Benjamin, 217
Cochran, John, 162, 163
Cockell, Commander William, 421, 426–427, 439–440, 487
Colbert, Admiral Richard, 141–142
Cold Dawn (Newhouse), 283, 348, 349

Cold War, 61
Common Market, 484
Congo, Republic of, 308–310
Conquest, Robert, 28
Constellation (aircraft carrier), racial disturbances, 221–235, 240–250, 253, 257, 259, 312, 376
Coral Sea (aircraft carrier), 385
Corcoran, Thomas, 117–118
Cousins, Admiral Ralph, 182, 195, 251, 476
Coutelais-du-Roche, Mouza, *see* Zumwalt, Mrs. Elmo R., Jr.
Cox, Archibald, 118, 438
Crawford, Commander, 86
Crete, 133, 306, 354, 437
Cronkite, Walter, 302
Cruise missiles
    U.S.S.R., 61–62, 76, 78, 381
    U.S., 74, 75, 81–82
        Harpoon, 74, 75, 81–82
        Regulus, 81
Cuba, 33, 323, 397, 428
    Kissinger and, 310–312
    U.S.S.R. and, 310–313
Cuban missile crisis, 29–30, 69, 287, 290, 293, 302, 344, 444
    Nitze and, 29–30, 69
    U.S.S.R. and, 69, 83
    Zumwalt and, xiii, 29–30, 45, 69
Cunningham, Randy, 388
Cushman, General Robert, 254, 418
CVA carriers, 77–78
CVAN carriers, 73, 74, 101, 105, 107
CVS carriers, 77
Cyprus, 297–298

Daniel, W. C., 245, 247, 252, 253
Daniels, Josephus, 66
Dardanelles, the, 297
Darrow, Clarence, 90–92
Davey, Captain Jack, 54
DD-963 (Spruance) destroyers, 73–75, 102, 150–151
DE-1052 escort, 73, 75
Dean, John, 420
Decatur (destroyer), 372
Defense Program Review Committee (DPRC), 335–336, 339–340, 342
DELTA class submarines, 500
Demeaning and Abrasive Regulations, Elimination of, 182–196
Democracy, Zumwalt on, 69–70

Denmark, 62, 357
Denmark, Straits of, 466
Denton, Jane, 389, 390
DesRon 12, 132, 133, 135
DesRon 15, 132, 133, 135
Détente, xii, 486
    Kissinger on, 482, 483
    Zumwalt on, 161
Dewey (guided-missile frigate), 95, 96, 102, 185–186, 189, 215, 391–393
DiBona, Charles, 289
Diego Garcia, 363, 454–456, 458–459, 472
Dirksen, Everett, 100
Discrimination
    Chafee on, 201–204
    McNamara on, 255
    U.S. Navy, 168, 197–216, 261–265, 268–269
        Minority Affairs Programs, 204, 219, 220, 223–224, 237
        report on Subic Bay/San Miguel area, 205–210
        women, 168, 201, 203, 207, 261–265
    Zumwalt on, 168, 197–216, 254–255, 261–265, 268–269
    See also Racial disturbances
Distinguished Service Medal, 52
DLG escorts, 102–103
DLGN escorts, 73, 74, 81, 101–103, 105, 121
DMZ, 379–380
Dobrynin, Anatoly, Kissinger and, 310–311, 348–349, 351, 400, 404, 486–487, 506
Dominican Republic, 290
Dominick, Peter, 160, 409
DPRC, *see* Defense Program Review Committee
Dress regulations, 168, 173, 178–179, 182–185, 190–191, 193, 195, 257–258
Driscoll, Lieutenant Bill, 388
Drug problems, 269
Du Poix, Admiral Vince, 444
Dulles, John Foster, 302
Duncan, Admiral Charles, 190, 191
Dunford, Captain, 86–89, 91

Eagleton, Thomas, 149–150
East Bengal, 363–364, 367, 368
Ecuador, 470

Egypt, 276, 279, 294, 306, 483
  Israel and, 292–293, 361, 432, 433,
    438, 439, 444, 448–449
  Seven Days War, 361
  U.S.S.R. and, 292, 439
  Yom Kippur War, 432–434, 438,
    444, 448–449
Ehrlichman, John, 373–375, 395, 420,
  457, 479
Eighteen Nation Disarmament Confer-
  ence, 30
Eisenhower, Dwight D., xiii, 245
Eisenhower (aircraft carrier), 73, 120,
  455
Ellsberg, Daniel, 373
Emerson, Captain Dave, 385
Enterprise (aircraft carrier), 102, 105,
  150, 325–327, 360, 367
Enthover, Alain, 101
Equal Rights Amendment, 263
Ervin, Sam, 419
Escorts, 452
  DE-1052, 73, 75
  DLGs, 102–103
  DLGNs, 73, 74, 81, 101–103, 105,
    121
Esso a.g. of Hamburg, 449
Ethiopia, 454
Ewell, General Julian, 38, 50
Exxon Corporation, 449, 450

F-4 aircraft, 78, 144, 146, 148, 384,
  389
F-14 aircraft, 77–79, 136, 140, 143–152,
  162, 284
  U.S. Congress and, 136, 140, 143–
    152
F-14A aircraft, 80, 146–147
F-14B aircraft, 146–147
F-15 aircraft, 146, 147, 149–150
F-111 aircraft, 144
F-111A aircraft, 79
F-111B aircraft, 79, 146
Fairbrother, Lieutenant Commander,
  20
Filipinos, discrimination against, 168,
  198
Finland
  Iceland and, 466
  U.S.S.R. and, 467–468
First Fleet, 44, 82, 173
Fitzgerald, C. R., 21
Flag Officers News Letter, 262

Flanagan, Peter, 457
Ford, Gerald, 425, 465, 480, 511
Forward Based Systems, 313, 350–351,
  353, 400, 429, 487, 488
Foster, Dr. John, 288
Fowler, Rufus, 14, 16–17
Foxbat aircraft, 78
France, 29, 305, 354, 357, 484
  Indian Ocean and, 360–361
Franco, Generalissimo Francisco, 457
Franke, William, 95
Franklin D. Roosevelt (aircraft carrier),
  436, 437, 443, 447
Freeman, Nelson W., 117
Friedheim, Jerry, 509
Fulbright, William, 130, 162–163
  SALT and, 407

Game Warden (code name), 37
Gandhi, Indira, 365, 369
Gates, Thomas, 95, 285, 286
Gayler, Admiral Noel, 110, 251
Gelb, Leslie, 434
Germany, 52, 303, 355, 357
Ghana, U.S.S.R. and, 331–332
Giant Slingshot (code name), 38–39
Gibraltar, Straits of, 436
G-I-UK gap, 467
Goldwater, Barry, 32–33, 159
Gooding, Admiral Robert, 108–115
Goodpaster, General Andrew, 52, 128,
  302, 303, 357
Gorbunova, Colonel, 19
Gorbunova, Mrs. 19
Gorshkov, Admiral, 69, 70, 72
Great Britain, 53, 300, 301, 305, 307,
  357
  Iceland and, 467, 469–471
  Indian Ocean and, 360–363, 367–
    368
  Malta and, 354–356
  Persian Gulf and, 453–454
Greece, 62, 214, 293, 296–298, 318
  anti-Americanism, 133
  homeporting, 125, 128–136, 305,
    353–354
  Military Facilities Agreement
    (1953), 131
  Yom Kippur War, 442
Greenland, Iceland and, 466, 467
Gromyko, Andrei A., 483
Grooming regulations, 168, 169, 182,
  191, 192, 195, 248, 493, 494

Grumman Aircraft Corporation, 78, 144–149, 151
Guam, 379
Guam (amphibious ship), 116, 298–299, 300
Guinea, U.S.S.R. and, 332, 333
Gulf of Siam, 38
Gulf of Tonkin, 36, 75, 214, 217–218, 222, 290, 367, 378
Gulf of Tonkin Resolution, 458
Gutzloff Island, 6

Habarova, Anna Mihailovna, 18
Haig, Alexander, 29, 242, 255, 289, 327, 329, 445, 459, 506, 507, 510
    "Admirals Spy Ring," 372, 374, 375
    budgets and, 341, 347
    Kissinger and, 309, 318, 319, 397–399, 419, 420, 474
    Mediterranean crisis (October 1973), 448
    Nixon and, 396, 398–399, 419, 448, 474, 479
    PFIAB, 465
    SALT and, 490, 491
    Vietnam War, 384, 412
    Watergate affair, 420
    Zumwalt and, xii, 45–46, 355, 397–399, 493, 498
Haiphong Harbor, mining of, 81, 384–389, 393, 400, 417
Haldeman, H. R., 374, 375, 395, 420
Halperin, Lieutenant David, 54, 171–172, 199, 201, 319
Hamilton, Lee, 131
Hancock (aircraft carrier), 455
Hardy, Porter, 254
Harpoon cruise missiles, 74, 75, 81–82
Hassayampa (fleet oiler), racial disturbances, 218–222, 235, 248, 249
Hayward, Admiral Thomas, 244
Hazard, Lieutenant Commander Bobbie, 53
Heagy, Commander, 11
Heath, Edward, 470, 471
Hébert, F. Edward, 100, 124, 245
    Zumwalt and, 245–247, 251, 253–254, 257, 259
Helicopters, 71, 75, 80–81, 116
    CH-53, 80
    LAMPS (Light Airborne Multi Purpose System), 80

minesweeping by, 81
operational advantage of, 80–81
SH-2, 80
SH-3, 80
Helms, Richard, 322, 329, 365
Henkin, Daniel, 234, 251
Hicks, Floyd, 245, 247, 248, 251–253, 258, 259
High-Low concept, 72–84, 102–107, 116, 120, 121, 124–125, 284, 474
Hijacking, 276, 294, 295
Hill, Robert, 457
Hiss, Alger, 32
Ho Chi Minh Trail, 37, 38
Hoffman, Martin, 374
Holloway, General Bruce, 286–287
Holloway, Admiral James L., Jr., 177
Holloway, Admiral James L., III, 77, 176, 243–244, 476, 506
    Change of Command Ceremony, 510–511
    selected as Zumwalt's successor, 475, 477, 478
    Zumwalt and, 475, 478, 485
Holmes, Admiral Eph, 102
Holmquist, Carl, 96
Homeporting, 125–136, 453
    Australia, 132
    Chafee and, 128, 129
    Clarey and, 127, 128
    Greece, 125, 128–136, 305, 353–354
    Italy, 129, 131
    Japan, 132, 135
    Laird and, 128, 129
    Mediterranean Sea, 125–136, 305, 353–354
    Pacific Ocean, 126, 127, 132, 133, 135
    Portugal, 131
    Sardinia, 132
    Spain, 131
    U.S. Congress, 125–126
    Zumwalt and, 125–136, 305, 353–354
Hopkins, Harry, 139
Hormuz, Strait of, 362, 452–453
House Appropriations Committee, 124–125, 333
House Armed Services Committee, 124, 157, 245, 333, 452
Hughes, Senator, 162

Human Relations Council, 224–225, 257
Human Resources Development Center (San Diego), 226
Humphrey, Hubert, 160, 163, 377
Hungary, 344
Hussein, King, 293–294, 298
Hwangpoo River, 6–9
Hydrofoil patrol boat (PHM), 74–75

ICBM, see Intercontinental ballistic missiles
Iceland, 62, 276, 466–474
    communism, 470
    Finland and, 466
    fishing rights controversy, 470–471
    Great Britain and, 467, 469–471
    Greenland and, 466, 467
    NATO and, 466–469, 472–473
    Norway and, 466–469
    opponents of the Keflavík base, 469
    Schlesinger and, 473, 474
    Scotland and, 470
    Sweden and, 466
    U.S.S.R. and, 466, 468
    Zumwalt and, 466–474
Ignatius, Paul, 41
Incidents at Sea, 391–394
Independence (aircraft carrier), 135, 298, 299, 435–437, 443
India, 290, 372
    China and, 364
    Kissinger and, 365–368
    Nixon and, 365, 367, 368
    Packard and, 365, 366
    Pakistan and, 360, 363–369
    U.S.S.R. and, 364, 366
Indian Ocean, 360–369
    France and, 360–361
    Great Britain and, 360–363, 367–368
    the Netherlands and, 360–361
    Schlesinger on, 455
    U.S.S.R. and, 361–368, 456
    U.S. Navy and, 367–369, 454–456
    Zumwalt on, 360–368
Indo-China, 158, 413, 424–426
    Nixon and, 424–426
    U.S. Congress and, 424–426
    See also names of countries
Indonesia, 52, 62
    Zumwalt in, 214–215

Industrial College of the Armed Forces, 264
Inman, Commander Ray, 53
Inter-Agency Oil Task Force, 450
Intercontinental ballistic missiles (ICBM)
    U.S.S.R., 333, 349–350, 407
    U.S., 500
International Security Affairs, 28–33, 131
    Director of the Arms Control Division, 30
Ionnides, Colonel Demetrios, 135
Iran, 454
Iranian Air Force, 150
Iraq, 298, 300
    U.S.S.R. and, 360, 362, 454, 456
Ireland, 301
Irving, Frederick, 472–474
Irwin, John, 365, 450
Israel, 136, 276, 278, 279, 282, 292–293, 353, 354
    Egypt and, 292–293, 361, 432, 433, 438, 439, 444, 448–449
    Jordan and, 295–296, 300
    Kissinger and, 432–441, 446
    as military benefit to U.S., 442
    Moorer and, 441
    NATO and, 442
    Seven Days War, 361
    U.S.S.R. and, 292, 363, 439
    U.S. commitment to, 441–442
    Yom Kippur War, 432–442, 444, 448–449
        U.S. airlift, 433–435, 454, 465
Italy, 52, 141, 214, 301–302, 305, 354, 355
    homeporting, 129, 131
    Yom Kippur War, 442
Itaya, Admiral, 52
Iwo Jima (amphibious ship), 443

Jackson, Henry, 33, 51, 125, 160, 161, 163, 409, 435, 443, 452, 490
    SALT and, 395, 409–410, 427, 429, 504–505
    Zumwalt and, 32, 403
Jackson, Richard, 85–86, 95
Jackson Amendment, 486, 488
Jane's Fighting Ships, 315
Japan, 52, 62, 126, 150, 200–201, 360, 361, 363, 378, 484
    homeporting, 132, 135

oil and, 450, 451
World War II, 4–20
Jewell, Commander Dick, 270, 271
Johannessen, Admiral Folke, 355, 357, 358
John F. Kennedy (aircraft carrier), 298–300, 302, 436, 437, 443, 447
Johnson, Alexis, 355, 365, 457
Johnson, Bennett, 160–161
Johnson, Hiram, 24
Johnson, Louis A., 26, 27
Johnson, Lyndon B., xiii, 33, 100, 108
Vietnamization, 36
Johnson, Admiral Nels, 277
Johnson, U. Alexis, 65, 296–298
Johnston, Admiral Means, 110–115, 251
Joint Chiefs of Staff, 275–295
"Admirals Spy Ring," 369–376
budget discussions, 280–282, 284, 287–291, 313–317, 333–348, 407, 411, 461
Chapman, 276, 293–295, 314–315, 338
Laird, 278, 280, 287–290
Moorer, 277–281, 288, 289, 293, 295, 297, 314–316, 329, 348, 440
Nixon briefing, 288–291
Ryan, 276, 277, 342, 343, 347, 348
strategic arms discussions, 282–288
Westmoreland, 276, 277, 296–297, 315–316, 341–343, 347–348, 375
See also Zumwalt, Admiral Elmo R., Jr.
Joint Committee on Atomic Energy, 98
Joint Forces Memorandum, 341
Joint Strategic Targeting Planning System, 286–288
Jordan, 293–294, 298–301, 344
Israel and, 295–296, 300
Syria and, 298–301
Jordan crisis, 70, 126, 129–130, 139, 353, 354, 445

Kauffman, Admiral Draper, 268–269
Kelley, Roger T., 221
Kennedy, Edward, 160
Kennedy, John F., xiii, 32, 98, 310, 311, 344
Khrushchev, Nikita, 28, 31, 310, 311, 444
Kidd, Admiral Isaac, 44, 45, 254, 256, 302

Laird and, 476
Packard and, 476
question of Zumwalt's successor, 476–478
the Swanson conflict, 110, 112, 115
Zumwalt and, 136, 138, 139, 476
Kidnapping, 293
Kinkaid, Admiral, 15, 20–21
King, Admiral Jerry, 52
King, Dr. Martin Luther, Jr., 205
Kintberger, Commander Leon S., 184
Kissinger, Dr. Henry, 45–46, 108, 127, 242, 255, 275, 284, 287, 292, 302, 329, 355, 459, 506
"Admirals Spy Ring," 370, 373–375
on American decline, xiv–xv, 319–321
Brezhnev and, 404, 438
budgets and, 281–282, 313–317, 335–336, 340–341, 348
Chile and, 321–328
China and, 364, 368, 482, 484
Cuba and, 310–312
on détente, 482, 483
Dobrynin and, 310–311, 348–349, 351, 400, 404, 486–487, 506
on foreign policy, 481–484
Haig and, 309, 318, 319, 397–399, 419, 420, 474
India and, 365–368
Israel and, 432–441, 446
Joint Chiefs of Staff briefing, 289–291
Laird and, 241, 309–310, 314, 335–336, 373, 385, 408
Mediterranean crisis (October 1973), 448
Middle East and, 295–296, 298, 432–441, 483
National Security Council system, 317–320
National Security Decision Memorandums (NSDM), 314, 404, 421, 496–498
National Security Study Memorandums (NSSM), 322, 362, 421, 450
NATO and, 483–484
Nixon and, xii–xv, 309, 310, 319, 335, 396, 397, 405, 419, 421–423, 448, 474, 480, 486, 490, 507
Option Echo, 283

Packard and, 315
PFIAB, 465
POW/MIA families, 390–391
racial disturbances, 239–241
Robinson and, 318, 319
Rogers and, 311, 320
SALT and, xii, 320, 348–352, 400–410, 427–432, 472, 479, 480, 483–491
Schlesinger and, 485
study of world oil situation, 450
TTB and, 495–497
U.S.S.R. and, xiv, 310–312, 319–320, 323, 348–349, 362, 400–410, 438, 440, 445–446, 482–484, 505
Vietnam War, 379–381, 384, 385, 388, 390–391, 395, 404, 411–418, 426, 482
Yom Kippur War, 432–439
stalls U.S. airlift, 433–435
Zumwalt and, xii–xiii, 308–328, 340–341, 395–423, 493, 508–509
personal relationship, 396–397
Kissinger, Nancy, 318–319
Kitty Hawk (aircraft carrier), 215
racial disturbances, 217–224, 233, 235, 248, 249, 257, 476
Kleindienst, Richard, 395
Korea, 126, 279, 280, 414
Korean War, 62–63, 84, 290
Zumwalt, 65, 185
Korry, Edward, 326
Korth, Fred, 32, 99, 176
Kosygin, Alexsei N., 352–353
Kunle, Admiral Heinz, 357

Laird, Melvin, 56, 66, 84, 243, 255, 265, 267, 302, 311, 329, 367, 418, 422
"Admirals Spy Ring," 370, 374, 376
budgets and, 155–157, 335–338, 342, 347, 348
Chile and, 326–328
"fly before buy" principle, 146, 158
homeporting, 128, 129
as Joint Chiefs of Staff member, 278, 280, 287–290
Kidd and, 476
Kissinger and, 241, 309–310, 314, 335–336, 373, 385, 408
Nixon and, 305–307
racial disturbances, 228, 234, 241–242

SALT and, 350, 407–408
Vietnam War, 41–42, 45, 377–383, 385, 388, 411, 416
Vietnamization, 361, 377
on women, 262–263
Zumwalt and, 46–48, 70, 137, 154, 168, 194, 239, 244, 251, 253, 267, 310, 371, 412, 457
Lalor, F. M., 21
LAMPS (Light Airborne Multi Purpose System), 80
Lancy, Captain, 86
Laos, 35, 37, 344, 384, 425
Law of the Sea, 470
Le Boureois, Admiral Julien, 251
Leahy, Admiral William D., 66
Leaky (guided-missile frigate), 298
Lebanon, 290, 344
LeMay, Curtis, 294, 399
LHA (amphibious ship), 72–74, 150–151
Libya, 438
Light Airborne Multi Purpose Systems (LAMPS), 80
Lin, Loo, 9
Lincoln, Abraham, 194
Litton Industries, 74, 150–151
Lobbying, 123–124, 160–163
by U.S.S.R., 162–163
Lockheed Corporation, 78
Lon Nol, 424
Long Beach (cruiser), 95
Lundvall, Admiral Bengt, 357
Luns, Joseph, 357
Lurquin, Commodore Leon, 357

Maas, Admiral Johnny, 355, 358
McCain, Admiral John, 209–210, 384, 387, 475
McClellan, John, 120, 125
McCord, James, 395, 418
McDonald, Admiral David, 34, 44, 63, 99, 103, 250
McDonald, Lieutenant Colonel Dick, 53
McGovern, George, 160, 389, 408, 409
McIntyre, Thomas, 158, 159, 160, 162
Mack, Admiral Bill, 251
McKee, Captain Frances, 263
McKee, Captain Kinnaird, 286, 385, 421

McNamara, Robert, 32, 33, 35, 65, 79, 100, 144, 397
   discrimination, 255
Maginnes, Nancy, *see* Kissinger, Nancy
Mahon, George, 118, 120, 124, 409, 418
Mahon Committee, 120
Major Fleet Escort Study, 101–104
Malacca, Straits of, 367, 368
Malaysia, 52
Malta, 276, 303, 305–307, 318, 354–356, 421, 468
   Great Britain and, 354–356
   NATO and, 354
   Nixon and, 355
   U.S.S.R. and, 305, 307
Mankiewicz, Frank, 389
Mansfield, Mike, 160, 472
Mao Tse-tung, 484
Marijuana problems, 205
Mark 46 torpedoes, 78, 80, 82
Market Time (code name), 37
Marshall, General George C., 26–27, 276
   Zumwalt and, 26–27, 321
Marshall, Mrs. George C., 26
Martin, Lieutenant Ed, 17, 20
Matsu, 290
Mediterranean Sea, 75–76
   crisis (September 1970), 292–307
   crisis (October 1973), 432–437, 443, 446–448
   homeporting, 125–136, 305, 353–354
   strategy in, 297–307
   U.S.S.R. and, 130, 292–307, 444–447
"Meet the Press" (TV show), 507–510
Mekong River delta, 36–37
Mexican-Americans, discrimination against, 168, 197–198
Meyer, General John, 316
Mickey Mouse, Elimination of, *see* Demeaning and Abrasive Regulations, Elimination of
Middendorf, J. William, II, 115
Middle East, 126, 275–276, 280, 283, 284, 292–307, 360–369, 432–459
   crisis (September 1970), 292–307
   Kissinger and, 295–296, 298, 432–441, 483
   Moorer and, 303, 367, 443, 445–446

Nixon and, 294–295, 298, 299, 301–307
Packard and, 295–296, 300
U.S.S.R. and, 292–307, 433–438, 444–447
U.S. Department of Defense and, 295–296, 300
Zumwalt and, 292–307, 360–368, 432–459
See also names of countries
Midway (aircraft carrier), 135, 215, 216
Miles, Admiral Milton E., 10–14
   guerilla action, 11–12
Military Facilities Agreement (1953), 131
Minesweeping, 3–4, 81, 384–389, 393, 400, 417
   by helicopters, 81
Minh, General, 378
Minority Affairs Programs, 204, 219, 220, 223–224, 237
Mintoff, Dom, 305–306, 354–356
Minuteman sites, 156, 284, 349–351, 400, 495
MIRVs (Multiple Independently Targetable Reentry Vehicles)
   U.S.S.R., 161, 407, 488
   U.S., 153, 157, 320, 407, 487, 488, 499–503, 505–506
Missiles
   U.S.S.R., 153, 428–431
      ABM, 349, 350, 352, 400, 402, 487
      ASM, 147
      cruise, 61–62, 76, 78, 381
      ICBM, 333, 349–350, 407
      MIRV, 161, 407, 408
      SAM, 292
      SLBM, 401–407, 428–429
      SSN 8, 403
   U.S., 141, 153, 428–431
      ABM, 284, 320, 349–352, 402, 487
      cruise, 74, 75, 81–82
      ICBM, 500
      MIRV, 153, 157, 320, 407, 487, 488, 499–503, 505–506
      Phoenix system, 78, 147
      Safeguard, 349–353, 400
      SAM, 372
      SLBM, 333, 400–407, 428, 429
      Trident, 403, 500
      ULMS, 154–157

Mitchell, John, 420
Mobile Riverine Force, 37–38
Mobutu, Sese Seko, 308–309, 370
Mod Squad, 34, 175–176, 182–196
Montero, Admiral Raul, 324–328
Moorer, Admiral Thomas, 44, 46, 47,
    56, 64, 181, 209, 302, 306, 311, 418,
    419, 505, 510
    "Admirals Spy Ring," 369–376
    budgets and, 337, 339
    as Chairman of Joint Chiefs of
        Staff, 227–281, 288, 289, 293,
        295, 297, 314–316, 329, 348, 440
    Chile and, 326–328
    on grooming, 191
    Israel and, 441
    Middle East and, 303, 367, 443,
        445–446
    National Security Council system,
        318
    Nixon and, 506–507
    SALT and, 352, 402, 407, 409
    TTB and, 496–498
    Vietnam War, 379, 380, 382, 384–
        387, 413, 415–416
    Yom Kippur War, 434, 436
    Zumwalt and, 41, 51, 52, 71, 310,
        330, 402
Moorer, Mrs. Thomas, 51
Morocco, 192
Mozambique, U.S.S.R. and, 333
Mullikan, John, 256
Multiple Independently Targetable
    Reentry Vehicles, see MIRVs
Murphy, Admiral Daniel, 242, 243, 244,
    255, 347, 435–437, 439, 447–448
Murphy's Law, 222, 224
Muse, Admiral George, 205
Mutual and Balanced Force Reduction,
    313

Narva, Dr. William, 54
Nasser, Gamel Abdel, 302
National Aeronautics and Space Ad-
    ministration (NASA), 64, 145
National Command Authority, 349–352
National Security Council system, 317–
    320
National Security Decision Memoran-
    dums (NSDM), 282, 314, 404, 421,
    496–498
National Security Study Memorandums
    (NSSM), 322, 362, 421, 450

National Steel Corporation, 117
National War College, 27–28, 96, 264
NATO (North Atlantic Treaty Organi-
    zation), 129, 130, 136, 139, 276, 277,
    280, 297, 301, 305, 357–358
    China and, 484
    Forward Based Systems (FBS),
        313, 350–351, 353, 400, 429, 487,
        488
    Iceland and, 466–469, 472–473
    Israel and, 442
    Kissinger and, 483–484
    Malta and, 354
    Mutual and Balanced Force Re-
        duction, 313
    oil embargo and, 449–450
    relevant power, 344, 345
    U.S.S.R. and, 332–333, 353
    U.S. commitments to, 466
    Zumwalt and, 136, 305, 344, 345,
        357–358, 466–469, 472–473
Naval Investigative Service Office, 205–
    207
Naval Ordnance Test Station (China
    Lake), 49
Naval War College, 27, 54, 141, 356
NAVMINS (Navy Minority Informa-
    tion messages), 237–238
NAVOPS (message to the entire Navy),
    170, 172, 192, 195, 261–272
Nelson, Gaylord, 161
Netherlands, the, 355, 357–359
    Indian Ocean and, 360–361
    Yom Kippur War, 442
New Jersey (battleship), 82
New York Times, The, 221, 229, 239,
    434
Newhouse, John, 283, 348, 351–353,
    404
Newport News Shipbuilding Company,
    117
Nicholson, Captain Richard, 175–176
Nimitz, Admiral Chester, 245
Nimitz (aircraft carrier), 73
Nitze, Paul, 27–34, 73, 75, 78, 98, 101,
    154, 155, 254, 397, 410, 506
    appointed Secretary of the Navy,
        32–33
    Cuban missile crisis, 29–30, 69
    Nixon and, 490
    Nuclear Test Ban Treaty, 29, 30
    Personnel Retention Task Force,
        170

on question of Zumwalt's successor, 477
Rickover and, 97, 100, 101
SALT and, 30, 282, 283, 427, 487, 488, 490–492
Separable First State Disarmament Agreement (SFSDA), 30–32
terminates his appointment, 491, 505, 507
Zumwalt and, 27–35, 41, 52, 65, 68–69, 79, 96, 97, 105, 275, 285, 510
Nixon, Richard M., 46–48, 118, 126, 137, 157, 214, 229, 238, 241, 275, 287, 293, 317, 329, 388
"Admirals Spy Ring," 369–371, 375, 376
Brezhnev and, 429, 445, 481, 500
budgets and, 281–282, 313–314, 348, 463, 494
Chile and, 322, 323, 327–328
China and, 368, 481
deteriorating health of, 479
Diego Garcia issue, 458
Haig and, 396, 398–399, 419, 448, 474, 479
India and, 365, 367, 368
Indo-China policy, 424–426
Joint Chiefs of Staff briefing, 288–291
Kissinger and, xii–xv, 309, 310, 319, 335, 396, 397, 405, 419, 421–423, 448, 474, 480, 486, 507
Laird and, 305–307
Malta and, 355
Middle East and, 294–295, 298, 299, 301–307
Moorer and, 506–507
National Security Council meeting (January 1974), 479–481
Nitze and, 490
Option Echo, 283
PFIAB, 464–465
POW/MIA families, 413–415
question of Zumwalt's successor, 478
racial disturbances, 240, 242
reaction to Zumwalt's Annapolis speech (1974), 493–495
review of 1972–1973 events, 395–396
SALT and, xii, 351–353, 402, 408–409, 426, 429, 486, 489, 490

memorandum from Zumwalt, 499–504
Schlesinger and, 505–507
"State of the World" message, 330–331
U.S.S.R. and, 429, 444–446, 480–481, 500
Vietnam War, 377–382, 384, 386, 387, 393, 395, 411–417, 424, 426
visits Sixth Fleet, 301–307
Watergate affair, xiv, 395, 419, 420, 424, 427
on women, 265
Yom Kippur War, 434, 435, 438
Zumwalt and, xii–xiii, 303–307, 318–320, 405–406, 412, 493–495, 506–508
personal assessment (1973), 459–460
Nixon, Mrs. Richard M., 493
Nixon Doctrine, 128, 289, 300, 305, 330, 334, 356, 358
relevant power, 346
Norman, Lieutenant Commander William, 199–201, 204, 205, 211, 267–268
racial disturbances, 227, 228, 234
North Atlantic Treaty Organization, see NATO
North Carolina, University of, 26
Norway, 62, 355, 357, 358
Iceland and, 466–469
U.S.S.R. and, 466–468
Norwegian Sea, 466
NSDM, see National Security Decision Memorandums
NSSM, see National Security Study Memorandums
Nuclear Test Ban Treaty (1963), 29, 30, 405
Nitze and, 29, 30
Zumwalt and, 29, 30
Nuclear-propulsion systems, 63–65, 85, 93, 97, 100–108, 121
Nunn, Sam, 161, 505
Nutter, Warren, 131

October War, see Yom Kippur War
Oil, 360, 363
Arab embargo, 449–452
China and, 451
Japan and, 450, 451
Kissinger's study of world situation, 450

Posture Statement on, 452
U.S.S.R. and, 442, 449–451, 453
Yom Kippur War and, 433, 434
Zumwalt on, 452–453
Oman, 362
Operation Pegasus, 132
Option Echo, 282–283, 308, 348, 349, 429
Orientals, discrimination against, 168
Oriskany (aircraft carrier), 455
Overkill, 286–287, 430

Pacific Ocean, 76, 126, 214–216
homeporting, 126, 127, 132, 133, 135
Packard, David, 65, 70, 289, 326, 327, 330, 353, 418
budgets and, 336
India and, 365, 366
Kidd and, 476
Kissinger and, 315
Middle East and, 295–296, 300
military procurement, 146–148
SALT and, 154, 156, 350
Zumwalt and, 70, 147, 281, 310
Pakistan, 70, 362
India and, 360, 363–369
Palestine Liberation Organization, 449
Palestinian commandos, 276, 293–294, 295
Palmer, General Bruce, 293, 341
Panama, 398
Panama Canal, 322
Papadapoulos, George, 135, 297
Parsons (destroyer), 372
Pastore, John, 120
Patrol Frigate (PF), 75, 102, 106, 121
Pearl Harbor Shipyard, 108–115
Peet, Ray, 87, 95–96
Pell, Claiborne, 418
Persian Gulf, 333, 360, 361, 362, 451–453
Great Britain and, 453–454
U.S. Navy in, 453–456
Zumwalt on importance of, 453–456
Personnel Retention Task Force, 170
Peru, 421
Petersen, Forrest, 102–103
PFIAB (President's Foreign Intelligence Advisory Board), 464–465
PG gunboats, 75
Philip (destroyer), 20, 94, 179

Philippines, the, 37, 41, 62, 205, 378
PHM hydrofoil patrol boat, 74–75
Phoenix missile systems, 78, 147
Pirnie, Alexander, 245, 247, 252–253, 255
Planning, Programming, Budgeting System (PPBS), 334–336, 341
Plato, 91–92
Polaris-Poseidon submarines, 59, 83, 106, 153–154, 156, 159, 284, 351
Pollack, Admiral Michael, 357, 471
Porter, William, 473
Portugal, 29, 62, 318, 456
homeporting, 131
Yom Kippur War, 442
Posture Statements, 452, 461
POW/MIA families, 389–391
Kissinger and, 390–391
Nixon and, 413–415
Zumwalt and, 389–391
PPBS (Planning, Programming, Budgeting System), 334–336, 341
President's Foreign Intelligence Advisory Board (PFIAB), 464–465
Preston, Ralph, 118
Price, Admiral Frank, 75
Pringle, Captain Don, 53, 231, 385, 444, 445
Pritzlaff, John J., Jr., 305
"Problem of the Next Succession in the USSR, The" (Zumwalt), 28
Programs for People, 174–175, 265, 267–272
Project 60, 66–84, 104–108, 126, 154, 177, 211, 284, 306–307, 340, 444, 475
Providence, 216
Proxmire, William, 125, 136–149, 151, 160
Zumwalt and, 136–149
Pueblo (intelligence gathering ship), 279
Puerto Ricans, discrimination against, 168
Pursley, Brigadier General Robert, 47

Quemoy, 290
Question and Answer Book, 249
Quigley, Captain Robin, 262–264

Racial disturbances, 217–260, 412
Anderson and, 233–234
Clarey and, 219–220, 223, 227, 228, 230–231, 242

Constellation, 221–235, 240–250, 253, 257, 259, 412, 476
Hassayampa, 218–222, 235, 248, 249
Kissinger and, 239–241
Kitty Hawk, 217–224, 233, 235, 248, 249, 257, 476
Laird and, 228, 234, 241–242
Nixon and, 240, 242
Norman and, 227, 228, 234
television and, 229, 239, 240, 242
U.S. Congress and, 245–260
Warner and, 227, 228, 230–234
Zumwalt and, 217–260, 412
See also Discrimination
Radford, Yeoman First Class Charles, 369–376, 385, 477
Rauch, Admiral Charles F., Jr., 105, 175, 190, 194–195, 199, 211, 309
on alcohol problem, 269–271
Ray, Dixy Lee, 496
Rectanus, Admiral Rex, 38, 39
Red Cross, 53
Red Sea, 75
Regulus cruise missiles, 81
Relevant power, 344–346
Replogle, Luther, 470
Republic, The (Plato), 92
Reserve Officers Training Corps (ROTC), 172
women, 264
Zumwalt and, 26
Retention study group programs, 170–173, 220–221, 262
Richardson, Elliot, 118, 267, 337, 395, 418, 419, 422, 438
Rickover, Admiral Hyman, 63, 72–74, 124, 154, 160, 329, 474
Division of Nuclear Propulsion, 85
length of tour, 98, 158
Major Fleet Escort Study, 101–104
Nitze and, 97, 100, 101
on nuclear-propulsion systems, 63–65, 85, 93, 97, 100–108, 121
passed over for promotion, 98
reappointments, 99–100, 108
retirement, 98–99
ULMS, 154–156
U.S. Congress and, 85, 97–100, 103–104, 107–108, 123
Zumwalt and, 85–122, 477, 478
first meeting, 85–95

nuclear power conflict, 93, 100–108, 121
Sea Control Ships, 106, 116–121
the Swanson conflict, 108–115, 118
Riverine warfare, 37–38
Rivero, Admiral Horacio, 52, 103, 141, 302, 305
Zumwalt and, 456–457
Rivers, L. Mendel, 100, 124, 254
Robertson, Captain H. B., 385
Robinson, Admiral Rembrandt, 289, 299, 311, 340, 375
"Admirals Spy Ring," 369, 374
Kissinger and, 318, 319
Robinson (destroyer), 3–4, 15, 20, 21
Rockefeller, Nelson, 465
Rogers, William P., 289, 302, 303, 305–306, 329, 416, 419, 457
Kissinger and, 311, 320
Roosevelt, Franklin D., 66, 139
Rosenthal, Benjamin, 125, 130–136
Zumwalt and, 125, 130–136
Rosenthal's Subcommittee on Europe, 130, 131
ROTC, *see* Reserve Officers Training Corps
Ruckelshaus, William, 118, 438
Rumsfeld, Donald, 449
Rush, Kenneth, 148, 149, 415, 416, 418, 486
Rush, Myron, 28
Russell, Richard, 32–33, 100
Rutherford Preparatory School, 24
Ryan, General Jack, 70, 316, 418
as Joint Chiefs of Staff member, 276, 277, 342, 343, 347, 348

S-3 aircraft, 78
Safeguard missiles, 349–353, 400
SALT (Strategic Arms Limitation Talks), 142, 152–157, 160, 161, 276
Assurances, 405–408
the budget and, 407–410
as a codification of rules, 157
Fulbright and, 407
Haig and, 490, 491
Interim Agreement, 406–407, 410, 487–489, 499, 501–503
Jackson and, 395, 409–410, 427, 429, 504–505

Kissinger and, xii, 320, 348–352, 400–410, 427–432, 472, 479, 480, 483–491
Laird and, 350, 407–408
Moorer and, 352, 402, 407, 409
Nitze and, 30, 282, 283, 427, 487, 488, 490–492
Nixon and, xii, 351–353, 402, 408–409, 426, 429, 486, 489, 490
 memorandum from Zumwalt, 499–504
Option Echo, 282–283, 308, 348, 349, 429
Packard and, 154, 156, 350
Schlesinger and, 430–432, 487–491
throw-weight issue, 431–432
TTB and, 495–497, 500, 503
U.S.S.R. and, 348–352, 400–410, 427–431, 486–492, 495–497, 499–504
U.S. Congress and, xii, 407–410, 427–428, 430, 486
U.S. Department of Defense and, 154, 156, 350, 407–408, 430–432, 487–491
Zumwalt and, 30, 52, 107, 282–284, 287, 308, 348–349, 400–410, 426–432, 485–492, 495–505, 509, 510
 Memorandum for the President, 499–505
Salzer, Admiral Robert, 269, 378
SAM (surface-to-air missiles), 292, 372
Sanctuary (hospital ships), 131, 132, 264
Saratoga (aircraft carrier), 215, 298, 299, 302
Sardinia, 132
Saudi Arabia, 438, 449, 454
Saufley (destroyer), 3, 20, 26
Scandinavia, *see* names of countries
Schlesinger, James, 116, 120, 157, 314, 395, 418, 440, 443, 445–446, 481
 "Admirals Spy Ring," 373–374
 budgets and, 116, 120, 157, 463, 464
 Iceland and, 473, 474
 on importance of Indian Ocean, 455
 Kissinger and, 485
 Nixon and, 505–507
 PFIAB, 464–465

question of Zumwalt's successor, 475–478
SALT and, 430–432, 487–491
TTB and, 496, 498
Yom Kippur War, 443–435
Zumwalt and, xi, 121, 422–423, 459, 473–475, 492–495, 498, 508–511
Scotland, 159, 313, 351
 Iceland and, 470
Scoville, Dr. Herbert, 161, 163
Sea Control Ships, 75–76, 106, 116–121
Sea Float (code name), 39–40
Second Fleet, 44, 436
Seignious, Lieutenant General George, 277
Selden, Armistead, 253, 324–327
Senate Appropriations Committee, 125, 140, 333
Senate Armed Services Committee, 125, 140, 148, 150, 157–159, 333, 409
Senate Foreign Relations Committee, 130
Separable First Stage Disarmament Agreement (SFSDA), 30–31
Seven Days War, 361
Seventh Fleet, 36, 37, 44, 45, 52, 76, 127, 205, 214, 222, 379, 388, 455
 Zumwalt visits, 215–216, 378
SFSDA (Separable First Stage Disarmament Agreement), 30–31
SH-2 helicopters, 80
SH-3 helicopters, 80
Shah of Iran, 150
Shanghai Power Company, 16, 20
Shepherd, Captain Burt, 53, 371, 372
Shikoku (Japanese carrier), 5
Shultz, George, 291, 314, 329, 347, 420
Sicily, 185, 306
Sigmond, Commander Arie, 53–54, 309
Sikes, Bob, 418
Singapore, 52
Sisco, Joseph, 296, 297, 473
Sixth Fleet, 44, 45, 52, 76, 126, 127, 130, 139, 173, 176, 185, 296–307, 353–354
 Mediterranean crisis (October 1973), 435–439, 443, 446–448
 Nixon's visit to, 301–307
Skjong, Admiral Hans, 357
SLBM, *see* Submarine-launched ballistic missiles
Smith, Gerard, 408–409
Smith, Admiral Levering, 154, 155

Smith, Margaret Chase, 125, 155
Somalia, 356, 456
    U.S.S.R. and, 333, 361
Sonnenfeldt, Helmut, 399, 448, 491
Southwest Africa, 421
Spain, 29, 62, 296, 301, 303, 305
    homeporting, 131
    U.S. bases in, 159, 214, 313, 351,
        456
Spiers, Ronald, 130
Spiro, Lieutenant Colonel Mike, 53
Spivak, Laurence, 507, 509
Springfield (cruiser), 299, 302, 307
SSN 8 missiles, 403
SSN-688 Class submarines, 72, 74, 83,
    105, 106, 155
Stalin, Joseph, 28, 184
Standard Oil Company, 16
"State of the World" message, 330–331
Stennis, John, 51, 125, 150, 159–160,
    251, 407, 409, 418, 505
    Vietnam War, 382–383
Stockdale, Admiral Jim, 195–196
Stockdale, Sibyl, 389, 390
Strategic Arms Limitation Talks, see
    SALT
Strauss, Robert, 448
Strong, Captain Jim, 53
Subic Bay/San Miguel area report, 205–
    210
Submarine-launched ballistic missiles
    (SLBM)
    U.S.S.R., 401–407, 428–429
    U.S., 333, 400–407, 428–429
Submarines, 61, 153–156
    communications problems, 83
    DELTA class, 500
    Polaris-Poseidon, 59, 83, 106, 153–
        154, 156, 159, 384, 351
    SSN-688 Class, 72, 74, 83, 105, 106,
        155
    Trident, 107, 140–141, 152, 157–
        163, 284, 350, 403, 495, 500,
        503
Suez Canal, 81, 276, 344, 358, 361, 417,
    432, 438, 456, 457–458
    importance of, 456
    U.S.S.R. and, 449, 456, 458
    Zumwalt and, 457–458
Suharto, President, 214
Surface-to-air missiles (SAM), 292, 372
Surface-effect ships, 76–77
Swanson, Anne, 108–110

Swanson, Captain Charles O., 108–115,
    118
Sweden, 150, 357
    Iceland and, 466
    U.S.S.R. and, 468
Symington, Stuart, 125, 149–150, 159,
    163, 418, 505
Syria, 276, 279, 298, 300
    Jordan and, 298–301
    U.S.S.R. and, 300–310, 483
    Yom Kippur War, 432–434, 438

Taft, Robert, Jr., 505
Taiwan, 52
Talley, Admiral George, 443, 444
Tasca, Henry, 305
TASS, 311–312
Taylor, Commander, 113–114
Technology
    U.S.S.R., 153, 156, 401
    U.S., 153, 156, 487–488, 499
Television
    racial disturbances and, 229, 239,
        240, 242
    Zumwalt on, 388, 507–510
Tenant, Captain, Ray, 53
Tenneco Corporation, 117
Terihese, Captain, 6
Thailand, 52
Thieu, President, 413–416, 426
Thompson, Captain Bill, 54
Thompson, Llewellyn, 28
Thompson, Sir Robert, 426
Thornton, Tex, 151
Thostrup, Admiral Sven, 357
Threshold Test Ban (TTB), 495–498,
    500, 503
    Clements and, 496
    Kissinger and, 495–497
    Moorer and, 496–498
    SALT and, 495–497, 500, 503
    Schlesinger and, 496, 498
    U.S.S.R. and, 495–497, 503
    Zumwalt and, 495–498, 500, 503
Throw-weight issue, 431–432
Thurmond, Strom, 32–33, 505
Thuy, Xuan, 416
Tidd, Admiral Emmett, 54–55, 211–
    213, 259, 283, 324, 373
Tills (destroyer), 185
Time, 178, 256
"Today" (TV show), 242, 388
Tower, John, 409, 505

Towl, Clint, 148
Train, Harry, 462
Trident missiles, 403, 500
Trident submarines, 107, 140–141, 152, 157–163, 284, 350, 403, 495, 500, 503
  U.S. Congress and, 157–160
Truman, Harry, 199, 204
Tsushima, Straits of, 368
TTB, *see* Threshold Test Ban
Tucker, Gardiner, 342, 343
Tulare High School, 24, 89
Tunney, John, 161
Turkey, 62, 214, 293–297, 299, 306, 307, 318, 354, 421
  Yom Kippur War, 441
Turner, Captain Stansfield, 67, 104

Uchida, Admiral Kazutomi, 378
Underwater long-range missile system (ULMS), 154–157
Uniform Code of Military Justice, 240, 242
Union of Soviet Socialist Republics, 154–163, 279, 290, 344, 391
  Angola and, 333
  Arabs and, 363, 432–439, 441, 442, 445–449
  oil embargo, 449–451
  Chile and, 322–324, 326, 328
  China and, 31, 363, 484
  Cuba and, 310–313
  Cuban missile crisis, 69, 83
  Egypt and, 292, 439
  Finland and, 467–468
  Foxbat aircraft, 78
  Ghana and, 331–332
  G-I-UK gap and, 467
  Guinea and, 332, 333
  Iceland and, 466, 468
  India and, 364, 366
  Indian Ocean and, 361–368, 456
  Iraq and, 360, 362, 454, 456
  Israel and, 292, 363, 439
  Kissinger and, xiv, 310–312, 319–320, 323, 348, 349, 362, 400–410, 438, 440, 445–446, 482, 484, 505
  as a land power, 60, 62, 347
  lobbying by, 162–163
  Malta and, 305, 307
  Mediterranean and, 130, 292–307, 444–447

Middle East and, 292–307, 433–438, 444–447
  military expenditures, 314
  missiles, 153, 428–431
    ABM, 349, 350, 352, 400, 402, 487
    ASM, 147
    cruise, 61–62, 76, 78, 381
    ICBM, 333, 349–350, 407
    MIRV, 161, 407, 488
    SAM, 292
    SLBM, 401–407, 428, 429
    SSN 8, 403
  Mozambique and, 333
  NATO and, 332–333, 353
  Navy, 69, 72, 75, 82–85, 289, 330, 444–447
    compared to U.S. Navy, 59–65, 84, 105, 140–144, 275, 291, 303–304, 315–316, 333, 337–338, 345–346, 462–465
    Incidents at Sea, 391–394
    modernization of, 59
    Sea Control Ships, 120
    submarines, 61, 153–156
  Nixon and, 429, 444–446, 480–481, 500
  Norway and, 446–468
  oil and, 442, 449–451, 453
  possible nuclear exchange with U.S., 286–288
  relevant power, 344–346
  SALT and, 348–352, 400–410, 427–431, 486–492, 495–497, 499–504
  Somalia and, 333, 361
  strategic weapons compared to U.S., 276, 280, 282, 287–288
  Suez Canal and, 449, 456, 458
  Sweden and, 468
  Syria and, 300–301, 483
  technology, 153, 156, 401
  TTB, 495–497, 503
  Vietnam War, 381, 382, 384, 400
  world hegemony, 25, 152
  World War II, 60–61
  Yom Kippur War, 433–439, 442, 445–449
  Zumwalt and, 25–26, 30–31, 35, 48, 330–331
    "The Problem of the Next Succession in the USSR," 28
United Arab Republic (UAR), 458

United Kingdom–Iceland gap, 116
United Nations, 365, 438
United States
  dependence on the seas, 60
  Kissinger on decline of, xiv–xv, 319–321
  Minuteman sites, 156, 284, 349–351, 400, 495
  missiles, 141, 153, 428–431
    ABM, 284, 320, 349–352, 402, 487
    cruise, 74, 75, 81–82
    ICBM, 500
    MIRV, 153, 157, 320, 407, 487, 488, 499–503, 505–506
    Phoenix system, 78, 147
    Safeguard, 349–353, 400
    SAM, 372
    SLBM, 333, 400–407, 428–429
    Trident, 403, 500
    ULMS, 154–157
  possible nuclear exchange with U.S.S.R., 286–288
  strategic weapons compared to U.S.S.R., 276, 280, 282, 287–288
  support to straits nations, 62
  technology, 153, 156, 487–488, 499
  See also names of military branches
U.S. Air Force, 64, 70–71, 221, 249, 276, 277, 280, 282, 283, 297–299, 316, 401, 456, 497–498
  B-52, 156, 384, 389
  budget, 334, 337, 411
  F-15, 146, 147, 149–150
  F-111A, 79
  lack of access to airfields, 70
  training agreement with U.S. Navy, 70
U.S. Army, 37, 221, 246, 249, 276, 277, 280, 284, 299, 314, 401, 497–498
  budget, 334, 337, 341, 342
U.S. Coast Guard, 270
U.S. Congress, 70, 74, 78, 123–163, 295, 371, 454
  budgets and, 336–339, 342, 407–411, 463–466
  Diego Garcia issue, 458
  F-14 controversy, 136, 140, 143–152
  homeporting, 125–136
  House Appropriations Committee, 124–125, 333
  House Armed Services Committee, 124, 157, 245, 333, 452
  Indo-China policy, 424–426
  lobbying, 123–124, 160–163
  racial disturbances, 245–260
  Rickover and, 85, 97–100, 103–104, 107–108, 123
  SALT and, xii, 407–410, 427–428, 430, 486
  Sea Control Ships and, 120
  Senate Appropriations Committee, 125, 140, 333
  Senate Armed Services Committee, 125, 140, 148, 150, 157–159, 333, 409
  Senate Foreign Relations Committee, 130
  Subcommittee on Disciplinary Problems, 252–259
  Subcommittee on Europe, 131
  Subcommittee on the Near East, 131
  Trident appropriations, 157–160
  Vietnam War, 378, 381, 382, 410–411, 413, 416–417
  on women, 261, 263, 264
  Zumwalt and, 107, 123–163, 245–260
U.S. Department of Defense, 70–71, 148, 149, 278, 314, 333–335
  budgets and, 116, 120, 155–157, 336, 463, 464
  Distinguished Medal, 498, 511
  Middle East and, 295–296, 300
  military procurement, 146–148
  SALT and, 154, 156, 350, 407–408, 430–432, 487–491
U.S. Marine Corps, 70–71, 144, 218, 246, 270, 276, 290, 303, 314, 316, 338, 379, 493, 497
  CH-53 helicopters, 80
  F-4s, 384, 389
  LHA amphibious ship, 72–74
U.S. Maritime Administration, 71
U.S. Naval Academy, 23, 24, 56, 66, 89–90, 96, 201
  women, 261
  Zumwalt at, 24, 89–90
U.S. Naval Guerilla Forces in China, 10
U.S. Navy
  "Admirals Spy Ring," 369–376
  aircraft

A-6, 78
BACKFIRE bomber, 500
F-4, 78, 144, 146, 148, 384, 389
F-14, 77–79, 136, 140, 143–152, 162, 284
F-14A, 80, 146–147
F-14B, 146–147
F-111, 144
F-111B, 79, 146
S-3, 78
VSTOL, 71, 75, 77, 116
aircraft carriers
CVAs, 77–78
CVANs, 73, 74, 101, 105, 107
CVSs, 77
Sea Control Ships, 75–76, 106, 116–121
alcohol problems, 269–271
amphibious ship (LHA), 150–151
ANG-9 fire control system, 147
Backup Book, 249
budget, 281, 284, 289–291, 315–317, 333–348, 411, 461–466, 494
Captor mines, 82
communications systems, 82–83
compared to U.S.S.R. Navy, 59–65, 84, 105, 140–144, 275, 291, 303–304, 315–316, 333, 337–338, 345–346, 462–465
DD-963s (Spruance), 73–75, 102, 150–151
Demeaning and Abrasive Regulations, Elimination of, 182–196
DesRon 12, 132, 133, 135
DesRon 15, 132, 133, 135
discrimination, 168, 197–216, 261–265, 268–269
Minority Affairs Programs, 204, 219, 220, 223–224, 237
report on Subic Bay/San Miguel area, 205–210
double mission of, 60
dress regulations, 168, 173, 178–179, 182–185, 190–191, 193, 195, 257–258
drug problems, 205, 269
escorts, 452
DE-1052, 73, 75
DLGs, 102–103
DLGNs, 73, 74, 81, 101–103, 105, 121

family separation, 126, 168, 176–178
Flag Officers News Letter, 262
grooming regulations, 168, 169, 182, 191, 192, 195, 248, 493, 494
helicopters, 71, 75, 80–81, 116
LAMPS (Light Airborne Multi Purpose System), 80
minesweeping by, 81
operational advantage of, 80–81
SH-2, 80
SH-3, 80
homeporting, 125–136
Human Relations Council, 224–225, 257
hydrofoil patrol boat (PHM), 74–75
Incidents at Sea, 391–394
Indian Ocean and, 367–369, 454–456
job satisfaction, 168
leaves, 184
marijuana problems, 205
Mark 46 torpedoes, 78, 80, 82
Mediterranean crisis (October 1973), 443, 446–448
Middle East crisis, 292–307
Mod Squad, 34, 175–176, 182–196
NAVMINS, 237–238
NAVOPS, 170, 172, 192, 195, 261–262
obsolescence since World War II, 59
Patrol Frigate (PF), 75, 102, 106, 121
in the Persian Gulf, 453–456
personnel policies, 167–196
PFIAB, 464–465
PG gunboats, 75
Programs for People, 174–175, 265, 267–272
projection by, 63
Question and Answer Book, 249
racial disturbances, 217–260, 412
recruitment, 210–214
reenlistment rate, 222, 266, 271
1970 and 1975, 167
relevant power, 344–346
retention study group programs, 170–173, 220–221, 262
strength of (current), 465–466

submarines, 155–156
   communications problems, 83
   DELTA class, 500
   Polaris-Poseidon, 59, 83, 106,
     153–154, 156, 159, 284, 351
   SSN-688 Class, 72, 74, 83,
     105, 106, 155
   Trident, 107, 140–141, 152,
     157–163, 284, 350, 403, 495,
     500, 503
surface-effect ships, 76–77
training agreement with U.S. Air
   Force, 70
union system in, 63–64
Vietnam War, 34–44, 169–170,
   190, 377–378, 383–389
World War II, 3–25, 60–61, 183–
   184
Yom Kippur War, 435–437
Z-grams, 172–196, 202–204, 213,
   220, 237, 248–251, 261–272
See also names of ships
U.S. Office of International Security
   Affairs, 296
U.S. Office of Management and the Bud-
   get, 48
U.S. Office of Strategic Services, 11
U.S. Strategic Air Command, 286–288
U.S. Supreme Court, 204–205
Uruguay, 324

Vance, Cyrus, 397
Very Short Takeoff or Landing
   (VSTOL) aircraft, 71, 75, 77, 116
Vice Chief of Naval Operations, 54–55,
   103
   code designation for, 53
Viet Cong, 37, 38, 39
Vietnam, 127, 276, 279, 280, 290, 291
Vietnam War, 33–44, 84, 142, 146, 167–
   168, 205, 212–214, 218, 242, 377–389,
   395
   Abrams, 378, 379, 383–384, 388
   Bunker, 383–384
   Cau Mau Peninsula, 39
   Chafee, 380, 381
   China, 388
   Clarey, 381, 382, 384, 386–387
   the DMZ, 379–380
   Game Warden (code name), 37
   Giant Slingshot (code name),
     38–39
   Haig, 384, 412

Ho Chi Minh Trail, 37, 38
Kissinger, 379–381, 384, 385, 388,
   390–391, 395, 404, 411–418, 426,
   482
Laird, 41–42, 45, 377–383, 385,
   388, 411, 416
Market Time (code name), 37
mining of Haiphong Harbor, 81,
   384–389, 393, 400, 417
Mobile Riverine Force, 37–38
Moorer, 379, 380, 382, 384–387,
   413, 415–416
Nixon, 377–382, 384, 386, 387,
   393, 395, 411–417, 424, 426
POW/MIA families, 389–391,
   413–415
Sea Float (code name), 39–40
Stennis, 382–383
U.S.S.R., 381, 382, 384, 400
U.S. Congress, 378, 381, 382, 410–
   411, 413, 416–417
U.S. Navy, 34–44, 169–170, 190,
   377–378, 383–389
Vogt, 379
Zumwalt, 34–44, 65, 67, 169–170,
   190, 377–389, 405, 410–415
   ACTOV, 36, 40–42, 44, 47
Vietnamese Navy, 377–378
Vietnamization, 377, 378, 426
   Abrams and, 378
   Johnson and, 36
   Laird and, 36, 377
   Zumwalt and, 46–47, 426
Vinson, Carl, 124, 245, 247, 253–254,
   259
Vinson (aircraft carrier), 73, 120
Vogt, General Johnny, 277, 425
   Vietnam War, 379
VSTOL aircraft, 71, 75, 77, 116

Wages, Commander Jerry, 53
Walker, Admiral Thomas, 227, 228,
   230, 232, 233
Waller (destroyer), 20
Walt, General Lewis, 316
Ward, Captain J. D., 223–230, 253, 257
Warner, John, 115, 116, 118, 149, 160,
   249, 253, 254, 330, 393, 418
   "Admirals Spy Ring," 369, 371–
     372
   Incidents at Sea, 393
   question of Zumwalt's successor,
     477–478

racial disturbances, 227, 228, 230–234
Zumwalt and, 44–49, 243–244, 256, 265–267
Warner, Mrs. John, 393
Warsaw Pact, 313, 351, 356
Washington *Post,* 370
Washington Special Action Group (WSAG), 294, 295, 298, 364–366, 369–370, 440
Watergate, xii, 157, 260, 395, 418–420, 424, 426, 427
 Haig, 420
 Nixon, xiv, 395, 419, 420, 424, 427
WAVEs, 172, 193
 retention study group program, 262
Weinberger, Caspar, 291
Weisner, Admiral Mickey, 227, 228, 239, 243, 244
 question of Zumwalt's successor, 475–478
 Zumwalt and, 475–476, 478
Weiss, Seymour, 399
Welander, Admiral Robert, 369, 370, 372–376
Wendt, Admiral Wallace, 302, 357
Western Carolines, 3
Westmoreland, General William, 276, 277, 296–297, 315–316, 375
 budgets and, 341–343, 347–348
Wheeler, General, 46
Whittet, Master Chief Petty Officer Jack, 215
Wickham, General, 508, 509
Wikner, Fred, 487
Wilson, Woodrow, 66
Wisconsin (battleship), 185, 188
Wolfe, Colonel Tom, 30
Women, 172, 251
 black, 201, 203, 207
 discrimination against, 168, 201, 203, 207, 261–265
 Laird on, 262–263
 Nixon on, 265
 ROTC, 264
 U.S. Congress on, 261, 263, 264
 U.S. Naval Academy, 261
 Zumwalt on, 216–265
Woodbury, Dave, 53
World War II
 China, 6–22
 guerilla action, 11–12

Japan, 4–20
 U.S.S.R., 60–61
 U.S. Navy, 3–25, 60–61, 183–184
 Zumwalt, 3–25, 65, 183–184
Wright, Christina, 26–27, 49–50, 321
WSAG, *see* Washington Special Action Group

Yangtze River, 4, 6–7
Yemen, People's Republic of, 362, 456
Yew, Lee Quan, 52
YMS (mine sweeper), 9–10, 12–15
Yom Kippur War, 70, 118, 279, 432–449, 454, 455, 456, 465, 475
 Egypt, 432–434, 438, 444, 448–449
 Greece, 442
 Israel, 432–442, 444, 448–449
  U.S. airlift, 433–435, 454, 465
 Italy, 442
 Kissinger, 432–439
  stalls U.S. airlift, 433–435
 Moorer, 434, 436
 the Netherlands, 442
 Nixon, 434, 435, 438
 oil and, 433, 434
 Portugal, 442
 Schlesinger, 433–435
 Syria, 432–434, 438
 Turkey, 441
 U.S.S.R., 433–439, 442, 445–449
 U.S. Navy, 435–437
 Zumwalt, 432–449
Young, David, 319
Young, Milton, 120, 125, 338, 464
Yugoslavia, 301

Zaire, 308–310
Zeller (destroyer), 26
Z-grams, 172–196, 202–204, 213, 220, 237, 248–251, 261–272
Zumwalt, Ann, 33, 49, 52
Zumwalt, Elmo R., 3, 23, 25, 48–49, 94, 239
Zumwalt, Mrs. Elmo R., 23, 24
Zumwalt, Admiral Elmo R., Jr.
 Abrams and, 34, 36, 39, 43–44, 47
 Arnold J. Isbell (destroyer—second command), 185–189
  voice call sign, 187–189
 awarded Distinguished Service Medal, 52
 background of, 23–24

Bagley and, 475, 478, 485, 506
in Belgium, 52
Chafee and, 43–46, 167–169, 172, 194, 211, 239, 243, 271, 310, 457
Chapman and, 276–277
as Chief of Naval Operations
  on air power, 70–71
  on alcohol problems, 269–271
  appointment as, 43–52
  basic philosophy, 55
  Change of Command Ceremony, 56, 510–511
  on construction contracts, 136–137
  Demeaning and Abrasive Regulations, Elimination of, 182–196
  Department of Defense Distinguished Medal, 498, 511
  on discrimination, 168, 197–216, 254–255, 261–265, 268–269
  dress regulations, 168, 173, 178–179, 182–185, 190–191, 193, 195, 257–258
  Executive Panel (CEP), 84, 286, 329
  F-14 problems, 143–151
  on family separation, 126, 168, 176–178
  first staff meeting, 55–56
  Flag Officers News Letter, 262
  grooming regulations, 168, 169, 182, 191, 192, 195, 248, 493, 494
  High-Low concept, 72–84, 102–107, 116, 120, 121, 124–125, 284, 474
  homeporting, 125–136, 305, 353–354
  on job satisfaction, 168
  on leaves, 184
  lobbying, 123–124, 160–163
  Mod Squad, 34, 175–176, 182–196
  NAVMINS, 237–238
  NAVOPS, 170, 172, 192, 195, 261–272
  personnel policies, 167–196
  PFIAB, 464–465
  Posture Statements, 452, 461
  Programs for People, 174–175, 265, 267–272
  Project 60, 66–84, 104–108, 126, 154, 177, 211, 284, 306–307, 340, 444, 475
  racial disturbances, 217–260, 412
  retention study group programs, 170–173, 220–221, 262
  speech at Annapolis (1974), 493–495
  Subcommittee on Disciplinary Problems, 252–259
  "Taking Stock of Naval Personnel Management," 265–266
  Trident appropriations, 157–160
  TTB, 495–498, 500, 503
  ULMS, 154–157
  WestPac Trip Observations, 215–216
  on women, 261–265
  Z-grams, 172–196, 202–204, 213, 220, 237, 248–251, 261–272
Chile and, 321–328
in China, 6–22, 25
Clements and, 418, 448
comparison of U.S. and U.S.S.R. Navy, 59–65, 84, 105, 140–144, 275, 291, 303–304, 314–316, 333, 337–338, 345–346, 462–465
"Course for Destroyers, A," 72
Cuban missile crisis, xiii, 29–30, 45, 69
on democracy, 69–70
on détente, 161
Dewey (guided-missile frigate—third command), 95, 96, 102, 185–186, 189, 215, 391–393
Division of Systems Analysis, 34
education, 23, 24, 27–28, 89–90, 96
favorite war story, 3–22
on general-purpose (conventional) forces, 59–60
in Germany, 52
in Great Britain, 53
Haig and, xii, 45–46, 355, 397–399, 493, 498
Hébert and, 245–247, 251, 253–254, 257, 259
Holloway and, 475, 478, 485
Iceland and, 466–474

on importance of a fighting command, 34–35
Incidents at Sea, 391–394
on Indian Ocean, 360–368
in Indonesia, 214–215
International Security Affairs, 28–33, 131
   Director of the Arms Control Division, 30
Italy and, 52, 141, 305
Jackson and, 32, 403
as Joint Chiefs of Staff member, 275–295
   "Admirals Spy Ring," 369–376
   budget discussions, 280–282, 284, 287–291, 313–317, 333–348, 407–411, 461
   European trip (1971), 357–359
   National Security Council system, 317–320
   Nixon briefing, 288–291
   oil embargo, 449–452
   South American trip (1971), 321–328
   strategic arms discussion, 282–288
   turnover in associates (1972–1973), 418
Kidd and, 136, 138, 139, 476
Kissinger and, xii–xiii, 308–328, 340–341, 395–423, 493, 508–509
   personal relationship, 396–397
Korean War, 65, 185
Laird and, 46–48, 70, 137, 154, 168, 194, 239, 244, 251, 253, 267, 310, 371, 412, 457
Major Fleet Escort Study, 101–104
marriage of, 19–22
Marshall and, 26–27, 321
Mediterranean crisis (October 1973), 446–448
Middle East and, 292–307, 360–368, 432–459
on military procurement, 136–152
on military strength, 25–26, 32
Moorer and, 41, 51, 52, 71, 310, 330, 402
at National War College, 27–28, 96
NATO and, 136, 305, 344, 345, 357–358, 466–469, 472–473

at Naval War College, 27
Nitze and, 27–35, 41, 52, 65, 68–69, 79, 96, 97, 105, 275, 285, 510
Nixon and, xii–xiii, 303–307, 318–320, 405–406, 412, 493–495, 506–508
   personal assessment (1973), 459–460
on Nixon Doctrine, 289, 300, 305, 330, 334
on Nixon's "State of the World" message, 330–331
on Nuclear Test Ban Treaty, 29, 30
on nuclear-propulsion systems, 63–65, 101–103
on oil, 452–453
Packard and, 70, 147, 281, 310
on Persian Gulf, importance of, 453–456
Personnel Retention Task Force, 170
POW/MIA families, 389–391
preparations for successor, 461–464, 474
promotions, 34
Proxmire and, 136–149
on question of his successor, 474–478
on rapid turnover in top leadership, 474–475
reasons for remaining in Navy, 25–27
reasons for retirement, xi, xii
relevant power, 344–346
religion, 20
retirement ceremony, 498
Rickover and, 85–122, 477, 478
   first meeting, 85–95
   nuclear power conflict, 93, 100–108, 121
   Sea Control Ships, 106, 116–121
   the Swanson conflict, 108–115, 118
Rivero and, 456–457
Rosenthal and, 125, 130–136
ROTC program, 26
SALT and, 30, 52, 107, 282–284, 287, 308, 348–349, 400–410, 426–432, 485–492, 495–505, 509, 510
   Memorandum for the President, 499–505

Schlesinger and, xi, 121, 422–423, 459, 473–475, 492–495, 498, 508–511
SFSDA, 30–31
in Singapore, 52
on strategic (nuclear-missile) forces, 59–60
Suez Canal and, 457–458
in Taiwan, 52
on television, 388, 507–510
Tills (destroyer—first command), 185
U.S.S.R. and, 25–26, 30–31, 35, 48, 330–331
"The Problem of the Next Succession in the USSR," 28
U.S. Congress and, 107, 123–163, 245–260
at U.S. Naval Academy, 24, 89–90

Vietnam War, 34–44, 65, 67, 169–170, 190, 377–389, 405, 410–418
ACTOV, 36, 40–42, 44, 47
Vietnamization, 46–47, 426
visits Seventh Fleet, 215–216, 378
Warner and, 44–49, 243–244, 256, 265–267
Weisner and, 475–476, 478
working habits, 33, 67–69
World War II, 3–25, 65, 183–184
Yom Kippur War, 432–449
Zumwalt, Mrs. Elmo R., Jr., 18–22, 25, 26, 33, 49–50, 52, 56, 67, 141, 320, 358, 389–390, 393, 511
Zumwalt, Elmo R., III, 25, 33, 52
Zumwalt, Jimmy, 33, 298
Zumwalt, Mouzetta, 33, 49, 52
Zumwalt's Gold Watch, 118
Zuska, Captain Joseph, 270, 271